Wallace Reid

Wallace Reid

*The Life and Death
of a Hollywood Idol*

E. J. Fleming

McFarland & Company, Inc., Publishers
Jefferson, North Carolina, and London

ALSO BY E.J. FLEMING
AND FROM MCFARLAND

*Paul Bern: The Life and Famous Death of the
MGM Director and Husband of Harlow* (2009)

Carole Landis: A Tragic Life in Hollywood (2005)

*The Fixers: Eddie Mannix, Howard Strickling
and the MGM Publicity Machine* (2005)

*The Movieland Directory: Nearly 30,000 Addresses
of Celebrity Homes, Film Locations and Historical Sites
in the Los Angeles Area, 1900–Present* (2004; paperback 2009)

*Hollywood Death and Scandal Sites: Sixteen Driving
Tours with Directions and the Full Story,
from Tallulah Bankhead to River Phoenix* (2000)

Frontispiece: Albert Witzel's signed master photograph of
Wallace Reid. This original would be left with the photographer,
and reproductions with the signature "in" the picture
were made to order by the studio (courtesy Cecil Jones).

*The present work is a reprint of the illustrated case bound
edition of* Wallace Reid: The Life and Death of a Hollywood
Idol, *first published in 2007 by McFarland.*

LIBRARY OF CONGRESS CATALOGUING-IN-PUBLICATION DATA

Fleming, E.J., 1954–
Wallace Reid : the life and death of a Hollywood idol /
E.J. Fleming.
p.   cm.
Includes bibliographical references and index.

ISBN 978-0-7864-7725-8
softcover : acid free paper ∞

1. Reid, Wallace, 1891–1923.
2. Actors—United States—Biography.   I. Title.
PN2287.R4F64   2013   792.02'8092—dc22 [B]   2006039476

BRITISH LIBRARY CATALOGUING DATA ARE AVAILABLE

© 2007 E.J. Fleming. All rights reserved

*No part of this book may be reproduced or transmitted in any form
or by any means, electronic or mechanical, including photocopying
or recording, or by any information storage and retrieval system,
without permission in writing from the publisher.*

On the front: Cover art of Wallace Reid from
the December 1922 issue of *Classic* magazine

Manufactured in the United States of America

*McFarland & Company, Inc., Publishers
Box 611, Jefferson, North Carolina 28640
www.mcfarlandpub.com*

Another one for my family—
Barb, Abby, Teddy and Colin

Acknowledgments

Wallace Reid's closest friend, writer Adela Rogers St. Johns, once wrote, "It always seemed to me that only one who knew Wally could write the story of his life."[1] After spending several years trying to write the story, I've come to believe that St. Johns was correct. Wally's friends are long dead; deciphering the real Wally from the legend was difficult, but I believe I have. I could not have done it without the assistance and support of literally hundreds of writers, researchers, archivists and friends who deserve my thanks.

As always, a special thank you goes to the staff of the Herrick Library at the Academy of Motion Pictures Arts and Sciences in Hollywood, especially Barbara in the Special Collections area, for their unflinching goodwill and assistance. Barbara and the staff are always ready to dig up something from deep within the files without warning (usually something I've forgotten).

Thanks again to Marc Wanamaker for allowing me access to his fabulous Bison Archives and for providing some of the photographic record that helps make the stories of early Hollywood come alive. Marc is unfailingly helpful and willing to share his vast resources.

In Santa Barbara, Dana Driskel at the University of California, Santa Barbara, Department of Film Studies reviewed the materials about Wally's time at Flying A in Santa Barbara and offered invaluable insight, and introduced me to Linda Schad, whose bulldog-like detective work uncovered a trove of previously undiscovered Reid stories in Santa Barbara and Los Angeles. Thanks also for the introduction to the Friends of Flying A. Thanks also to Deb at the Humboldt County Historical Society for her help researching the 1919 train wreck and subsequent *Valley of the Giants* filming, and to Ray State for his assistance hunting records of a forgotten, elusive 1919 train wreck.

In Los Angeles, Michael Kirley at the History & Genealogy Department of the Los Angeles Public Library offered his cheerful assistance in locating Wally's homes, offered good advice on my address searches, and referred me to Chris Aprato. Chris did an excellent job hunting through dusty Los Angeles City Directories and searched through the voluminous probate records to complete the legal side of the story. Sally Dumaux shared her Selig research materials with me and helped me to confirm much of Wally's filmography. Gary Hamann provided some of his wonderful books containing years of newspaper and press articles, as he has for past work. He can be found at www.gdhamann.blogspot.com.

In St. Louis, thanks to Lisa Johnston for her wonderful photos of beautiful Lafayette Square and of the 1896 "cyclone," and for driving around looking for Wally's birthplace at the request of a stranger.

In Chicago, thanks to the staff at the Chicago Historical Society for their help, and to Craig Pfannkuche, Memory Trail Research, for trying to find Wally in Chicago in 1910. Jerry Schneider introduced me to Jeff Look, who provided a number of wonderful early William Selig photos and background on Wally's time in Chicago. A special and overdue thank you to Bruce Long for his amazing historical record of early Hollywood contained at www.taylorology.com, the most complete record pertaining to the murder of William Desmond Taylor and a wonderful repository for innumerable interesting silent-era stories.

Diane Weir-Smith, Director of Alumni Relations at the Perkiomen School in Pennsylvania, provided information about Wally's prep school days and, with her assistant Janet Wampole in the Alumni Affairs office, managed to dig up a copy of one of Wally's yearbooks.

Thanks to Tom Meyers at the Fort Lee Film Commission for his continued support of my work. Bob Monsees graciously offered one of his collection of Wallace Reid photos, and Matthew DuBois his photo of his Echo Park house when Wally lived down the street.

In addition to the multitude of researchers and other writers who have continued to keep my work up to date are the friends who continue to keep my spirits up and my interest fresh. Boze Hadleigh, a wonderful writer of tremendous talent, offered his candid opinions and criticisms on structure and writing, for which I am always grateful. And Scott Michaels at www.findadeath.com has been one of my greatest supporters since the early days. Thanks to both of you.

And thanks to Liz at www.classicactresses.com, fellow writer Michelle Vogel and my publicist Tommy Garrett. Thanks guys.

My family continues to support this, whatever it is. My brother Tony still takes care of everything computer and web-related, and there's nothing to describe coming home to Barbara and our wonderful children, Abby, Teddy, and Colin. I love you all.

Wally Reid's story is a wonderful story, and thank you all for helping me tell it.

Contents

Acknowledgments	vii
Preface	1
1. Family and Youth	3
2. Finding "the Movies"	22
3. Dorothy and the Davenports	35
4. Santa Barbara and Marriage	47
5. The Birth of a Star	64
6. Lasky's "Diamond"	78
7. Stardom	90
8. War and Work	102
9. Where's Wally?	118
10. Accident, and Addiction	134
11. "Good-Time Wally" Faces the Abyss	152
12. Barely Hanging On	167
13. The Industry Teeters, and Wally Falls	192
14. The Curtain Falls on a Tragedy	210
15. Human Wreckage	226
Filmography	241
—*Actor*	241
—*Director*	257
—*Writer*	258
—*As Himself*	258
—*Archival Footage*	259
Chapter Notes	261
Selected Bibliography	281
Index	289

Wally Reid was a 180-pound diamond...
—Cecil B. DeMille

He can act and is, moreover, apparently not conscious
of the fact that he is disturbingly good looking.
—Kitty Kelly, 1915

In all of Hollywood history one man—*one man only*—
was the Prince Charming, the idol,
the irresistible man to all women—*all women*.
His name was Wallace Reid, the handsomest man any of us ever saw.
—Adela Rogers St. Johns

He was the most handsome, charming and magnetic man I've ever met.
—Jesse Lasky

Wally Reid was like Peter Pan. He never grew up.
—Adela Rogers St. Johns

This is a tough town, and even the toughest don't survive without scars.
—Dorothy Davenport Reid

Preface

Fame's fleeting nature is a truism rather than a cliché, applicable to all those in the public eye—athletes, politicians, and perhaps most of all, entertainers. Over the course of movie history, many actors and actresses have enjoyed popular success, fame and critical acclaim, often for years, only to quickly and surprisingly vanish from public view. Darlings of the industry for a time, they were beloved and recognized the world over. And then they were gone. In the public consciousness, it's as if they never existed.

Many early stars as far back as the silent era have retained their worldwide acclaim. Men like Charlie Chaplin and Buster Keaton remain in the public consciousness, although even Keaton was forgotten for a half-century until being "rediscovered" in the 1960s. Douglas Fairbanks and Mary Pickford are still remembered by the nom de guerre they enjoyed for decades, the "King and Queen of Hollywood." And directors like D.W. Griffith and Cecil B. DeMille are still recognized for their varied contributions to the development of the filming art. But for every Chaplin, Keaton, Fairbanks or Pickford, for every Griffith, there is a Roscoe Arbuckle, an Olive Thomas, a Mabel Normand, or a William Desmond Taylor. Names and faces who have somehow vanished from the public's memory.

Almost unearthly beautiful Olive Thomas was known as the loveliest girl in the world and was one of cinema's rising stars. During her 1920 honeymoon after a fantasy wedding to Jack Pickford, younger brother of Mary, she committed suicide amidst rumors of drug addiction and syphilis given to her by her husband. Roscoe "Fatty" Arbuckle earned $3,000,000 in 1921 before scandal ended his career and reduced him to menial on-set jobs using the pseudonym "Will B. Good."

William Desmond Taylor, one of the best known and respected directors in Hollywood, was murdered in a case that still baffles police 80 years later. His closest friend and an early suspect, Mabel Normand, was perhaps the screen's best-known and most beloved comedienne. Like her mentor and alleged lover Taylor, she too was embroiled in a tortuous love affair; hers was with Mack Sennett, "the King of Comedy." After Taylor's death she also quickly disappeared and quietly died in a sanitarium, wracked by the effects of drug addictions and tuberculosis.

Perhaps the most famous of these falls, though, was that of Wallace Reid. For a decade "Wally" was the most recognized face in silent film, the most successful and most universally beloved actor in the movies. Wally was famous the world over, idolized by tens of millions of fans.

Like a rocket he soared into the public consciousness, and like a meteor fell to earth equally fast. But incredibly, today Wally is almost totally forgotten except by movie historians. Many of his 200-plus films—most lost forever as silver nitrate versions slowly turned to dust in forgotten film canisters in dusty storage closets—are known only to researchers and biographers. All that is remembered of Reid is that he died in a sanitarium, the victim of a morphine addiction.

Writer Adela Rogers St. Johns described Wally after he died, reminding fans, "The important thing about Wallace Reid is not that he was the greatest and most popular star the motion picture has produced. It is that he was, beyond dispute, the best loved man of his generation. He woke in the heart of the multitude a great affection, a lasting affection, that still gives off fragrance, like crushed lavender. It wasn't only women who loved him, though they did—and often not wisely but too well. Men loved him, boys, old people, children. There was something about Wally Reid that fitted into the dreams in every heart. His life story is important because of that love and because his death grieved and bewildered and shocked the whole world."[1]

His death rocked Hollywood to its foundations. It was the straw that broke the proverbial camel's back. The huge new industry, making millionaires out of common men, almost died with Wally. Coming on the heels of the scandals of Thomas and Pickford, Arbuckle, and Taylor and Normand, Reid's agonizing death in a padded cell at a private sanitarium sent Hollywood reeling. The studios were forced to step in. The changes they were forced to make altered the landscape of the movies forever. Wally's death proved that they had to rein in their wealthy stars that obviously determined the studio's commercial and financial destinies. Wally's death was the birth of the "studio system."

Reid's life and catastrophic fall has somehow been forgotten. His story has never been told. This is Wally's story. Wally was a true Renaissance man. Onscreen, he was a talented actor equally adept at drama and comedy. He was a gifted writer, an accomplished director and a skilled cameraman. Away from the movies, he was a musical prodigy; self-taught, he could play any musical instrument, from the saxophone to the piano. He also wrote music. He could sing, so well that his one-time co-star Geraldine Farrar, herself an opera legend, suggested he leave the movies and step onto *that* stage.

He was a talented painter whose landscapes hung in the mansions of some of Hollywood's elite. He did remarkable caricatures of his cast-mates. He could have been a professional athlete; he played football and ran track in school, and stood his own boxing with his instructor, the former trainer for heavyweight champion Jack Dempsey. He drove cars like a racer, setting the speed record on the most dangerous road course in California and earning a racecar driver's license. He could also take apart and rebuild an engine.[2] And as a person, he was a loving father and husband that everyone seemed to adore. There was nothing that Wally couldn't do.

Wally's story is the story of a protected and wealthy youth amidst the turn-of-the-century theater world, a dazzling rise to film stardom and the wealth and status that it begat, and a love story that lasted 55 years. And it's a story of tragic death, a death that had less to do with drug abuse than with medical ignorance, an addiction orchestrated by an unknowing studio that turned a happy, well-adjusted man with a loving family into a drug-wracked corpse in less than three years.

But this is also the story of the near-death experience of an entire industry. Of an industry almost crushed beneath the weight of its own excesses. Wallace Reid was as much a victim as an example. Wally Reid was "Dashing Wally Reid." He was "Handsome Wally Reid." He was "Wally Reid, the All-American Boy." In the end, *being* Wally Reid killed Wally Reid. And almost killed the movies.

Barrington, Illinois
January, 2007

1

Family and Youth

It's probably no wonder Wally Reid was such an interesting person, talented and intellectual, a "Renaissance man" before the term was fashionable. It may have been his bloodlines, stories by themselves. Qualities that made him the most popular star of the silent era were in his background. His family trees include arenas as diverse as the English monarchy, first Virginia settlements, Revolutionary War, American politics, and late 1800s American theater. And, of course, the movies. Wally's weaknesses probably also had their birth in his ancestry, which was burdened with excess, scandal, and failure. It is this marvelous but frightening dichotomy from which young Wally emerged.

His father's family can be traced to James Reid, among the first Pennsylvanians to enlist in the Revolutionary Army. On January 6, 1776, James was commissioned a Lieutenant in the 4th Pennsylvania, paid $80 a month in U.S. currency and 30 pounds British.[1] He fought with Moses Hazen's 2nd Canadians in Major General William Alexander Lord Stirling's 5th Division, called "the Infernals" for their bravery. During the Battle of Brandywine, Reid's valor earned him a field promotion to Major.[2] In 1778–1779 the Infernals fought at places like Trenton and Princeton, and in 1781 marched down the Hudson to take part in the siege at Yorktown.

Reid mustered out in June, 1783, and returned to Carlisle, in Cumberland County, Pennsylvania, but by 1790, he and son John[3] were in Miami County near present-day Dayton, Ohio.[4] By the mid–1800s the Reids were prosperous farmers and merchants in the area between Cedarville and Xenia. Wally's great-grandfather John, John's brother Robert and several uncles farmed there.[5]

Robert's son Whitelaw was born on October 27, 1837, and became one of the most famous men in 19th century American politics. In 1859 he was editor of the *Xenia News*, the largest newspaper in Ohio, and during the Civil War was correspondent and aide-de-camp to Generals Thomas A. Morris and William S. Rosecrans. He moved to Washington for the *Cincinnati Gazette* and in 1866 to New York, where *New York Tribune* owner Horace Greeley hired him as an editorial writer. Greeley's death left Reid the Editor-in-Chief of the biggest newspaper in New York.[6] In 1880 he was sharing a fashionable brownstone with two live-in servants and his 22-year-old niece Ella at 271 Lexington Avenue.[7]

On March 3, 1881, society pages announced "Whitelaw Reid will marry $300,000. Her other name is Mills. An Ohio man of luck anyhow."[8] Elizabeth Mills was the daughter of Darius O. Mills, a millionaire banker among the wealthiest land-owners in California, who lived on a huge Millbrae estate with 15 servants.[9] Lizzie met Whitelaw during an 1880 New York visit and they married in 1881. In 1892 he was the unsuccessful Republican vice-presidential candidate with Benjamin Harrison[10] and later served as an advisor to President Garfield. During those years he also apparently performed a greater, but less public, service for the Reid family.

The Ohio Reids flourished. John Reid's son Hugh was the only dentist within a day's carriage ride of Cedarville and Xenia, and the gifted teacher was also Professor of Dentistry at the Ohio Dental College.[11] He was quiet and unassuming, but his friends were men like John Hay, William McKinley, and Theodore Roosevelt.[12] Hugh lived in a large house with his wife America and twins Sarah S. and John E., born in 1859, Kate, born in 1861, and James Halleck, born on April 14, 1862.[13] James was nicknamed "Hal."

Hal Reid was a contradiction. Writer Adela Rogers St. Johns later described him as "a picturesque and brilliant figure, a veritable mass of contradictions, an erratic and lovable genius. A man who could hold any gathering spellbound with his wit and his extravagant flow of language ... yet, with all of it, as unstable as the wind, a prey to his own love of the pleasures and passions of life."[14] This contradiction had a profound effect on his son Wally, who loved his mother but *idolized* his father. St. Johns wrote that "no doubt the most important factor in shaping Wally Reid's youth was his father. He believed that his father was the greatest of men."[15] His father's flaws broke his heart, but he was inconsolable when he died.

At 18, Hal moved to Cincinnati and worked as a reporter at the *Cincinnati Times Star*. The publisher was Charles P. Taft, brother of future President William Howard Taft. Hal's forte became turning one-paragraph "fill" stories into long yarns derisively referred to as "sob stuff," and he began writing plays and acting with theater groups.

The man St. Johns called a "whole-souled, big-hearted gentleman, clever and interesting"[16] was also an inveterate womanizer. In 1882, 20-year-old Hal had a brief dalliance with 16-year-old Mae Withers, the daughter of a farmer who lived ten miles from town.[17] A few weeks later the couple eloped, and eight months later Mae gave birth to a girl they named Hazel. Mae and Hazel stayed with her family while Hal toured with a theater company.

At the time, what was known as "legitimate theater" was the most popular entertainment in cities both large and small. The earliest references to staged productions for paying audiences in the U.S. date to the Revolutionary War, and permanent theaters first arose in the 1700s. American theater is usually dated to the arrival of Londoner Lewis Hallam's troupe in 1752 at Williamsburg,[18] and the first permanent theater was built in 1767.[19] Between 1800 and 1850 the number of playhouses and touring companies increased dramatically, and through 1850 New York and Philadelphia were the centers of U.S. theater. Theaters held 250 to 3,500 people, and in the 1860s technologies improved offerings. New York's Booth Theater (owned by Edwin Booth, brother of John Wilkes) advertised "special facilities for scenic effects; the wide stage could be made to sink, and hydraulic rams were introduced for the handling of the sets."[20] Theaters had in-house companies, and by the 1870s American and British troupes were passing each other in the mid–Atlantic, steaming to each other's shores. At the same time, plays were becoming available even to remote locations—St. Louis in the 1820s, New Orleans in 1835 and Indianapolis and Chicago in the 1850s.

Touring was not glamorous. The players provided their own costumes. Charlotte Smith and Mary Gish sewed costumes for their daughters, Gladys and Lillian and Dorothy.[21] Small companies traveled by carriage, and small-town theaters lacked heat and running water. The companies stayed in cheap hotels, usually paying $1 for a grimy room with a thin mattress, a chair, and communal bathrooms. A bath was 25¢; the tin tub was scoured with steel wool first. The travel was grueling. Shows lasted one or two nights;

any longer, there were no locals left to come. Gladys Smith once endured 19 *weeks* of one-night stands, each night a different town. When they traveled by train they took the cheapest runs on late-night trains and slept sitting in their seats. Gladys spent so many nights sleeping that way that for her entire 87-year life she could only sleep with her arms over her head.[22] She became Mary Pickford.

From 1884 into 1887 Hal lived this nomadic life, returning to Cincinnati every few months. In the fall of 1887 he was at the West St. Paul (Minnesota) Opera House. Maud Compson was a young actress in the company,[23] living with her sister in Mrs. Kimball's Rooming House near the theater. She had worked for Hal less than a week when she accused him of assaulting her on September 5th. Headlines screamed "MORE MINNEAPOLIS DEPRAVITY: An Innocent Girl Victim of Villain's Lust."

It was mentioned that Maud might die, and Hal's guilt was assumed when he fled after a confrontation with her sister, who said, "I said I would like to go to Minneapolis to see my ill mother. He [Hal] said 'I want to send a note to my father. If you will take it I will pay for your travel expenses,' but ... when I returned I found my sister on the bed in delirium."[24] She told police Maud was a virgin and did not call them until Monday so as not to upset their mother. The argument with Hal was witnessed by the company. She attacked him, scratching his face and throwing a pot of hot tea at him. Hal then fled to Ohio but first offered to marry Maud if criminal actions ceased.

Arrested in Alliance, Ohio, on the 6th—reported as "THE DEVIL'S DOING. Hal Reid, the Minneapolis Fiend, Held by Authorities at Alliance, Ohio"—Hal was charged with rape and criminal assault and returned to Minneapolis on the 9th. Papers called him "Reid the Rapist,"[25] but he denied everything, saying, "People do not wait four days to make a complaint in a case of rape, do they? I am innocent." Oddly, he added, "I did tell Mrs. Williams that my wife would be glad to get any excuse to get rid of me and that I could give her a good excuse and then I would marry Maude [sic]."[26] Hal wired his father for the $8,000 bail.

A few days later a letter Hal wrote his wife from his Ohio hotel surfaced that seemed like an admission and asked for a divorce so he could marry Maud and avoid prison. "REID'S CONFESSION!"[27] read, "Don't let Hazel's papa become a convict. If you had only stuck to me this never could have been as it is. Take the baby and save me from the penitentiary for your own sake and Hazel's."

Hugh Reid initially refused to pay Hal's bail, but Hal appealed to Whitelaw, who convinced Hugh to wire the $8,000. On December 1st "Hal Reid's Trial for Committing Rape on Maud Comson [sic] Began in St. Paul,"[28] and he "made his appearance in court looking as nonchalant as ever."[29] Maud tearfully repeated her story and Hal's defense asserted the relations were consensual, but his patronizing demeanor and seeming indifference alienated his blue-collar jury. Even though Maud's landlord testified "people of questionable reputation visited the girls' room often until she forbade it,"[30] and Hal's lawyers made a compelling case, he was convicted and sentenced to 15 years in prison. For the next year his lawyers argued appeals. Mae divorced Hal in Cincinnati.

Hal was taken to the Stillwater State Penitentiary, built in the 1700s for 500 incorrigible prisoners but often crammed with 2,000. The fearsome-looking stone compound squatted on a windy plateau near the St. Croix River north of Minneapolis. Inside, it was either bitterly cold or unbearably hot. From November to April it rarely climbed above 30° and during the summer hovered above 80° for weeks, made more humid by the nearby river and hundreds of lakes. But amid the misery was some comedy. Warden "Bull Beef" Webber allowed murderers to leave without guards to hunt deer for him and let imprisoned prostitutes work inside the prison as long as he received a percentage.

On October 23, 1888, Hal's final appeal was denied[31] and it appeared he would spend ten years inside the squalid facility, but just three months later he was pardoned. He was simply exonerated and released. It was rumored Whitelaw Reid struck a deal since at the time he was being considered for an ambassadorial appointment from President Harrison. Help from Whitelaw is unconfirmed, but it isn't likely Hal received a full pardon without it. Even the paperwork was rushed; he was in Cincinnati before Christmas as something of a celebrity, with parties held in his honor as he was welcomed back into the social whirl. On March 19th Whitelaw was named Ambassador to France and he took over as "Envoy Extraordinary and Minister Plenipotentiary to France," a post he held until February 27, 1892.

Audiences were becoming more demanding as theaters offered plays, ballet, opera, and emerging vaudeville and burlesque. In 1889, 400 touring companies traveled the U.S.[32] and plays drew big crowds everywhere. Every town had a theater, an "Opera House" or an "Academy of Music." *The New York Dramatic Mirror* was the industry guide to which theater managers telegraphed two-line reports of ticket sales and local reaction.[33] Big-city theaters charged $2.00 for tickets, but in medium-sized cities like Atlanta or Reno, "Dress Circle Reserved Seats" were $1, "Regular Balcony Reserved Seats" 75¢, and a "Balcony" seat 50¢.[34] In smaller towns like Sandusky, Ohio, or Trenton, seats cost 75¢, 50¢ and 25¢.[35] The more remote, the cheaper. The only theater in Fort Wayne, Indiana, offered seats for 30¢, 20¢ and 10¢ for a prime Saturday performance.[36]

By 1889 the stars earned fame equal to their plays. The biggest, like Maude Adams, Ethel Barrymore, and John Drew, were treated like later movie stars. It was the birth of celebrity. Amidst the plays were rare viewings of short films shown with Thomas Edison's "Projectoscope." The fascinating new technology helped fill theaters.

Just months after his release, Hal joined Agnes Herndon's company. She was said to be from a wealthy Virginia family and a cousin of the wife of ex–President Chester A. Arthur, but her real name was Agnes Jessel and she was born in New York in 1849.[37] Hal began an affair with the 40-year-old and became her lead actor. In February the Herndon-Reid troupe opened *La Belle Marie* in Mansfield, Ohio, at the Memorial Theater,[38] then traveled to Cincinnati, then south to the Charlotte Opera House and Charleston (South Carolina) Theater.[39] During the tour Hal wrote a play about life in the Arkansas backwoods titled *Human Hearts* that debuted in Charlotte on November 19th. Hal was among the first writers to inject humanity into a play, and his plays became popular in the far-off markets, "the sticks."[40] Wally later described his father's style as "the kind of play in which the attempts of the black-mustached villain to tie the golden-haired and tearful heroine to the railroad tracks were foiled by the splendid young hero, ably assisted by the soubrette and the comedian."[41] The humanity and his lurid (for the time) love scenes attracted huge crowds. *Human Hearts* was the most famous play of the 19th century and made Hal famous.

During the fall of 1889 the Herndon troupe traveled through Minnesota, Illinois and Missouri. They were performing in St. Louis during December when Hal met 21-year-old Bertha Westbrook just before Christmas. Like the Reids, the Westbrooks had a storied history. Bertha's background is dotted with glory, suffering and tragedy going back 1,000 years. Her father's family consisted of hard-working American farmers, and her mother's was among the earliest Virginia colonists. Bertha carried herself with the vanity and superiority to which she felt her bloodline entitled her. Wally made fun of her obsession with her family tree and bristled each time she put the family crest on a new set of silver, telling her, "It doesn't matter what a man's grandfathers were; it only matters what he was himself."[42] But Bertha constantly bragged about family, describing gentile surroundings layered with the trappings of wealth. She said her great-grandfathers cultivated plantations "with the work of dozens of slaves,"[43] and were among the most important families in the Virginia colonies.

Bertha's family actually did have regal beginnings, going back 25 generations to English King Alfred "the Great," who ruled in the 800s. Among her ancestors were Edgar "the Peaceable," the first King of a unified England (he was the first to use the title "King of England"). Henry II ruled an empire that stretched to the Pyrenees and introduced the concept of trial by jury. His grandson John Lackland signed the Magna Charta at Runnymede in 1215, and his great-grandson was Edward II, the first Prince of Wales. From the 1300s to the 1600s descendents of this line of Edwardian Kings owned baronial estates as Dukes and Earls until 20-year-old William Strother, IV boarded a boat for Virginia in 1650.

Strother and his wife Dorothy Savage arrived from Northumberland and settled in a tiny Richmond County, Virginia, trading post called Port Conway. The family then moved onto farms in the lush, remote western Shenandoah Valley. Some lived in Culpeper and by the 1700s others were in mountain towns like Millwood and Winchester. In the 1760s descendents of Strother married into the Rice family and, like James Reid, fought in the Revolutionary War. James Rice left his farm in Millwood, near Frederick, to serve under his uncle Henry Brown in a Virginia regiment marching with the Marquis de Lafayette. In 1806, James' son Thomas B. Rice was born, and in 1835 Thomas moved to rural southern Illinois with his wife Mahala Farrow and their three children. He settled in Macoupin County on a large tract of land in the long-vanished village of Rhoads Point, and by 1850 he had 10 children, five boys and five girls born between 1829 and 1850. The family later moved to another disappeared town, Medora, 50 dusty miles from the nearest large city, St. Louis.[44]

By the 1860s Thomas Rice owned 5,000 acres and several grist and flour mills. The 1870 census records support Bertha's description of wealth; his land was worth $25,000 ($3,000,000 today[45]) and his home $27,000.[46] Among his five daughters was Mary Virginia, born in 1839. Some 25 years later she married Henry Westbrook, one of four children of Chester Westbrook, who farmed in remote Hardin County, Ohio, in a tiny settlement called Goshen near present-day Macksburg in southeastern Ohio. The area is hard to reach even today, 40 miles northwest of Parkersburg, West Virginia, in the Appalachian foothills.

Chester and his wife had four children, David, born in 1934, Maloma in 1836, Henry (called "Harry") in 1839, and Levy in 1841. Their mother died in childbirth in the mid–1840s and the children were shuttled off to local families; by 1850 all were living on farms owned by family friends, and used as laborers. David, 16, and Maloma, 14, were taken in by farmer Miles Van Fleet on his large farm in Dudley, 10 miles away.[47] Levy, barely 9, was taken in by Nathan Smith. Harry was the only child who stayed in Goshen, moving in with farmer John Kinsley.[48]

As a teenager, Harry worked on the Kinsley farm and later for Joshua Coke.[49] Maloma would marry and move near Cincinnati, and Levy and David bought farms 150 miles north in Claiborne. In her 1923 book about Wally, Bertha offered almost no information about Harry. That he worked hard is all but ignored by Bertha, and while effusive in her praise of the Rices, the Westbrooks merit one sentence: "their daughter, Mary Virginia, married Colonel 'Harry' Westbrook of St. Louis, formerly of New York City, who told of the days when corn fields flourished at 23rd Street."[50]

Bertha hinted that her father served in the Union Army, hence the "Colonel" title.

But his only military record is an 1890 Veteran's Census form he filled out listing his rank as "Colonel" and his assignment as "Press Command."[51] The listing was crossed out. After the war Henry lived in New York, a traveling book salesman. During a trip to Illinois he met Mary Virginia Rice and they were married in 1866 or 1867. Bertha wrote that they wed in St. Louis, where they were living in 1880.

Harry and Virginia had three daughters between 1867 and 1873—Bertha in 1868, Maud in 1870, and Emma in 1872. In 1880 they lived at 2940 Jefferson Avenue and Henry was listed as a "book agent."[52] The house was an unimpressive two-story brick home on a busy thoroughfare in a working class neighborhood a half mile from the massive railroad yards and crowded docks along the Mississippi River south of downtown.

Harry was hard-working and became the General Manager of the St. Louis News Correspondence Bureau, a publishing company at 407 North Broadway. By 1890 the family moved to a more impressive, large three-story 1870 Victorian town house at 30 Nicholson Place. It was a lovely street lined with stately homes and town houses, two-story brick homes topped by a third floor mansard roof and dormer windows. The Westbrook house had a stone façade, beautiful arched doorways and windows, ornate cornices and bay windows.

The street ended at the southern edges of Lafayette Park at Lafayette Avenue.[53] The upscale neighborhood was full of large Victorians, Second Empire townhouses, and 1850s Federal style homes. The wide tree-lined streets encircled the 30-acre park that was a Civil War encampment turned into a Victorian showplace with five acres of gardens, dozens of gazebos, a bandstand, an aquarium, and a boathouse surrounding a large lake. Nearby lived Abraham Lincoln's Postmaster General, Montgomery Blair, and U.S. Supreme Court Justice Louis Brandeis, and at 1532 Mississippi Avenue was the imposing 1877 mansion of riverboat captain Horace H. Bixby. Among his maritime students was Samuel Clemens.[54]

The Westbrooks were closer to St. Louis society but still a distance from where Bertha aspired. Even so, her accounts painted a picture of affluent life among the elite. Although educated in public schools, she said she "enjoyed two social seasons when she became a member of the old McCullough Club for amateur theatricals."[55] The Club was a prestigious theater group, and a fellow member was Augustus Thomas, who enjoyed the social status Bertha dreamed about as the son of a wealthy doctor, and who spent summers as a Congressional page and wrote for New York and St. Louis papers. He began writing plays at 14, and during her summers Bertha appeared in several of his plays at the Club.

During the summer of 1883 he wrote a play called *The Burglar*.[56] When Maurice Barrymore and Della Fox agreed to play the leads it became a monstrous success and he was hailed a prodigy. He became among the most successful playwrights in theater and wrote 60 plays during a 35-year career. Bertha's experience made her desire to become a stage actress stronger, and during the 1880s she appeared in local companies. She was but a small part of regional theater, but in her mind she was already a star when Hal Reid and Agnes Herndon arrived in late 1889.

Late that December, Hal was riding a wave of success from *Human Hearts*. Audiences loved the play and he was celebrated as a writer. Fame also eliminated the need for his relationship with Agnes. Hal was introduced to Bertha before Christmas and just five days later, on December 26 or 27, shockingly, they were married. The troupe was heading to Kansas City and Hal convinced Bertha to elope and marry there, where they did at the home of the only Southern Methodist Episcopal minister in the city.[57] Agnes Herndon was understandably upset and the elopement caused uproar in St. Louis theater circles. Hal's wedding to "St. Louis debutante Bertha Bell Westbrook, on five days acquaintance" became a scandal. It was fueled by stories planted by Hal and Agnes.

Headlined "THEATRICAL SCANDAL—Hal Reid, an Ex-Convict, Tells a Bad Story on Agnes Herndon," Hal said he "left the company because Agnes, or Mrs. Jessel as she is known off the stage, kept importuning me to elope with her and desert my wife. When she learned I had married she went into high tragedy and offered me $400 a week as leading man for life if I would elope."[58] His position in the company was understandably compromised; on January 3rd he left and settled with Bertha's parents at Nicholson Place.

For the next year and a half Hal was not interested in finding steady work and concentrated on writing. The couple moved to Chicago, then Cincinnati, back to St. Louis and briefly to New York in the summer of 1890. Hal sold another backwoods love story, *The Home-spun Heart*, a typical Hal tale of a manly farmer and an old playmate separated by the efforts of a miserly banker and a "heartless adventuress,"[59] only to overcome both with the help of the adventuress' half-witted brother.

In late 1890 it became the first play offered by Hal's new company and debuted in Cincinnati, with Bertha playing the cruel adventuress. They then went to Minneapolis, a surprising choice given his notoriety there, appearing together in *Two Orphans*. Bertha was billed as "Bertha Belle Westbrook," the stage name she used for the rest of her theatrical life. Hal wrote the play *Daughter of the Confederacy*, based on an *Orphan* character, that became a Broadway success, and the couple toured the Midwest with that play for the next year. During the tour in the summer of 1891 Bertha became pregnant.

Bertha's single-minded obsession with her child began prenatally, as she later wrote that she "knew that the great responsibility of a human soul-flower, an incarnated spiritual entity out of the fathomless mystery of No-where, was to be entrusted to my care, and the sacredness of that trust, was ever present with me from that time—months before Wally came to me—until the terrible and tremendous day when he went from me."[60] She and Hal moved back to St. Louis and she immersed herself in her pregnancy. She "believed in the immeasurable power of pre-natal influence"[61] and was excessive, but her beliefs were ahead of their time in 1890. Thinking that her activities developed the baby's personality, she dedicated daily hour-long periods to various activities: painting, music, singing, writing, and reading aloud to the fetus. She surrounded herself with photos of beautiful children, believing the imagery would develop an attractive child.

Early on the morning of April 15, 1892, Bertha gave birth to an 11-pound 12-ounce boy, a beautiful child with blond hair, piercing blue—almost violet—eyes, fair skin and rosy red cheeks. He was named William Wallace Reid after the Scottish hero in Sir Walter Scott's *Scottish Chiefs*[62] and nicknamed "Cotton-top" for his blond hair. Bertha called him "Cotton-top" his entire life, but everyone else called him Wally. Wally later suggested he was born in a St. Louis hotel,[63] but he was born at Nicholson Place. From the start, the Westbrooks worshipped the child. He later said, "To hear Mother tell it, I recited Shakespeare at six months and went to the grocery store alone before I was a year old."[64] His crib was a shrine; he was never left unattended.

Shortly after his birth he was brought to Minneapolis to visit Hal's father, then at the University of Minnesota as Dean of the School of Dentistry. Dr. Reid had an immense tub installed in the living room so the entire family could witness the child's daily bath, attended by parents, grandparents, servants, and two aunts. While there, Hal supervised a production of *Human Hearts*. From Minnesota the family traveled to Cincinnati and then to New York, where Hal and Bertha appeared in the Milton Nobles play *The Phoenix*. For Wally the trip was the first experience of a life spent traveling with his parents or staying in St. Louis with the Westbrooks when his parents toured.

For his first two years Wally spent most of his time cared for by nannies. He would later fictionalize his life, saying he spent those years on family plantations in Virginia[65] where he "spent a good many happy days."[66] But there is no record he ever visited his Virginia ancestors.

In 1895, well-known producer Harry C. Miner paid Hal to offer *Human Hearts*, with Hal and Bertha in the leads. Critics described Hal as "a very handsome, noble-looking fellow" and Bertha as "an advanced type of female villain; an elegant, dashing woman who behaves so heartlessly and so naturally as Miss Westbrook is seldom seen."[67] The play sold out theaters for over a year. Hal continued to write; in September 1893 he sold *The Lilly and the Rose* to producer A.Y. Person,[68] and a play written with Bertha entitled *The Prince of Peace*.

Miner sent the *Hearts* troupe on the road in 1895, and for the next two years Hal and Bertha toured the Midwest and South. The fall of 1895 was spent in Illinois, Wisconsin and Minnesota, and the winter and spring of 1896 in the Carolinas. During the 1896 tour Wally made his stage debut, when, just after his fourth birthday, he appeared in *Slaves of Gold* with his parents, playing a young girl.[69] A later *Washington Post* obituary recorded his first appearance as being a role in his father's play *The Girl and the Ranger*,[70] but that did not occur until 1909 or 1910.[71]

When not traveling, Wally was with the Westbrooks at Nicholson Place. Bertha romanticized his childhood to excuse her frequent absences, writing, "At times we were away on business when he would be left in his grandparents' care."[72] She understates the truth; she and Hal were rarely with Wally at all. His childhood was not normal. He grew up apart from his parents, in the care of grandparents. His personality was developed during a childhood without any real male presence. St. Johns described a protected childhood, an upbringing devoid of harshness or punishment of the "Fairy Prince." His parents adored him and never punished him for anything, and he was a docile child. But she warned "the note of sternness, of a certain kind of *hardness*, was missing."[73]

Although the street has been renumbered, fire department maps and census records indicate that this Nicholson Place house was Wally's birthplace, and the place where the terrified youngster rode out the terrible 1896 tornado that destroyed much of the surrounding neighborhood. Most of the original house remains, including the original facade, but at the time of Wally's birth, there was another house between these two (courtesy Lisa Johnston).

Wally was the center of attention. The missing fatherly presence was replaced by the strong female presence of his aunts and grandmother, whom he called "sweetheart Virginia."[74] Even at four, the women made his every bath a command performance. The missing "hardness" described by St. Johns would eventually help kill him.

During the 1895–1896 stay at Nicholson Place, Wally almost died when the "Great Cyclone of 1896" destroyed much of St. Louis on the afternoon of May 27th. A huge funnel cloud touched down near Lafayette Park and plowed east toward the river, ripping homes off of their foundations and laying waste to entire blocks. As Wally and his grandfather struggled to get to the cellar, the chimneys were ripped off the roof and the bay windows blown in around them. Wally later remembered the day, happily saying, "I remember the cyclone just as well as I remember what happened yesterday. And the thing I remember is that my aunt had just baked a lot of cherry pies and they blew out of the window and started raining cherries everywhere."[75] But he was terrified.

Hundreds of mansions and nearby buildings were destroyed. Houses across the street were flattened and a row of two-foot-wide oak trees lining Nicholson Place were reduced to matchsticks. By the time the cloud crossed the river a half mile away over 300 people were dead. The damage and people's hesitance to rebuild led to an exodus to the West side, and within ten years the once elegant Lafayette Square was known as "Slum D."

For the rest of his life Wally hated wind. Even the slightest breeze made him uncomfortable. When the seasonal "Santa Anna" winds blew through the L.A. basin when he was older, he rarely left his house. After the tornado Bertha and Hal took Wally on tour. He made his second appearance in *Human Hearts*, this time playing a boy.[76] After a few months they dropped him back at Nicholson Place and continued touring. The play was advertised as "The Greatest Production of Modern Times! With a Full Railcar of Scenery and Properties!"[77] Sold-out theaters meant infrequent visits home. The Westbrooks took Wally to visit his parents more often than they visited him.

One thing the childhood solitude left Wally with was a love of books. He immersed himself in literature. His wife later said, "The only real rival I ever had after marriage was our library. Thanks to Wally, I acquired a literary education I never acquired in my youth."[78] Wally grew up a thoughtful, intelligent boy, but more a boy than a man.

Hal was virtually incapable of a monogamous relationship, which Bertha learned quickly. Their son's birth tempered her misgivings about Hal's affairs, but she reached her limit during the 1897 summer tour when young actress Beatrice Winship, Hal's latest "other woman," contacted her. On August 7th Bertha filed for divorce, as newspapers noted, "Mrs. Reid has taken under her protection Miss Beatrice Winship, the co-respondent in the case, whom Reid had deserted penniless and friendless in New York."[79] Winship was also reportedly pregnant with Hal's child. Bertha and Wally moved to an apartment Hal had earlier rented on West End Avenue just off Central Park.

For most of 1898 Bertha and Wally lived there. Her ever-protective father moved the family from St. Louis and rented an apartment about four blocks away at 17 Manhattan Avenue, a block west of Central Park and 101st Street. Bertha's sisters, Maud and Emma, worked as stenographers for the Miner Theater, and Harry listed himself as an "orator."[80]

With Bertha gone, Hal contacted his long-neglected daughter Hazel and convinced her to join the *Hearts* company. Still in Cincinnati with mother Mae, the beautiful 16-year-old agreed. Hal's successes as a playwright and actor had erased the memory of the Maud Compson scandal; both Hazel and her mother were using the Reid name again after years of using Mae Withers' maiden name.

Hazel joined the troupe in September 1897 and first appeared on stage in February 1898. In January, papers reported "H.L. Dunkinson was in Fort Wayne [Indiana] in advance of Hal Reid's 'Human Hearts.'"[81] Dunkinson (real name Harold Leopold) was a 19-year-old who joined the group in the fall. In a scene eerily similar to Hal and Bertha's romance, Hazel and Hal eloped a week after meeting. But she divorced him on September 11, 1899, after less than ten months, described in newspapers as a "case of marry in haste and repent at leisure."[82] Dunkinson appeared in 100-plus movies from 1912 to 1925 before dying in Hollywood in 1936. Hazel was divorced before her father; Bertha had yet to formally divorce Hal.

In late 1898 the Miner troupe began production of the Hal play *Knobs o' Tennessee*, co-written with Lincoln J. Carter. It debuted in Nashville in September with Hal in the lead and Margaret Elsmere replacing Bertha. It was a story of a family's battle with moonshiners. The cast included a trained dog who finds his master's dead body in the woods, licks his face and mournfully wails, something audiences had never seen. A reviewer wrote, "Never has the curtain risen on this beautiful masterpiece of stage scenic art but that it has been met with rapturous applause."[83] Hal said, "Anyone buying a ticket for my performance who wants their money back after the second act, I will refund them the full price of admission out of my own pocket."[84] The play was another hit.

By 1898 Hal was writing more than acting. *Human Hearts* and *Knobs o' Tennessee* were hits, and he wrote plays for popular stars. Chuck Connors starred in *From Bowery to Broadway*, Bob Fitzgibbons in *A Fight for Love*, and "Gentleman Jim" Corbett appeared in another. Hal returned to New York to try to reconcile with Bertha, renting an apartment near Columbia University on East 103rd overlooking Morningside Park. By year's end he had convinced her to move there with Wally, and on April 1, 1899, theatrical pages noted, "Mrs. Hal Reid and her husband have kissed and made up. Their divorce proceedings have been dismissed."[85]

Hal also purchased a large house on a hilltop above the shoreline borough of Highlands, New Jersey, a hilly and densely-forested promontory six miles directly south of Manhattan. Young Wally loved the remoteness of the Highlands estate but hated the often turbulent boat rides there. Like his memories of the 1896 tornado, he was never comfortable on boats, though he spent time sailing as a child.

The Highlands house was called "Glory View" for good reason; it was a three story mansion with large porches on the highest hill above Highlands Township. It was on Bay Street, a narrow road winding through the woods above the ocean. James Fenimore Cooper's book *Water Witch* was set down the street. The ruins of the 18th century inn Cooper called "The Rust-in-Lust" stood on the edge of their property, as did a natural spring said to have been used by Hendrick Hudson during his first exploration of the Hudson River. The family spent the week in the city, but most weekends found Wally and his friends exploring the woods around Glory View. As an adult he spoke fondly of "the time I spent at Glory View."[86] He was seldom seen around Highlands without his two Llewellyn setters.

In April 1898, Hal and Carter wrote a play about the sinking of the battleship *Maine* in Havana harbor that caused a sensation. Reid-Carter productions were known for lavish, expensive backdrops, but theater-goers were amazed at simulated explosions, the destruction of the Spanish fort, and the simulated sinking of several Spanish ships.[87] At the same time, Hal formally sold *Human Hearts* to Harry Miner, who offered the play for years afterward. Hal sold it for $500, and the play grossed over $2,000,000 for Miner.[88] Hal was wealthy from selling plays, and in early 1899 he and Bertha formed a company to perform his latest, *The Night Before Christmas*, touring the Midwest and south through 1899.

In early 1901 a Hal Reid play, *At the Old Crossroads*, toured the west coast with a young actor named Thomas Ince, while Hal took another on the road—*The Little Red School House*, with him and Bertha in the leads. In early April the company was in Toronto at the Valentine Stock Cabin and Hal saw a production of *East Lynne*, about which papers noted "Gladys Smith, the little tot whose work has been so much admired."[89] Gladys' father died from a head injury suffered unloading a ship in Toronto when she was four, and to make ends meet, her mother pushed her on stage at six. When Hal saw her, she was already a local favorite and he hired her for the fall *School House* tour,[90] which began in November in Ontario and wound its way through Detroit, Grand Rapids, and Ohio. Unfortunately for Gladys, the show closed in Cincinnati when Hal went off with friends and missed four days.

During the next few years, Hal frequently hired the Smith family—Gladys, mother Charlotte and younger siblings Jack and Lottie. In 1902–1903 they worked for him in *In Convict Stripes*, in 1904 *The Gypsy Girl*, and in 1906–1907 *For a Human Life*. Hal knew Gladys would become a star, which she did as Mary Pickford. Hal also hired another beautiful waif named Lillian Gish.

During the tours around 1900 Wally stayed in New York with his grandparents and aunts, separated from his parents. In mid–1901 Bertha again became estranged from the philandering Hal, but when she went to the Midwest to visit family she left Wally in New York. Bertha was recognized during her travels and mentioned in local papers like the April 25, 1901, Elyria, Ohio, paper that noted, "Bertha B. Westbrook, a prominent actress and wife of Hal Reid, the playwright, stopped off in Elyria on Monday to be the guest of her friend, Miss Ethel Kelbe of this city."[91]

When she returned, she and Wally moved to Highlands while Hal remained in the city and churned out hit plays like *Cripple Creek*, *A Mountain Romance*, *To Serve the Cross* and *The Confession*. Many of his earlier works, like *Home-spun Heart* and *Human Hearts* were still performed everywhere, with papers often mentioning a "Third Year!" or "Fourth Year!"[92] But he was still Hal and had a huge ego. A later review of *To Serve the Cross* said he was credited as "John Halleck Reid" and that "When Mr. Reid writes for the popular price houses [less expensive theaters] he is known as plain 'Hal Reid.'"[93]

In 1904, Hal and Bertha reconciled again and purchased a home across the street from Glory View called "River Rest." They kept the old house and rented it to Perriton Maxwell, publisher of *Cosmopolitan* and *The American Magazine*. River Rest was even larger than Glory View—twelve rooms in three-plus stories, with almost 100 feet of porch on two levels above the large lawn. It was 80 feet above the Shrewsbury River, which ran between the estate and the ocean.

Wally later wrote of his summers: "There was a sort of a cave in the neighborhood where we lived—there's always a cave where boys are concerned. Well, anyway ... we used to build our stories around it. Sometimes they were Indian stories and sometimes they were detective stories."[94] Wally dreamed of becoming a detective, "Not one of those soup-and-fish slick boys with a waxed French mustache. I wanted to go about with my eyes half-closed, a knowing half smile lurking about my mouth, and a long, monogrammed cigarette in a gold holder ... the regular, aristocratic upper class stuff."[95] Wally loved Highlands and usually claimed it as the place he grew up rather than St. Louis or New York.

He also learned how to drive there, which bred a love for speed that remained for the rest of his life. In the early 1900s, automobiles were rarely seen on country roads, a curiosity only the wealthy could afford. To see a teenager driving a car was unheard of, but at 12 Wally roared up and down the steep inclines and flew around the wooded corners in Highlands.

Just after his parents purchased River Rest, Wally was sent to military school. Why he was sent to Freehold Military School depended upon who was asked. Bertha said he was too tall (at almost six feet) to go to school with his shorter friends, but Hal hoped that a military environment would toughen up his son. Having Wally away also made it easier for his parents to travel.

The Reid family's "River Rest" estate in the hills above the Shrewsbury River and Highlands, New Jersey, during his childhood. It burned to the ground in the 1920s.

Freehold, New Jersey, location of the military school, dates to the 1600s and was the site of a Revolutionary War battle that gave birth to the legend of town resident Molly Pitcher. In 1845 the school was called the Freehold Young Ladie's (sic) Seminary and later, the Freehold Institute for Boys, but in 1900 Colonel Charles J. Wright closed the Freehold Institute and re-opened it as the New Jersey Military Academy. Shortly after, the Freehold Military School was added. In 1904, after four years, girls were prohibited from both institutions.

The schools offered "Select home school, limited to 40 [students]. Small classes. Military training and discipline, but not a reformatory nature.[96] Refined surroundings. Gymnasium. Athletic sports. We prepare for any college. Rates $450 to $500. Reply to Major C.M. Duncan, Principal." It was "designed to meet the needs of a military school for young boys only—an institution where the boy of tender years can benefit by the unquestionable advantages of military training and be free from influence of boys of maturer years.... Every cadet is the subject of individual care and tutelage."

Class and dorm rooms filled three large colonial buildings next to a park in the middle of Freehold, dominated by the main classroom building, 3-stories with a large steeple. Next door was a 3-story house with a barracks wing where students lived and ate. There were parade grounds on all sides for drills and precision marching, and athletic fields in the glade below.

Freehold was almost exactly halfway between New York and Atlantic City, so a steady stream of visitors stopped at one of the two hotels. There was the American Hotel, a strange combination of Spanish mission style and New England colonial which dated to 1824, and the three-story Belmont Hotel, which Bertha preferred. The stately Belmont dominated the main square, filling the corner of West Main and South Streets two blocks deep. The hotel's flagpole soared 100 feet above the town square, and huge wrap-around porches with sun-shades and dozens of rocking chairs offered surprising luxury amid the bucolic surroundings. On both sides of the dirt streets nearby were shops and restaurants.

When Wally arrived in 1904 there were 150 students at the two schools. It was a strict military environment, with daily drills and inspections. In the morning the boys had exactly three minutes to get up, make beds and dress for inspection. It was more discipline than Wally expected, wanted, or knew. The Wally Reid who arrived at Freehold was spoiled and wealthy, had not yet grown into his athletic body, and more at ease writing than playing sports. At first he did not fit in with the mix of boys, most of which were there for disciplinary reasons or from military families. It was a tough crowd and he was an easy target for abuse from upper classmen of higher rank. He was placed "on guard" almost weekly for real or imagined infractions, and bristled at the regimentation and abuse. The rancor between Wally and some of his classmates culminated in a brawl his first semester. A classmate Bertha described as "a hot head of Latin blood"[97] stabbed Wally in the thigh, landing him in the infirmary for a week, one of several such skirmishes.

Nearby Lake Topanemus offered a refreshing break when the boys could sneak from the barracks. Wally got caught sneaking out several times and was almost expelled, and his attempts to fit in were not helped by weekly visits by his mother and Aunt Maud. He missed his mother as much as she missed him, which added to his misery. His feelings for her are evident in a poem he wrote at Christmas:

Wally, and his adoring mother, at 4, 13 and 18.

As I sit by the rain-lashed window
Looking out at the dreary day,
The vision comes before me,
And drives the rain away,
To leave but the glorious sunshine
Of a love so pure and good,
I deserve not, tho' it is mine
The love of motherhood.

That love so great and glorious,
That the waters as they swirled-
Sang, "The hand that rocks the cradle,
Is the hand that rules the world."
The poets sing of heroes
And martyrs great and good,
But none so pure as thou dear,
With thy love of motherhood.

Wally signed it, "Christmas, 1904, Dedicated to My Mother. W. Wallace Reid." To the card he added an inscription that indicates that even at 12 he was aware of her difficulties with Hal, writing, "She who has stood by her two erring boys with the patience of Job and the forgiveness of the Saviour." Attached to a poem given his father, who recently reconciled yet again with Bertha, Wally wrote, "To My Father, He who deserves great admiration for a wonderful change."

Wally made some friends at Freehold but had chronic disciplinary problems, and his grades were poor, described even by his mother as "appallingly low."[98] He was ranked among the lowest of the 150 students, and at the end-of-year ceremony the only award he earned was for public speaking. After a year Wally was sent to another school. Later writings by Wally and Bertha suggested the move was brought on by his desire to attend Princeton medical school, and she said he passed entrance exams for the prestigious school, but that is doubtful.[99]

Bertha chose the Perkiomen Seminary, a boarding school in Pennsburg, Pennsylvania, founded in 1887 by followers of 16th-century German theologian Kaspar von Schwenkfeld, who believed in divine guidance and was a supporter of daily "Quiet Time" for reflection. The campus was 50 miles northwest of Philadelphia and 120 miles from Highlands. A history of Bucks County, Pennsylvania, described the school in 1906 as "30 teachers and an enrollment of 361 ... equipped with new modern buildings, chemical and physical laboratories, gymnasium, athletic field, etc. Pure fresh air and an abundance of excellent spring water supply the school which is heated by steam and lighted by electricity."[100] Unlike Freehold's military bearing, Perkiomen's was college prep in a gorgeous setting in the Pennsylvania hills, much like Highlands. Graduates went to colleges like Harvard, Yale, Princeton, and many of the best institutions in the East. And Perkiomen was co-ed. Academy Award–winning songwriter Al Dubin attended while Wally was there (two years behind), and playwright John Cecil Holm later attended.

Enrolling in 1906 in the Call (class) of 1909, Wally thrived and spoke glowingly of the school and his time there. He had grown to over six feet tall and his natural athleticism and creativity were developing. He played football and ran track and was pop-

Top: Early postcard view of students doing marching drills at the New Jersey Military Academy at the time of Wally's attendance, ca. 1905. *Above:* The Belmont Hotel in Freehold, New Jersey, ca. 1915, where Bertha stayed while visiting Wally at the New Jersey Military Academy.

ular with the girls. On team rosters in his junior yearbook (1908–1909) he was listed as "W. Wallace Reid."[101] He was a right offensive tackle on the football team that won four of their eight games against teams like Allentown Prep., Villanova, and Drexel Institute. Even though he was thin, Wally competed in strength events on the track team. Listed among "RESULTS OF THE JUNIOR-SENIOR CLASS MEET '08," Wally placed second in his three events— the high jump, hammer throw and shot put—finishing behind an older senior in each. His creative talents also expanded. He was an editor of the school newspaper and yearbook; he gave the yearbook its name "The Griffin," which is still used today; and he designed the Griffin logo, also still in place. Wally is visible in football and track team pictures, and the books' sketch illustrations were all done and signed "WWReid."

More specific records of Wally's years at Perkiomen were lost in a 1990s fire that destroyed most early 1900s records. A 1908 yearbook in the school's possession is the only record of his time there. During his 1908 summer vacation Wally allegedly

Top: The 1908 yearbook photograph of the Perkiomen Football Team, with Wally top row center. *Above:* The 1908 yearbook photograph of the Perkiomen Track Team, with a lanky Wally top row left (both courtesy Diana Weir-Smith, Perkiomen School).

made his first adult stage appearance, in a Robert Edeson vehicle, *Unto the Fourth Generation*. In the opening night audience were two of New York's biggest theatrical producers, Daniel Frohman and Henry B. Harris (who later died in the sinking of the RMS *Titanic*). There is doubt Wally actually performed, though. He tried out but there is no confirmation he appeared,[102] even though Frohman and Harris later recalled offering him contracts. Their stories may be apocryphal; in any event, Wally wasn't interested.

Wally's educational history is contradictory. According to Bertha, he attended Perkiomen for four years preparing for Princeton. Wally's later writings mentioned "most

Perkiomen graduates go to Lafayette, their college alma mater, so I trailed along with them." Both Bertha and Wally later hinted that he attended college, but he did not. In fact, he didn't even graduate with his 1909 class at Perkiomen and wasn't mentioned in the 1909 yearbook at all. There was no academic or disciplinary reason for Wally's departure, but after his junior year he simply left.

Later writings by Bertha and Wally offered clues to his sudden departure. At Perkiomen, Wally dated often and said himself that he fell in love for the first time while there. He was a talented athlete and creative writer but was an immature 17 year old. Coddled by his family and brought up in a dysfunctional environment, he seemed to fall in love with every woman he kissed. He introduced Bertha to a classmate at a luncheon at New York's Knickerbocker Hotel in the spring of 1908. Bertha described her as a beautiful young girl that Wally had asked to marry, but when "he offered her his heart and his name, she declined."[103] She told Wally she "was too young, only 15,"[104] indeed much too young to marry. But for Wally, who didn't understand, it was heart-wrenching.

Title page of the 1908 Perkiomen Yearbook, with Wally's name and signature listed as "Chief Illustrator" (Diana Weir-Smith, Perkiomen School).

Above: One of Wally's drawings in the 1908 Perkiomen Yearbook. *Right:* The Perkiomen School Griffin logo, designed by Wally during his school days and still in use today (both courtesy Diana Weir-Smith, Perkiomen School).

Wally spoke sentimentally of his years at Perkiomen and of his "school-boy love affairs"[105] there. But apparently the rejection of the young woman led him to run away. At least he had an interesting place to go. "Buffalo" Bill Cody and Hal were friends; Hal wrote a play for him in 1908. During a visit to Highlands that summer Wally mentioned to Cody his wish to visit the West, fueled no doubt by the end of his first love affair.

Wally told Cody, "I'd like to go west for awhile, Mr. Cody. I think it would do me a lot more good than going to college." Cody replied, "I'll write a letter to my sister. If you ever get out to our town, I reckon she'll see you get cakes, anyhow."[106] Within days Wally was on a train for Wyoming, against his parents' wishes. In the remote outpost Wally would try to get over his lost love, in a place he could also just be Wally, not "Hal Reid's son."[107] As Wally headed west in the spring of 1909, Hal and Bertha finally, mercifully, divorced. She lived at River Rest and Hal stayed at a New York apartment.

Wally arrived in Cody with his introduction letter from Bill Cody. Such letters were commonplace; it assured a place to stay, perhaps a job, or whatever help might be needed in a strange place. The town of Cody was founded in 1896 to service the tourists expected to visit the newly-opened Yellowstone National Park. Bill Cody invested in the area after learning about it from his son-in-law (the original park surveyor) and opened the first hotel—the Hotel Irma—in 1902. It was named for his daughter, run by his sister May and her husband Lou Decker. Wally sought out May, later writing, "When I arrived, I had 15¢ in my pocket. I went to the hotel, registered and strolled into the dining room. There was a pretty waitress and I tipped her and the next day went to work."[108] He was hired as the night clerk and manager and allowed to live at the hotel. It was a grimy frontier place described by National Park Director Stephen Mather as "the dirtiest, most unsanitary

Cody, Wyoming, at the time of Wally's visit, as seen from the front of the Irma Hotel.

The Irma Hotel, where Wally lived and worked for six months during his sojourn in the remote Wyoming wilderness.

place I had ever seen," with "horrible, greasy, inedible food served by loud, boisterous, grimy ... waitresses."[109] May paid Wally $30 a month, with free food ("cakes") and a room.

Like the Irma, in 1909 Cody was a free-for-all full of plainsmen, Indians, prospectors and people trying to make a living off the new park. The hotel's brown leather lobby chairs were usually full of cowboys trading stories and drinks during the warm Wyoming evenings. Wally soaked in the dusty atmosphere for three months before deciding he needed a change. He hadn't come west to be a clerk so he bought a horse and ventured out. May told him, "I reckon it won't do you no harm. You're too young to stay put yet awhile."[110]

For the next nine months Wally roamed Wyoming on his horse, finding work as a ranch hand for a few weeks at a time. Eventually he hired on as a pick-and-shovel laborer with a surveying company working in the mountains on the Shoshone Dam irrigation project. He also did some surveying. The project was one of Bill Cody's investments; his company brought water down the mountain to irrigate 6,500 acres of farmland. Wally spent seven months in the mountains and learned horsemanship, hunting, shooting, and mountaineering. He became an expert outdoorsman.

During a weekend hunting jaunt in the Big Horn basin, Wally shot an antelope. When he located the carcass, darkness prevented him from leaving the remote, rocky canyon so he used the remains for warmth. He would field dress the animal the next morning, and slept under a tree next to the body. When he awoke there was little left but bones; a mountain lion had eaten his kill during the night. "I never knew why he didn't eat me too," Wally said years later, "I guess he filled up on antelope and didn't want dessert."[111]

Wally recalled his 11 months in Wyoming as "the happiest time that ever came to me."[112] He was independent and, more importantly, anonymous, just Wally. Just another guy on a horse. He never enjoyed the attention brought on by his looks or athleticism. In Wyoming he was just another dirty cowboy riding a horse along a fence. He was enthralled with the beauty of the landscape, enjoyed the camaraderie of his cowboy pals and thirsted for the physical work. He would have stayed had his father not intervened. In retrospect, it would have helped his development as a man had he been allowed to stay. It was one of the few times he lived on equal footing with other men, but Hal had other plans.

In the spring of 1910 Hal put an end to Wally's peaceful interlude. Wally wired that he intended to stay in Wyoming, so Hal replied via a telegram telling him that his mother was near death. Frantic, Wally boarded a train for New Jersey. When he arrived in Highlands pale and anxious he was told Bertha was out riding with his aunt. When she returned he discovered the ruse, but it was too late to return west and he regretfully stayed in New Jersey. Bertha maintained she knew nothing of Hal's treachery. Wally was at another crossroads and yet again retreated to indecisive ways. Wanting to return to Wyoming, he nonetheless stayed in Highlands.

With nothing else to do, he took a job as a reporter at the Newark *Morning Star* earning $10 a week reporting police stories and an occasional morgue assignment. He was talented, and in a few months was writing the daily column "As Told in Essex"[113] and was hired as Atlantic Coast correspondent for the *New York Journal*. But he did not like reporting and didn't have what St. Johns described as the "ferret quality of diving down deep and bringing up what was hidden."[114] His disinterest in glamorizing the pathos in a story cost him his job when he refused to print personal details about one of his subjects, details that found their way into another paper. When St. Johns asked him about the firing years later, he told her, "What the hell is a newspaper? Maybe I'm wrong, but I could never throw down a human being for anything as abstract as a newspaper."[115]

Wally was unconcerned. Hal nagged him to appear in a play touring small Midwestern theaters, a western Wally helped Hal write entitled *The Girl and the Ranger*. When a juvenile actor got sick Wally took the role. Bertha and Hal fought viciously over this. She had experienced the emotional roller coaster that was Hal and theater, and although they were wealthy because of his work, Bertha didn't want Wally involved with Hal. She believed that life with Hal would be bad for Wally, that the glittery, careless stage life would harm her son. But Hal won and Wally went. In a later writing Wally suggested he "persuaded my father to get me a small role in one of his sketches,"[116] but that was not true according to Bertha.

With virtually no experience, during the spring of 1910 Wally traveled the Midwest with Hal's *Ranger* troupe. The play ended in Chicago in April or May. Wally didn't know it but he was on his way to "the movies." But he didn't want to act. He told St. Johns, "I've seen so much. I've really been close to and had a lot of experience with all sorts of interesting people and unusual places. When they let me quit acting I'm going to write my own scenarios and direct them myself."[117] If only it were that easy.

2

Finding "the Movies"

The "movies" were not born of creative parents. It wasn't writers or actors who dreamt up the idea of projecting images onto a screen. Movies' parents were scientists, men with ideas. Entrepreneurs became rich and famous from the idea, but it was scientists who directed the birth.

The first image on a screen occurred in 1659 when Dutchman Christian Huygens devised a lantern projector using a candle to light glass transparencies through a simple lens. By the mid–1800s the illusion of motion was created, first by the 1826 "thaumatrope," which rotated a card with two images printed on opposites like a bird and a cage, then the 1834 "Phenakistiscope," similar to "flip books" made by children today.[1] The first successful motion photography grew out of a $25,000 bet in 1877, when California governor Leland Stanford hired Eadweard Muybridge to prove that a galloping horse lifts all four hoofs off the ground simultaneously. Muybridge lined up 24 cameras next to a track with strings attached to shutters, and when the horse tripped the shutters, 24 closely-spaced pictures proved Stanford's contention. The seminal moment in the birth of the movies came about on a bet.

Thomas Alva Edison and William K.L. Dickson designed early cameras at the first movie studio, a darkened New Jersey building with a movable roof called the "Black Maria." In 1891 they built free-standing wooden boxes with an eyepiece called "Kinetoscopes" that let viewers watch a short movie for 5¢. His first was his friend Fred Ott sneezing.[2] In 1895, Thomas Armat patented a projector called a Vitascope that put Edison's films onto a screen. The Edison Manufacturing Co. built cameras and projectors and made films, but French inventors Louis and Auguste Lumière patented the first real projector and camera, the Lumière Cinématographe, in 1895. On December 28, 1895, they held the first public screening of a 20-second film of employees leaving the Lumière Factory.[3] Lumière films showing a steam engine chugging toward the camera before swerving away or a cowboy firing a gun caused viewers to dive to the floor or scream in fear.

On April 20, 1896, at Koster & Bial's Music Hall in New York, the first paying customers watched Edison films, such as the surf breaking on a beach, a comic boxing exhibition, or two young women dancing, an experience *The New York Times* described as "wonderfully real and singularly exhilarating."[4] We take technology for granted, but barely a year earlier, T.L. Tally opened an L.A. "phonograph parlor" in a tiny storefront where patrons paid 10¢ to hear "canned music" on phonographs. One at a time, 15 people listened through ear tubes attached to a speaker.[5] People paid just to *listen*. *Seeing* something move was unfathomable.

Harry Carr, a Mack Sennett publicity man, recalled "old man Tally's peek-for-a-nickel show in a booth under the old Ramona Hotel, on the corner of Spring and Third streets downtown. One day he rushed out in great excitement and stopped me as I was ambling along the sidewalk. 'Come in here,' he said, 'I've got the darndest thing; they call it a moving picture.' I went in and saw my first movie, James J. Corbett, the champion of the world, punching the nose of one Courtney, on a screen that leaped and flickered and jumped."[6]

Dickson and Edison filmed everyday events, like dancer *Carmencita* or *Sandow* lifting weights. There was little craftsmanship, but that changed by accident when Frenchman Georges Méliès' camera jammed and caused an object to disappear. He used the mistake in films, and suddenly they were stories with effects, like the fade-in and -out, dissolve, and even animation. Méliès' 1902 *A Trip to the Moon* was a sensation, showing a rocket ship landing in the eye of the man in the moon and disappearing space creatures. Inspired by Méliès, Edison lengthened his movies, and in 1902 his chief cameraman Edwin S. Porter took nine 50-foot-long films (all about fires, a favorite Edison theme) and spliced them into a 450-foot *The Life of an American Fireman*.[7]

By the late 1890s, studios were popping up all over New York. Edison made films in the Bronx. Biograph was in a converted brownstone at 11 East 14th Street in Manhattan, and others operated in the wilds of Fort Lee, New Jersey. In 1897, J. Stuart Blackton and Albert E. Smith opened American Vitagraph on the roof of the Morse Building in Manhattan,[8] and by 1910 the Europeans arrived. By 1912, J.A. Berst, U.S. manager of Pathé Frères, was making the most popular films in the world, including the later *The Perils of Pauline* (from 1914) with Pearl White.

In 1908, Edison organized the Motion Pictures Patents Company (MPPC), "The Trust," a merger of Edison, Biograph, Vitagraph, Essanay, Lubin, Selig, Kalem, Méliès and Pathé, to try to take control of the new industry. He obtained 16 patents for cameras and projectors, and made a deal with Eastman Kodak for raw film; filmmakers had to pay a licensing fee to the MPPC for everything,[9] and exhibitors could only offer films made by members. Edison hired hundreds of spies to sneak into studios and onto sets looking for unlicensed or copied products. If they found an illegal camera they simply took it. His "patents' goons" also destroyed negatives, stole film, and beat up directors and actors. Early movie directors carried sidearms for more than just appearance. The MPPC hired snipers to shoot cameras from afar—cameras rather than actors or cameramen because cameras were harder to replace.[10] Director Allan Dwan routinely posted sentries armed with rifles.[11]

It wasn't just the weather that brought studios to California; Edison's private army contributed to an exodus from the East Coast. It was easier to hide unlicensed equipment in L.A., and Jesse Lasky mentioned another benefit—"the Mexican border handy for emergencies."[12] Unlicensed studios were everywhere, Florida, Cuba, Texas, and even Oregon, escaping the goons.[13]

Films were from 750 to 1000 feet long and lasted 8 to 10 minutes. From 20 to 50 copies of a finished film might be sold, usually at 12¢ to 15¢ a foot, or about $150 a copy. In 1908 and 1909, a typical Biograph short brought in about $2,800.[14] People became "actors" simply by walking into a studio. Most came from vaudeville circuits or the legitimate stage. As Minta Durfee[15] later remembered, "the stage seemed to be losing its glamour ... the Orpheum Circuit and the Sullivan-Considine Circuit, or the legitimate plays, they would all quit and everybody just meandered over to the [studios]...."[16] Usually movie players were *not* the upper strata of stage performers, but local stock players.[17] Their inexperience and exaggerated pantomime usually ended up on film. Dorothy

Davenport explained, "If you toured in stock and *then* went into films you brought a little extra besides a face. You could do scenes, and handle lines." But she added, "You hoped what looked natural in the theater didn't register on the big screen as something grotesque."[18]

In 1910, when Wally Reid entered the movies, the industry was in upheaval. There were 13,100 U.S. movie theaters and 26,000,000 people a week paying an average of 7¢ a ticket to see a movie. New studios and stars were born every day. The patent wars were ongoing. Edison became even more powerful; he formed a subsidiary of the MPPC, General Film Company, that bought up regional film exchanges and by 1910 owned every film exchange in the U.S. except one. But the sheer number of independent production companies meant too many small battles for the MPPC, and by 1915 Edison's monopoly was legislated out.

Amid this tumult Wally traveled to Chicago with Hal in April 1910. Hal's troupe was performing *The Girl and the Ranger*, and Hal met with William Selig's Polyscope Film Company and Selig's rival Essanay Studios.[19] Hal was trying to sell *The Confession*, a scenario written by Wally from one of Hal's plays. Its controversial theme—a priest's insistence on keeping a confession inviolate—made it difficult to sell.[20]

Wally fell under the spell of the movies. He wanted in, but as a cameraman, not as an actor. When the Reid troupe left Chicago, he stayed to work for legendary "Colonel" William N. Selig. Selig was born in 1864 in Chicago, but as a chronically sick child was sent to California for the milder climate. In the 1880s he joined a minstrel show as magician "Colonel Selig, Conjurer," but during an 1895 trip to Dallas he saw a Kinetoscope, quit the show and moved back to Chicago to open a movie studio. He altered a Lumière camera and a Latham projector, named his "inventions" the Selig Standard Camera and Selig Polyscope Projector, and formed the Mutoscope & Film Company on April 9, 1896. He sold his equipment through the Sears & Roebuck mail-order catalog. Selig Polyscope Company later rented a warehouse on the northwest corner of Byron and Claremont Avenues and engraved his trademark "Diamond S" in marble over the entrance. Selig soon owned the entire block and connected buildings with underground tunnels.

The studio was on Chicago's north side, not far from present-day Wrigley Field near the large Revere and Horner Parks, with the Chicago River nearby. The area offered excellent exterior venues. Selig filmed local life, like *Chicago Police Parade* (1901) and *A Trip Around the Union Loop* (1903), the huge Chicago stockyards and visits by Theodore Roosevelt, Admiral George Dewey and President William McKinley. By 1905 Selig was "The biggest motion picture company in the country,"[21] and William Selig was wealthy. He lived with eight servants in a mansion at 398 Garfield Boulevard in Chicago's elegant Hyde Park,[22] and later a larger mansion at 5356 North Magnolia.[23]

Selig made the first feature-length films and the first American serial, Kathlyn Williams' *The Adventures of Kathlyn*. He made one of the first animated serials, the "*Seligettes*," and was among the first to make westerns. He hired "Broncho Billy" Anderson, found cowboy Tom Mix at a Wild West show, and Edward "Hoot" Gibson at the Dick Stanley Congress of Rough Riders show. In 1909 Selig began making films with a marvelously-talented 300-pound comedian named Roscoe Arbuckle. "Fatty" films like *Ben's Kid, Mrs. Jones' Birthday* (both 1909) and *The Sanitarium* (1910) made both men world-famous. Selig was also among the first to use California settings when he sent Francis Boggs and cameraman Thomas Persons to La Jolla to film exteriors for *The Count of Monte Cristo* in 1907.

Hal sold several scenarios to Selig during the 1910 visit with Wally. Hobart Bosworth's[24] *A Tale of the Sea*, released in late 1910, was based on one of his poems, as was the June 1911 film *Jim & Joe*. Hal also sold *Human Hearts*, but Selig didn't use it for another year. Wally joined Selig in April or May 1910 and was paid $25 a week as an assistant to lead director Otis Turner. Everyone called Turner "Daddy" or "the Governor." Wally worked as an assistant director, scenario writer, cameraman and utility man,[25] but preferred camera work. Selig cameraman Charles Rosher said Wally, "playing small parts, could also crank the handle, and sometimes we changed places. While he shot the film, I was made up with side whiskers and a beard and I acted with the rest of the players."[26]

Cameramen cranked a handle on the side of a box to move and expose the film. The best filmed without ever varying pace; pace filmed was pace on-screen. If the cameraman lost *his* pace, the film pace suffered, but steady timing was difficult since cameramen were often in harrowing positions like atop a moving car or wagon. And Selig loved animal films so his cameramen sometimes filmed *inside* cages with live animals. Wally worked hard at everything except acting. He had no interest in that job.

Wally later said he joined "more from curiosity than anything else,"[27] and that he "had all sorts of varied experiences with Selig. I was character actor, director, and cameraman. There were days when we made up the stories as we went along. I would start directing the picture, jump in front of the camera in the lead, paste on a moustache to play the villain, and turn the camera crank if the regular cameraman became tired or went to lunch."[28] In the early years a "movie star" life was not glamorous, as Harry Carr recalled:

> Jack Pickford used to tell me ruefully that picture acting would be all right if you didn't have to do so much freight carrying. He and Bobby Harron were the two youngest actors so they had to ride to location on bicycles and carry the props for the other actors. In the mornings, they would be wild Indians marauding around on war ponies. In the afternoon ... change clothes and chase over the hills as U.S. cavalrymen. The girls of the company were required to be no less versatile. Dorothy Gish ... in the morning, she had to be an innocent country girl fleeing the demon Sioux. In the afternoon, she was a vicious gun man with a long beard—which tickled her neck.[29]

Wally made light of acting because he had no desire to be an actor. He was happiest behind the camera. St. Johns wrote, "Wally tried hard to be everything in motion pictures *except* a star. He was a cameraman, a writer, and a director, and preferred any of them to acting."[30] Wally undoubtedly acted in dozens of Selig's 1910 films because extra crew always appeared on camera, but his only credited role was his debut film *The Phoenix*, filmed in late April and released July 18. It was a typical single-reeler, with Wally credited as "the reporter." The movie was an adaptation of a play written by Milton Nobles, who starred with his wife Dolly. They had appeared in the stage version; coincidently, in the 1890s so had Hal and Bertha. Wally played a young newspaper reporter who rescues the heroine from drowning and from being burned to death. *The Phoenix* illustrates the pace of production. Scenarios written during morning coffee were filmed after lunch. Wally said, "I landed my first job because I could swim ... with the Selig Company in Chicago. I saved a heroine from the icy waters of Lake Michigan and then from a burning building in the same movie, 'The Phoenix.'"[31]

Other than that role, there is no record of Wally on any other 1910 films. During that time, Selig made the first versions of L. Frank Baum's popular *Oz* books, including *The Wonderful Wizard of Oz, Dorothy and the Scarecrow of Oz, The Land of Oz*, and *John Dough the Cherub*. The last three were made while Wally was there and directed by Turner, so Wally doubtless worked on them, but that isn't confirmed. It's hard to confirm films Wally worked on, but he probably worked *somewhere* on all of Turner's films between April and

October, 1910. Wally stayed until November, later saying he learned "the camera, use of crepe hair—I was the utility man and *always* wore variegated whiskers—and how to write scenarios. At the time I had no idea of sticking with the business so returned to New York that winter and went to work as an assistant editor of *Motor Magazine*."[32]

Wally actually returned because Bertha was seriously injured when her car was struck by a streetcar. She, of course, wired Wally and he left Selig to be at her side, caring for her through the winter. He was hired at *Motor Magazine* by publisher Perriton Maxwell, who was renting the Reid's old Highlands Glory View estate. It was a perfect job for Wally, obsessed with cars since he was young. He went to car shows and races, test-drove new cars and wrote reviews. Wally enjoyed the job, but as he remembered, "springtime came and life in 'the office' became a nightmare so I went over and knocked on the Vitagraph gates and said, 'Please let me in.' They did, and here I am."[33]

He arrived at Vitagraph with his *Confession* script. Later biographical materials credit Wally as appearing in the film, and adding to the confusion, *he* mentioned appearing in the film along with Hal, Jimmie Morrison, Maurice Costello, and Harry Morey.[34] But it isn't likely Vitagraph even *made* the film; it had the same controversial theme that prevented Hal from selling it earlier. Vitagraph purchased the scenario but didn't make the movie for five years; also, Morrison, Costello and Morey never worked together as far as we know.

Wally had several jobs at Vitagraph—writing, camera, and playing the violin or viola during filming as background to help the actors emote. Geraldine Farrar is credited with being the first to ask for musical accompaniment to work up emotion, but at Vitagraph as early as 1910 director Dick Rosson picked up a violin to help Florence Lawrence do the same.[35] Wally began taking small unbilled roles, his first in *The Leading Lady* with John Bunny, a 47-year-old, short (5'4"), 300-pound former stage actor. *Lady* was a one-reel gag comedy directed by Ned Finley, with Bunny playing the female lead alongside Wally and Van Dyke Brooke. The film did little for Wally's image. He played a female.[36] *Lady* was Bunny's twentieth Vitagraph film and he made 225 more during the next four years, most of them with Flora Finch. Movie theaters were named after him and had rabbit figures carved in granite over marquees. When he died, his *New York Times* obituary noted, "John Bunny's name will forever be linked to the movies."[37] But in five years he was forgotten and today is absent from most movie history books. He just disappeared, like Wally years later.

When Vitagraph released *The Leading Lady* on April 11, 1911, Wally had fallen in love again. The New York opening of Hal's play *The Confession* was at the Bijou Theater at 1239 Broadway, on March 13, 1911. Among the cast was Theodore Roberts, who later worked with Wally in dozens of movies.[38] After the performance the cast and well-heeled audience members gathered for an impromptu lobby celebration. Among attendees were wealthy L.A. theater patrons Charles and Mamie Modini-Wood and their daughter Elizabeth.

Like Wally, she was 19, "beautiful of character and disposition, marvelously beautiful to look upon, talented, cultured and altogether fascinating."[39] She was a talented singer; the family was on their way to Italy where she would study opera in Florence. She looked almost Spanish, with long black hair and glowing brown eyes, wore jeweled hair combs and lace mantillas and affected a romantic look even standing still. She was breathtakingly beautiful. For two months the doe-eyed beauty and Wally were inseparable.

Her father was a California real estate investor whose family was among the first to settle in the state. His love of music led him to open one of the first opera houses in the state; he changed the family name from Wood to "Modini-Wood" to sound Italian. There were no Modinis in the family. They were both Midwesterners. The couple, daughters Elizabeth, Hanna, and Mona, and son William, were prominent among L.A.'s social elite. They lived in a 25-room mansion at fashionable 20 St. James Park with a half dozen servants, and had one of only a dozen handmade Estey pipe organs in the state (all others were in large churches).

From March into May, Wally and Elizabeth were rarely apart. They attended plays, toured the city's museums and parks, and spent weekends at Highlands, Wally speeding down the roads with Elizabeth at his side. In early May 1911, Wally and Elizabeth announced they would marry. Bertha was thrilled; she had no idea the Modini-Woods were not really opera royalty and felt Elizabeth a perfect wife for her son. But Charles Wood had other ideas. Even with his own faux background, he looked on Wally's job in the movies with disdain. In 1910 the movies were still snubbed by the legitimate stage as an art form beneath them, and when Charles learned of his daughter's engagement he quickly packed up the family and left for Europe early. By the end of May, Wally's fiancée was gone.

It may have had something to do with Hal, whose reputation as a womanizer had gotten worse. His forgotten rape problem was replaced by dozens of stories of infidelity, illegitimate children and tawdry affairs. His brilliance as a writer hid his personal problems. Hal or not, Wally's Elizabeth was gone. Later, Mona became a successful opera writer and Wally's ex-fiancée married James Langford Stack. Their second child—Charles Langford Modini Stack—became better known as Robert Stack.

It was the summer of 1911. Wally's engagement was over and his fiancée gone. He was again shattered, his heart broken, and again he ran. When his Perkiomen love turned down his proposal he fled to Wyoming. When Elizabeth was taken from him he went farther west, to California. Wally headed toward L.A. and back to Selig.

At this time he was credited with another film that is difficult to confirm. Some filmographies—including one confirmed by Dorothy in the 1960s[40]—include the Selig short *The Reporter*, which featured Fred Woltan, Sam Pickens, Karl King, and Barbara Swager. It was released June 26, 1911; most of that April and May he had squired Elizabeth around New York, which was noted by his mother, who made no mention of film work. Had he done a film she probably would have mentioned such. And Selig did not have a New York operation. His studios were in Chicago and Hollywood, and there was a small one in New Orleans. Further, *The Reporter* was a split reel short, meaning it had other material included, action from *Scenes from Our Navy*. But Dorothy later wrote that he played an assistant to a reporter writing a story "How It Feels to Be a Burglar."

In June he headed west, intending not to act but to work as a cameraman. He told St. Johns, "I was never going to act again."[41] Later he wistfully told her, "When you put grease paint on the face, something goes out of the heart."[42] Wally felt acting was more natural for women than men, that it was more natural for women to make something out of their looks and charms (what he considered an unnatural act for men). He often quoted Arnold Bennett,[43] who said, "A great actress is something more than a woman, but the greatest actor is something less than a man."[44]

Wally met his mother for lunch at the Knickerbocker Hotel to break the news. Bertha recalled him saying, "Mother dear, I will not have the time nor opportunity to come down home before I go ... and I cannot go, 'sweetheart mother,' without seeing you before I do."[45] Normally, we would assume such a saccharine remembrance to be exaggerated, but Wally did indeed speak with his mother like that. Around her, his actions were very different from his image. He often grabbed her in his arms and picked her up over his head, crowing, "Darling little mother, sweetheart mother mine!" It was lucky that his fans didn't hear these stories until after his death. Image, as they say, is everything.

As tough as he was handsome, as athletic as he was manly, Wally did not appear to be a "man's man." He had few close male friends. Some men likely found him effeminate. His own lack of conceit added to this image. From his youth, Wally's self-effacing attitude was sometimes off-putting. St. Johns described the predicament, saying, "His truthfulness about himself gave people the ammunition to attack him. He admitted his faults to people too readily, and people who did not understand the humility of the boy's soul misjudged him cruelly."[46] But beyond that, even at 19 he had not developed much as a person. More time in Wyoming may have helped that internal growth, but Hal ended that. The acting career he was about to embark on led to self-contempt that washed over him like a tide later in life.

His life had been affected by a number of influences. His overly protective mother left him psychologically weaker than he may have been otherwise. His decision not to go to college stunted development that may have taken place there. Hal's telegram that brought him back from the Wyoming life he loved and his decision to stay in Highlands further stifled development that probably would have left Wally a different man. It would have at least made him stronger. He had two serious relationships and in both cases immediately asked the woman to marry him. When the first refused and the second was taken away, Wally ran. The first time to Wyoming. The second, to the movies.

His inability to assume control or take a lead in his friendships with men eventually led to his death. But in the interim he would meet another woman. And he would almost immediately ask her to marry. In fiancée number three, Wally luckily found a woman who ignored his indecision and didn't mind controlling the relationship.

Selig built a California studio in 1908 and moved everything there in 1911. During his 1911 trip west he stopped in Canyon City, Colorado, to visit one of his companies above the Rocky Mountain timberline making *Told in Colorado* (1911) with Tom Mix, Tom Carrigan, Myrtle Stedman, and William Duncan. When Mix asked Selig where they were going, he was told, "in some foothills near L.A. It's just a bare little place, and you've probably never heard of it. It's called Hollywood."[47]

Wally's old boss Otis "Daddy" Turner had gone to Edendale the previous March and was producing three or four one-reelers a week. As an inducement to join him, Turner gave Wally a raise from $25 to $40 weekly, and when he arrived in June, Selig's Edendale operation was the largest in Hollywood. Only 319,198 people lived in L.A.

During Colonel William Selig's 1911 studio move to California, the group stopped for this photograph taken at the Continental Divide in Colorado; Wally joined the studio shortly after their arrival in Hollywood (courtesy Jeff Look).

county; in Edendale about 5,000. Compared to the other studios in Edendale it was a palace. When D.W. Griffith arrived in January 1910, he rented a vacant lot at Georgia and 12th streets, lined it with dressing room tents and made movies with Henry Walthall, Owen Moore, and Jack and Mary Pickford.[48] Selig, the first permanent movie studio in Hollywood, was at 1845 Allesandro Street (now Glendale Boulevard). The first film was the Francis Boggs–directed *In the Sultan's Power*, which starred Hobart Bosworth and Tom Santschi, and is often credited as the first movie filmed entirely in California. The studio was making popular westerns and did well with their *Oz* films, and when Selig's 1909 film of Teddy Roosevelt, *Hunting Big Game in Africa*, became a hit he changed his billing to "Colonel" and purchased a huge menagerie of African animals for exotic jungle movies using authentic location footage.

The Selig troupe arrives near their Edendale studio site (courtesy Jeff Look).

He settled his 700 animals at the "Selig Jungle Zoo," just below the main studio, and opened it to the public, that wandered beautiful walkways, picnic areas surrounding man-made ponds, and gazebos overlooking the largest private collection of wild animals in the world. It was a beehive of activity when Wally arrived. There is little confirmation of exactly what he did that summer. No Selig records survive that describe Wally's work, but later interviews indicated that Wally went to Edendale to work for Otis Turner. We do know that the Selig world was torn apart later that year. If Wally were there, it would explain his sudden, surprising departure from Selig.

The Edendale operation was run by Francis Boggs, a former Chicago actor who was Selig's most trusted assistant. Boggs first came to California for the 1908 *Count of Monte Cristo* filming, and Selig tapped him to oversee construction. In four years Boggs produced, directed or wrote 200 films. He is virtually forgotten today but Boggs was one of the most important men in silent film, and when Wally arrived he was General Manager and lead producer.

On October 27, 1911, Boggs was murdered at the Selig offices, shot to death by 29-year-old Frank Minematsu,[49] a Japanese immigrant studio gardener.[50] Early that morning, Minematsu left the bungalow he shared with three friends at 1240 Irolo Street, just three miles south of the studio, and rode

Long forgotten murder victim Francis Boggs was responsible for much of the early success of the Selig operation and one of the influential men of the early movies.

the streetcar from the end of the block the short distance up Allesandro. He calmly walked into the office and opened fire on Boggs and Selig, who just happened to be there. Boggs was shot twice in the heart and died before he hit the floor. Selig was almost killed, shot through the right arm and chest as he dove for cover. Under a headline "MILLIONAIRE SELIG SHOT!!!" it was reported that Selig was expected to die.[51] He nearly bled to death but survived. Minematsu tried to flee but was chased down by employees a block away. Stories mentioned he "ran amuck without provocation," but Boggs had fired him several months earlier for smoking cigarettes on the job.[52] He died in Folsom Prison in the mid–1930s. The Selig operation would never truly recover. Otis Turner directed a final Selig film—*A Counterfeit Santa Claus*—just after the murder. It was released in January 1912, but within a month of the shooting Turner had joined Carl Laemmle's Independent Motion Picture (IMP) studio at Vitagraph and Reliance studios. Wally joined him there.

At Vitagraph, Wally's work environment was the highly disorganized world of silent filmmaking. The first challenge was weather. Movie companies came to California to take advantage of good weather but had not considered the *fog*. The L.A. basin was covered in fog until mid-day, so no filming could be done until noon. Filming was done quickly to ensure two to five films were made each week. Mack Sennett made 150 during his first ten months in Hollywood. Rarely did it take longer than a day and a half to complete a movie. They were called "shorts" for a reason. At 750 feet they lasted about seven or eight minutes. Filming was not unlike what appeared on film—Keystone Cop—disorganized and done by the seat of the pants. Seldom was a script finished beforehand. Usually a scenario writer simply offered a possible plot line, and it was up to a cameraman and director to produce a story *around* the story using the disinterested locals and events that happened to be available to them at the moment.

Minta Durfee recalled, "Because we didn't have any scenery, all you had to do was to lift the lock on the great big wooden fence, or gate, and come in. We made everything in parks, Echo Park ... Griffith Park ... and we worked in the streets ... or if there was a fire, somebody went to the fire with a camera, and some cop and one girl would usually run along, and then we'd make the picture up, the story up, afterward. See, we didn't have any picture writers for years ... for the first two years we were there, each comedian worked out his own gags."[53]

Directors took advantage of scenes and people they could exploit. Houses were "borrowed" for background. Banks, closed for weekends, were rented for $5 or $10. Locals were corralled for crowd scenes and streets illegally blocked to film automobile crashes.[54] Often, scenario ideas were the product of necessity versus creativity. Sennett writer Harry Carr remembered his first Universal writer's meeting:

> I arrived at a time of stress and storm. Mr. Isador Bernstein, the general manager, had just received a bill for hay. "Who eats all this hay?" he cried, "The actors?" "The elephant," was the subdued reply. "The elephant!" he thundered, "I don't see any stories about elephants!" "That's because we can't think of one," was the meek reply. Mr. Bernstein turned to me with an intense look, "Do you mean you can't write a story about an elephant?"[55]

Carr quickly wrote a story about an elephant. The birth of Sennett's "Keystone Kops [sic]" was equally fortuitous. Directors like Sennett always knew what was happening around town. Auto races or parades were used as settings for that day's small plot line. Sennett learned a Shriner's Parade was marching up Main Street in downtown L.A. with groups of soldiers, so he put a shawl on Mabel Normand and told her to hold a baby (doll) and act distressed as her "husband" marched off to an imaginary war. Ford Sterling was ordered to start an argument with a marcher, and as cameras rolled several local policemen stepped in to stop what they considered a disrespectful display. They chased the actors through the parade, cameras kept rolling, and the Cops were born. The first Keystone Kops were actual Los Angeles policemen.[56]

The moth-eaten uniforms in Sennett's always-barren wardrobe shack made the policemen *look* even funnier, so they were used. The Cops became the most famous faces in the movies—Mack Swain, who owned a pig farm; Carnival taffy-puller Ben Turpin's crossed eyes; Chester Conklin's droopy mustache. At the outset of their careers, many well-known stars appeared as Cops, including Ramon Novarro, Malcolm St. Clair, Harold Lloyd, and Wallace Beery.[57]

Amidst the confusion, cameramen and directors were daily improving the quality and art. D.W. Griffith's cameraman, Billy Bitzer, was experimenting with lighting variations, discovering the dissolve shot and inventing the close-up. New ideas and technology made it an exciting time to be in the movies when Wally arrived in Edendale.

Most of the information about movies—not just Wally's but any films made pre–1914—is murky. The studios often did not keep detailed cast records; this was long before the studios identified actors. There were no acting credits for another five years. And most information has been lost, unfortunately, along with most of the films. What information is available is hard to confirm and subject to question. The Selig materials are a perfect example. At the Academy of Motion Pictures Arts and Sciences Herrick Library—the best repository of film history in the world—the Selig files contain fifteen feet of papers that begin in 1911 and end in 1917. Some of the production files go back farther but contain almost no individual film records or cast lists; the studio didn't think it was important. When a cast was listed it usually only noted highly paid or important stars. We know that Wally worked on Selig films during that time, but his name does not appear in any of those records.

Making confirmation even more difficult is the plethora of erroneous casting information produced in the years since. There are several excellent sources, like Ephraim Katz's *The Film Encyclopedia*, but others, like Einar Lauritzen and Gunar Lundquist's *American Film Index: 1908–1915*, contain information that is often suspect. For these reasons, the text describing Wally's films from 1911 to 1915 are mostly of review in nature. It was not until 1915 or so that he was a name star and his films earned public note.

Wally's late 1911–early 1912 schedule was as expectedly hectic, given the vagaries and volume of silent filming, and the upheaval at Selig. He worked on at least a half dozen movies in November and December alone, all released between that December and early spring 1912. During 1912 Wally appeared in almost three dozen films. Unlike most actors, he worked continually from the first days he arrived in Hollywood.

His first Hollywood film was *War,* alongside Charles Kent and Rose Tapley, filmed within weeks of the Boggs murder and released December 8th. He then appeared with Florence Turner in *A Red Cross Martyr*, released January 2, 1912. She was the biggest star at Vitagraph. She debuted in 1908, was one of the "Vitagraph Girls" and already famous. *Martyr* was her 65th film, and among three or four Wally films made in November and released in January.

As much as the studio wanted Wally in front of the camera, he tried to get to the other side. He wrote his first scenario in November, a John Bunny comedy entitled *Chumps* that was released in early January. Subtitled *A Fairy Story for Overgrown-ups*, it starred Bunny with Leah Baird, William Shea, and Marshall P. Wilder. Wally played "George, the Denouement," a flying trapeze artist married to the heroine. During spring 1912 Vitagraph released over a dozen films with Wally in a variety of roles. It was telling that he worked with Vitagraph's top directors, apparently being groomed for leading man status. Several roles were opposite Florence Turner, assignments that were a coup for a young actor. He also had an extra role in *The Seepore Rebellion* and worked with his father and Turner in several others.

The two Reids starred with Turner in *The Course of True Love*, which was released January 6th, and *Jean Intervenes*, released January 23rd. "Jean" was "the Vitagraph Dog," a trained collie who appeared in numerous films. In *Intervenes*, which also featured Edith Halleran, Turner is jealous of Wally's dog, which leads to a quarrel and a reconciliation arranged by the collie. After *Jean*, Wally and Turner led in *Indian Romeo and Juliet*, directed by Larry Trimble and released January 30th. It was an Indian-themed version of the Shakespeare play, written by Hal; Wally's Huron Romeo was named Oniatore, and Turner's Mohawk Juliet, Ethona. Wally's next film was with another Vitagraph lead, Edith Storey. *The Telephone Girl* was her 40th film for the company after making a name for herself in early classics like *King Lear, Oliver Twist* and *Les Miserables* (all 1909) and *A Tale of Two Cities* (1911). Storey is a telephone operator who remains at her switchboard warning occupants of her burning building; she is nearly trapped before being rescued by her fireman boyfriend, played by Wally. *Telephone Girl* was released March 12th.

During that spring Wally worked on several films directed by Hal. The first was *The Seventh Son*, which Hal also wrote, which starred Mary Maurice, Earle Williams, James Morrison, William R. Dunn, Robert Gaillard, Tefft Johnson, Ralph Ince, and Wally. Maurice plays a widow who gives six of her seven sons to the Union cause, and when the seventh is condemned to the firing squad for cowardice during battle she goes to President Lincoln seeking mercy and is told, "You have given six sons for your country; I am going to give you the seventh." *Son* was released April 3rd, after which Wally worked with director Charles Gaskill on *The Illumination*, released April 5th and starring Tom Powers, Helen Gardner, Rosemary Theby, Harry Northrup, and Rose Tapley. The drama centered on a spiritual light emanating from a statue of Christ and its effect on those upon whom it shines. Wally then worked with Bunny again on the Hal-directed *At Scrogginses' Corner*, released April 9th, then took the lead in the George Field–directed *Brothers*, released April 24th for Champion films, and another Hal-directed film, *The Victoria Cross*, released the 27th. *Cross*, subtitled *The Charge of the Light Brigade*, also featured Edith Storey, Tefft Johnson, Julia Swayne Gordon, and Tapley. Wally plays a young soldier who saves the life of his colonel, winning the heart of the colonel's daughter and the Victoria Cross. After *Cross*, he worked with Gaskill again on *The Hieroglyphic*, with Tom Powers, Zena Keefe, and Harry Northrup, playing a man-about-town the villain tries to use to swindle a wealthy young woman. It was released May 4th.

Then he worked on a Bunny-Finch serial, *Diamond Cut Diamond*, released May 24th. The Bunny-Finch serials—this was among the second dozen—were the most popular films in the U.S. at the time. Supporting Bunny and Finch were Dick Rosson, (Miss) Ray Ford, Jack Standing, and "Mrs. Costello." Then there was another Hal film, *Curfew Shall Not Ring Tonight*, released May 29th, and a starring role with Gertrude Robinson in *His Mother's Son*, released June 1st by Reliance.

Wally wrote his next film for Reliance, the Indian-themed love story *Kaintuck*, filmed in early 1912, directed by Hal and also starring Robinson, Robert Tabor, and Virginia Westbrooke. "Westbrooke" debuted a few weeks earlier in Hal's *Beaucliare*, but no Virginia Westbrooke appears in census, birth or L.A. directories. This Virginia, 68 at the time, may have been Wally's grandmother, Virginia Rice. Wally plays a mountaineer jealous of the city artist painting his girlfriend; all ends well when Wally saves his life and learns he is actually in love with her younger sister.

Much of Wally's early work was in westerns, the dominant genre at the time. Viewers were fascinated by western scenery most had never seen, and the low cost and effort needed to produce westerns made them popular for studios. *Real* cowboys were hired from Wild West shows, and authentic Native American performers, such as James Young Deer and Lillian Red Wing, filled Indian roles. It was a desire for western locales that prompted Selig to send Boggs west in 1907 and to move to Edendale in 1909. By 1911 there were six studios operating full-time in Hollywood making westerns: Selig, New York Motion Picture, Kalem, Nestor, American, and Pathé West Coast.[58]

Next was *Virginius,* adapted by Hal from the James Sheridan Knowles novel of Virginia history. It was made for Reliance, and Hal starred with Wally. It was released June 15th. A week later Wally made *The Gamblers* for Vitagraph, with Julia Swayne Gordon and Zena Keefe, released June 22nd. Next was Wally's third script, directed by Otis Turner for Reliance, *Before the White Men Came*. Wally plays the Indian Waheta, whose love (Gertrude Robinson) is killed protecting him, after which he kills himself so he can be with her in the "Happy Hunting Ground."[59] It was released June 29th.

Next was the Civil War drama *A Man's Duty*, directed by Hal for Reliance. Wally was supported by Charles Herman, Hector Dion, Sue Balfour, and George Siegmann. He plays a Union spy caught and brought before his own father, who is forced to sentence him to death before a reprieve arrives. It was released June 3rd and followed by the film version of Hal's play *At Cripple Creek*, made for Reliance and released July 17th. Two films were released in August, *Making Good* for Carl Laemmle's IMP Studio on the 26th, with Jane Fearnley, and *The Secret Service Man*, back at Reliance on the 28th, with co-star Rodman Law. Wally is the villain who is chased (by Law) by horse, motorcycle, automobile, train and airplane.

Another film credited to Wally and in dispute is a D.W. Griffith Biograph short released in September. *An Unseen Enemy* starred Lillian and Dorothy Gish, Harry Carey, Lionel Barrymore, and Wally allegedly in a small role as the "brother's friend." The film was typical Griffith; orphaned children of a doctor lose their inheritance to the family housekeeper and a burglar friend, but the two daughters and a brother organize a rescue party to save the girls' money. Wally was allegedly among the group of friends, but circumstances seemingly prevent him from having been there.

All of the numerous conflicts must be resolved before it can be realistically considered that Wally made this film. Most important, the interiors were filmed at Griffith's 11 East 14th Street Manhattan studio and exteriors near Fort Lee, New Jersey, at his Shadyside township properties.[60] But Wally was not in New York during July, 1912, when *Enemy* was filmed. He was in Edendale making *The Indian Raiders* for Bison and Universal, and there was no break in his shooting schedule; he probably filmed *Making Good* and *The Secret Service Man* in July, too. There was no two-week period when he was *not* working that allows for travel to New York. And it is unlikely Griffith would bring Wally to New York at considerable expense for a minor role unless he used him in other films, which he did not. Most Griffith biographers don't credit his first work with Wally until 1915's *Birth of a Nation*. If Wally was in *Enemy* it probably would have become part of the Griffith–Wally Reid discovery myth, which has always mentioned *Birth of a Nation*. Finally, and probably most conclusively, Bertha Reid never mentioned visiting with Wally that summer, which she would have if he had been in New York. She and Wally both wrote that it was six years from the time of his 1911 departure until they saw each other again. He returned to New York in 1916, so it's almost impossible that Wally appeared in a 1912 Griffith movie.

After *Secret Service Man* Wally's next confirmed picture was *The Indian Raiders* for director Tom Ricketts (made while Griffith made *The Unseen Enemy*). At the same time, in July or early August, Wally directed for the first (confirmed) time. But, interestingly, his directorial debut was not for Vitagraph or Reliance, nor was it in Hollywood. It was in Santa Barbara, up the coast from L.A. Before leaving for Santa Barbara, Wally worked on two films that figured prominently in his life and career. *His Only Son* and *Every Inch a Man* were both made during the summer of 1912. During one of these assignments Wally met Dorothy Davenport.

Dorothy insisted she met Wally on *His Only Son*. In fact, she usually referred to the film incorrectly as *His Son* (which added to the confusion). But though she is not listed in credits for *Every Inch a Man*, for his part, Wally insisted it was on *that* film that he first laid eyes on the teenager he would marry.

3

Dorothy and the Davenports

In 1922 Dorothy said, "It was in 1911 that I first met Wally. I was then working for the Universal Film Company. While the pictures were restricted to one reel, 'Dorothy Davenport' was a star. I am, as many of the fans know, a niece of the famous Fanny Davenport."[1] She also said, "We weren't faces hired off the street. The Davenports and the Reids were *of the theater*."[2] Dorothy was very proud of her family's theatrical heritage, which was even more impressive than that of the Reids. Hal and Bertha were successful stage actors, and Hal wrote popular plays, but Dorothy's parents were stars of the "legitimate stage." And unlike the Reids, the Davenports were famous globally, as well-known on European stages as in America.

Dorothy's grandfather, Edward Loomis Davenport, was born in Boston in 1819 and made his stage debut in Providence, Rhode Island, with English legend Junius Brutus Booth, father of John Wilkes. By the early 1840s E.L. was in large New York theaters, and in the late 1840s traveled to England to work with the famous Anna Cora Mowatt (Ritchie) and Macready companies. At Macready he met lovely 18-year-old Fanny Elizabeth Vining.[3] Fanny's theatrical family traced its lineage to the 1700s and famed Irish actor Jack Johnson. Her father Frederick managed the renowned Haymarket Theatre in the 1820s and 1830s. When she met Harry she was married to actor Charles Gill.

In 1849 Fanny divorced Gill and married E.L. at St. John's Church in London. The following April 10th their first child, Blanche, was born there, and a second, Lilly, was born in Scotland in 1852 just before the family returned to New York, where the parents were booked at the prestigious Drury Lane Theater. They arrived that fall and E.L. soon became so popular that his face appeared on etched cigar bands, along with other actors like Ethel Barrymore and John Drew. For the next few years they traveled through the U.S. appearing in large theaters, but when Fanny became pregnant in 1855 they returned to Boston and E.L. took over as director of the Howard Athenaeum (theater). Over ten years the family grew with daughter Marion ("May"), born in 1856, Florence ("Flo") in 1858, Adele in 1861, Edgar in 1862, and Harry, on January 19, 1866.

E.L. earned a huge following traveling with a Howard friend, James W. Wallack, Jr., performing versions of Dickens novels and Shakespeare's *Hamlet*. He also worked with Fanny. A December, 1862, Walnut Street Theater playbill noted "Mr. and Mrs. Edward Loomis Davenport in Anna Cora Ritchie's FASHION: OR LIFE IN NEW YORK." E.L.'s fame even reached the White House. In the National Archives there is an 1863 letter to President Lincoln from Leonard Grover inviting him to a performance by the Davenport-Wallack troupe at the opening of his new theater:

419—13th St.
Monday Sep 28th 63.

Your Excellency,

I desire very earnestly to have the honor of the presence of your Excellency at the opening of my new Theatre on Monday Oct 5th. The piece in view for the occasion is Shakespeare's Othello as adapted to presenting Messrs. Wallack and Davenport in parts of nearly equal strength.

James W. Wallack was a British-born actor and member of a well regarded theatrical family who spent most of his career in the U. S. Edward L. Davenport considered one of the finest American actors of his day. Both men were known for portraying the roles of Othello and Iago.

I have the honor to submit for your acceptance a double box with connecting door or any box or boxes in my theatre for the accommodation of your Excellency and the party accompanying you. Should your Excellency prefer any of the other plays of Shakespeare within the repertoire of Messrs Wallack and Davenport: Hamlet, Richard III, Macbeth: it will afford me, as well as those gentlemen, the greatest pleasure to concur with such preference. Should the date above mentioned conflict with any different arrangement your Excellency may have in view, I will gladly with your permission postpone the day of opening one or two days to have the gratification of your presence.

It may not be amiss to state that Grover's Theatre is under the management of one who ever has and ever will do all that may lie in his power to strengthen the devotion of his audiences to the cause of the Union and your Excellencies Government in which purpose he has ever been warmly seconded by the artists in his employment.

I have again to renew the expression of my desire of last season that your Excellency will at any time avail yourself of the services of my Theatre; and any play or artist acceptable to your Excellency will meet with my immediate consideration.

Have the kindness to permit Mr. Nicolay to acquaint me with your wishes, of which no public use will be made, and sincerely oblige.

Your Servt
Leonard Grover[4]

E.L. Davenport, famed stage actor, in the 1870s.

Theater buff Lincoln asked E.L. and Wallack to perform *Othello* for him and asked that Grover postpone the opening one night, so on Tuesday evening, October 6, 1863, President and Mrs. Lincoln took a carriage to the Grover Theater, sat in a private box and watched E.L. perform *Othello*. The Grover Theater became the Lincolns' favorite venue, and during the next seven months they attended a dozen plays. On April 14, 1864, Lincoln accepted an invitation from Grover, but at the last minute Mrs. Lincoln opted to see *Our American Cousin* at Ford's Theatre, leaving their son Tad to play with Grover's son Leonard. E.L. had debuted with Junius Booth, the father of John Wilkes Booth, who also appeared at Ford's Theater that night.

E.L. and Fanny's children each became famous; of them, Lilly and Blanche world-renowned. Theater historians have assumed Blanche was the famous 19th century actress "Fanny Davenport," but evidence confirms that younger sister *Lilly* was actually "Fanny," not Blanche. When actress "Fanny Davenport" died in 1877, her beneficiaries were three living sisters,

May D. Seymour (Marion), Florence C. Tiers (Flo), and, strangely, *Blanche Davenport*. The remaining un-named sister was Lilly (Adele died in childhood). Lilly was Fanny. Also, a later newspaper story noted, "May is with her sister Fanny, and Blanche (known as Bianca la Blanche), the prima donna, is in Italy."[5] Blanche could not be Fanny. This writer also uncovered archival opera listings that confirm Blanche Davenport was indeed "Bianca la Blanche," prima donna for the Max Strakosch Italian Opera Company, and unearthed a photograph of Bianca dating to an 1870s U.S. visit. Blanche was "Bianca" and Lilly was "Fanny." For over a century it has been wrongly assumed that the actress Fanny Davenport was Blanche Davenport.

Lilly re-arranged family names for her stage name "Fanny Lily Gypsy Davenport" and at 16 joined a Louisville, Kentucky, company before working with prestigious companies like the Arch Street Theater Company in Philadelphia (run by the "Grande Dame" of American Theater, Louisa Drew) and Augustin Daly's Fifth Avenue Theater Company in New York. Sister Blanche became an opera star, hired by Max and Maurice Strakosch, the biggest American opera promoters. During the late 1800s she toured the world, visiting England, France, Italy, Monte Carlo, even Russia. She was as famous in opera as her parents were on stage.

Blanche Davenport as opera diva Bianca La Blanche in 1878.

In 1870 the rest of the Davenports lived in one of the largest mansions in Boston. At home were May (14), Flo (12), Adele (9), Edgar (7) and Harry (4).[6] In 1871, Harry debuted in a Howard production of *Damon and Pythias* at the Globe Theater.[7] In 1874, E.L. moved to rural Canton, Pennsylvania, 50 miles north of Williamsport. It was remote and beautiful, with verdant green hills covered with trees and broken up with squares of farmland and dotted with tiny villages like Beech Flats and Windfall. Fanny actually purchased the property, with a large house that had been "The Half Way House Tavern," built in 1826 over a 1768 log building. The Georgian mansion was made with bricks burned on the property and beams hand-hewn and assembled with wooden pegs; no nails were used. The intricate woodwork was hand-carved; the front door alone took 22 days to construct.

E.L. and Fanny opened a tea room in the lower level called the Boars Head Inn in homage to a pub in her native London,[8] and they lived quietly there until September 1, 1877, when E.L. died. He was only 58. A later history of Boston entitled *Massachusetts Gazetteer* listed 50 "eminent people whom Boston may claim for her own by birth and education," and among the names were Samuel Adams, Cotton Mather, Gen. Henry Knox, and Edward L. Davenport.[9]

In 1881, papers noted, "Members of the family of the late E.L. Davenport are nearly all on stage. Mrs. E.L. (Fanny Vining) and son Harry are with Frank Mayo. Edgar is with the Curtis troupe in 'Samuel of Posen.' May is with her sister Fanny and Blanche (known as Bianca la Blanche), the prima donna, in Italy. May paid her a visit this summer. Florence is married and lives in Philadelphia."[10] In 1882, Harry joined Edgar in the Hazel Kirke Company, and in 1883 at the Madison Square Theater Company. Into the 1890s he spent the winters on the west coast and returned to Canton each summer. In the summer of 1891 Fanny Vining Davenport died there at age 62.

Soon after, Harry joined the Charles Dickson Company with well-known actors Charles Dickson, Robert Edeson, Louis Mann, and Ned Moreland.[11] The female star was 27-year-old New Yorker Alice Shepard. For two years Harry toured with Dickson and on January 26, 1893, papers reported "Fedora's Brother Marries" (referring to Fanny's latest role), noting, "Harry Davenport, youngest brother of Fanny Davenport, was married today to Miss Alice Shepard."[12] That summer was the hottest New York summer in 25 years and led to the worst year in theater history, with ticket sales at the lowest level in decades. Many theaters simply closed[13] so Harry and Alice escaped to Boston.

Lilly Davenport, better known to stage crowds as "Fanny Davenport."

It was there on March 13, 1895, that Alice gave birth to a daughter they named Dorothy. Harry was working with the Askin Opera Company at Boston's Globe Theater. Later that summer he moved to New York's Herald Square Theater at Broadway and 35th[14] to join George Musgrove's production of *The Belle of New York*. In the cast was Phyllis Rankin, who, like everyone else in the extended Reid-Davenport families, came from an acting family. Harry and Phyllis began an affair while Alice was home caring for Harry's newborn daughter Dorothy.

Phyllis Rankin's father was actor McKee Rankin, who inherited passion and temper from his own father, who once fought a duel with Canadian novelist John Richardson.[15] Young McKee left home at 16 and briefly enlisted in the Union Army before resigning in 1861. He married actress Caroline Henri but divorced and married more famous actress Kitty Blanchard. He performed across America, traveling by train to "San Francisco in 1869 just after the railroad was completed"[16] and to L.A. in 1870. Working in western theaters was not glamorous. In 1871 the Virginia City, Nevada, vigilante "601 Gang" lynched a murderer and hung his body from the rafters at Piper's Opera House, riddling his dangling corpse with bullets and filling the theater with the stench of gunfire and death. McKee was appearing there with Annie Adams, mother of actress Maude. McKee built dozens of theaters from New York to San Francisco and was called the "Father of Los Angeles Theater" for his work there. He was one of the first Broadway impresarios.

McKee and Kitty eventually separated in 1899. Their daughters married into the theater. Gladys married Sidney Drew, son of Louisa Drew, and Doris married Lionel Barrymore, Sidney's nephew. Lionel later wrote that his family "first appeared on the stage in 1752 ... the 250 years since, the Barrymore-Drew clan has been accused of more nepotism than any other performers. My grandmother Mrs. John Drew Sr., my father Maurice, my mother Georgiana Drew Barrymore, my uncles John and Sidney Drew ... we all played together."[17]

Phyllis Rankin's tiny stature earned her the nickname "Pixie," but she was as passionate and unpredictable as her father. Her affair with Harry was heated. Within a few months she was pregnant with Harry's child. Harry divorced Alice Shepard and married Phyllis in early 1896. At the same time, his sister Fanny suddenly died. At the time, her Fanny Davenport Company was presenting *Gismonda* with a young actor named Cunningham Deane. His real name was William Desmond Taylor.

Alice Shepard Davenport remained in New York raising Dorothy, who in the early 1900s was growing into a lovely teenager, a tiny, doe-eyed, dark-haired beauty even at 13. She began working with small stage companies before trying films in 1910. Like most, she simply walked into a studio one morning and asked for work. Dorothy chose Biograph Studios, located in a four-story brownstone at 11 East 14th Street not too far from her own home.

Biograph had leased the building from the Steck Piano Company just a few months earlier. A large Singer Sewing Center sign hanging next door reflected into all the first floor windows, and the layout of the once-private home was labyrinthine. Dorothy entered up a short flight of stairs, through large double doors, and up another short flight to the first floor offices. In the front were small rooms on either side of a long hallway that ran the length of the building. At the end of that hall was a large ballroom used for interior filming. In darkened second and third floor rooms, film was prepared for shipment to J.J. Kennedy's film development lab in Hoboken, New Jersey.

Biograph was managed by ex–stage actor David Wark Griffith, born in 1875 on a rural Kentucky farm, the sixth of seven children of cantankerous Confederate Army hero Jacob "Roaring Jack" Griffith. Too poor to attend school, he became a voracious reader of the classics and ardent supporter of the South's version of post–Civil War Northern transgression.[18] He became an actor, traveling with Melbourne McDowell's company in California. Coincidently, McDowell was the widower of Fanny (Lilly) Davenport. The McDowell outfit folded and Griffith joined the Nance O'Neill Company in San Francisco, replacing leading man McKee Rankin.[19] When he tried selling a script to Edison in

Biograph Studios' 1910 location at 11 East 14th Street in Manhattan.

1906 he was instead hired to act, and in 1908 the same thing happened at American Mutoscope & Biograph Company, managed by Edison's ex-partner William Dickson.

Griffith joined Biograph as an extra for $5 a day plus a bag lunch, and in six months appeared in 21 films. He also sold scenarios like *Old Isaacs the Pawnbroker*, *The Music Master* and *The Stage Rustler*.[20] Biograph films were directed by Wallace McCutcheon, but he was too old and ill to produce the quota needed by the studio, so desperate owner Henry Marvin let Griffith direct. Griffith had been pestering him for months, and Biograph director Gene Gauntier recalled, "Every time I came through the studio he waylaid me with the same query, 'Why don't they give an actor a chance to direct?'"[21] Griffith's first assignment was *The Adventures of Dolly* in June, 1908, filmed at Sound Beach (now Sound View) in tiny Niantic, Connecticut. Griffith's independence was visible on this, his first film:

> Griffith did not rush into his first picture unprepared; he took several days to mull over the script; disappeared for three more, keeping his people at Sound Beach. An air of mystery enveloped the proceedings. Waiting in the office I grew anxious. Three days for a simple picture Olcott would have taken in less than a day! Even after his return I did not see Griffith for several days. Then I received a message to come to Mr. Marvin's office and I found them together. [The film] was a lovely little thing ... a feeling of poetry. It moved along as smoothly and gently as the river which played such a large part in it. [Griffith's cameraman Billy] Bitzer had given it the finest photography I had yet seen, and the short six or eight scenes of the original had been elaborated into some thirty or more by means of a new technique, unknown, undreamed of up to that hour—the use of the flashback.[22]

Marvin offered Griffith a director contract paying $50 a week and $1/20$ of a cent for every foot of film sold. Griffith churned out 1- and 2-reelers at an unheard-of rate, often five a week. His output saved Biograph. From 1908 to 1910 he made 206 films for $1,000 apiece that earned $2,000,000, and from 1910 to 1912 another 104 that cost $2,000 per and earned $2,100,000 ($200,000,000 today).[23]

Griffith was an innovator and technical genius. He and cameraman Billy Bitzer[24] used new technical devices like close ups, slow motion, fade-ins and -outs, and lighting effects to change the way movies told stories. They showed time passing and simultaneous events, also new techniques. His actors avoided overdone theatrics; he was the first to make them ignore the camera and focus on the role. He did not walk around the set with the script; he carried no notes. He directed with his right hand, which always held a large, black, usually burned-out cigar that he lit every day at breakfast. In his left hand was a megaphone. He waved either the megaphone or the cigar, which served "as the baton serves an orchestra director."[25]

When Dorothy Davenport walked in that July, Griffith had directed 275 films for Florence Lawrence, Mary Pickford, Mack Sennett and Mae Marsh. Griffith saw something in Dorothy because he hired her and paid her $25 a week, excellent pay considering experienced actors earned $40 to $75. The dark-haired Dorothy was a strange pick; Griffith liked blondes like Pickford, Lawrence, Blanche Sweet and Lillian Gish.[26] Two weeks later he added Dorothy to a company traveling to New Jersey for two weeks. Griffith filmed there often. The area was cheap to access; Fort Lee was a 10¢ ferry ride and the company escaped the mugginess of the city. Also, it was cost-efficient to bring a group and make multiple films and Biograph only had the single indoor stage, the original 14th Street ballroom, and no exterior stages.

Griffith liked the area around Cuddebackville, New York, near Port Jervis in far northwest New Jersey. The mountainous region had beautiful rocky cliffs, meandering rivers, and lush forests and farms full of abandoned stone buildings dating to the 1700s. The Neversink River passed south of the tiny settlement, and a mile north was the gorgeous Basher Kill, a pristine two-mile lake surrounded by 100-foot pine trees. Griffith first went there in 1909 and returned every summer after.

On July 20, 1910, Dorothy joined the 30 people on the 10¢ ferry to Weehawken, New Jersey, where they boarded an Ontario & Western train to Summitville and took a branch line through Port Jervis to Cuddebackville. Cuddebackville station was less a station than a small shack next to the rails where trains simply stopped, a half mile down the hill from the Caudebec Inn.

The Caudebec Inn, located in remote Cuddebackville, New York, rented every summer by D.W. Griffith for his summer Biograph filming.

The inn was a converted farmhouse owned by the Predmore family on Oakland Valley Road, originally built for boaters using the Delaware & Hudson Canal. It was a large three-story building encircled by a big porch and meant to hold a dozen guests. It defined "rustic": spotlessly clean thanks to Mrs. Predmore, but only one bathroom, a tiny parlor, and a large dining room overlooking an apple orchard. Across the dirt street was the small Tammany Hall tavern where crew-members held nightly card games and played craps.

The 1910 company included Griffith (with his wife Linda Arvidson), Bitzer, Henry Walthall, Bobby Harron, Gertrude Robinson, Mabel Normand, Jack Pickford, Mack Sennett, Claire McDowell, Henry Lehrman, George W. Morris, and young Dorothy. Getting off the train, most trudged up the hill on foot, but the Griffiths and Bitzer were driven by the innkeeper's son Lester in the family's large red Thomas Flyer the Griffiths nicknamed "the Red Devil."[27] Even in remote Cuddebackville, Griffith was wary of vandalism and theft of film, so Sennett hired a local policeman as a $2 a day watchman and paid a neighbor $3 to use her house as a backdrop and store-room.[28]

Dorothy appeared in backgrounds and crowd scenes in the 1910 New Jersey films, like *In Life's Cycle* with Charles West, *Willful Peggy* with Pickford and Normand, *A Summer Idyll* with Walthall, and *The Modern Prodigal* with Mary's brother Jack. But Dorothy didn't receive cast credit for this group of films. Her first acknowledged role came weeks later when Griffith took another group to the Delaware Water Gap region in western New York twenty miles south of Cuddebackville. Her first significant role was in the Indian-themed *A Mohawk's Way* with George Nichols and Claire McDowell. It was filmed from August 9th to the 12th and released September 12th. Returning to New York, Griffith stopped in Patterson, where Dorothy and Harry Walthall made *The Oath and the Man* from August 16th to the 19th. It was released September 22nd. From Patterson, Griffith stopped at a small school in Westfield to film *Examination Day at School*. Dorothy worked with W. Chrystie Miller and Kate Bruce, one of the ten "students" in the credits. Filming lasted from August 23rd to the 31st and it was released September 29th. When filming ended, the company returned to 14th Street.

Dorothy next had a small role in another Walthall film, *The Iconoclast*, filmed on August 25th and 26th. Almost the entire Biograph family appeared in this movie, including McDowell, Nichols, Kate Bruce, John Dillon, Gladys Egan, Frank Evans, Henry

Lehrman, and Jeanie Macpherson (who became a legendary screenwriter and Cecil B. DeMille's confidante). It was released October 3rd. After *Iconoclast* it was back to Cuddebackville on August 28th with Griffith, Bitzer, Mary, Lottie and Jack Pickford, Kate Bruce, Sennett, Edward Dillon, "Pathé" Lehrman, MacPherson and Dell Henderson. Dorothy's first film there was the Mary and Lottie Pickford vehicle *A Gold Necklace*, filmed during the first few days of September and released October 3rd. *Necklace* was one of the few movies done by Biograph in Cuddebackville that was not directed by Griffith; Frank Powell directed the Frank Woods vehicle. Dorothy was back with Griffith in *The Broken Doll* on September 2nd. Filming lasted until the 7th and the movie was released October 17th. Gladys Egan starred as a young Indian girl and Linda Arvidson had the other lead. Dorothy played one of several dozen townspeople.

She was already considered a Griffith "regular"[29] and on the 16th she boarded a train for Greenwich, Connecticut, along with Grace Henderson, Kate Bruce, and William J. Butler. From the 16th to the 22nd Griffith filmed *Two Little Waifs*, released October 31st, and *Waiter No. 5*, which featured Claire McDowell, Mary and Jack Pickford, and Charles West, released November 3rd. Dorothy played a restaurant diner.

The Fugitive began filming on September 24th in Fishkill, New York, a Kate Bruce and Edward Dillon Civil War vehicle. Filming lasted four days and it was released November 7th. Dorothy was then assigned a comedy starring William J. Butler and Flora Finch. Coincidently, the early October filming of *The Troublesome Baby* took place in Highlands, within a half mile of the Reids' River Rest estate. Dorothy appeared in a scene filmed at the train station. *Baby* was released November 17th. Between October 19th and the 29th Dorothy worked on *The Golden Supper*, a Renaissance drama based on an Alfred Lord Tennyson poem. It was an elaborately-costumed film starring Dorothy, Charles West and Claire McDowell. The interiors were filmed at 14th Street and exteriors back in Greenwich. Dorothy had a role as a flower seller in *Supper*, which was released December 12th.

Just after filming *Supper*, Griffith announced the roster for the studio's annual winter trip to California in December. The actors who made the two-month trip were all of higher status than Dorothy, like Mabel Normand, Dorothy West, Grace Henderson, Kate Bruce, MacPherson, Sennett, Donald Crisp, and Blanche Sweet, but she was still bitterly disappointed at what she considered a snub. When Griffith left for California without her, she left Biograph and signed with Reliance, a small studio in Bayonne, New Jersey, that was part of the Nestor Motion Picture Company. Nestor was run by Englishman David Horsley, a coal miner's son who came to this country in 1884. He lost most of his left arm when he was run over by a trolley car at 11 but still owned a successful bicycle business and a small pool hall on Avenue

Dorothy about the time she met Wally, ca. 1911.

D in Bayonne by 1908. Biograph director and scenarist Charles Gorman was a regular at the Horsley Pool Parlor; Gorman and Horsley formed the Centaur Film Company. The mythical centaur was half man (Gor*man*) and half horse (*Hors*ley).[30]

Centaur was a shoestring operation. Cameraman Charles Rosher said, "I wouldn't call it a studio. It was really nothing but a shop with a lot of bathtubs for developing film."[31] Even so, by October, 1911, the studio was making three or four films a week. Horsley and his brother William went to California looking for a location when they met Murray Steele at their downtown L.A. hotel. Steele took them to a place called Hollywood because he knew of a bar named the Blondeau Tavern at the northwest corner of Sunset Boulevard and Gower Street that was closing due to a new ban on alcohol. There was a tavern, a corral and barn behind, several small buildings and a bungalow. The Horsleys rented the site from Mr. Blondeau for $35 a month and moved in on October 27, 1911.[32] A few years later Cecil B. DeMille moved in after the Horsleys abandoned it.

Horsley's California operation was called Nestor Films and was managed by Al E. Christie, who was in charge of the studio's popular *Mutt & Jeff* comedies. The Horsleys returned to New Jersey to handle production and distribution. Centaur was the first film company to locate permanently in California but within three months another 15 studios were there. At Nestor, Christie handled comedies, Milton Fahrney westerns, and Thomas Ricketts dramas, all under the Nestor Films label. The day's filming was developed on the tavern's screen porch during evening darkness and sent back to Bayonne for printing and distribution.[33]

It isn't known exactly when Dorothy arrived in California. She is credited with three 1911 Reliance or Nestor films—*His Son, His Dream,* and *The Best Man Wins*—which were filmed in June, July and October and released August 5th, September 9th, and December 25th respectively. *His Son* has long been credited to Henry B. Walthall, but independent confirmation of the production is impossible. Dorothy mentioned working on a film with that title, but she may have confused *His Son* with *His Only Son*, a film she did with Wally in 1912. It seems *His Son* is more myth than reality. Like much of silent film history, it is impossible to confirm.

Since Fahrney supposedly did not arrive in California until late October it appears *His Son* (if it was made) and *His Dream*, both Fahrney-directed and starring Walthall, were filmed in New Jersey. Dorothy may still have been in New York as late as August, 1911, working on these films. She *was* in *His Dream* with Gertrude Robinson. Made in July and released in September, *His Dream* was probably made in New York (since Robinson was with Biograph crews in New Jersey at the end of July). As late as August, 1911, Dorothy was evidently still in New York. She said the Horsleys first sent her to California with *New York Journal* writer Harry Herschfield[34] for a serial adaptation of his story *Desperate Desmond*[35] but once in California the lead was given to Betty Miller. Nestor released seven versions like *Desperate Desmond Abducts Raymond* (1911) and *Desperate Desmond at the Cannon's Mouth* (1912) but we don't know if Dorothy appeared in extra roles since cast lists do not survive.

It seems that Dorothy and her mother Alice arrived in Hollywood during September or October, 1911. Her film, *The Best Man Wins,* was filmed in California; the backgrounds were western and though Biograph had thousands of feet of archived western footage, Nestor-Reliance probably did not have any. *Best Man* was filmed in October by Tom Ricketts and starred Harry Lockwood and Dorothy, supported by Russell Bassett and Alice. Dorothy played an Easterner who wins the man of her dreams at a Western rodeo competition. It was unusual that Ricketts directed since Fahrney made the company's westerns. It was released December 25th.

Dorothy and Alice rented a bungalow in what was then called the Cahuenga District of Hollywood. The area is up in what is today the Cahuenga Pass where the 101 Freeway bisects the hills into the San Fernando Valley. In 1911 it was a rutted dirt road running from one dusty town—Hollywood—to another dusty town—Cahuenga—and beyond to a 40 mile valley of orchards, wild flowers, and farms. The Davenport's house with the sun porch in front was a short ride from the Nestor offices at Sunset and Gower at the bottom of the hill.

In 1911, Los Angeles was a contradiction. It was a remote outpost but was dotted with thousands of wells remaining from the 1890s oil boom. Scattered around a very small downtown were 40 small towns within a 30-mile radius. It was impossible to tell where one ended and another began. The landscape was a patchwork of lemon and orange groves, pueblos, a few hotels, a few small business blocks, and large houses built by retirees in California escaping winter. The entire area was a grid of dirt roads. Only a few major streets around downtown were paved but there was a well-organized trolley system. The famous L.A. "Red Car" Line ran from downtown to the San Fernando Valley and Glendale (then called "Tropico"), down the coast to Newport Beach, and out as far as Riverside.

Hollywood was not the Hollywood of today. There was one main street, Prospect Avenue (Hollywood Boulevard today), a long dirt boulevard shaded by pepper and palm trees, and only two large buildings. One was the massive wooden Hollywood Hotel and the other the estate of famous artist Paul de Longpre, a Moorish castle at Prospect and Cahuenga. There were no other buildings taller than a single story. To get to Hollywood from downtown was a 40¢ streetcar ticket and passengers had to change cars three times.[36]

Every morning dozens of real cowboys and authentic Indians gathered near Nestor at the bottom of Gower at Sunset hoping for employment,[37] which led to the nickname the "Gower Gulch." Another gathering place was a row of benches in the middle of Vine Street. At the time Vine was a dirt road with a row of pepper trees down the middle; between the trees were dozens of benches usually full of people looking for work.[38] Between 1900 and 1910 the population of Hollywood surged from 500 to 6,000. Along Prospect and the side streets scores of fashionable clothing stores opened, as did restaurants, cafes, and, to the horror of locals, taverns. The Boulevard was a promenade filled most sunny evenings by locals wandering among the new shops.[39] But Hollywood was still farmland; Nestor actors often snuck under fences to help themselves to the figs, apples, and lemons growing in the orchards surrounding their lot, much to the disgust of the rancher next door.[40]

From their little bungalow Dorothy and her mother sometimes walked a few blocks and boarded the Red Car line down to Sunset. From there it was a short stroll over to the studio. Most days they rode one of the three horses Alice purchased when they arrived. Her first days in Hollywood certainly were far from the glamour she might have expected! The studios did not resemble modern-day studios; sound-stages were a few years away. The locations were usually office space and a gathering place for crews to meet in the morning and be carted off somewhere in the San Fernando Valley to make movies.

Most Nestor filming was done in an area known then as "Warner's Ranch," which was reached by traveling through Dark Canyon to an area near Burbank and present-day Lankersham Boulevard where Carl Laemmle constructed some open stages, dressing rooms and a commissary. Later all of the buildings were moved to what became Universal City. It was remote; when the writing staff moved there in 1913 the howling of the coyotes was so annoying they fired pistols out the windows to quiet them down. The appointments were spartan; tents, covered wagons, or the back of an automobile served as dressing rooms and lunch was served picnic-style in the open under large oak trees. A decades-old adobe baking oven across the road, said to have been built by General Pio Pico, was used for cooking.

Filming itself was a helter-skelter affair, with three, four, and sometimes five films made on a single unchanged stage. While filming was underway, hammers banged as carpenters erected or knocked down sets, saws buzzed and people yelled. Property men were expected to carry large gongs; if noise got so loud actors couldn't hear directors the prop man banged the gong loudly to command silence.[41]

All of the actors working with Dorothy called Alice "Mother Davenport."[42] As emotional as Dorothy was quiet, Alice had a brusque manner, and young players all came to her for advice and counsel.[43] The Davenport bungalow was something of a boarding house, with usually two or three actors sharing the spare bedroom or using what Dorothy called her "sleeping porch."[44] While Dorothy worked for Nestor, Alice worked for Sennett, who had come to Hollywood with the January, 1910, Biograph crew and stayed to make his own movies at his new Keystone studio. It was the California group Dorothy had been left out of.

It is assumed *The Best Man Wins* was Alice and Dorothy's first California work. When it was finished in October or early November, Alice went to Keystone and during the next five years was one of Sennett's most popular supporting actresses. From 1911 to 1922 she appeared with Keystone stars Harry McCoy, Fred Mace, and Ford Sterling, and appeared in nine Mabel Normand films like *A Spanish Dilemma* (1912) and *The Engagement Ring* (1912).

Dorothy became one of Nestor's most dependable stars. The list of Centaur-Nestor actors was not full of Biograph names like Pickford and Sennett. Nestor had names like Harold Lockwood, Howard Davies, Jack Conway, Eugenie Forde, and Jefferson Osborne. A few, like Lockwood and Forde, were well-known but most were not. But Dorothy was a lead actress and she worked a lot. During her first six months in California, she made twelve films, dramas and romantic comedies. In each of her first ten she starred opposite Harold Lockwood. Lockwood was a salesman turned vaudevillian who did a few films for Edison director Edwin S. Porter before joining Nestor in late summer, 1911. He was among the cinema's romantic stars when he died tragically during the worldwide 1918 influenza epidemic.

Dorothy and Lockwood did four films during November and December, 1911. *The Lost Address*, a comedy directed by Al Christie, was filmed in early November and released January 8, 1912. Next was *Brave Little Woman*, listed as a romantic comedy, though the title and the fact that Ricketts—who handled dramas—directed, indicate otherwise. *Woman* was filmed in November and released January 15th. Next followed two romantic comedies directed by Christie, *A Matinee Mixup*, filmed in late November and released January 22nd, and *Inbad the Count*, filmed in December and released February 2nd. Both also starred Lockwood and also evidenced a change in Nestor films.

Most studio executives believed films wouldn't hold audience attention for more than four or five minutes. A year earlier Griffith asked Henry Marvin if he could make a two-reeler but was turned down. Marvin was convinced an audience could not pay attention for fifteen minutes.[45] In late 1911 Nestor began lengthening Dorothy's films from 600 feet, or about eight minutes, to 900 feet or longer, lasting ten minutes, beginning with *Matinee* and *Inbad*.

Dorothy was back at work as 1912 dawned, still playing opposite Lockwood. In early January she filmed *The Feudal Debt*, a Ricketts drama released March 18th. The film was a love story set amidst a Hatfield-McCoy–type backwoods feud.[46] Next was *The Bachelor and the Baby*, a comedy, which normally meant Christie directing; but Tom Ricketts' wife Josephine had a small role, so he directed. Dorothy and Lockwood played newlyweds dealing with a newborn baby Lockwood discovers in his car. The film was released March 30th. In late February Dorothy was back on three Ricketts films. *The Cub Reporter's Big Scoop* was filmed late that month and released April 6th, followed by *The Torn Letter*, released April 12th, and *A Pair of Baby Shoes*, released April 15th.

In addition to longer films, Ricketts and Christie films also became more complex. They were done on larger scales, with bigger casts and more intricate plots. Dorothy's first such film was *Her Indian Hero*, a longer western. It is regarded incorrectly as the first full-length motion picture filmed in California; it was one of the first done in the larger scale, but not the first full-length film. Directed by Jack Conway, the film starred Conway, George Gebhardt, Dorothy and Victoria Forde (Eugenie Forde's daughter). It was filmed in mid–February and released April 17th.

For some reason Dorothy didn't work much from early March until June. Production records of the time being what they are, it's possible she had any number of extra roles, but after working leads for six months it would be odd to have been given small uncredited roles. It is not known what she was doing but we know that from the April 17th release of *Her Indian Hero*, Dorothy doesn't appear in cast lists until the following August 28th release of *Uncle Bill*.

Dorothy's lack of work may have had something to do with the upheaval within Nestor and Universal. In May the Horsleys joined Carl Laemmle's new Universal Film Manufacturing Company, which included Laemmle's IMP and a group of independents including Horsley's Centaur, Nestor and Reliance, Joe Engel and Ed Porter's Rex Motion Picture Company, Fred Balshofer's 101 Bison Films, Edwin Thanhauser, and Ludwig Erb and Pat Powers' Powers Motion Pictures. The merger caused some fractious relations and power squabbles so David Horsley sold out to Laemmle for $300,000, making him fill the back of a touring car with bundles of one, two, five, ten, and twenty-dollar bills.[47] Universal would distribute all of Dorothy's films.

Dorothy was assigned *Uncle Bill*, directed by Fahrney and another of Nestor's more lavish offerings, with a large cast including Howard Davies, Jack Conway, Dorothy, Eugenie Forde, Jefferson Osborne, William Ryno and Victoria Forde. It was filmed in mid–June. Most of that cast moved to *The Boomerang*, which was released October 2nd.

Dorothy's next film would not be the most famous of her career nor the most successful. But it would be the most important. The movie was *His Only Son*. Dorothy's co-star was one of the rising stars in Hollywood, working on his 30th film. He had also written several screenplays, directed, and done camera work. On that set, Dorothy met Wally Reid.

4

Santa Barbara and Marriage

Wally made his 31st and 32nd films in July and August, 1912, but two of the last dozen are of note. *His Only Son* was made by Nestor, directed by Jack Conway and Milton Fahrney, and starred Wally and Dorothy. He made Vitagraph's *Every Inch a Man*, directed by William Humphrey and co-starring Hal and Rose Tapley. And he met Dorothy.

Dorothy said they met on the Henry Walthall film *His Son* which she recalled making in July, 1911, and that "Wally Reid had come to the coast with the late Otis 'Daddy' Turner; 'The Governor' he was called. Wally was assistant director, scenario writer and general utility man. My director Milton Fahrney was making a one-reel picture entitled *His Son*, a western. We were without a leading man. Turner was not ready to start, and Wally, on the company payroll at $40 a week, was assigned to us as leading man. At that time I was being paid $35 a week."[1] She said Wally worked with Tom Mix "as a stunt man. Mix was in charge of horses for Selig."

Parts of her recollection are true. Wally came west to work with Turner and was a stunt man with Mix but her timing is wrong and also, *His Son* was probably never made. Walthall is the only actor credited when the film *is* listed, it is in few legitimate filmographies, and she is never mentioned. Even Wally filmographies that include doubtful entries don't include the film. He said they met later and they both agreed that they met in California, but in July, 1911, Dorothy was still in New York with Biograph. Dorothy was probably remembering the Nestor 1912 western *His Only Son* which was directed by Fahrney.

She was not impressed with Wally, writing, "my impression of him was that he was all hands and feet, and very much embarrassed. My impression when the picture was completed was he was a very poor actor. When I came home I complained to mother because I had to play with 'this boy' when I had been playing with actors as Harold Lockwood, Henry Walthall, James Kirkwood.... After *His Son* [sic] Wally ... did several pictures with Margarita Fischer, Ella Hall and others." Writer St. Johns echoed Dorothy: "This big, overgrown boy ... knew nothing whatever about acting. Wally was annoyed because he was once more in front of the camera, and he sulked openly. In fact, they glared at each other from across the set between takes."[2]

On the third day of the *His Only Son* shoot Dorothy conspired with her cowboy friends to "fix" the newcomer. Men like Hoot Gibson, Caryl Eagles, and Tom Mix were *real* cowboys, expert riders that looked down on actors *playing* cowboys. Actors got the most ill-mannered horses, and Mix did this to Wally without knowing about Wally's year in Wyoming. He was an excellent rider, and when Dorothy arrived she saw Wally battling a bad-tempered mount given him by Gibson. St. Johns wrote that Wally was "easy, cool, and graceful, took everything this horse had to offer, corkscrews, tailspins, and sunfishes, before trotting him back to the corral sweating and conquered."[3] Bertha recalled, "The cowboys, among them Hoot Gibson, were waiting eagerly to show up this good-looking greenhorn from the East. They gave him a very frisky horse to ride, and then stood aside, expecting him to be thrown. They never tried any other tricks—he had proven himself one of them."[4] After watching Wally, Mix asked that he be used as his stunt double.

Wally didn't harbor any misgivings about Dorothy. The 16-year-old was beautiful, with dark eyes framed by red-brown hair falling over her shoulders and according to St. Johns, an "exquisite figure" and was blessed with "clear common sense, an amazing sense of humor, and a fierce loyalty."[5] Wally began childlike flirting. The company dressed in a converted barn nicknamed "the Ranch" and each morning Wally rode by, making sure Dorothy saw him. Alice liked Wally and lobbied on his behalf. Dorothy recalled, "Mother used to rave over his handsome appearance. It was my daily practice to slam the door when he appeared because I knew he knew that he was good looking, and I was not going to let him think I had succumbed to his good looks."

A movie magazine photo of Wally and Dorothy, taken just after their first film together in 1911.

Even though he was 20 and she barely 16 the two began dating. Wally took her to a weekly movie in Glendale or downtown on what he called "Dorothy nights" and became serious quickly. Within a month Wally and friend Gene Pallette rented Alice's extra room, joining Selig actress Phyllis Gordon, who had rented the "sleeping porch." Wally and Gene built a corral behind the house for everyone's horses, and each morning they rode to their studios. Another Hollywood newcomer lived in a bungalow nearby; Cecil B. DeMille also rode his own horse to work.[6] On weekends the group rode their horses into the mountains. It wasn't long before Wally asked Dorothy to marry him.

After *His Only Son*, Wally and Dorothy didn't work together for two years. For a few months Wally worked primarily for Bison Film Company. Six of Wally's next eight films were Bison westerns directed by Frank Montgomery, Bison's principal western director. All eight were done in August and September. The first was Vitagraph's *Every Inch a Man*, directed by William Humphrey with Wally in the lead supported by Hal (who wrote the scenario), and Rose Tapley, Robert Gaillard, and Morris McGee. It was released October 12th and it was during *this* film that Wally insisted he met Dorothy, writing, "I shall never forget this [movie] for it was ... [when] ... I met Dorothy Davenport. Miss Davenport had the role of the heroine in the picture ... a wild western.... It wasn't long before I was re-enacting the proposal scene from the movie in real life."[7] But Wally adds confusion too. In *His Only Son*—not *Every Inch a Man*—Wally's character proposed. *Every Inch a Man* was about a son saving his family and the lead was 40-year-old Tapley, playing the mother.

Wally's next role was the lead in Bison's *Early Days in the West*, with Dolly Larkin, George Field, Ray Francis, and W.G. Rice, released October 19th. *West* was followed by four westerns with Charles Inslee; Wally starred in one and played support in three. He supported *Hunted Down*, with Inslee, William Clifford, Margaret Manners, and Lizette Thorne, released October 22nd. *A Daughter of the Redskins* featured Inslee and Wally, with Harry Tenbrook and William Messick, and *The Cowboy Guardians* paired the two with Sylvia Ashton. These three were released October 22nd, 26th, and 29th, respectively.

Wally starred and Inslee played support in the next two. *The Tribal Law*, released November 16th, featured Margarita Fischer. In *An Indian Outcast*, released November 26th, Wally and Inslee worked with Fischer, Edward H. Philbrook, William Steele, and *real* Indians Chief Harvey and Ravena. Wally's final 1912 role was a Vitagraph lead in *All for a Girl*, released December 14th. He appeared with Dorothy Kelly, Leah Baird, Harry T. Morey, and Kate Price.

After *All for a Girl* Wally ran again, leaving in November for Santa Barbara to work for Allan Dwan, who had moved his "Flying A" company there from San Diego. Flying A—the American Film Manufacturing Company—was founded in Chicago in 1910 by film exchange owners Samuel S. Hutchinson, John Freuler, Charles Hite and Harry Aitken, whose lofty goal was to "Make American Film for American People."[8] They had less lofty methods of staffing, though. They raided nearby Essanay Film Manufacturing Company studios for cameramen and directors to film westerns they made in southern Wisconsin. In December, 1910, Frank Beal's unit was sent to Tucson, Arizona,[9] to avoid Edison's patent goons.

A month later, after the company had moved on to Southern California, Dwan replaced Beal. Dwan recalled, "There were about eight actors, cowboys, some horses, everyone sitting doing nothing. I said, 'Why aren't you working?' They said, 'Our director has been away on a binge for two weeks in Los Angeles so we haven't made any pictures.' It looked like a pretty bad situation and I wired Chicago, 'I suggest you disband the company. You have no director.' They wired back, 'You direct.' So I told the actors, 'Now either I'm a director or you're out of work.' And they said, 'You're the best damn director we ever saw. You're great.' I said, 'What does a director do?' So they took me out and showed me."[10]

Dwan was born in Toronto in 1885 and studied electrical engineering and played football at the University of Notre Dame. He then taught engineering and was an assistant football coach before joining Essanay in 1909 and Flying A in 1910.[11] He was feisty, opinionated, and always battling bosses, actors, or censors. He hated stage people, described his lead J. Warren Kerrigan as "quite a lady himself," and felt movies were full of "'pansies and poseurs because 'Hollywood sucked them all in.'"[12]

In May, 1911, he moved Beal's unit to San Diego to a makeshift studio near the Lakeside

Legendary director Allan Dwan was one of Wally's early mentors.

Hotel where they lived. In August he rented quarters in nearby La Mesa[13] and the next year made 125 films in the El Cajon valley and nearby beaches. Unfortunately, San Diego scenes had been filmed so often they were recognizable; Kerrigan described it as "worn out."[14] Dwan's assistant Marshall Neilan suggested Santa Barbara[15] and in July, 1912, Flying A relocated there and rented at 14 East Cota Street. It was a five-block walk to the beach and the huge Stearns Wharf. The building was 30 by 40 feet and held a few small offices and a developing room for five large circular developing tanks. Completed films were shipped to Chicago where 100 copies were made and sold. On November 5th, Hutchinson announced a second company would be added to Dwan's lead company, and papers announced, "PERMANENT HOME, 2 TROUPS, FOR AMERICAN FILM COMPANY HERE!"[16] Dwan hired Wally to lead the second company, a prestigious job for a young director. A second company was a production unit responsible for making films. Wally's company's payroll exceeded $100,000.[17]

Wally wanted to direct more than act but the main reason for his move was Dorothy having declined his proposal. She remembered it taking place "early in 1912" during a Sunday ride through Griffith Park when Wally said, "I guess it would be nice if we got married."[18] Dorothy said, "At the time I did not want to marry anybody. I told him I cared for him but did not love him. I replied curtly, 'I am not going to marry you or anyone.'" According to Wally, she "spurred up her horse and left me flat."[19] Dorothy's 1912 timing is again wrong. Wally's proposal occurred perhaps two months after they met, and she said it happened after he "accepted a place with the American Film Company at Santa Barbara and wanted me to go along as his bride. He wanted me to play leads but I did not want to break up house-keeping, and besides, I was not particularly anxious to be with him. We had a quarrel one day. Afterward we did not correspond for a long time, fully six months." It appears that his proposal actually took place not in 1912 but in July, 1911.

Whenever women failed him Wally ran. He first ran to Wyoming. The second time to Chicago. The third time, Dorothy failed him so he accepted Dwan's offer and went to Santa Barbara. Dwan's was not the safest of offers. Wally was an established actor and was joining a small studio in a new location—a major risk. But he likely wasn't thinking of it as such. Dorothy recalled it as a working vacation: "Wally directed the second company at Santa Barbara, with Vivian Rich, George Field, Ed Coxen and others.... Wally lived with Alan Dwan and Alan's mother. He came to Los Angeles occasionally to see me...." Actually, he didn't speak to her for six months and didn't live with Dwan; he lived at a hotel and then an apartment.

The Flying A company had well-known actors Pauline Bush, J. Warren Kerrigan, Jessalyn Van Trump, Marshall Neilan and Louise Lester.[20] Dwan's principal cameraman was Roy Overbaugh.[21] On November 15th Santa Barbara papers announced, "PRINCIPALS FOR SECOND 'FLYING A' WILL ARRIVE SOON—Wallace Reid, Miss Christie, and Ed Coxen Are Due Tomorrow." Lillian Christie[22] and Coxen[23] were established stars and it was noted they would stay at the Arlington Hotel and "between the two companies three plays will be produced each week.... Jack Kerrigan will take the lead in two, leaving the lead for one western play to Reid."[24]

Wally's unit arrived on the 17th. There were now 42 Flying A employees in Santa Barbara. A week later Wally, Dwan, Bush, Kerrigan, and Van Trump rented at the Edgerly Arms Apartment Hotel, which was built on nearby Sola Street for movie people.[25] Marion Davies, Lottie Pickford and Mary Miles Minter later lived there.[26] *Motion Picture Magazine* announced, "W. Wallace Reid Joins Producing Staff of American," in early December.[27]

Dwan rented a bungalow near an ostrich farm at State and Islay Streets and converted it to business and director's offices, the scenario department and two large dressing rooms.[28] The 2nd company—Wally, Christie, director William J. Bauman, publicity man Omar F. Doud, and cameraman A.G. Heimerl—began work on November 20th[29] and when Bauman realized Wally could direct *and* act he returned to Chicago.

Wally's first assignment was directing and acting in the western *Hidden Treasure*, filmed November 20th and 21st. Some records indicate a release date of November 12th, but period papers confirmed filming didn't start until the 20th. Three earlier versions of *Hidden Treasure* were made—by Selig and Urban-Eclipse in 1908 and Great Northern in 1910—but no material about Wally's version has been uncovered until now. Period newspapers confirm that Wally and Christie appeared in the film. *Hidden Treasure* is often credited as Wally's first directing assignment but research points to an earlier film. He is sometimes credited with co-directing *The Pathfinder* for Vitagraph, with Laurence Trimble,[30] in 1911.[31] Trimble was working at Vitagraph with Hal, and Wally was there during filming but his involvement can't be confirmed. He appeared with Hal in another James Fennimore Cooper adaptation, 1913's *The Deerslayer*, which may have caused the confusion. At the end of the *Hidden Treasure* shoot, a photograph of both companies was taken in front of the new offices, and before leaving for Chicago, Hutchinson purchased three acres at Mission and Chapala Streets at State for a permanent site.

Lunch break for the 1911 filming of *The Deerslayer* near Otsego Lake, New York. Director Larry Trimble stands far right; front right in black coat is Evelyn Dominicus (Hetty Hunter); Hal Reid (Hurry Harry March) is seated at left, in fur cap, and Wally (Chingachgook) is seated front left; Harry Morey (the Deerslayer) stands far left, in fur cap; Florence Trimble (Judith Hutter) stands left rear, wearing kerchief.

During September or October, Wally supposedly wrote and starred in a Vitagraph film, *All for a Girl*, with Dorothy Kelly, Leah Baird, Harry Morey, Kate Price, and Earl Foxe. It's included on some filmographies but given the December 14th release date it's not likely Wally did the movie unless it was actually shot much earlier. He would have had to return to L.A. almost as soon as he got to Santa Barbara and given the recent break with Dorothy it's not likely he would return.

In Santa Barbara, Wally directed, wrote, worked cameras, and acted (in that order). Writing scenarios was good money. Dorothy wrote, "Everyone took a crack at writing in those days. A writer got $25 for every scenario reel."[32] That was more than some actors earned in a week.

After *Hidden Treasure* he directed and starred in *Love and the Law* with Christy and Ed Coxen, and *A Rose of Old Mexico*, directing with Dwan and starred with Christy, Coxen, and Chester Withey. Both were made in December and released in January, 1913. Between December 10th and 12th he co-starred in a J. Warren Kerrigan film directed by Dwan entitled *Their Masterpiece*, released January 13th. On the same day, *Pirate Gold* was released by Vitagraph in New York. The Wilfred Lucas–directed effort featured Blanche Sweet and Charles Hill Mailes and Wally is sometimes listed in a small role, but it's doubtful he made this film. Filming was apparently done in New York in the fall of 1912 and the role was small for him.

Rare early studio still from Wally's 1913 film *Love and the Law*, made for Allan Dwan's Flying A troupe. With Wally is Nell Franzen (courtesy Dana Driskel, University of California Santa Barbara).

Wally next starred with and directed the three biggest Flying A names—Dwan's girlfriend Pauline Bush, Vivian Rich, and Murdock MacQuarrie—in the romance *The Ways of Fate*. It was made on December 26th and 27th and released April 21st. A 25-year-old Colorado Springs native debuted in *Fate*. Though his parents were deaf-mutes Leonidas Frank Chaney became an actor and started a theater company with his brother John. As "Lon" Chaney he made 158 films, including dozens of classics, before cancer killed him at age 47.

Dwan's crews made two pictures simultaneously with three days to finish both, at a cost of $10,000–$12,000. He'd "pile everyone into two buckboards, a wagon for our equipment, cowboys on horses—actors if they were riding in the picture—and off we went out into the country. On the way out, I'd try to contrive something to do. I had a heavy named Jack Richardson, so we'd send Kerrigan up there to struggle with Richardson and throw him off the cliff. Now, having made the last scene, I had to go backwards and try to figure out why all this happened."[33]

As the film made its way to Chicago for distribution the crew moved to another assignment. One surprising result was that "many of us never even saw the pictures we made. We simply shot them in California, cut off the scene numbers, and shipped the negative east, where it was printed, edited and sub-titled. Half the time the Eastern office fastened a new title so there was no way of our identifying it when it was released. By the time we'd made another dozen anyway, and the pictures playing at movie houses seemed ancient history."[34]

The Chicago office sold the films on a "state rights" basis: an exhibitor bought the rights to a state for resale to theaters. Track records determined price. Jesse Lasky later explained, "A print was sold for a flat sum to service a specified territory and could be rerun in its assigned region till it wore out. A small state got only one print, a large state two, and a block like New England, four or five."[35] It was often a gamble. Distributor J. Frank Hatch offered Mack Sennett $8,000 for Mabel Normand's *Mickey* for Ohio but refused to pay $9,000. Rival Pittsburgh distributor Harry Grelle paid $12,000 for Ohio and $10,000 for Pennsylvania for three years and in 2 years resold prints for $350,000 ($7,000,000 today) and $60,000 in Pittsburgh alone.[36]

Flying A began building their new Mission Street studio in the nicest neighborhood in Santa Barbara, across from the summer retreat of jeweler Louis Comfort

Tiffany.[37] A 3-story mission-style building topped by a 70-foot tower would house offices for Dwan and Wally, business offices, a projection room, and scenario offices. There would be 12 buildings: large concrete and glass sets 25 feet tall and 40 by 60 feet long with removable walls; a prop building; carpentry shop; garage; development plant; and a large livestock corral. A large building would hold private, heated dressing rooms, each with running water. It would cost $50,000 ($4,000,000 today). The entire site would be surrounded by an ornamental iron fence, and the manicured grounds would be covered with flowers surrounding a 36-foot pond. The grounds could be sets, framed by mountain peaks above.[38]

On December 28th, after completing *The Ways of Fate,* Wally was injured in a freak accident. Papers reported, "Wallace Reid, director of one of the 'Flying A' companies, sustained severe injuries to his left leg when, on horseback, he was giving chase to a runaway on the boulevard one afternoon recently. His horse fell with the rider beneath it. Mr. Reid and Miss Lillian Christy had been at the plaza and were about to return uptown. The two horses were untied when Miss Christy's dashed away. Mr. Reid was immediately astride his own and giving chase to the runaway. He was in a wild gallop about a block from the plaza when the animal lost its footing on the pavement and fell, carrying its rider with it. Mr. Reid's left leg was pinned beneath his mount and he suffered a severe sprain or break of the left ankle."[39] Papers noted, "he will not be able to wear a shoe on the foot for several days,"[40] and he remained on crutches for two weeks before a doctor made a plaster cast so he could move about.

During the week of the accident Wally's great-uncle Whitelaw Reid died in his New York mansion at age 82. He left an estate worth $15,000,000 to $20,000,000.[41] On January 18, 1913, the *Santa Barbara Morning Press* began a daily "NOTES FROM THE 'FLYING A' STUDIO"[42] column, with film notes and updates. Wally was a daily feature and already receiving more fan mail than anyone at Flying A. Among his mail was a "weekly message from a feminine admirer in Alabama. The first came in the form of mistletoe, mailed from New York."[43]

Wally's injury kept him from working in early January. He returned in mid-month in the Dwan-directed *When the Light Fades,* starring with Christy, Gene Pallette, and Ed Coxen. It was released February 24th. During *Fades* filming studio President Hutchinson began orchestrating the eventual ruin of Flying A, for reasons unknown. Christie was a very popular actress but after *Fades* filming finished Hutchinson announced that Vivian Rich[44] would replace her as the female lead in the 2nd unit. He also brought in Jean Durrell,[45] a San Francisco stage actress, and Dorothy Brown[46] as the new "engenue [sic]."[47] Dwan was furious at Hutchinson's interference.

At the same time, Wally's reckless driving almost led to tragedy on January 22nd when he lost control of a car ferrying his crew up the narrow Mountain Road near remote Parma Park. Papers noted that while "making a turn late [in the] afternoon the car was stopped when a few more inches ahead would have resulted in a plunge to the bottom of the ravine. It was impossible to extricate the car and it had to be abandoned overnight."[48] Nobody was injured but the car had to be pulled from its spot hanging over the cliff the next day.

Several films attributed to Wally during January and February 1913 don't match either his location or the work he was doing. The first, almost certainly incorrectly credited is *Near to Earth,* a Griffith-Biograph film. Griffith arrived in California after New Year's 1913 and he made some 30 films there during 1913, among them Lillian Gish's *The Mothering Heart* and the Blanche Sweet classic *Judith of Bethulia* (Wally's favorite film). *Near to Earth* was Griffith's third film but was not made near Santa Barbara. Griffith's 1913 films were produced in the San Fernando Valley or the mountains near Sierra Madre.[49] Additionally, production coincides with the time Wally was hobbled on crutches.

Another film of doubtful pedigree is *The Eye of a God*, released April 13th. It was written and directed by Joseph Golden for Pyramid Film Company, a small group at Warner Features. There is no evidence Wally participated though he is often included in cast lists.

According to Dorothy early in 1913 she and Wally began communicating again. It may have been stories of Wally's day on horseback with his leading lady, or of fan letters and gifts that prompted her change of heart. For whatever reason, by late February their relationship had been rekindled.

Flying A was doing well; Hutchinson even spent $3,000 for new cameras for each unit[50] and ground was broken for the new site even as he was dismantling his company. Each morning Dwan put a camera at the corner of Mission and Chapala and a cameraman cranked once; the result was a 15-minute quick-motion recording of the four-month construction. In February, Wally received a gift from Hal, who borrowed equipment and filmed the family back in New Jersey. Bertha, Grandmother Virginia, and the family's servants went "through a number of interesting antics before [the] camera for the special benefit of the son. Naturally, it made Mr. Reid a bit home sick [sic], but when he feels the 'heimway' too strong again he can have another run at the film." Wally gathered his entire crew for a special viewing.[51]

From February through April, Wally acted, wrote and directed. When new ingénue Jean Durrell arrived on March 2nd he was writing, directing and playing the lead in *When Jim Returned* with new cast-mate Vivian Rich and his roommate Gene Pallette. It was released April 24th. He followed it with *The Tattooed Arm* and the same cast, released May 1st. He then directed and starred in three Theodosia Harris scenarios. The first, *Youth and Jealousy*, with Rich and newcomer Frank Borzage, was released May 10th. The second was *The Kiss*, with Rich and Pallette, released May 15th. The third was *Her Innocent Marriage*, with Rich and George Field, released May 19th.

Wally then directed four films in which he starred, the first three with Rich and Field. The first was *A Modern Snare*, released May 24th, after which Wally convinced Dwan to buy one of Hal's scenarios, *When Luck Changes*, which he directed and was released June 2nd. The third was *Via Cabaret*, released June 7th. Wally's next assignment was *The Spirit of the Flag*, with Bush, Van Trump, Arthur Rosson, Neilan, and David Kirkland. It was filmed April 10th and 11th and released June 7th. Wally, Rich and Field were back together on *Hearts and Horses* on April 15th and 16th; it was released June 12th. *Hearts and Horses* was high-budget for Flying A; Wally had a barn built in the hills that was burned to the ground during filming.

Wally's next film was the war movie *In Love and War*, directed by Dwan and Thomas Ince for Ince's 101-Bison Films, so named because Ince hired 100 cowboys and Indians from Miller Brothers' 101 Ranch & Wild West Show. *Love and War* featured Wally opposite Bush and Neilan in a story of a young man who, after being rejected for military service, volunteers as a war correspondent and becomes a hero. It was released June 17th.

Wally wrote his next two films, starring with Bush in *Woman and War*, which also featured Van Trump and Neilan and was released June 21st. Then followed *Dead Man's Shoes*, a film he wrote, directed and starred in. Rich and Field worked in *Shoes*, which was released June 28th. Wally's next film was another Hal scenario, *The Pride of Lonesome*, which Wally directed and starred in with Borzage. It was released July 3rd. Next was the Dwan-written and directed *The Powder Flash of Death*, made for 101-Bison. Bush starred, with Neilan, Van Trump and Kirkland. It was released July 8th.

While the company gathered for a surprise birthday party for Dwan at his De La Vina Avenue bungalow on April 4th, something was afoot with Hutchinson. The first hint was the sudden hiring of Rich, Durrell, and Brown, which led to the abrupt exit of Wally's lead actress Lillian Christy. On May 11th Hutchinson returned from a month-long visit to Hawaii but stayed only one day before returning to Chicago. As cryptic notes in "NOTES FROM THE 'FLYING A' STUDIO" suggested, he was preparing to replace much of the Santa Barbara staff.

On April 15th he announced Albert A. Hale would join as a director and would make his first film immediately. There was no third unit, so he was replacing *someone*. The paper noted, "Hutchinson held a conference with players and heads of departments at the Arlington last night when questions of future policies were discussed." Surprisingly, also noted were "unfounded rumors that the retirement of Allen [sic] Dwan as director had resulted in much dissatisfaction within the company," and that Dwan was starting "a Santa Barbara company for a Los Angeles production concern ... borne out by the fact that Mr. Dwan is at present in Los Angeles."[52]

That Dwan missed Hutchinson's staff meeting is telling. Also significant was the fact that Vitagraph was looking for Santa Barbara studio property at the time and that director Francis J. Grandon and writer Wallace C. Clifton were in town scouting locations for Lubin Film Company.[53] They stayed at the Arlington with the Flying A people.

It's possible Hutchinson, knowing of the Vitagraph and Lubin rumors, thought Dwan was quitting and reacted preemptively by bringing in new players and a new director. It's also possible Hutchinson bristled at Dwan's relaxed production schedule of three films a week from two companies, thinking Dwan was not producing enough. A secret then—and not well known even today—Hutchinson fired Dwan that April. Dwan confirmed this in a 1978 interview with documentary producer Dana Driskel.[54] After he was fired, Dwan telegrammed William Selig, inquiring about employment.

Hutchinson's moves angered most of the Santa Barbara crew, including Wally and the soap opera was played out in the newspaper's "NOTES" column. Hale was important; an April 17th column described him as the top new director at Flying A "in the market for good scenarios, with locations in mind that are readily accessible to the company."[55] He completed his first film—*Reward of Courage*—on April 18th and the next day Hutchinson took him to L.A. for the "purpose of engaging new players" and to "take players to Venice to make scenes of a 'Calamity Jane' film...."[56] The same day it was announced that Van Trump and Bush (Dwan's girlfriend) were leaving "at the end of the coming week for Los Angeles. Both have been with American for two years. Since coming to Santa Barbara they have made many friends, and their modest and pleasing personalities have impressed the folks here. There is nothing definitely known about their future plans."[57] A few days later papers reported they were joining "Universal Film Company ... glad to know they are leaving because the opportunity to better themselves is too great to be resisted."[58] There was clearly a major power shift afoot.

Bush and Dwan were dating (they married in 1915) and Hutchinson had already fired Dwan by the 18th, but it is unclear if Hutchinson wanted Wally out, too. He continued to direct the 2nd unit but some articles listed Ed Coxen as the 2nd unit director. Given Wally's personality it is doubtful he would have stayed after his friend Dwan left. On May 7th, as Wally was considering leaving, Vitagraph released *The Deerslayer*. This release evidences the difficulty of quantifying silent film history, specifically timing and locations. The movie was directed by Hal,[59] who also starred with Harry Morey, Ethel Dunne, Edward Thomas, Evelyn Dominicus, Florence Turner, and Wally as the second lead Chingachgook. The film was made near remote Otsego Lake, New York; Hal even hired two dozen local Indians and area hunting guide "Caribou Bill."[60] Wally was in the film; cast photos survive with Wally visible.

But it was made two years earlier. On July 5, 1911, local papers had noted "Vitagraph Company of America to Take Moving Pictures of Cooper Tales Here,"[61] and *Moving Picture World* announced, "Vitagraph has under production the 'Leatherstocking Tales,' by Fennimore Cooper [sic] including ... 'The Deerslayer.'"[62] On September 6, 1911, papers reported, "Vitagraph Folks Are Here!"[63] The film was not made in 1913 as reported in some filmographies, but was probably a re-release of the 1911 film which may have had limited original release around New York.

In late May, after starring in *A Foreign Spy* with Rich and Borzage (released July 10th) Wally left Flying A. He returned to L.A. and Hutchinson's dismantling of the Santa Barbara company was complete. Hutchinson immediately increased production to a film a day, a pace that continued until 1916 when his ongoing meddling, the inability to produce quality features in large numbers and the War's impact led to the company's demise.

The company's output began faltering during the War though some of their films—particularly those featuring William Russell, Margarita Fisher, and Mary Miles Minter—were indeed successful. A combination of the collapse of Mutual Film Corporation in 1918 and a lack of additional studios in Santa Barbara also hurt Flying A. Mutual's shift to "Big Films With Big Stars" in late 1916 meant a reduction in the number of day-player jobs in Santa Barbara, so many of the bigger names were forced to return to Los Angeles to find sufficient work.

Back in Los Angeles, Wally rented at the Reiter Arms Apartments in the middle of Hollywood. The Spanish stucco building was on the corner of Sunset and Hillhurst Avenue and many of its residents were film people. Frank Borzage lived there, as did actors George Marshall and George Siegmann (Barrabus in DeMille's *The King of Kings* [1927]), and young director Tod Browning. The first month after his return eight Wally films were released including the *Deerslayer* re-release.

While Wally was in Santa Barbara, Dorothy was busy at Universal's Selig and Nestor units. During the last months of 1912 she appeared in seven films playing leads in all of them. That work included *The Border Parson*, with William Clifford; *Fatty's Big Mixup*, with Howard Davies and Jefferson Osborne; *In the Long Run* for Nestor lead director Jack Conway, with William C. Dowlan and Osborne; *Almost a Suicide*, with Eddie Lyons; *Home and Mother*, with George Field; *A Black Hand Elopement*, opposite Herbert Rawlinson; and *All Rivers Meet the Sea* (released in 1913). She appeared in a number of films during the first half of 1913, like *A False Friend* for Lubin and *Toplitsky and Company*, directed by Henry Lehrman and starring Alice. Her final film before Wally's return was *The Failure of Success*, with Charles Edler, for Kay-Bee Pictures and Mutual.

Dorothy was doing well professionally, having made 36 films by that June, but Wally far surpassed her in output and popularity. In addition to playing 71 roles, he directed another 16 films and wrote 12. We can only guess at the number of movies he filmed, but it was in the high dozens. Dorothy recalled that it was after Wally's return she realized she might be in love: "Gradually I must have fallen in love with Wally, although it was a long time before I would admit it even to myself. He was so sweet, so thoughtful one could not help liking him."[64]

As Dorothy returned his affections he began wearing her down. When he left Hollywood in a huff he told Alice, "I'll make her care for me. I've never been licked yet—and I'm not licked now." His efforts were comical, certainly not what we'd expect from a movie star. Even Dorothy found him clumsy: "Now here is an odd thing. Wally had returned with the determination to make *me* propose to *him*. Wally would come to our house. The telephone would ring. 'Is Wally Reid there?' a voice would ask. Wally would go to the phone and say importantly, 'All right, I'll be right over.' I learned later he was having people call him up just to make me jealous. Once he said to me, 'You are going to marry me this fall!' 'Oh,' I replied, 'I suppose I have nothing to say about it?' 'No, you haven't,' he said, 'Your mother and I have decided it.'" Once he took Dorothy to the train station and picking up a magazine with the picture of a bride on the cover told her, "That's the way you are going to look this fall."[65] Dorothy was weakening.

Wally went right to work after his return to Hollywood. Carl Laemmle had taken control over his Universal cartel and almost all of Wally's subsequent films were done for one of Laemmle's studios. Wally first reunited with Dwan and Bush in *The Picket Guard* along with Neilan, Van Trump and Kirkland, for Bison. It was released July 12th. Next was *Mental Suicide* for the Powers Picture Plays unit, with Wally, Bush, Neilan, Van Trump and Kirkland, released July 25th. Then followed several Dwan films for Rex Motion Pictures with the same cast. The first was *Man's Duty*, released August 10th, then *The Animal*, in which Wally plays an animal who becomes human when he reunites a couple (Van Trump and Donald Barlow) and their lost child and wins the love of Bush. Mickey Neilan also appeared in the film, released August 17th. Wally later said he thought *The Animal* was "the one he thinks was his best" work.[66]

The next film was also made for Rex, written and directed by Wally. William Walters and Bush starred in *The Harvest of Flame* with Wally and Neilan supporting. It was released August 21st. A film attributed to Wally at this time is in doubt. *The Picture of Dorian Gray*, made for New York Motion Picture Company by Phillips Smalley, starred Lois Weber. Wally's participation can't be confirmed.

Wally next directed *The Spark of Flame* for Powers, requesting Dorothy as his co-star in the film, released August 22nd. Of the ten films he made between June and early October he starred with Dorothy in six. After *Spark* was Bison's *The Mystery of the Yellow Aster Mine*; directed by Frank Borzage, it paired Wally with Bush and Arthur Rosson. The film was made in June and released August 26th.

Wally directed *The Gratitude of Wanda* for Bison and was again teamed with Bush, Rosson, and Van Trump. It was released August 30th. Dwan directed Wally in *The Wall of Money* for Rex with a Flying A cast: Bush, Neilan (who wrote the screenplay), Van Trump and MacQuarrie. The film was made in late June and released September 21st.

After *Wanda*, Wally wrote a serial about a gentleman crook, the Cracksman. The first was *The Heart of a Cracksman* which he directed for Powers. Wally starred with Cleo Madison, supported by James Neill, Ed Brady and Marcia Moore. It was filmed in July and released November 7th. *The Cracksman's Reformation* followed, again directed by Wally. He replaced Madison with Dorothy and backed her with the same supporting cast as the original. The film was released November 14th.

Dorothy worked on 8 films that summer, 6 with Wally, and decided to marry him. In August, Dorothy finally answered "yes" to his repeated proposals, recalling, "At Pine Crest I began to develop symptoms of being in love, so mother has since told me.[67] I would not dance when the others danced, and I spent much time alone, thinking, thinking. Following my return to Los Angeles, Wally said one evening, 'You are going to marry me Saturday.' This time I did not say I would not marry him. I was not through protesting, however."[68] She told him, "If it is to be at all it must be on the thirteenth. Thirteen, I have always believed, is my lucky day, because of a series of three and thirteens in my life. I was born March 13, the third month of the year and the third day of the week." So the date was set for October 13, 1913. The truth had less to do with numerology, was less romantic, and involved the other woman in Wally's life, Bertha. She disagreed with Wally's plans.

Originally a Christmas wedding was planned and Wally wired Bertha with the news; he found "the only girl in the world"⁶⁹ for him. Bertha did not dislike Dorothy. She disapproved of *any* woman marrying her son. She wrote they should wait, that they were too young—he 19 and she barely 17—taking "the liberty of advising them not to be in too much haste." But she "grossly offended these mettlesome young things."⁷⁰ Dorothy was furious. Her response to Bertha's meddling was to move the marriage *up* three months to October, and to exclude Bertha, who read about the wedding in the newspapers. It would be six years before Wally saw her again. Dorothy and Alice arranged the October 13, 1913, wedding at the Church of the Holy Cross in Hollywood. In the meantime, Wally and Dorothy had to work.

Wally was becoming an established name for Universal as a director, writer *and* actor. His movies did well at the box office and fans liked the tall, handsome blonde with the piercing blue eyes. Laemmle's publicity department proclaimed Wally and Dorothy a team in *Moving Picture World*, which had already dubbed Wally one of the handsomest men in the movies. Of Dorothy, it observed, "In Dorothy Davenport he has a delightful leading woman, for Dorothy is a great favourite [sic] with a discerning public...."⁷¹

This rare early studio photo of Wally was taken about the time he married Dorothy. It was taken by a relatively unknown photographer—Albert Witzel—who was an industry favorite through the mid–1920s.

Wally's next five films were directed by himself, either co-directed with Willis Robards or by Robards alone. Wally wrote *The Fires of Fate*, directed by him and Robards for Rex. Dorothy co-starred and Brady played support in the film, released November 20th. Wally and Robards teamed to direct *Cross Purposes*, with Cleo Madison co-starring in a film released December 5th. The team then directed *Retribution* for Nestor with Wally and Dorothy in the leads, supported by Brady, Phil Dunham, Borzage, and Anna Q. Nilsson. The film was released December 10th. English-born vaudevillian Dunham met Wally on the *Retribution* set, which was Dunham's debut. The two became friends and remained so the rest of Wally's life. Dunham's first 20 films were all directed by or starred Wally, who requested his new friend be assigned to his films.⁷²

Wally followed with the third in his *Cracksman* series, *A Cracksman Santa Claus*, again for Powers. It was directed by Robards with Wally and Dorothy starring, supported by Gertrude Short, Borzage and Brady. It was released December 19th. On Monday, October 13, Wally began work on *The Lightning Bolt*, with Dorothy supported by Brady and Dunham. Wally directed the 3-day shoot; the film was released Christmas Eve, 1913.

On Monday evening after the first day of *Lightning Bolt* filming, Wally and Dorothy were married. At 6:30 P.M. a small group gathered at the Church of the Holy Cross and the couple were wed by Rev. Baker P. Lee. The only people present were the film's co-stars Ed Brady and Phil Dunham, Ruth Roland, Universal manager Isidore Bernstein, and Alice Davenport.[73] Dunham stood as best man and Ruth Roland was maid of honor. Vaudevillian western star Roland was Dorothy's best friend.

Wally's friendship with Dunham exhibits the contradiction that was Wally. Evolving into the on-screen symbol of masculinity, he was decidedly un-manly in lots of ways. The Renaissance man who loved fast cars, did his own stunts, and played every musical instrument evidently had trouble cultivating friendships with men. His best man was an actor he had known less than a month. He had no close friend to ask. He had plenty of friends— everyone at his studio loved him, it seemed—but no *real* friends.

The wedding party celebrated at Isidore Bernstein's home at 1525 North La Brea.[74] Several friends stopped by, including actors Charles Worthington and Kerrigan, who came with his mother. Bernstein forbade alcohol in his home so the guests drank lemonade. The story of the marriage made all of the movie magazines. *Moving Picture World* announced, "Universal Film Director Marries Leading Woman,"[75] though they mentioned Christ Episcopal Church rather than Holy Cross. Photos of the newlyweds in Wally's new Stutz coupe ran in West Coast papers.

Wally said, "My wife comes from one of America's best and oldest theatrical families, one that is aligned in marriage to the Rankins, Drews, and Barrymores."[76] Not the most romantic reaction but for Wally the marriage was more about conquest than acquisition. The honeymoon had to wait. They had to be on the set the next day so they spent their wedding night at Wally's Reiter Arms apartment. The next morning it was back to finish *Lightning Bolt*. *Moving Picture Magazine* described the welcome the newlyweds received at the studio entrance on Sunset: "The young couple are held in the highest esteem by their professional associates, and their reception at the Hollywood studios Tuesday morning attested to their popularity. There was the popping of guns and cheers as the couple was heralded down the street...."[77] Hollywood was still enough of a cowboy town that actors could stand outside the Nestor office at Sunset and Gower and fire pistols into the air!

A month later Wally and Dorothy rented a small apartment in a bungalow court on North Las Palmas Avenue above Hollywood Boulevard. Hundreds of similar courts filled Hollywood, usually containing four to eight units around a courtyard. They were inexpensive—a nice one cost $40 a month—and popular among actors who tended to be transient.

Alice Davenport had become Mack Sennett's and Keystone's most dependable supporting actress. She appeared in over 50 films from 1913 to 1915 alongside the great names like Ford Sterling, Charlie Chase, Roscoe Arbuckle, and Charlie Chaplin. She appeared in famous Keystone films like the Arbuckle classics *The Telltale Light* and *A Quiet Little Wedding* (both 1913) and the Chaplin films *Making a Living, Tillie's Punctured Romance* and *The Property Man* (all 1914).

Wally and Dorothy were also busy the rest of 1913. He made another 10 films, beginning with writing, directing and starring with Dorothy in the Nestor film *A Hopi Legend*, supported by Brady, Borzage and Dunham. The picture was released December 31st. He worked with Reliance director John B. O'Brien on two films, the first being *Sierra Jim's Reformation* with Gertrude McLynn supported by Raoul Walsh and Native American actors Eagle Eye and Dark Cloud. It was released in late December and was immediately followed by *The Second Mrs. Roebuck* in which Wally starred with Mary Alden, Blanche Sweet, and Walsh.

Then followed three Reliance-Mutual films released in January, 1914. *A Mother's Influence* featured Wally with Billie West; *Moonshine Molly*, directed by Christy Cabanne, co-starred Mae Marsh, Dorothy's Biograph pal Robert Harron, Fred Burns, and Native American Eagle Eye; *The Little Country Mouse* was directed by Donald Crisp and starred Wally with Sweet, Alden and Walsh. Wally then did two films directed by Cabanne, *Her Awakening* with Sweet and Ralph Lewis, and *For Those Unborn* with Sweet, Harron, and Irene Hunt. Both were released in January.

He did a final non–Nestor film for Powers, *Whoso Diggith a Pit* with Lurline Lyons and his friends Ed Brady and James Neill, released January 9th. After completing *Pit*, Wally and a Nestor group traveled to the mountains above Lake Arrowhead. Between late November, 1913, and mid–January, 1914, Nestor made several trips there and shot a dozen films.[78] Led by Wally and Dorothy the group included friends Ed Brady, Phil Dunham, Lucile Wilson, Frank Borzage, and Gertrude Robinson, and new faces Raoul Walsh, Fred Gamble, and John Blystone.

The first trip also served as a honeymoon, Dorothy remembering "months after our marriage, our own small unit went up into the Sierras to film several scripts, all of which had a mountain background. This location jaunt gave Wally and me a belated honeymoon—and for free, which was important."[79] It was a working honeymoon since the couple filmed non-stop. They stayed at the secluded Squirrel Inn, a beautiful and rustic private lodge in the Twin Peaks area of Lake Arrowhead near the present-day intersection of routes 18 and 189. In 1913 the lake was called Big Bear Lake and was not a resort destination.

The Squirrel Inn was built in 1892 on 40 acres owned by the Arrowhead Mountain Club and James Mooney, a wealthy financier who ran Arrowhead Reservoir & Power Company with his partner James Morris Gamble (of Procter & Gamble). Intent on building the Lake Arrowhead Dam, Mooney started buying land and water rights in the 1890s for a project to provide water to San Bernardino County. The Inn was originally named the Squirrel Inn Club and was only available to Mooney investors who paid for the thousands of nearby acres of virgin timber land. Eight-hundred-acre Big Bear Lake was surrounded by a magnificent forest of pine and cedar at an altitude of 5,000 feet. Film companies used the woodlands as early as 1910 but it was difficult to reach. It was only 90 miles from L.A. but it took a full day to make the dangerous journey.

The only access was the Two Mile Road that snaked down the Arrowhead Mountain from the summit into Lake Arrowhead village, part of a winding road carved by Mormon loggers through the San Bernardino Mountains in the 1850s. The Mormon Road followed Hot Springs Canyon (now Waterman Canyon) over the summit. It was dangerous, straight up the mountain.[80] Mooney re-routed the 2½ miles near the summit with thirteen switchbacks. The only other route was from the east, the Bear Valley Toll Road, which was even more dangerous than the Mormon Road. There were too many fatal accidents to count on the roads toward the Inn.

The Inn was beautiful, more a hunting lodge than an inn. The large cabin was crafted from logs cut from nearby stands. Two large wings flanked a four-story main structure. The first-floor lobby was dominated by a twelve-foot wide fireplace at the rear and a long porch out front. The large two-story gable above the second floor was made by joining hundreds of perfectly matched round log-ends, stacked with a stunning display of craftsmanship. The second and third floors of the middle section had half a dozen guest-rooms. Two large two-story wings flanked the main section, each with its own six-foot-wide stone fireplace. One was a communal den and the other a dining room and kitchen area. The Inn was surrounded by pine trees soaring 100 feet in the air. It was a half mile down into the small Arrowhead Village next to the lake. Wally and Dorothy returned several times and later bought property in the area for a planned vacation retreat.

Early postcard view of the Squirrel Inn, site of the Reids' honeymoon, often rented by film studios filming in the Lake Arrowhead area.

Mooney's project fell apart in 1913 and in 1921 his land was sold to Arrowhead Lake Company, a syndicate led by L.A. developer J.B. Van Nuys. The group renamed Lake Arrowhead after a large rock outcropping in the shape of an arrowhead and built dozens of luxury lodges, a golf course, and marinas. They spent $10,000,000 tearing down the Little Bear Resort (downtown Lake Arrowhead) and replacing it with a Norman English–style village that opened on June 24, 1922.[81] But it was still remote; only 100 families lived within ten miles. The Squirrel Inn closed in the 1930s and was demolished. The acreage where it stood is owned by the Church of Scientology and is reportedly the site of a secret vault.

The 1913 Nestor crew made a dozen movies during their visits that fall. The films were released between January 14 and March 10, 1914. This group of films was dominated by Wally. He starred in each and wrote or directed also. The first seven were directed by Wally and starred him and Dorothy. *The Intruder* featured Brady and Dunham, followed by *The Countess Betty's Mine*, with the same cast; *The Wheel of Life*, with Brady, Borzage, Lucile Wilson, and John Blystone; *Fires of Conscience*, with Gertrude Robinson and Brady; *The Greater Devotion*, with Fred Gamble, Brady and Dunham; *A Flash in the Dark*, with Brady and Borzage; and *Breed o' the Mountains*, with Brady and Wilson. Dorothy played a waif abandoned at the door of a young woodsman's cabin that leads to a Hatfield-McCoy type of mountain feud. The eighth film, *Regeneration*, featured Wally and Helen Taft in the leads, supported by Brady and Dunham. Then Wally and Dorothy did *The Voice of the Viola*, with William Steele, Brady, and Dunham, released March 4th.

Just after *Regeneration*, Dorothy's aunt, Gladys Rankin, daughter of McKee Rankin, died suddenly in New York at age 39. She was married to actor Sidney Drew when she died January 9th. They entered movies in 1911 and were popular Vitagraph stars. Their son, S. Rankin Drew, left a promising acting career to fly for the famed Lafayette Esquadrille in World War I but on May 19, 1918, he was shot down over France and killed. Sidney never recovered. In perfect health when his son died, within a year he had withered away, dying on May 9, 1919, of uremic poisoning (friends believed a broken heart killed him). Just months after Gladys' death he had married 24-year-old actress Lucille McVey. In 1925, she died of cancer at age 35.

Regeneration was Wally's first 2-reeler. In late 1913 studios began moving from single-reelers lasting about five minutes to longer two- and three-reelers that lasted ten to fifteen minutes. Longer films meant more creativity and better plots. Almost all of Wally's subsequent films were 2 reels or longer. Wally wrote his next Nestor film and directed and starred. *Heart of the Hills* was a 2-reeler featuring Wally and Dorothy, Dunham, Brady and Wilson. It was released March 12th. He then directed and starred with Dorothy in a Bess Meredyth scenario, *The Way of a Woman*, which featured Nestor players Edna Maison and Antrim Short and was released March 18th. Next he wrote, directed and starred in *The Mountaineer* with Dorothy, Dunham, Wilson, and Brady, released March 25th. It appears *The Way of a Woman* was the final Nestor film done at Lake Arrowhead. Wally's next film, *The Spider and Her Web* for Rex, was directed by Phillips Smalley and Lois Weber, who had just started her own production company. Dorothy co-starred with Weber and Wally supported along with Smalley and Rupert Julian. The film was released March 26th.

Wally and Dorothy were primarily Nestor players at Universal. With the exception of a few films their output the rest of the first half of 1914 was for Nestor. Wally starred and/or directed all of them and wrote two scenarios. Dorothy appeared in all but one and Wally's friend Phil Dunham in all of them. Wally still preferred directing and writing to acting and complained, "My damn face kept me from becoming a director and a writer." St. Johns said, "Nothing so incensed Wally more than feeling that he was just 'getting by' on his looks."[82] Fans knew him as an actor but his peers knew him as a director more than an actor. That was fine with him.

Returning from Lake Arrowhead, Wally was thrilled at an invitation to join the Photoplayer's Club, the first group formed in the new industry. Founded in December 1912 for production types, actors were allowed in later if they paid $6 a year in dues. The club leased two floors at 349 South Hill Street, with a library and a wide fireplace, a Dutch stein room, a dining room and kitchen to serve up to 500, a billiard room, an English tap, lockers, showers and guest rooms. The original officers were directors Fred Mace and George H. Melford and members included Al Christie, Thomas Ince, Henry Lehrman, and Mack Sennett.

By January 4, 1913, there were 150 members[83] and the first public event was a St. Valentine's Ball at the enormous 6,000-seat Shrine Auditorium. The group held a parade through downtown on the 8th to publicize the party.[84] William Selig provided animals, including his prized elephant "Big Otto" and a lion named "Duke," while Ince sent 100 cowboys and Native Americans. Kathlyn Williams led 150 automobiles filled with stars like Mabel Normand and Wally. The ball allowed fans to mingle with 2,000 actors; 9,856 of the 10,000 available tickets were sold.[85] *The Los Angeles Times* announced, "THEY REALLY HAVE VOICES! Photoplayers Meet Audience and Say 'Hello.'" It was the first time "friends of years standing heard one another speak ... as actors mingled with their audience that had long wondered what the voices of their favorites sounded like and how these men and women of a make-believe world really looked in the flesh."[86] Wally and Dorothy joined attendees like Charles Murray, Theodore Roberts, Ann Little, Bessie Eyton, the Gish sisters, Carlyle Blackwell, Herbert Rawlinson, J. Warren Kerrigan, and Tom Mix.

During that February, Wally directed five Nestor films starring him and Dorothy.

He wrote an adaptation of a Bess Meredyth scenario, *Cupid Incognito*, which also featured Dunham, John Blystone, and William Wolbert. He then directed and starred with Dorothy in *A Gypsy Romance* with Ed Brady and William Steele and did the same for *The Test*, with Frank Lloyd, Tom Santschi, Brady, Antrim and Gertrude Short. *The Test* was a fascinating story by Allan Dwan, a "grim parallelism of the lot of two homes...."[87] One wealthy couple (Lloyd and Short) lives in a mansion but the husband is absorbed with business, while across town a poor couple lives in a tenement, the wife (Dorothy) dreadfully ill. There is no money for food or medicine so her desperate husband (Wally) tries to rob a mansion and breaks into the wealthy couple's home, finding the husband in the library with a gun and poison, having just learned his wife has run off with another man. He laughs as Wally begs for mercy, saying, "Weren't you afraid you might be killed trying this?" Wally replies, "Wouldn't you be willing to die for those you loved?" to which the wealthy man answers, "No, and you wouldn't either," and proposes a test. "Here is poison that doesn't prove fatal for an hour after it's taken. Drink it, and I'll give you $1,000." He draws out a wad of bills. Wally struggles with the offer before saying, "I'll take it," and drinks; but the rich man had removed the pills and Wally received his $1,000 and the rich man a renewed appreciation for life.

The only non–Nestor film was Wally's next, for Powers. *The Skeleton* was a radical departure, a comedy that featured him and Dorothy with Dunham and Wolbert. Wally's only previous comedy experience was Hal's *At Scrogginses' Corner* in 1912. *Skeleton* showed he could not only *direct* comedy but was a gifted comedy actor with perfect timing and a knack for expression. Wally avoided the pitfall of most early actors, the overdone pantomime of the stage. Keystone Kops and pratfalls were comedic standards but Wally offered subtle comedy. His ability to do any role soon placed him in front of the camera forever. The public also noticed; he and Dorothy were described in ads as "Well-known Stars!"[88]

After *Skeleton* it was back to Nestor for an adaptation of the Elaine Stern magazine story *The Fruit of Evil*. He directed and starred with Dorothy, Brady, Gertrude Short, and Gladys Montague.[89]

Dorothy learned that McKee Rankin died on March 17th in San Francisco at 69. He had been transformed from a once-handsome actor to an obese alcoholic, the affliction that led to his death.

That same month Wally appeared in five movies, the first with Phyllis Gordon for Victor Film Company, entitled *The Daughter of a Crook*. The rest of his spring work consisted of Nestor films that he directed and starred in with Dorothy. First was *Women and Roses* with Lillian Brockwell and Vera Sisson, then *The Quack*, a comedy with Wolbert, Dunham, James Robert Chandler and Lucile Bolton, *The Siren*, with Brockwell, David Kirkland, Page Peters, and Lucile Bolton, and *The Man Within*, with Dunham, Steele, and Clarence Burton.

Wally made three films in April, directing them all, with him and Dorothy in the leads. The first was *Passing of the Beast*, which featured Joe King, John Blystone, Steele, Dunham, Edgar Keller and William Wolbert. Then followed *Love's Western Flight*, written by James Oliver Curwood and originally entitled *Children of Fate*. The supporting cast included King, Dunham, Wolbert and Frank Borzage. Next was *A Wife on a Wager*, with King and Blystone, and *'Cross the Mexican Line*, with friends Dunham, Steele, and Keller.

In May, 1914, Wally made his last film as a Universal contract player. He directed and starred with Dorothy in a western drama by F. McGrew Willis entitled *The Den of Thieves*. The supporting cast included Lillian Brockwell, Kirkland, Wolbert, and Phil Dunham. The film was released June 24, 1914. By then Wally was working for D.W. Griffith.

5

The Birth of a Star

The month of May 1914 marked several milestones for Wally. On the personal front he and Dorothy moved into the first house either had ever owned, leaving the Las Palmas bungalow court for a house at 1390 Allison Avenue in the hilly and winding streets above Echo Park. The park is a still-gorgeous property surrounding a 33-acre lake that got its name in 1895 when workers building bridges and walkways heard their voices echoing off the bluffs and hillsides around them.

The lake and its park, which featured a huge boathouse, the Echo Park Clubhouse, and a giant bed of lotus plants that survive to this day, were used as film sets for literally hundreds of early films when studios on Allesandro Street—now Glendale Boulevard—borrowed the park and lake. At one point city leaders barred Mack Sennett's Keystone crews from shooting any comedies at the lake because too many flowers were being trampled.

When Wally and Dorothy bought the Allison house the streets above Echo Park were largely empty and still unpaved dirt. The hills were criss-crossed with stairwells allowing residents to walk down to catch the trolleys at Sunset Boulevard, hillside bungalow courts and apartment buildings. Small houses, like the Reids', were just beginning to appear. Even as late as 1920 most of the hills around the lake were still untouched and farmhouses still lined the northern edge of the lake even as new four-unit, Craftsman-style apartment flats began rising on Echo Park Avenue and Alvarado Street.[1]

Adela St. Johns described the Allison house as "a little vine-covered cottage"[2] but it was a good-sized two-story craftsman-style with a porch across the front. Two large dormers rose above the roof (one remains). Allison was a quiet street above the lake but over the top of the hill from the park, leaving the lake not visible. A large hillside across the street towered above their porch but it was only about 50 yards from Sunset Boulevard and a trolley ride. The couple often relaxed on the porch that Dorothy filled with large wicker chairs, tables and flowers.[3] Alice lived with them and was listed in the 1914 Los Angeles City Directory, although strangely, Dorothy is not.

The neighborhood was crowded with film people though the neighbors in Wally's block were school teachers, city workers, and bricklayers.[4] In the 1914 Directory, Wally was listed as "director, Universal Film Company."[5] Echo Park and Silverlake (just on the other side of Sunset) were already teeming with movie people: Herschel Mayall lived at 1426 Allison, Ethel Teare—who worked in several dozen films with Wally's pals Phil Dunham and Charles Inslee—was at 1133 Laguna, J. Park Jones at 1128 Laguna, Marie White at 1072 Laguna, and Charlie Chase in the 1200 block of Echo Park. Coincidently, at the bottom of the hill, Los Angeles District Attorney Thomas Woolwine—remembered as one of the most corrupt in California history—lived at 1040 Kensington.

May 1914 also marked a milestone in Wally's career. Wally left the relative security of Universal for D.W. Griffith's smaller Mutual Film Corporation, which included Majestic and Reliance. For years Griffith wanted to make longer films like the European studios. In 1913 Italian director Enrico Gauzzino released *Quo Vadis*, a lavish eight-reel, two-hour spectacle and though American audiences loved it, the studios were determined to keep domestic films short. Griffith believed audiences were hungry for better movies with more complicated narratives.

A current view of the Allison Avenue bungalow purchased by Wally and Dorothy in 1914, the first home the couple owned.

It's surprising Griffith's Biograph bosses didn't listen to him. His films were their most popular and his results tangible; in his two years at the studio Biograph stock value increased from 50¢ to $112 a share![6] The studio stubbornly refused to let Griffith make 4- or 5-reel films and when he threatened to make one anyway he was threatened with firing.[7] Knowing his days were numbered he did it anyway. In June 1913 he built a huge set in Chatsworth for the Biblical epic *Judith of Bethulia* starring Blanche Sweet as Judith,

A nearby Echo Park street about the time that Wally and Dorothy moved into the Allison Avenue house. Note that the streets are all still dirt, and few houses cover the hillsides (courtesy of Michael DuBois, who lives in the house shown in the photograph).

a widow who agrees to pose as a courtesan to enter the camp of the Assyrian General Holofernes (Henry Walthall). Filming took two months and when Griffith returned to New York to edit the six reels that cost $36,000—twice the approved budget—he was stripped of his duties. He walked away from the studio he made famous and to punish him the film was not released.

Ever the showman Griffith went public, buying an ad in the December 3rd *New York Dramatic Mirror* with the simple headline "D.W. GRIFFITH." He listed his 151 films and a resume that read:

> Producer of all great Biograph successes, revolutionizing motion picture drama and founding the modern technique of the art. Included in the innovations which he introduced and which are now generally followed by the most advanced producers, are: the large or close-up figures,

distant views as represented first in *Ramona*, the switchback, sustained suspense, the *fade-out*, and restraint in expression, raising motion picture acting to the higher plane which has won for it recognition as a genuine art. For two years from the summer of 1908, Mr. Griffith personally directed all Biograph motion pictures. Thereafter as general director he superintended all Biograph productions and directed the more *important* features until October 1, 1913.[8]

Griffith's notice precipitated the end of Biograph. Adolph Zukor offered the out-of-work filmmaker $50,000 a year to direct but Griffith had eyes on Harry Aitken's new Mutual and Reliance-Majestic studios, which were moving to California. He went to Mutual with Wally close behind. St. Johns recalled Wally's reasons for leaving Universal for Mutual as his "beginning to have high ideals of what might be done in pictures, and wanting to work with D.W.,"[9] but it probably wasn't Wally's idea to leave. He was happy where he was, directing and earning $75 a week while Dorothy made $50, when Griffith invited him to Mutual's 651 Fairview Avenue offices (his new studio at 4516 Sunset Boulevard would not be finished until late 1914).

Wally's introduction to Griffith was not an auspicious one. When he and Dorothy arrived the eccentric director was in what Dorothy described as "a playful mood." While Wally stood amidst the confusion of the set Griffith joked, shadow-boxed, and ignored him. "Wally came out boiling mad.... [He] thought that he'd hardly been given even a courteous reception by the 'great master,' and was sure that he could charge the whole incident to time wasted."[10] It was a Griffith tactic to test potential employees; he called Wally back and Wally made his way through the maze of buildings and down a series of meandering hallways to Griffith's office buried in the back. The office probably surprised Wally, as it did everyone. It looked like a bank president's office, with expensive furniture, oriental rugs, hardwood floors, and tasteful art.[11] After a short meeting Wally joined Mutual, and he took a cut in pay, from $75 to $50, to do so.[12]

The move was a turning point in Wally's career but the decision has the marks of a Dorothy decision. Wally made no decision—no matter how trivial—without consulting her. She was in awe of Griffith, probably moreso since his renown had grown. Perhaps she saw a chance for better roles for herself. Wally didn't know it but it was virtually the end of his career as director and writer. From that moment on he was an actor. Griffith didn't hire him for anything else. Wally perhaps thought he would direct for Mutual but it is clear Griffith did not think so. Wally had directed 20 movies in the previous six months but he directed just 3 during the remaining nine years of his life. Wally probably would not have moved had he known that.

Wally knew Mutual people, particularly Griffith's lead director Christy Cabanne. In late 1913 Wally worked with Cabanne at Universal on *Moonshine Molly*, *Her Awakening*, and *For Those Unborn*. He liked him, probably because of their similar backgrounds. Cabanne was also born in St. Louis (in 1888) and also sent to private schools, St. Rose's Academy and Culver (Indiana) Military Academy. Cabanne worked at Fine Arts Film Company on early Fairbanks films and when Griffith came to California the quietly efficient Cabanne was his chief of staff and a trusted aide. Actors appreciated Cabanne because he was organized and had no ego; he did not interfere by over-directing.

Griffith started Wally slowly. His first three films were directed by Cabanne, the first an Anne Tupper Wilkes scenario entitled *Arms and the Gringo*. Wally starred with Dorothy Gish, Fred Kelsey and F.A. Lowery. Next was *The City Beautiful*, again with Gish, and then one of Wally's stories, entitled *Down by the Sounding Sea* with Robert Harron and Mae Gaston. In June, July and August, Wally did one film a month. In June he had an uncredited role in *The Avenging Conscience; Thou Shalt Not Kill*, directed by Griffith with an all-star cast of Henry Walthall, Spottiswoode Aitken, Blanche Sweet, George Siegmann, Ralph Lewis, Mae Marsh and Robert Harron. *Conscience* was among a group of Griffith's early Mutuals—including *Home Sweet Home*, *The Battle of the Sexes*, and *The Escape*—described as "dramas of the sort that few motion picture directors would attempt to handle, presenting in the scenario such difficult tasks as would take the heart out of the most ambitious producer."[13] *Battle* cost less than $2,500 and grossed over $400,000.[14] In July Wally starred in *Down the Hill to Creditville*, directed by Donald Crisp, co-starring with Crisp, Dorothy Gish, and Kate Price. In August he made the John B. O'Brien–directed *For Her Father's Sins*, with Blanche Sweet, Billie West and Al F. Wilson.

The fall was busier, with about a dozen films from September through December. Seven were released in 1914 and the rest in January–February, 1915. In September, Wally made three, the first the Donald Crisp–directed *The Niggard*, starring Crisp, Billie West and Cora Drew. Then he was with Cabanne on *The Odalisque* in a supporting role with Blanche Sweet, Miriam Cooper, Harron, and Walthall. Last, Crisp directed *Another Chance*, written by Hal, in which Wally starred with William Lowery, Mary Alden, Maxfield Stanley, and Crisp.

In October, Wally worked with director Fred Kelsey, who directed 35 films from 1914 to 1917,[15] on *Over the Ledge*, starring with Irene Hunt, Ralph Lewis, and Crisp. Next was the Hal scenario *At Dawn* starring George Siegmann, Billie West, Lowery, Claire Anderson, and Native American actor Eagle Eye. His final October film was with Kelsey, *The Exposure*, starring with Irene Hunt, Howard Gage, Ralph Lewis, Lowery, and his old friend Raoul Walsh. It was Wally's last 1914 release. The next five were all released in 1915. Two were directed by Cabanne and another by Kelsey. Griffith directed the last, a film that became Hollywood history and made Wally a star.

In late 1914 Wally and Dorothy were becoming well-known enough to earn special mention in newspapers. In November at a Photoplayers Club event attended by 2,000 famous faces, papers noted, "everybody in filmland was there," and singled out in a list including the Gish sisters, Mabel Normand, Tom Mix, and Griffith, were the Reids.[16]

There were major changes underway in the manner studios sold films and stars. Almost all films made before 1914 have either been lost or turned to dust as silver nitrate film deteriorated. Few survive; in most cases little beyond basic cast, director or release dates are in archive materials. Some information can be gleaned from early movie columns, the first of which dated to June 1908 when Frank Woods began reviewing films in a back-page column for the *New York Dramatic Mirror* titled "The Spectator."[17] But by late 1914 movie stars were no longer anonymous faces. The anonymity was due to a combination of factors. Most film historians blame the studios. Indeed, it was not in their best interest for actors to earn power from popularity, but most thespians were anonymous by choice. They welcomed security and weekly paychecks movies offered but stage actors still believed it was a passing fancy and that they would eventually

A studio postcard of Dorothy, ca. 1914, around the time the couple moved to Echo Park.

return to the stage. They worried that producers wouldn't re-hire them if they had worked in "the movies."

The studios happily kept actors' names a secret, for their part worrying that acclaim meant leverage to demand more money; but even early on, audiences clamored for information. While studios remained mum local exhibitors furnished names in their ads and lobby cards. This popularity index resulted in the star system and led to studio publicity departments and movie fan magazines. Griffith was inadvertently at the forefront. His insistence that actors *play* roles and not simply play for the camera meant his actors were *up front* on screen. His technical innovations brought attention to his actors, often making them more important to the movie than previously.[18] By focusing on actors Griffith encouraged a star system. He and Carl Laemmle both knew the importance of producing movies *featuring* certain stars.

As one writer put it, "In the 'star' your producer gets not only a 'production' value ... but a 'trademark' value, and an 'insurance' value which are ... very potent in guaranteeing the sale of this product."[19] In 1910, Laemmle created the first real star by luring Florence Lawrence away from Biograph. Ontario-born Florence Annie Bridgwood was the daughter of vaudeville star Lotta Lawrence. She made her first movie in 1907 and 38 Vitagraph films in 1908. Learning she earned $20 a week but had to make her own costumes, Griffith stole her for $25 and studio-supplied attire. Fans bombarded Biograph with requests for her name but she was just "the Biograph Girl." In 1910, Laemmle, needing a star for his new Independent Motion Picture (IMP) Studio, lured her away by promising to identify her publicly. A master marketer, Laemmle than arranged the world's first publicity stunt.

Once out of Biograph she was sent into hiding while Laemmle planted rumors she had been killed in a streetcar accident. A paper's location determined where the accident took place; a New York paper mentioned L.A. while the L.A. paper mentioned New York. Laemmle ended the public frenzy with ads—with her photo—introducing his "IMP Girl" and her film *The Broken Oath*. She emerged at a grand St. Louis press conference, but left IMP in 1911 to form Victor Film Company with her director-husband; they later sold it to Laemmle and Universal.

It took several years but studio fears came to pass as actors demanded and received more money. By 1915 salaries were set in a free-market system but few made astronomical amounts. Studios sometimes paid for short periods. Keystone paid the (Joe) Weber & (Lew) Fields comedy team $100,000 for six months and Broadway star Billie Burke $40,000 for two. Marguerite Clark earned $50,000 from Famous Players–Lasky for three and Ethel Barrymore and Lillian Russell $12,500 each for a single film. Weekly salaries climbed for a select few. Mary Pickford, Charlie Chaplin and Marguerite Clark later earned $1,500 a week but most salaries were well below that figure.

Mabel Normand was one of a few earning $500 weekly. Recognized faces like Clara Kimball Young, Blanche Sweet, and Anita Stewart earned $200 to $500 a week. In 1913, Pickford earned $500 weekly from Adolph Zukor for 3 Lasky films over 14 weeks.[20] When writer Harry Carr suggested a publicity picture of Pickford sitting on a pile of silver dollars representing her salary, she slyly replied, "I should say not, I am working for money, but it is just as well to let the public think I am working for art."[21] Early male stars earned less than female stars. Leading men like King Baggott, Francis X. Bushman, and Carlyle Blackwell earned $100 to $400 a week, J. Warren Kerrigan $400, John Bunny $350, and Earle Williams $300.[22] Wally's earnings had risen to $75 a week.

Increasing salaries was a slow process but by early 1915 the names were public. Wally was well-known but not a full-fledged star. That would change quickly. He was a popular face as early as the latter part of 1914. A popular syndicated column entitled "The Frame of Public Favor" featured a photograph/drawing of an actor with a short biography and was reserved for more popular stars. Wally made his first appearance in December 1914 as "the popular leading man of the Mutual Company, appearing in Majestic and Reliance releases. He's an American, is 24 years old, is six feet, two inches tall, and 190 pounds. He has light brown hair and hazel eyes. Before going into pictures, Mr. Reid was a newspaper man and did some magazine work.... He is a college man and fond of sports, such as swimming, tennis, baseball, and polo." His favorite movie was *Judith of Bethulia*, and Wally added that his best work was in *The Animal*, and:

> I liked reporting all right, but pictures sure did make an appeal to me and so I went in for them. I have been with a lot of companies, Selig, Vitagraph, Old Reliance, Bison 101, American, and Universal. My wife is as well known as I am, and people love her, including myself. She's Dorothy Davenport. My ambition is to live my parts instead of acting them. To be thoroughly and entirely natural. To do nothing on screen that I would not do under similar circumstances in real life.[23]

Wally was receiving consistent press attention at the end of 1914. Two of his last five films were directed by Cabanne and one by Kelsey. The first Cabanne film was *The Three Brothers* starring Wally with Allan Sears, William Hinckley and Claire Anderson. Set in the French Canadian countryside, it is the story of a beautiful adopted country girl (Anderson) who is pursued by three brothers, a dour and villainous elder (Sears), the middle sibling (Wally), and the honorable younger (Hinckley) who gives up his pursuit of the girl for the handsome middle brother. Writer Kitty Kelly described the film in her "Flickerings from Filmland" column:

> The way of coming is obstructed by the boulders of human passions, conflicting loves, jealousy, trickery ... loyalty, protectiveness, and final claiming of the love apparently forfeited by the younger brother ... heroic renunciation by the middle brother ... the little girl is of the cameo faced type of Griffith specials, and she plays in the regulation Gish-Sweet manner, wearing effectively those quaint little clothes that nobody else in the world but Majesticites[24] could wear and preserve their picturesqeness [sic].

Of Wally, she wrote:

> ... of course Wallace Reid is Wallace Reid, which is sufficient definition, except to add that he is one of the successful young men of the hero caliber who has not been so unduly puffed up by the adulation as to be unable to submerge Wallace Reid into Jean or whoever he is interpreting for celluloid purposes.[25]

Kelsey directed Wally's next film, *Station Content*, a romantic drama revolving around a lost doll. The plot was typical Griffith, playing on emotion and family tension. The title described the happy life of Jim Manning (Wally), who worked at a train station and lived with his wife and daughter. His employees gave his daughter a doll, which, broken, was lost at the station, and when the child tragically dies, Mrs. Manning (Catherine Henry) learns telegraphy and works on the line to try to forget. When Station Content is abandoned Manning buries himself in work and neglects his suffering wife so while he is gone on a trip she leaves him and takes a train away. Through a series of coincidental storms and wrecks she takes shelter in the ruins of their old station, where she discovers her dead child's doll. Memories bring with them a desire to hear the telegraph again and she cuts in to listen. She hears warnings that a nearby bridge has washed out and the "Special" has already left the last open station—with her husband aboard—on its way to certain doom at the missing bridge. She flags the train down and saves her husband, and seeing his wife and the doll he realizes his mistakes and determines to start anew.[26] Griffith expertly wove such complicated story lines together in his movies.

After *Station Content*, Wally made two films about which little is known. *Sheriff for an Hour* paired him with Arthur Mackley and *The Craven* cast him opposite Seena Owen, William Hinckley and Allan Sears. Then Wally worked on a picture that propelled him to stardom, but the film was a winding path of opportunity, disappointment and ultimately, discovery. The film became Griffith's most famous. It was titled *The Clansman* when it debuted in L.A. on February 8, 1915, but when it opened in New York on March 3rd the name was *The Birth of a Nation*.

Griffith and Harry Aitken formed Epoch Producing Corporation to produce a movie based on Reverend Thomas Dixon's racist book and 1905 play, *The Clansman*. The book was the second in a trilogy consisting of *The Leopard's Spots: A Romance of the White Man's Burden 1865–1900*, *The Clansman: An Historical Romance of the Ku Klux Klan*, and *The Traitor*. Griffith witnessed the pain of Reconstruction first-hand and identified with the racist Dixon, a North Carolinian Baptist minister who said he would "allow none but the son of a Confederate soldier to direct the film version of 'The Clansman.'"[27]

Theater poster for D.W. Griffith's controversial *The Birth of a Nation* with the original title, *The Clansman*.

The Birth of a Nation is perhaps the most influential film in American cinema. It was Griffith as Griffith. Shooting was done with no script except his visualization of the film in his head that wove four complex narratives using fifteen times as many shots as the longest film ever made to that point. The initial cut ran 48 reels, and the final version was 12 reels, running 13,058 feet and lasting three hours.[28] He used 17,500 actors and 3,500 horses. Rehearsal and shooting took fifteen *weeks* and film editing three months, when films usually took three or four *days* to make. It was an unprecedented financial gamble with the largest budget ever considered: $40,000, which ballooned past $60,000 so quickly that Griffith begged investors to finance the film. He had no takers. At one point he needed $8,000—maybe $200,000 today—and asked dozens of friends to invest in exchange for a *quarter interest* in the film! Still there were no takers. He made a last-minute states rights deal with Sol Lesser without giving up the quarter interest and Lesser eventually made millions. Had anyone given him the $8,000 they would have made over $25,000,000. In 1915. Almost everyone involved became wealthy, except Griffith.

Dozens of studio employees took stock or a percentage in lieu of salary. Writer Harry Carr recalled "a costume maker who grudgingly took stock as part pay rolling around in expensive limousines and living in a Hollywood palace."[29]

Griffith was plagued by financial shortfalls during shooting. One day on location in the San Fernando Valley he only had enough money to pay the hundreds of cowboys through noon, and cowboy extras were notorious for demanding their $5 ($10 with a horse) in cash as soon as shooting ended. "Pay or no ride" was their motto but the afternoon shot was the climactic rescue scene in the first half of the film. An assistant director got an inspiration and moved the food wagon a half mile down the road and blew the dinner horn. Hundreds of riders made a mad dash down the road for food past six whirring cameras.[30] Even with such creativity the film eventually cost *ten times* more than any film ever made—$120,000 for 100 prints. Few thought the ambitious project would succeed.

Henry B. Walthall, an Alabaman who had done 200 films, was cast in the lead. But he thought he was too short for the role at five foot seven and told Griffith he wanted to play a different part. But Griffith wanted him because of his expressive eyes and because he was an expert horseman and Civil War buff who could help direct intricate battle scenes. But after Walthall took the role Griffith announced that an "illness" would prevent him from doing the film. Magazines reported that Walthall "had to be operated upon"[31] and was "not expected to live"[32] but the mystery illness was never identified. Dorothy recalled a "kidney ailment"[33] but similar absences plagued the alcoholic actor throughout his career; he often disappeared for days. Griffith usually assigned bodyguards to follow Walthall and make sure that he got to work.[34]

Every actor in Hollywood knew about Griffith's planned film and wanted a role. Wally was no exception and when Griffith offered him the plum lead after Walthall disappeared he excitedly accepted what he knew would be his biggest role. Griffith was said to have cast Wally in his original small role in the advent of just this occurrence. Dorothy said Wally "thought the Gods were smiling on him when Griffith called him in one day that ... [he] ... was to get the role."[35] According to St. Johns the couple celebrated and "costumes were fitted to the boy. Tests were made. Shooting began, and then Walthall recovered. Before 500 feet of the film was shot, Walthall was back and ready to go to work. It almost broke Wally's heart. They gave him instead the part of the young blacksmith who cleaned out the gang of Negroes. They told him in the end it would do him more good. And it did. Few who saw the film ever forgot Wally, stripped to the waist, smiling, a white, avenging god of strength among those mad colored men. But it was difficult to see that then, and Wally only took it because he was so disappointed he just didn't care." Recognizing later the tremendous impact the role had on Wally's career, St. Johns added that it was "the first and only disappointment of his career, and even that proved in the end a golden boomerang."[36]

At the moment though, Wally couldn't see the future. All he saw was fury at Griffith, who tried to assuage his disappointment by saying he "had him in mind for another role in the picture, one which would undoubtedly make him star material."[37] When he was given the role of Jeff, a blacksmith murdered near the film's climax, he was even angrier. According to Dorothy, Griffith *wanted* Wally angry, knowing his emotion would play on screen. Dorothy felt every person he beat up in the huge fight scene and "every poor guy that Wally threw out of the blacksmith shop was D.W. Griffith."[38]

Filming began in early September. Sets were built across the street from Griffith's studio and crews filmed in the mountains around Big Bear, in the Calexico desert and the San Fernando Valley. Two villages were built across Sunset from the studio. One was a Southern village during Reconstruction, a street lined with houses with a church in the background and hundreds of trees and bushes bordering a half-mile picket fence. Lining the street were lamps and hitching posts. Another set re-created a group of slave cabins, described in period articles as "the negroes quarters of the old south."[39]

Filming was typical Griffith; no film outline and no script, just his mental pictures. His ever-present cigar and megaphone in hand, Griffith sat under his straw hat next to whatever camera he directed. His attention to detail was mind-boggling. Writer Selwyn Stanhope was amazed watching a large crowd scene with 250 African American extras jammed into a street scene choreographed by cigar. Stanhope described the scene:

> Two hundred people were before him ... negroes of every age. Mule carts driven back and forth. Banjo players, barefooted negro dancers, old colored men, and pickaninnies under foot. His eyes watched them all. Now he looks down the street and spies an aged negro man. He sends a sub-director for the old darky, looks him over from head to foot and smiles. This aged negro, but an extra, has struck Griffith's eye. He is placed in the foreground with the dancers. The music and the dancing begin again. Griffith tells the camera man to get busy. The aged negro dreams of the days of his youth. He dances better than the young men. He dances the old plantation steps. He pats the top of his bald head with the palm of his hand. He forgets he is working before a movie camera—he is back in the old days and these folk around him are his people.[40]

Griffith picked the old man—the perfect old man—from a crowd of 250 dancing extras from 100 yards away. Watching the scene even today one is taken by the old man's unrehearsed passion and expression. In another scene, to get a group of a half-dozen young African American extras to ignore cameras and act like kids Griffith sat in the dirt tossing dimes on the ground, exhorting them to "Scramble for 'em! That's it! Laugh and cut up! Now, there's another dime for each of you if you do it again, and do it right. That's it!"[41]

Filming the most important scene in the film—an emotional homecoming when the lead returns to a ruined plantation and greets his sister—Griffith abruptly stopped filming and peered down the street into a crowd of 100 extras. He asked, "Who is that pretty girl? Have her step out to the front." Every eye turned with looks of envy, jealousy, and interest, knowing Griffith had seen something in the anonymous girl. Seena Owen became a great star, one of the great beauties in film.[42]

The film follows two Southern families during the Civil War. In Piedmont, South Carolina, the Camerons are led by "Little Colonel" Ben (Walthall), and in Washington, D.C., the Stonemans by politician Austin (Ralph Lewis). In the pre-war years the families were friends but politics put them on different sides of the conflict. The first half of the film chronicles the Civil War and its impact on families, with massive battle sequences and love scenes closing with a perfectly-staged recreation of Lincoln's assassination. The second half follows Reconstruction and the anarchy resulting from free blacks allowed to govern, when Ben Cameron founds the Ku Klux Klan to protect his hometown and restore decency.

The film's prologue depicts slavery's introduction in the 17th century with a prediction that the practice will reap discord and a title card reading, "The bringing of the African to America planted the first seed of disunion." Dixon based Austin Stoneman on Pennsylvania Senator Thaddeus Stevens, a radical Republican anti-slavery leader. Stoneman's three children, Elsie (Lillian Gish), Phil (Elmer Clifton), and Tod (Robert Harron) are friendly with the Camerons, a plantation family with five children: Margaret (Miriam Cooper), Flora (Violet Wilkey), Ben (Walthall), Wade (Andre Beranger), and Duke (Maxfield Stanley). The Cameron plantation is a peaceful place where happy slaves work contentedly, get two-hour dinner breaks and happily dance for the family.

Romances arise. Phil Stoneman falls in love with Margaret Cameron and Ben with Elsie Stoneman, whom he has only seen in photos but loves just the same. In Washington the Senator is sexually obsessed with his mulatto housekeeper Lydia Brown (Mary Alden) who is portrayed as a sex-crazed negro. A title card describes the Senator's "great weakness that is to blight the nation."

At the outbreak of the War, Phil and Tod Stoneman enlist in the Union army and three Cameron boys march with the Confederates. War arrives at Piedmont in the face of a black guerilla horde led by a ne'er-do-well white Captain that ransacks the town and terrorizes the Camerons before being driven off by Confederates. It is inevitable the sons will meet on the battlefield and when Duke Cameron raises his bayonet to kill a wounded soldier only to see his old friend Tod Stoneman, he pauses. At that ironic moment Tod dies of his wounds and Duke is shot dead, falling peacefully next to his best friend's body. Wade Cameron dies in the battle for Atlanta and the last Cameron and Stoneman sons meet on the battlefield when Ben leads an infantry charge toward Union forces commanded by Phil. Ben is wounded but saved from death by Phil, who sends him to a military hospital where Elsie Stoneman is a nurse. Ben awakens to meet the girl from the photographs he had fallen in love with.

The conclusion of the first half begins with the surrender at Appomattox and Ben's return to Piedmont, arguably one of the finest scenes ever put on film. As he wearily approaches the front steps of his ruined home his younger sister Flora bounds out happily. Both hesitate and fall into each other's arms, he kissing her hair and she crying. From the side, the hand of his unseen mother is shown slowly pulling him into his home. It is a marvelous, moving, Griffith moment.

Lincoln argues against Stoneman's urge to punish the South but leniency is derailed when he is killed. The assassination marks the start of the South's descent into chaos. The second half of the film describes "The blight of war [that] does not end when hostilities cease." At the start of the second half Griffith naively offered a mea culpa to any appearance of bigotry or racism. Title cards read, "This is an historical presentation of the Civil War and Reconstruction Period, and is not meant to reflect on any race or people of today."

The South is overrun by Northerners pillaging and getting rich as they "cozen, beguile, and use the negroes...." In Washington, Stoneman appoints mulatto protégé Silas Lynch (George Siegmann) the leader of the blacks. Portrayed as evil and sexually attracted to every white woman, Lynch comes to Piedmont to help blacks and carpetbaggers organize black voters. Slaves are induced not to work and black militia is paraded in front of horrified whites. When the blacks win the election they rampage through town in a drunken orgy of celebration. Their juries render unjust verdicts against whites while a Cameron slave is whipped for not voting with the blacks. Blacks in government are shown as power-hungry, stupid, and lazy, sitting with bare feet on desks, but they pass a law that whites must salute negro officers in the street. The white minority is helpless until Ben Cameron has an inspiration while watching white children wearing sheets and pretending to be ghosts. He is stirred to form a secret vigilante group, the Ku Klux Klan, to avoid being "under the heel of the black South." Their first nighttime visit is harmless; they frighten two blacks who quake in fear and run away.

Wally appears at the highest point of tension in the film. After blacks kill three Klansmen and Flora Cameron has a run-in with former family slave Gus that ends in her accidental death Ben seeks revenge as Gus takes refuge in a tavern. Burly and shirtless blacksmith Jeff (Wally) confronts the men hiding Gus and a fight ensues, during which he is shot twice in cold blood, the coup de grace provided by Gus. Gus tries to flee but is caught, quickly tried, and lynched. In Griffith's original version Gus was castrated prior to hanging but he removed the scene when some initial audience members became ill. A symbolic battle between Lynch's black militia and Ben's hooded Klan fills the end of the movie as blacks chase the remaining Cameron family from their home. When they find refuge in a small cabin with two Union veterans title cards note, "the former enemies of North and South are united again in common defence [sic] of their Aryan birthright."

The imagery in the second half of the movie is monstrously racist. Lynch tries to force Elsie Cameron to marry him and become the Queen of his "Black Empire." Klansmen race up on horses to prevent the forced marriage carrying torches and crosses, rescuing white women from the black plague. The Klan drives Lynch's militia from Piedmont after a bloody gun battle. Griffith concludes with the ultimate victory of the whites over the black insurgency as gun-toting Klansmen supervise elections and blacks are put back in their place. Phil and Margaret are together, as are Ben and Elsie, seen sitting next to the ocean's edge as the movie closes. A tableau with a Christ-like figure emerges from the background, fading to a final title card: "Liberty and union, one and inseparable, now and forever!"

It took three months of editing to trim 48 reels and 12 hours down to a final release of 12 reels and just over 3 hours. From a technical standpoint the movie is a masterpiece. Griffith and cameraman Billy Bitzer used dozens of techniques never seen before, all of them common today. Among the innovations:

- night photography (using magnesium flares)
- the still-shot
- scenes filmed from different and multiple angles
- the camera "iris" effect (expanding or contracting circular masks to either reveal and open up a scene, or conceal part of an image)
- the use of parallel action and editing in a sequence
- extensive use of color tinting for dramatic or psychological effect
- moving, traveling or "panning" camera tracking shots
- total-screen close-ups to reveal intimate expressions
- the use of vignettes in "balloons" or "iris-shots" in a dark screen
- the use of fade-outs and cameo-profiles (a medium close-up in front of a blurry background)
- the use of lap dissolves to blend or switch from one image to another
- high-angle shots and panoramic long shots
- extensive cross-cutting between two scenes to create a montage-effect and generate suspense[43]

The film's battle scenes were also remarkably authentic given their grand scale; but even before the release controversy swirled around Griffith and the film's racism. Local censors approved the final cut but the L.A. City Council ordered it suppressed. Griffith obtained a court injunction to release it,[44] debuting the picture at Clune's Auditorium Theater in L.A. on February 8th as *The Clansman*. Before its New York debut at the Liberty Theater on March 3rd Griffith re-titled it *The Birth of a Nation*. In 1906 the same theater had presented Dixon's play. The film then toured the country.

The New York opening was a huge event. Tickets began at $2 ($50 today) and special trains brought attendees from all over the East coast. Even though the racial undertones aroused the public Griffith lined Times Square with billboards of hooded Klan night-riders. President Woodrow Wilson, a Princeton classmate of Dixon and a dedicated historian, personally endorsed *Birth*. It became the first film ever screened in the White House.

The film was a huge hit, particularly in the South. Even with exorbitant ticket prices crowds were so large that it was the first movie to require the use of ushers inside theaters. The actual box office for *Birth* isn't known though it took in over $20,000,000 (about $350,000,000 today). Jesse Lasky thought the figure was closer to $30,000,000.[45] Because states rights had been sold outright exact figures can't be confirmed but the gross was probably $75,000,000 to $100,000,000 (over a *billion* dollars today).

The financial success was tempered by public outcry. Griffith tried to head off controversy by prefacing the film with title cards reading, "A PLEA FOR THE ART OF THE MOTION PICTURE— We do not fear censorship, for we have no wish to offend with improprieties or obscenities, but we do demand, as a right, the liberty to show the dark side of wrong, that we may illuminate the bright side of virtue—the same liberty that is conceded to the art of the written word—that art to which we owe the Bible and the works of Shakespeare." His naïve belief that the public would ignore the racism and bigotry was not helped by his pleas. At its core the film was just too racist.

When the film was released nationally, it was released as *The Birth of a Nation*, the title with which it is remembered today as one of the most influential films in history.

The pure scope of *Birth* and the technical innovations were a brilliant accomplishment, as Griffith for all intents and purposes invented a new film genre: the feature film. Its status as a cinema classic came with a cost. It was met with protests and in many states screenings were prohibited. Riots broke out in Boston and Philadelphia and the film's release was denied in Chicago, Ohio, Denver, Pittsburgh, St. Louis, Minneapolis, and in eight entire states. Demonstrations followed the film for decades, arising again each time it was re-released (1924, 1931, and 1938). By 1921 Griffith had to release a further-edited version without reference to the Klan.[46] But the original was not rejected everywhere. It ran in sold-out Atlanta theaters for almost five years.

The movie is a contradiction, a source of both pride and shame. At its core it is atrociously, explicitly racist. Griffith blamed every American problem before, during, and after the Civil War on the presence of African Americans in the U.S. The depiction of African Americans is horrifyingly racist: sub-human and born with the worst kinds of depravity in their being. The only evil whites are those in league with blacks. The political and moral ideals presented by Griffith are appalling and his naivety cause for wonderment. Dixon never hid his message, telling a Boston paper, "that one purpose of his play was to create a feeling of abhorrence in people, especially white women, toward colored men," and, "he wished to have Negroes removed from the U.S., and hopes to help in the accomplishment of that purpose by 'The Birth of a Nation.'"[47] What Griffith was really thinking remains a mystery.

The deleted scenes were disturbing and not removed until *after* the L.A. premier. A graphic love scene between Congressman Stanton and his mulatto mistress and maid was removed as was the vivid depiction of the castration of Gus before his lynching. Another offered "Lincoln's Solution" to the slavery issue: all African Americans are shipped back to Africa while Lincoln and Jesus Christ look on approvingly. Interestingly, Griffith chose Wally to portray Christ in the missing scene.[48]

Wally filmed several scenes as Christ in allegorical tableaus. Filming another scene that was deleted, Wally spent a bitterly cold morning hanging virtually naked on a cross. He was fed brandy to keep him warm and by the time the scene was acceptable to Griffith, Wally was so drunk that he quite literally looked dead.[49] He passed out and had to be carried from the set.

Birth contributed to a rebirth of the Klan, which had been effectively dissolved since 1869.[50] Membership reportedly swelled by 500,000 between 1915 and 1920. For its part, the National Association for the Advancement of Colored People (NAACP), only formed in 1909, mobilized African Americans and organized boycotts and marched outside thousands of theaters. As late as the 1940s the NAACP still organized boycotts when the film was shown.

A group of independent African American filmmakers spent $500,000 of donated funds and stock sales[51] to make *The Birth of a Race* in response. Filmed in New York, Florida, and Chicago, the 1918 film was directed by John W. Noble, written by Noble and Rudolph de Cordoba, and starred John Reinhardt, Jane Grey, George Le Guerre, Ben Hendricks, and Gertrude Braun. It was panned by critics. *Variety* declared it "replete with historical inaccuracies, gross exaggerations, and bromidic appeals to patriotism."[52] Later efforts by prolific black filmmaker Oscar Micheaux like *The Homesteader* (1919) and *Within Our Gates* (1919) more effectively countered *Birth*'s message.[53]

The Birth of a Nation is at once vulgar, racist, brutal, repulsive, cinematically breathtaking and innovative. But amidst the controversy and noise, one thing that emerged from the movie was the obvious screen presence of a tall, handsome actor—shirtless blacksmith Jeff—that everyone seemed to notice even in a small role.

Wally's assignment on *Birth* lasted past the summer of 1915 as production and editing were all Griffith did that fall. Other than perhaps a week's work Wally enjoyed a relaxing break. Dorothy continued to work but it was less satisfying. She obviously thought Wally going to Mutual would mean opportunity for both but while it proved true for Wally it did nothing for her. At Mutual she was Wally's leading woman on the verge of nationwide popularity. Had they stayed there she would have become a much bigger star.

As a solo performer she was not in the great demand she anticipated. After a final Universal film together in the summer of 1914 (*The Den of Thieves*) she didn't work until October. She took lead roles in a number of films but they were unimportant titles like *The Toilers of the Sea*, *$500 Reward*, and *A Voice from the Sea*. She was also working with small independents like Paragon Films and Balboa Amusement Producing Company, alongside the likes of Phil Lee, Philo McCullogh, Joyce Moore, and Fred Whitman. It was a big step down from the actors she worked with at Universal.

She described her work, while offering a hint of the disparity between their assignments, by saying, "it seemed that Wally always got jobs on pictures to be shot at the studio, while I got the sleeper-jump locations. That meant getting up at dawn, taking the red electric car downtown, racing from Hill to Main on foot, and catching another Pacific Electric car out to Long Beach, or some place like that, where I had to be ready to start shooting by eight o'clock."[54] Dorothy's career was probably a disappointment. But Wally's stardom hadn't arrived, and, returning to work, he hadn't forgotten the anger at having the Cameron role taken from him. In fact, in his 1922 serial autobiography he barely mentions Griffith and doesn't mention *Birth* at all, even though he knew the film catapulted him to fame.[55]

6

Lasky's "Diamond"

In 1913, Jesse Lasky formed the Jesse L. Lasky Feature Play Company in New York with Samuel Goldfish (later Goldwyn), Arthur Friend, and Cecil B. DeMille. They lured Dustin Farnum from Broadway for a film version of his popular play *The Squaw Man* to be filmed in Arizona. Farnum demanded he be paid in cash in advance; DeMille offered $250 a week or a quarter of the film's profits.[1] Thinking the venture would be a failure Farnum took the cash. After stopping briefly in Flagstaff, Arizona, and deciding the area was unsuitable, the DeMille group went to L.A. DeMille visited the same Hollywood barn that had been used by the Horsley brothers two years earlier.

After viewing the property DeMille and Lasky traded prophetic telegrams. DeMille wired Lasky, "Flagstaff no good for our purpose. STOP. Have proceeded to California. STOP. Want authority to rent barn in place called Hollywood. STOP. $75.00 a month. STOP. Cecil." From New York, Lasky replied, "OK to rent barn on month to month only. STOP. Don't make any long commitments. STOP. Regards Jesse and Sam."[2] Owner Jacob Stern retained the right to leave horses and a carriage in the barn. "After all," DeMille said, "he was there first." When Stern washed horses the water ran through DeMille's office, forcing him to raise his boots to let the water drain.[3] Horse stalls were turned into offices, dressing rooms and a projection room. A tack room became a storage closet. A wooden platform stage was built in a clearing amid the orange and lemon groves out back. Filming in these primitive surroundings began on December 29, 1913.

The Squaw Man was a sensation after its February 17, 1914, premier at the Longacre Theater in New York. It grossed over $225,000 after costing $12,000.[4] Had Farnum taken a percentage he would have earned $50,000 ($1,500,000 today). When Lasky and DeMille first saw Wally in 1915 their studio was one of the most successful in Hollywood. Lasky boasted that they "ground out films like sausages."[5]

Most studios believed the only way to make features was to pay fees for rights to existing properties and that a scenario writer used to producing short scripts couldn't create interesting pieces an hour long. Lasky was the first studio to hire writers to produce feature-length scenarios in-house and he convinced DeMille's brother William C. de Mille,[6] a successful New York playwright, to assemble the first studio story department. William not only convinced Lasky to script his own movies but to script the filming, a radical idea. His daughter Agnes remembered, "Coming from legitimate theater my father suggested it might be useful to write out in detail before-hand what they planned doing. He wrote complete little synopses for Cecil. Then he asked a writer friend, Margaret Turnbull, to come west to help him. The two wrote synopses sitting at desks in a small wooden house with screen doors on the lot. Pop got a studio painter to make him a sign he hung on the doorknob, SCENARIO DEPARTMENT ... the first time those words appeared in Hollywood."[7]

William hired writers and convinced name scribes like Margaret's brother Hector and Robert E. MacAlarney to join.[8] They held classes for the young writers and the studio soon had the most talented writing crew in Hollywood. It was in this evolving environment that Lasky and DeMille attended the L.A. premier of *The Clansman*. From among the 250 listed cast members and 17,500 actors they were both drawn to the barechested blacksmith Jeff. Lasky wrote of the moment in his memoirs, describing a "young man who played a bit part as a blacksmith [and who] had a perfect physique, large expressive eyes, and flawless features. He was over six feet tall and weighed in

On December 29, 1913, Cecil B. DeMille sits on the running board of a Lasky truck before the first day of filming of Lasky's first Hollywood movie, *The Squaw Man*. Co-director Oscar Apfel sits above DeMille, and star Dustin Farnum is standing among the Native American cast members with Art Acord (courtesy Bruce Torrence, the Bruce Torrence Hollywood Photograph Collection).

the neighborhood of 180 pounds. Seeing him was just like finding a 180-pound diamond...."[9]

The men set about what Lasky described as "larcenous inspiration" and contacted Wally to steal him from Griffith. With Wally still seething after having his *Birth* role pulled and Dorothy probably looking for better roles too, he was an easy target. Wally was close to stardom that spring when he quietly returned to work at Mutual. The Chicago movie magazine *Motography* described the annual Photoplayer's Club Gala at the Shrine Auditorium on February 13th, noting "every prominent star and player of California's famed motion picture colonies attended the grand ball.... Mary Pickford led the grand march with Dell Henderson, President of the club,"[10] followed by director William Desmond Taylor, Cleo Madison, Henry B. Walthall and Wally and Dorothy. The march indicated the "pecking order" and behind the Reids were Lillian Gish, Mabel Normand, Charlie Murray, Tom Mix, Ford Sterling, and Roscoe Arbuckle. Wally and Dorothy shared a private box with Griffith and Billy Bitzer.

Wally worked on a half dozen Griffith films in early 1915. The first two were Christy Cabanne 4-reelers, *The Lost House* and *Enoch Arden*. *Lost House* was filmed in late January–early February and released March 25th. Wally starred with Lillian Gish, supported by F.A. Turner, Elmer Clifton, and Allan Sears. The story was based on the short story "The Lost House" in the Richard Harding Davis book *The Man Who Could Not Lose*.[11] It is the tale of beautiful young Dosia Dale (Gish), who is mistreated by a conniving uncle (Turner). Unbeknownst to her, her uncle spent most of her expected inheritance and as she nears legal age he tries to cover his tracks by convincing her to marry. When she refuses he conspires with evil Dr. Protheroe (Sears) and has her declared insane and committed to an asylum. Dosia manages to drop a note from her window that is found by handsome young reporter Ford (Wally), who feigns insanity to gain admittance. Protheroe locks Ford up with Dosia but Ford has already entrusted his story to his friend Cuthbert (Clifton), who brings the police. Dosia's uncle and Dr. Protheroe are killed in a gun battle with police and the asylum is set ablaze, but Ford and Dosia escape. The couple leaps from the roof into a fire net and in the final scene are engaged.[12]

Enoch Arden was filmed in March, a D.W. Griffith–written adaptation of the 1864 Alfred Lord Tennyson poem. The leads were Alfred Paget and Lillian Gish with Wally co-starring along with Griffith. The story takes place in an 1800s English fishing village and centers on orphan Enoch Arden (Paget) and his two best friends, Annie Lee (Gish) and Philip Ray (Wally). Both boys grow up loving Annie but she married Enoch, and through the years the dejected Phillip remained a close friend to the pair and their two children. When poor fisherman Enoch hires on to a commercial ship he is gone for ten years. Phillip, now wealthy, cares for Enoch's family. After a decade, believing Enoch dead Annie marries Philip, but unknown to the pair, Enoch was stranded on a desert isle after a shipwreck. After he is rescued he returns and sees his family and Phillip happily together and leaves without being seen. In the film's final scenes, taking place years later, on his deathbed Enoch entrusts an old woman to tell Annie his story before dying.[13]

The first reel was released on June 12th, the second on June 14th. Playing one of Enoch's children was lovely Wyoming teenager Mildred Harris. Just 13, she had an impressive resume, working as a child at Fine Arts with Douglas Fairbanks and William S. Hart. She was barely 15 when she began an affair with Charlie Chaplin; her resulting pregnancy forced the pair to marry in 1918.[14]

Following *Enoch Arden* (often called "Enoch Garden" in ads) was another 4-reeler, *A Yankee from the West*. *Yankee* was directed by George Siegmann and adapted by Mary O'Connor from a novel by Opie Read.[15] Wally starred opposite Seena Owen, who had been pulled from anonymity during *Birth of a Nation* by Griffith just a few months earlier. Their co-stars included Tom Wilson, Josephine Crowell, Chris Lynton, and William H. Brown.

Wally played Billy Milford, a Harvard graduate working as a stationmaster in a Western town in love with pretty Norwegian immigrant Gunhild (Seena). His excessive drinking gets him fired and he retaliates by robbing the company with his friend Jim Dorsey (Wilson). Jim runs off with the money and Billy is forced to leave town and his love in shame. Two years later Gunhild stumbles upon Billy operating a farm in the East and love is rekindled but Jim reappears and tries to win Gunhild's attentions. Under threat of blackmail Billy is forced to fight Jim, whom he knocks out. He then confesses to the railroad superintendent (Filson) his part in the original robbery and gives the man his life savings as restitution. Moved by Billy's honesty the superintendent refuses the money and instead gives it to Gunhild as a wedding present.[16] *West* was released that August. Wally's next assignment was the lead in *Old Heidelberg*, which began filming in late May or early June.

Just after completing *Yankee*, Wally's chronic careless driving almost ended his career and almost killed both him and his passenger, Thomas Ince. Both were lucky to survive but the family in the other car was not so lucky. Wally and Ince had spent a relaxing and alcohol-fueled Friday night in Santa Monica. Neither may have known the others' pending good fortune; Wally was considering Lasky's offer to join Universal and Ince was negotiating an agreement with Harry Aitken to form a new studio. Aitken made a fortune from *Birth* and organized Ince, Griffith, and Mack Sennett to run a studio at his triangular Culver City lot. The Triangle Film Corporation would not open for two months but was probably arranged when Ince and Wally went out the night of April 30th.

Speeding up the Pacific Coast Highway near the beach in his Marmon coupe, Wally slammed into a small car carrying a family of five. Both cars were demolished; the Marmon rolled over into a ditch. Miraculously, Wally walked away with minor cuts and bruises but Ince suffered a broken collarbone and internal injuries. In the other upturned car the driver was dead and his wife and son seriously injured; two other children suffered broken bones. Wally was arrested and booked into the Santa Monica jail charged with manslaughter and several driving violations. Griffith arranged for his bail and he was released the following Monday.[17]

Interestingly, no record of the accident was found in Los Angeles newspaper archives. The only mention were small notes in the movie magazines *New York Dramatic Mirror* and *Moving Picture World*. It would not be surprising for the studio to solve a problem like this outside of court; cover-ups were becoming common. No definitive proof exists but something was done while Wally remained in seclusion at Allison Avenue. On May 17th the Grand Jury refused to indict Wally for anything (even the driving violations of which he was clearly guilty). The *Dramatic Mirror* announced on May 19th, "REID EXONERATED: AUTO ACCIDENT KILLED ONE AND INJURED TWO." Wally probably owed his good fortune to Griffith's intercession.

The next day Wally began *Old Heidelberg*, a 5-reeler directed for Griffith's Fine Arts Film Company by John Emerson and starring Wally with Dorothy Gish. Emerson got the job because his wife Anita Loos was one of Griffith's favorite writers. The scenario was based on the novel *Karl Heinrich* by Wilhelm Meyer-Förster.[18] Wally and Gish were supported by Karl Formes, Erich von Stroheim, Raymond Wells, J.W. McDermott, James Gibson, and Franklin Arbuckle. Emerson used von Stroheim—who also had a minor role in *Birth*—as an assistant director and technical advisor. It was his big break.

Wally plays Karl Heinrich, the heir apparent to the principality of Rutania, who leads a lonely existence in the royal palace with no friends and no life outside. He longs to become part of the exciting life in town and when he is finally sent to the university, there he enjoys camaraderie with friends and falls in love with Kathie (Gish), his only childhood friend and an innkeeper's niece. But Rutania is on the verge of a war that it does not want and Karl must return. Though palace courtiers and the military suggest that war is the only answer, Karl escapes to speak with his subjects, none of whom want war. Unfortunately, the only way for Karl to avoid war with the neighboring country is for him to marry its princess. He knows he must desert his true love Kathie and during a final sad visit to Heidelberg bids her farewell and assumes his lonely duties.[19]

On November 14th the film was released to middling reviews which described it as a "pleasantly done little story, but no master picture." Critics took aim at "the old theme elaborated into undue length, showing the maid's and prince's childhood, and there is overmuch of student frolic and a great deal of anti-war propaganda. It is no Griffith product, which Triangle had led us to expect."[20] One innovation moviegoers enjoyed about *Old Heidelberg* was an idea first used by Griffith for *Birth* screenings: a musical score written for the film.

Heidelberg was Wally's final film for Griffith. When filming ended Wally left Griffith and signed with Lasky and DeMille.[21] Stealing the young actor perched on the edge of stardom was a major coup. Griffith was so angry he refused to release *Heidelberg*, doubtless feeling Wally disloyal after he probably helped save Wally's career after his car accident. Although *Heidelberg* was filmed in the spring it wasn't released until November.

While Griffith stewed over losing Wally, Lasky told a writer that Wally "inherited his father's gift for story-telling, had a keen sense of humor, good singing voice, played the saxophone and piano, and was altogether the most charming, personable, handsome young man I've ever met. And the most cooperative."²² He signed his contract with the Jesse L. Lasky Feature Play Company on June 26th. Wally's salary was $75 a week. That is perhaps $4,000 today and Wally was earning more than most actors. John Gilbert earned $15 a week, Frank Borzage $12, Charles Ray $15, and Lew Cody $35. William S. Hart, the biggest western star, earned the same amount as Wally, $75.²³

Lasky knew the moment he saw his "180 pound diamond" that he had something special, and in an unprecedented move announced that Wally would not be loaned to any studio for any amount. He was among the studio's primary stars and Lasky and DeMille set about turning their unpolished gem into the first great American idol.

DeMille was Lasky's primary director. Cecil's brother William also directed but each had a different approach. Louella Parsons described the two as "curiously unlike in their method of presenting the photo-drama. Cecil specializes on the spectacular and emphasizes it to the nth [sic] degree at every opportunity. William makes the spectacular only incidental, and seldom thinks it necessary in his type of film drama. He is more of a dreamer and a poet, unconsciously seeking the more subtle problems of life as material for his photo-dramas."²⁴ The DeMilles had a profound effect on Wally's career.

In a photo probably taken in 1918 or 1919, Wally and DeMille discuss a script.

Cecil B. DeMille was a brilliant filmmaker whose body of work is among the most prodigious and prestigious in movie history. Volumes have been written describing his creative and technical expertise and his talent for picking stars. But Adolph Zukor described DeMille's *real* talent: "DeMille didn't make pictures for himself, or for critics. He made them for the public. He chose stories if he thought the public might like them. He was a showman to his smallest finger. He never started shooting until he had completed every detail of the script, and he followed through as he had prepared."[25]

Wally's first film was a major Lasky production, a remake of the play *Carmen* to star Geraldine Farrar. There is much confusion as to when films were made given the limited production records available. Frequently we have only release dates to reconstruct a filming record. This is the case with *Carmen*. Film historians usually list *The Chorus Lady* as Wally's first Lasky film because it was released on October 15th, followed by *Carmen* on October 31st, but *Carmen* was produced first. Wally later wrote, "My first picture for Mr. Lasky was 'Carmen.' ... After a couple of pictures in which I was co-starred with Cleo Ridgely, I was made a star in my own name...."[26] During June and July, Wally actually made two films with Farrar—*Carmen* and *Maria Rosa*—before *The Chorus Lady*.

Lasky did not like to pay fees for rights but he had no hesitancy paying huge amounts for talent. He first lured Farnum west and in 1915 paid stage legend Sarah Bernhardt $30,000 for six weeks, the largest sum ever paid a stage performer for a movie. He knew Bernhardt would end up not coming, but believed that paying her would make it easier to hire *other* stage stars. If it were not beneath the dignity of Bernhardt, who wouldn't participate, he wondered. Lasky actually wanted Geraldine Farrar.

She was to opera what Bernhardt was to stage, the most famous performer in the world. She was described by St. Johns as "the most brilliant figure among American women. Famous as a beauty, as an artiste, as a wit, she occupied a dazzling position."[27] Her millions of male fans were known as "Gerry-flappers." Getting her on film would be a major coup and Lasky was willing to pay dearly for it, offering her $35,000 for three films in eight weeks, along with amazing perks. Lasky knew Farrar had other incentives. The beginnings of World War I had already closed many European cultural centers where Farrar appeared but she was still not interested after seeing her first film featuring an opera star, a 1914 European short of Czechoslovakian soprano Emmy Destinn[28] in a lion's cage. She said, "in Berlin, I had been asked to consider an appearance in the films. I witnessed a few hundred feet devoted to the ample figure of Destinn, in a lion's cage which had caused an uproar in the august circles ... of our musical prestige. This circus stunt was awful. Of course, I refused to consider such a peculiar ... activity."[29]

Lasky traveled to New York and retained Morris Gest, the well-respected son-in-law of Broadway impresario David Belasco, as an intermediary. Farrar knew Gest well and took his advice; he was more or less her manager. Lasky sat through several performances, and met her after one. Knowing *Carmen* was her favorite role and that she was afraid movies would hurt her stage following he said, "I don't know whether you've seen a motion picture, but my company makes them, and I'd like to persuade you to do the story of Carmen for us. I could see by the ovation you got today that your prestige is such that whatever you do, your public will accept it as right." When Farrar replied, "Do you think I could turn the tide?,"[30] Lasky knew he would get her. But it took more than $35,000 and compliments.

Lasky's final package limited her workday to six hours—two three-hour periods with a two-hour rest period between. Nothing could be done that might impair her voice, meaning Farrar ultimately controlled when and *if* she worked. Lasky also paid for a private railcar between the coasts and all living expenses, renting a mansion in Whitley

Heights on two manicured acres of gardens[31] and staffed by a maid, cook, and butler. Every room was bedecked with flowers. A private studio bungalow dressing room, the first of its kind, was built. Hers contained a living room, dressing room and fully-equipped bath. Since Farrar never allowed visitors to watch her the area around her sets was boxed and a private enclosed corridor built between the set and the bungalow. She wrote in her 1938 memoirs, "Though every possible comfort and convenience had been provided, I still had to use my legs in a short promenade to and from the various sets."[32]

The contract's terms were unheard of and extravagant even by today's standards. Lasky also bought an insurance policy for $2,000 against "damage" to Farrar from the time she left New York until her return.[33] When her railcar arrived in L.A. she was met by Los Angeles' Mayor Henry Rose and 500 children who tossed a pathway of flowers from the car to her chauffeured limousine.[34] She brought her parents,[35] Gest and his wife Reina, a press agent, two maids, secretary, butler, personal chef, hairdresser and chauffeur.

Studio employees were worried about Farrar after hearing stories of the supposed eccentricities of opera divas. They expected a difficult and temperamental star. The cowboy actors were the most dubious and announced they would live away from the studio during her stay but Farrar proved a much more accepting fellow employee than they imagined.[36] The employees awaited her arrival nervously even as her massive car entered the studio but any doubts were allayed when she was escorted into her elaborate bungalow. Seeing the huge reception room with its grand piano and walls hung with chiffon and large mirrors, she was overwhelmed.[37] Right away she called the architect who designed it, the interior decorator who ordered furniture and drapes, and the secretaries who filled the house with flowers, thanking each. She then led her entourage on a walk around the studio, introducing herself to employees of all levels.

Opera star Geraldine Farrar at the time she was being wooed to Hollywood by Lasky and DeMille.

When rehearsals for *Maria Rosa* began she introduced herself to the crew and insisted they call her "Gerry." At lunch she told DeMille, "Let me give a party" and sent out for lunch for everyone. And though she almost *never* sang in public except on stage she had a piano brought to the set and serenaded her crew.[38] Almost none of these workers had ever heard an opera, but Lasky described "everyone on our payroll—the cast, carpenters, grips, cowboys and office staff—standing bareheaded in a transfixed circle" listening to the greatest singer in the world.[39] A few days later the cowboys appeared. As they ambled onto the set Farrar chatted with them and within a few days knew and remembered the stories of each. They so enjoyed her that, during a break in filming in Griffith Park, a group put on an exhibition of bronco and rough riding. When they were done they gifted Farrar with a pony she rode almost every day.

Maria Rosa filming began on June 14th.

It was based on an 1890 Spanish play by Ángel Guimerá and had been a Broadway success for Lou Tellegen.[40] Tellegen, who Lasky said "looked like a Greek god," was hired just before Farrar arrived. Most *Maria Rosa* filming took place in the hillsides in and around the Cahuenga Pass. It is a tragic love story of Catalonian peasant Maria Rosa (Farrar), who is in love with handsome fisherman Andreas (Wally). But another villager, Ramon (Pedro de Cordoba, playing the role Tellegen made famous on Broadway), uses a knife belonging to Andreas to murder another fisherman (Horace B. Carpenter). While Andreas serves ten years in prison for Ramon's murder, Ramon convinces Maria that Andreas died there so she agrees to marry him. But on the day of their wedding Andreas returns from jail and an enraged Maria stabs Ramon to death. James Neill, Ernest Joy and Anita King appeared in supporting roles in the 5-reeler filmed from June 14th to the 26th, but not released until May 7, 1916.

Farrar and Wally hit it off immediately. She was captivated by her handsome co-star, and he with her. St. Johns described her impact on Wally: "she swayed the boy as no other personality with whom he had come in contact in his life up to that time had ever swayed him."[41] It is interesting that St. Johns, Wally and Dorothy's closest friend, left Dorothy *out* of the comment. It was obvious Farrar was attracted to Wally. They spent hours together at each other's homes and socially. Sometimes with Dorothy, but usually without. Rumors of an affair swirled around Lasky. Stories of Wally and other women were already frequent, and intensified the more famous he became; and Wally's history of becoming emotionally involved quickly made Farrar risky for him.

Their intense chemistry played out on film. Wally's work with Farrar exhibited an intensity he had not shown before. He was a different actor with her. According to St. Johns, Wally was demanding directing work until he met Farrar. "It was the charm of Geraldine Farrar and his desire to work with her and know her," wrote St. Johns, "that persuaded Wally to continue acting."[42] The two had much in common beyond acting, the most basic being music. The pair spent hours at her home or the Reids' playing, singing or talking about music. Farrar sang arias to Wally's violin accompaniment during private gatherings. St. Johns inferred something more than a professional friendship when she described the relationship as "a friendship that stimulated Wallace Reid in many ways," noting that he "accepted her words as the utterance of an oracle," and also that "the flattery of her interest gave him a new self-confidence and a new ambition."[43]

Interestingly, Dorothy studiously avoided mention of Farrar in her prolific writings and later interviews. She was usually effusive in details of his films, but rarely mentioned *Carmen, Maria Rosa*, or his later films with Farrar. Given the impact Farrar had on his career, this omission seems telling.

On June 28th, just days after concluding *Maria Rosa*, filming began on *Carmen*. This movie was among a short list of films that made Wally a star. *The Birth of a Nation* brought him to Lasky's attention; *Carmen* brought him to the world. Farrar had starred in the Broadway version the previous year and William de Mille wrote the scenario for the 5-reel film based upon the original 1845 Mérimée novella instead of the better-known Bizet opera, which made a more suspenseful film. Farrar and Wally played the leads, supported by de Cordoba, Carpenter, King, and newcomers William Elmer, Milton Brown, and DeMille scenarist Jeanie Macpherson.[44]

Like *Maria Rosa*, *Carmen* is another tragic love story set in Spain. After beautiful gypsy Carmen (Farrar) gets into a vicious fight with another gypsy (MacPherson) at the cigar factory, she is given to the custody of dashing Spanish military officer Don Jose (Wally). He falls in love with her but when he takes her to the city she falls in love with bullfighter Escamillo (de Cordoba). Unknown to him the deceitful Carmen is using him so her gypsy smugglers can pass through town safely. Carmen completely bewitches Don Jose while her real love, the toreador Escamillo, waits for her in the shadows. In Pastia's (Carpenter) tiny tavern Carmen dances for Don Jose and Escamillo in a brilliantly-filmed sequence that highlights Farrar's earthy sensuality. Carmen and Escamillo escape and flee toward Seville with Don Jose in hot pursuit, willing to do anything to win her, while enduring a progression from love to jealousy to obsession to insanity. His misguided passion finally overtakes him when he stabs her to death outside the Seville bullring where Escamillo is performing. His life ends in disgrace because of his obsessive love. The final bullfight scene features DeMille trademarks: huge crowds and dramatic visual scenery that evoke a moody atmosphere of high drama and vengeance.

Writer Macpherson offered to play the gypsy girl that has a realistic and brutal fight with Carmen. During filming Macpherson began an affair with DeMille that lasted the rest of her life. She became his most trusted advisor and confidante; he never made a movie decision without consulting with her.

During shooting, which lasted until July 13th, Farrar asked for music to help her emote. She recalled, "I was so accustomed to orchestral accompaniment for certain tempi and phrasings, I felt I could better pantomime the rhythm of the effects. A little piano was hastily wheeled on the set and the talented Melville Ellis, who knew every kind of music, Broadway jazz as well as the classics, by heart, inspired all my scenes with his impromptu playing."[45] She is often credited with this inspiration, but several directors had used the same method earlier.

Farrar was impressed with DeMille, saying, "DeMille's long and varied experiences in the legitimate theatre gave him an uncanny reading into his actors' psychology. Thus, with me, he outlined briefly the scenes and with the minimum expenditure of precious energy in preliminaries, set his cameras at all angles to catch the first enthusiasm of a scene, which spontaneous impulse was always my best interpretation. We were not cautioned to beware of undue emotion, disarranged locks, torn clothing, etc. We were allowed free action as we felt it; so we acted our parts as if we were engaged in a theatre performance, and I believe, for this reason, we had real expression and feeling, which I find so often lacking in the beautiful but monotonous faces of so many of the screen stars today."[46]

Lasky rushed *Carmen* into release. Though it was filmed after *Maria Rosa*, *Carmen* was released on October 15th while *Maria* stayed in the canisters until the following year. *Carmen* was a critical and financial success. The *Chicago Daily Tribune* noted, "*Carmen*, which has been so long coming, has come and conquered. The result of their weeks of work and mountains of money is a high powered illuminator."[47] *The Atlanta Constitution* followed, "One of the year's greatest events in the motion picture realm will be the appearance at the Grand Theater the first three days of next week, at the present price, of Geraldine Farrar in the celebrated Lasky production of 'Carmen.' All the alluring witchery the role calls for has been put into 'Carmen' by Miss Farrar with the result being the picture has been declared one of the greatest ever shown here."[48]

Again Wally was singled out, one reviewer noting the "slim and good-looking" star was "putting it over his operatic predecessors and a lover to match Carmen's own vintage of emotion."[49] When *Carmen* was completed Farrar took a month off before starting *Temptation* on July 27th. Filming lasted until August 10th. Farrar's co-star was Theodore Roberts, supported by de Cordoba, King, Joy, Elsie Jane Wilson, Raymond Hatton, and Sessue Hayakawa. During filming she began dating Lou Tellegen, whom she knew from Broadway. They were married February 8, 1916. The marriage lasted four years.

Farrar stayed in Hollywood for a month after her commitment concluded, leaving in October for the New York opera season. The experiment was a resounding success for Lasky and Farrar, who bid farewell to virtually every studio employee she had met, addressing each by name. Her contract was eclipsed a few months later when Billie Burke was paid $40,000 by New York Motion Picture Company to leave Broadway for the seven-reeler *Peggy*.[50] Production was limited to five weeks, $5,000 specified for a wardrobe she kept, and she had the same bungalow and mansion arrangement as Farrar.[51]

All three of Farrar's films were windfalls for Lasky. *Maria Rosa* cost $18,574.53 to make and grossed $102,767.81, *Carmen* cost $23,429.97 and grossed $147,599.81, and *Temptation* cost $22,472.25 and grossed $102,437.47.[52] In today's dollars, the films cost about $1,500,000 combined and grossed over $8,000,000. Considering Farrar's portion of the $65,000 cost was probably $40,000, the results are impressive. Also, the grosses are below actual grosses with states rights fees excluded. During subsequent trips to Hollywood in 1916 and 1917 Farrar would accept no other leading man. She demanded and was given Wally.

Geraldine Farrar and Wally became very close friends when they worked together during the summer of 1916.

After Farrar's departure Wally went back to more typical Lasky fare. He starred with Cleo Ridgely and Marjorie Daw in the Frank Reicher–directed romantic comedy–drama *The Chorus Lady,* a 5-reel Marion Fairfax adaptation of a 1906 James Forbes play. Richard Grey and Mrs. Lewis McCord supported in the film, released on October 18th. Ridgely plays chorus girl Patricia O'Brian, who is engaged to detective Danny Mallory (Wally). Pat wants to leave Broadway and live on a farm but is forced to stay to protect her star-struck younger sister Nora (Daw), who is being seduced by philandering theatrical producer Dicky Crawford (Grey) and given a role in a play with Pat. Crawford also makes a play for Pat not knowing that Danny had been hired by Crawford's wife to gather evidence for a divorce. When Danny walks in at the moment Crawford tries to kiss Pat he thinks she's having an affair with Crawford and walks out. But Nora clears the air, Crawford's wife divorces him, and Danny and Pat—along with Nora and her new boyfriend—move to the country to live on a farm.[53]

Wally and Cleo Ridgely next teamed in the six-reeler *The Golden Chance*, directed by DeMille, who wrote the story with protégé-mistress MacPherson and featured Ernest Joy, Edythe Chapman and Raymond Hatton. It is the tale of Mary Denby (Ridgely), who becomes a seamstress for the wealthy Hillarys (Joy and Chapman) after her shiftless husband Steve (Horace B. Carpenter) spends their money on liquor. Mrs. Hillary, impressed with Mary's beauty and charm, gives her an opportunity to escape poverty and enjoy life's luxuries. Posing her as unmarried, she assigns Mary to assist one of her business associates, millionaire Roger Manning (Wally). During their travels Manning falls in love with Mary but she has to hide her true identity and marriage status and refuse her "golden chance." But her husband tries to blackmail and kill Manning; their battle ends when Steve is killed in a police gunfight. Mary tells Roger her secret and the pair quickly marries.[54]

Chance was filmed between October 26th and November 26th. It was a challenging production for DeMille. While filming *Chance* he was also making *The Cheat* with Fannie Ward, Jack Dean, and Sessue Hayakawa. And *Chance* had casting problems. Edna Goodrich, better-known than Ridgely, was to play Mary Denby but caused production delays due to her alcoholism. DeMille halted production on November 1st and restarted on the 5th after replacing Goodrich with Ridgely. He had to redo the Goodrich footage but the change helped the movie since Ridgely brought a vulnerability to the role that is both winsome and haunting.[55] Mary Denby is a classic DeMille heroine who turns her back on privilege only to find tragedy when afforded "the golden chance" to gain social status.[56]

Chance, advertised with "The Lasky Co. claim that this is the finest picture they have released up to this time,"[57] grossed $80,000 at a cost of under $18,000. It is long-forgotten but is an early DeMille masterpiece. He and art director Wilfred Buckland used a sort of visual short-hand. Mary's boss' office is shown only as a desktop and a wall. The bar frequented by her husband is a back-lit silhouetted "beer" sign. The Denby's apartment is a one-room set and the boss' mansion is suggested more than seen. Cameraman Alvin Wyckoff's use of the dark "Rembrandt lighting" favored by DeMille added moodiness.[58]

More remarkable was the fact that DeMille filmed *Chance* simultaneously with *The Cheat*. *Cheat* filming took place during the day, and *Chance* at night. DeMille used the experiment to prove by example to Lasky directors that they were not overworked (a common complaint). *Cheat* was released on December 12th and *The Golden Chance* on January 31, 1916. *Chance* was described by critics as a "thrilling society drama ... full of thrills that make the picture quite a production," and "Jeanie MacPherson's greatest love story success."[59] Wally and Ridgley were also featured in a November issue of *Moving Picture World* in an article entitled "Cleo Ridgley and Wallace Reid Co-Stars."[60] It was an upgrade in the scope and type of publicity and photos featuring Wally. The film's European release in the spring of 1916 began Wally's jump to stardom on that continent as well.

Wally's final 1915 films were two 5-reel historical dramas. The first was a George Melford adaptation of the Mary Johnston novel *To Have and to Hold*[61] written by Margaret Turnbull. Wally starred opposite Mae Murray,[62] with Tom Forman, Ronald Bradbury, Raymond Hatton, James Neill, Lucien Littlefield, Bob Fleming, and Camille Astor. Beginning with this film Wally worked with "all-star" casts; his co-stars were the best Lasky had to offer. The movie was a faithful depiction of the early history of the Virginia colonies. Lasky's librarians, historians and writers spent six months researching and confirming historical accuracy before filming began. It was described as "a glance into the days when strong men and brave women fought for the rights of existence on a new continent."[63]

Lady Jocelyn (Murray), a member of the court of England's King James, escapes an arranged marriage to the hated Lord Carnal (Forman) by fleeing to the American colonies with a shipment of brides. Soon after arriving she agrees to marry Captain Ralph Percy (Wally) though she doesn't love him, but Carnal follows her to Virginia and orders she and Percy imprisoned. Percy and Jocelyn join other prisoners, escape and overpower Carnal on his own ship. They flee, with Carnal aboard, but the ship is forced onto a remote island inhabited by pirates. Trying to save himself and take Jocelyn, Carnal convinces pirate leader Jeremy Sparrow (Bradbury) that he is himself an infamous pirate and tells him that Percy is a British Naval officer. As Percy is about to walk the plank the pirates turn their attention to an approaching British ship carrying the Governor of Virginia. Percy's small group foils the attack and Carnal, knowing he will hang, commits suicide. Percy and Jocelyn, now in love, return to Virginia with the governor.[64]

The movie was released on March 5, 1916. Lasky did a remake just five years later in 1922 with George Fitzmaurice directing an adaptation written by his wife Ouida Bergère and starring Betty Compson and Bert Lytell.

Wally's final 1915 assignment was the Frank Reicher–directed western *The Love Mask*, written by DeMille and Macpherson. According to period newspapers Paul Dickey was originally supposed to direct, although that is not confirmed by studio archives. Wally starred opposite Cleo Ridgely, supported by Earl Foxe, Bob Fleming, Dorothy Abril and Littlefield. The film, made in the Mojave Desert, takes place during the days of the California gold rush.

Wally plays Sheriff Dan Deering, who is in love with feisty female prospector Kate Kenner (Ridgely), whose claim is stolen by four miners. Kate takes the law into her own hands and, after disguising herself in the trademark black mask of the bandit Silver Spurs, holds up the saloon where the men who stole her gold hid the booty. But when she tries to get away Dan catches her and is stunned; he assumes his girlfriend really *is* Silver Spurs. Kate is tried and a guilty verdict seems assured until the real Silver Spurs, who admired the masquerade, steals the gold himself and leaves a note exonerating Kate. Instead of pursuing the escaping bandit, Dan makes plans to marry Kate.[65] Early studio releases noted Wally and Cleo rehearsing "the original Cecil B. DeMille–Jeanie MacPherson vehicle *Behind the Mask*."[66] The title was again changed to *Under the Mask* before DeMille settled on *The Love Mask*.

In the six months since Wally joined Lasky, he jumped from popular actor to full-fledged star, but during the same time Dorothy's career was idling at a much slower pace. She was making single-reelers like *The Witness* and *In Humble Guise* and still toiling at smaller studios like Paragon and Balboa. The small studios were taking advantage of Wally's popularity by casting Dorothy. Likewise, her crews and co-stars were of lesser quality, and she worked for lesser directors like Donald MacDonald and Lee Hill. After a single-reel western, director Rupert Julian's *The Wolf's Den* for Navajo Films, in which Dorothy starred opposite Ben Horning, Wally intervened. In August, he asked Lasky to hire Dorothy, a request that Lasky could not decline.

Lasky gave Dorothy her first feature, the 5-reeler *The Explorer*. It was directed by George Melford and featured a story adapted by William de Mille from a Somerset Maugham novel. Dorothy starred opposite Lou Tellegen and Tom Forman, supported by James Neill and Horace B. Carpenter. The film was released on September 27th. The rest of her 1915 films were either Lasky features or longer films on loan-out to Universal companies Carl Laemmle was also using Dorothy to piggy-back on Wally's name. At Lasky, Dorothy starred in *Mr. Grex of Monte Carlo*, another 5-reeler directed by Frank Reicher, with Theodore Roberts, Carlyle Blackwell, Frank Elliott, Lucien Littlefield, Carpenter, Robert Gray, and Gertrude Keller. This was as close Dorothy had ever come to an all-star cast. She followed *Grex* with *The Unknown*, directed by George Melford and co-starring Tellegen and Roberts. Her Universal loan-outs were shorter 2-reelers but of higher quality than her other previous films. They included *One Hundred Years Ago*, starring with Rupert Julian and Elsie Jane Wilson, and *The Phantom Island*. *Island* was made by Bison and Thomas Ince, and she starred with Jay Belasco and Francis Ford. Dorothy would benefit from Wally's popularity in 1916 and beyond.

7

Stardom

By 1916 almost 70 percent of the world's movies were made in Hollywood. Over 10,000,000 people saw a movie weekly. European immigrants dominated the movie industry. Unlike conservative American Protestants, men like Zukor, Lasky, and Laemmle were attuned to public desires and were willing to exploit the ribald humor people liked in films. The Europeans came from business backgrounds and were sensitive to customer needs and changing the product if needed. They knew marketing. Goldwyn once said, "If the audience don't like a picture, they have a good reason. The public is never wrong. I don't go for all this thing that when I have a failure, it is because the audience doesn't have the taste or education, or isn't sensitive enough. The public pays money. It wants to be entertained. That's all I know."[1]

In January, Adolph Zukor merged his Famous Players studio with Lasky's to form Famous Players–Lasky. The new entity was led by Zukor, with Lasky second in command and DeMille lead director. Samuel Goldwyn was the odd man out. The new studio was large, capitalized with $12,500,000. It would make the 80 features a year that Zukor wanted, using well-known names like Marguerite Clark, Pauline Frederick, Blanche Sweet, Mary Pickford, John Barrymore, Victor Moore, and Wally.[2]

The studio's well-organized film distribution system was assembled by San Franciscan William W. Hodkinson,[3] who organized 20 film exchanges into one large entity called Paramount-Publix Pictures. Soon, Zukor was forced to buy Paramount[4] so Hodkinson couldn't control Zukor-Lasky production. When he did so he also instituted a "block-booking" requirement that forced theaters to buy multiple films. To get a star feature lesser movies had to be purchased. Paramount Pictures/Famous Players–Lasky was fully vertically integrated; it produced, distributed, and owned the theaters that showed their films.[5] Zukor's innovative 1916 strategies redefined the industry.

The merger came at the right time for Lasky. Movies were getting longer, as long as ten reels. A typical 5-reeler cost $12,000 to $20,000 and took six weeks to make. In 1917, the *New York Dramatic Mirror* detailed the average cost to produce a feature:

Star ($1,500 weekly)	$6,000
Leading man ($400 weekly)	$1,200
Principal actors	$1,300
Extras	$300
Director ($750 weekly)	$3,000
Assistant Director ($75 weekly)	$300
Cameraman ($75 weekly)	$300
Assistant Cameraman	$100

Scenario work	$1,000
Transportation	$500
Studio sets	$1,000
Film stock for negative	$1,000
Renting locations	$200
Costumes	$1,000
Incidentals	$500
Total	$17,700

The combined studio could better afford these high costs and film historians often point to Zukor's production needs as the impetus for the merger. But there was a more pressing need. An event now largely forgotten and ignored, a September 11, 1915, fire at Famous Players' 26th Street studio in Hollywood destroyed virtually the entire site.[7] The fire threw production into chaos, but worse it destroyed negatives including the only copy of the Alan Dwan–directed Mary Pickford film *The Foundling*. The Saturday morning fire was so fierce that the safe containing unreleased negatives couldn't be found in the rubble until Tuesday.[8] The loss of unreleased films was not publicly discussed but it would have been a catastrophe for Zukor. The merger likely saved the studio.

Zukor was instrumental in developing the producer system, in which managers are delegated responsibility for segments of the movie process. His production strategies, Lasky's creative strength, and Paramount's distribution capacity made for a formidable studio. Wally was in the perfect place at the perfect time with better roles and more publicity.

On January 1st he joined Lasky's top stars Theodore Roberts, Victor Moore, Cleo Ridgely, and Anita King in a vaudeville performance to benefit a local church. Ridgely auctioned a kiss, and King donated her small Kissel-Kar coupe. Wally got the most applause simply by dancing with Camille Astor.[9] Including Wally at the event indicated his bankability to Lasky.

The industry was committed to feature-length films. Comedy fillers were the only shorts being produced. But features meant more work with more complex plot-lines and shooting that could take two months instead of two days. Between 1912 and 1914, Wally made 125 films[10] and in 1915 he made 12 five- or six-reelers. Today that would mean perhaps a dozen films in a year. His was an impressive body of work. In 1916 he released just 9 and three were filmed in 1915—*To Have and to Hold*, released on March 5th, *The Love Mask* on April 16th, and *Maria Rosa* on May 7th.

Wally's first 1916 work was on the E. Mason Hopper–directed western *The Selfish Woman*, filmed in March (also called *The Taming of Helen*). Trade papers listed George Melford as directing and 1941 studio records listed he and Hopper as co-directing. The 5-reeler paired Wally with Cleo Ridgely, supported by Edythe Chapman, Charles Arling, Joe King, Horace B. Carpenter, Bob Fleming and Milton Brown.

Wally plays Tom Morley, a civil engineer on a railroad expansion whose wife Alice (Ridgely) married him for his family's money. An independent sort, Tom eschewed working for his father to work for a railroad but to entice him to return to work with him the elder Morley (Arling) promises Alice $1,000,000 if she can help Tom's railroad fail. Alice quietly convinces Tom's men to go on strike. When Tom finds out he leaves her, but when the strikers burn their camp Alice realizes her mistake and that she loves Tom. She returns to the burning camp to stop the riot, admits to the men she invented the reasons for the strike, and convinces them to return to work. Alice loses her million dollars but makes up with Tom.[11]

During filming Ridgley dashed through the burning camp on horseback at the head of a sheriff's posse. A half dozen houses had been set ablaze surrounded by burning sul-

With Cleo Ridgley in *The Selfish Woman*.

phur pots billowing smoke. As she galloped up the street she was overcome by the fumes and fell off her horse, unconscious. In the dark melee the other horsemen were about to trample the star when one of the riders jumped from his horse and threw himself over her. The anonymous extra saved her life.[12] *The Selfish Woman* was released on July 9th.

Ridgely and Wally teamed up again on *The House with the Golden Windows*, a 4-reeler directed by Melford. Also called *The House of the Golden Windows*, it was filmed in April or early May. Supporting were Billy Jacobs, James Neill, Mabel Van Buren, Marjorie Daw and Bob Fleming. The movie was released on August 3rd.

Wally plays shepherd Tom Wells, living in poverty with his wife Sue (Ridgely) in the shadow of the palatial Peabody mansion. Sue, tired of being poor, convinces Tom to join a check fraud scheme she organizes when the Peabodys (Neill and Van Buren) go on vacation. She discovers a loophole in the Peabody's lease allowing her and Tom to take ownership of the estate but living a wealthy life does not make Sue happy. When Peabody returns and discovers what she and Tom have done, he shoots Tom. As he prepares to shoot Sue, she wakes up from her dream. While the newly-repentant Sue and Tom share a meager meal, Peabody returns and announces that Tom is his new estate overseer, ending Sue's money worries.[13]

Wally's next film was the romantic drama *The Yellow Pawn*, probably filmed in May. *Pawn* was based on the short story "A Close Call" by Frederic Arnold Kummer. A brief item in studio records mentions that the story first ran in *All-Story Magazine* in 1914, but it may be in error; it isn't in any publication records. The film was released domestically on November 23rd as either a 4- or a 5-reeler depending on the market. It was directed by Melford and Claude Mitchell, and again paired Wally with Cleo Ridgely. They were supported by William Conklin, Tom Forman, Irene Aldwyn, Clarence Geldart, George Webb and George Kuwa.

Kate Turner (Ridgely) marries shady district attorney Allen Perry (Conklin) so she can care for her younger sister, but to marry him she must reject her real love, struggling artist James Weldon (Wally). Years later, Weldon has become a successful and wealthy portrait painter and Perry becomes jealous. Hoping to catch his wife in a compromising position, Perry commissions a portrait of his wife. After Kate leaves his studio late one evening James's sleazy brother Tom (Webb) arrives and quarrels with the artist. When Weldon's servant Sen Yat (Kuwa) sees Tom stealing money, he and Tom fight and he stabs and kills Tom, but Perry has Weldon arrested for the killing. In the film's suspenseful climax, as Perry questions Weldon, Kate reveals she was at the studio that night. As Perry flies into a jealous rage and threatens to kill Weldon and his wife, Sen Yat rushes in, stabs Perry to death and admits to the first murder as well. Finally free, Kate and James reunite.[14]

During *Golden Windows* and perhaps as he began work on *The Yellow Pawn*, Wally spent a few days working with D.W. Griffith. Lasky had a firm "no loan-out" policy for Wally but if Wally made the request it would have been granted. The role was small and like his last Griffith role in *The Birth of a Nation*, his character was killed. But *Intolerance: Love's Struggle Through the Ages* was another important Griffith masterpiece. It was his answer to critics of *Birth*. *Intolerance* was an expansion of *The Mother and the Law*, an indictment of social injustice he began in 1914. A critique of capital punishment and business' brutal suppression of labor, it included four stories, each set in a different historic era. They illustrated man's inhumanity to man, religious hatred, discrimination, and injustice, all resulting from intolerance.[15] Like *Birth*, *Intolerance* is among the greatest American films, and beyond Griffith's message of tolerance the sheer spectacle of the production has never been matched.

Studio financial backers were hesitant about the project, knowing the costs would be enormous and that the film was personal to Griffith. To avoid them entirely Griffith financed the film himself, buying out backers with notes and using *Birth* profits to finance shooting.[16] Costs are hard to confirm. Griffith mentioned $385,000,[17] an absurdly low estimate. Archival records suggest $1,600,000[18] but that may have been orchestrated in response to the reported $1,750,000 gross. More reasonable estimates put the cost between $2,000,000 and $3,000,000. Replacing sets like the Babylonian temple that took craftsmen a year to make would cost $500,000,000 today. Over 10,000 extras were each lavishly costumed individually and entire cities built as backdrops.

Griffith's film graphically showed intolerance as the cause of each of the most destructive events during 2,500 years of history, including the fall of Babylon due to intolerance of a new religion, the crucifixion of Jesus Christ, the mass murder of thousands of innocents by French noblemen and Catholic clerics, and an evil economic system ruining a country.[19] Each vignette is a film within the film. The director's cut was eight hours long and he considered releasing it at that length. Lillian Gish was one of the few who saw the full eight-hour version and said it was the finest film she ever saw. The final release was 14 reels and 3½ hours long. Each segment was tinted a different color. The "Babylonian" story, taking place in 539 B.C., is gray-green. The "Judean" Story, in A.D. 27, is blue. The "French" story, in 1572, is sepia, and the "Modern" Story, in 1914, is amber.

The lavish Babylonian story is the tale of peace-loving Prince Belshazzar's Babylon during the conquest by King Cyrus the Persian,[20] made possible by the treachery of his High Priests. It was told amidst a mountain girl's vain efforts to avert the tragedy. The Judean story is the story of Jesus Christ's struggles with the Pharisees, his betrayal by Judas and the crucifixion. It is the shortest but most powerful of the four. The French (or Medieval) story takes place during the Renaissance in 16th century France and describes the slaughter of the Huguenots by rulers Catherine de Médicis[21] and her son King Charles IX.[22] It culminates with the atrocities of the St. Bartholomew's Day Massacre,[23] showing its effects upon the planned wedding of an innocent Huguenot couple. The Modern story depicts labor and social unrest in California as ruthless employers and zealous reformers battle. A young Irish Catholic boy, an exploited worker, is wrongly sentenced to hang for a murder he did not commit and is saved from execution by the last-minute arrival of his wife with a Governor's pardon.

Griffith used a moving visual technique to weave stories together as he cut between the four, showing a simple image of Lillian Gish rocking a baby's cradle as the link between them. It was her only role in the film although she is often incorrectly credited as the female lead. Griffith borrowed liberally from the Walt Whitman poem "Out of the Cradle Endlessly Rocking" and Anita Loos used poem text for title cards.

Griffith put together a vast collection of creative and artistic talent. Each segment had all-star leads and hundreds of stars in smaller roles. It's impossible to list every "name" star that appeared. The Babylonian story starred Constance Talmadge, Elmer Clifton, Alfred Paget and George Siegmann. The Judean story featured Bessie Love, Lillian Langdon and William H. Brown. Director Woodbridge Strong Van Dyke[24] made his acting debut as a wedding guest. The French story had Margery Wilson, Eugene Pallette, Allan Sears, Spottiswoode Aitken and Frank Bennett. The Modern story starred Mae Marsh, Robert Harron, Walter Long, Ralph Lewis and Edward Dillon. Another director, Tod Browning,[25] also debuted in a small role. Huge stars took uncredited roles, among them Wally, who appeared in the Babylonian battle segment. Others included Seena Owen, Tully Marshall, Douglas Fairbanks, Carmel Myers, Elmo Lincoln, Erich von Stroheim, King Vidor, Monte Blue, Marguerite Marsh, Alma Rubens, Pauline Starke, Ernest Butterworth, Carol Dempster and Owen Moore.[26]

The massive 1915 Babylonian set built by D.W. Griffith for his classic *Intolerance*, which covered ten square blocks and was visible for miles around. It stood for years decaying in the sun before being demolished (courtesy Marc Wanamaker, Bison Archives).

The outdoor Babylonian set was the largest ever created for a film and the crowd shots of 15,000 extras the grandest in cinema history.[27] Designed by Frank Wortman and Walter L. Hall, the most famous was an amazing Great Wall of Babylon temple erected at the corner of Sunset and Vermont. It covered almost twenty *acres*, with a massive temple entrance three football fields wide and 200 feet tall. Flanking a huge courtyard standing atop ten 100-foot-tall, 40-foot-wide carved pillars, were ten 60-foot-tall statues of rearing elephants. Ornate carvings covered every wall and thousands of statues filled niches or stood on columns. The other massive set was a lavish banquet hall, the backdrops still the largest ever built.[28] A spectacular panorama view of the banquet Feast of Belshazzar was accomplished with the first crane shot,[29] attaching a camera to an elevated platform three stories high mounted on a dolly that tracked through the scene.

The courtyard and banquet sets cost well over $1,000,000 and it cost $200,000 just to *film* the banquet. The Great Wall was a Hollywood landmark that stood rotting across from the studio for years. Griffith had no money to dismantle it even though the L.A. Fire Department cited the remains as a fire hazard and ordered them demolished. It was finally removed in 1920.

Directors had always feared that plot movements confused audiences but Griffith used over 50 transitions to cut back and forth over great gaps of time.[30] The film was shown on August 5th in a Riverside theater after which Griffith repeated his *Birth* process and removed scenes thought too offensive or confusing. The film was released September 5th but the technical brilliance couldn't carry it financially. It was considered a failure even though it earned somewhere near $2,000,000. In 1919, trying to recoup his investment, Griffith re-cut the modern and Babylonian stories and released them individually as *The Mother and the Law* and *The Fall of Babylon* in 1919. The film's pacifist message was buoyed by America's antiwar mood in 1916 and it did well internationally, running for five years in Japan and ten in Russia.[31] Griffith publicist Harry Carr recalled, "'Intolerance' was a flop. Griffith expected to make a fortune and an imperishable name by it. I don't know why it failed."[32] Over the decades since, though, it has become a cinema landmark.

Wally took the small role because stars were clamoring for any role in the film and it was obviously good publicity for Lasky. When Wally returned, Geraldine Farrar was on her way and demanding to work with him again.[33] During this visit they made a single film, *Joan the Woman*, and this time Dorothy welcomed Farrar into her home. She was no longer a threat; in February, Farrar had married Lou Tellegen.

Lasky employees looked forward to her arrival and as with her earlier visit, Farrar threw herself into her work. The film was based on the martyred Joan of Arc and when she learned Joan wore her hair bobbed, rather than use a wig she had her famous long red hair cut off. After her suit of armor was finished she clumped heavily around the studio getting used to the 100-pound costume.[34] It was made to her exact measurements and "fit her like a sardine can fit its contents."[35] Farrar was deathly afraid of horses; just being near one left her "shaking with apprehension"[36] but she tried to ride even with her cumbersome armor, sword, gauntlets, a heavy banner, and what she described as her "crucifying helmet." Two men were needed to lift her on and off her horse and during filming the animal sped away toward nearby meadowlands with her aboard. She was rescued when actor Jack Holt grabbed the reins while riding alongside at a full gallop. Thereafter, DeMille hired female stuntman Pansy Perry to stand in for the greatly relieved Farrar.

Joan the Woman was a major project that Lasky described as "more pretentious than anything we had attempted before."[37] DeMille wanted to make spectacles like Griffith, and gave up his responsibilities as Vice President to direct full-time. *Joan* was a DeMille propaganda film based on Friedrich von Schiller's *Die Jungfrau von Orleans*.[38] It was DeMille's first historical epic, produced at a time when the outcome of World War I was uncertain. It was a grand-scale tribute to the spirit of the French, whose country was awash in blood. Wally and Farrar were supported by Raymond Hatton, Hobart Bosworth, Theodore Roberts, Charles Clary, James Neill, Tully Marshall, Lawrence Peyton, Cleo

Ridgely, Lillian Leighton and Marjorie Daw. It had a $300,000 budget ($7,000,000 today), ran 10 reels (3 hours),[39] and was written by Jeanie Macpherson and William de Mille. Alvin Wyckoff directed 17 cameramen, who began on June 19th amidst Wilfred Buckland's massive sets.[40]

After a month of shooting, work continued in fits and starts until October 7th. Exteriors were done in massive Griffith Park. The film's preamble described the lavish epic as the story of "The Girl Patriot Who Fought with Men, Was Loved by Men and Killed by Men, Yet Retained the Heart of a Woman." DeMille used Griffith's multiple-plot technique, telling Joan's story as a metaphor to provide a petrified soldier (Wally) with the bravery needed for a suicide mission. It is divided into two epochs. The first follows young Joan's leadership of the French against British troops occupying France. The second shows the betrayal of Joan by Erich Trent (also Wally) and her eventual martyrdom at the hands of the Church, headed by evil Bishop Cauchon (Roberts) and the mad Monk L'Oiseleur (Marshall).

Wally's frightened English soldier is fighting in France but volunteers to carry a bomb across a bloody, body-strewn field and heave it into a German trench. Readying himself for impending death, he is filled with fear until he finds the decayed sword of Joan of Arc, whose life then unfolds before him in a dream. He sees Joan's humble beginnings as a peasant milkmaid in the mid–1400s to her divinely inspired fight against the British, empowered by divine visions and voices telling her to fight in the name of God. She joins France's rightful king Charles VII (Hatton), and leads his impoverished and disorganized army to victory at the battle to retake Orleans. She is then betrayed by her British lover Eric Trent (Wally) and is captured, tried and burned at the stake. Joan tells the terrified soldier to die for France to atone for English sins against her, and inspired by his visions he sacrifices himself.[41] In the touching climax Wally's character places a small cross of twigs onto Joan's death pyre.

DeMille highlights Joan's dreams and death scene using hand-tinted frames and double exposures of surreal ghost-like images only she can see. Flames surrounding her as she dies were hand painted in deep reds that bounce off the black-and-white screen to great effect.[42] The coloring process was new, and according to copyright registrations was called "the Wyckoff Process." In his autobiography DeMille credits himself, Alvin Wyckoff,[43] Max Handschiegl and Loren Taylor for the new technique.

DeMille staged massive scenes using thousands of extras battling in swarming masses, with swords flying. The danger was evident on film.[44] During the Battle of Orleans, men fall from the La Tourelle castle walls, fighting soldiers splash through moats and scalding liquid is poured from cauldrons above. To ensure realism, DeMille offered a $20 bonus to each English soldier if they captured Joan and each Frenchman if they prevented her capture.[45] The determination to claim the bounty is evident on-screen.

Farrar arrived before nine and rarely left before eight in the evening and often remained until two A.M. During the battle scene she stood in a castle moat for four hours and when De Mille asked her if she'd like a break she replied, "If the boys can stand it, I think I can."[46] Filming the French capturing the upper parapet of the castle, DeMille offered another $20 bonus if several men would fall from the parapet 40 feet into the moat. The frightened men jumped instead of falling, and after numerous attempts DeMille said to Farrar, "I guess the men are afraid to do it. We'll have to cut out that scene." She said to him, "Yes, I am afraid so, but it would be very effective." The men heard her, and DeMille later received a note signed by 25 extras promising to fall, not jump and that they would continue until Farrar was happy with it. And they would do it for free. The next morning the parapet literally rained men falling in twos and threes into the moat. Several were injured when other armor-clad extras fell on top of them.

She engendered fierce loyalty from the extras. During a battle scene one of her own men accidentally knocked the heavy steel helmet off her head. Later that evening a group of his fellow actors grabbed him from bed, wrapped him in a blanket and beat him. As she was filmed atop a cart heading to her execution an extra said, "I don't think she's so much." He was beaten so severely he was hospitalized.[47]

The film premiered on Christmas Day 1916 and opened nationally on January 4th, 1917. It grossed over $600,000, though Farrar's performance received lukewarm reviews. She was then 34 but playing a teenager (Joan was 16 or 17) and the physical disparity between Farrar's wide hips and middle-aged appearance and a teenager was obvious. She is simply not believable as a young girl, and combined with her operatic over-acting the results were predictable. Wally, however, received glowing reviews and was credited with saving the film:

> Was there an Eric Trent in history who loved Joan? If so I have forgotten. There is such a person in the picture, and he is Wallace Reid. Mr. Reid has done much good acting in his life, but he has never done anything better than the role of the English officer who is saved from death by Joan, loves Joan and betrays her—still loving her. He is not afraid of his emotions. He lets them have their sway despite the fact that he is handsomer far when he is smiling, thereby placing himself in a niche all his own far and above the rank and file of so many of the handsome heroes.[48]

Lasky hired California portrait artist Stiles Dickinson to paint Farrar in costume for a backdrop in the film. Wally so liked the result that he sat for Dickson; the result hung in his home. Seeing Wally's, dozens of other stars also had portraits made, including Mary Pickford, Douglas Fairbanks, Vivian Martin, Julian Eltinge and even Jeanie Macpherson.[49]

As opposed to the previous summer, in 1916 there were no rumors of an off-screen relationship between Farrar and Wally. They remained close friends and Farrar often visited the Reid home with her husband Tellegen, but Dorothy still avoided contact with Farrar when she was able.

When crew-members learned DeMille was getting a gift for Farrar, 250 laborers and extras purchased a jeweled mirror engraved with images from her *Joan* role. A solid gold fleur de lis was inlayed on the back and the front inscribed with the autographs of all the principal members of her company. The handle was a sterling silver base relief of Farrar in her armor with the cast at her feet. It cost over $1,000, donated by crewmen making $\frac{1}{1000}$ of what Farrar earned working with them. Handed the gift as she left, she burst into tears.[50]

As filming was ending, mentor Otis Turner asked Wally to join his new Director's Association. Still hoping he would be allowed to actually *do* that job, he happily accepted. The group met at the downtown Alexandria Hotel to play cards and socialize. Turner—then Universal's lead director—ran the group with Allen Curtis and Eddie Dillon, other friends of Wally's.[51] Unfortunately, Wally was already too popular *not* to act. Turner's group evolved into the Screen Director's Guild by the mid–1930s and eventually the Director's Guild of America.

Wally was ambivalent about his stardom. He complained that people saw only his looks, that "scenario writers lie awake nights devising new methods of getting him killed."[52] Critics often chided him saying his acting relied on "his chief stock in trade for facial expression—the arched eyebrow,"[53] but he was less overt in expression than most actors. He brushed aside the thought that acting ability was worthy of great praise. The idolatry of his fans bewildered him. He told St. Johns, "Why? I haven't done anything. I haven't accomplished anything."[54] She later lamented that Wally tried to laugh off popularity and hide behind modesty that prevented him from doing things he could have done because he didn't want to appear conceited. During his rise to stardom he was in terrific conflict.

But his name and face appeared in papers and movie magazines regularly. On July 12th he and Dorothy attended a surprise birthday lunch for director Tod Browning, coincidently at the ballroom of the Reiter Arms where they lived when they first married. A *Moving Picture World* story noted that 300 "notable film people from the studios in the motion picture colony" attended and among the names singled out were Mabel Normand, Christie Cabanne, Bessie Love, Marguerite and May Marsh, Keystone stars Charlie Murray and George ("Slim") Summerville, Wally and Dorothy.[55]

In the late summer 1916 Wally returned to Lasky for two features, *The Golden Fetter* and *The Prison Without Walls*. *The Golden Fetter*, filmed in August, was a 5-reel western directed by Edward LeSaint, based on a Charles Tenney Jackson story adapted by Charles Maigne. Wally starred opposite Anita King, supported by Tully Marshall, Guy Oliver, Walter Long, Clarence Geldart, Lawrence Peyton and Lucien Littlefield.

Wally plays young mining engineer James Ralston, in love with beautiful Faith Miller (King), a Massachusetts school teacher relocated west for health reasons. She unwittingly purchases a half-interest in a worthless mine from unscrupulous Henry Slade (Marshall). When it's discovered she was duped the townspeople take pity and give her a job as the schoolmistress. Her only two pupils are a "half-witted boy" and Ralston. Ralston, in love with Kate, is suspected of train robbery because he inadvertently befriended the real robbers, Edson (Oliver) and McGill (Long), after they nursed him back to health following an illness. When Edson kills the sheriff Ralston is arrested and sentenced to hang. As Faith pleads for Ralston's life a deathbed confession from Edson prevents the hanging and all ends happily when Ralston "salts" her mine and tricks Slade into buying back her interests.[56]

Lasky records note LeSaint's co-director on *Fetter* was a "Capt. Ford." The anonymous man was probably minor Lasky director Sterrett Ford,[57] who worked on five or six films in the pre–1920s, but there is conjecture that it may have been the legendary John Ford.[58] Ford arrived in Hollywood in 1915 as a writer and actor and began directing Universal westerns in 1917. He assisted numerous other studios, often uncredited. Some historians credit this film to John Ford but more likely it was Sterrett behind the megaphone. *Golden Fetter* critics fawned over Wally following its January 25th release, writing, "The star, Wallace Reid, is one over whom fans have always raved—and with quite good excuse. It's pretty safe to say that, even could Mr. Reid not act as well as he does, much would be forgiven on account of his smile. However, he can act and is, moreover, apparently not conscious of the fact that he is disturbingly good looking."[59]

After *Fetter*, Wally made *The Prison Without Walls*, a 5-reel prison movie directed by E. Mason Hopper, with a scenario written by Beulah Marie Dix based upon a Robert E. MacAlarney story. Wally starred with Myrtle Stedman, supported by William Conklin, William Elmer, Marcia Manon, James Neill, Leighton and Geldart. The plot follows heiress and prison reformer Helen Ainsworth (Stedman), whose estate executive and fiancé Norman Morris (Conklin) pretends to assist her but is actually involved in prison graft and uses Helen to visit prisons and collect bribes. The Governor brings Huntington Babbs (Wally), an authority on prison reform, in to enact reforms that are assailed by Morris and his friends. Babbs goes undercover as an ex-con named Conroy, who is hired by Helen to then spy on Morris. When Morris discovers Babbs' deception he convinces Helen's maid (Leighton) to frame Conroy and have him jailed. Morris arranges for Helen's safe to be burglarized and the tools found in Conroy's possession but Morris' accomplices fess up and Morris is imprisoned. With Morris gone Babbs reveals his true identity and ends up with Helen.[60]

Prison was released on March 15, 1917, to reviews that described Wally and Myrtle as "the popular young artists who score such a pronounced success in the Lasky-Paramount production."[61] His growing popularity was evident to everyone, including Carl Laemmle, who re-released several of Wally's old films in late 1916 and early 1917 to take advantage of his growing fan base and the anticipated release of the earlier-done *Carmen*. On December 3rd Laemmle released *The Wall of Flame* (1913), a short starring Wally and Pauline Bush made at Laemmle's Independent Moving Pictures Company (IMP). On December 15th he released *The Wrong Heart*, another short romance drama written and directed by Wally and released for Big U Films at Universal. Wally co-starred with Dorothy. It's not known when these films were actually made.

Shocking everyone at the studio, on September 14th Zukor forced Samuel Goldwyn to quit. Lasky did the dirty work, a difficult task since Goldwyn was married to Lasky's sister. Just two days later Goldwyn signed Mabel Normand, stealing her from Mack Sennett. A *Motion Picture Magazine* poll had recently named Normand the world's favorite female comedian. Zukor and Lasky would never have fired Goldwyn had they known of his relationship with Normand. The combination of Mabel Normand and Wally would have been incredible but Goldwyn used his $900,000 severance to form Samuel Goldwyn Pictures with Edgar Selwyn on November 19th. It's difficult not to wonder how Wally's career would have evolved had he been paired with Normand.

Away from the studio Wally and Dorothy were still living at Allison Avenue. She had become his de facto personal manager and correspondence secretary. Virtually all of Wally's mail was from females—a magazine noted that his mail bore "undeniably the stamp of feminine manumotion [sic]"[62]—and Dorothy was keeping an eye on things. Sam, a page responsible for delivering mail, tied Wally's mail into little bundles and left them at Wally's dressing room. He was given $1 a day by Wally, who dutifully brought the bundles to Dorothy at home. Wally's 5,000 letters a week was more mail than anyone else at the studio was receiving.

Dorothy was working at Universal and still on higher-quality films, Laemmle still piggy-backing on Wally's popularity. She was earning $250 a week and no longer running to far-flung sets. She had a studio dressing room and all the perks and her films were usually directed by Laemmle's favorite director Lloyd B. Carleton, and released through Universal's Red Feather or Rex units. Dorothy made over 20 films in 1916, all of them with bigger names.

She starred in the Thomas Ince–Bison film *The Phantom Island* (released February 12th) and *Doctor Neighbor* with Hobart Bosworth (May 1st). Her Universal films were mostly 2-reelers with Johnson, like *Her Husband's Faith* (May 11th), *Heartaches* (May 19th), and *Two Mothers* (June 1st). But in late spring she began working in features, the first, *The Way of the World*, with Bosworth (5 reels, released July 3rd). In early summer Laemmle paired her with rising star Emory Johnson, son of scenarist Emilie Johnson.[63] Laemmle thought Emory could become a leading man like Wally and paired him in a dozen 1916 films with Dorothy. The pair made films like *A Yoke of Gold* (released August 14th), *The Unattainable* (September 4th), *Black Friday* (September 18th), *The Human Gamble* (October 8th), *Barriers of Society* (October 16th) and *The Devil's Bondwoman* (November 20th). The Davenport-Johnson films did well but the on-screen chemistry between Dorothy and Wally could not be duplicated so Laemmle tried other men. In the fall Dorothy made *The Scarlet Crystal* with Herbert Rawlinson (released February 5th, 1917) and *The Girl and the Crisis* opposite Charles Perley (February 26th, 1917).

In the midst of this major upturn in her career Dorothy learned in early October that she was pregnant. Both she and Wally adored children and were ecstatic. Hearing the news her father came to L.A. for the holidays. Bertha stayed in New Jersey; it's not known if Wally and Dorothy even told her as she later inferred she first learned from newspaper stories. Wally had not laid eyes on his mother—his "sweetheart mother mine"[64]—since 1911, and had not spoken to her since the 1913 feud between Dorothy and Bertha erupted.

The pregnancy—and Wally's increasing prospects—meant they needed a bigger house so they bought an impressive four-bedroom, two-story California bungalow at 1822 Morgan Place. It was a quiet street on the east side on Hollywood, north of Franklin. A 1917 fan magazine incorrectly identified the location as Elevado Avenue.[65]

Locating a period site in modern-day L.A. can be difficult with so many neighborhoods bulldozed for freeways, aqueducts, or apartments. The often-conflicting historic descriptions add to the confusion. The Morgan Place house was also described as being at the corner of DeMille Boulevard and McGaffey Drive, neither of which was an actual street name (nor was the house on a corner). Today the only remaining section of what was then Morgan Place is a short circular block at the top of Taft Avenue now named Morgan Hill Drive. According to area residents, in the pre–1920s the area was fig and olive orchards owned by the original Morgan family who lived in a house near the top of Taft. Everything beneath the small neighborhood at the top of the hill has been renamed and renumbered. Just below Morgan Hill is the northern end of Taft but in 1916 the circle led down onto what is now the upper reaches of Gramercy Place two blocks east. Wally's house at 1822 Morgan Place was located eight houses below Franklin Avenue on the east side of the street. It was the largest house on the street according to 1920s Sanford Fire Insurance Map records.

Wally in a late 1916 studio still colorized for a 1917 *Motion Picture Magazine* cover (see page 103) indicating his already growing popularity. The photo was taken about the time the Reids moved to the Morgan Place house.

Wally was earning $750 a week and could afford a bigger mansion but that was not his style. Under Dorothy's influence Wally rarely spent extravagantly. His only weakness was cars; he already owned several, including a Marmon coupe, one of the fastest cars available. A 1917 magazine story about the Morgan house noted "his 90 horsepower car is paid for, and his only expenses were his monthly dues at the L.A. Athletic Club and his cooks and maid."[66] Wally's expenses totaled $200 and he and Dorothy allocated $100 a month for a house.

The house was a good-sized two-story mission-style house with a porch running the length of the front. Behind were a guest house and a garage for Wally's cars. The house had three large awning-covered windows on the second floor and a large yard. Alice Davenport moved into the guest house. In the 1917 and 1918 L.A. City Directories the Reids and Alice were listed as "photoplayers" [sic].[67] The block was comprised of retirees and working people, mostly immigrants like German newspaper lithographer Fred Kaiser at 1816, and the three elderly spinster Larter sisters—Lucy, Anne and Gertrude—at 1812. The only movie people lived across the street. At 1809, 24-year-old cameraman Ellsworth Rumer lived with his mother. At 1815, pharmacist Otto Ayres rented rooms to 19-year-old studio scenario writer Edythe Fink and Wisconsin transplant Harry A. Grinde, who described himself as a "director of motion pictures."[68] The Reids moved in during November, 1916. An unknown named Rudolph Valentino would rent across the street in November, 1918.[69]

8

War and Work

The war raging in Europe in 1916–1917 closed European film markets but U.S. studios still pumped product out that was a barometer by which the world measured America.[1] The shattered economies left by the war ended European movie industry growth and Hollywood gained a dominance it never relinquished, but the prevailing attitude in America was isolationism. President Wilson admonished that the U.S. was "overwhelmingly neutral and determined to stay so ... with no ... intervention."[2]

From 1900 to 1910 over 50 peace groups organized like the World Peace Society and Andrew Carnegie's Endowment for International Peace. In 1911, Carnegie hosted a four-day New York peace conference that drew 40,000 observers and 1,253 delegates from around the world.[3] Business wanted to stay out, led by Carnegie and Henry Ford, who launched a "peace ship" in 1915 to broker an end to fighting. Ford spent $500,000 on a variety of anti-war efforts.[4] But other factors were moving the U.S. to war. A covert British propaganda ministry run by diplomats and military personnel courted U.S. reporters so "American papers would see through British eyes."[5] When Wilson allowed loans to allied countries a foundation for U.S. economic ties to war was laid. Supplies bought from American companies meant war was good for the economy. In February 1915 Germany announced that ships traveling to England would be torpedoed, an outrageous violation of neutrality rights that angered Americans. In May, German submarines sank the Cunard passenger ship *Lusitania* without allowing passengers off first, killing 1,200 of the 2,000 aboard, including 124 Americans. A few days before, two U.S. merchant ships were sunk.[6]

As the U.S. began active preparation for war in late 1915 an execution in France galvanized public opinion. Edith Cavell was a Red Cross volunteer in occupied Belgium found guilty in a German military court of assisting French and British soldiers to escape to neutral Holland. She was shot by firing squad. Few events had the same emotional impact as Cavell's brutal murder. By 1916 it was clear the U.S. was going to war.

In Hollywood, Carl Laemmle released more old Wally films. The first, released on January 6th to coincide with *Joan the Woman* opening, was a re-release of *The Wall of Money*. *Wall* was a 1913 Allan Dwan–directed film for Rex and Universal that starred Wally and Pauline Bush, Mickey Neilan, Jessalyn Van Trump and James McQuarrie. On March 4th Laemmle released *Buried Alive*, directed by Wally and starring him and Dorothy, and on April 26th *A Warrior's Bride*. On April 30th he released the Wally-directed *The Penalty of Silence* (all 1917), which featured Wally, Dorothy and Ed Brady.

Lasky built up Artcraft Pictures, the distributor and principal financial backer of his bigger films. He bought Triangle, bringing in Douglas Fairbanks, William S. Hart, Charles

Ray, and the writing team of John Emerson and Anita Loos. The Realart Pictures brand was formed to produce lower-cost films for younger actors like Bebe Daniels and May McAvoy. Lasky's 1917 schedule was for 104 films—52 Paramount, 18 Artcraft, and 34 Realart—most made at Vine Street but a few at the New York studio, a converted riding stable on 56th Street.[7] Wally was the linchpin to the schedule.

In January, Wally traveled to Fort Bragg, a coastal town 175 miles north of San Francisco, for two westerns filmed in the hills still lined with empty mining towns, relics from the 1849 gold rush. The first film was *The World Apart* for Paramount's Oliver Morosco Productions, a 5-reeler directed by William Desmond Taylor. It was a George Middleton[8] story adapted by Julia Crawford Ivers and filmed by Homer Scott. Wally appeared with Myrtle Stedman, John Burton, Eugene Pallette, Florence Carpenter, Henry A. Barrows and Phyllis Daniels (Bebe Daniels' mother).

Wally played hard-working Bob Fulton, a mine superintendent whose boss Roland Holt (Burton) thinks Bob can transform his son Clyde (Pallette) from a worthless ne'er-do-well into a working man. But Clyde spends his time losing money in poker games, forging company checks, and finally robbing the company safe. The only way Bob can prevent the robbery is to shoot Clyde, who loses his wedding ring while making his escape after shooting and wounding Bob. Bob keeps the ring so that his boss won't learn of his own son's treachery. A few days later Clyde's new bride Beth (Stedman) arrives and learning that her husband has disappeared, nurses Bob to health. She falls in love with him but when she finds her missing husband's ring among Bob's possessions she assumes that Bob killed him. All appears lost until Clyde returns and is killed in a gunfight with the sheriff, leaving Bob and Beth together.[9]

The February, 1917, magazine cover using his popular 1916 studio still.

The film was released on June 4th to mediocre reviews. *Exhibitors Trade Review* described it as "inconsequential to the point of thoroughly insipid," with the only positive being "the settings."[10] *Motion Picture News* "liked the acting and the production, but the story is weak. Without the clever Morosco titles and big mining camp scenes and other things that make us forget it is only an average story ... it was a very ordinary offering...."[11] Pre-release publicity concentrated on "Wallace Reid and Myrtle Stedman, the popular young artists who scored such a pronounced success in the Lasky-Paramount production of 'The Prison Without Walls' ... now in 'The World Apart' an unusual and exciting story of western life...."[12] But critics loved Wally. "Wally, as he is better known by his thousands of admirers, is said to be the best example of young American manhood now on the screen. Tall, clean-cut, good-looking and powerful, he is equally popular with both sexes, and with Myrtle Stedman, the two make a combination of stars that are hard to equal."[13] And "Wallace Reid is good looking, manly, and, as far as I have ever seen without pose or affectation."[14]

As Wally fought local extras filming the first scene the on-screen brawl escalated from choreographed to real; it took the entire crew to break it up. It was impossible to tell where the film fight ended and the real fight began, so cameramen kept filming. Amusingly, *Moving Picture World* noted that "by some inexplicable oversight an excessively vulgar picture has been used as a wall decoration."[15] A large painting of a nude woman was hanging prominently in the saloon.

Wally's next film was *Big Timber*, another 5-reeler directed by Taylor, this one adapted from the Bertrand W. Sinclair novel by Gardner Hunting. Wally starred with Kathlyn Williams, Joe King, Alfred Paget, Helen Bray and John Burton. Williams plays Stella Benton, a concert singer so traumatized by her father's death that she loses her voice and wealth and is forced to move to a lumber camp run by her brother Charles (Paget). Woefully overworked, she accepts a marriage proposal from neighboring lumberman Jack Fyfe (Wally), even though she does not love him. The loveless union produces a child and the couple begins to love each other until wealthy lumberman Walter Monahan (King) arrives and turns his attention to Stella. When the infant dies Stella leaves Jack and returns to the stage. Monahan, jealous of Jack's success (even though Jack's wife has left him), sets fire to his lumber holdings. When Stella learns this she immediately returns to the camp, where she offers her own money to rebuild. At that moment a huge rainstorm develops and saves Jack's forest and marriage.[16] *Big Timber* was released on July 5th.

Filming was difficult. For a week Taylor took his crew to a remote mountain setting 50 miles away above Clear Lake. To get there the crew took cars to a stage stop outside Fort Bragg, then a stage over rutted dirt roads to the lake, a two-mile trip via motor launch, and a logging train to the set. The long trip meant filming was limited to two hours a day and it rained the entire week.[17] Crews often hitched rides on rickety lumber trains that usually hauled only wood. Later, a similar ride would lead to tragedy.

After *Big Timber*, Wally made an uncredited appearance in a film that is not in any other Wally filmographies. However, period newspapers confirm his involvement in a 5-reeler filmed in Santa Cruz in early March. Santa Cruz is between Fort Bragg and Hollywood. *Mothers of Men* was a Robards-Reid Production directed by Hal and Willis Robards and filmed by Walter Lundin.[18] On March 9th a local paper noted, "Hal Reid graciously introduced different members of the company to the people, including his son, W. Reid, director Robard [sic], Hobart Bosworth, a member of the Lasky Company and one of its stars, Dorothy Davenport and others."[19] Dorothy played the lead opposite Robards, supported by Marcella Russell (recently married to Hal), Katherine Griffith, Arthur Tavares, Billie Bennett, Harry Griffith, George Utell and Grace Blake.

Wally's name is absent from records of this film but daily updates in local papers described the filming and repeatedly noted his work and visits to local businesses. If he asked to do a film with Dorothy on his way back to Hollywood his request would have been granted. Hal's small company couldn't afford a loan-out and perhaps Lasky required the appearance be uncredited. Hobart Bosworth is also absent from filmographies but was also involved.

Dorothy plays a suffragette leader who becomes a judge, and spent the movie draped in judges' robes that hid her six-month pregnancy. During filming Marcella Russell— playing Dorothy's blind sister, coincidentally—was struck by "Kleig eyes."[20] Caused by the excessive heat and brightness of early lights it was a painful condition that led to temporary blindness, headaches, swelling and often permanent vision damage. She spent a week recovering at the home of a local family.[21] Filming ended March 9th or 10th and Wally and Dorothy returned home.

On March 12th, Wally attended the opening of Griffith's *Hearts of the World*, a World War I film set in a small French village. Griffith brought Lillian and Dorothy Gish and his crew to the actual French battlefields for the first war movie.[22] The Clume Theater premier meant "the theatrical world was represented by many of its leading directors and stars—Jesse L. Lasky, Cecil de Mille [sic], William de Mille, Jeanie Macpherson, Wallace Reid, Dorothy Dalton...."[23] Wally was mentioned before dozens of names like Pickford, Ince, Chaplin, and Fairbanks.

The next evening Wally appeared at a benefit for the family of Maitland Davies, the *Los Angeles Tribune* drama critic who had died the previous week.[24] Davies left his family in "poor circumstances" and the "profession rallied to the aid of the family." Among performances by Chaplin, Theda Bara, Fairbanks and Mary Pickford and William S. Hart, Wally played the saxophone. No personal detail of Wally's life seemed uninteresting.

Wally's next assignment was a sequel to Lasky's 1914 *The Squaw Man* entitled *The Squaw Man's Son*. The 5-reeler was directed by Edward LeSaint and Sterrett Ford and written by Charles Maigne. Like the original, it was based on the 1910 Edwin Royle novel *The Silent Call*. Wally starred with Anita King[25] supported by Dorothy, Donald Bowles, Clarence Geldart, Frank Lanning, Ernest Joy, Lucien Littlefield, Mabel Van Buren and Raymond Hatton.

Wally played Hal, Dustin Farnum's infant son in the original version,[26] now the grown Lord Effington and living with his wife Edith (Dorothy) at the ancestral English home of his father. When he returns to the Colonies to visit his mother he sides with Indians in a land deal against David Ladd (Geldart), the wily reservation agent secretly working with an asphalt trust trying to swindle them. Hal falls in love with Wah-na-gi (King), a college graduate who returned to teach at the Indian school, but his honor means telling her of his marriage. Learning of his father's death, Hal returns to England to discover his wife has fallen in love with Lord Yester (Littlefield) and wants a divorce. Hal gladly agrees but when the family physician informs him Edith is addicted to morphine and if he stays she might live, he stays. Returning to America for a climactic courtroom scene involving the Indian lawsuit, Hal sadly tells Wah-na-gi he cannot leave his wife. Wah-na-gi walks off into the snow to kill herself near the grave of Hal's mother but Hal receives a message that Edith has died of her addiction and rushes to find Wah-na-gi and asks her to marry.[27]

The film was released on July 26th to excellent reviews. It was "a stirring sequel to 'The Squaw Man,' written in response to the demand from the great army of readers to tell the story of young Hal," and the "all-star cast was headed by popular Wallace Reid."[28] It was also the last film Dorothy made for three years. When filming ended she returned to Morgan Place to await the birth of their child. Her next film would be *The Fighting Chance*, in 1920.

By that spring of 1917 the studios were already assisting government fundraising and propaganda efforts. On March 31st the industry organized a baseball game at Washington Park in L.A. to benefit the Red Cross. The teams were the Tragics and the Comics. The Comics were Charlie Chaplin (pitcher), Eric Campbell (catcher),[29] Charlie Murray (1st base), Slim Summerville (2nd), Bobby Dunn (SS), Hank Mann (3rd), Harold Lloyd (left field), Ben Turpin (center), and Chester Conklin (right).[30] The Tragics were led by Wally (pitcher), William Desmond (catcher), George Walsh (1st), Gene Pallette (2nd), Antonio Moreno (SS), Franklyn Farnum (3rd), Jack Pickford (left), George Beban (center) and Hobart Bosworth (right). The umpires were race car driver Barney Oldfield and boxing champion James J. Jeffries.

Over 5,000 people filled the stadium for a 2-inning game but it was an embarrassing day for Wally. Reversing teams, Walsh, who once played professional baseball (a fact Wally didn't know), hit a Wally pitch 400 feet out of the park. *Photoplay* described Wally's at bat: "The carnage was terrible. In the blood, dust and grand confusion the game broke up after two innings and Lord knows who won. The one really dreadful holocaust was the fanning of Wallie Reid."[31] He struck out in front of 5,000 fans and was mortified, but Chaplin's Comics stole the show. After hitting a long foul ball Chaplin none the less ran straight to second base and then straight back to home. When Umpire Oldfield called it a foul, 50 costumed Keystone Kops tumbled out of the dugout and rolled Oldfield in the dirt until he called it fair.

Amusements like the baseball game couldn't hide the fact that the U.S. was on the verge of war. On January 31st Germany increased the scope of their submarine blockade.[32] Then British agents intercepted a telegram from German Foreign Minister Zimmerman to his Ambassador to Mexico warning him that U.S. involvement was inevitable and directing him to obtain Mexican support in exchange for New Mexico, Texas and Arizona. The public was outraged and President Wilson declared war on April 6th.[33]

Hollywood became an important cog in the war machine. It had happened before. On April 21, 1898, the day war was declared war on Spain, J. Stuart Blackton and Albert E. Smith watched from their New York Vitagraph offices while a crowd filled the streets waving American flags. They raced outside and filmed *Tearing Down the Spanish Flag*, a battle film that attracted thousands of viewers to makeshift showings anywhere there was a blank wall.[34] It was the movies' first propaganda film.

When the U.S. entered World War I the industry had already produced propaganda-themed movies. DeMille's *Joan the Woman* was one, and others like *The Little American* and *Till I Come Back to You* depicted Germans as barbaric and uncivilized. Louella Parsons wrote, "films have been raising the temperature of the Allies' patriotism to blood heat."[35] Millions of moviegoers watched hundreds of films supporting U.S. war efforts, films writer Emily Leider described as "beat the drum features."[36] In addition to making films the studios offered that "every individual in this industry" has promised to provide "slides, film leaders and trailers, posters ... to spread that propaganda so necessary to the immediate mobilisation [sic] of the country's great resources."[37] Wilson established the Committee of Public Information (CPI) targeting women, African Americans, German-Americans, Irish-Americans, pacifists, and socialists. CPI's Division of Four Minute Men gave speeches during movie intermissions; it took four minutes to change a reel, so theater owners supported the idea. The name evoked Revolutionary War "minutemen" and during the war, 75,000 Four Minute Men gave 755,000 speeches to 315,000,000 people.[38]

Studio illustrators joined the Division of Pictorial Publicity to make posters. A News Division coordinated information releases, pioneering the news release handout. Studios later used similar handouts for films. Scenario writers assisted the Division of Civic and Educational Cooperation, producing the famous *Red, White and Blue* and *War Information Series* pamphlets.[39] The Division of Films distributed Signal Corps photographs and war films through studio distribution channels and produced the weekly newsreel *Official War Review*. Unlike World War II when hundreds of stars joined the military, few stars served in World War I.

Wally's studio was very involved. When the California State Defense Guard was formed (known as the California Home Guard), Lasky organized his "Lasky Home Guard

No. 51," led by DeMille, the group's Captain.[40] It was a strange scene, the Lasky Company marching down Vine Street on Sunday afternoon in full military uniform shouldering prop rifles.[41] Unlike Army olive green, Home Guard wore dark grey. DeMille and a brass band made up of prop men, grips, and actors led by talented cornet player Tully Marshall led the marches.[42] Wally was listed in studio materials as a member but never participated in any Company activities.

DeMille's wife Constance toured Hollywood in a nurse's uniform with her friend Anna Beth Fairbanks (Mrs. Douglas). On Wednesday night stars visited the Hollywood Red Cross tea shops.[43] When the Governor reviewed the Lasky Guard, Mary Pickford presented the colors, a silk flag with hand-embroidered stars made by her and her mother Charlotte.[44] The *California Home Guard News* profiled the Lasky unit in December, 1917:

> ... Home Guard Company No. 51, known as the Lasky Home Guard Company ... are certainly setting the pace in their part of the State. Commanding Officer is Cecil B. DeMille; First Lieutenant and drill master ... Lt. [Henry] Woodward, assisted by his Second Lieutenant, James Neill, has raised the entire company to a point of efficiency ... and ... of the noteworthy larger number of men who have enlisted in the regular branches of the service of the Government at this time, all but two or three have won rank as non-commissioned officers. A number of the members of the Lasky Home Guard were formerly in the United States service.[45]

Stars made thousands of personal appearances, led by Pickford, of whom *Photoplay Journal* noted, "Since Uncle Sam started measuring his sons for uniforms ... various persons prominent in the public eye have devoted much of their own time to help brighten up the lives of the boys in khaki.... Conspicuous ... is none other than our own Mary Pickford, known throughout the land as 'America's Sweetheart.'"[46] Pickford biographer Eileen Whitfield wrote that she "seemed to be everywhere at once, speaking through megaphones, posing for posters, collecting cigarettes to send to the doughboys ... and if anyone gave a donation, they received a note autographed by Pickford. The 143rd California Field Artillery wore her photograph in lockets; they made her their honorary colonel."[47] A 1918 *Photoplay* ran a full-page photo of Mary in doughboy uniform with knee boots as "Colonel Mary of the 143rd Field Artillery, U.S.A."[48]

In 1918, he joined Chaplin, Fairbanks and William S. Hart for Liberty Loan drives. Hart toured the west, Chaplin the south, Fairbanks the mid–Atlantic and Pickford the north. She and Fairbanks—both married—were in the midst of a torrid affair so Fairbanks had his schedule revised to join Mary in New York.[49] She also organized a benefit that raised $40,000 to buy ambulances as gifts from picture stars.[50] DeMille cast Mary in *The Little American*, a blatant propaganda film portraying Germans as barbarians who raped and pillaged anywhere they went. It was released on July 2nd just after the U.S. entered the war. *The Little American* borrowed from the nurse Cavell story and included a graphic sinking of the passenger ship *Veritania*, an obvious reference to the *Lusitania*. A DeMille title card read, "I stopped being neutral and became a human being."

With America at war less than nine months Adolph Zukor wrote, "In giving the best within us, we shall best be serving ourselves and our industry."[51] He knew the war would reap huge studio profits hidden behind the guise of patriotism. But conspicuous in his absence was Wally. As the biggest star at the biggest studio he should have been front and center; his absence made him look weak and even afraid.

In May the Selective Service Act authorized registration and the draft of men between 21 and 30; from summer 1917 to fall 1918 men from 18 to 45 signed up. Registration days were patriotic events, with parades, business and school closings, and ringing church bells. Entire families often accompanied sons to register. Almost 24,000,000 registered, a quarter of the population.[52] Wally filled out and signed his card on June 5th.[53] He was a perfect specimen for the military. He was 26, six foot two, athletic and an expert marksman. He attended military school and was familiar with regimentation. But he didn't want anything to do with it.

A July, 1917, newspaper article entitled "DRAFT HITS MOVIE MEN" noted, "Watching the 'score board' ... is the favorite occupation of movie stars ... and 'Are you called?' is the common salutation between actors, managers, directors, and 'extras.'" Fox Studios reportedly lost comedy star George Walsh; Fairbanks Production, cameraman Victor Fleming; and Universal, George Marshall, director Francis MacDonald and comedian William Franey. The paper mentioned Lasky employees "ready to serve" were Marshall Neilan, Ray Marshall, director Claude Mitchell, and Wally."[54] Seeing his name on a list of men who actually might serve must have been embarrassing.

Wally's fears would result in years of self-doubt. He had reason to feel stress at the time. Dorothy was in the final days of her pregnancy and he was finally making movie-star money, reportedly $1,250 a week.[55] He did not want to lose his new spot as the top matinee idol in the movies. And a final concern never discussed publicly but evident to his friends, was the onset of a serious alcohol problem that would have made service difficult. His answers on his registration form confirmed his unwillingness to serve. To a question of whether family prohibited him from serving, Wally wrote, "Wife/Expectant Mother." To "Do you claim exemption from health/family grounds?" Wally responded, "Yes. On grounds of dependent family."[56] Wally regretted his lack of will for the rest of his life. Lasky pressured him not to serve while showing him publicly as *wanting* to enlist. He assuaged his guilt by appearing at War Bond drives and opening his home to visiting soldiers. St. Johns was more succinct; she believed he hated himself for not serving and that guilt affected him deeply. She felt it was the "beginning of the end ... when he didn't put on a uniform ... he never forgave himself ... [it] was a soul problem of which few people knew. On the face of things, in the eyes of the man in the street, even according to the judgment of the fervent patriot, Wally Reid's war record is not subject to attack from any source or angle. In the boy's own eyes that record was stamped indelibly with the black "S" of slacker. He himself felt that he had failed, that his manhood was smirched, that he had fallen below his own standard and the standard of the Reid family."[57]

Wally didn't hide his feelings of inadequacy. In 1919 he gave St. Johns a publicity portrait in a British military uniform taken during *Joan the Woman*. He signed, "Just a so-and-so who never got into uniform except when he put on his grease paint."[58] She wrote, "Those who did not enlist he despised. And he was one of them! Nice company! As far as he could see, he just wasn't worth a damn. I do not think he was ever criticized to any extent for not donning khaki. But he believed that everybody else thought the same things he was thinking. We winced every time he passed a man in uniform. His confidence in himself faded to zero." The event "shattered the idealist" in Wally and she inferred that he secretly worked for the government but that the story "is and must continue to be part of the unwritten history which belongs to every war. Many of the details I do not know myself, but I do know that Wallace Reid served the Secret Service of his government and was of exceptional value to it all through the days of fighting." There is obviously no evidence at all to support that story.

Wally's conflict affected his taste in music. He was talented; a visit to the Sunset Inn café was chronicled in *Motion Picture Classic*, "when he wasn't dancing, he was borrowing the musicians' instruments. First, he substituted at the drums, and then took a turn at the saxophone, and last played the violin with one arm around his wife's neck."[59] He was a gifted self-taught violin player who said, "with one of those tucked under my chin, the director can shout his head off—I'll never hear him."[60] He taught himself the saxophone in two weeks. After the war, though, he rarely played the violin, as if it reminded him of his failings. Saxophone became his favorite and the one with which he was identified. He owned two dozen of all types, brass, gold and silver.

All of this turmoil disappeared at least temporarily on June 18th. The 17th was a miserably hot southern California day and Dorothy spent most of it in the shade in the back yard at Morgan Place being fanned by Wally. She refused a hospital (she had begun studying Christian Science a year earlier), so Wally hired a live-in doctor and two nurses in early June. She went into labor the evening of the 17th and early on the 18th, William Wallace Reid, Jr. was born. During the final stages of Dorothy's labor Wally sat outside the bedroom and played his violin to calm her.[61]

It was evident "Billy" would be pampered and spoiled like his father had been. New grandmother Bertha heard the news from reporters. Dorothy invited *Photoplay* to the house for a photo shoot a month later. The headline read, "Oh, Look Who's Here—It's Wallie [sic] Reed, Jr."[62]

New father Wally began spending money like the star he was.[63] After Billy's birth he hired Oscar and Nora Smith (he a 29-year-old Kansan, she a 25-year-old Alabaman). Oscar was a handyman and valet and Nora cooked and cleaned. They moved into the guest house and Alice into the main house. Wally and Oscar became good friends and Wally put him on the studio payroll as his valet, introducing him as "the Cute Kid." The nickname stuck for his 30-plus years at Paramount where he ran the shoeshine and newsstand Lasky gave him at Wally's request. He later founded a talent agency for black actors, the Harlem Casting Agency, and for years after Wally's death cried when customers mentioned his name.[64] The relationship with Oscar was a window to Wally's personality, described by Dorothy as lacking "pretense and ostentation or show ... he never made a class distinction in life except against those in high places he felt had no business there ... [he was] the most democratic man ... that ever lived."[65] A private nurse was hired, 61-year-old Luella Bauchens, who hailed from Missouri and took a small upstairs room near the baby's. The three servants stayed with the Reids for six years.

Wally's first love was still cars. St. Johns said he "adored automobiles. I have seen him sit on a curb and gaze at a new roadster for hours, pointing out its lines, emphasizing its beauties, explaining its mechanical perfections. He was the finest driver that I've ever ridden with."[66] He owned a series of expensive cars, including Marmon Speedsters, Stutz roadsters, Duesenbergs, a Frontenac and McFarlans. In her memoirs Louella Parsons described him as "one of the most attractive and lovable men who ever lived, [but] drove the streets of Hollywood as if he were on the last lap of the chariot race in *Ben Hur*—only Wally's chariot was a low-slung robin's-egg blue car with a horn that played 'Yankee Doodle Dandy.'"[67] Wally was often seen in one of his cars—his blue Stutz convertible and a later favorite, a jet black Marmon coupe—racing around Hollywood on roads still unpaved and rutted. He already had survived a near-fatal accident in 1915 but said, "I love to speed. If I always drove myself I'd probably spend half my money on fines for breaking the road laws.... Whether speeding down an open road or through the air, [I] feel a surge of blood through [my] veins that prompts [me] to ever increasing speeds."[68]

He was a serious racing fan and attended events frequently. He was reportedly the godfather to driver Roscoe Sarles[69] and lifelong friends with drivers he hired as extras in his films. Among his best pals were Eddie Hearne, Jimmy Murphy and Eddie Miller, the top drivers of the era. He dreamed of becoming a racecar driver but Lasky would never allow him to do anything so dangerous. Even driving a street car was dangerous. None

Wally's good friend, racecar driver Roscoe Sarles (right, with cigarette), standing next to his car after an accident at the Santa Monica road course Wally often drove, ca. 1920.

had safety features of any kind; even racing cars had no seat belts. Model T's could speed at 50 miles an hour and Wally's cars were much more powerful.[70] Lasky tried unsuccessfully to force Wally to use studio chauffeurs.

Around this time rumors first arose about Wally's nightlife. A new nickname—"Good-Time Wally"—popped up in gossip columns and rags like *Captain Billy's Whiz Bang*. Even his appearances at legitimate social functions made gossip columns. The week after Billy's birth he attended the wedding of British boxer and Fairbanks actor Spike Robinson and Stella Dominguez. Wally stayed at the reception until the "wee hours," along with other well-known partiers Mabel Normand, Charles Murray, Charlie Chaplin and Jack Mulhall,[71] a fact that made the papers.

When Billy was born Wally was already filming the Robert Thornby–directed *The*

Hostage. Beulah Marie Dix adapted the scenario for Wally based on her story "We and They."[72] His co-star was Dorothy Abril, supported by Gertrude Short, Clarence Geldart, Guy Oliver, Marcia Manon, Noah Beery, George Spaulding, Lillian Leighton and Lucien Littlefield. *Hostage* was "A thrilling drama of love 'over there' so intensely human, so tenderly loving, that you'll hold your breath 'till the end."[73]

The theme was social biases, the story of the Lowlanders and the Mountaineers. Each accuses the other of barbarism and cruelty but when both unite to fight the Coast people their attitudes change. They are sworn enemies until Lieutenant Ivo Kemper (Wally), son of the militaristic Lowlanders' leader (Geldart), is held hostage by the Highlanders to force his father's army to retreat. To his surprise Ivo is treated with kindness and consideration, especially by Boyadi (Beery) and his beautiful daughter Nathalia (Abril), whom he learns to love. So instead of obeying his father's command to secretly escape when the Lowlanders plan to violate a pledge and storm the fortress he remains a prisoner. The Highlanders, inflamed by the Lowlander deception, are ready to kill Ivo when news comes of the approach of the Coast people, and the two former enemies unite to defeat the new foe.[74] *The Hostage* was released on September 10th as "The Biggest Hit of His Phenomenal Career."[75]

Just after, Geraldine Farrar returned with husband Lou Tellegen and DeMille hosted a welcome luncheon attended by Wally, Jeanie Macpherson, Julia Faye, St. Johns and magazine writer Herbert Riley Howe. Wally showed his childish side when the waiter forgot to serve MacPherson her salad. He told the Chinese waiter—who spoke no English— "Mr. DeMille doesn't sleep with Jeanie any more. He sleeps with Julia." St. Johns was shocked silent, but far from being angry, DeMille laughed and said, "To debauch any kind of innocence is one of the last and greatest pleasures of the sophisticate. When you become jaded, my boy, with the overripe charms and activities of the experienced, always find the innocence to corrupt. There's nothing like a good orgy to cleanse the palate or the prick."[76] Wally looked upon him as a mentor but St. Johns believed him the worst possible counsel for Wally.

Wally and Farrar made *The Woman God Forgot* between July 2nd and August 10th at the vast Inceville property in Santa Ynez Canyon and at Yosemite National Park. It was a 5-reeler (period records mentioned it went to theaters in six)[77] directed by DeMille, Charles Whittaker and Cullen Tate. The story was from Macpherson and William de Mille and the massive Aztec sets designed by Wilfred Buckland. His art direction and set design were magnificent as were the intricate feathered costumes worn by hundreds of extras. Exquisite hand-woven rugs covered sets, each painstakingly copied from authentic Mayan designs. In a poolside scene hundreds of birds fluttered inside fine wire netting with which Buckland encased a large studio filled with lush tropical plants. Farrar and Raymond Hatton led with Wally, supported by Hobart Bosworth, Theodore Kosloff, Walter Long, Charles B. Rogers, Olga Grey and James Neill.

A Spanish expedition led by Cortez (Bosworth) lands in Mexican territory and Cortez sends Captain Alvarado (Wally) to approach Montezuma (Hatton), the King of the Aztecs. Montezuma throws Alvarado in a dungeon, only to be rescued by Montezuma's daughter Tecza (Farrar), who has fallen in love with him. Her lover Guatemoco (Kosloff) finds Alvarado hiding in her chambers and recaptures him. To save Alvarado from sacrifice at the altar of the war god Tecza opens the city gates to the Spaniards, who storm the castle and rescue Alvarado. The Aztecs are defeated in the ensuing battle and Tecza cursed by her dying father, High Priest Taloc (Long); but Alvarado offers love and religion and Tecza finds salvation in both.[78]

During a battle scene Wally re-injured the leg he hurt in Santa Barbara. Acciden-

Left: Wally was among 52 silent stars immortalized in a deck of playing cards produced in early 1918, along with his friend Geraldine Farrar. *Right:* Farrar's card from the same 1918 deck.

tally clubbed by an extra he also injured his shoulder and suffered a severe thigh strain. He limped for a month. *Woman* was a DeMille blockbuster, costing $125,000 but earning $350,000 after the October 28th release. Trade papers noted some scenes were colored to give a pastel effect using the DeMille-Wyckoff process.[79] Lasky remembered nothing of the film, writing in his memoirs, "I'm afraid I've forgotten The Woman God Forgot."[80]

After a week off Wally and Gerry began *The Devil-Stone* on August 18th, filming until September 14th. The 6-reeler was directed by DeMille and Whittaker and the scenario written by Macpherson from a story suggested by DeMille's mother Beatrice over Sunday dinner at her apartment.[81] Wyckoff was the cinematographer, and the realistic French fishing village and Breton countryside sets built by Buckland were on the beach north of Malibu. Farrar remembered "a holiday on the beaches while filming...."[82] She and Wally were supported by Hobart Bosworth, Tully Marshall, James Neill, Mabel Van Buren, Lillian Leighton, Gustav von Seyffertitz, Horace B. Carpenter, Ernest Joy, Burwell Hamrick, Raymond Hatton and Theodore Roberts.

The romantic drama begins in a picturesque French Brittany coast fishing village and ends in New York. Beautiful, young Breton Marcia Manot (Farrar) finds a priceless emerald which harbors a devil's curse which will remain until returned to the Christian monastery from which it was stolen. Silas Martin (Marshall), avaricious American owner of the Brittany fisheries, marries Marcia to obtain the stone and its evil power. She realizes this and accepts the sympathies of Martin's general manager Guy Sterling (Wally). Silas steals the jewel and when he and Marcia struggle she strikes him with a candlestick and kills him. Sterling is accused of the crime and exonerated after hiring criminologist Robert Judson (Bosworth). When Judson discovers Marcia's role—she and Sterling are by then married—she pleads self-defense and returns the emerald to the church, ridding herself of the curse of the devil-stone.[83]

DeMille used his colorizing process whenever the jewel was shown[84] and Wyckoff used extraordinary stock footage of the Breton coast that added to the film's visual beauty. Wally was visibly immobile, in pain from the injury from *The Woman God Forgot*. In the small portion that remains—the film is lost except for two reels in the American Film Institute Collection in the Library of Congress—he hardly moves. The film was released on December 16th. Critics loved it, calling it "one of the great mystery superfeature [sic] stories ever produced."[85] It was relatively inexpensive at $67,413, but earned $300,000.

Unlike other Hollywood faux–Europeans like Erich von Stroheim[86] and Henry Lehrman, who invented aristocratic backgrounds, supporting actor Gustav von Seyffertitz was from Austrian nobility. Born in Bavaria on August 4, 1862, his father was a prominent politician and his brothers military men, but Gustav entered the theater and wound up in New York. During World War I theater and film producers were reluctant to employ Europeans. Erich von Stroheim was often heckled walking in Hollywood.[87] Lasky suggested Gustav change his Teutonic name so he used his mother's maiden name and became C. Butler Clonblough, a pseudonym he used until 1918.

After *Devil-Stone*, Wally went to the mountains to make *Nan of Music Mountain* and *Rimrock Jones*. He later recalled that *Nan* was filmed in the Sierra Nevadas near Truckee, northeast of San Francisco, but Paramount archives suggest *Nan* was filmed near Big Bear. It was directed by George Melford and Claude Mitchell and filmed from September 19th to October 25th. DeMille directed several scenes in the Beulah Marie Dix adaptation of the 1916 novel by Frank H. Spearman, which had been serialized in *Everybody's Magazine*. Wally was paired with Ann Little and supported by Theodore Roberts, James Cruze, Charles Ogle, Raymond Hatton, Hart Hoxie, Guy Oliver, James P. Mason, Henry Woodward, Ernest Joy, Horace B. Carpenter and Alice Marc. Lasky was searching for an on-screen partner for Wally and found it in the gorgeous Little and their on-screen chemistry was obvious.

Little was Wally's type. She was born Mary Brooks near Black Butte at the foot of Northern California's Mt. Shasta in 1891 and grew up on a ranch. Like Wally (but unlike Dorothy), she loved the outdoors, camping and swimming, and rode a horse and shot from the saddle as well as her male co-stars. And strangely she bore a striking, almost startling, resemblance to Dorothy. Wally later said, "She suits me better as to type than any leading women I have ever had,"[88] which is interesting since his first leading lady was Dorothy. Little grew up fiercely independent and after finishing high school at 16 joined a San Francisco company where she was hired by Bronco Billy Anderson to make westerns. She debuted in Essanay's 1911 *The Indian Maiden's Lesson*[89] and then worked for Anderson and Thomas Ince at Bronco, making 25 films from April, 1911, to October, 1912, like *A Young Squaw's Bravery* (1911) and *The Indian Maid's Elopement* (1912). She appeared in 70 films and six different serials before working on *Nan*.

Wally plays Thief River Stage manager Henry de Spain, who is battling the Morgan gang, a notorious band of thieves (Roberts, Hatton and others). De Spain sets out to find the gang responsible for his father's murder and the robberies, fearlessly entering the gang's hideout and arresting Sassoon (Ogle), one of the leaders. But when the sheriff, fearing reprisals, allows him to escape, de Spain chases Sassoon into the mountains where de Spain is ambushed and wounded. He wanders to Music Mountain where he meets Nan (Little), who nurses him back to health while they fall in love. But Nan's uncle and guardian is gang-leader Morgan. When he learns of Nan's assistance he orders her to marry Gale Morgan (Cruze), a cousin and gang member. Nan writes to de Spain, who risks death to rescue her. In the ensuing battle Sassoon is killed after de Spain learns that he, not Morgan, killed his father, and the Morgans and de Spain are reconciled.[90]

DeMille reportedly aided the technical production of the realistic blizzards although existing studio records don't confirm this.[91] The film was released on December 12th to excellent reviews for Wally, described as "The Adonis of the Screen." A patriotic theater offered "Soldiers and Sailors Admitted Free!" and asked "Other theaters please copy!"[92]

After *Nan*, Wally and Little traveled five miles into the mountains to an old mining village named Doble, above Baldwin Lake, where director Donald Crisp had sent location managers searching for the original Gold Mountain Mine. The Holcomb Valley, called Rancho Santa Anita, was the site of a massive 1860s gold rush. It was owned by Scottish-born Mexican Hugo Reid, but Elias Jackson ("Lucky") Baldwin bought it in 1875 and built the Gold Mountain Mine.[93] Gold spilled and huge mills provided wood to build the mine and nearby towns of Shadow Ranch and Clapboard Town.[94] The mine operated for 40 years, and with the nearby town, both abandoned for ten years,[95] was the setting for *Rimrock Jones*.[96]

Rimrock Jones was a 5-reeler written by Frank X. Finnegan and Harvey Thew based on the 1917 Dane Coolidge novel set at the fictional Big Top Mine. Crisp was assisted by Louis Howland and Faxon Dean did the filming. Wally and Little were supported by Charles Ogle, Paul Hurst, Guy Oliver, Fred Huntley, Edna Mae Cooper, Gustav von Seyffertitz, Ernest Joy, George Kuwa and Mary Merch.

In the mining town of Gunsight, Rimrock Jones (Wally) loses his copper mine to unscrupulous lawyer Andrew McBain (Oliver) after McBain applies an obscure "Apex Law" to trick Jones out of his claim. Undaunted, Jones finds a richer mine and borrows $2,000 from stenographer Mary Fortune (Little) for his new Tecolote strike. When part-owner Mary is stricken with sudden deafness she travels to New York to meet a specialist followed by the love-struck Jones, but when he arrives her train has already left to return to Gunsight. Wall Street financier Stoddard (von Seyffertitz) wants Rimrock's new mine and hires prostitute Hazel Hardesty (Cooper) to detain Rimrock but Mary returns in time to prevent the takeover. Rimrock, free from Hardesty's grasp, reappears to save Mary from Stoddard's gang. The movie ends with Wally and Little in a passionate embrace.[97]

Wally in a studio still taken before filming of *Nan of Music Mountain* and *Rimrock Jones*. He wore this same hat and costume in both films.

During filming around the abandoned Gold Mountain site a party of surveyors arrived to re-open the mine.[98] The area was used for episodes

Wally confronts Gustav Von Seyffertitz in *Rimrock Jones*, with Guy Oliver in the background left; back right is unidentified.

of the television series *Bonanza* from 1950 to 1965.[99] *Nan* was released on January 21, 1918, and the public was captivated by the on-screen chemistry between Lasky's popular new couple. Wally and Little were paired repeatedly for the next year while rumors swirled of off-screen chemistry and that the two were having a heated affair.

It appears that Wally again was injured or still bothered by leg and shoulder injuries from *The Woman God Forgot* because papers reported that "Wallie [sic] Reid probably will undergo an operation before he goes east shortly. His doctor has diagnosed his case as a dislocated verterbrae [sic]."[100] It doesn't appear he had any surgery but he did stay home for most of the fall before a December trip to New York for *The Things We Love*.

The Reids spent Christmas at Morgan Place. His son was his greatest joy and, according to Dorothy, he "took tremendous pride in his boy—regarded him more as a pal than a father usually does. He wanted above all things to make a man of him, to instill manliness into him from his first months."[101] Perhaps to make the man of him that Wally's family had failed to make of him. Indeed, when Billy was an infant Wally sat him in the passenger seat of one of his cars and sped around Hollywood while his son bounced about. Wally described Billy as "my chief hobby ... William Wallace Reid, Jr., and folks, he's a pippin! A bouncing young blonde kid, like his dad. I don't know whether or not Wallie, Jr., will be a movie star. At present, his inclinations tend toward direction ... of his mother and father. And he's going to be an excellent automobile racing driver. When

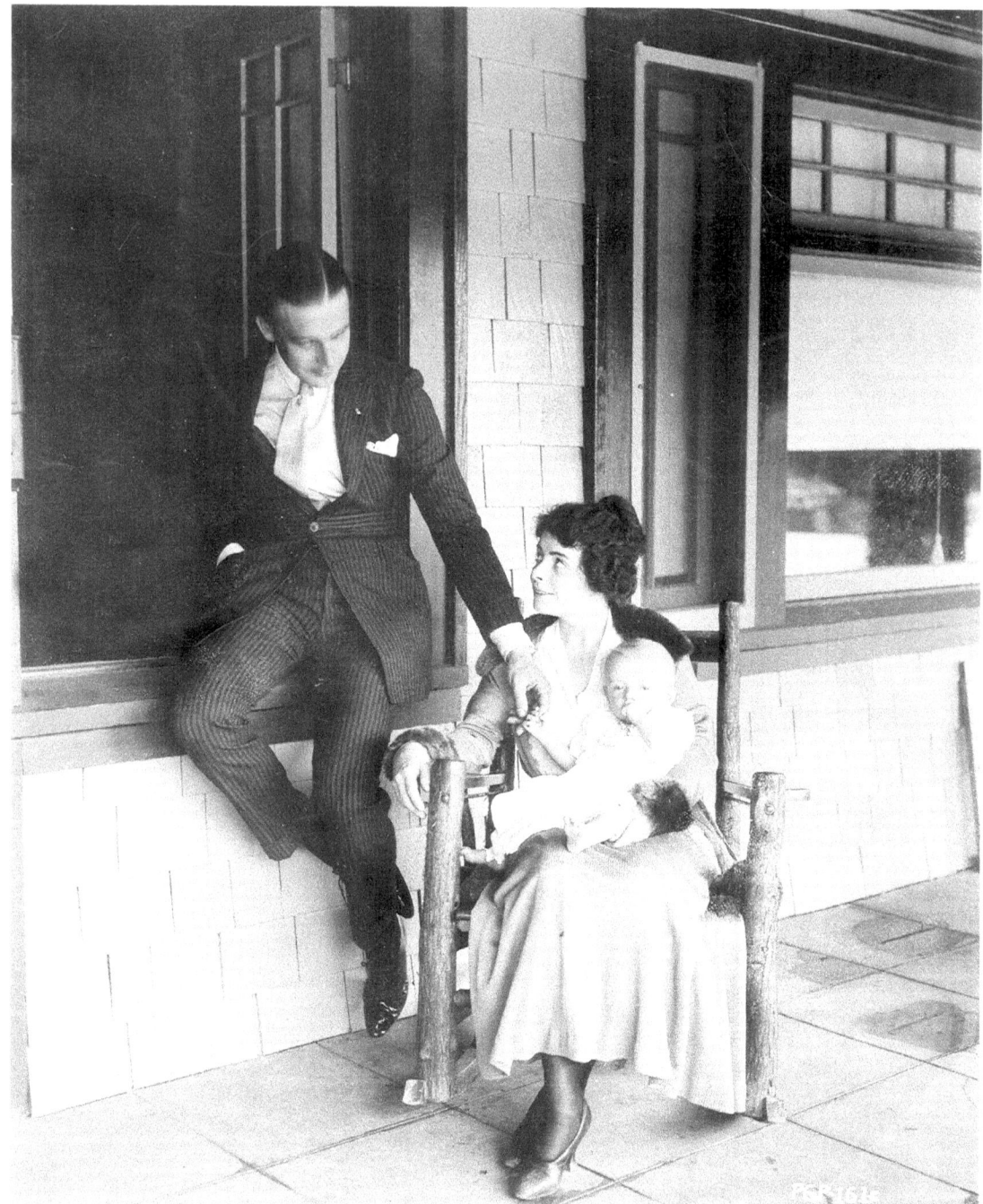

The Reids and infant son Bill Jr. on the porch of the Morgan Place house in the fall of 1917.

I take him out in the car with me, he sits up straight and fairly eats up the wind and dust. 'Faster, Daddy!' he keeps saying to me."[102] When the boy was barely four Wally bought him a .22-caliber rifle and let the infant shoot by himself![103]

On December 20th the family boarded a train in Burbank for New York and *The Things We Love*. In Chicago he made an unannounced visit to the Motion Picture Editor at the *Chicago Daily Tribune*, who was amazed to look up and see Wally Reid! The writer, who used the pseudonym Mae Tinee, described the unaffected star:

> Last week was one of those weeks when a motion picture editor is glad of her job and all the feminine fans wish they had it. Wallace Reid came to town. He came unheralded and unsung. No brass band greeted him at the station. Neither did we. The office door opened quietly and three men came in. Two of them looked like just men. The other—yes, you have guessed it— was Wallace Reid, completely surrounded by greatcoat, looking every inch of his six feet—and six feet shy. I gasped, and so did every other mere woman in the office. It was, indeed, almost too much. Mr. Reid disposed of his hat and overcoat in the wastebasket, seeing no other receptacle handy.[104]

Wally was still bothered by his injuries and "settled his exceedingly well-proportioned self slowly in the chair by my desk, so slowly that I frowned in some perplexity and asked 'Rheumatism or something?'" Wally rubbed his shoulder in pain and explained, "In one of those strenuous scenes I strained a ligament. It was getting all right when I had a little fracas with a horse. That put it on the blink again. The minute I got to the hotel I sent for a bone twister. Thought he'd sort of fix me up so I could come and see you, but when I got rubbed some more, *ouch!*"

Wally described his blasé attitude towards stardom, "I never wanted to be a moving picture actor, anyhow. I wanted to be a director. Just because I'm young and a blonde though, I suppose I'll have to be one—at least until the years have touched my hair with grey and etched my face with wrinkles—how's that, poetic, huh? Well, anyhow, I'm thankful I'm on my way east again. Been on the coast for a year." He was resigned to his status but disregarded the thousands of letters asking for photos by describing the variations on the request:

> They say three things and only three. They say, "Dear Mr. Reid, I think you are so handsome. You have such lovely hair and eyes and such nice manners. Now just for that, don't you think you should send me an autographed photograph?" Or they say, "'Dear Mr. Reid, Kindly send me your autographed picture by return mail and oblige.'" Or they say, "'You don't know how you affected me—you look just like somebody who had died.'" That's what they say.

He honestly didn't want to be a star.

9

Where's Wally?

Even though the war had closed once-vast European markets after 100 films in 1917, Lasky planned 120 in 1918. He believed providing theaters two pictures a week would force owners to buy only his films. His illegal block-booking tactics also meant selling to different owners at different prices. If a theater refused Lasky implied that the studio would build its own theater in that area. His distributors, especially North Carolinian Stephen A. Lynch, were notorious for these terrorist tactics.[1]

Ads evidenced this power. A 1916 *Golden Chance* ad read, "This is a guarantee to Superba patrons[2] of good pictures and good pictures only. You may come week after week and be absolutely sure of splendid music and clean, intelligent Paramount pictures."[3] A similar ad touted "two great [Paramount] pictures each week."[4] The studio had to revamp production for Lasky's "mass production with a vengeance"[5] to meet this need so Lasky created a new position—Production Supervisor—to oversee individual films. Frank Woods, who learned from D.W. Griffith, and Hector Turnbull were hired to lead the group. Woods was close to retirement so Ben "B.P." Shulberg was also hired. He was an ex–Famous Players publicist making movies with his discovery Clara Bow. Shulberg was paid $25,000 for Bow's contract ($2,000,000 today). He and Turnbull were each responsible for half of the studio's production.

The supervisors were the link between production and studio managers and were among the brightest and most talented men in the movies, like Tom Geraghty, Lucien Hubbard, E. Floyd Sheldon, Ralph Block, Julian Johnson, William LeBaron, Howard Hawks and Louis "Buddy" Lighton. Woods, Turnbull and Shulberg took charge of the often-frenetic pace of filming.

Wally's arrival in New York for *The Things We Love* was an event. Over 1,000 fans were at the train station when Wally, in tweed coat and tie, disembarked. Photographers were everywhere. *Things* was filmed in early January and was his first wartime propaganda film. Some period records mention a fall filming and suggest Hollywood locations but the filming schedule for Wally's other fall productions leaves no time for a film before his arrival in New York. *Things*' January timing was also confirmed by the publicity of his visit and magazines like *Moving Picture World* noting, "Wallace Reid in New York," in late December.[6]

It was directed by Geraldine Farrar's husband Lou Tellegen, who she said switched to directing due to a "none too successful career in his screen activities, [so] Jesse Lasky suggested he take over a post as director."[7] Lasky copyrighted the movie as *The Things We Love* but it was released as *The Thing We Love* and scenario records in the Paramount archives refer it as *Money Mad*. It was a 5-reeler (released in some theaters at 4) written by Harvey Thew from a story by H.B. and W.B. Daniel. The cast was led by Wally and Kathlyn Williams, with Tully Marshall, Mayme Kelso, Charles Ogle and Billy Elmer supporting.

The film is a powerful drama set in a wartime munitions plant. At the outbreak of World War I, Margaret Kenwood's (Williams) family owns the Kenwood Manufacturing Company but she retools to produce munitions for the war effort. Her boyfriend and vice president Rodney Sheridan (Wally) is unimpressed with her patriotism and suspects that president Adolph Weimer (Ogle) is a spy. Rodney goes undercover as a laborer and discovers Weimer has agreed to blow up the factory in exchange for a payoff from the Germans. Rodney pretends to be a German loyalist and gains entry to the plotters and his apparent loyalty earns him the job of planting the bomb. Coincidently, unaware of Rodney's true intentions a detective observes him acting suspiciously and arrests him. Even with the false evidence against him he proves Weimer and a cohort (Elmer) are the real conspirators.[8]

One of numerous portraits taken by Nelson Evans, this one probably ca. 1918–1919.

The film followed Rodney's voyage from idealistic pacifist to self-sacrificing, high-hearted volunteer. Papers described his process as recognizable "by many a loyal American as exactly the fight they fought, the battles they had with themselves, until they came to the realization of 'The Thing We Love.'"[9] It must have been a difficult role for Wally given his personal turmoil over his lack of service.

It was released on February 11th and though Wally was praised, the film was not. Lasky blamed that on Tellegen's direction. Farrar did not work for Lasky again, saying "the picture he directed was not satisfactory to the officials, no reflection on either party. However, [Tellegen] chose to get very upset ... my support was his, and whether right or wrong I did not renew a further engagement with Lasky on his account."[10] Had she not sided with her husband she would have done more films with Lasky. Her final eight films were done at Goldwyn or Pathé and none were as successful as her Lasky films.

Wally was with Ann Little for his next three films, the first, *The House of Silence*, a 5-reeler directed by Donald Crisp and assistant Nat Deverich. The scenario was written by Margaret Turnbull based on the 1906 novel *Marcel Levignet* by Elwyn Alfred Barron. Wally and Little were supported by Adele Farrington, Winter Hall, Ernest Joy and Henry A. Barrows. Wally's character was a "man of leisure accidentally involved in a murder case which he resolves to solve, regardless of the consequences."[11]

Wally plays wealthy partier Marcel Levington, who has a Sherlock Holmes–like hobby investigating mysteries. In his town there is a shadowy mansion called "the House of Silence" that police suspect is a rendezvous for criminals led by owner Mrs. Clifton (Farrington). She had avoided police efforts to confirm the criminal activity but as Levington passes by one evening a disheveled and distressed woman stops him and begs him to find a doctor for a man who is dying inside. He and his friend Dr. Henry Rogers (Hall) enter to find prominent Judge Carter (Barrows) dead, stabbed in the heart with a hatpin that Rogers realizes he had given to his daughter Toinette (Little). Rogers tells Levington and police that the death was from a heart attack and returns home to confront Toinette. Unknown to Levington she confesses to her father that she was enticed to the house by Mrs. Clifton, who lied and said she was ill. Once inside she was attacked by Carter and in a desperate attempt to salvage her honor stabbed him and fled. The next day Levington notices Toinette and Clifton on a rooftop garden chatting, Clifton holding Toinette's purse that she kept as blackmail to keep the secrets of the house. Toinette believes she is about to be uncovered and tries to jump from the roof as Levington is sneaking in. Knowing then that Toinette killed the judge to defend her honor, Rogers and Levington agree to protect her. When Levington sneaks into the house he fights a group of Clifton's thugs, finds bags of stolen money and jewels, and prevents Toinette from suicide. Levington retrieves Toinette's pocketbook, gives police his solution, and returns to Toinette, with whom he has fallen in love.[12]

Silence was released on April 8th. Wally's character was named "Marcel Levignet" (from the novel) in period reviews and some ads, but Paramount archives continuity records list the name "Marcel Levington."[13] Lasky probably was still avoiding European- or Teutonic-sounding surnames that audiences associated with Germans.

In February, Wally and Little made a film that further accelerated his stardom, *Believe Me, Xantippe*, a 5-reeler directed by Donald Crisp. Olga Printzlau wrote the screenplay based on a 1913 Frederick Ballard Broadway play that was one of the first "Harvard Prize" plays. Lasky assigned his top cameraman, Henry Kotani, to the production, as well as his best supporting actors—Henry Woodward, Noah Beery, James Cruze, Winifred Greenwood, James Farley, Charles Ogle and Clarence Geldart.

Wally plays George MacFarland, a wealthy adventurer who bets his friends Thornton Brown (Joy) and Arthur Sole (Woodward) $20,000 that he can commit a crime, tell the police, and elude capture for a year. George forges a check, heads west, and escapes arrest for nearly a year despite the dogged pursuit of Detective Throne (Farley) and thousands of wanted posters with his picture and his favorite expression, "Believe me, Xantippe." In the mountains of Colorado, George meets Dolly (Little), the lovely daughter of local Sheriff Kamman (Beery). Working at the remote hunting lodge where George lives, Dolly recognizes and tries to arrest him but the terms of the bet dictate that he must be captured by a genuine officer of the law, which Dolly is not. At the stroke of midnight the year elapses and George wins the bet, and as expected, the love of the sheriff's daughter.[14]

Xantippe was a change for

Hotel employees recognize Wally (note the drooping disguise moustache) hiding from police in the 1918 film *Believe Me, Xantippe*.

Wally. He carried the romantic comedy. Dorothy compared Wally's comic talents to Chaplin's: "Wally could do comedy, but not the type Charlie did. Charlie was *physical*. Wally's humor was gentler."[15] After the film's June 2nd release, reviews raved about Wally as a comedian, noting, "fans of Wally Reid will be thrilled to learn that he is as talented at comedy as he is a leading man."[16] Another said, "We always knew Mr. Reid could make love, and we always knew he's good to look upon, but we never realized before that he was a born comedian. Ten chances to one Wally's infant son will turn out to be a clown."[17]

Ann Little was a beautiful actress, and loved the outdoors as much as Wally.

Rumors of a Wally-Little affair that started on *Nan of Music Mountain* grew with the sexual energy apparent on this film. Wally and Dorothy denied the rumors; Wally had been the subject of similar stories before, but the Little relationship was probably the most visible, and of the rumors the most likely true. Dorothy was smart enough to suspect affairs and this story was all over the papers. She later rationalized, "There were always rumors about Wally having romances on the set. I expected that. He was a *man*, a *real* man, and a lot of girls were attracted to him ... if you see his brief scenes in *The Birth of a Nation*[18] you knew why there was such a strong reaction from the ladies. If the stars of any era, silent or sound, had as many romances or affairs as were reported in the papers and movie magazines, they wouldn't have the time or the strength to stand in front of a camera!"[19]

When she was younger Dorothy's personality was as well known as her beauty. She was intelligent and funny and had many friends but even after a short tenure as "Mrs. Wally Reid" the change in her personality was obvious. Once bubbly and funny, by 1918 she was often distant and aloof. The price of being Wally's wife was taking a toll on her as she developed "an outer shell which at times made people think her cold."[20] The rumors and Wally's increasing alcohol problem exacerbated the change in Dorothy. Sadly, it would only get worse.

Dorothy tried to keep Wally on a tight leash but his social life and reputation were well-known. He was already known as "Good-Time Wally." It was interesting that, as with Farrar, Dorothy avoided any contact with Little. She was among the few co-stars who never visited the Reid home. During the war Wally made few public appearances, but he and Dorothy were rarely seen out. Just a single 1918 appearance as a couple could be uncovered, on March 9th at Pasadena's Huntington Hotel.[21] The benefit for the War Camp Fund at the hotel's Georgian ballroom featured stars like Theodore Roberts, Constance Talmadge, Norman Kerry, Jack Pickford and Olive Thomas, and coincidently, Little.

Charlie Murray and Franklyn Farnum were masters of ceremonies for the party that lasted literally until breakfast. A charity auction featured animals donated by the stars, everything from an Airedale to a donkey. Wally and Dorothy were not going to donate any of his beloved pets, but he got caught up in the moment and offered his Boston bull terrier. The dog fetched almost $3,000![22] "Good-Time Wally" was among the guests that stayed past breakfast.

Wally was saddened when Otis Turner was found dead at his Hollywood home at 1612 Curson Avenue on March 28th. Only 56, Turner died of chronic heart disease after a brief career that lasted from 1908 to 1917. But he wrote over forty scenarios and directed more than 150 silents, including the earliest versions of *The Wonderful Wizard of Oz* (1910), *Robinson Crusoe* and *Uncle Tom's Cabin* (both 1913). Turner taught Wally to direct and Wally had followed him to L.A.[23] Turner also directed the movie version of Hal's *Human Hearts* (1912), and he and Wally were close friends. Wally and Dorothy attended Turner's funeral. Though Turner is virtually forgotten today he was a major force during the early years. In a 1943 column "25 YEARS AGO TODAY" the 25th anniversary of Turner's death was noted: "Otis Turner, known as the father of the motion picture industry in Hollywood, died at his home, one of the first directors."[24]

At the same time an obscure Kansas death set off one of the great tragedies of the 20th century. On March 4th a group of young inductees took Army physicals at Fort Riley and within hours hundreds were deathly ill. Company cook Albert Gitchell was the first to die and in 48 hours 525 men were sick.[25] One of their vaccinations was a shot for influenza. Vaccines cause a mild case of the disease they are to prevent but in 1918 there was no way to predict the severity of the reaction. There was something wrong at Fort Riley. Seven soldiers died in a doctor's office and so many during the next days that there were not enough coffins. Even so, hundreds of other infected soldiers were shipped overseas carrying the deadly flu.

Within ten months 675,000 Americans and an untold number worldwide died in the "1918 Spanish flu" epidemic. Doctors knew it originated in the U.S. but called it *Spanish Influenza* to deflect any notice. It had no Spanish origin, but the name stuck (angry Spaniards called it "French Flu"). Over 20,000,000 died in India; the worldwide total may have been 50,000,000.[26] By summer an even more deadly strain broke out on the East Coast.[27] Hollywood victims included Harold Lockwood, a former vaudevillian who was Dorothy's leading man during her first year in Hollywood (they starred in 10 films together in 1911–1912). He died in New York on October 19th at age 31. In July, Robert Harron's sister Tessie died at age 19. She and another brother, Johnnie, appeared in small roles with Robert in Griffith's *Hearts of the World* in 1918 but Tessie was incorrectly billed as "Jessie Harron."[28] Other lesser-known movie casualties included George Binns, John Hancock Collins, Dale Hill, Chester Ryckman and Rex Webber.[29]

Movie production was spotty that spring as fear kept employees away for days and weeks at a time. Rudolph Valentino left for a month in San Francisco but after catching a slight cold returned to L.A. in a panic. He was living across the street from Wally and Dorothy on Morgan Place at the time. Wally stayed home most of that period and his late-night saxophone playing became a constant irritant to Valentino.[30] Wally rarely ventured from the house before returning in April for his second war film, *The Firefly of France*.

Wally was again paired with Little, who coincidently had recently separated from Allan Forrest, her husband of just 15 months.[31] *The Firefly* was a 5-reeler directed by Donald Crisp and Nat Deverich. Margaret Turnbull wrote the scenario based on the 1918 Marion Polk Angellotti novel which was serialized in *The Saturday Evening Post*. Henry Kotani did the filming that began in mid–April and lasted through early May.[32] The supporting cast was led by Charles Ogle, Raymond Hatton, Winter Hall, Ernest Joy, William Elmer, Clarence Geldart, Henry Woodward and Jane Wolfe.

Masquerading as a chauffer, Wally listens to Ann Little as Charles Ogle eavesdrops in the background in the 1918 film *The Firefly of France*.

Wally plays Devereux Bayne, a wealthy American who travels to Europe to fly for the Lafayette Esquidrille. During his trip he meets beautiful but secretive Esme Falconer (Little) and a mysterious man calling himself Jenkins (Ogle) who tells him Esme is a German spy. Esme won't reveal why she is going to France but Bayne won't believe she is a spy and follows her to a small French inn. That night her chauffer is killed so Bayne takes his place to take her to the Falconer family chateau, followed by Jenkins and his spies (Joy, Elmer and Geldart). There, Jenkins reveals he is really Von Blenheim, a German agent and demands Esme obtain secret war plans which had been carried by her brother-in-law, a famed pilot from America known as "the Firefly" (Hatton). Ads for the film described the Firefly: "in truth is the daring aviator, who, far above the battle-scarred lands, darts hither and thither upon his mission, as the eyes of the army below."[33] Unknown to Von Blenheim the Firefly is hiding in a concealed chamber at the castle so Esme and Bayne escape to the hidden room. While the Firefly and Esme escape Bayne turns over fake documents to Von Blenheim. The Germans take Bayne and drive toward their own lines but he is able to signal French forces and the Germans are captured. During the heroic struggle he is shot and wounded but Esme returns to lovingly nurse him to health.[34]

Firefly was released July 7th and after a three-day break Wally and Little began the comedy *Less Than Kin*. It was a Marion Fairfax adaptation of a 1909 Alice Duer Miller[35] novel done by the same technical crew as *Firefly*—Donald Crisp and Nat Deverich directing and Henry Kotani filming. Wilfred Buckland did the art direction. Wally and Little were supported by Hatton, Ogle, Oliver, Noah Beery, James Neill, Jane Wolfe, James Cruze, Calvert Carter, J. Herbert and Gustav von Seyffertitz.[36] Although featuring gloomy themes like murder, arson, thievery and marital desertion, the film was a comedy tour de force for Wally, who stole the movie.

He played two roles, Robert Lee, a ne'er-do-well disowned by his family, and Lewis Vickers, who accidentally kills a man in defense of a woman, escapes jail and finds refuge in Central America. Vickers is involved with revolutionaries led by Señor Cortez (Beery) and Dr. Nunez (Neill) and they form a motley army to battle the oppressive government. In town Vickers has a chance encounter with Lee, who bears him a striking resemblance. When Lee is killed during a robbery Vickers assumes his identity and returns to New York the prodigal son. Lee's father Endicott (von Seyffertitz) and beautiful ward Nellie Reid (Little) are convinced that Lewis is Robert but soon Vickers is haunted by Robert's unsavory past. A local bank demands money stolen by Lee 12 years earlier and Lee's abandoned wife Maria (Wolff) appears with their children demanding support, so Vickers ends the masquerade. He reveals his true identity to Nellie and saves the family and their animals from a barn fire. She realizes she loves him and breaks her engage-

Wally as wealthy ne'er-do-well Robert Lee, with the lovely Ann Little, in *Less Than Kin*. Gustav Von Seyffertitz played his wealthy father.

Wally tells Gustav Von Seyffertitz, playing the father of his look-alike, that his son is dead in *Less Than Kin*.

ment to James Emmons (Hatton). They marry and Lewis is cleared of the murder charge.[37]

Little's character's surname was changed to Reid from Jacobsen, the name used in Miller's book. Wally may have suggested the change. It can only be imagined how Dorothy reacted. By the release of *Less Than Kin* on July 29th the supposed Wally-Little relationship was something of an open secret in Hollywood, true or not. The rumor mill went into overdrive just before the film's premier when Little left her husband and moved with her mother to an apartment at 945 South Orange. Also living there was William S. Hart and actresses Florence Oakley and Mary Alden.[38]

The U.S. was fully involved in the war and that involvement was turning the tide against Germany that spring. Hollywood continued supporting the military but a common question was, "Where was Wally?" On May 25th the new Motion Picture War Service Association met at Clune's Theater with Griffith as Chairman and Mack Sennett the treasurer. The board included Lois Weber, Charlie Chaplin, Mary Pickford, Douglas Fairbanks, William S. Hart, Marguerite Clark, Maurice Tourneur, Cecil B. DeMille, Frank Woods, Billy Bitzer and William Desmond Taylor.[39] No Wally, though.

After Griffith read the famous speech by patriot Patrick Henry and DeMille announced a fund for a 1,000-bed hospital, the event became a fundraiser.[40] Mary Pickford autographed her membership card and with Charlie Murray as auctioneer sold it to Dustin

Farnum for $2,500. Chaplin paid $2,600 for Murray's, Sennett $2,400 for Clara Kimball Young's, Griffith $2,500 for Mae Murray's, Sessue Hayakawa $2,000 for De Mille's, and on and on until $40,000 was raised.[41] Coincidently, the group evolved from Otis Turner's Directors' Association. That made it doubly interesting that Wally was absent while virtually every other name star was there. The group held numerous fundraisers, none of which Wally attended.

That spring, papers described a training center for balloon aviators at a local Y.M.C.A. that had a theater offering films and vaudeville shows. The entire corps of 350 crowded into the small building to listen to musicians (usually women) and see films. The first movie shown was Wally's *Big Timber*[42] but he did not attend though it was reported he would. Lasky was correctly worried about the potential public relations nightmare. His most virulent star and most popular leading man was never mentioned patriotically in the press, so he sent him on a three-week tour with studio publicist Kenneth McGaffey for *Photoplay Magazine*.[43]

Dorothy and Billy stayed home, which was unusual. Spouses normally came along on trips like this but Dorothy may have been smarting over the Little rumors and the fact that Wally had said he was "eager to make a trip to New York to attend the opera season." His old friend Geraldine Farrar would be performing.

A *Photoplay* picture of Wally on the train platform during his 1918 publicity tour.

Traveling first to Salt Lake City, Wally had no idea what to *do* on a publicity tour and asked McGaffey, "What have I got to do?" McGaffey told him at each of the dozen stops the train would be met by a delegation of prominent officials who would take them to visit theaters in town, followed by a dinner. When McGaffey said *his* job was to "find postcards for friends" while Wally performed, Wally said, "'No, it *ain't*!' You will appear on stage with me each and every time or I'll be awfully hard to catch." Wally got his way but was still at a loss about what to talk about. McGaffey suggested, "Tell them how good an actor you are." Wally replied, "No, I've got to talk longer than that." He mused, "How pictures are made is old stuff and would take too long. I must talk about something that won't take too long, because after three or four minutes out there, I am going to pass away, and besides, I can't stand long on this bum hip."[44]

Even backstage at the first

Salt Lake theater Wally implored McGaffey, "*What* am I going to talk about?" But once on stage he was the charming Wally that people knew from the screen. Just in case, McGaffey brought along a violin without telling Wally. They went to Denver, Kansas City, Chicago, Pittsburgh, Philadelphia and New York. Lasky made sure Wally sold War Bonds or collected Red Cross donations. During the trip Wally entertained passengers in the lounge car with his saxophone. They returned to Hollywood in late June. When he was in New York, Wally did not contact Bertha in New Jersey. Dorothy still prohibited any contact.

McGaffey's story of their travels ran in June, 1918 and was titled "Wandering with Wally." Apart from a single photo of Wally on the train's observation platform there are no photographs, but there are ten of Wally's sketches of McGaffey and people they met during their trip. He was traveling on June 8th and missed a benefit hosted by Paramount, a fundraiser featuring stars from every studio. Douglas Fairbanks offered to fight boxer "Kid" McCoy[45] but the "fight" ended before the second round when Fairbanks fell into a nearby pool. Booths were set up offering candy, flowers, and small items, manned by stars like the Gish sisters, Gladys Brockwell, Constance Talmadge, and Carmel Myers. William S. Hart and his cowboy actors ran the bar.[46]

Clara Kimball Young auctioned off the clothes from what the auctioneer called her "warm, pulsating body." Standing behind a screen she slowly removed items, beginning with her hat and gloves and ending with lingerie. Her dress went to a film distributor.

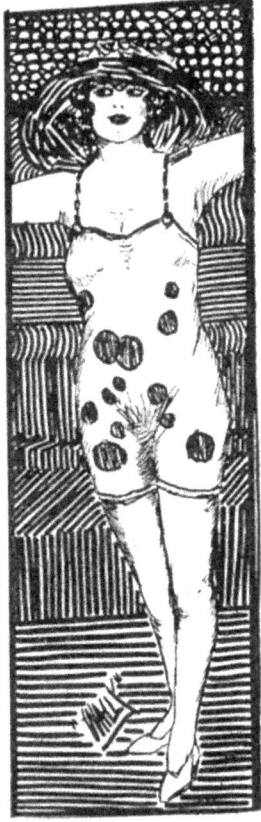

Three of Wally's drawings published in the *Photoplay Magazine* story detailing his 1918 publicity trip.

DeMille bought her stockings. Her lingerie went to Hart, Fairbanks, and Chaplin for $80 to $150 (several thousand dollars today), described as "censored, slightly censored, and heavily censored." Chaplin spent the evening with Kimball's panties around his neck.[47]

Continuing his public relations blitz, Lasky arranged a loan-out of Wally to Fox Film Corporation for a Liberty Bond drive propaganda film. It was a single-reel film produced in July and released on November 1st featuring Wally, Dorothy Dalton, William Farnum, William Faversham, Pauline Frederick, Dorothy Gish, William S. Hart, Sessue Hayakawa, Madge Kennedy, Harold Lockwood, Mae Marsh, Tom Moore, Mae Murray, Mabel Normand, Mary Pickford, Edith Storey and Norma

Talmadge. Each spoke briefly or waved during the film, a filler shown between features. Wally's absence from almost all things war-related was, and remains, a mystery.

After his tour and Liberty Bond appearance, in early July Wally and Little traveled to the San Bernardino Mountains to film *The Source*. It was a Monte M. Katterjohn adaptation of a 1918 novel by Clarence Budington Kelland that was serialized in *The Saturday Evening Post* the previous fall. It was directed by George H. Melford and Claude Mitchell, filmed by Paul Perry, with art direction from Wilfred Buckland. The supporting cast included Theodore Roberts, Raymond Hatton, James Cruze, Noah Beery, Nina Byron, Charles West, Gustav von Seyffertitz (still listed as G. Butler Clonblough), and Charles Ogle. Paramount archives note that James Neill appeared in a supporting role also.

Wally plays Van Twiller Yard, the alcoholic son of a prominent Bostonian, kidnapped during a drunken spree and taken to a lumber camp in Vermont's Green Mountains. Forced into hard work he is beaten up by his foreman Langlois (Cruze) when Langlois realizes the superintendent's daughter Svea Nord (Little) has eyes for Van Twiller instead of him. When Van Twiller offers no resistance Svea casts a contemptuous glance at him, thinking him a coward. She doesn't know his cowardice stems from his physical weakness and liquor. The events lead Van Twiller to spend two months off liquor getting into shape and earning respect from his fellow lumbermen. When yard owner Big John Beaumont (Roberts) witnesses a fight in which Van Twiller prevents Langlois from inciting the men to strike, beating him soundly in the process, Van Twiller is given Langlois' job—to the displeasure of Svea's father, John Nord (Beery). Langlois is secretly in the employ of a Swedish power company owned by German spies and bribes Nord to stop a dam that will allow Beaumont's logs to be taken to mills. Van Twiller organizes the lumberjacks and after a fierce battle the dam is opened. As a result of his courage Van Twiller is made the General Manager of the lumber company and wins Svea's heart.[48]

The film was released on September 8th. Wally and Little stayed in the mountains for *The Man from Funeral Range*, a western directed by Walter Edwards and filmed by James C. Van Trees.[49] The movie was another Monte M. Katterjohn adaptation, from the 1917 play *Broken Threads* by W. Ernest Wilkes. The cast included Lottie Pickford (Mary's younger sister), Willis Marks, Tully Marshall, George McDaniel, Phil Ainsworth and Tom Guise. Pickford played a prostitute described in ads as "an entertainer of a different sort."[50]

In one of his favorite roles Wally plays prospector Harry Webb, who returns to town from the Funeral Range Mountains and falls in love with cabaret singer Janice Williams (Little). But he makes enemies of sleazy lawyer Mark Brenton (McDaniel) and his partner Frank Beekman (Marshall) when he refuses to sell them his mine. Brenton lures Janice to his hotel with a forged note from Webb, where they are met by his jealous former sweetheart Dixie (Pickford), who shoots and kills Brenton. Hearing the shot, Webb rushes in and believing his love is the killer assumes the blame to shield her. During the trial Beekman kidnaps Janice and holds her prisoner on a tramp steamer to prevent her from testifying; consequently, Webb is convicted and sentenced to hang. En route to prison Harry escapes to the desert and later returns to town to sell one of his mines to Freddie Leighton (Ainsworth). Beekman recognizes him, and when they fight a gun is discharged, mortally wounding Dixie, standing behind a screen. Before her death she confesses that she killed Brenton, which clears Harry's name and allows him to marry Janice.[51] The movie was released on October 6th.

Wally's popularity meant he would probably never again direct, which was a disappointment. But he helped his friend James Cruze get that assignment. Jens Vera Cruz

Wally and Ann Little filming *The Source* near Lake Arrowhead.

Bosen was a Utah-born Mormon and part Ute Indian whose first job was a "snake oil" salesman with a traveling medicine show.[52] He arrived in Hollywood in 1911 and his acting resume included *The Last of the Mohicans* (1911), *Dr. Jekyll and Mr. Hyde* (1912), and *Robin Hood* (1913). But his only directing experience was on the 1914 Thanhauser short *The Cat's Paw*. Cruze worked with Wally in 1917 on *Nan of Music Mountain* (Cruze's 84th film), *Believe Me, Xantippe*, *Less Than Kin* and *The Source*. The entire summer of 1918 Wally pestered Lasky to let Cruze direct one of his films[53] and Lasky relented and Cruze was assigned the 5-reel comedy *Too Many Millions* in September. He would direct 12 of Wally's final 30 films, including Wally's last—*Thirty Days*, in 1923.[54]

The *Millions* scenario was written by Gardner Hunting based on the 1917 novel *Someone and Somebody* by Porter Emerson Browne. Lasky produced (keeping an eye on Cruze) and assigned top cameraman Charles Rosher. Wally's co-star was Ora Carew, supported by Tully Marshall, Charles Ogle, Winifred Greenwood, James Neill, Noah Beery, Percy Williams, Ernest Pasque and Richard Wayne.

Wally plays Walsingham Van Dorn, a poor young man who makes a meager living selling books before inheriting $40,000,000 when his two skinflint uncles (Beery and Williams) die in an auto accident. Van Dorn asks his personal secretary and lawyer Wilkins (Marshall) to manage the fortune and retires to his uncle's mansion. He is awakened one evening by beautiful Desiree Lane (Carew), who tells him his uncles swindled her family out of $2,000,000. She refuses to leave until money is repaid. Van Dorn agrees to give

Desiree the money but the next morning they discover Wilkins has stolen it and fled. The couple set out to find him and stay at an inn, which catches fire and burns. Barely escaping with their lives they are left standing in front in their pajamas; to avoid a scandal they marry. When they stop to get gas their car is stolen and they decide to simply settle where they are. Van Dorn takes a job at the gas station and they live happily in the small town. After two years living poor but happily Wilkins returns out of nowhere and restores the money to Van Dorn. The couple hesitate taking the money, worrying it will ruin their peaceful existence, but end up rich and happy.[55]

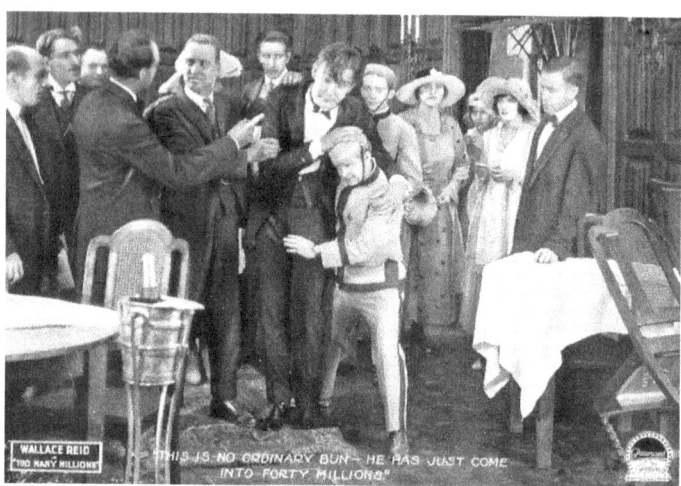

A drunken Wally learns he has inherited $40,000,000 in this amusing lobby card for the 1918 film *Too Many Millions*.

Too Many Millions was released on December 8th. Wally's film ads had gradually grown in size and they now featured Wally's face. Lasky ran quarter- and half-page ads for Wally's films, not the usual smaller sizes.

As *Too Many Millions* was going to theaters the war came to a merciful end. By the end of the summer it was apparent to Germany the war was lost. Battling a mutiny within their once-proud Navy and a public revolution in Munich the Kaiser abdicated and an armistice was signed in November. The war had cost 10,000,000 lives. Among the dead was an extra from *Joan the Woman*, one of the cowboys Geraldine Farrar so liked. She remembered in her memoirs, "One of my ablest riders was found dead among five German soldiers, having taken a machine-gun nest alone."[56]

The end of the war was a confusing time at the studios. Dozens of war films in various stages of completion were abandoned, costing millions, and entire production schedules were reworked and new product begun. The good news was that the European markets would soon be re-opened. It's difficult to underestimate the potential; in postwar London the *Daily Mail* listed 24 films showing in London. Of that, 22 were American.[57] Before the war Europe was years ahead of the U.S. in movie development but as economies were ravaged by governments diverting money toward war efforts, U.S. studios expanded and gained an unassailable foothold. The industry would never be seriously challenged by international competition again.

The timing of the armistice coincided with a resurgence of the Spanish flu epidemic. Lasky closed Paramount for weeks at a time that fall, laying off hundreds and idling actors. Although the worst of the resurgent epidemic was in the East people in Hollywood were terrified the disease would return. *Moving Picture World* noted that "Hollywood was full of doom and germs."[58] It took months to get back to normal production.

James Cruze directed Wally's next film, *The Dub*. Lasky assigned William Horwitz as Cruze's assistant for the October filming. The scenario was by Will M. Ritchey based on the short story "The Dub" by Edgar Franklin[59] that had appeared in the June 17, 1916, *All-Star Weekly*. *Motion Picture Weekly* described the film as a re-issue of one of Wally's

Wally and Ora Carew in *Too Many Millions*.

earlier films, but no archival confirmation exists in archives.[60] Charles Rosher did the cinematography. Wally was paired with Nina Byron and supported by Charles Ogle, Ralph Lewis, Raymond Hatton, Winter Hall, Guy Oliver, H.M. O'Connor, Billy Elmer, and Clarence Geldart. Wally played against his public character in the role of a young soldier known as a coward and a "dub" (slang for a loser).

The movie's theme posits that chance happenings change the direction of one's life. When the brokerage firm of Blatch, Markham & Driggs dissolves, George Markham (Ogle) steals company papers that include the option on a valuable mine owned by Phineas Driggs (Hatton). Meanwhile, Frederick Blatch (Lewis), who wants the option to expire so he can then purchase the mine himself, hires attorney Burley Hadden (Hall) to convince Driggs that he is trying to recover the papers. Hadden sees contractor John Craig (Wally), who desperately needs $800 for his payroll, shake nervously from the pop of a paper bag, thinking it was a gunshot. Assuming him to be a "dub" Hadden offers Craig $1,000 to retrieve the papers assuming he will fail. After Markham tries to dupe Craig, he meets Markham's lovely ward Enid Drayton (Byron), who is being held a virtual prisoner in Markham's mansion. Craig and Drayton meet a friendly burglar who retrieves the papers that prove that Markham and Blatch had been cheating Driggs. Driggs rewards Craig and tells Enid she owns a $1,000,000 estate, and the film ends as she and John embrace.[61]

Wally retrieves important papers and wins the love of the beautiful Nina Byron in *The Dub*.

The Dub was released on January 19, 1919. Reviewers mentioned similarities between the character and Wally's reputation, one noting John's courage as similar to Wally's "natural heritage. In real life Mr. Reid has met difficulties in the same way that he does in this picture, surmounting them with the same determination. He has been newspaper reporter, surveyor, cowpuncher, writer and director, and always his quick thinking and courage have been his greatest assets."[62] But the role was no doubt troubling to Wally, given his wartime experiences or lack thereof.

In November, Wally began his final 1918 film, *Alias Mike Moran*. He was happily back with Ann Little in the 5-reeler directed by Cruze. It was written by Will M. Ritchey based on the Frederick Orin Bartlett short story "Open Sesame," which ran in the *Saturday Evening Post* in August, 1917. Frank Urson did the camera work and Wally and Little were supported by Emory Johnson, Charles Ogle, Edythe Chapman, William Elmer, Winter Hall, Jean Calhoun and Guy Oliver. The film was an interesting choice for Wally, about a slacker who allows an ex-convict to take his place in the military after he is drafted. Given his ongoing personal struggles over this theme it must have been a challenging role for Wally, especially after a similar role in *The Dub*.

Wally plays Larry Young, who sells ribbons at a department store but is looking for a wealthy society bride. When lovely maid Elaine Debaux (Little) visits his shop on an errand for her wealthy employer Young believes her to be the daughter of a millionaire shipbuilder and falls in love with her. At the same time, Young is drafted into the Army.

Out to dinner one evening he and Debaux are rescued from a bunch of drunken gangsters by ex-convict Mike Moran (Johnson), who is injured in the fight and taken home by Young. Young complains he has been drafted and Moran complains the military refused him because he was once in prison. They agree to switch identities and Young moves away and works as Moran in a shipyard while Moran enters the military under Young's name. Moran, as Young, dies gloriously in battle, and when she learns that the man she thinks is her lover is dead, Debaux goes to France as a Red Cross nurse. Ashamed and humiliated, Young joins the Canadian forces to save Moran's name, awaking in a field hospital with wounds that cost him his arm. But he was a hero. Both confess their deceptions and they marry. His heroism leads the War Office to overlook his draft evasion.[63]

The film was released on March 2, 1919. Gossip writers noted that the divorced Little and Wally were an on- and off-screen couple. As with their last movie together (when her character name was changed to "Reid") her character name in *Moran* was revised to "Debaux," which sounded suspiciously like "the beau."

By the end of 1918 theaters were handing out flyers like this one by the millions. Wally's star was on the rise.

10

Accident, and Addiction

By 1919 Wally had become the movies' first "idol." His films made more money than those of any other actor. Papers often just announced, "WALLY REID NEXT!"[1] and often mentioned when his movies *ended* runs, one reading, "WE HAVE JUST CONCLUDED A THREE DAYS' RUN OF THE BEST PICTURE WALLY REID EVER MADE."[2] *Motion Picture Magazine* called him "the screen's most perfect lover."[3]

Responding to a reader's request for some stars' addresses, of Wally a columnist replied, "just address Wally at Hollywood, California. Everybody knows him there."[4] He had "an everlasting place in the hearts of the movie patrons. A big, powerful, handsome, clean-cut young man with years of dramatic experience, without affectations or poses, he has given the world the best example of straightforward young American manhood."[5] He was "tall, clean-cut, good-looking and powerful, equally popular with both sexes...."[6]

St. Johns summed it up: "The important thing about Wallace Reid is not that he was the greatest and most popular star the motion picture has produced. It is that he was, beyond dispute, the best loved man of his generation. It wasn't only women who loved him ... men loved him, boys, old people, children. There was something about Wally Reid that fitted into the dreams in every heart."[7] Lasky knew a "Wally Reid picture" meant money from men and women. Women threw themselves at him. St. John's recalled a beautiful society woman who bombarded Wally with letters and gifts for over a year, along with nude photos and a key to a secret apartment. She also gave his valet jewelry worth $25,000[8] just to get a look into his dressing room. Another young girl secreted herself under a blanket in the back seat of his car, and was not discovered until Wally and Dorothy left the studio.[9]

Dorothy and Wally found dozens of girls hiding in every imaginable space at home. "Dorothy dragged them out from under the bed, from inside the closets, from inside the music cabinets, from the attic, the cellar, even from the car pits" in the garage.[10] Wally's make-up man, a squat middle-aged Italian named Kelly, made a handsome living taking bribes (including the famous necklace) for access to Wally's dressing room or cars.

He was among the first actors with endorsements, paid $5,000 by Buescher Saxophone, and by hat, shirt and shoe makers. But Wally had simple goals:

> There are only a few things worth while [sic] in this world—and they are so easy to get. An open fire, books, a little music, and a friend you can talk to or keep silence with. I think that everything you get beyond just that is in the end a burden and a temptation. The happy lives are the quite lives, aren't they? And yet it's so hard to be quiet! Never to hurt anyone, to do good to others when you can, to keep your own code of honor unbroken, your soul unstained

by lust or greed or pride, your mind unsullied by lies and pretense, your body strong and clean—those are the things you must do. You believe in God. Sometimes I do too, though I can't always give him a name. But I do believe in good. I know there isn't any happiness possible for me without self-respect, and I could never respect myself if I fell below the standard I *know* to be right.[11]

His sense of self showed on-screen. Above his desk was the framed sentiment, "I shall pass through this world but once. Any good thing therefore that I can do, or any kindness that I can show to any human being, let me do it now. Let me not defer it nor neglect it, for I shall not pass this way again."[12] He was friendly with everyone, from the office boy paid an extra $2 to bundle his mail, to the men in his crews.

Wally had no ego. During the publicity trip with Ken McGaffey two young female reporters showed up unexpectedly at their hotel. Wally was still sleeping but gave an interview in his pajamas, hair and teeth un-brushed, sans makeup.[13] He didn't care. Dorothy said, "I never heard him express an egotistical thought or do any act

A 1919-era publicity still of the man becoming the most popular actor in the movies.

that suggested that he thought himself above or different in any way from others. He hated above all things to think that his physical looks helped him to his success and popularity. He didn't let me have pictures of him in the house. The only time in his life he showed someone else a picture of him was [one] from 'Forever' as an old man in wig and makeup. He had in the fullest sense of the word charity for all—charity not only in his acts but in his thoughts ... no matter what it cost him of time and effort. Nothing was too big or too little for Wally to help a friend, or an enemy."[14]

Wally's friends in everyday life, like Levi's Tavern owner Al Levy, felt it. Wally was Al's favorite customer, a compliment from a man who owned the Tavern for 50 years and knew Hollywood notables from Valentino to Chaplin. Columnist Herman Morin recalled:

> [A] tall young fellow with blue Irish eyes and a contagious smile, comes in. He stops to exchange a joke with Al. Something funny that happened on the set today. "Did I tell you the one Teddy Roberts told me," says the young fellow, "The one about...." "You did, yesterday," says Al, "I've saved a nice quiet place for you, Mr. Reid." But Wallace Reid never sits alone. His friends call to him, and make a place at their table. He has a lot of friends, Wally Reid, too many. Al brings him a bowl of tomato soup. He knows, in advance, what Wally will order. Then there will be steak. And coffee ... two or three or maybe four cups. Wally Reid is Al's pet and favorite customer.[15]

He never acknowledged his talents. He told St. Johns, "My damn face kept me from getting a chance to be a writer or director,"[16] and "Sometimes I think it's a shame I can't write. I've seen so much. I've really been close to and had a lot of experience with all sorts of unusual people and places."[17] When he said that, he had written 25 scenarios.

Dorothy saved hundreds of poems he give her "shyly."[18] Written just months before he died, Wally penned a letter to his son called "Lullaby":

> You cry for your Daddy, baby o' mine
>   Can't you see that I'm crying, too?
> You're asking me and I'm asking God
>   For I'm just a baby like you.
> You want to know when, O Baby o' mine,
>   He'll be coming home to you.
> And O how I'm longing and longing dear
>   To be able to tell you true.
> I want to sob with you, Baby o' Mine,
>   But I must be brave for us three—
> For you with your childish sorrow, dear,
>   For daddy, who's fighting—and me.
> So come to my heart, dear Baby o' mine,
>   Let me comfort your baby woes.
> And we'll trust in God to stay with the Flag
>   And with daddy, wherever he goes.[19]

Fans would probably have been most surprised at his intellect. He was a voracious reader, devouring up to six books a week. His library was not decorative; he read the books he purchased, enjoying history and favoring Macaulay, Carlyle, and Swift. He rarely appeared on set without books Dorothy described as "tattered and torn."[20] He was also keenly interested in science, with a fully-equipped lab in his cellar. "When you missed him from parties, you were pretty certain to find him down there, messing around with all kinds of stuff. New inventions and discoveries of which he read always interested him enormously and he liked to investigate them."[21]

But amidst the fame, dark clouds were forming over "Wally Reid, the All-American Boy." By 1919 he had a serious alcohol problem. The nickname "Good-Time Wally" was well-deserved. Dorothy described a "gaiety that was of the heart, that sweet and simple gaiety that fell upon everyone around him like sunshine, that shone in his eyes and his smile, a real cheerfulness of the heart. The 'kid' in him adored all surprises."[22] The kid would never intentionally hurt anyone but was himself sensitive, easily wounded. He was effusive in gift-giving, particularly to Dorothy, rarely coming home without something. He was generous with friends, a soft touch for anyone needing a loan. He gave freely, never asked why, and was loath to ask to be repaid. He kept a small black book St. Johns described as a "haphazard record of the money he had loaned to people. The names amazed me ... all you had to do was ask and Wally gave."[23] Bertha also worried about Wally's largesse, noting his "appallingly large" loans and that "greater and more frequent were the calls for 'loans' and more numerous the applicants ... from all callings and with every excuse." But Wally lived by his grand-

This was the face Wally's friends most often saw; but by early 1919 he had developed a serious drinking problem.

mother's motto; it was better to help nine unworthy cases than miss the single worthy one.[24]

Friend Buddy Post remembered, "Wally was always lending and spending, not much on himself, though his greatest personal expense was his motor-cars ... he gave money to a fellow he disliked ... broke and out of a job and Wally supported the fellow and his family. Wally came home one night with a carload of paintings purchased from a local artist 'to keep the poor fellow going.'"[25] He also gave freely of his home, which sped his downfall. St. Johns said he just couldn't say "no" to anyone and his door was always open to guests. He was afraid that his "friends" would be somehow disappointed at his rejection.[26]

Dorothy said, "Wally loved to keep an open house, and if others sometimes abused that great-hearted hospitality, still he would not shut anyone out."[27] St. Johns described the challenge faced by Wally's chief protector: "If ever a girl tried to stem a rising tide, Dorothy Reid tried. If ever a woman upheld her husband's hands, she upheld Wally's."[28]

Lasky knew any Wally film meant money for Paramount; the studio growth had been because of him. In 1919, Lasky and DeMille rushed Wally from picture to picture. When stars usually took a week or two between features, Wally was given three or four days. Chronic exhaustion and an increasing need for alcohol spelled disaster. That year was the beginning of the end for "Good Time Wally," but nobody had an inkling as he began *The Roaring Road*. The role became his image—a fast-driving, reckless hero. It was the first of the racing movies that spiraled Wally's popularity, the films with which he was most identified. He became the first action hero.

He loved his cars. He cruised to the studio in one of his convertibles with the top down every day and to ward off the chill usually wore a fur coat that made him look "like a grizzly bear."[29] He said, "I must admit I enjoy working in [racing movies] best of any, because I'm fairly nuts about motor-cars, and it's combining business and pleasure when I get to play a racing driver role."[30] A story titled "Wallace Reid Is a Speed Demon" noted he'd "always been a speed demon. The Paramount star has trouble in keeping within the speed laws, even in his own car, such is the impulse to crowd on the juice and only hit the high spots."[31]

He frequently ran the Santa Monica Road Race route. The summer races held between 1909 and 1919 took place on unpaved Santa Monica roads with drivers like Barney Oldfield, Ralph DePalma, Jimmy Murphy, "Terrible Teddy" Tetzlaff and even Eddie Rickenbacker racing in super-charged Marmons, Stutzes and Duesenbergs. The dangerous course ran south along Ocean Avenue to Wilshire Boulevard, east to San Vicente, and back to Ocean. The 90-degree left-turn from Ocean to Wilshire was called "Dead Man's Curve" because of the numerous horrible or fatal accidents that happened there as open-cockpit cars careened around at 100 miles per hour.

The Roaring Road was filmed in Jan-

The Roaring Road was the first of the racing films that catapulted Wally to even greater popularity.

uary and directed by James Cruze and James Barranger. Frank Urson filmed and Wilfred Buckland did the art direction. The scenario was written by Marion Fairfax (Mrs. Tully Marshall) based on a series of Byron Morgan racing stories published in the *Saturday Evening Post* during the fall of 1918.[32] Wally and Ann Little starred, supported by Theodore Roberts, Guy Oliver and Clarence Geldart. Studio archives note that Gustav von Seyffertitz appeared and with the war over, he was able to abandon his Americanized pseudonym, G. Butler Clonblough, and use his real name.

Wally plays "Toodles" Waldron, the best salesman at a car company owned by J. D. Ward (Roberts). Ward's Darco racers compete with Rexton Motors. Waldron and Ward are at odds because Ward doesn't feel the young man is a suitable store manager and won't let him race in the Santa Monica Race. Nor will he let him marry his daughter Dorothy (Little). Just after Waldron quits Darco in a huff, a train carrying three new Darco cars crashes and the cars are damaged. Waldron and Dorothy secretly salvage enough parts to build one racer, enter and win the race. After Waldron wins Ward gives him the general manager position and consents to the marriage if the couple waits five years. But Waldron doesn't want to wait and refuses his boss's request to go after the Los Angeles–to–San Francisco speed record so Ward arranges to take his daughter to New York for a year. Put in jail for speeding, Waldron learns that Dorothy and her father are to stop in San Francisco, breaks out of jail and goes in pursuit. With the help of a friendly Darco mechanic he speeds to San Francisco, racing the train carrying his love. Beating the train and setting the record his future father-in-law so coveted in the process, Waldron wins the girl.[33]

During filming, racing drivers hurtled around the Santa Monica course with their mechanics in the second seat.[34] Wally sped around the course exceeding 90 miles an hour with his terrified co-star Guy Oliver beside him.[35] At one point, Wally's car slid sideways and almost tipped over but Wally made a deft steering correction and maintained control. Had he not, both men would have been killed.[36] Papers described the thrilling race sequences: "The big feature of the story is a race in which the handsome star does some of the most sensational driving ever seen on the screen."[37]

When not working, Wally borrowed the racing cars and snuck onto the course. During the week of the real races he set the track speed record around Dead Man's Curve—110 miles per hour[38]—at a time when the top speed at Indianapolis was *under* 90! Wally screamed away pursued by crew members checking to see if any locals had seen him pass by. The area was rural and crew members came upon a farmer standing next to a fence along the road. Asked if he had seen Wally and if he was heading toward L.A. the incredulous farmer replied, "Well, the last time I saw him he was headed that way, but I wouldn't bet a barley straw that he'll get there alive."[39]

One of the professional drivers in *Road* was California race team owner Omar Toft. His film car was the "Darco Special," a name Toft kept for his real car during the Indianapolis 500 that May 30th. He and Wally became good friends and Toft was so impressed with Wally's driving he suggested that Wally enter the Indianapolis race. The studio rented a Duesenberg racer for Wally in the movie which he raced around L.A., outrunning underpowered policemen who tried to give chase.[40] But the car seemed cursed. Just a week later a professional driver rolled the car at Dead Man's Curve. The car was rebuilt and ran the Indianapolis race, where it rolled again during the 18th lap, killing rookie driver Arthur Thurman. Wally's friend Toft brought the car back to California and rebuilt it and Wally drove it in *Excuse My Dust* in 1920.

The Roaring Road premiered in New York on April 13th and nationally on the 27th. Fans loved the movie, but, aside from the racing sequences, the critics were ambivalent.

Motion Picture Magazine said the "picture is supposed to star Wallace Reid, but according to the number of close-ups of Theodore Roberts smoking a cigar, it was starring a new brand of tobacco.... I cannot but admit the production as a whole is a mighty interesting piece of work ... suspense, interest and thrill is maintained until the very end, while all the comedy possible is extracted from the conflict of the two men's hot tempers. Some of the photography is unnecessarily harsh on Ann Little and Wally Reid is conspicuous because of the distance they keep him from the camera...."[41]

Omar Toft pilots a 1915 racecar around Dead Man's Curve in Santa Monica, where Wally later set the speed record, tearing around the dangerous corner in a similar car at over 100 miles per hour!

Byron Morgan adapted his other two stories for Wally with characters named "Speed Carr" and "Dusty Rhoades" in the later films *Excuse My Dust* and *Too Much Speed*. Lasky wrote, "The audience couldn't get enough of him behind the steering wheel. We virtually turned these road-racing movies out on an assembly line, and every one was a money-maker. But even that couldn't type Wally. He was believable in almost every role we gave him."[42] His racing movies were his most popular, though.

In February, Wally was again with Cruze, assisted by Cullen B. Tate in the comedy *You're Fired*, a Clara G. Kennedy adaptation of the O. Henry story "The Halberdier of the Little Rheinschloss," originally published in *Everybody's Magazine* in May, 1907. Wally's leading lady was Wanda Hawley. The Scranton, Pennsylvania, native began in movies in 1917 and was a star in a year, getting more fan mail than studio principal Gloria Swanson. The tiny 5'3" Hawley briefly billed herself as Wanda Petit and had interests similar to Wally—she composed music, played the piano, and was an athlete who excelled at swimming, golf, and basketball.[43]

The *You're Fired* supporting cast consisted of Theodore Roberts, Henry Woodward, Lillian Mason, Herbert Pryor, Raymond Hatton and William Lesta. Wally again demonstrated his comedy talent playing devil-may-care playboy Billy Deering, who proposes to wealthy Helen Rogers (Hawley). Her railroad magnate father Gordon Rogers (Roberts) agrees to the marriage if Deering can keep a job for one month without being fired. If he gets fired he cannot marry Helen, who knows nothing of the wager. Wally shows perfect slapstick timing in several vignettes when he "learns" to use a typewriter as an office clerk and plays the xylophone in an oom-pah band run by kapellmeister Hatton. He fails at everything. On the verge of getting fired from his office job he takes the second position before he's fired from the first. He repeats the process several times, each effort more unsuccessful than the previous. One reviewer noted the comedy comes from Deering's seemingly bottomless vat of ineptitude, as he's incapable of any type of labor. With blisters on both hands, Wally executes a perfect slapstick gag when Roberts enthusiastically grabs his hand and shakes it, and Wally jumps a foot in the air.

Costumed as a knight in his job as a restaurant doorman, Wally is tormented by Theodore Roberts, playing the father of his love, Wanda Hawley (seated at right) in *You're Fired*. **William Lesta (with mustache) and Raymond Hatton are at left.**

Eventually Deering gets an easy job in the restaurant of a ritzy hotel as halberdier, donning a medieval knight's costume and posing as a statue in the lobby, a decorative doorman. The final night of the wager, Rogers, Helen, and her friend Tom (Woodward)— who also wants to marry her—enter. Rogers has just merged his railroad with a competitor of a railroad owned by Tom's uncle, and, unknown to Rogers, Tom has arranged for the documents to be stolen. When Helen recognizes Deering she jokingly demands from the proprietor (Lesta) that he serve them dinner even though she knows he can't. She still knows nothing of the wager and she and her father have Deering running pell-mell trying to keep up with their orders, Mr. Rogers hoping he gets fired and Helen laughing.[44] Deering nearly gets fired but stumbles upon Tom's cronies and foils their attempt to ruin the Rogers' deal.

The movie was a box-office smash after its June 8th debut, and after a 3-day break Wally was back for *The Love Burglar*, this time with Anna Q. Nilsson. She was a Swedish beauty and among the first female stars to achieve worldwide acclaim. She debuted for Kalem in 1911's *Molly Pitcher* with Guy Coombs, a coupling so popular the studio paired them in 58 films from 1911 to 1915! *Burglar* was her 87th film.[45]

The Love Burglar was directed by Cruze and Tate, photographed by Frank Urson, and written by Walter Woods, based on the 1918 Jack Lait play *One of Us*. Wally and Nilsson were supported by Raymond Hatton, Wallace Beery, Wilton Taylor, Edward Burns, Alice Terry,[46] Dick Wayne, Henry Woodward and Loyola O'Connor. Filming was done in late February.

Wally plays wealthy David Strong, who stumbles on his wayward brother Edward (Burns) about to be robbed in a seedy gangster bar. David takes his brother's money and sends him home before fighting a gang led by notorious "Coast-to-Coast" Taylor (Beery). Beating Taylor, the other people mistake him for recently released convict "the Colt Kid" and he goes along with the charade. Joan Grey (Nilsson), the torch singer in the bar, blurts out that David is her fiancé to ward off the advances of Taylor. To support their story David marries her right there. Without consummating the marriage, they fall in love. As revenge for the beating Taylor arranges for David to be arrested for a faked robbery at the wedding of David's sister Alice (Terry). The police think they've arrested "the Colt Kid," and when Joan warns him she too is arrested and jailed. When police identify Taylor and his gang as the real criminals and arrest them, David's mother (O'Connor) confirms his true identity and in a wonderful plot twist, David's sister identifies Joan as a college friend and writer who was masquerading as a singer to infiltrate the gang for her stories. It is then that she agrees to a real marriage with David.[47]

The Love Burglar was released July 13th. Wally's ads were now at least ¼-page and most at least ½, describing the film as "love, romance and thrills interwoven with comedy."[48] The huge Clune's theater in Los Angeles ran the film every two hours from 7 A.M. until midnight, with seats costing 15¢, 20¢ or 30¢.

Shortly after finishing *Burglar*, Wally and his crew boarded a train for northern California to make the film that changed his life. *The Valley of the Giants* was a Marion Fairfax adaptation of a 1918 Peter B. Kyne novel serialized in *Red Book Magazine* in August. Cruze, Tate, and cameraman Urson led a group of 20 actors and several dozen crew. Wally and Grace Darmond were supported by Will Brunton, Charles Ogle, Alice Terry (using her real name, Alice Taafe), Ralph Lewis, Kay Laurel, Jack Hoxie (listed as Hart Hoxie), Noah Beery, Guy Oliver, William H. Brown, Richard Cummings, Virginia Foltz, Odgen Crane, Lillian Mason and Speed (Ariel) Hanson.

The crew traveled to the small but bustling coastal town of Arcata, 100 miles south of Oregon. They settled at the Hotel Arcata—40 rooms that overlooked a circular plaza filled with tall palms and ringed by colorful plants. Arcata is along the coast near Humboldt Bay and the Pacific Ocean, and a mile from the edge of 1,000 acres of towering redwoods in the majestic South Fork Mountains. The Klamath River flows through gorges and the verdant Hoopa Valley.

For hundreds of years the region was home to Native American Wiyot and Hoopas, which were among California's first cultures.[49] In 1828 the first American trappers and miners

A 1920s view of the town of Arcata, California. At the time of Wally's 1919 accident, the Lasky crew stayed at the Hotel Arcata, the three-story building behind and left of the center of the town square.

came up the Trinity River and in 1850 a settlement rose near Fickle Hill named "Union" after the Union Company. By the late 1850s it was renamed Arcata and had a deep-water wharf connected to the Plaza by the first horse-drawn railroad in California. Ships full of gold-seekers had arrived weekly but dwindling gold supplies left two huge 1870s mills, the Jolly Giant and Dolly Varden Mills, to sustain Arcata into the 1900s. By 1919, 1,500 people lived there.[50] The Hotel Arcata was built in 1914 with in-room claw-foot tubs with running hot water, a restaurant and a tavern. Two doors down was the Minor Theatre, also built in 1914 and still open, the longest operating movie theater in the U.S. The crew's parties at the hotel were the talk of the town.

Valley of the Giants interiors were filmed at the exquisite Sumner Carson mansion in Eureka[51] but exteriors were filmed near the tiny lumber settlement of Korbel, just east up in the mountains. From the hotel the crew took a 3-mile carriage ride over dirt roads through the tiny town of Alliance to Indian Junction, a railroad interchange at the foot of the mountains where the Arcata & Mad River and North West Pacific Railroads met. Small lumber company railroads carried logs down the mountain to the spot. These short lines, notoriously unsafe and unregulated, had badly-maintained equipment and track, but movie companies used them because they were cheap; often a few signed photos or a few roles for extras was enough.

On Monday morning March 2nd, 40 Lasky crew members and their equipment filled a lumber car and small caboose. They left Indian Junction and traveled past another tiny camp town, Blue Lake, headed to Korbel. The trip covered six dangerous miles of rickety track straight up the mountain, crossing several large creeks that fed the Mad River.

Giants was the most important film Wally made. But not for the movie. Indeed, it is lost but for written records. What was important happened *before* filming. On the dangerous train ride from Indian Junction to Korbel there was an accident. As the train lurched out of Indian Junction and across the trestle over Lindsay Creek the passengers crowded onto the two cars—especially the 12 or 15 crammed in the caboose—must have been nervous. They were about a mile out of Indian Junction, slowly crossing the shaky trestle over Noisy Creek when disaster struck. As the caboose traveled over the narrow trestle it groaned, jerked and somehow tipped, and simply fell off the bridge, rolling 15 feet down into the 50-foot-wide creek and landing on its side. Lumber track was narrower than long-haul track so tipping was common. The trains traveled slowly to maintain jittery balance; the overloaded caboose simply fell off the track.

Papers reported, "Nearly every member of the Wallace Reid company was injured in an accident last Monday [March 2, 1919] in northern California, when a train caboose, carrying the Reid company of players, jumped the tracks on a trestle bridge near Arctas [sic] and turned over. Wallace Reid sustained a three-inch scalp wound, which required six stitches to close. Grace Darmond and others in the company suffered similar cuts and bruises...."[52] Dorothy later described the accident:

> ... in the middle of the smelly old caboose sitting side by side on the long leather-padded seat to the right. Wally is in the center, strumming his guitar and singing lustily. On one side is Speed Hanson with his inescapable banjo. On the other is Grace Darmond, in a fluffy dress ... the old caboose groans and jerks and sways along over the narrow-gauge mountain railway. All of a sudden the caboose swayed perilously. The car bumped over the ties of a little trestle and then, with a sickening lurch, careened and toppled into space ... with the piercing screams of Miss Darmond. Wally crawled out of the door, dragging Miss Darmond, whose fluffy dress was drenched with blood. When he reached the open, he collapsed, but his wonderful stamina came to his aid. With the back of his skull scraped from the blow of a falling [rail section] and his left arm sliced to the bone by glass, he still was strong enough to lurch among the other members of the party, attending to their wounds. Twelve hours later they reached town and a

doctor and then, for the first time, Wally's wounds were dressed. Against the advice of the physicians he went to work next day and the picture was made on schedule.[53]

The injuries could have been much worse. Wally was the most seriously injured. He had a deep, bloody gash at the base of his skull (which required six to twelve stitches), another cut in his arm that went to bone, and he re-injured his back with a severe strain.

When they finally arrived back at the Hotel Arcata late that evening Cruze sped to the telegraph office and wired Lasky, who had a dilemma. Wally was in agonizing pain and unable to work but halting production and bringing the crew back would cost $10,000 ($450,000 today). Not willing to bear that cost Lasky sent word to find a doctor and dispatched a studio doctor there. Wally was to be given morphine so he could work.

Moving Picture World reported, "REID COMPANY IN WRECK!"[54] It was reported that Wally valiantly threw himself over Darmond to protect her and then helped injured friends while ignoring his own injuries. Wally was frightened to death of, and took sick at, the mere *sight* of blood,[55] but responded well in emergencies. St. Johns witnessed two examples: "On location in the high Sierras, he set four broken fingers for one of the prop boys and did a perfect job, according to the Hollywood surgeon who examined the hand." On another occasion, they came upon a wrecked car and badly injured woman near the beach: "It wasn't a pretty sight, but Wally, with extraordinary coolness ... did everything that could be done with the contents of his first-aid kit, and then Dorothy drove to the hospital while he held the woman as motionless and comfortable as possible. The doctor told us Wally saved the woman's life."[56]

With the help of morphine Wally returned to the set. Morphine was discovered in Germany in 1805 when 22-year-old pharmacy apprentice Friedrich Sertuerner concentrated opium in poppies into a crystallized form that eased everything from coughs to pain to insomnia. It helps the brain release dopamine, responsible for pleasurable sensations. It makes users feel good, is highly addictive and works no matter how it enters the body: taken in pill form, dissolved under the tongue, injected into muscle or into the bloodstream. By the late 1800s it was used for anything from calming crying babies to relieving headaches to treating Civil War injuries.[57] Versions like Dr. Flannery's Teething Syrup and Children's Comfort flowed unregulated off store shelves but by 1906 its addictive powers were known and the Pure Food and Drug Act required morphine to appear with drug labels. In 1914, due partly to the thousands of U.S. opium dens, the Harrison Narcotics Tax Act regulated use.[58] Morphine was the drug of choice in Hollywood and getting some was as easy as a phone call. With Wally mobile from studio-supplied morphine the crew was back on another train from Indian Junction three or four days later.

In the film Wally plays a young man "called upon to fight with brain and brawn against an unscrupulous foe who would seek to gain control of the property."[59] Bryce Cardigan (Wally) returns from college to find his nearly blind father (Ogle) being swindled out of the beautiful glade ("the Valley of the Giants") where his mother is buried. The cheat is rival lumberman Colonel Pennington (Lewis), an unprincipled Easterner, and when Bryce learns the redwood that guarded his mother's grave was felled by Pennington foreman Jules Rondeau (Hoxie), Bryce beats him unconscious. Bryce then meets Pennington's beautiful daughter Shirley Sumner (Darmond) and saves her and her father from a runaway logging train. Even so, Pennington ungratefully refuses to haul Cardigan logs; that means failure for the Cardigan Company. But Bryce schemes with railroad agent Buck Ogilvy (Brunton); they pretend to build a railroad connecting to a transcontinental line, bypassing Pennington. Backers agree to finance it as long as they can cross Pennington tracks, so Shirley, in love with Bryce, helps them secure that part

Wally comforts his father (Charles Ogle) beneath a painting of their beloved forest in *The Valley of the Giants*. Camera angles hid the bad gash at the base of Wally's head; morphine got him through filming.

of the deal. Although her father tries to bribe the mayor (Crane) to stop the deal his dishonesty is exposed and the valley remains the Cardigans'. Shirley is now Mrs. Bryce Cardigan.[60]

Wally liked the role, telling *Picture-Play Magazine* he enjoyed "growing a beard, smoking cigars and acting like a man would in the woods. But the studio ordered no more beards. No more cigars. From henceforth I was to appear as is. So they doll me up and shove me on screen."[61] The film was released August 31st described as "A picture of the great outdoors, of the logging camps of the West, of giant men and redwoods. See a log train, running wild down a mountain plunging into a river! See Wallace Reid as the daredevil son...."[62]

Wally's mettle was tested in the runaway train scene. Huddling in a railcar he and Darmond hurtled down the same winding track where he almost died a week earlier. The studio doctor made sure Wally was pain-free and gave him morphine any time he complained so shooting could continue. But Wally was plagued by blinding headaches and according to Agnes de Mille, daughter of William and niece of Cecil, "The next day Wally had a dose of pain, and a dose of morphine was given. The pattern was established: pain, morphine, pain, morphine. Before the film ended shooting Wally's morphine addiction was well-known back at Paramount."[63]

Lasky kept Wally working by providing him unlimited morphine. Paramount couldn't wait for him to heal. Not surprisingly, Lasky did not mention the movie or the accident in his 1957 memoirs. Neither did Wally in his own 1922 life story, Dorothy in an extensive 1925 *Photoplay* article, or St. Johns in her 1928 *Liberty Magazine* serial, which went into minute detail on every *other* aspect of his life. The seminal moment in Wally Reid's life goes unmentioned in anything written about him. Nobody wanted to talk about it.

The train wreck story has some doubters but it is virtually confirmed that the accident traveling to the *Giants* filming site was the start of Wally's drug addiction. Doubters point to alternative stories about Wally's alleged first use of drugs. A 1922 story blamed it on a *filming* accident when "a large rock falling from an overhanging bank struck Reid on the back of the head and knocked him out. Eleven stitches were taken by physicians in the actor's scalp."[64] Her father told Agnes de Mille that Wally "accidentally stepped on a rusty nail. My uncle [Cecil] knew what happened but he had a doctor there, as he always did because of the insurance policies ... accidents took place all the time, they were taken care of and the shooting resumed ... no need to send dozens of people home. The doctor was there quickly to administer an injection of morphine.[65] Wally returned to the set after an hour or so...." She was told it took place during *The Affairs of Anatol*, which was not until 1921.

Dorothy told so many conflicting stories that she added even more confusion. In November, 1921 she blamed emergency dental work and studio-prescribed morphine: "Between pictures he went to a dentist to have work done. Work was started on the picture ... while Wally's mouth [was] raw swollen gums ... the dentist could not understand how Wally had been able to do any work. The pain, the dentist said, was even greater than that which comes with appendicitis."[66] Wally did endure three days of painful dental surgery to remove (incredibly) nine teeth but it took place two years later and was worsened by his then chronic morphine use. A month after the November article she revised the story as an accident *during* filming:

> Wally and Miss Darmond [were riding] down an incline in a logging car. While this scene was being taken an accident occurred. An iron block swung toward Wally and Miss Darmond. It appeared inevitable that Miss Darmond would be injured. Seeing this, Wally threw himself directly in front of her. The iron block struck him on the head. Wally was painfully injured. To ease his pain morphine was prescribed by physicians. He was unable to sleep and sleep-producing potions of an apparently harmless nature were given to. The pain he suffered in his head gave him almost continuous trouble. All of this time he was working at the studio, unmindful of his suffering.[67]

Dorothy's new version added sleeping pills to the mix and Wally is shown as even more courageous. The conflicting stories are hard to wade through and some doubters also point to a lack of an accident report on file at the Department of Transportation for an event near Arcata in March, 1919. The D.O.T. kept extensive records of even minor rail accidents. In the D.O.T. Archives Investigations of Railroad Accidents 1911–1966 are 5,000 summaries, 83 from 1919 for 50 companies in 35 states. The reports are minutely detailed but there are none for the large railroads serving Arcata—North West Pacific and Arcata & Mad River—or for the smaller Redwood Lumber Line or the Humboldt Redwood lumber lines. But the lack of records is explainable. The D.O.T. never investigated short-line accidents since they occurred frequently, were in remote areas, and didn't impact larger lines.

Before the accident Wally was probably an active alcoholic and likely had tried recreational drugs. In any case, when he returned to Hollywood at the end of March he was addicted to morphine. "Good-Time Wally" was in trouble. Dorothy did not see it, saying, "When he came back to Hollywood, in six or seven weeks, he apparently had fully recovered. His eyes were bright and his health above normal. He had gained weight. It was months before I realized that the change in his disposition dated from that wreck in the lonely mountain wilderness."[68] Wally was hurtling toward disaster while his films were the most popular the world over. In England and Europe, magazines like *Picturegoer* touted his every move and film. In U.S. magazines a lengthy feature in *Picture Show Magazine* in May described "Film Favourites in New Parts: Wallace Reid!"[69]

The most telling evidence that something was wrong was his absence after he returned to Hollywood. He virtually vanished from the end of March until early June. Given how much Paramount needed Wally films to survive financially Lasky would have continued moving him from film to film if he could have. But he could not. Unable to work due to still-severe pain, he was home in bed calmed with studio-supplied morphine. Tragically, after those three lost months he was well past the point of normal withdrawal and the addiction was probably already fatal. Paramount had turned their most profitable asset into a hopeless morphine addict. Making it worse, Wally had always been in perfect health and believed he could control his use.

A formal Wally in an early 1920 publicity still, one of several from the same sitting with photographer Nelson Evans, who is credited with invented the "cheesecake" photo taking pictures of Mack Sennett's "bathing beauties."

Dorothy never blamed Wally or let him take responsibility. She usually blamed doctors. "What happened to Wally happened to many a soldier released from hospitals after World War One, and happened to patients, men and women, released from hospitalisation [sic], cured perhaps of their ailments but made into hopeless addicts through the then abysmal ignorance of the medical profession."[70]

Wally's painful injuries healed but chronic leg and hip pain from the Santa Barbara accident returned.[71] He was also plagued by insomnia that kept him up all night reading or chain-smoking. He usually fell into fitful sleep at sunrise. Then he often had to work. Dorothy had yet another excuse: "Insomnia came next. I remember only too clearly the night I watched the doctor give Wally his first 'shot' to quiet his nerves and its astonishing effect. The old doctor ... for half an hour tried to reason Wally into sleepiness ... the argument failed. I lay in bed and watched with a fascinated horror as the doctor opened his little black bag and took out a smaller case. The reading light at the head of Wally's bed glinted from the steel and glass tubes which lay in the little case in orderly rows. Silently, with a slight frown, the doctor prepared the 'shot.'"[72]

For Wally insomnia was an excuse to find a party. "Occasionally he would awaken me in the small hours ... as he stamped about the room getting into his clothes. 'Where are you going at this time of night?' He would mutter, 'Any place; any old place; out to get some air.' The lights of his car would flash across the windows and I would hear the roar of the motor as he raced down the drive into the night."[73] Wally's favored haunts were the Ship, a bar near the Venice Pier, and the Sunset Inn, near the beach in Santa Monica. Both had crowds and free-flowing liquor: "The real cutups go to ... the Sunset Inn on the road to Santa Monica, miles from Hollywood...." The Ship was "a bootlegger's paradise."[74] Another favorite was Nat Goodwin's Café in Santa Monica. When he went out, Wally was normally gone all night.

Some mornings Dorothy recalled, "He would get into his shooting clothes before daylight, telephone some friend out of bed, take his gun and drive to the ranch to shoot rabbits at dawn. He would return fresh, apparently rested, just in time to bathe, change clothes and rush off to the studio for work."[75] He was probably "fresh" from drugs but even so he rarely appeared at Paramount before 9:00 or 10:00 in the morning after his accident.

His various injuries continued to bother him. He complained of painful lumps at the base of his skull on the spot of the original gash. His right leg troubled him and sometimes was numb all night.[76] His psyche was also affected. Dorothy recalled, "Unpleasant thoughts and fears crowded his mind. Sometimes he shrank from some horrible danger he never confided to me. But times without number he awakened me and sitting on the edge of my bed, clasped my hand nervously and whispered: 'Don't leave me alone, mamma. I feel so strange. I don't want to be left alone.' He was just a child and I soothed him as I would my baby. Sometimes he pattered downstairs and I would hear him in the dining-room mixing drinks. He found that very often drinking enabled him to sleep and he chose whiskey as the lesser evil. But Wally wasn't drinking to excess. Prohibition was still new and everyone, I suppose, was drinking to some extent."

Wally's combination of liquor and morphine was deadly. When he realized he "couldn't put a stop or even a check to the morphine, he began to use liquor as a cover-up for what he was really doing. Before that, he had only drunk for relaxation and fun. Drinking now made things even tougher for him. There were times when he behaved badly in public."[77] Wally was a heavy drinker and perhaps an alcoholic and his drug addiction offered an excuse to drink even more. He was using morphine for pain and to sleep and mixing it with alcohol and staying up for days. His work suffered immediately.

During his three-month sabbatical Wally still raced around L.A. in his cars. Omar Toft suggested he race in the Indianapolis 500 in May and offered Wally one of his cars. Wally entered using an alias, telling Lasky he was attending as a spectator. But Lasky discovered the ruse. When Wally refused to withdraw, studio lawyers threatened legal action. Lasky knew he was barely mobile during March and April and already addicted to morphine. He clearly couldn't drive a racecar, and an angry Wally was forced to capitulate. Dorothy was relieved; even she was not aware how serious he was, later saying, "He had talked about it, but I didn't dream he was seriously thinking of so dangerous a stunt."[78]

From the accident until his death three years later Wally's production steadily shrank, even with increasing supplies of studio-provided morphine. During 1916, he made 10 features, and in 1917 and 1918, 22. *Giants* was his fourth 1919 release, and filming ended in March. From that point, his production decline is startling. He made only two more films in 1919, and from 1920 to 1923 averaged six yearly. To the public it was reasonable, but it was disaster to Lasky. Their most popular star was slowly becoming unable to work.

In June, Lasky coaxed Wally back in work for *The Lottery Man*, surrounding him with a cast and crew of familiar faces. Cruze directed, with Tate assisting, and Frank Urson did the camera work, assisted by Elmer Harris. The scenario was based on the

Wally is caught between Carolyn Rankin (left) and Marcia Manon in *The Lottery Man*.

1909 Rida Johnson Young play. Lasky was remaking a little-known 1916 film by Leopold and Theodore Wharton's F. Ray Comstock Company. Among the cast in that film was a heavy-set 23-year-old from Georgia named Oliver Hardy. Lasky starred Wally opposite Wanda Hawley, supported by Harrison Ford, Fannie Midgley, Sylvia Ashton, Carolyn Rankin, Wilton Taylor, Clarence Geldart, Marcia Manon, Winifred Greenwood, Fred Huntley, Tully Marshall, Lila Lee, Charles Ogle and Guy Oliver.

Wally plays broke newspaper reporter Jack Wright, who borrows $500 from his college pal, newspaper owner Foxhall Peyton (Ford). The money is lent on the condition that Jack write a story to increase circulation but Jack loses the money in the stock market and decides to hold a lottery with the prize being him as a husband. Jack prints flyers and tickets "GET A HUSBAND FOR $1" but the plan gets out of hand and hundreds of thousands of tickets are sold. While tickets are selling Jack falls in love with Foxhall's cousin Helen Heyer (Hawley) who, when she learns of the lottery, leaves Jack. Intending on going through with it, Jack is mobbed by hundreds of women at the drawing, won by old spinster Lizzie Roberts (Carolyn Rankin). Somehow Jack's maid Nora (Manon) proves Lizzie stole the ticket from *her* and because she loves Jack's butler (Huntley) she sells her winning ticket to Jack for half the proceeds. Jack rushes to Helen and they embrace as her suitcase pops open to reveal hundreds of tickets she had purchased.[79]

The role reminded Wally of his newspaper jobs in New Jersey and a paper noted,

"One morning about ten years ago a youth entered the newspaper office and asked for a job as a reporter. The editor liked his looks and put him on the staff for $10 a week. The 'cub' made good but after a few months wanderlust attacked and he left for the west."[80] Wally remembered, "I still haven't given up that old ambition to write and some of the happiest days of my life were those I spent as a reporter. That's one of the reasons I liked making 'The Lottery Man' so much."[81]

The film premiered in New York on September 28th and nationally on October 12th. During filming Wally became friends with another famous face. Both were recognized everywhere, both at the top of their careers and both loved a party. William Harrison Dempsey had just beaten 6'6", 250-pound Jess Willard to retain his World Heavyweight Championship, knocking him down four times in the first round and breaking Willard's jaw. In 16 years Dempsey won 64 of 70 fights, 53 by knockout. His real record is not known. As a dirt-poor teenager "Kid Blackie" spent 1911–1916 visiting Colorado mining towns fighting hundreds of unsanctioned bouts. Astra Film Company and Pathé paid Dempsey $1,000 a week to come to Hollywood and make action shorts. Boxing historian Mel Heimer wrote, "The Big Names of the movies became his friends. Wallace Reid was closest to him but Douglas Fairbanks was another good 'pal.' He sparred with Rudolph Valentino—whom Dempsey noted 'couldn't knock your hat off.' He and Charlie Chaplin were on a first-name basis."[82] Dempsey and Wally hung around together constantly. That summer Dempsey filmed Woodridge Van Dyke's *Daredevil Jack* and visited bars with Wally at night.

In June, Wally's contract was up for renewal, which worried Lasky. Wally was less able to work but the public knew nothing and his films were still box office gold. He offered Wally a five-year contract at $1,750 a week, which was signed in July. Some articles suggested that Wally earned $2,500. It was a huge contract but not what Wally could have commanded had he been healthy. He easily could have demanded $5,000 a week if he could have worked.[83] The contract had escalators through a fifth year but Lasky probably knew they were a moot point.

It was a month after *Lottery Man* before Wally returned to work with Lila Lee on *Hawthorne of the U.S.A.* in August. Lasky again assigned Cruze and Tate. Paramount archives list Charles E. Schoenbaum as cameraman, but period records and the actual credits identified Frank Urson and William Marshall. Wilfred Buckland did the art direction. The scenario was written by Walter Woods based on a popular 1912 James B. Fagan play that starred Douglas Fairbanks. The supporting cast included Harrison Ford, Tully Marshall, Charles Ogle, Guy Oliver, Edwin Stevens, Clarence Burton, Theodore Roberts, Ruth Renick, Robert Brower and Frank Bonner.

Jesse L. Lasky's Famous Players Studio at the time Wally signed his contract in late 1919 (courtesy Bruce Torrence, the Bruce Torrence Hollywood Photograph Collection).

Wally plays law clerk Anthony Hamilton Hawthorne, visiting the casino at Monte Carlo with his pal Rodney Blake (Ford) when Anthony breaks the bank. Anthony and Blake drive through the impoverished kingdom of Bovinia (in Wally's own two-seat roadster which he used in the film), where he meets a beautiful girl (Lee) when he stops after the wind blows off his cap.[84] Unbeknownst to Hawthorne the pitiable-looking girl is Princess Irma, daughter of King Augustus (Brower). Hawthorne is smitten and stays in Bovinia. To help the local populace Hawthorne uses some of his winnings to fund the local healing spa and is persuaded to finance a revolution instigated by conniving Prince Vladimir (Stevens) and crazed local Nitschi (Marshall). They convince him the King is evil; in truth he is as poor as his subjects, forced to beg cigarettes from his guards. While Hawthorne's group plots the coup Anthony learns the girl is the King's daughter and in danger of being assassinated. Anthony thwarts Nitschi's attempt to shoot the King and Irma during a parade but is himself accused of the crime and sentenced to death. But he bribes the guards, escapes and rushes to the palace and stops the mob by giving soldiers their back pay from his casino winnings. The revolution over, Anthony opens the spa at the medicinal springs and Bovinia prospers. When King Augustus declares the country a republic, Irma and Hawthorne are free to marry.[85] Their kiss—in the garden where they met—is the final scene.

Changes in Wally's appearance are evident from certain camera angles. He looks drawn and thin but when he first meets Lee, he is still able to easily pull himself ten feet up a tree and throw himself over a high wall to enter her garden. Leaving, he jumps up and easily re-scales the wall.

The film was released November 16th to tepid reviews. One reviewer didn't "care for this, in comparison to Wallace Reid's recent vehicles.... It simply does not measure up to the very high standard Reid's producers have set for him."[86] Viewing the film today it's difficult to find fault. It is well-paced and the story told adroitly; perhaps, as *Photoplay* noted, the bar for Wally's films was getting too high. For the large parade scene, Cruze employed hundreds of uniformed soldiers, dozens of horsemen and carriages, and 2,500 extras lining the streets waving flags. There are excellent comedic moments also. Wally offers several wonderful Chaplinesque bits mimicking the body motions and steps of his guards, and exhibits his flair for magic during a delightful scene in which he makes money "appear" to bribe his guards. But overall, he looks lifeless and visibly tired in many scenes.

The role seemed perfect for Wally but for the first time he could not carry the film. The *Photoplay* critic even suggested, "Douglas Fairbanks [,who] played it on the stage ... with his indisputable charm and personality, probably would have played it a lot better in pictures." Even such a mild criticism was a stinging rebuke for Wally.

Lasky knew he had a problem so he went back to a role he knew Wally would enjoy and would inspire him. It involved cars. Wally still owned a half dozen and was a silent partner in a Chicago dealership he visited that August.[87] He had Stutz and Marmon roadsters, a Sunbeam racer, and a LaSalle sedan custom-made by the Earl Carriage Works that made unique cars for Mary Pickford and Douglas Fairbanks, DeMille, and designed Roscoe Arbuckle's $250,000 cruiser.[88] In 1919 Wally bought his first McFarlan, "the American Rolls Royce" and the most expensive car in the U.S. Only 175 were made annually at the Connorsville, Indiana, plant. Wally's first was a McFarlan Sport Roadster, a 2-seater that cost $5,000 ($150,000 today), replaced in 1920 with a $6,000 Sport Touring Car. Only 25 McFarlans are known to still exist.

Lasky assigned Wally *Double Speed*. Fans expected a racing film like *Roaring Road* but it was a romantic comedy, not a racing movie, which disappointed many. It was originally titled *Speed Carr*, but that became Wally's character's name. Sam Wood, DeMille's assistant on 1918's *The Squaw Man*,[89] was given his first directing job. The first of five Wally films directed by Wood, it was filmed by Alfred Gilks in November between L.A. and San Francisco. Wood found ways to get Wally to work; Cruze had trouble getting his good friend motivated. Clara Genevieve Kennedy based the scenario on a J. Stewart Wodehouse story, and Wally starred with Wanda Hawley, Tully Marshall, Theodore Roberts, Lucien Littlefield, Guy Oliver and Maxine Elliot Hicks.

Wealthy heir Speed Carr (Wally) is driving from New York to L.A. to meet with his uncle, banker John Ogden (Roberts). Still 1,000 miles away, he is robbed of his belongings by highwaymen and when he arrives in L.A. is filthy. He is thrown out when he enters his uncle's bank in rags and since his uncle is away the destitute Speed takes a job as a chauffeur for Effie McPherson (Hawley),[90] daughter of the bank president (Marshall). Effie's father is awaiting his boss's nephew and is anxious to find Speed before Ogden returns. When the return is imminent Macpherson persuades Speed to pose as Speed not knowing he *is* Speed. Effie has already fallen in love with Speed over her father's objections, but when Uncle John returns everyone is happy.[91]

The movie was released February 1, 1920. Fans wanted a racing movie but apart from regular driving scenes Wally drives only as a chauffeur! The film still did well. Wally is noticeably thinner in surviving photos but his prankster side was still there. Mysterious—but excellent—sketches of the crew suddenly began simply appearing, first Hawley's pinned to her chair. Roberts found his tacked to his mirror, and pictures of Wood, Gilks and others also appeared. Wally was unmasked when Hawley crept up as he furiously sketched a portrait of a prop man. Once exposed, everyone requested and received a picture by Wally.[92]

Double Speed was the last time Wally worked in 1919. By December his parties had replaced social outings with Dorothy or publicity work for Lasky. He avoided industry functions and his name was absent from press stories about events like the Director's Ball, held in the opulent Rose Room of the Alexandria Hotel on Thanksgiving eve. It was "the biggest social event in the motion picture world...."[93] Among the 450 guests were Roscoe Arbuckle, the Pickfords, Bebe Daniels, Edna Purviance, Mary Miles Minter, Wally's *Double Speed* co-stars Hawley, Marshall and Roberts, Viola Dana, Bert Lytell, Antonio Moreno and Anna Q. Nilsson. Everyone except Wally.

Wally preferred hosting almost-nightly parties at Morgan Place, going to the beach bars or visiting a remote Laurel Canyon house off Wonderland Avenue that he rented just for parties. Dorothy stayed home trying to avoid watching Wally and his pals indulge in cocaine, morphine, and even heroin. St. Johns wrote, "Mrs. Wallace Reid cried on my shoulder because she was so bored sitting home every night in front of the fire with only an occasional dinner at the Hollywood Country Club to brighten her existence."[94] The story was probably true but the tears weren't from boredom.

Amidst it all Wally was still a doting father. He adored Billy. Bertha said his feelings for fatherhood and "happy pride can better be imagined than described."[95] Without Dorothy's knowledge Wally had begun sending letters to his mother. As they neared their third Christmas at Morgan Place he sent Bertha photos of them in the living room decorated with a huge tree and presents. One toy car he bought for 3-year-old Billy was big enough for Wally to sit in, and a second had glass windows, rubber tires, a starting crank, horn and lights! Christmas, 1919 would be the last somewhat normal holiday the Reid family would enjoy.

11

"Good-Time Wally" Faces the Abyss

As 1920 began the Reids were at Morgan Place with servants Oscar and Nora Smith, nurse Luella Bauchans and 21-year-old Pennsylvanian Vernon Peck, who Wally hired as a mechanic for his cars.[1] Alice had moved to a bungalow nearby at 1748 North Western.[2]

Weekly movie attendance had risen from 10,000,000 in 1916 to 35,000,000 in 1919, virtually destroying vaudeville and the legitimate stage. The movies drove most regional theaters out of business; adding insult to injury, most were then converted into movie houses. Movies forced stage producers to concentrate on themes movies couldn't reproduce, like sophisticated dramas and musicals that silent films couldn't duplicate. The result was a return to innovative stagecraft and a rebirth of creative local theaters, like the Washington Square Players (1915) and Provincetown Players (1916).[3] Only a few vaudeville troupes still toured, visiting mostly small, remote towns. As late as 1923, amid a dozen movie ads, was a notice reading, "SUNDAY VAUDEVILLE—SIX BIG ACTS!!!"[4] But it was dying.

The public was long-tired of patriotic war movies and sentimental post-war themes; they wanted fun. Stories of Hollywood excess—money, mansions, sex and parties—were embraced, along with Jazz Age excess as a whole. Writer Vicki Botnick noted the "'new morality' showed up onscreen in spicy yarns about infidelity, wild parties, sexual hijinks and criminal pursuits."[5] The public appetite for scandal was insatiable. "Anything goes" was the theme.

Wally's first 1920 assignment was a racing movie but unlike *Double Speed, Excuse My Dust* was a real "Wally Reid Racing Picture." *Dust* was the sequel to *The Roaring Road* that Lasky rushed into production in January, reuniting Wally with Ann Little and Theodore Roberts, both of whom played in the original. Filming would take place in San Francisco. When the pairing was announced gossip writers recalled the couple's 1918 meeting, her subsequent divorce, and the rumors. Dorothy suggested to Lasky that Billy play the role of Wally's son, a breach of her oath that he would not appear onscreen. Lasky readily agreed. She also requested a role in a Lasky film being made in San Francisco at the same time and was given a co-star role in Anna Q. Nilsson's *The Fighting Chance* even though she hadn't worked since 1917. She would appear with Nilsson, Conrad Nagel, Clarence Burton and Frederick Stanton.[6] It was a big assignment for someone who hadn't worked for three years and whose star power was limited. But she may have gotten the filming moved as well! The plot did not require the locale; the film was almost all interiors, but filming was moved to San Francisco—where Wally was filming with Little.

Sam Wood was able to keep Wally focused on *Double Speed* so Lasky assigned him *Excuse My Dust* over James Cruze, who did the original *Roaring Road*. *Dust* was written by Will M. Ritchey and based on a Byron Morgan story from the July, 1919, *Saturday Evening Post* entitled "The Bear Trap" (also the original U.S. release title). Assisting Wood was Robert Lee, and Alfred Gilks did the camera work. Supporting Wally, Little and Roberts were Guy Oliver, Tully Marshall, Walter Long, James Gordon, Jack Herbert and Fred Huntley. Writers Morgan and Ritchey had small roles.

Wally loved his racing movies. St. Johns recalled, "The movies that Wally loved were the ones where he had to do stunts—where he could ride, or drive a racing car...."[7] He was certainly excited about working with Little and was reunited with the Duesenberg from *Roaring Road* that had been brought back to L.A. by Omar Toft.

Wally reprised the "Toodles" Walden character and Little again was his wife, Dorothy. Toodles is trying to settle down but racing is in his blood. He is still managing the Darco Racecar Company owned by Dorothy's

Paramount distributed this still in 1919 and 1920, and it became one of Wally's most popular photos. Taken by popular portrait photographer Melbourne Spurr, the signature was stamped by a studio secretary, and this was probably the most-used of all of his studio photographs.

father J.D. Ward (Roberts) and testing a revolutionary engine that rival Fargot Racing is trying to steal. Two slimy Fargot managers, company president Mutchler (Marshall) and Ritz (Long), entice Toodles to enter an illegal race, where he is arrested. J.D. must sell three cars to raise money for Toodles' release and Mutchler purchases two, wrongly believing they have the secret engine. Toodles buys the last unit, nicknamed "the Cyclone." The Fargo group suspects Toodles' Cyclone has the new motor and plans to sabotage it during an L.A. to San Francisco race and steal the engine. But J.D. learns of the plot and when Toodles is summoned to San Francisco to save his sick infant they enter the new Darco car to speed there, foil the plot, and win the race.[8]

The film had what the public wanted—Wally racing across the countryside. After its March 21st release it set box-office records at theaters that ran it for a month. Some owners used dangerous publicity stunts, like W.D. Harwell of the Empress Theater in Wichita Falls, Texas, who hired a local man to drive a yellow Stutz coupe through town to promote the premier. Early on March 26, 1920, young T.B. Noble, Jr. removed the muffler from the car and donning goggles, a tam cap and scarf like Wally's, roared down the main street while hundreds of passersby looked on in terror. Noble reached 100 miles per hour before screeching to a halt in a cloud of dust in front of the theater. When police came to arrest him, 100 locals stood gaping at what reporters called "the flying meteor."

A furious judge fined him $100, paid by Harwell, who mused, "It was good publicity. We had the biggest crowd we've ever had at the Empress."⁹

Dust was so popular that writer Morgan combined the three short stories into a novel *The Roaring Road* in 1920. Director Woods turned out a great picture, not an easy task given that the physical effects of Wally's addiction were, for the first time clearly visible on camera. Even with makeup, his eyes were surrounded by dark circles and his face gaunt to the point that when he appeared in profile the outline of his cheekbones clearly visible.¹⁰

Anna Little's career has always been a Hollywood mystery. *Excuse My Dust* was the last of 11 films she made with Wally, including some of his best, like *Believe Me, Xantippe* and *The Roaring Road*. *Dust* was her 116th film in 8 years. But she made only 7 more before inexplicably exiting the movies in 1924. She lived in Hollywood until her 1984 death but never once offered a public explanation for her sudden departure. According to movie archivist Marc Wanamaker, a friend of Little's in the 1970s, "She left the film business because she became a Christian Scientist. Someone got to her and convinced her that Hollywood was sinful and being an actress was not the right thing to do, so she quit for Religion [sic]. She never mentioned Reid at all when I asked her about leaving the film business."¹¹

Wally was Hollywood's biggest international star, particularly popular in South America. A Brazilian theater chain held a contest and Wally was voted "Most Popular Actor" by a large margin, noted in *Moving Picture World* in April under the headline, "Paramount Stars Lead in Rio de Janciro [sic] Contest."¹² He was also the biggest star in Europe, his every move noted in film magazines. In England there was something about Wally in every issue of the magazine *Picturegoer*.¹³ In March he spent two weeks performing the lead in an English comedy satire, "The Rotters," at Los Angeles' Little Theatre. Papers noted Wally was "a success in vaudeville and Paramount [is] anxious to see how his voice translated into scenes."¹⁴ His appearances were all sell-outs.

During March and April, DeMille assigned Wally several light romantic comedies and another racing movie. The effects of his addictions made serious roles difficult; he could handle a romantic lead more than the exertion of a dramatic role. DeMille paired him with Bebe Daniels for the comedies *The Dancin' Fool* and *Sick Abed*, both filmed in March and April. She was an old Selig friend. Her first roles were 1910 Selig Chicago films—*The Courtship of Miles Standish* and *The Wonderful Wizard of Oz*. She made 50-plus Harold

Wally was equally popular around the world, as evidenced by this postcard from Hungary, ca. 1920.

Lloyd *Lonesome Luke* serials from 1915 to 1917, and from 1917 to 1919 she and Lloyd made another 70-plus before DeMille brought her to Paramount for *Male and Female* in 1919.[15]

The Dancin' Fool was directed by Wood and Robert Lee with a scenario by Clara G. Kennedy based on a serial from the previous May *Saturday Evening Post* written by Henry Parson Dowst. Alfred Gilks did the camera work and Wilfred Buckland the art direction. Wally and Daniels were supported by Raymond Hatton, Willis Marks, George B. Williams, Lillian Leighton, Carlos San Martin, William H. Brown, Tully Marshall, Ruth Ashby and Ernest Joy.

Wally plays country bumpkin Sylvester Tibble, who comes to New York and works for his uncle Enoch Jones' (Hatton) jug company for $6 a week. One night he wanders into a cabaret and meets dancer Junie Budd (Daniels), who teaches him some steps and takes him on as a partner after he saves her from a drunken customer. They perform at the Garden of Roses dancehall but his uncle doesn't agree with his hobby and when Wally tries to save the company from being stolen from his uncle, the man won't listen. Returning home from a lengthy trip, Sylvester discovers that rival manufacturer Charles Harkins (Marshall) is about to buy out his uncle. Denounced as a "dancin' fool" by his uncle, Sylvester nonetheless saves the business with new orders obtained by use of his modern business techniques. Sylvester enters into partnership with his uncle and is able to marry Junie.[16]

A Paramount publicity flyer described the movie: "Yes, Ves Tibble is his name; Hicksville his station. But the Gods had given him syncopated feet. One day he struck N.Y. He worked for his uncle Enoch brushing dust from moth-eaten jugs for a dollar a day and the experience until one night, while passing a little Cabaret, he smelled fresh country eggs cooking. Then a regular meal—a regular fight—a regular girl; then the dancing fool landed a $200 a week job, the uncle's jug business and the girl all won on jazz. You'll see the latest steps and fads in dancing, and then some, with watching Bebe Daniels and 'Wally' Reids [sic] own Jazz band!"[17]

The movie introduced several new dance steps. Wally was an excellent dancer; he and Dorothy were versatile ballroom dancers. His specialties were the tango and the hesitation waltz, two very difficult forms. They won dozens of dance contests popular at the time, held at the Sunset Inn, the Vernon Country Club, and Nat Goodwin's. A *Motion Picture Classic* writer who witnessed the Reids at the Sunset Inn wrote, "Wally is *some* stepper. Let me tell you the boy can dance. And when he wasn't dancing he was borrowing the musicians' instruments."[18]

When *Dancin' Fool* was released on May 2nd theaters offered a movie and a dance contest. In Chillicothe, Missouri, the Renraw Park Theater offered a "Dancin' Fool Dance" with "the best dance this season, introducing several new and novel dances and a special solo Apache Dance by the clever little toe dancer Miss Lahunta Selsor...."[19]

As soon as Wally was able Lasky pushed Wally into *Sick Abed*, another Wood-directed effort with Daniels that was filmed in April. *Sick Abed* was another breezy romantic farce offering Wally an un-challenging role. Gilks was the cameraman, and Clara G. Kennedy adapted a play by Ethel Watts Mumford. Wally and Bebe were supported by John Steppling, Winifred Greenwood, Tully Marshall, Clarence Geldart, Lucien Littlefield, Robert Bolder, Lorenza Lazzarini and George Kuwa.

Wally plays Reginald Jay, who is over 30 but still lives in the care of his guardian, real estate agent John Weems (Steppling). Traveling through Madrid, Weems spends time with a local woman and the story finds its way to his wife Constance (Greenwood). Later, while showing a female customer (Lazzarini) some property his car breaks down and he has to stay in a roadhouse with her during a storm. Constance, bored with her

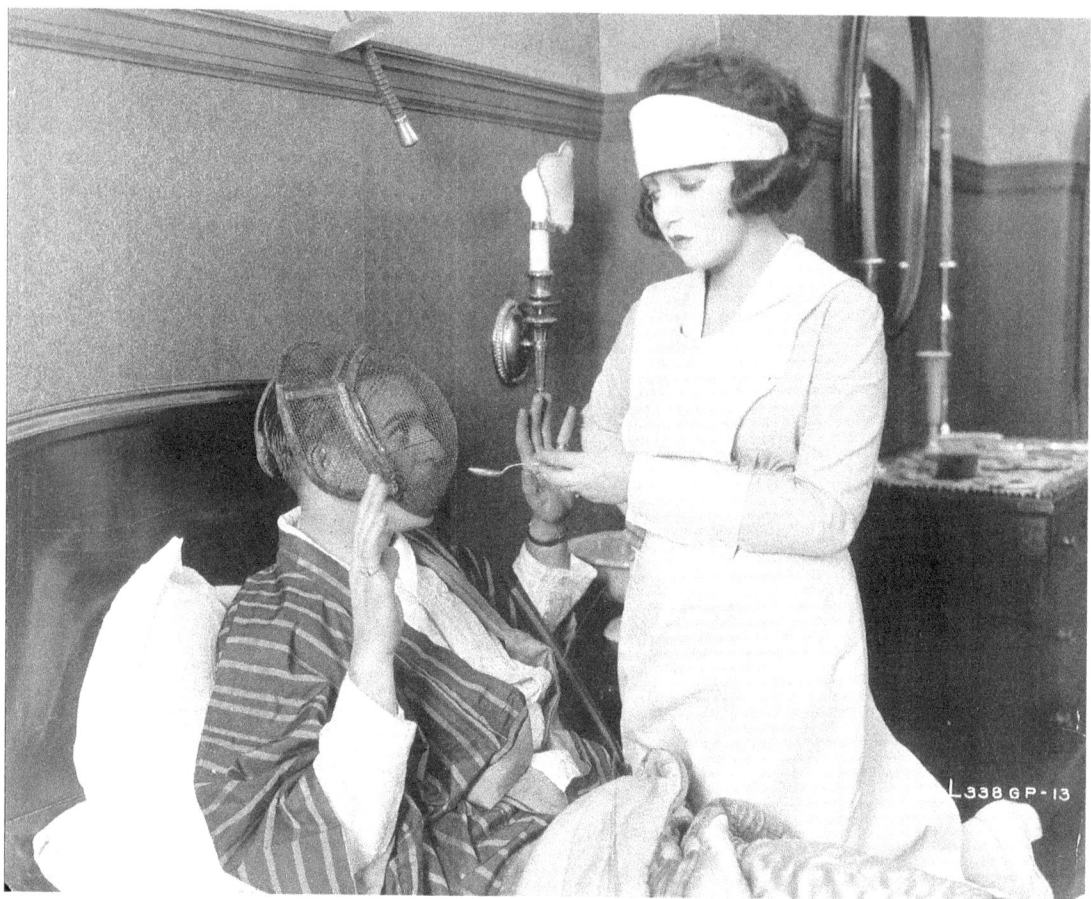

Feigning illness, Wally refuses medicine from his beautiful nurse Bebe Daniels in *Sick Abed*.

marriage, decides to divorce John and calls Reginald to testify about the incidents. Jay does not want to testify and fakes illness so he will be hospitalized and unable to appear. He hires a lawyer to gather witnesses to confirm he is suffering from nervous prostration and promptly falls in love with his caregiver, Nurse Durant (Daniels). The film centers on the farcical lengths to which Reginald goes to act sick. After several funny incidents involving Jay trying to convince doctors of his malaise to avoid testifying against his friend, Weems finds out about Reginald's plan and gives him something to make him really sick. During these machinations the Weems are somehow reconciled and Jay wins the love of his nurse.[20] The film was released on June 27th.

As he completed *Sick Abed*, Wally's father died. Just 59, on May 20th Hal suffered a fatal heart attack in New York. He was living in a mansion on Tom Hunter Road in Fort Lee, New Jersey, a fashionable area across the Hudson from New York City. In late 1917, 56-year-old Hal had married 22-year-old actress Marcella Russell. In February, 1918, they had a son, John Harold Reid, nicknamed "Hal Jr." Marcella's mother Alva lived with them.[21] Hal's death was agonizing for Wally. He called it a "source of profound sorrow to me,"[22] but he had always known of his father's weaknesses, earlier saying, "I sometimes wonder which of us is the father and which is the son. Sometimes I feel that he is my son, not I his. That's funny, isn't it? But I've had to look after him a great deal. Of course, you can't expect a man with a marvelous brain like Hal's to be just normal.

Wally with John Steppling in *Sick Abed*, with Winifred Greenwood in the background.

Genius is always overbalanced."[23] Wally took a two-week break to travel East for Hal's funeral. Fan magazines announced, "Wally Reid Back in Hollywood,"[24] when he returned in June.

A few days after returning from his father's funeral the Reids broke ground on a new home. Dorothy had spent three months working with architects designing a Hollywood mansion befitting the most popular star in the movies. They purchased a 500 foot-long lot near the western end of DeLongpre Avenue, a long boulevard running the length of Hollywood.[25] The acre-plus at 8327 DeLongpre was on a hillside below Sunset, bordered on the east by North Sweetzer. Next door, to the west, was the colonial mansion of William S. Hart.[26] Ruth Roland lived around the corner at 1446 Sweetzer.

Dorothy helped design the magnificent stucco and tile–roof mansion in a Moorish-Spanish mission style. The long, rambling two-story mansion, visible above the foliage from Sunset Boulevard above, had two large wings—each the size of a large home—connected by an atrium-like foyer filled with large arches. The entire rear of the house was large French doors opening onto the backyard gardens. The main (west) wing was for family, with bedrooms upstairs, large living and dining rooms below and servant's quarters to the rear. The master bedroom and children's bedrooms had their own private porches crowned with hand-made sun-shades.

The huge living room had a concert grand piano that could be converted into a pipe organ. In racks and cases were dozens of instruments—guitars, banjos, saxophones, a concert drum set and a case of violins and violas. In the arm of one of the over-stuffed sofas was an electric Victrola, a rare convenience in 1920 that cost $1,000. Wally owned six—there were others in the dining room, one in the master bedroom shaped as a table lamp, at the pool, and in the den. One of the music boxes played continually when Wally was home.

Off the living room was a large library, four walls of floor-to-ceiling bookcases filled with Wally's books, each marked with a bookplate he designed. He spent hours there in his favorite rocking chair. Dorothy later said, "Whenever he sat down with a book in the rocking chair he favoured, he would lose himself so completely in what he was reading that when he came to later, he would seem a bit surprised to find he'd rocked himself into the adjoining room—about forty feet from his starting point!"[27] The library opened to the living room through large French doors. A movie screen was installed so guests could sit in the living room and watch films through the doors into the den. The screen covered one of the walls and extended to the floor. Chauffer Vernon Peck picked up current movies at the studio but Wally rarely showed his own. If Billy was awake, Wally's comedies or cartoons were shown, and he was put to bed before adult features began.

The eastern wing was dominated by the large first-floor den, featuring a two-story fieldstone fireplace with an 8-foot opening. Wally called it his "bumming room."[28] In the middle of a dozen comfortable chairs was a hand-made mahogany pool table and at one end a fully-stocked restaurant bar and upright piano. On the walls hung several of Wally's pastel landscapes and one of his electric Victrolas stood in a corner. He used the den for reading and writing; his drop-head desk and typewriter stood next to the Victrola. Over his desk was a small framed card that prophetically read, "I shall pass through this world but once. Any good thing therefore that I can do, or any kindness that I can show to any human being, let me do it now. Let me not defer it nor neglect it, for I shall not pass this way again."[29] Inside a specially built closet was a movie projector and screen.

Cases held more of Wally's books and a gun cabinet his collection of 50 firearms, described by his mother as "an arsenal of fine guns and pistols for all sorts of uses—for big game and little."[30] Off the den was a combination studio–science lab where Wally indulged his fascination with all things science. He spent hours in the dark room staring into his expensive microscope and he also painted there. His landscape oils and pastels hung in some of the nicest mansions in Hollywood.

Wally had a huge in-ground pool put in the large backyard. Bordering the west side of the pool in front of the cabana was a large, sandy "beach" that fed into the pool, reportedly the first in Hollywood. There is some disagreement with that oft-made claim; Francis X. Bushman's huge

A rare early postcard view of the Reids' impressive DeLongpre mansion estate; usually pictures only offered half of the huge house (courtesy Marc Wanamaker, Bison Archives).

The back of the DeLongpre house, with Wally's beloved pool, as seen from the sidewalk on Sunset Boulevard. Fans often watched the family at play in the yard.

Whitley Heights estate was also said to have had the first in-ground pool in California when it was built some years earlier. In the 1920s pools were all the rage in Hollywood. Cowboy star Tom Mix was so proud of his he had it installed in *front* of his Benedict Canyon mansion rather than in the private acreage behind. The water in Mix's pool could be scented, or the pool drained and/or filled, by pressing buttons next to his bed.[31]

The DeLongpre house had a garage for 5 cars with a fully-equipped mechanic's station and fuel storage tanks. There were also repair pits so Vernon Peck and Wally could get beneath the cars to work on them. The house would be ready in the fall, reportedly at a cost of about $25,000 (over $1,000,000 today).

Lasky had to carefully consider Wally's assignments due to the actor's worsening health. Wally's next film was another easy assignment, a romantic comedy car movie called *What's Your Hurry* filmed in June. *Hurry* was another Byron Morgan racing story taken from the last of his three *Post* stories, "The Hippopotamus Parade." The working title of his original screenplay was *Too Much Speed* but Lasky used that on a later film. *Hurry* was directed by Wood and filmed by Gilks. Wally's co-star was Lois Wilson, with support from Charles Ogle, Clarence Burton, Ernest Butterworth, Ernest Joy and Jack Young.

In the tradition of Speed Carr and Toodles Walden, Wally plays Dusty Rhoades, a driver in love with Virginia (Wilson), the daughter of truck builder Pat MacMurran (Ogle). MacMurran won't let his daughter marry the reckless Rhoades so Dusty makes a deal with MacMurran to make his Parko Truck famous in exchange for Virginia's hand. Dusty learns that the nearby Cabrillo Dam is about to burst and flood the valley and town so he recruits racers to drive a fleet of Parko trucks full of sand and explosives. He leads them through mountain roads to the dam, drives the truck into the breach and saves the valley. The Parko Trucks become famous, and MacMurran offers Virginia to Dusty and a position of company General Manager.³²

The film premiered August 15th and nationally September 20th, and like every Wally car movie was a hit. Ads, still half or full-page with drawings of Wally behind the wheel, trumpeted, "A story that goes like blue blazes! From the Great Saturday Evening Post story "The Hippopotamus Parade" by Byron Morgan! Another Wally Reid racecar film!"³³ Wally again hired driver buddies Toft, Ralph DePalma and Jimmy Murphy for racing scenes filmed at the new Beverly Hills Speedway. On farmland north of Wilshire Boulevard between Lasky and Beverly Drives, the 1¼-mile oval made out of two-by-fours had turns banked 35 degrees. Sunday races drew 70,000 fans but the last race was in early 1924 and by 1928 the Beverly Wilshire Hotel was on the site of the second turn.

Wally's output concerned Lasky. Even though his films were 5-reelers that took a month to complete most stars made 10 or so a year. It was work to get Wally to do half that. As hard as Dorothy tried to rein in Wally he had a new problem, a growing number of hangers-on described by St. Johns as his "court, a gang of admirers, none of whom were his equals ... a gang of flattering sycophants.... The strong, cold winds of honest male companionship with men of his own class and mental caliber did not blow upon him, only the breezes of perfumed words and self-seeking adulation."³⁴

Another problem was women. It is fairly clear that Wally had numerous affairs, among them in all probability relationships with Geraldine Farrar and Ann Little. St. Johns vaguely referred to this problem as one that was difficult for him to deal with, noting that the story touched "the living, and since they must not be hurt, the subject is one of extreme delicacy. But unless it is honestly dealt with you cannot get a fair estimate of the hurricane of temptations sweeping the boy. He was not a man who cared especially for women. He had sowed no wild oats. He had passed through one sweet and worthy young love affair to a happy and complete marriage."³⁵

But he had affairs. St. Johns believed that Wally loved three women during his life—Bertha, Dorothy, and her—but even as she rationalized his temptations she opened a door to truth. Wally never *did* sow his "wild oats." He ran away from two women he loved but couldn't have and married the first woman he could. As his star rose, innumerable women threw themselves at him, and during the 1920s—tired, overworked, weakened by addictions—he was most vulnerable.

Wally still employed his personal driver Vernon Peck, but Lasky assigned him a studio driver, Benjamin "Benny" Frazee.³⁶ Wally couldn't be trusted to drive himself and Frazee was responsible for getting Wally to the studio.

Wally's physical appearance had deteriorated such that Lasky cameramen had to alter camera angles and lighting to make sure he didn't look ill on film. In the late spring of 1920, Pola Negri

An introspective Wally posed for this studio portrait, probably mid–1920, already showing the physical toll of his addictions.

wanted Wally to star in *Sumurun*,[37] which would film in July in Germany. But when she visited him and saw his condition she decided against hiring him.[38] The role of hunchback clown Buckliger went to Ernst Lubitsch. Just a year earlier, Wally had been acknowledged as the best-looking man in Hollywood.

Lasky assigned Wally three light comedies during the remainder of 1920, the first two—*Always Audacious* and *The Charm School*—directed by Wally's pal Cruze, and the last—*The Love Special*—by Frank Urson. *Always Audacious* was adapted by Thomas J. Geraghty from a Ben Ames Williams serial published in the *Saturday Evening Post* as "Toujours de L'Audace" in January, 1920 and was something of a sensation.

Although the film was a comedy Wally's role was not easy. It was a dual role, two characters with divergent personalities—a wealthy man-about-town and a petty crook, both born on the same day and as identical as twins. Cruze directed, assisted by Cullen Tate, and Wilfred Buckland did the art direction. Charles E. Schoenbaum and Karl Brown did the photography, and the film featured several of the earliest uses of camera-over technique. Scenes had audiences gasping when Wally shook hands with himself, knocked himself down and pushed himself through a doorway. He starred with Margaret Loomis, supported by Clarence Geldart, J.M. Dumont, Rhea Haines, Carmen Phillips, Guy Oliver and Fannie Midgley. The July filming was in San Francisco in August and September, with interiors at the St. Francis Hotel and at several Knob Hill mansions.

Perry Danton (one of Wally's roles) is an irresponsible scion of a wealthy San Francisco family who must prove his business acumen before he can take over the family's interests. He works for the family's lawyer Theron Ammidown (Geldart) and is earnestly trying when his fiancée Camilla (Loomis) mistakes petty criminal Slim Attucks (also Wally) for him. Slim sees he can take advantage of the resemblance and concocts an elaborate plan, installing cohorts (Dumont, Haines and Phillips) in positions close to the family. Slim has Perry shanghaied onto a steamer bound for Honolulu and takes over Perry's job and fiancée. Attucks becomes so familiar with Perry's affairs that Perry can't make anyone believe him when he escapes and returns. Perry enlists the help of a newspaper editor (Oliver) who knows the family and confronts Slim in Ammidown's office, but his own feeble understanding of his family's affairs is apparent when Slim does better on the test. To further confuse matters Perry is spotted by a banker whom Attucks robbed, and is arrested. With his reporter friend's help Perry confronts Slim in the family mansion and is again doing poorly until the family dog recognizes his true master and exposes Attucks. As Slim is led away Camilla tells Perry she knew of the deception but would not speak up until Perry proved true to the Danton motto: "Always Audacious."[39]

The press was not told Wally would be in San Francisco and for a time the crew went unnoticed among the wealthy hotel guests. One morning, Wally, dressed as a rough-looking sailor in blue overalls, a dingy black sweater, a knit sailor's cap and a three-day growth of beard, sat in the elegantly appointed St. Francis lobby. One of the guests complained to the hotel manager, "What a nerve, that creature coming in here. He should not be allowed in here." As the manager was trying to oust Wally a guest approached and told them, "Excuse me, but that's Wally Reid!"[40]

Wally's nightly parties did not endear him to the staff, either. Late one night he moved the party from his room to the roof and from atop the most glamorous hotel in San Francisco dropped eggs on unsuspecting pedestrians. Walking past a well-dressed man with an egg on his expensive bowler hat complaining to the manager, Wally mentioned to them he had seen flying chickens on the roof and walked away.[41]

The film was released on November 14th. From the U.S. to Europe audiences thrilled to the camera-over scenes. Films opening new theaters were expected to be blockbuster, especially at theaters as big as the Howard Theater at Peachtree and Pryor in Atlanta. Every studio wanted their film used for the December 13th opening of "the most beautiful picture playhouse in America," which cost $1,000,000 and offered leather seats, ornate decorations, a $30,000 pipe organ and a 35-piece orchestra.[42] *Always Audacious* was chosen with ads touting, "Wallace Reid shall have the honor of being the first star to appear on the new Howard screen, and who could have been selected to please a greater number of people than 'Wally,' as he is affectionately called by his millions of admirers all over the world." Studios took these openings seriously. The opening was attended by Governor Hugh Dorsey, Mayor James L. Key and a Paramount contingent led by Adolph Zukor, finance chief H.D. Connick, film exchange head Al Lichtman, Secretary Ralph Kohn and Publicity Director Jerome Beatty.[43]

Wally had a week off after returning from San Francisco and then began work on *The Charm School*, a comedy directed by Cruze and filmed by Charles Schoenbaum. The screenplay was written by Thomas J. Geraghty from a 1919 Alice Duer Miller novel serialized in *The Saturday Evening Post* during June and July, 1919. Filming was done at Pomona College, about 25 miles east of L.A. in Claremont, in early August. Wally starred with Lila Lee, supported by Adele Farrington, Beulah Bains, Edwin Stevens, Grace Moore, Patricia Magee, Lincoln Steadman, Kate Toncray, Minna Redman, Snitz Edwards, Helen Pillsbury and Tina Marshall.

Charm School was another light romantic comedy. Wally plays likable and fun-loving car salesman Austin Bevans, who inherits a finishing school for girls when his Aunt Polly dies. The Bevans School is failing because it is too old-fashioned. After Austin becomes Headmaster, he decides that "calculus and higher learning is antediluvian and tends to develop girls with masculine characteristics," and the greatest asset a woman can have is charm, so he replaces the previous curriculum of classics with instruction in swimming, dancing, and lessons on how to leave a room and pick up a handkerchief. Then he falls in love with beautiful student Elsie. Teachers and parents disagree with Austin and want him removed, and when a disputed will is found, the school is taken from him. Elsie's grandfather takes pity on Austin and

A mini-biography published for Wally's fans in 1920, including photos of Wally with his cars, his musical instruments, and his family.

gives him a job, and after first resenting him for accepting a job with people who thought him undesirable, Elsie later relents and takes him back.[44]

The film was released in January, 1921. One reviewer wrote, "Never was there a picture better calculated to display the endearing charms of the king of moviedom than 'The Charm School.' It picks him up and sets him down, right in the midst of a bevy of girls and shows him in all of his adorable phases. How daring, considerate, and all the rest that he is!"[45] The role was no challenge for Wally, whose films were becoming increasingly formulaic, but his millions of fans didn't care. Lasky had no choice, and churned them out. Wally's next assignment was an adventure to begin filming just after the New Year in the mountains near Yosemite. Wally was thrilled; he still loved the outdoors.

But things were going badly at home. Just days after her return from the *Always Audacious* shoot, Dorothy took Billy to San Francisco for three weeks without Wally. She waited for him to return and then traveled to where he had been, tired of her fight to prevent what had become nightly parties at Morgan Place. She later said, "Wally did not drink heavily until the following July, when I took Billy and went away for a vacation. Late in June it became very warm and the first of July I took the youngsters and went to the mountains for a month, leaving Wally at work."[46] If she wanted to punish him her strategy failed miserably. With Dorothy gone, he partied more, usually three or four nights a week, and worse, allowed a childhood friend (one of his party pals) to handle his financial affairs in her absence. When she returned the unidentified man left the family's financial affairs in disarray.[47]

In late November the Morgan Place house was sold and the family moved to the new Delongpre mansion. Wally was now living like the movie star he was, in a huge house with servants, chauffeurs, gardeners and nurses. The location changed but the evenings didn't. Even in the impressive setting Wally still couldn't say "no," and now had bigger quarters. The house-warming was a harbinger of things to come, which Dorothy called "the most terrible evening in my recollection":

> I have never on any picture lot seen so strange an assembly of humanity as gathered in our drawing room and overflowed into our kitchen that night. It was the most terrible evening in my recollection. I often wondered whether I would live to see another day. Guests began arriving about 8 or 9 o'clock. They were our friends, the people we knew. Wally's jazz band, in which he alternated with the saxophone and violin, was in full swing. There were three other boys and one girl in the organization. And, of course, there was liquor. What Christmas-time housewarming would be complete without it? Later in the evening, guests began to come from all directions at once—people neither Wally nor I had invited. They had been to other Yuletide affairs, and most of them were already under the influence of liquor. Several young men became hostile and one or two girls were ludicrous. One of the strangers barely entered the house when he insulted a young man and the two prepared to do mortal combat in our [foyer] ... to save the furniture, I was forced to ask the uninvited guest to leave the house. His wife, who had not been drinking, was more embarrassed than I, but she whispered to me that she understood.[48]

It's hard to believe a house-warming at Wally and Dorothy Reid's new mansion would be full of drunk, uninvited guests getting into fistfights. Even more incredible, Wally's only concern was that his guests had a good time:

> ... 1 or 2 o'clock in the morning I felt a touch on my arm and found Wally, hair rumpled and all out of breath from his saxophone calisthenics, standing at my elbow. "Do you think everybody's having a good time?" he whispered anxiously. He seemed very much concerned about it. I assured him I thought the party was a howling success. "Good," he said, and dashed back to his band. When we went into the kitchen to hunt some cold turkey about 4 o'clock, his arm was around my shoulders and he had to be assured, over and over again like a child, that the party had been successful, that everyone had gone away happy. My evening was completed at 4:30 when one young man came wandering back to demand a turkey sandwich.

Few people knew the death grip that morphine already had on Wally. In Hollywood in 1920 drugs were tacitly approved of and most were still legal. Mack Sennett biographer Simon Louvish wrote, "Cocaine was praised as therapeutic by Sigmund Freud and acceptable in literature as used by Sherlock Holmes ('a seven percent solution, Dr. Watson!'). Cocaine Toothache Drops were advertised openly in the 1880s ('Instantaneous Cure! Price 15 Cents!'). Coca-cola, marketed from 1886, was said to contain cocaine until 1903. Heroin, a brand name of the Bayer Company, was introduced in 1898 and used to counter the addiction to morphine, which was becoming a growing social problem in the early 1900s."[49] Cocaine was prohibited by the Harrison Act in 1914 but marijuana wasn't outlawed until 1937.

Drugs were plentiful and inexpensive. Stars used them to cure hangovers from "bathtub gin" or from fruit punch laced with 200-proof alcohol. The bigger dealers concentrated on a single studio and used a network of low-level studio employees as paid couriers. "Mr. Fix-it" served Fox, "the Man" and "Captain Spaulding" at Lasky. "Spaulding" was once arrested for selling drugs but when he threatened to name names the charges were dropped.[50] The best-known dealer was "the Count," who put heroin in peanut shells and sold them by the bag. He served the Sennett Studio and gave customers their first bag free. His most famous clients were Mabel Normand and Wally. Director Eddie Sutherland identified him as Keystone employee Hughie Faye.[51]

Faye was apparently a likable fellow. Sutherland told *Photoplay*, "Everyone who [sic] took drugs in the industry was started by this man, one of the quietest, nicest actors I've ever known. He put Mabel Normand on the junk, Wallie Reid, Alma Rubens. All three died as a direct result. Somebody would have a hangover, and he'd say, 'I'll fix it for you,' and that was that."[52] Historian Kevin Brownlow also identified Faye as the dealer that hooked Wally and described him as "one of the most dangerous men ... [but] a charming, apparently inoffensive actor on the Sennett lot."[53] Faye played minor roles in 20 Keystone films from 1915 to 1927 and lived quietly with his wife Elsie in the upscale Las Palmas Apartments at 1775 North Las Palmas. Las Palmas rents were between $55 and $100 monthly[54] ($1,500–$3,500 today), pricey for a $25-a-week bit player. Ominously, the Las Palmas Apartments were barely a mile down Sunset from DeLongpre.

In late 1920, Hollywood excess that had so enthralled moviegoers began to turn them away. Events unfolded that shook Hollywood to its foundation. Strangely, they began with two seemingly unrelated events involving "America's Sweetheart," Mary Pickford. The public was gleeful when Pickford divorced Owen Moore on March 2, 1920. Everyone wanted her and onscreen lover Douglas Fairbanks together. On March 28th a fairy tale wedding took place just weeks after her divorce, followed by honeymoon trips around the world with hundreds of thousands of adoring fans following them everywhere. But rumors swirled that the wedding was preceded by an adulterous affair. The (true) story would have ended both careers if it was public but it would have been worse had fans known Moore threatened to kill Fairbanks and that Fairbanks fled to Arizona for a month and considered going to South America for six.[55] The public also didn't know Pickford paid Moore $100,000 for a divorce. Then Mary's sister-in-law killed herself.

Olive Thomas' death offered the first public inkling that something was wrong in Hollywood. Violet-eyed Thomas was an incredible beauty born in a grimy mining town near Pittsburgh. She was a runaway bride at 14, was named "the Most Beautiful Girl in New York" at 16, and was a Ziegfeld Follies star by 17. Alberto Vargas called her "the Most Beautiful Woman in the World" and painted her as his first "Vargas Girl." She appeared in a few movies and on October 26, 1916, married Pickford's little brother Jack, a philandering drug addict. In August, 1920, in the midst of the stormy marriage Jack and Olive went to Europe and checked into the Royal Suite at Paris' luxurious Hotel Crillon. On September 20th maids found Olive nude on a pile of some of her 150 furs near an empty bottle of bichloride of mercury she swallowed in a glass of whiskey.

Friends knew the couple was in Paris looking for drugs and that Olive was despondent over her and Jack's worsening addictions and that he had infected her with syphilis, then considered untreatable. Olive had used the mercury bichloride to treat the disease for three years. Jack was a sometime actor who lived off his sister's money and was known by female studio workers as "Mr. Syphilis."[56] He brought Olive's body home and on September 24th, 4,000 people attended her New York funeral. A month later Pickford auctioned off his wife's belongings for $26,931. Mabel Normand purchased a 14-carat gold cigarette case for $50, a 20-piece toilet set for $1,425, a diamond pearl brooch and sapphire pin for $500, and a platinum set with star sapphire for $425.[57] The pathetic Pickford lived off of a $500,000 life insurance policy, married and divorced twice, and died of a drug overdose in 1933.[58]

There were by then growing murmurs that the "All-American Boy" had his own addiction. By 1920 it was an open secret in Hollywood. Just a few days after the Reids moved into DeLonpgre and Thomas' belongings were auctioned a small item appeared in *Variety* under a headline "HAD DOPE FOR SALE":

> Thomas H. Tyner, alias Claude Walton, alias Bennie Walton, was taken into custody here on a local lot with seven bundles of heroin on his person, according to the arresting officer. He was arraigned before U.S. Commissioner Long and held for $1,000 bail for a preliminary examination. It is said Tyner declared he was delivering the dope to one of the best known male picture stars on the coast and that it had been the second time he was engaged to deliver to the same star, whose wife, in the hope of having him break the habit, informed the authorities.[59]

Tyner was arrested as he attempted to enter the secured Lasky lot. Everyone in Hollywood knew the delivery was to Wally and that Dorothy had called the police. Apparently Tyner first tried to deliver the drugs to Wally at DeLongpre and when Dorothy sent him away he went to Lasky. It would have taken an astute movie fan to figure it out, but Hollywood knew. Dorothy's recollection of the Tyner incident was quite different:

> When Tyner was arrested, he admitted that he "was going to see Wally Reid." The explanation was true but the innuendo was false. Gossips immediately said the young man was taking the drugs to Wally. That was not true. Wally was not then addicted to drugs. Wally was fond of French magazines. Our chauffeur knew this young man had a large collection of such magazines. One night he brought the boy to the house and Wally bought about $20 worth ... little paper-wrapped packages fell out—bindles, they are called. "What's the idea?" Wally demanded. The boy professed innocence ... [Wally said Tyner] found "the drugs behind the moulding [sic] of the bathroom at his home and brought them here believing [Wally[would buy them." He heard stories about drug addicts among picture people. "He's coming to the studio tomorrow and I'm going to try to get him a job." So Wally arranged to meet him at the studio next morning, promising him work in the pictures. The boy was arrested "going to see Wally Reid." His wife was expecting a youngster. They were in financial straits. I helped the wife with the baby things. Wally was anxious to visit the young man at the jail, but his friends advised him against it. So gossips decided the boy's story was true.[60]

Dorothy's explanation was almost laughable. Even if one accepts that Tyner was going to see Wally about a job there is no reasonable explanation why he had drugs with him, nor how the police knew. As the story swirled and the year ended Lasky prepared to star Wally in a movie about a railroad. DeMille announced that Wally would have "an opportunity to exercise his speed propensities on something else besides an automobile, for he drives a locomotive through a thrilling episode of speedy scenes."[61] He and Lasky were using their most successful formula: Wally, speed, and thrills. Hopefully, they could keep him healthy enough to work.

Wally and Dorothy prepared for Christmas at Delongpre. Wally loved Christmas. He was, after all, just a big kid. Dorothy later remembered, "Christmas was a great time for Wally. When we were poor, or when success had lightened and removed the financial stress, it was all the same. He loved to give and loved others to give to him."[62] Writer DeWitt Bodeen later noted ominously that 1920 "would be the last Merry Christmas Wallace Reid had in that house—or any other."[63]

12

Barely Hanging On

Wally's uneven work in 1920 led Lasky to wonder whether Wally could handle *any* role heading into 1921 after his output fell from 13 films in 1917 to just 6 in 1920. And, he hadn't worked at all since September. His first 1921 assignment was *The Love Special*, a romantic drama directed by Frank Urson, filmed near Yosemite.[1] Eugene B. Lewis based the screenplay on the 1903 Frank Spearman novel *The Daughter of a Magnate*, and Charles Schoenbaum filmed. Wally starred with Agnes Ayres, supported by Theodore Roberts, Lloyd Whitlock, Sylvia Ashton, William Gaden, Clarence Burton, Snitz Edwards, Ernest Butterworth and Selma Maja.

Wally plays Jim Glover, a civil engineer for a railroad ordered to act as guide for the company's new president, Gage (Roberts), traveling with his daughter Laura (Ayres) and Allen Harrison (Whitlock), a new manager. Predictably, during their trip Jim falls in love with Laura, but Harrison is also infatuated with her. After Jim successfully arranges for Gage to get an option on the property of hermit Zeka Logan (Edwards) for a needed right of way, Harrison uses the situation to steal Laura. Harrison persuades Logan he was cheated by Jim's deal and offers a larger sum for an option himself. When Laura accidentally overhears the backhanded dealings she and Jim take a wild ride in a locomotive from the hamlet of Sleepy Cat to Medicine Bend to tell her father. The storm strands them all, coincidentally in the same hotel together, and Wally gets the girl.[2]

Ads described, "When the daughter of his boss breezed into camp she soon learned who was her engineer!" Wally actually piloted the locomotive through a Yosemite mountain pass in a blinding real-life blizzard, which must have been frightening after his accident, but he said, "It was great sport to feel the big engine pick up as I pulled the throttle but I felt lost without a steering wheel. At times when we went around a sharp curve, I would instinctively grab for the wheel, only to remember that I was in a locomotive and didn't have to do any steering."[3]

The film was released on March 20th in Los Angeles, and April 17th nationally to strong reviews and big box office. Lasky assigned Wally another film without a break, knowing that inactivity invariably led to increased drug and alcohol intake due mainly to what Dorothy described as "the convivial evenings at our new home":

> More and more friends added themselves to our evenings at home ... some barely acquaintances. They would come romping into the house ... and make themselves very much at home. Wally's liquor supply diminished rapidly during this period. The strangers sometimes ... walked out with whole quarts in their pockets. In effect, our home became a wayside inn during these months, with no cover charge and everything free. Wally would not stop them;

he was "hail fellow well met" with them all. One cold night in April, an unusually boisterous crowd came in late and demanded Wally go swimming. They all found bathing suits and splashed into our ice-cooled pool. They came out blue—but cold sober. That was one of the few nights during these months Wally slept soundly.[4]

As always, Dorothy absolved Wally of responsibility, blaming the guests:

All this time he was working, taxing his strength in the studio or on location, playing with his guests until all hours. His heart wasn't in any of this, he didn't get any "kick" out of it. He simply had the open, generous heart of a child. So when acquaintances dropped in, he would not drive them away.

Wally at the controls of the real train he piloted in *The Love Special*, with Agnes Ayres.

Movie magazines often described Wally's perfect home life, with stories about hobbies, Billy, and Dorothy. A 1921 story noted his "penchant for shooting irons and his three pet rifles the pride of his heart next to his saxophones and musical instruments."[5] Another described his fondness for golf: "Wally likes to chase the golf ball around all over the place."[6] He started playing during Dorothy's pregnancy and by 1921 was out several times a week at Griffith or Rancho Park with Oscar Smith or Benny Frazee. Fans walking along Sunset above the house often saw Wally hit golf balls from one end of the yard over his pool to the other.

After womanizing became an issue the publicity people orchestrated several *Photoplay* stories from November, 1920 to January, 1921. Dorothy allegedly wrote the first, "How to Hold a Husband." Wally's response was "How to Hold a Wife" and Dorothy's rebuttal "Coming Back at Friend Husband." The three offered insights into their real relationship. While Dorothy offers practical insights Wally's take is ill-conceived. In "How to Hold a Wife" he offered, "Tell all mankind that you have the dearest, sweetest, most charming and tolerant little wife in the world and you have put her in a position from which she cannot retreat gracefully." He also opined, "If you can get your wife to go on record that she 'believes it is a wife's duty to give her husband all the freedom he desires, to pet him, and baby him,' you'll find she'll stay put and consequently manage to be happy about a lot of things that would otherwise open the tear ducts."[7] Other platitudes offered:

- "Never question the 'seven veils' that symbolize how women look at themselves— her danger to and from men, her beauty, her intellect, her dependence, her independence, her slavery, and her liberty."
- "The most indulgent wife is the one most successfully flattered."
- "Woman is still pagan enough to want her love-life symbolized [with gifts]."
- "If a man is unfortunate enough to find his wife in the arms of another man, he shouldn't run for a gun; he should run for another woman."

Given his normal desire to please, his comments are surprising. A third installment was not originally planned but Dorothy was so angry she wrote "Coming Back at Friend

Wally with Theodore Roberts and Agnes Ayres in *The Love Special*.

Husband." To Wally's suggestion that wives are easily duped by flattery and gifts, Dorothy began, "Not so long ago, my husband undertook to tell readers how to hold a wife. He didn't say whose, but let that pass."[8] She suggested that the success of a "marriage rests entirely with the women," compares husbands to children, and advises a "School of Pre-Marital Training" where brides could study child psychology "since taking a child to raise and marriage are identical in most respects." She offers some interesting insights:

- "Don't worry about the woman who walks out of the room and slams the door. But beware the woman who shuts it quietly."
- "The greatest of all pleasures is to give pleasure to those we love. That's the reason women are happier than men if they love."
- "The woman who encourages a man's infidelity to his wife encourages his ultimate infidelity to herself. A man will nearly always be unfaithful *to* the woman he has been unfaithful *for*."
- "I like to see a self-respecting woman who can speak her little piece if she isn't properly treated."
- "The wife who does not make friends of the friends of her husband deliberately refuses the most potent bulwark of defense against outside interference."

Dorothy took dead aim at Wally saying he was "very nice. He's a lot of bother and a great deal of care ... and has a bad habit of making plans and forgetting them and leaving me holding the sack. But outside of that, he is a pretty good husband, if there is such a thing." A "pretty good husband" who needs "a great deal of care" was all Dorothy could muster, and interestingly she mentions infidelity a half dozen times in three pages. She also noted that Wally "always has and always will call" her "Mama" and her two photos of him were inscribed, "To our Mama" and "To my Mama-Dot, with all my love, Wally-boy." Not the most attractive picture of the biggest star in the movies but things weren't peaceful at home. And Wally was already appearing in public sans Dorothy.

Wally often appeared with other women, usually actresses, which wouldn't raise eyebrows outside of Hollywood. On February 14th he attended a black-tie charity event; Dorothy was conspicuous by her absence, and Wally by his date:

> It was a prize Saturday night Mardi Gras at the Ambassador.... Mary Pickford looked lovely in a pale blue silk with Douglas Fairbanks.... Rudolpho Valentino wore a Spanish cavalier's costume. Oh, but there were some devils present! Some dressed for the part, some not. Take Wally Reid, for instance. That nonchalant gentleman didn't bother advertising. He just wore evening clothes. Besides, he was in a protective mood. Had he not brought Mary McIvor Desmond?[9]

Even a *hint* that Wally was out with another woman shocked readers, as did the note that he attended a formal function in casual clothes. But fans didn't know; he still received 10,000 letters a week, now sorted by a dozen clerks. In early 1921, *Moving Picture World* voted Wally and Norma Talmadge the most popular stars in America.[10] Wally's 25,916 votes was twice the nearest competitor.

Following a short break after *The Love Special*, Wally went to work on *The Affairs of Anatol*. The film's working title was *Five Kisses*, and it was not released until September 25th, after two others—*Too Much Speed* and *The Hell Diggers*—that were made later. *Five Kisses/Anatol* is sometimes listed after those two but period papers confirmed that during February filming, "a tame leopard is featured in a scene from 'Five Kisses,' a Cecil B. DeMille picture based on 'The Affairs of Anatole [sic].'"[11] The reason for the delay is unknown; perhaps the 9-reeler took longer than expected.

Five Kisses was a massive undertaking and at $175,000 one the most expensive films ever made. DeMille directed and assigned his 12 most popular stars, led by Wally and Gloria Swanson. It was among the first advertised as having an "ALL-STAR CAST!!! The roster reads like a Who's Who!"[12] Filming took almost six weeks. Co-stars included Wanda Hawley, Theodore Roberts, Elliott Dexter, Theodore Kosloff, Agnes Ayres, Monte Blue, Bebe Daniels, Lucien Littlefield, Julia Faye, Raymond Hatton, and Polly Moran. In supporting roles were Alma Bennett, William Boyd, Elinor Glyn, Winter Hall, Fred Huntley, Ruth Miller, Charles Ogle, Guy Oliver and Maude Wayne. Alvin Wyckoff and Karl Struss filmed, Howard Higgin was the production manager and Paul Uribe the art director. The Jeanie Macpherson scenario was only loosely based on the 1893 Arthur Schnitzler novel. The film was controversial, risqué and full of jaw-dropping jazz-age decadence. DeMille was pushing censors.

Swanson had misgivings though. Just a month earlier she had given birth to her first daughter and was still carrying 20 (visible) extra pounds on her tiny frame. Her husband Herbert Somborn[13] didn't want her to do the film but DeMille begged her.[14] Ben Hecht was told by a mutual friend that she was extremely concerned about Wally's increasing instability and became even more worried after watching him work.[15]

Wally plays socialite Anatol de Witt Spencer, on his honeymoon with coquettish bride Vivian (Swanson). Visiting the Green Fan speakeasy he sees his grade school sweetheart Emilie (Hawley), who has become the sex toy of flamboyant older man Gordon Bronson (Roberts). To Vivian's dismay, idealistic Anatol tries to rescue the seductive

Emilie, taking her from Bronson and putting her in an apartment and introducing her to culture. But he realizes she just wants his money, deceiving him into thinking she will leave Bronson and throw his expensive diamond gifts into the river. When she returns to Bronson, Anatol destroys the apartment and then takes Vivian to the country, "where people are honest and decent." But once there, he repeats the process with Annie Elliot (Ayres), who has been thrown out by her husband Abner (Blue) for stealing church money to buy lingerie. Despondent, she jumps from a bridge.

With Bebe Daniels as the seductress "Satan Synne" in *The Affairs of Anatol*.

She lands next to the Spencer's canoe and Anatol saves her, but she repays his kindness by stealing his wallet. As she kisses him good-bye Vivian returns with a doctor (Ogle) and sees the kiss. At a party, jealous Vivian allows herself to be hypnotized, and Anatol, convinced she is being unfaithful seeks out New York's most amoral woman, Satan Synne (Daniels), for his own affair. The mysterious Synne uses men and keeps a leopard as a pet but is really a loving wife of a disabled soldier trying to gather $3,000 to pay for a needed operation. When Anatol learns the truth he gives her the money and returns to make peace with Vivian, finding that she has been carrying on with his best friend (Dexter).[16] But he realizes he loves her, and they reconcile and embrace.

The sexual themes and decadence were uncommon for the time. DeMille offered women smoking, drinking during Prohibition, aggressively pursuing men and exposing their bodies, and presents open debauchery. Swanson's and Daniels' costumes barely concealed their breasts and Daniels lies across a couch with a single hand over a breast. Wyckoff and Struss filmed exotic double-exposures that showed a waterfall that a hypnotized Swanson "sees" at her feet, and Wally peering into a mirror at a skeletal image of himself. Art director Uribe was assisted by artist Romaine de Tirtoff Erte, who provided a visual feast of exotic and opulent costumes, and almost orgiastic, elaborate speakeasy and party scenes. No expense was spared. When Anatol wrecks Emilie's apartment he destroyed $30,000 worth of furniture, smashing a set of original Louis XVI chairs, a grand piano, lamps, mirrors, tables, a desk and a magnificently carved phonograph. He tossed a sofa through a set of ornate French windows.

The film was released on September 11th at 9 reels and 117 minutes, almost twice as long as typical films. Originally it was even longer; the original title (*Five Kisses*) referred to the number of Anatol's affairs. A fifth sequence with Dorothy Cumming was cut by DeMille. After Zukor saw the film he told reporters it was "undoubtedly the best thing we have ever done with the greatest cast ever assembled for one picture," but it received mixed reviews. *Motion Picture Classic* skewered the film and criticized the "crudity and even clumsy vulgarity. We look upon 'The Affairs of Anatol' as the worst massacre since Custer's forces were wiped out by the redskins."[17] But it grossed $1,191,789.19.[18]

A pensive Wally with Ruth Miller in *The Affairs of Anatol*.

Lasky described some of the challenges faced during filming and indirectly ascribed them to the Wally problem:

> It was no easy task for the photographers to get the best effects from their cameras with a picture which includes such famous stars as Wallace Reid, Gloria Swanson ... every one of these luminaries offered an individual problem. Wallace Reid has certain lighting arrangements under which he appears to best advantage. Gloria Swanson requires an entirely different gradation of lights ... a seemingly impossible task of synchronizing lighting effects ... showing each to their best advantage ... [and] each important character had his or her favorite make-up style. One ... has a decided preference for yellow grease paint while another favors pink.[19]

Wally never before worried about camera angles but his rapidly declining physical appearance was obvious. Cameramen Wyckoff and Struss were hard-pressed to find an angle that showed a healthy-looking Wally. For the first time he looked weak and drawn, especially around the face. He was also heavily made up, with painted eyebrows and lipstick. *Anatol* showed that Wally was sick and getting worse. Swanson wrote in her memoirs, "although I never saw him take drugs, his behavior never seemed quite right during 'Anatol.'" His behavior and demeanor "gave [her] the jitters."[20]

Wally made a rare public appearance in late February at the Washington's Birthday races at the Los Angeles speedway. St. Johns described the visit for *Photoplay*[21]: "Everybody was at the Washington's Birthday races at the Los Angeles Speedway...." Attending were May Allison, Tom and Nell Ince, Elinor Glyn, Mabel Normand (St. Johns noted her recent return from a "rest cure" which was likely a rehab stint), DeMille and his wife, Jack and Lottie Pickford, Tom Mix, Hoot Gibson, Douglas Fairbanks and Antonio Moreno. Wally spent the afternoon in the pits with his driver friends, with a Lasky cameraman getting exteriors for his next film.

Lasky used Wally for publicity when his health permitted but it was often difficult finding an opportunity. But on March 12th Wally attended the opening of a theater in Vancouver, British Columbia, taking the train up the coast. Magazines noted, "Wally Reid Given Ovation at Opening of Vancouver Theater"[22] and local papers reported:

> On opening night of the Capitol Theatre, March 12, 1921, famous silent film star Wallace Reid, "the most popular screen idol in America," burst through a paper screen singing and dancing to great applause. The Roaring Twenties were ready to roar.[23]

Wally returned to L.A. for the much-anticipated March 15th premier of *The Four Horsemen of the Apocalypse*, the film that rocketed Rudolph Valentino to fame. Wally's popularity was again evidenced in the attendee list; he was the third name mentioned behind Tom Moore and Mabel Normand, among Tom Mix, Louis B. Mayer, Mack Sennett and Charlie Murray.[24] Conspicuous by her absence was Dorothy, who remained at home. Again.

Lasky next returned to Wally's most popular genre with a sequel to *What's Your Hurry*. *Too Much Speed*, another adaptation from a Byron Morgan *Saturday Evening Post* story, was filmed in late March. This time the magazine story was based on the movie instead of the other way around; the *Post* published the story on May 28th before the movie premiere. The original title was *Watch My Smoke*.[25]

The theme—racecar driver trying to win the girl's heart over the objections of her curmudgeon father—repeated the formula from *Roaring Road* and *What's Your Hurry*, with Theodore Roberts again the "grouchy old duffer with a heart as big as a house."[26] Agnes Ayres replaced Ann Little and co-stars included Jack Richardson, Lucien Littlefield, Guy Oliver, Henry Johnson and Jack Herbert. Frank Urson directed and Charles Schoenbaum did the filming. The racing background scenes were filmed by Wally and a cameraman during the Washington's Birthday races.

Wally is again "Dusty" Rhoades, now engaged to Virginia (Ayres), daughter of Patrick MacMurran. Dusty has retired from racing to please his future father-in-law but his ego allows him to be goaded into a race by Tyler Hellis (Richardson), the owner of the competing Ronado Car Company. He is trying to secure the same South American order that MacMurran's Pakro Company desires. Rhoades' car ends up in a ditch, and worse the elder MacMurran had seen the two cars careen down the road and refused to let his daughter marry the reckless Rhoades. With the wedding cancelled, Dusty and Virginia elope in a Pakro car pursued by MacMurran. Dusty and MacMurran are both arrested for speeding and Dusty spends two nights in jail after MacMurran bails (only) himself out. Dusty secretly buys a Pakro car that has been idle for two years and enters the big race. A furious MacMurran is powerless to stop him and Dusty and mechanic Jimmy Rodman (Littlefield) defeat the Ronado entry and win the South American contract. MacMurran then allows Virginia to marry Dusty.[27]

Wally did his own driving and again Santa Monica streets and the new Speedway provided backdrops. Dangerous race scenes required cameraman be tied to the inside or outside of the cars, and as Wally raced at 110 miles per hour these poor souls furiously cranked their cameras. *Too Much Speed* was released on June 5th,[28] advertised as "A story of love and racing cars and a daredevil driver who proved a fast worker in both." It was well-received by fans and another financial success for Lasky's biggest star.

Wally in a popular role, as Dusty Rhoades in *Too Much Speed* alongside good friend Lucien Littlefield.

Every night Wally either partied at his favored beach bars or hosted an open house at DeLongpre. Correctly sensing he had to get as much out of Wally as he could before his movie star collapsed, Lasky assigned Wally to back-to-back films. During the first six months of 1921, Wally would make four films and began shooting a fifth, all taxing shoots done without a break. *The Love Special* meant bitter cold in the Sierras, *The Affairs of Anatol* was a lengthy 9-reeler, and *The Hell Diggers* meant a month in searing northern California heat. Though later 1921 assignments *Don't Tell Everything* and *Rent Free* were 5-reelers and less strenuous fare, the year taxed Wally's emotional and physical strength.

By the end of the year he was dying but that was apparently of little concern to Lasky as he continued the 1921 schedule. The reality was that he had to use his most popular asset even if it meant killing him. From *Too Much Speed*, Lasky rushed Wally into *The Hell Diggers*, which began in mid–April with a trip to Northern California along the Sacramento River near Lodi. *Hell Diggers* was written by Byron Morgan based on his *Saturday Evening Post* story of October 2, 1920. Wally starred opposite Lois Wilson in the Frank Urson–directed film, supported by Alexander Brown, Frank Leigh, Lucien Littlefield, Clarence Geldart and Charles A. Post (as "Buddy" Post).[29] Charles Schoenbaum filmed.

The title *Hell Diggers* described the enormous dredges used to find gold. The massive machines were great floating ships that winnowed gold from the ground's surface down to bedrock and then moved on, leaving in their wake an environmental disaster. Soil was left at the bottom, with huge stones on top, the land unfit for agricultural use. The mining companies turned once-lush farmland into miles-long gravel pits.

Wally plays Teddy Darman, construction superintendent of the Continental Gold Dredging Company managed by Calthorpe Masters (Leigh), a bitter, miserly old man who lent money for a dredging operation. Darman falls in love with Dora Wade (Wilson), the daughter of John Wade (Brown), leader of a group of farmers (including Geldart, Littlefield and Post) bitterly opposed to the destruction done by Darman's machines. As he falls for Dora and becomes sympathetic to the farmers' plight he is caught between his job and love for Dora. Darman designs a machine that will re-soil the land as it digs. Masters won't have anything to do with it so Teddy takes his invention to Dora's father, who along with fellow farmers mortgages land for a prototype. But Masters arranges for one of his employees to blow it up which means the farmers may lose their gold claim. Wally leads them in a fierce battle with Masters and his miners, climaxing in a thrilling gunfight after Wally converts a dredging machine to a moving fortress to storm and capture the men intent on stealing their claim. Teddy and Masters face off in the middle of the epic battle, Teddy winning as the sheriff arrives. Masters agrees to use the new machine while Ted wins Dora and is made general manager of the company.[30] *Hell Diggers* was well-received after its September 4th release.

Earlier in April Lasky had announced that Wally would "go to New York to appear with Elsie Ferguson in Paramount's screen adaptation of 'Peter Ibbetson.'"[31]

Wally during filming of *Hell Diggers* before leaving for *Forever* filming in New York.

After *Hell Diggers*, Wally had a week off before leaving for a two-month *Ibbetson* shoot but had to attend the American Society of Cinematographers ball at the new Ambassador Hotel, "THE social event of the season."[32] Every major star attended. Roscoe Arbuckle led the orchestra and the audience howled at his final dance, described by St. Johns in *Photoplay*: "with a lovely little Follies girl. The rotund comedian had had a hard day, the evening had been long and rather wet[33] and Roscoe went to sleep on the floor, resting his head gently against his partner's rosy cheek and continuing to move his feet occasionally to the music." Attendees included Pauline Frederick, May Allison, James Kirkwood, Lois Wilson, Thomas Meighan and Frances Ring, Alla Nazimova, Elinor Glyn, Gloria Swanson and Jack Mulhall. "Mr. and Mrs. Wallace Reid were guests of May Allison," but amidst the hoopla there were more rumblings that something might be amiss with Wally Reid.

On May 25th, L.A. papers ran a story of the arrest of a small-time drug courier delivering product to a "prominent actor" everyone knew:

> Trailing a suspect in a taxicab to the home of a prominent actor in Hollywood, officers arrested Joe Woods, 34, a notorious narcotic distributor, and confiscated $1000 worth of morphine.... They followed him in a police automobile to Hollywood and took him into custody in

the pretentious home of the actor while he was attempting to sell his wares. Woods, who is well known to them as a narcotic peddler ... but ... officers declined to reveal the name of the actor. It was explained by them that the actor was neither an addict nor a distributor, and played no part in the arrest of the suspect.[34]

Woods was arrested *in* the DeLongpre house on the eve of Wally's departure for New York. The story quickly circulated through the Lasky lot where everyone knew Wally was leaving for New York and that an addict would need a lot of morphine—at least $1,000 worth—for a two-month shoot. Wally went to New York alone. Dorothy later explained, "I wanted to accompany him, and now I wish I had. But I feared the hot weather would be hard on Billy and couldn't bear to leave him behind. So Wally went alone."[35] St. Johns wrote that Dorothy changed her mind at the last moment, that "Bill had had a hard siege of whooping cough and it didn't seem safe to take him East into the summer heat. Nor could his mother leave him. So she stayed. And Wally went alone."[36]

Wally didn't want to go, for reasons real and imagined. His alcohol and drug intake had been prodigious and his health was suffering. For the first time in his life he was rather desperately ill. St. Johns said his nerves "were strung to the breaking point by the continual rebellion within ... over the life he was leading. His physical condition was beginning to show the result of the pace he was living...." To make matters worse, just before leaving he had nine teeth removed (done over three days) and his weakened system didn't respond well. He was home for over a week recuperating and when he left was in constant pain.

Summer in New York was insufferably hot and humid, weather that he despised, and he knew there would be no privacy and much unwanted attention. The latter worsened his insomnia, making him more willing to party. He loved a party but didn't particularly enjoy the clamor of New York; he preferred the relaxation of California. And he did not want to work with Fitzmaurice or Elsie Ferguson, both of whom he disliked. His attitude would mean reciprocal feelings from his director and co-star, so filming would be tense. When people didn't like him and he felt it, he responded by "putting his worst foot forward," according to St. Johns.

Lastly, he didn't like the role. He abhorred having his hair marcelled (jelled) every day, which St. Johns said made him feel "overpowered once more by the nature of his profession, the futility of his work, and the unmanly quality of the things which he was doing." He described his concerns to Louella Parsons, who, like St. Johns, loved Wally:

> Mr. Reid is a little worried over his part in "Peter Ibbetson." "They have me dissolved in tears most of the time. My public expects to see me in comedy and I wonder how they are going to like this tragedy. I am not very fond of gloom myself and I think I understand how my friends in the small towns feel." These Main street habitués are very important to Wallace Reid. Whereas the average motion picture favorite is more interested in what Broadway thinks of him. Mr. Reid is far more concerned with Keokuk, Iowa, or Oscaloosa [sic], Mich. These are the people who are responsible for his popularity, and he does not forget it.[37]

Wally stopped at St. Johns' Hollywood home on his way to the train. He had promised her young daughter Elaine that he would say "good-bye" and she and "Uncle Wally" spent several hours playing on the floor. St. Johns recalled, "He looked thin and drawn, ill and unhappy. A premonition of danger and disaster hung over him. 'I wish I hadn't agreed to go,' he said but he promised he was 'going on the wagon for the whole trip.'"

One interesting piece of the Wally puzzle is his apparent self-awareness that he did indeed have a problem. While he never controlled it he was not like many addicts who pretend they are in control. He knew he was a prisoner and powerless to stop it. Perhaps Wally had the same foreboding about the trip as St. Johns. He left Dorothy a photo that

Left: Wally and Bertha during his short, and last, visit to his beloved Highlands family home, on his way to film *Peter Ibbetson* in New York City. Though he was there for almost two months, he rarely saw his mother. *Above:* Wally during his last visit home to Highlands.

Dorothy hung over her desk for the rest of her life, signed "To our Mama, Wally's and Bill's, with all my devoted love, Your Wally-Boy."

Wally traveled with a male secretary, a publicity person, and several large steamer trunks. One contained clothes and the other was full of toys: violins, saxophones, magic tricks, books, and the Victrola he took to every set on which he worked. Unbeknownst to Dorothy but probably in desperate need of family, Wally visited Highlands during the trip. He was still in the middle of the feud entering its second decade, but wired Bertha he was coming and also several times during the trip. When he disembarked at Penn Station and saw her he picked her up like one would a little child and kissed her. Driving to Highlands, their car was followed by several cars of reporters and photographers. The locals recognized their old neighbor, waved and yelled, "Wally! Wally!" It was like a parade as he waved back. He described his homecoming to Parsons:

Mr. Reid said he had been at Sea Gate with his mother ever since he came to town. "Mother never stopped talking from Sunday night until Tuesday morning," laughed Mr. Reid, "She hadn't seen me in three years and she had so much to say. Last time Dorothy and the baby came with me and she directed her attentions to them; but this time she had me alone and she made up for lost time." [Parsons said,] "You look like you enjoyed her long conversation." Wally replied, "The best time I have had in months. It's great to be with your own people and of course there isn't any one like one's mother."[38]

He spent several days at Highlands with his favorite aunts, Maude and Emma (who cared for him like a child), his uncle Fred, and his 82-year-old grandmother he called "sweetheart Mary Virginia."[39] He left for New York on the 20th for the *Ibbetson* shoot. His arrival was timed to coincide with the second annual Paramount Eastern Studio distributors meetings, which Lasky ordered him to attend. On the evening of the 20th he and Elsie Ferguson were masters of ceremony at a dinner in the Commodore Hotel ballroom with Thomas Meighan, Alice Brady, Constance Binney and Reginald Denny also attending. Wally played the saxophone with the orchestra and performed with Binney and Wallace McCutcheon in a movie satire by director Kenneth Webb.[40] He played a cameraman. There was a dancing contest "from which Wally was barred from competing"[41] and Lasky set up a film processing lab in the basement that produced a half-hour movie of the evening that was played for the people.[42]

Wally took a suite at the Commodore for a week before renting a furnished apartment on 5th Avenue. On his piano was a framed photograph of Dorothy and Billy. For the first time he was mobbed everywhere he went. When the address of his rented apartment was publicized he wading through crowds just to go out, but even though he was physically falling apart he was still nice to all. A Parsons *New York Telegraph* column described his conflict:

> Wallace, mobbed on Fifth avenue [sic] by female shoppers when he strolled last week, was not in the least impressed at the commotion he caused. He was much more thrilled over Pat Casey, a traffic cop, who threatened to arrest the cameramen for taking his picture. "It's against the law for us to take a man's picture against his will," said Pat, "and us Irish has to stick together. Ain't it right, Mr. Reid?" Mr. Reid explained the cameraman was Famous Players–Lasky and ... it was part of his business. He did agree with Pat that the women who congregated to gaze upon him were a nuisance ... how bored this all makes the man who thinks being called a matinee idol is a deadly insult.[43]

Wally honestly believed that women liking him was "bunk," as he called it. He was not flattered with the fawning; he was much more interested in whether his films were accepted.

Forever was an adaptation of the George De Maurier novel *Peter Ibbetson*[44] and the 1915 London play by John Nathaniel Raphael. George Fitzmaurice directed and Wally starred with Elsie Ferguson.[45] The all-star cast included Montague Love, George Fawcett, Dolores Cassinelli, Paul McAllister, Elliott Dexter, Barbara Dean, Nell Roy Buck, Charles Eaton and Jerome Patrick. The scenario was adapted by Fitzmaurice's wife Ouida Bergère and Constance Collier, the art direction was by Robert M. Haas, and Arthur Miller filmed. The film's budget was $200,000.

Wally plays Gogo Pasquier, son of a Parisian chemist (Dexter) and childhood sweetheart of Mimsi Seraskier (Ferguson). He is adopted by English rake Colonel Ibbetson (Love) after the death of his father and mother (Dean).[46] Taken to England and re-named Peter Ibbetson he grows up in a self-indulgent, loveless environment repulsed by the Colonel's debauchery-filled lifestyle. He becomes an architect and is hired by the Duke of Towers (Patrick) to design a building. When the Duke invites him to the theater he is reunited with Mimsi, who is now the Duchess of Towers. In the dressing room of a dancer (Cassinelli) Peter quarrels with his uncle Seraskier (McAllister), who asserts that Peter is actually *his* son and in a later encounter Peter accidentally kills him in self-defense. Although he is tried and sentenced to hang the sentence is commuted to life imprisonment through the influence of the Duchess. Both grow old but their dream life continues on film. After Mimsi dies saving children from a burning orphanage she returns to Peter after his death and the two are reunited forever.[47]

Bertha visited the set, the first time she had even seen Wally act.[48] *Forever* premiered in New York on October 16th (nationally the following March) and did well but critics panned it. Wally's concerns about the role were well-founded. Cameraman Miller's work was called "photographically the best that ever graced the silver screen"[49] but the *Atlanta Constitution* questioned whether fans could accept Wally in a wig, asking, "Can you imagine Wally Reid in a wig? Well, prepare for the worst. In 'Peter Ibbetson' ... he hides his sleek hair with a mane that will make picture fans of the feminine gender shudder when they view it.... It is certain that Wally will not satisfy them in 'Peter Ibbetson' but Wally says that he is going in for the art and he doesn't care a fig if his wig doesn't make a hit."[50] His acting was described as "his most pretentious attempt at romantic acting wherein he had to rely on his chief stock in trade for facial expression—the arched eyebrow." But other reviewers, blaming "unfortunate casting for Wallace Reid," said that "all-in-all he does unusually well."[51]

One particularly unflattering review led to oft-mentioned rumors about Wally's sexuality. A reviewer noted derisively, "Wally Reid climbs into a fighting arena at the Dock Wolloper's Sporting Club and knocks out a professional pug twice his size. And, later he overcomes five stagehands. If all of that isn't bunk, what is?"[52] The off-handed insult to Wally's masculinity led to other stories and more questions. His coterie of male buddies at his always open house was usually noted and St. Johns herself casually described how the "manliness of his predesessors [sic] may have been 'bred out' of him."[53] It's easy to question sexuality and Wally did indeed appear un-manly at times. His childhood was marked by instability and missing parents, the care of nannies, and often living in hotels. From age 2 to 4 his parents left him with his grandparents and he went to boarding school as a teenager. As a child he was a social misfit—he spoke with grown-up language inappropriate for and usually misunderstood by his fellow children. But the circumstantial evidence doesn't come near proving that Wally was anything but heterosexual.

Like most of Wally's films no print of *Forever* (which was also known as *Peter Ibbetson*) is known to exist. Dorothy held the only print until late in life and generously donated it to a proposed museum in Hollywood along with a copy of *Roaring Road*. Incredibly, when the museum failed to materialize and the collection dispersed the films had disappeared.[54]

Wally couldn't keep his promise to St. Johns to "stay on the wagon" in New York. Dorothy deluded herself that Wally first used drugs during this visit but it's impossible to believe she didn't know earlier. His New York life varied little from his Hollywood life. Like DeLongpre the 5th Avenue apartment was an open house with nightly parties and he frequented illegal speakeasies and legitimate clubs, like Club Richman, Barney Gallant's, the Silver Slipper, Texas Guinan's, Perona's or Jerry Docker's. There was Harlem too, when things closed downtown, and Connie's Inn, Small's and the Cotton Club.

Wally also attended several sporting events. On July 2nd he watched the championship fight between Jack Dempsey and Georges Carpentier in New Jersey. Writer Alfred Cohn later recalled the evening and Wally's sense of humor, writing, "One incident which

Wally left an inscribed copy of this photo with Dorothy when he left for the *Forever* shoot that he did not want to do. Her favorite image of him, she kept it with her for the rest of her life.

was both funny and tragic sticks in my memory. The scene was Boyle's 30 Acres in Jersey City during the famous Dempsey-Carpentier fight. When the handsome Frenchman landed his one effective blow on the then unpopular champion, the crowd rose to its feet and demanded Jack's knockout. At this moment Ivan St. Johns and Wally Reid, members of our party, arrived. Both had stopped en route for a few snifters. The handsome and lovable Wally smiled happily as he sat down, turned to me and said, 'Gosh, that was a great hand they gave me, wasn't it?'"[55]

Ivan was Adela Rogers' writer husband but they spent most of the time apart. He was the west coast editor of *Photoplay* and owned a successful advertising agency, arranging Wally's endorsements including a string of free Stutz Bearcat coupes. He also arranged for Gloria Swanson to use face creams and Stan Laurel and Oliver Hardy to smoke Omar cigarettes, all for large fees.[56] He was one of Wally's close friends and traveled to New York at his wife's request to check up on Wally but was quickly caught up in the party life (note Cohn's comment that they arrived under the influence).

If he wasn't working or partying Wally had to do publicity work. On June 21st, in the middle of filming Wally and several Lasky stars took a three day trip to Cleveland for of all things, the closing of the Ziegfeld Theater. Wally led "a coterie of Paramount stars for a gala evening at the Theater roof gardens, along with Thomas Meighan, Elliott Dexter, Agnes Ayres and French comedian Max Linder. Wally performed an impromptu 20-minute Terpsichord recital for the 200 revelers."[57] Wally was physically and mentally exhausted when he returned to Hollywood at the end of July. Before leaving New York, though, he bought a $48 battery-operated pool motorboat for Billy, one of 50 of all sizes that Wally bought for his son's fleet.[58]

Dorothy offered her version of the New York sojourn in a later interview with William Parker just before Wally died. Parker noted, "Wallace Reid ... contracted the morphine habit in New York City.... It had been the public belief, and a conviction which had spread nation-wide, that the handsome actor had become a narcotic addict in Hollywood."[59] Dorothy described his New York nights as "all sorts of people began dropping into his apartment, from the studios, from the newspapers and from everywhere. It must have been a perpetual open house. Wally ... was too thorough a gentleman to show his annoyance. And so elaborate parties were given in Wally's apartment without his consent. Friends who came back from the East told me they had seen Wally slip out of the house at the height of the festivities and remain away until his 'guests' had gone."[60]

Wally's insomnia was awful during his stay and was worsened by drugs, which left him exhausted. His weakened condition led to a cold that almost resulted in pneumonia, but he still worked. Dorothy used this illness as the linchpin for her theory, saying, "During this severe cold he was attended by a New York physician ... who kept Wally on his feet by administering drugs. I imagine that Wally, believing his will power stronger than the insidious ravages of the drugs, bought morphine and administered it to himself. Please understand Wally did not desire a 'kick.' He was not maliciously drugging himself. He used drugs, then and always, simply to keep on his feet and to be able to go about his work ... that is the terrible thing that Wally began to fight in those weeks in New York." St. Johns offered a similar story, that a "doctor in New York had given Wally some 'sleeping powders' to help him conquer the 'white nights.' He had come to depend upon them."[61]

When he arrived home in July the physical and mental tolls were evident. Dorothy and St. Johns met him at the train station and St. Johns said the horrific change "in him appalled me. It was like meeting a stranger or seeing a dear friend through a thick veil. Dorothy had sensed the thing, naturally much more quickly and deeply than I had. A little white mask seemed to have slipped over her radiant face. The change in Wally after that New York trip was apparent to everyone close to him. An indescribable, baffling something surrounded him which no one could understand. It was as though some malignant fairy had transformed him with one wave of her want into a distorted image of his former self ... suddenly he had crashed. The gradual decline of the next few months, the crumbling of the physical man, the dimming of the things in him that were so wonderful and so lovable, were enough to make the angels weep."

Dorothy, heartbroken and concerned, said, "When Wally returned from the East he was not the same Wally Reid I had known when he left Hollywood. He seemed to possess a dual nature. To me he had been always the affectionate suitor. Now there was a change. For no apparently accountable reason he would become irritable, morose, strange ... a complete metamorphosis of his former self. He was undergoing agonies of mental suffering. He grew sullen, dogged, miserable, unhappy. His outlook on life was distorted. He spoke spitefully of his friends, accusing them of caring for him 'only for what they could get out of him.' He appeared to doubt my love. His opinions were very biased. He suspected everybody of ulterior motives. It was a nightmare of distrust."[62]

Wally was exhibiting the paranoia of a person under a terrible siege of drug addiction. Friends also approached Dorothy wondering if "Wally isn't using drugs?" And when she intercepted telegrams from New York written in "mysterious terms" containing notes about "shipping" she realized he was receiving drugs at the house and confronted him. She said, "I was deeply puzzled. Before long rumors began to reach me. A wife, as every one knows, is oft times the last to hear the truth about her husband. I determined this should not be the case in the Wallace Reid family. I went to Wally and asked, 'Wally, are you using drugs?'"[63] She said she had "never seen emotions flash so swiftly over a man's distorted face. Trapped fear, doubt, dumb questioning and sorrow all were written there. He flew into a childish tantrum of rage. He paced the floor, denying his addiction, firing questions at me, accusing me of all sorts of things. 'You don't love me any more,' he cried. After a while he quieted. But I had seen the guilt written in his eyes." But he still denied it, saying "Don't believe a word you hear. I am not."

Dorothy probably knew he was lying but she was "not convinced ... knew something was wrong and was resolved to get at [sic] the bottom of it." But she was also in denial, saying, "I do not think Wally really meant to lie to me. I think it was more of an effort on his part to deny to himself the possibility of his ever allowing the drug to gain a definite foothold."

Wally grew more fitful. According to Dorothy, "All of his life Wally has been intensely restless. I don't believe he has ever had what would be termed a good night's rest. In reading he is constantly crossing one leg over the other and shifting about in his chair. This restless condition became accentuated. The realization must have dawned on him that he had fallen into the pit. He began to drink. He had never been a steady drinker, his drinking being confined to social occasions. Now, however, he seemed suddenly to have an appetite for whisky. What was really going on in his consciousness, no doubt, was the awakening to his danger from the drug. Eventually he confessed to me he was using morphine."

Dorothy was tender and considerate after that first confrontation. She said, "The argument for me was closed. I never mentioned drugs again until ... months later, when he confessed to me and begged for help in fighting back." She recalled the night that Wally confessed: "It had been such a terrible day; he had been so unreasonable. As usual he was awake far into the night. I was aroused by the soft touch of his hand on my hair. He was sitting on the edge of my bed, beside himself with grief. His eyes were terrible."

It came flowing out of Wally, who told her, "'I didn't want you to know, mamma. I thought I was big enough to fight my own battle and win. I thought I could come back alone, and you would never have to know.' I can't remember what he said, all of what he said. I don't want to remember. I want to forget all that, if I can, and live for the future he and I sketched that night—the future we would have when he was well again. We talked until morning and I tried to soothe him, to drive his fears away. Late in the morning he slept. I can't begin to tell you the happiness I felt that day. It was like a re-awakening. I felt that our old confidence, our old mutual affection, had been restored. The servants must have marveled at my soaring spirits." When Dorothy told her mother of Wally's confession Alice suggested they arrange for Wally to be forcibly kidnapped and brought to a sanitarium to be cured.[64]

According to Dorothy, during this time Wally often "harped to his friends and acquaintances on the drug evil. 'Keep off the stuff!' I heard him time and again ... he seemed to have a horror that others might fall into the clutches. He preached long sermons to Bill, our boy; tender, whimsical sermons I am sure the youngster didn't understand. He seemed his old personality only when he was with Bill. Time after time I have heard him say: 'Remember this, Bill; Every time daddy does something he shouldn't do, he must pay for it. Remember son.'" Dorothy correctly surmised that the 2-year-old "didn't have the slightest idea what it was all about."[65]

Studio publicity photo, "received October 26, 1921," according to handwritten note on reverse. While Wally had plunged into a morass of drugs and alcohol, his fans still saw him as the erudite star in his library, smoking a pipe.

It is baffling that neither sought medical assistance. Doctors weren't consulted nor did Wally enter a sanitarium for treatment, common at the time. He and Dorothy returned to their lives as if nothing was wrong but Wally could not work, exhausted after his return.

Lasky had another problem. Just before making *The Affairs of Anatol*, Gloria Swanson made *Under the Lash*, which Lasky and director Sam Wood knew would bomb. Both films were about to be released, *Anatol* and then *Lash*. Lasky knew *Anatol* would be well-received so he decided to sandwich *Lash* between *Anatol* and another Wally picture. Unfortunately he didn't have another Wally film ready so he made one off the cutting room floor, literally. He used footage that DeMille had cut from *Anatol* and made a feature with it.

The result of this cut and paste effort was the romantic comedy *Don't Tell Everything*. Shooting filler scenes took a week in late July or early August.[66] *Don't Tell Everything* was the fifth of the original "Five Kisses" that made up *The Affairs of Anatol*, released with only four. The last of Anatol's five affairs was to have been the temptations of Dorothy

Cumming's outdoorsy, athletic woman. Instead, the segment became the base for *Don't Tell Everything*; scenario revisions were done by Lorna Moon and Albert Shelby LeVino and Wood simply blended the *Anatol* footage with some new footage shot by Al Gilks.

Wally, Cumming, Swanson, Elliott Dexter and Genevieve Blinn appeared in the film, along with several children. Wood used his own infant daughter Gloria[67] in a child role; others were done by a set of twins, Charles and Raymond De Briac. Wally's Anatol character is wealthy Cullen Dale, who along with best friend Harvey Gilroy (Dexter) is in love with beautiful Marian Westover (Swanson). Gilroy's loyalty to his best friend prevents him from acting on his feelings for Marian, who notices the kindness Cullen shows Harvey after both men are injured in a polo accident. She accepts Cullen's marriage proposal but is overcome with jealousy of his old girlfriends like Jessica Ramsey (Cumming), who coincidently arrives and tries to steal him away. Jessica is athletic and Marian can't match her skills with horse or gun and is certain her fiancé will leave her. When Jessica invites the couple to a mountain lodge and Marian refuses to go. Cullen grabs her, throws her in his car and takes her to a justice of the peace and they are married. For some reason he then drops her off and goes on to the lodge, keeping the marriage secret. When a fierce storm prevents him from returning, Marian enlists Gilroy to drive to the lodge where all is explained away. All are happy except Jessica.[68]

The movie had the same thematic problem as *The Affairs of Anatol*. It is never clear if Wally's characters would act on the obvious impulse to have an affair. Like the other *Anatol* segments, in *Don't Tell Everything* Wally's character seemingly does the right thing but then does something contradictory. Cullen marries Marian to prove he loves her but then drops her off and goes to Jessica's lodge *without her*. Critics couldn't get past this major plot problem but fans loved the beautiful outdoor settings: pine woods, lush polo fields and a gorgeous California golf course. Wood staged a real polo game, probably filmed on the polo field at the Pacific Palisades ranch of Will Rogers. Rogers also had a three-hole golf course there; the golf sequence may have been filmed there as well. After its November 13th release it did as well as *The Affairs of Anatol*.

Wally was inactive for a month before starting the comedy *Rent Free* on August 23rd, which filmed through late September. Director Howard Higgin's only previous experience was as the Production Supervisor on *Anatol* but Wally liked him and Lasky knew Wally only did good work with people he knew. Elmer Rice wrote the scenario from a story by Izola Forrester and Mann Page. Charles Schoenbaum filmed. Wally starred opposite Lila Lee, supported by Henry Barrows, Gertrude Short, Lillian Leighton, Clarence Geldart, Claire McDowell and Lucien Littlefield.

Wally plays Buell Arnister, Jr., an artist who rebels against his father's (Barrows) wishes that he become a lawyer. When his father takes away his money and he loses his studio he takes refuge in a tent on the roof of an abandoned mansion. One day he looks up and sees Barbara Teller (Lee) and her friend Justine Tate (Short), also homeless. Barbara's father once owned the mansion but she was cheated out of her inheritance by her stepmother (McDowell). During a rainstorm the three take shelter in an unoccupied bedroom where Buell finds in the pocket of an old dressing gown a note addressed to his father and signed by James Teller giving Barbara his estate. As he and Barbara fall in love, Buell begins producing newspaper sketches, among them one of the well-known Count de Mourney (Geldart). The Count is sufficiently impressed that he invites the young artist to dinner, but unknown to Buell or Barbara, her stepmother has since married the Count and become the new Countess de Mourney. When Buell and the girls arrive for dinner the Countess has them arrested, but Buell produces the note which leads to the discovery of a second will by which Barbara regains her property.[69]

Wally during the 1921 filming of *Rent Free*. At the height of his fame, he was beginning to show the physical effects of his addiction.

The film was released on January 1, 1922, and was another box-office success for the studio.

The year had been difficult for Wally personally, but Lasky and Paramount had problems beyond their star's drug use. On August 30th the Federal Trade Commission charged the studio with restraint of trade for their block-booking policy, coercing distributors into buying unwanted films to get popular titles. Studio ownership of theaters also came under scrutiny. The case would not be resolved (Lasky would lose) for almost six years but the studio probably knew in 1921 that it was a loser.

But there were even bigger concerns. By September almost 40 states were considering censorship measures. Matters that had previously been kept private were discussed openly in papers. The public it seemed would no longer turn a blind eye to activities previously accepted. Lasky remembered, "Churches, women's clubs, and reformers had blood in their eyes over Hollywood's sinfulness and the moral laxness in some films."[70] The six months commencing September, 1921 was the most important period in movie history. Three events would dictate a new public perception of movies and the stars. Three events would cause a realignment of the industry. Three events—the trial of Roscoe Arbuckle, the murder of William Desmond Taylor, and the destruction of Wally Reid— would be forever intertwined, forever remembered for almost ruining the industry.

Roscoe Arbuckle was "Fatty" to his fans. In 1913 he was a $3-a-day extra. In 1921 he earned $3,000,000 ($100,000,000 today), had a mansion at fashionable 649 West Adams and a custom-made Pierce-Arrow that cost $250,000. It was three times the size of a normal car and had a bar and a toilet. He had worked for Joseph Schenck, who distributed his films through Lasky, but Lasky and Zukor outbid Schenck's contract and stole him. He made over a dozen Lasky films up to 1921 and they made millions but Lasky, Zukor and B.P. Shulberg bristled that they had to pay him the biggest contract in history: $7,500 a week, over $3,000,000, for three films. They felt like they had been extorted even though Arbuckle deserved it, so when "Fatty" got in trouble they had a chance to punish him. Without getting their hands dirty.

Arbuckle was exhausted after finishing three films in a row without a break and told Lasky he would spend the Labor Day weekend in San Francisco.[71] Arbuckle drove his huge car up the coast and took a three-room suite on the 12th floor of the St. Francis Hotel overlooking Union Square. The party began Saturday and lasted all weekend. When uninvited guests showed up Arbuckle, like Wally, never turned them away. One party-crasher was young actress Virginia Rappe, an acquaintance of Arbuckle, who became violently ill during the party and had to be rushed to nearby Wakefield Sanitarium at 1065 Sutton Street. Arbuckle was concerned and telephoned Maude Delmont, who brought Rappe to the party, to see if she was all right, telling her, "She'll be all right. I'm leaving by steamer for Los Angeles tomorrow morning. If everything doesn't go smoothly you know where to call me. And send the bills to Anger."[72] After paying his $611.43 hotel bill he left for L.A. on the S.S. *California*.[73] But Rappe was not all right. On Friday afternoon she died from peritonitis that an autopsy revealed was caused by a seriously infected bladder. It was likely the result of a botched abortion (her sixth); coincidently the doctor who probably performed the illegal procedure cared for her and later assisted in her autopsy!

When Arbuckle got out of a cab taking him home from the Long Beach pier police were there to bring him back to San Francisco. When he entered the police station he casually straightened a wall calendar but almost fainted when they told him he "was to be held without bail for the murder of Virginia Rappe." The trumped-up charge shocked people everywhere, but he was pilloried in the press. Unfounded rumors—many still held as true today—arose that he violated Rappe with a Coke or Champagne bottle or a piece of furniture! He also allegedly infected her with gonorrhea. All were untrue although she did have gonorrhea when she died.[74]

He was vilified in the press. "TORTURE OF RAPPE CHARGED," screamed the *San Francisco Examiner*, and "ARBUCKLE DRAGGED WOMEN TO ROOM" the *New York Times*.[75] St. Johns was among many who knew Rappe was a whore, that Mack Sennett had his studio fumigated *twice* after her visits to remove "crab" infestations she left behind. Hollywood knew the truth as Arbuckle sat in jail for three weeks but instead of rallying behind him—which Lasky was recommended to do by the other studios—Paramount left him hanging. They had millions of potential dollars in movies ready to release but Lasky, Zukor and Shulberg used studio publicists to work *against* him. They even encouraged stories they knew to be untrue. Lasky's only comment was, "Every man is innocent unless proven guilty in a court of law."

The Grand Jury indicted Arbuckle for manslaughter and even before his first trial began in November the backlash was formidable. His blockbuster *Gasoline Alley* was pulled from 3,200 theaters. Drunken cowboys in Themopolis, Wyoming, shot up the screen at the Maverick Theater when the manager didn't stop an Arbuckle feature. He was not the only person caught up in the fiasco; his best friend Lowell Sherman was fired by his studio even though he wasn't involved. Rappe, whose insignificant career totaled

11 films in 5 years, somehow became a star. Her forgettable films suddenly filled theaters. One Atlanta theater offered a "SPECIAL ADDED ATTRACTION!!! VIRGINIA RAPPE in 'A Twilight Baby' with WALLACE REID in 'Too Much Speed.'"[76] Rappe's film had been out of theaters for two years, Wally's for several months.

Arbuckle's grand jury proceeding and November trial were mockeries; every prosecution witness lied embarrassingly. A coroner said he bumped into an orderly with a bottle containing Rappe's internal organs heading to the incinerator. Arbuckle's chief accuser was ugly, disagreeable Bambina Maude Delmont. She was a con-woman with a record of 50 arrests for prostitution and bigamy who offered herself to lawyers as "bait" to trap married men in adulterous situations.[77] She lied outrageously, saying Roscoe "grabbed Miss Rappe by the hand and dragged her against her will into the bedroom." She was one of 40 alleged guests who implicated Arbuckle; the jury never saw the telegram she sent to her attorney saying, "WE HAVE ROSCOE ARBUCKLE IN A HOLE HERE. STOP. CHANCE TO MAKE MONEY OFF HIM. STOP."[78] The final witness was director Henry Lehrman, who became obsessed with Rappe after a few dates and let her live in his home while he pretended she was his fiancée. Though he married actress Jocelyn Leigh on April 28, 1922, in the middle of Arbuckle's trials, he later arranged to be buried next to Rappe.[79] He was among 40 witnesses who testified even though most weren't at the party!

Even with the perjured testimony the jury did not convict Arbuckle; the trial ended December 2nd with a hung jury voting 10 to 2 for acquittal. One of the guilty voters covered her ears with her hands during deliberations and said, "I was certain Mr. Arbuckle was guilty and I'd vote that way until hell freezes over." But the foreman said, "The facts or evidence were an insult to our intelligence. I was disgusted with all of them." But the D.A. announced he would try Arbuckle in January.

Even today outrageous stories are passed on as true. For example, the Fathom Archives at Columbia University contain an otherwise well-written article entitled "American Film Institute; The First Fifty Years of American Film" that contains the comment, "In one of his infamous days-long parties, teeming with chorus girls and bootleg whiskey, a minor actress named Virginia Rappe died in a hotel room of peritonitis. Her ripped clothing and other circumstantial evidence suggested rape and murder, and pointed to Arbuckle as a possible

One of the last studio portraits of Roscoe Arbuckle, taken by L.A. photographer Albert Witzel. This rare photographer's original was kept by Witzel and used to make reproductions as ordered by the studio for fans (photograph courtesy Cecil Jones).

suspect.... He was indicted for manslaughter and the public convicted him at once, especially after newspapers revealed that the Massachusetts district attorney had received a suspiciously generous $100,000 donation after one of Arbuckle's earlier parties in that state."[80] In addition to the ridiculous Rappe comments, Arbuckle was not involved in the Massachusetts incident; it was a gathering of studio executives at a local brothel and he had nothing to do with the bribe paid by a Boston distributor.

That fall Wally was barely able to function, only able to stand for brief periods and prone to crying jags and emotional breakdowns. He couldn't attend studio or industry functions and his health was the subject of press innuendo. He was virtually invisible in Hollywood, missing events like the well-attended premier of *The Three Musketeers* during that Labor Day weekend. Negative stories appeared that described Wally though they never identified him by name. In September, the *New York American* described a Hollywood drug party noting, "Nero, whose lurid orgies have been a byword of history, would have turned his head in shame at some of the modern-day ribald gatherings in ... the Hollywood motion picture colony...."[81] The story detailed the antics of a group dubbed "the Live Hundred," allegedly stars who attended or hosted lavish parties fueled by illegal alcohol and drugs. One party was allegedly viewed by policemen hiding in the bushes at DeLongpre:

> Concealed in a hedge below the windows detectives viewed excesses so extreme as to nauseate some guests and impel them to leave the party in disgust. Decorators installed furniture and settings at a cost of $20,000. The entrance to the palatial house was converted to a cavern entrance, "The Grotto of Good Fellows." As the group sat down at the long table a maid pushed a wheeled tea tray in after extensive indulgence in drinks ... with an assortment of needles, opium pipes, morphine, cocaine, heroin and opium. Each guest hilariously helped himself or herself to drugs and selected needles or pipes ... they injected morphine into one another or helped the next-seat neighbor to "sniff" his or her selection. A motion picture actress standing on the stairs called ... interrupted as she turned to the white powder in her palm. "I want the most beautiful man here. I am his." A dozen men staggered and stumbled and ran, to gain the prize. She commanded that those clamoring for possession of her submit to a vote. Thus was chosen "the prettiest man of the bunch." What followed proved too much for those at the hedge to endure. They pounded at the doors. Lights went out. In some manner the host got out ... drugs and needles and pipes had been destroyed or concealed in the brief few minutes. The host came back, ringing at the front door. He had driven up in an automobile. He wore a cap, a motoring ulster and goggles. He had, was his explanation, been out driving. The host angrily denounced the invasion. He demanded search warrants. He was not arrested, but the guests were. They were not prosecuted, however. It was learned that the host had made a practice of leaving his automobile a few blocks away during these parties so that he might establish just such an alibi....

Describing the host with "cap, a motoring ulster and goggles" was the same as naming Wally so identified was he with the race car driver image. Just a week later a story in the trade magazine *Variety* mentioned, "It is known the wife of one of the most popular of the younger male stars has time and again had the peddlers of dope supplying her husband arrested, but she has been unable to get her husband to break his habit...."[82]

St. Johns tried her best to put Wally and Hollywood in a better light. In the October *Photoplay* she described the parties at the DeLongpre house in a much different light, describing a Hollywood "overrun with swimming parties." According to her the only parties at DeLongpre were pool parties hosted by Dorothy and attended by stars like Wanda Hawley, Mabel Normand, T. Roy Barnes and his wife Bessie Crawford, Bill Hart and May Allison.[83]

Amidst all the negative stories Wally was secluded in the mountains above Pasadena. After finishing *Rent Free* he took a "short vacation in the California hills."[84] Lasky actually hid him at a remote cabin with studio guards, Dorothy, and Teddy Hayes.[85] Lasky would later remember Wally's first big collapse in June, 1922 but it obviously occurred in late 1921, after which the Pasadena interlude was arranged. On the way to Pasadena, Wally told Dorothy, "Nothing can lick us. We're going to win. I'll shake this thing."[86]

Wally and Bill Jr. enjoy the pool at the DeLongpre house.

Barely 30, Teddy Hayes was a well-known trainer who had coached boxer Jack Dempsey.[87] He and Dorothy spent a month nursing Wally to health for his next film in which he was to play a feisty boxer. Several photos remain from the mountain retreat. Wally is thin and pale and wears heavy sweaters to look bigger. The sweater, out of place in the heat, can't hide his emaciated appearance and thin, wan face. Wally's secret was out though. *Photoplay* ran a photo of Wally in his sweater sparring with Hayes with the surprising caption, "Wally, caught in the act of 'coming back.' After his breakdown several months ago, he went to the mountains accompanied only by Dorothy Davenport Reid and his trainer, Teddy Hayes, and there he rested and devoted his days to getting himself into condition."[88] Wally was also reported to be at a "foothill sanitarium near Los Angeles suffering from Kleig eyes and a serious nervous breakdown" and exhaustion from overwork. Dorothy said, "Wally's improvement is remarkable. He had us pretty well worried when we took him there but I am so pleased and happy over the way he is getting along. He's putting on weight, climbing mountains, sleeping twelve hours a night and beginning to look like himself again."[89]

The World's Champion was filmed after Wally's return from the mountains in early September. Lasky publicists wrote, "Wallace Reid's home in Beverly Hills resembled a prize fighter's training camp rather than a domicile for a motion picture star during the filming of 'The World's Champion.' In Wally's latest Paramount vehicle he dons the gloves and goes through several rounds with a professional ex-champ, and it was necessary that he be really able to hold his own to make the scenes realistic."[90] Phillip E. Rosen directed the Albert LeVino and J.E. Nash adaptation of the play by Thomas Louden and A.E. Thomas.[91] Charles Schoenbaum did the camera work with Thompson Buchanan, and Wally starred with Lois Wilson, Lionel Belmore, Henry Miller, Jr., Helen Dunbar, Leslie Casey, Stanley J. (Tiny) Sandford, W.J. Ferguson and Guy Oliver.

Wally is Englishman William Burroughs, who prefers the outdoors and athletics to philosophy studies ordered by his businessman father (Belmare). Even with his athletic bent William enjoys associating with nobility but when he meets Lady Elizabeth Galton (Wilson) he is thrashed by her cousin Lord Brockington (Sandford). Wally put Hayes' boxing lessons to use in a realistic fight scene during which he is knocked down three times. He is disowned after losing the fight and arguing with his father over the direction of his life he leaves for America intent on becoming a middleweight champion, which he does. Returning to England he discovers that Lady Galton, in poor circumstances, has become his father's secretary. His father is disgusted to hear of his son's career until newspapers describe his fame and he is visited by awestruck local nobles. Still, though she has refused marriage to Lord Brockington for the seven years, Lady Galton spurns William because of his fighting reputation. Brockington challenges William to a fight over her affections and is badly beaten by William, but when William promises to renounce the ring and become an attorney she relents and announces she is willing to go to America with him as his wife.[92]

The fight scenes were extremely realistic. The stuntman for Wally's opponent in the big fight was former middleweight champion Charles "Kid" McCoy.[93] Director Rosen was going to use a stunt double for Wally but Wally insisted on boxing McCoy for realism. For the climactic payback scene Rosen used a wonderful technique to frame the resolution. There is no fight footage; instead, after being challenged William slowly removes his championship ring and carefully places it in his pocket and follows Brockington outside. Rosen pans back as William returns and replaces the ring on his finger and walks away whistling. In the background Brockington is carried inside by six pals.

A very thin Wally (left) trains for *The World's Champion* in the driveway of the DeLongpre house with a man who appears to be "Kid" McCoy, a former boxing champion who trained Wally and appeared as a stuntman in the film. Behind the two is one of Wally's beloved Marmon coupes.

The movie premiered in New York in late February and nationwide March 12th. Reviews described it as a "furiously funny comedy with many humorous touches that Reid is master of...."[94] Wally took a month off when filming ended before starting *Across the Continent*. Finding it ever harder to find roles his increasingly unstable star could handle, Lasky knew a road racing film was a good choice.

Wally retreated to DeLongpre and was rarely seen in public that fall. He was absent from any Hollywood events. He missed the November opening of Marcus Loew's new State Theater at Broadway and 7th downtown even though papers noted "Everybody who was invited ... the blue book of the Coast film colony...."[95] was there. Stars like Rudolph Valentino, Buster Keaton, Gloria Swanson, Antonio Moreno, John Gilbert and Mabel Normand attended. The only name missing was Wallace Reid, the biggest star in the movies.

Wally's international fans were still oblivious to his problems. He was still a weekly feature in European film magazines. In October, November, *and* December the British *Picturegoer* had a feature article or photo feature of Wally. When German director Ernst Lubitsch released *The Loves of the Pharaoh*, his new lead Henry Liedtke was called "the

Wally and Mary MacLaren win the climactic transcontinental race in *Across the Continent*.

Wally Reid of Europe."[96] Wally was equally visible in the domestic press but remained out of the public eye as the holidays approached.

Across the Continent was a formulaic film Lasky knew Wally would enjoy making. He drives through a huge prairie fire and races a train to a crossing gate in a "flivver," a small sports car also called a "bug." They were dangerous—lighter than a Duesenberg or Stutz but powered by a racing engine that could cruise at 100 miles per hour, "as fast as could be gone while barely staying on the ground."[97]

Byron Morgan wrote the screenplay especially for Wally. Phillip Rosen directed and Charles Schoenbaum did the December filming. Wally starred with Mary MacLaren, supported by Theodore Roberts, Betty Francisco, Walter Long, Lucien Littlefield, Jack Herbert, Guy Oliver and Sidney D'Albrook. Wally plays Jimmy Dent, whose father John (Roberts) produces inexpensive but efficient cars. When John orders his employees to drive Dents, Jimmy rebels when Lorraine Tyler (Francisco), daughter of rival manufacture Dutton Tyler (Long), induces him to buy *her* father's expensive roadster. Jimmy learns Tyler is plotting to wreck a Dent entry in a transcontinental race and gives up his Tyler to drive a Dent in the race. His father's secretary Louise (MacLaren) tries to warn him of a sabotage attempt, disguises herself as a mechanic, and runs the race with Jimmy. They battle rival drivers, Tyler saboteurs, a prairie fire, and barely escape an oncoming train, but Jimmy wins the race and Louise.[98]

The film was a box-office bonanza for Paramount, but ads mentioned Wally's health. Ominously, one read, "Your chances to see Wallace Reid will soon be few, and this is the most thrilling and funniest of all the Reid racing romances!"[99] By this time Wally had difficulty completing scenes. He rested often and rarely stood for long periods during filming. He was completely out of the social press that fall. No specific mention of Wally or Dorothy appeared until the following February in a St. Johns piece defending Hollywood that described her 1921 holiday visit to DeLongpre.

Like her earlier "swimming pool party" defense St. Johns' Christmas story described a visit by eight or ten disabled soldiers from the Arrowhead Hospital for whom Wally had sent his car. The party was attended by Jeanie Macpherson and her mother, Mr. and Mrs. Bill Desmond and the St. Johns. After some dancing the group sat on the floor and according to St. Johns played card games.[100]

St. Johns' stories were obviously sanitized to the point of fiction, but in fact Wally was partying less in late 1921 because his health was so poor. His house wasn't as wild as some described but neither was it as clean as St. Johns' portrayal. An interesting omission in St. Johns' story was Bertha, who was actually there after Dorothy finally allowed her to visit her son and grandson. Maybe sensing the depth of Wally's trouble she allowed Bertha to spend three months with them. From December to March, Bertha witnessed several important events and chronicled them in her later biography without knowing their importance to help clear up Wally's story.

Wally wanted to meet Bertha when her train arrived in Barstow near the *Continent* filming, but he couldn't get away and when Bertha arrived nobody was there to greet her. While staying in L.A. she became good friends with Wanda Hawley and spent days sightseeing with her. Hawley and her husband Allen were among the Reids' close friends; Allen and Wally hunted, fished and played polo together. Wally's other close friends were his driver Benny Frazee and Charles Post. "Buddy" Post was a Utah-born, 6'6", 330-pound character actor who had worked for Pathé, First National, Haworth and Goldwyn.

That Christmas, Wally received hundreds of gifts but the one he was most excited about was his racing driver's license. He could now drive in any sanctioned race and planned to compete in the Indianapolis 500 in May. Wally wore the pin night and day.[101]

It had been a grueling year for Wally balancing fame, family, his increasing inability to work, and his addictions. Given that, his 1921 work was prodigious. Lasky cajoled 7 films from Wally and started an 8th (he released 8 but *Don't Tell Everything* was made from deleted *Affairs of Anatol* scenes). Lasky's 1921 assignments were a good mix: romantic adventures like *Love Special* and *Hell Diggers*, a comedy in *Rent Free*, a sports-themed *The World's Champion*, and road movies *Too Much Speed* and *Across the Continent*. For spectacle, DeMille offered *The Affairs of Anatol* and *Forever*.

Wally remained the number one box office star in the world but for the first time his work was uneven and some reviews unflattering. He had huge influence on the public. After appearing in *The World's Champion* without the stiff, detachable collar men wore with shirts, it was said that he single-handedly put collar companies out of business overnight. The story was probably apocryphal, but telling. Heading into 1922 his star power was unquestionable. His ability to survive was not.

13

The Industry Teeters, and Wally Falls

In early 1922 Paramount organized a publicity blitz to take some attention away from Wally. In January, *Picture Show* ran a four-part "Wally Reid's Life History—By Himself." His interesting life story was sprinkled with enough quotes that it appeared to readers that he may have written it. The story is fictionalized (medical school stories, among others, were included), and it addressed the Hollywood controversy. Wally described his acting friends as a most "loyal, congenial ... crowd. Nobody is quicker to lend a hand than a film player, male or female."[1]

After the holidays Wally completed *Across the Continent* and had a single day off before starting *Nice People*.[2] Meanwhile, Hollywood dominated headlines with the second Arbuckle trial beginning January 11th, the appointment of Will Hays to police the movies, and another death.[3]

During the first Arbuckle trial every prosecution witness had been impeached. At the second even *they* testified that D.A. Matthew Brady orchestrated illegal acts including holding witnesses hostage and forcing them to commit perjury. Star witness Maude Delmont couldn't testify, as unbelievable as she was. The other witness who had testified that Rappe identified Arbuckle as a rapist now testified Rappe never said it and that Brady forced her to lie. The jury began deliberations on February 1st and on the 3rd the trial ended with another hung jury. The first vote was 11 to 1 for acquittal; the tenth was 9 to 3 for conviction. Votes were changed only because Arbuckle's attorney waived his final argument! Brady said he would try Arbuckle yet again.

On the 2nd another scandal erupted. The day Virginia Rappe was buried the previous September, the new Motion Picture Directors Association President said Hollywood would be "cleaning house" and produce "the cleanest of films."[4] He was Lasky's chief director William Desmond Taylor. On the morning of February 2nd he was found dead in his Hollywood bungalow court home. The afternoon prior he had met with Lasky to discuss a Mary Miles Minter movie.[5] A policeman described Taylor as "a cultured, dignified gentleman with a charming personality and considerable magnetism." His Paramount bio said he grew up in Kansas, prospected in the Klondike, served in the Canadian Army, and earned medals for heroism at Dunkirk. He was among the most respected directors in Hollywood and his life a wonderful tale of a life well-lived, but the truth was less romantic. In 1900 New York he was known as William Cunningham Deane-Tanner, owner of a small antique shop, married to actress Ethel Harrison, and father of a daughter. In 1908 he simply vanished but in 1916 Ethel and their daughter saw him in a movie and tracked him to Vitagraph and he began secretly paying their expenses.

Most of the Lake Terrace units at 404 South Alvarado housed movie people. Chaplin's ex–leading lady and best friend Edna Purviance lived on one side of Taylor and actor Douglas MacLean and his wife Faith Cole on the other. The MacLean and Taylor homes were separated by a dark eight-foot alley leading out to the street. Police thought Taylor suffered a heart attack but two hours later detectives rolled his body over and found a pool of blood and a bullet hole in his back.[6]

Minutes after police arrived Taylor's best friend, Paramount manager Charles Eyton, arrived and began collecting items from the bedroom (police alerted Lasky, who called on Eyton to "clean-up"). After burning some papers in the fireplace Eyton took others and left. Faith MacLean told police the evening before, she had heard a gunshot and saw someone walk out the alley in a long coat with a high collar, a scarf and hat. The person appeared like a "man walking funny."[7] There were plenty of suspects. His first wife. Chauffeur Dennis Sands, who was probably his career criminal brother Denis. Disgruntled drug dealers who hated Taylor for public anti-drug posturing. Mabel Normand, the last person to see him alive. And Mary Miles Minter's mother Charlotte Shelby, who knew of a relationship between 50-year-old Taylor and her 16-year-old meal ticket. Two pictures were on his piano, one signed by Mary Pickford and the other, "For William Desmond Taylor, artist and gentleman, Mary Miles Minter."

Minter arrived from her 40-room mansion just blocks away in her robin's egg blue Cadillac roadster emblazoned on the door with her signature butterfly emblem in solid gold. Hysterical, she wailed over the body and disappeared upstairs where she was found rummaging through Taylor's desk. Police found a pink nightgown and a lace handkerchief both monogrammed "M.M.M." and in the toe of his riding boot love letters written in a schoolyard code and signed, "Mary."[8] All were on Minter's signature butterfly stationary, written in schoolgirl scrawl. Physical evidence linked to Minter was also found. Three strands of long blonde hair beneath the collar of Taylor's coat matched hair from a brush in Minter's dressing room.[9] Taylor's valet laundered his suits daily so police knew Minter was with him the day he was murdered.[10]

Budd Shulberg was the son of B.P. Shulberg and a successful producer. At a 1996 symposium at the University of Southern California he discussed corruption that allowed studios free reign, saying, "I always thought of Hollywood like a principality ... and the people who ran it really had that attitude.... Their power was absolutely enormous, and it wasn't only the power to make movies or to ... make someone a movie star or pick an unknown director and make him famous over night. They could cover up a murder. You could literally have somebody killed and it wouldn't be in the papers." The 1920s district attorneys were for sale. Thomas L. Woolwine was *paid* to speak at movie functions including a testimonial for Arbuckle before his arrest.[11] He was not the first dishonest D.A. but his tenure (1914–1923) coincided with great movie industry growth and he was involved in more cover-ups than any other D.A. The Taylor physical evidence was moved to his office and later to his home; he later told the Grand Jury it was "lost." What little evidence remained was kept in a briefcase and carried around by Woolwine's successor Asa Keyes. During a 1926 Chicago visit it was allegedly stolen.[12]

The Minter revelations were a bombshell but his friends knew of the friendship between the middle-aged director and the teenaged ingénue. Police quickly identified Shelby as the prime suspect. She knew the affair would end her daughter's career. She said the night of the murder she was playing cards but police remembered Faith MacLean's "man walking funny"—like a woman pretending to be a man. Shelby was never formally questioned, nor was Minter. Shelby testified before the Grand Jury but Woolwine lost the single copy of her testimony that was produced!

Even with a clear suspect, physical evidence, motive and opportunity, D.A. Woolwine never publicly solved the murder. When he was run out of office in 1923 his relationship with Shelby was uncovered. Her alibi was Jim Smith, Woolwine's investigator. The alibi didn't come cheap. Shelby told her accountant that Woolwine's replacement "would require a lot more money than Woolwine."[13] That successor was Asa Keyes, "Ace" to his pals. Coincidently the Wednesday before his death Taylor played golf with Antonio Moreno at San Gabriel Country Club. Keyes, a friend of Taylor, joined the two for dinner at the club. Minter's career was over and her mother was a pariah. If Shelby did indeed kill Taylor she inadvertently ended her daughter's career. For the remaining 50 years of her life Mary Miles Minter lived in seclusion in Santa Monica. Her mother lived with her until her death in 1957 and Mary died in 1984. Wally attended Taylor's funeral with Rudolph Valentino.

Between Arbuckle and Taylor, the industry was reeling. Cries to clean up Hollywood grew louder. With terrible timing, stories identified Wally as a drug addict. On February 9th the *Chicago American* mentioned, "Stars of the movies, idols ... beautiful women and athletic men, are being destroyed by the use of drugs."[14] The innocuous reference to "athletic" men hinted at Wally.

Newspaper articles demanded reform. Stars were no longer bullet-proof. The industry responded by decrying the rumors and offering another version of Hollywood. St. Johns offered a series of stories in February asking:

> What in the world is this Hollywood stuff? I certainly don't recognize the old home place from the lurid descriptions I've been reading.[15] It's pretty dull out here ... a good place to rest up. No cabarets. No place to dance nearer than six miles. An occasional party ... listening to Wally Reid and Wanda Hawley play duets on the saxophone and the piano.... The Hollywood Hotel ... has a nice family dining room where everybody has their own table and knows the waitresses ... nice old ladies from Iowa and Kansas come out for the winter.... Anita Stewart was there, dancing with her husband, Rudy Cameron. Mae Busch ... Marguerite de la Motte [sic], May Allison—and we all went to the drug store and had an ice cream soda between dances. I went to a dinner party at Charlie Chaplin's ... Charlie, Sam Goldwyn, Gouverneur [sic] Morris, Rupert Hughes and his wife and May Allison and Claire Windsor. Hughes and Chaplin ... discussed religion for three hours.... Mary Pickford lives the life of a recluse ... nothing else for her to do.[16]

St. Johns also described Lois Wilson's life with her father, Jack Holt and his children, Conrad Nagel's Sundays as a church usher, and Bebe Daniels living with her grandmother and aunt. There was a photo of Wally and Billy in the sandbox next to the pool, noting, "There are those who claim Wallie is about as 'wild cat-ey' as they come, but here he is taking orders from his youthful son, Bill."[17] In another story St. Johns offered her take on the Taylor-Minter relationship:

> But who shot Bill Taylor? Is there anything yet to convince you that he was killed for any immoral reason or ... a result of his connection with pictures? Suppose Mary Miles Minter was in love with him. She's an unmarried girl and her mother keeps pretty close tab on the family wage-earner. Bill Taylor was a big, fascinating, strong man. No wonder she fell in love with him.[18]

The stars' sanitized views of Hollywood life were also offered. In March, *Movie Weekly* offered Betty Compson's "What Is Hollywood Really Like: An Intimate Closeup of the Picture Colony," written by a Paramount writer but attributed to her:

> Mother and I live in a bungalow on a Hollywood hill-top ... so busy at work that none of my neighbors knew I was in motion pictures until "Bill," my terrier, got into a fight with another

dog.... The screen players ... have nothing to conceal. Bebe [Daniels] lives in a charming house with a charming mother and a quaint old grandmother perfectly happy under their chaperonage.... Mary Miles Minter ... is a very brainy and discerning girl.... Lois Wilson and Conrad Nagel stand by the Lasky bulletin board engaged in a "secret" conversation ... about their respective church work.... May McAvoy started out to be a school teacher, and is a little like one.... [It is] a peculiar, long-distance manifestation of the mob spirit, with Hollywood and its people as victims.[19]

The rebuttals didn't stem the tide of criticism though. A Missouri editorial offered, "It may be that the man who committed the Hollywood murder will escape, but Hollywood can't. Hollywood as a community, as a social condition, as a moral delinquency, stands indicted. Men and women intoxicated by money ... more money than your abilities or service entitle you to, to spend it in wild excesses, to reject the restraints of decency, was to be approved a member of this order." The headline? "THE DEFENDANT IN THE CASE."[20]

Money also created envy. In 1921 studios addressed salary issues not to appease the public but to survive. *New York Herald* writer Thoreau Cronyn described Hollywood as "an El Dorado for a few, a grub stake for many and a Dead Man's Gulch for most."[21] Few actors had fixed contracts like Wally's. Most earned a salary *only if they worked*. A $500 contract meant little if you didn't work. The highest salaried actors were Mary Pickford, Charlie Chaplin and Douglas Fairbanks. Pickford and Fairbanks earned $10,000 a week, but Chaplin's First National contract paid $1,000,000 that people still assume was paid yearly. But it was for 8 movies that took five years to complete. He actually earned $200,000 a year. William S. Hart earned $2,000 a week. Valentino's Paramount contract paid $1,000 a week in year one, $2,000 the second and $3,000 the third. Lasky paid Minter for five movies at $30,000, $40,000, $50,000, $60,000 and $70,000 per—$250,000 for two years.[22] Gloria Swanson made $3,500 a week, Pola Negri $2,000, and Agnes Ayres $2,500. Considering his value Wally was a bargain even with his limited ability to work. His 1922 contract paid $1,750 and Cronyn noted, "I heard Wallace Reid had been reduced from $1,750 to $1,250, but in view that he is one of the greatest drawing cards at the film theaters, it seems improbable."[23] It would have been reasonable for Lasky to reduce Wally's pay given his decreasing work but there is no archival confirmation. Wally was a steal at $1,750; it's surprising Dorothy didn't demand more.

Cronyn spent a month in Hollywood looking for drug stories but in his rambling and contradictory *Herald* serial at once diminishes the problem while exposing stories of such excess. One clearly described Wally apparently nearing rock bottom:

I went to Hollywood to find out the truth, good and bad ... talked with actors, directors, producers, screen writers, extras, merchants, doctors, ministers, bankers, detectives, newspaper men, publicity men, housewives, and others of high and low degree and varying standards of veracity. Scandalous stories may be heard in Hollywood and Los Angeles by any one who cares to listen. One of the stories I had heard was a handsome and popular actor puncturing himself in the stomach with a hypodermic needle at the peak of an exciting dinner attended by "stars" and crying, "This is the life." ... the actor in question was a morphine user.[24]

The needle story was first described by reporter Ed Doherty who allegedly spoke with the Japanese servant who witnessed Wally injecting himself with morphine, as:

[A] tale told by an [sic] humble Jap ... at the mansion home of one of the most beautiful and famous actresses in the world. "The guests came, two by two, man and wife, in great automobiles. They came in laughing, full of happiness. The greatest stars in the world! The guests sat down ... I served cocktails ... wine and highballs, green drinks, yellow, and orange, and purple ... the big man threw a plate of food at me ... hit me in the face. The gravies trickled down my vest and on to the rug worth thousands. Men threw things at women. Women threw things at men. Soon food was flying all over.... Costly china plates smashed against walls. Statues were thrown down and broken, pictures ruined. They threw whisky and wine at each other. They threw chairs at mirrors. One man, very graceful he was, turned cartwheels, and his feet struck a woman and knocked her down. She put her arms around him and kissed him and bathed his hair with half a tumbler full of whisky. Then the big man jumped on the table and pulled open his shirt and exposed his stomach. He held his stomach with his big left hand, and with the other he plunged a hypodermic needle into it. "This is the life!" he shouted, and jumped down and took a lady in his arms and went into another room. She was not the lady he came in with. Everybody left the room too, with everybody else's wife.[25]

It's hard to believe Doherty's tale of a bacchanal with actors in a food fight destroying the home and that the "big man" was Wally, who would never throw food at a servant. But DeMille admitted, "There's a sickness in Hollywood..." caused by "crumbling standards" and Gloria Swanson said scandal "drew the lightning on us all." The studios had to clean house so Louis B. Mayer quietly formed the Motion Picture Producers and Distributors of America which inserted morals clauses in contracts, wrote a "Code of Conduct," and brought Indianan Will H. Hays to run the MPPDA. The short unimposing ex–Postmaster General was accused of accepting bribes during the Teapot Dome scandal[26] but was paid $100,000 a year ($2,000,000 today), and his Hays Office opened January 14th. He believed the movie colony needed to become "mature enough to bear censure, conservative enough to value goodwill and shrewd enough to advocate middle class morals."[27] The studios really brought him in to avoid the looming state censorship.

The studios disagreed with Hays' suggestion that they could save money and earn trust if they made cleaner movies rather than movies they paid to redo after his censoring. His office had no real "teeth." It was symbolic. It would be five years before Hays released his famous list of on and off-screen behavior that included 11 "don'ts" and 27 "be carefuls,"[28] but one of Hays' first 1922 calls was to Jesse Lasky. It was about Wally.

Lasky suggested in his memoirs that he was unaware of Wally's drug addiction until the telephone call from Hays, an obvious lie. Wally had long been unable to work, was losing weight—he had dropped from 190 to 150—and could only stand on his feet for a few minutes. Even Lasky recalled, "He made a valiant struggle to get through his scenes, but it was obvious that something was wrong."[29] Employees knew Wally was in trouble, too. A group of directors and

Will Hays was brought to Hollywood to publicly "clean up" the movies, and his target was Wally; he tried to convince Jesse Lasky to drop Wally and remove his films after his addiction was publicized.

cameramen, writers and electricians formed the Federated Arts Group to boycott problem stars, targeting Wally and a few others. A delegation asked Lasky to remove Wally from films until he cured himself. Lasky promised to investigate but did nothing.[30]

Zukor called Lasky and said, "The entire country was teeming with the rumor that Wallace Reid was taking dope, and that if it were true we were sitting on a powder keg." Lasky worried about the scandals—Arbuckle, Taylor, and now Wally, all from within *his* studio—and wondered "if the studio could weather the loss of such a talented trio, especially under circumstances that stigmatized Hollywood in general and our studio in particular." Wally told him, "It isn't true, and don't you believe it," the same response he gave Dorothy. Lasky told Wally he needed a doctor to examine him and give him a clean bill of health and Wally said, "Go as far as you like."

Charles Eyton hired a friend from the Southern Pacific Railroad, Dr. Starr, who was ordered to live with Wally and not let him out of his sight, even to sleep and go to the bathroom with him. Nobody but Wally, Starr and the studio knew Starr was anything but a friend. Even the family wondered about the visitor who arrived on March 17th. Bertha remembered that his presence "seemed an unnecessary indignity ... was so much mystery about it all." Starr was to stay two weeks. His report to Lasky left no doubt that Wally appeared clean:

> In accordance with plans made March 16, 1922, I arrived at the home of Mr. Wallace Reid Friday morning, March 17th. From noon of that day until the present time, I have been constantly with him, and can state without reservation that Mr. Reid is not a drug addict. I have slept with him, eaten with him, been with him on the golf course and everywhere else he has been throughout the twenty-four hours of these days; and at no time has there been any indication of the use or need of any habit-forming drugs. Mr. Reid was examined by myself for morphine, dionin, codeine, heroin and peronin by the Kober test and for morphine by the Huesmann test, and found negative in both cases. Once while Mr. Reid was at his bath I carefully inspected his entire body, finding only a few puncture marks from injections of vaccine which had been prescribed by the family physician. From my knowledge and observation of addicts, I can state that Mr. Reid has none of the characteristics of one, and I believe that the reports of certain acts, said to have been committed by him, have been grossly exaggerated.

Wally was unfazed and cordial to Starr, who told Lasky, "I don't know anyone else that I could live with for two weeks like Siamese twins without wanting to murder, but he is unquestionably the nicest chap I've ever known."[31] With the whirlwind swirling around him, Starr tagging along, and being the subject of dozens of articles about drug addiction, Wally began *Nice People* less than a day after *Across the Continent* was completed. *People* was a Clara Beranger adaptation of a 1921 Rachel Crothers play. William de Mille directed and Guy Wilky filmed. Wally was teamed with his friend Bebe Daniels, supported by Conrad Nagel, Julia Faye, Claire McDowell, Edward Martindel, Eve Southern, Bertram Jones, William Boyd and Ethel Wales. Daniels plays Theodora "Teddy" Gloucester, among a group of 1920s jazz-era partiers called "nice people." During a storm she takes shelter in a secluded farmhouse with intoxicated companion Scotty Wilbur (Nagel) and stranger Billy Wade (Wally). Billy arrives in time to save Theodora from Scotty's unwelcome attentions but her furious father (Martindel) arrives the next morning and finds her and Scotty alone. When her party friends refuse to defend her she settles down to become an old-fashioned wife to Billy.[32]

The comedy jazz-age morality play—a heroine discovering the error of her party ways—premiered in Los Angeles July 2nd and nationally September 4th. Described as "A dramatic expose of the jazz-life of today. Played in a setting of lavish gowns and luxury by one of the greatest casts ever assembled,"[33] the 7-reel film was well received but an exhausting shoot for Wally.

In late February, Wally went right from *Nice People* to *The Dictator*; again Lasky gave him a single half-day off. In most scenes in his 1922 films Wally is seated. By early March he could only stand up for a few minutes and his weight had dropped below 150. *The Dictator* was a remake of a 1915 Famous Players film featuring John Barrymore, based on the 1904 Richard Harding Davis play *The Dictator; a Farce in Three Acts*. The 1922 scenario was written by Walter Woods and the film directed by Wally's old pal James Cruze. He starred with Lila Lee, supported by Theodore Kosloff, Kalla Pasha, Sidney Bracey, Fred Butler, Walter Long and Alan Hale. The story was similar to the 1919 Wally-Lee film *Hawthorne of the U.S.A.*

This photograph was used for theater handouts for *Nice People* in the summer of 1922, and barely six months later the reverse contained Wally's death notice. Lasky also used it for re-releases of *Thirty Days*.

Wally plays Brooke Travers, carefree son of a millionaire "Banana King" who controls prices in a small South American country. Chased by a cab driver (Long) for an unpaid fare, Brooke and a pal hide on a steamer which unbeknownst to them is going to the South American country where his father's company is located. There, they are caught in the middle of a revolution to bring democracy and replace the Travers family banana interests that control the economy. He falls in love with Juanita Rivas (Lee) and learns she is the daughter of Dr. Carlos Rivas (Kosloff), exiled leader of the revolution and self-styled "liberator" intent on removing Brooke's family business. Despite family loyalty Brooke helps revolutionaries depose his father's underhanded company manager (Butler) and earns his father's respect and Juanita's love.[34]

The film premiered in Los Angeles on June 25th and was released nationally on August 7th. In a strange coincidence, Thoreau Cronyn's story of the evils of Hollywood described a visit to Paramount during *Dictator* filming:

> Famous Players–Lasky covered two blocks near the center of town, one offices, stages, and permanent buildings, one for outdoor sets ... fringed with graceful pepper trees. The sealed door opened with a button because a friend left the password at the gate ... a sand street flanked on one side by the low office buildings, on the other by three or four monster stages.... We threaded our way among darkened sets until we came upon a patch of brilliant light. Moving closer we saw that the rays of the lights, fifteen, trained from an upper level at a spot where stood a stalwart young man in khaki breeches and cobalt blue, open throated shirt. He was in the act of defying a fat, epauletted, much medaled Latin American generalissimo. A director whom I couldn't see called "All ready." Epaulettes turned his head to blow out a lungful of cigarette smoke and then, while the handsome Gringo regarded him tensely, the camera began grinding.... I knew nothing except they were doing "The Dictator" and the hero with the blue shirt was Wallace Reid. The director, James Cruze, was getting whatever effects he wanted by speaking softly.[35]

The Dictator completion coincided with Bertha's return home after a three-month visit. Every night she was at DeLongpre Wally stopped by her room to kiss her goodnight. He had Benny Frazee drive her anywhere she wished; she traveled up and down the coast from Santa Barbara to Mexico, stayed at the Coronado Hotel near San Diego and visited racetracks in Tijuana. She also reconnected with an actress she knew as 10-year-old Gladys Smith when she worked for Hal. The two visited often and remained friends the rest of her life. For years Bertha and the now Mary Pickford corresponded monthly.[36]

Wally (center) with Kalla Pasha (left) and Sidney Bracey in *The Dictator*.

Bertha also witnessed the darker side of the Reid house and Wally's "friends" that frightened her. She described an open house with nightly parties but downplayed the merriment. Wally showed films in his den, putting out a "quart bottle of liquor with glasses, ice and cigarettes and a 10-pound box of candy." Among the questionable visitors she described was the son of a prominent actor who visited to borrow $40 and a gun, which Wally gave him even though the man mentioned he intended to commit suicide. Bertha denied ever seeing Wally under the influence of drugs and said he barely drank. She left via train in the middle of March which meant Wally was still partying heavily in early 1922.

Wally's next assignment evidenced how frantic Lasky was to find vehicles Wally could handle. Since the 1921 blockbusters *The Affairs of Anatol* and *Forever*, Wally's assignments were steadily less spectacular because he could not physically handle tough or trying roles. His 1922 assignments were mediocre movies. He barely survived *The World's Champion*. He enjoyed *Across the Continent* because he could drive cars. *Nice People* was an uninspired film and *The Dictator* a remake of a recent film.

The Ghost Breaker was another remake of a 1914 Famous Players film based on a 1909 Paul Dickey–Charles W. Goddard play *The Ghost Breaker, a Melodramatic Farce in Four Acts*. The 1922 version was directed by Alfred E. Green and the scenario was by Jack Cunningham and Walter DeLeon. Wally again worked with Lila Lee, supported by Walter Hiers, Arthur Edmund Carewe, J. Farrell MacDonald, Frances Raymond and Snitz Edwards. Three unknowns had uncredited roles as ghosts: Richard Arlen,[37] Mervyn LeRoy,[38] and George O'Brien.[39]

Wally plays Warren Jarvis, who with his servant (Edwards) flees a Kentucky feud and meets beautiful Spanish heiress Maria Theresa (Lee). She persuades him to help rid her newly-inherited castle of ghosts and find a treasure hidden in the walls. The three are unaware that the "ghosts" were actually hired by the Duke of d'Alba (Carewe) who hopes to find the treasure himself and use it to win the affections of Maria. Warren uncovers the plot, foils the Duke, and wins Maria's love.[40]

The 7-reel *Ghost Breaker* was a grueling shoot for the weakening Wally. Like most of his later assignments the film was uninspired. It premiered in New York on September 10th and nationally on October 15th, and was well-received by fans. A Wisconsin woman said, "I thought I'd die. It's the funniest film I ever hope to see. I nearly died laughing. Wally is wonderful!"[41] But reviewers noticed Wally's physical decline and mentioned an "illness," one in Chicago writing, "Though the star was much thinner the director thoughtfully omitted 'close-ups' so that, with Mr. Reid's cooperation and good work 'The Ghost Breaker' proceeds on its way with everybody happy, including the featured player himself."[42]

During filming Wally presented Lasky with a problem that was as ridiculous as it was potentially disastrous. He quietly began another attempt to drive in the Indianapolis 500. He had received a racing drivers' license the previous Christmas and was genuinely excited about entering a race, as originally suggested by Omar Toft. Lasky stopped him in 1921 but he came close to racing in 1922. He told Lasky he didn't care *what* Lasky did and registering under his own name. March 16th papers reported, "Wallace Reid, moving picture star, has leased a racing automobile and will try to qualify for the annual 500 mile race at the Indianapolis Motor Speedway, May 30, it was announced at the track today. Reid will drive the car which finished fourth in the 1921 race."[43]

Wally leased a Duesenberg Straight 8, the fastest car in the world, from Eddie Miller, who finished the 1921 race in the car just 10 seconds behind the winner. Tempting fate, Wally renumbered the car from Miller's number 5 to number 13. He told Lasky he would take the month of May off to go to Indiana and practice and on April 11th headlines noted, "WALLY REID TO DRIVE IN RACE—Movie Star Enters Indianapolis Speed Contests May 30 Despite the Protests of Jesse Lasky."[44] Track manager T.E. Myers confirmed, "His entry is on file at our office, and we have definite information that he will arrive here May 4 to start training and practicing for the big event. Reid, although a movie star, has many qualities and experiences that appear to make him worthy of a mount in the International sweepstakes. Jesse Lasky, head of the organization for which Reid has been filming pictures, has made an earnest effort to keep Reid out of the affair because of the dangers of automobile racing. But we are confident that Reid will be at the starting tape on Memorial Day."[45] Another story reported, "Wally Reid, fresh from winning a new series of moving picture races, will stake his chances for fame and additional fortune against the old masters."[46]

Lasky was adamant that Wally would not drive but Wally was determined in his delusion that he was capable of racing. The day before Wally was to leave Lasky again threatened to void his contract if he raced. Bitterly disappointed, Wally had no choice but to withdraw. On May 11 it was announced that Wally would "not drive the automobile he has entered in the 500 Mile International Sweepstake race to be run at Indianapolis Motor Speedway May 30. The reason given was that the holders of his long term picture contract refuses [sic] to permit him to compete."[47] A week later a writer noted, "The leading service rendered by the movies last week by Will Hays was the announcement that Wally Reid is too precious to be risked as a driver in that Indianapolis race Decoration Day."[48]

Wally's friends knew the reality; it was suicide for him to try to race. In the spring of 1922 he was a mental and physical wreck. St. Johns felt his determination to race proved how deep his problem was:

> The realization of the actual nature of the trouble mounted to a certainty, and his family, his real friends, his business superiors ... poised in horror and bewilderment [and] a pity that tore every heart. For, as a matter of fact, we had all known, deep down in our hearts.... Wally's determination to drive in the Indianapolis race forced our hands, drove us into the open. He had decided to drive his great English speed demon, the Sunbeam [an error by St. Johns] in the Decoration Day races. He was a licensed racing driver. The honor was one he valued

The death of Wally's close friend Roscoe Sarles—he bumped another car, crashed and was burned to death at a Kansas race track in September 17, 1921—didn't stop Wally from trying to enter the Indianapolis 500. Lasky was terrified that the same fate would befall his top star.

highly. The thing became an obsession with him. Arguments were powerless. The threats of the company that such an action would break his contract didn't touch him. The pleas of his friends were unavailing. Whether or not there was, deep down, a desire to die with his boots on, an almost subconscious hope that this would be a final, grand gesture, no one knows. He could not go there to drive. It was worse than suicide, in his weakened mental and physical condition. It might be murder.[49]

Wally's insistence on racing was nothing less than suicidal, which may have been his subconscious intent, as St. Johns noted. In Indianapolis 500 archives, the May 30, 1922, records list "Cars and Drivers Which Failed to Qualify in 1922." The first listing reads, "Car #13—Driver: Wallace Reid—Car: Duesenberg—Entrant: Wallace Reid—Engine: Duesenberg—Status: Withdrawn."

At the same tiem another legal battle was playing out in a San Francisco courtroom. Roscoe Arbuckle's third trial began March 6th as D.A. Brady continued his misguided effort to convict Arbuckle with his perjured case. Arbuckle, his career over due to Brady and the Zukor-Lasky decision not to back him, appeared thinner and sadder than he ever had and during the trial sat with his hands folded in his lap. The third trial was a joke. There were no facts, no evidence, and no witnesses. Brady offered nothing but theory, sentiment, and "San Francisco versus L.A. pride." It was another dismal failure.[50] The jury began deliberations on April 12th and was in the jury room for six minutes before filing back into court where the foreman read—almost yelled—"NOT GUILTY." Surprisingly, the foreman also read a statement into the record, saying:

Acquittal is not enough for Roscoe Arbuckle. We feel a grave injustice has been done him. We feel it is only our plain duty to give him the exoneration, under the evidence, for there was not the slightest proof to connect him in any way with the commission of any crime. He was manly throughout the case and told a straightforward story on the witness stand. The happening at the hotel was an unfortunate affair for which Arbuckle, the evidence shows, was in no way responsible. We wish him success and hope the American people will take the judgment of twelve men and women who have sat listening for 31 days to the evidence, that Roscoe Arbuckle is innocent and free of blame.[51]

Arbuckle sat and smiled weakly. The cases cost him $110,000 ($3,000,000 today) but the real cost was his life. Lasky issued a statement that the studio would release an Arbuckle feature but after a meeting on the 25th backed off and suggested Arbuckle take a six month European vacation to "let things quiet down." He did so and upon his return was surprised that Lasky and Hays felt it would be acceptable to make a film. But public backlash against *Fatty, Round the Clock* shocked everyone. Women's and church groups and the clergy flooded the studio and Hays with objections so Lasky decided against the film, kept his completed films out of theaters and bought out Arbuckle's contract. Fatty was finished. During the next decade he tried getting back into films, first quietly directing under the pseudonym "Will B. Good," and he opened a Culver City café called The Plantation Club. Not until 1933 did Warners feel safe enough to offer him a four-picture deal, but that evening he had a heart attack in his New York apartment. He was only 44. Just before her own death, Minta Durfee—at his side for the entire eight months of trials though they had been separated for five years—wrote, "My husband died of a broken heart over the persecution and prosecution he faced...."[52]

After the Indianapolis 500 debacle Wally was assigned the comedy *Clarence*, while his addiction was becoming more public. The public loved the new gossip columns. One of the first gossip books was *The Sins of Hollywood: An Expose of Movie Vice; A Group of Stories of Actual Happenings Reported and Written by a Hollywood Newspaper Man*. Rushed into production just weeks after the Taylor murder and released in early 1922, former *Photoplay* editor Ed Roberts' book included rumors about dozens of stars, only thinly disguising their true identities. For example, Rudolph Valentino was "Adolpho," a New York dance hall gigolo. But with every phony name was a photo of the actual star! Roberts promised readers his stories of "The sins of Hollywood are facts—NOT FICTION! ... the SINS OF HOLLYWOOD are given to the public."[53] His story about Wally was eerily accurate:

> ... a certain well-known and muchly [sic] adored heart-breaking star of the so-called "manly" type taught—who shall be called Walter—sought out several habitués of the underworld of Los Angeles and visited with them, consorted with them for the purpose of obtaining "local color." They induced him to try "a shot of hop." It was great, he told some of his friends and "Yes men." Yes, Walter smoked an opium pipe and went back for more. He then tried "snuffing" cocaine. He "took a few shots in the arm." Walter was a good sort. He wanted his friends to taste of the sweets of life ... he would give a "dope party." Obviously he could not hold this party at his own home. His wife—she, too, a star—would object. She didn't even know that Walter had been trying out various kinds of dope. Walter leased a cabin in Laurel Canyon and invited a few select friends ... Margaret and Mae, Vincent and Jay, Frank and Louise, Mary and Jack and Juanita. Oh, yes, there was a Chinaman there with his pipes and little pellets of opium. How they enjoyed that "shot in the arm." ... It was thoroughly a worthwhile party, his guests told Walter, and he was pleased. One by one they staggered homeward, vowing to return—any time—and partake of handsome Walter's hospitality. And they did. And once, not so long ago, the Federal officers called upon Handsome Walter and talked things over with him. They wanted to know if he was the go-between—the man who acted as middleman for the actors and the peddlers of drugs. Somehow he got out of it. At least, he is still in pictures and out of jail.[54]

Wally with his *Clarence* co-star May McAvoy. Robert Agnew is at left.

Roberts' piece was accurate. Wally was surrounded by "yes" men, his wife didn't like parties at their home and he always wanted friends to have fun. He was also caught in a drug den "looking for local color" for a role. The mob-owned bar was raided the previous summer while he was there but he was released. Friends knew of his Laurel Canyon hideaway and the party guests were friends: Margaret and Mae Marsh, Mary and Jack Pickford and Bessie Love (her real name was Juanita Horton; she had a house nearby at 2401 Laurel Canyon for *her* parties). It was also well-known that a Federal drug task force questioned Wally numerous times, assuming anyone doing the amount of drugs that he was *must* be involved in trafficking.

Picture-Play Magazine came to Wally's defense in July in a Hazel Shelley article entitled "Heroes I Have Known." Shelley wrote unpleasant details about stars she had known but of Wally said, "Wallace Reid came to the rescue of my lost illusions concerning heroes. Not knowingly, of course, because Wally would be the last person in the world to acknowledge himself a hero. His heart is almost too big and too generous for his own good."[55]

Wally and Lasky tried to ignore the firestorm as he began *Clarence* in June. William de Mille directed the Clara Beranger adaptation of the 1921 Booth Tarkington play *Clarence; a Comedy in Four Acts*. Guy Wilky did the filming. Wally starred with Agnes Ayres, supported by May McAvoy, Kathlyn Williams, Edward Martindel, Robert Agnew, Adolphe Menjou, Bertram Johns, Dorothy Gordon and Mayme Kelso. Wally's character was a "saxophone-playing ex-soldier who unconsciously becomes a domestic happiness expert and general fixer in the squabbling family where he lodges."[56]

Wally plays Clarence Smith, a penniless ex–Army mule driver who ambles up to the Wheeler home and is hired to do odd jobs by Mr. Wheeler (Martindel). Clarence is in the middle of a squabbling family but falls in love with the family nanny, Violet Pinney (Ayres). Mrs. Wheeler (Williams) believes Violet is the object of her husband's affections and with daughter Cora (McAvoy) conspires to ruin the supposed love affair by flirting with the disinterested Clarence. All the while Clarence settles petty family differences; unknown to them he was a college professor before his Army service. When he and Violet prevent Cora from eloping with the elder Wheeler's money-grubbing secretary Hubert Stem (Menjou), the family is in an uproar. Stem finds a clipping about a deserter named "Charles" Smith and tries to convince Mr. Wheeler that Clarence is this Smith, but a letter arrives revealing Clarence's background and inviting him back to teach and all are reconciled.[57]

The film premiered in New York October 15th and nationally November 9th. It was well received and fans were delighted to *see* Wally play his saxophone. The Beuchler Saxophone Company ran ads with Wally and their products, one of the deals arranged by Ivan St. Johns. Ads read, "Wally Reid is the mysterious hero who jazzes the flappers'

Wally with (from left) Kathlyn Williams, Edward Martindel and May McAvoy in *Clarence*. Fans were thrilled to see Wally with his saxophone, but didn't notice how sickly and thin he had become.

hearts away with his moanin' saxophone. Seven reels of pure joy."[58] But seven reels meant a demanding shoot for Wally, who was only able to stand for a few minutes at a time.

Wally's next assignment was *Night Life in Hollywood,* a propaganda film quietly made by Lasky to answer the public furor over Hollywood. It was officially made by A.B. Maescher's company and distributed by Arrow Films but Maescher was a minor producer and Arrow Film a tiny company that distributed independent films. Also it was directed by Fred Caldwell and Jack Pratt, directors with no studio affiliation and Maescher's wife has a producer's credit. There is no way these men could secure stars for small roles unless the studios were managing the project. There is no record of art direction, cameramen, or other credits typical for movies with actors like Wally, Theodore Roberts, Sessue Hayakawa, William Desmond, Bryant Washburn, Bessie Love and J. Warren Kerrigan. The "stars" were minor players J. Frank Glendon, Josephine Gale, Gale Henry, J.L. McComas, Elizabeth Rhodes, Jack Connolly and Delores Hall. Lasky no doubt produced the film; the name stars were all his employees.

This film is about a brother (Glendon) and sister (Henry) from Arkansas who set out for Hollywood, reputed to be a modern-day Babylon, but the town is quiet and full of unassuming stars who are not given to partying. When the boy falls in love with an actress (Hill) even his parents (McComas and Rhodes) approve since they know that "Hollywood people" are no different from folks back home. The name stars each appear in scenes supporting their quiet, boring lives. Cameras visit the homes of Wally and Dorothy, who sit quietly in the den with Billy running about, J. Warren Kerrigan (with his mother), Bryant Washburn and Will Rogers. Also shown are several stars attending Easter services at the Hollywood Bowl.[59] The film was released November 15th and was renamed *The Shriek of Hollywood* for European markets.

By the end of June, Wally's physical condition had declined to the point that he had trouble standing at all. Lasky had to surround him with name stars and fans openly wondered "why?" In June, *Photoplay* ran the story "Reid Does Not Think All-Star Casts Hurt Individual Player's Popularity" for fans who noticed he was no longer carrying his films alone.[60] In truth Lasky needed "All-Star Casts" with Wally. He could only get through a day of shooting with morphine, which left him unable to sleep. Always exhausted, he went from injection to injection. His weight was under 150; camera angles and lighting could no longer hide his astonishing decline.

That summer Wally and Dorothy rarely left DeLongpre. She was frantic, trying to find a cure for the addiction she knew was in its final stages. She sought cures everywhere, always secretly. She could not consult local physicians so was seeking alternative cures. She contacted Dr. C.P. Bryant, a Seattle physician and one of the country's earliest proponents of homeopathic medicine. Practitioners believe in treating patients with remedies that in crude doses would produce in healthy people symptoms similar to the disease being treated. But the remedies are natural sources without chemical toxicity.[61]

Bryant believed, "Medicine, based on pills and potion is becoming obsolete. Physiology has taught us many ways to deal with the human body ... successfully pursued by the drugless schools...."[62] In 1918 he allegedly successfully treated 500 Spanish flu victims and believed cancer was "the result of the use of vaccines and serums."[63] His treatment regimens for Wally for "Narcotic Drug Addiction–Disease" and "Alcoholism"[64] were both extremely simplistic and appear unrealistic. The treatment for drug addiction notes "no variation in the length of time required for the active treatment, regardless of the quantity of drug being used or the length of time the patient has been diseased." For alcoholism, treatment "is usually completed within 32 hours. It is advisable, however, to keep patient under observation at least 72 hours."

Bryant offered his "Crebo Method" for Wally's drug addiction. Crebo was described as "the lipoid of a non-toxic plant commonly found in India." The regimen was a daily mix of injections, enemas, and pills with crebo, curare, ephedrine, luminal, emetine hydrochloride, pilocarpine hydrochloride, adrenalin, avertin, and adreno-spermine. Curare was an interesting choice, a plant compound used in South America as an extremely potent arrow poison. It is prepared by combining the poisonous bark-scrapings and plants from which curare is derived and the venom from poisonout snakes and ants. Death results from asphyxia by paralyzing skeletal muscles and depending on the animal's size takes from seconds to 20 minutes. Contrary to rumor it was rarely used on humans, too expensive and scarce. Bryant's "General Rules" for his treatment seem ridiculously simple:

> The first requisite in the treatment of drug addicts is to gain the complete confidence of the patient and keep the patient's mind at ease. Assure him that he is free to leave the hospital at any time; that nothing is going to be forced upon him; that he is never going to be restricted in any way.... This takes away any fear that there is going to be any restraint or that he is going to be deprived of his drug at any time.... It is advisable never to mention or allude to narcotics.[65]

The protocol called for painful shots directly into the chest between the second and third rib near the sternum. Bryant suggested injections to "avoid old scar tissue," referring to Wally's old needle marks. Among side effects were severe twitching, cramps, nervousness, tension, insomnia, exhaustion, food and water cravings, and dysentery. Normally such treatment would occur at a private sanitarium but Wally took his at home. A handwritten note from Dorothy was found in the William Wallace Reid, Jr. materials at the Herrick Library.[66] In addition to what appears to be a sketch of locations for injections are notes about dosage and timing and ominously, instructions on what to do should Wally experience "heart collapse" or "unnatural results." Bryant's bizarre program had no effect and Wally's health worsened, which makes what happened in August that much more surprising. Or perhaps not.

On August 25th Wally and Dorothy petitioned the Superior Court to adopt 3-year-old Betty Ann Mummert. Papers announced, "Mr. and Mrs. Wallace Reid to Adopt Child" or "WALLY REID WILL ADOPT DAUGHTER,"[67] with a brief story that "Mr. and Mrs. Wallace Reid petitioned the Superior Court today for permission to adopt Betty Mummert, 3 years old, whose parents have consented to the adoption. Mrs. Reid is known to the screen as Dorothy Davenport Reid."[68]

Given Wally's health it was an odd time to adopt. Unless the child was his. Research and circumstantial evidence indicates that Betty Ann may have been Wally's biological child and was probably already living at DeLongpre. Both Dorothy and Bertha hinted at such. In a 1966 interview Dorothy described the first Christmas at DeLongpre in 1920: "there were three Christmas trees—a huge one for the grown-ups, and *two smaller ones for each of the children.*"[69] During her 1921 visit Bertha saw "the family Christmas tree, or rather three trees...."[70] One for the adults and *two for the children*. This can of worms has gone unnoticed until now.

How and when Dorothy and Wally brought Betty into their home is a mystery with no easy solution. The first "official" notice was the August 26th story, followed the next day by, "Mr. & Mrs. Wallace Reid expect to be presented with a bouncing baby girl soon, according to a petition on file in the Superior Court Friday, August 25, which asks the legal adoption of Betty Mummert, 3 years old."[71]

The articles mentioned that the child's parents consented to the adoption but where did Betty Ann come from? Extensive research of census records, city directories and period newspapers uncovered only one Mummert in California, a 1920 census listing for a successful physician with no children. Dorothy, Bertha, and St. Johns would tell different stories about Betty, which only added to the confusion. Dorothy said she found the girl in Long Beach:

> Wally always had wanted a baby girl. Playing in Long Beach one night, a tiny curly-haired youngster strayed into my dressing room. Her clothes were a sight. Her hands were black with the grime of the theater alley, her playground. But her face, beneath her tightly curled hair, was sweet and wistful. I found the old grandfather who cared for her and the next night I took her home—Betty, who is now our own. I wish you could have seen Wally's face that night. I carried Betty, still in her dirty clothes, out of the car and into the house. Some of our friends were there, but Wally forgot them. For an hour he sat on the floor with the youngster, and then, oblivious of his guests, took her upstairs and tucked her into bed. He refused to let the maid touch her. His face was working with emotion when he came back, but he said very little. I think that tiny Betty, with her curly hair and her dimpled cheeks, has played her great big part in Wally's comeback.[72]

Her story makes no sense. First, she made very few stage appearances (if any) in the 1920s and none in 1922.[73] Wally was dying and had she left him to do a play it would have been publicized. Also, bringing a child home who wandered into her dressing room defies reason. Lastly, the alleged grandfather contradicts accounts that mentioned that her "parents" consented.

Bertha's writings place Betty at DeLongpre during her 3-month visit in late 1921. She wrote, "Wally especially wanted a daughter, so that when Dorothy found little Betty and brought her home, Wallace received her with open arms...."[74] But she was clear that Betty was *there* during her "three month's stay"[75] and later recalled Billy was "four-years old" when Betty arrived, also indicating Betty was there in 1921. Interestingly, St. Johns didn't even *mention* Betty in the biography she wrote just five years later. Not a single mention, though there are dozens of mentions of Billy, including five photos.

A 1923 *Movie Weekly* story is perhaps the best description of how little Betty ended up at DeLongpre. The title was "REAL DRAMAS OF HOLLYWOOD":

> She heard of her dashing husband's affairs from time to time. She even indulgently answered his "mash notes...." But one night came something more serious. The wife was alone in the house, except for the children, who had gone to bed. The servants, Japanese, went home at night. Came a rap on the door, a timid rap, and the wife wondered why the visitor did not ring the bell.... She opened the door, and there stood a girl with a baby in her arms. It was so like a melodrama that the wife felt a horribly hysterical desire to laugh when the girl asked for her husband! "So it has come at last!" she said to herself, still with that awful clutching at her throat, the hysterical desire to laugh and weep. She ... had been expecting something of this sort to happen. The girl was crying, and looked so helpless, so utterly as a victim of her husband would look, she thought! The wife asked the girl to come in. The girl, young and very pretty and modishly dressed after a cheap fashion, brightened and came in. She felt no pang of jealousy when she looked at the girl, oddly enough, she thought to herself even then, but she felt a terrible, clutching feeling, half anger, half piercing pity, when she looked at the baby! It was all as the wife had expected from the first moment she looked at the girl. The baby was her husband's! She never thought to doubt the girl's story. It didn't occur to her until afterward that this was odd. But the girl was so evidently miserable, heart-broken, and her claim was made in such frank, genuine, if heart-broken, fashion, that the wife had to believe her. "I'm only an extra girl," the girl said hurriedly, after satisfying herself that her seducer was not at home, and that the wife had only pity in her heart for her. "I do love my baby so, but my mother died last week, and there is no one to care for him! Now you just must adopt my baby and..." The wife ... had expected a call for money, but not for this. "Yes," the girl said firmly. "There isn't any other way. My baby cannot go to a foundling asylum ... but his own father to have him! I'll kill myself if you don't!" the girl threatened desperately. "Yes, we'll do it!" the wife suddenly decided. Her husband would not dare refuse, she knew that. For the girl would certainly make a scandal. The girl promised never to see her baby again. She was only

This studio photo appears to show an infant clearly much younger than 3 or 4, Betty's supposed age at the time of her adoption. It also places her with the family two years earlier than alleged, since it was taken in 1920 or 1921.

one of many, she thought drearily. And the baby was a dear baby! So the little one found a home. And the child will never know the difference between its own mother and this foster one![76]

Betty's sudden appearance the lack of a plausible background, Wally's affairs, and the contradictory stories by Dorothy and Bertha, all point to the conclusion that little Betty was probably an illegitimate child fathered by Wally. She may have been at DeLongpre as early as late 1920 although the adoption process wasn't finalized until August, 1922. Adoption records are sealed so it's unclear exactly *when* or *how* she was adopted but Betty was apparently part of the family before August, 1922 although she was *never* mentioned in any story before 1922 and rarely after Wally's death. It's possible that Dorothy was starting the process of getting Wally's affairs in order in 1922, that she knew he would not survive the battle he was waging. Interestingly, photos of a four-year-old Betty show an uncanny resemblance to Bill Jr. and to Wally at age 4.

Finally, a rare family photo recently discovered shows Wally and Dorothy with both children. Little Betty is clearly much younger than the alleged age at the time of her arrival (3½). In the photo, she is clearly between 1 and 2, and Bill Jr. perhaps 5. And like other photos with both children the two youngsters look very much alike.

A final fascinating item was uncovered about Betty in the Letters of Guardianship and Letters of Administration records filed after Wally's death and signed by Dorothy. In the documents it was noted that her real name was not Betty Ann, but "Betty Anna."[77] Why nobody *ever* referred to her as "Betty Anna" is also unknown.

The infant had a profound effect on Wally. One of the few times Dorothy saw him angry was when someone referred to her as an "adopted child." His eyes flashed and he said, "Please never say that again. She is ours, our very own."[78] The first photos of Betty did not appear until the following year, after Wally's death. Sadly, many of the Reid "family" photos did not include Betty; just Wally, Dorothy, and Bill Jr.

14

The Curtain Falls on a Tragedy

As summer 1922 turned to fall, Wally's health was rapidly failing. Dorothy described the period: "Toward the last, just before he left the studio to recuperate, it would take only a few drinks to affect him. His breakdown came after he had reported back to the studio ready for work. A condition developed which baffled and is still puzzling doctors. It first manifested itself as an intestinal disturbance. He was ordered to a hospital. Every possible test ... was given him. Needles half a dozen inches long were driven into his spine. The pain he endured was terrible. Not a single test showed a positive result. In the midst of all this, influenza set in."[1]

In early September, Wally had a setback Dorothy blamed on "Kleig eyes," a painful condition caused by over-exposure to the bright white Kleig lights used on the interior stages. His "week of darkness" began one morning when Dorothy heard him bumping around the bedroom wailing, "Mamma! Mamma! Where is the door?" He was totally blind and terrified, crying like a child, "Mamma, please don't leave me; don't leave me alone in the dark." It took a week for him to regain sight and his vision was blurred for several more. She and Wally retreated back to the mountain cabin in Pasadena with Teddy Hayes. Wally told her, "No matter what comes now, mamma, thank God, I've bucked the drugs." Dorothy recalled a short stay in a sanitarium after the mountain retreat before the group traveled to Palm Springs.

They spent two weeks secluded in Palm Springs but Dorothy said, "His condition grew worse. We tried every known remedy without effect." So weak he could barely walk, perhaps due to abstaining from drugs, he was unhappy and talked constantly about home. So Dorothy brought him back. Hayes moved in and "rigged up a bicycle arrangement and forced Wally to exercise, much against his will. Still the dysentery persisted and Wally grew weaker. Toward the last, the trainer carried him in his arms up and down the steps and through the house." Dorothy may have again tried Bryant's Crebo cure; dysentery was a side-effect. She called this "Wally's second magnificent fight with death."

According to St. Johns though, during these weeks Wally was "himself again." His mind was clear for the first time in two years but with that came terrific remorse and daily crying jags. Trying to regain something from his old life he laid for hours listening to music on the Victrola. Dorothy also read to him, poets like Keats and Browning and the Shakespearean comedies.[2]

Fans weren't aware of Wally's deterioration as he began *Thirty Days* in September. He was emaciated—below 150 pounds—and barely resembled the actor of his earlier films. In one of the last candid photos from that set, the toll was glaringly evident. Gone

Wally on the set of his final film, *Thirty Days*, in the fall of 1922. He could barely stand, and in three months would be dead.

were his good looks, replaced by an older-looking gaze from hollow eyes. His face was fuller but his eyes deeper, lined with creases and large bags underneath. He looked 15 years older than he had just six months earlier. The studio caption read, "An exclusive photo of Wally Reid, made just before he collapsed and went in out of the 'snow'—into a sanitarium where the bootlegger can not break in and corrupt."[3] The "snow" reference was telling; the phrase was used to compare Kleig eye to snow blindness but was also a reference to drug use.

Wally certainly knew the gravity of his situation. In a letter to St. Johns just before filming began he admitted, "I don't know why I have failed like this. Sometimes I think you do. Pray for me that, somewhere in the strange land into which I am going alone, I may become at last the man I have always wanted to be."[4] She knew he was in danger, writing, "He worked—as he had always, faithfully and consistently, when he could hardly walk on the set ... but still he carried on. He played his part, but the old lovable, irresistible smile, that had won its way around the universe, was a shadow of itself. But the flame was gone. The shining light within, which had reached out and touched hearts, didn't burn any more."[5] He was contrite, weeping to Dorothy, "How did I happen to let myself go? Why couldn't I have stopped long ago? I thought I was so strong; I thought I knew myself so well; I can't understand it."[6]

Even as weak as he was, *Thirty Days* should have been an easy assignment, a comedy based on an A.E. Thomas and Clayton Hamilton play adapted by Walter Woods.[7]

Lasky assigned James Cruze to direct assuming only his old friend could get Wally through filming. Wally starred with Wanda Hawley, another close friend, supported by Charles Ogle, Cyril Chadwick, Hershel Mayall, Helen Dunbar, Carmen Phillips, Kalla Pasha and Robert Brower.

Wally plays naïve John Floyd, who has no idea how popular he is with ladies. He is at continuous odds with his jealous fiancée Lucille Ledyard (Hawley), who *is* aware. After being innocently friendly with beautiful Italian Carlotta Polenta (Phillips), John is pursued by her murderous husband Giacomo (Mayall), intent on avenging his honor. To escape the wrath of Giacomo, John has himself sentenced to thirty days in jail. But Giacomo is also sent to jail; John's efforts to elude Giacomo while both are imprisoned are the basis for the comedy scenes. After both are released the same day John explains matters to his fiancée and Giacomo is put on a ship before he can harm John.[8]

Wally barely survived filming. He couldn't even stand, let alone act. Stagehands helped him to his feet and in most scenes he either sat or leaned on furniture. It has long been stated that Wally suffered his final collapse on the *Thirty Days* set but that is not so. He completed filming and immediately started *Nobody's Money*. It was during *that* shoot that Wally's body finally gave out. Wally collapsed on the set of his "final film" and since *Thirty Days* was his final *completed* film historians incorrectly assume it was on *that* set he collapsed.

Nobody's Money was another light comedy, directed by Wallace Worsley. Wally was paired with Hawley, playing a young man who falls in love with the Governor's daughter while running a re-election campaign. On the first day of filming, Friday, October 19th, Wally collapsed on the floor in a heap. Henry Hathaway, the assistant director, witnessed the pitiful final breakdown and recalled, "He sort of fumbled about, and bumped into a chair, and then just sat down on to the floor and started to cry. They put him in a chair, and he just keeled over. They sent for an ambulance and sent him to the hospital."[9]

Wally was spirited to Dr. C.B. Blessing's nearby Los Angeles sanitarium that advertised the "Barker Cure" for drug addiction. He may have already visited the site between the last Pasadena visit and his trip to Palm Springs. Blessing was a follower of Dr. John Scott Barker, who ran a controversial Oakland drug treatment facility. His most famous client, actress Jaunita Hansen, said the "cure" consisted of a cocktail of unidentified pills and medicines and a rigid diet "to extract the poison that remained in my system." Rumors abounded that the pills were just replacement drugs that kept the addict off one but hooked on another. Hansen wrote an extensive story of her battle but was re-arrested in 1923 for drug use.[10]

Barker's site was raided numerous times, as was Blessing's (Blessing was arrested by Federal drug agents the following December). Wally entered the facility on the 19th; entry records gave his age (incorrectly) as 31, his height 6 feet 2 inches, and his weight 146, below his normal weight which was noted as 190. They also indicated his use of drugs at the time was three to six grains of morphine a day.[11] Wally remained there for six weeks.

Wally was aware of the severity of his plight but was still committed to beating the addiction on his own terms. He was probably past the point of surviving his morphine addiction even *with* some type of formal program and resolved to quit "cold turkey" and pray his body could survive. He told DeMille and Lasky, "I'll either come out cured or I won't come out."[12] Dorothy said he was "determined to go to a reputable sanitarium, and cure himself once and for all."[13]

The first public notice was a small Saturday morning story that "Wallace Reid's reported to be critically ill at his Hollywood home. An eye infection has recently confined the famous motion picture star to his home and yesterday it was said he was recovering. He suffered a sudden relapse last night and it was planned to remove him to a hospital. Today his condition grew so serious that it was found advisable to move him."[14] But Sunday headlines screamed, "WALLACE REID SERIOUSLY ILL IN SANITARIUM." Lasky publicists insisted Wally was suffering from exhaustion and Kleig eyes and identified the movie he was working on as *Nobody's Money* (and correctly that Jack Holt replaced him).

Drugs were not mentioned in any of the early articles, which noted the severity of his illness and that he was "waging a valiant battle against a combination of maladies" but "doing as well as could be expected." Dorothy was described as being at his bedside and told reporters that Wally was "a very sick man. It is true that his condition is serious but he is not dying, as was the rumor." She continued to blame the illness on "Kleig eye," but for the first time admitted that her husband had suffered a nervous breakdown after an illness that had lasted "several months," explaining that "because of overwork and the eye malady ... [the] combination ... proved too much for his physique Wednesday and he suffered a 'complete breakdown.'" Dorothy indicated that his eyes had never been strong (clearly not true) and that they had failed completely just before the breakdown.

It was admitted that "the climax came when he started work on the Lasky 'lot' a week ago on a picture 'Nobody's Money.' He was cast for the lead, but was unable to continue after the first day or so. Yesterday it was announced Jack Holt had been signed to play the lead. Reid requested and obtained a four weeks' vacation from the Lasky Corporation which ended Wednesday. During that period he camped and hunted in the mountains in an attempt to stem the onrushing nervous breakdown."[15] Though the stories usually tried to downplay the severity of the problem it was confirmed that he would be away from the studio for "at least a month."[16]

Coming on the heels of the Arbuckle and Taylor scandals Wally's problem was a huge Paramount problem. That fact ws not lost on Will Hays, who tried to convince Lasky to remove Wally's films from theaters. Lasky ignored the advice. As long as drug use was not confirmed Lasky believed the studio could avoid fall-out, correctly assuming most of the world was still unaware. On the day he collapsed *Moving Picture World* reported Wally as the most popular American actor in Europe.[17]

Articles running even weeks later still didn't grasp the enormity of the situation. A review of *The Ghost Breaker* chided moviegoers, "Don't go to see 'The Ghost Breaker' with any idea in your head that Wallace Reid has permitted his illness to interfere with his acting. I suspect him of having been a gallant gentleman in fact, as the role he plays, and while the photoplay was being made, keeping his discomfort to himself, doing his bit with a high and gay courage."[18] Lasky publicists added to the charade, writing, "Yes girls, Wally Reid is recovering rapidly, his press agent says. In fact he started work this month on 'Mr. Billings Spends His Dime' by Dona Burnett."[19]

No records survive of his stay at Blessing but it is assumed doctors spent the first weeks stabilizing Wally's health while he battled horrible withdrawal symptoms. Even in his weakened condition he somehow retained his sense of humor. When he was given some whiskey in medicine, so weak that he could literally not lift his head off of his pillow without fainting, he roused and said, "What are you trying to do? Get me started again?"[20]

Dorothy spent the first weeks at Wally's bedside. She did not immediately tell Bertha; perhaps she thought that he would weather the storm. Bertha wrote later she did not even know of Wally's illness until she was moving from Highlands to her New York townhouse the first of December. That was a fabrication; Wally's name was all over the papers for weeks and she was trading telegrams with Dorothy as early as October. She begged Dorothy to tell her the truth, pleading for "mercy," but Dorothy stubbornly refused even as Wally lay dying. She wired back, "Condition much improved—no cause for worry. Starting today for 10-day motor trip. Ignore all rumors. Love from all. Wallace and Dorothy."[21]

Bertha called him daily but most days he was incoherent. When he could speak he told her, "I'm winning the fight Momma."[22] Dorothy did not want Bertha coming west and also kept the truth from her own mother. Alice had moved into DeLongpre to care for the children and didn't share her daughter's contempt for Bertha; in fact the two became fast friends during Bertha's visit and corresponded weekly after Bertha's return home. Alice's first letter on October 26th, a week after Wally's collapse, said, "I was so upset at your telegram. I was so afraid the false reports would reach you. He has been quite sick but not in any danger, although we feared he may lose his sight. He will be better than he has in three years." On October 31st she wrote, "Wally grows stronger every day and goes back to work in two weeks. The reports were all wrong. We did not realize that you would get them. He will look better than he has in three years. The reports were just killing him, but it's all over, thank God. Now we can rejoice. He will write when he is able. His eyes are not right yet, but they will be in time. They are going out at least twice a week to nice places together. I'm so happy that things look so bright."[23] It's doubtful Alice would knowingly help Dorothy deceive Bertha, though her letters indicate she too underestimated the severity of the situation. Dorothy was apparently lying to her, too.

While he lay dying in the hospital, advertisements featuring the suave star still filled newspapers, like this one for Mallory Hat Company.

Lasky made no initial mention of Wally's illness, hoping the story would fade, and indeed after the first days he stayed out of the news for weeks. Papers were fed false reports in early November. On the 3rd it was reported Wally had been taken to the "Mayo Clinic in Rochester, Minnesota, where experts were examining the eyes of Wallace Reid, film star, reportedly seriously affected by the powerful studio lights. Reid is in seclusion here and visitors are barred. In public he wears heavy bandages over his eyes."[24]

On November 13th Alice wrote Bertha, "The children [Wally and Dorothy] are in Oakland for a day or two en route. Wally is gaining fast. P.S. Nothing to worry about *now*." But on December 10th she reported, "Poor Wally had a relapse and he can't go to work for two or three weeks yet, but we hope all will be well in a few days. I'll keep you posted. He is not in danger. He was better today. As soon as the dysentery stops he will begin to gain. His face is like a *kid's* now. He looks twenty-two. He gains quickly, so don't worry. The worst is past. You will be proud of your son soon. I shall miss you at Xmas, for I learned to love you, you were just so sweet and wise." Had Bertha had an inkling Wally was in danger Dorothy knew she would be on the first train. She made sure Bertha stayed in New York.

On December 6th Dorothy recognized the Blessing treatment was failing and that Wally was probably dying. She moved him to the best-known private sanitarium in Hollywood, Banksia Place. Blessing's exit record noted, "Treatment of morphinism for two weeks [sic] and partial withdrawal accomplished. Reid later entered another sanitarium, where he is recently reported as improved in health."[25] Banksia Place was in a quiet residential area at 5227 Santa Monica Boulevard.[26] The studios favored Banksia. Mabel Normand, Alma Rubens, W.C. Fields, and dozens of other ailing stars visited because it was secretive. It wasn't a rehab facility per se; it was a full-service hospital and in fact the unit that passed as drug treatment was not much. According to Agnes de Mille, "The so-called private sanitarium really was the bottom floor of one of the hospitals. In the basement there were padded rooms adjacent to one another. Each room had a single light [that] burned overhead constantly, a sink, a toilet without a seat, and a small mattress on the floor."[27]

In those awful surroundings Wally had two full-time male nurses monitoring him and two doctors watching his treatment, led by Dr. Gavin S. Herbert, who later said Wally "weighed but 120 when he came here and was in woeful shape."[28] The next day Universal ads for the 1922 version of *Human Hearts* were revised, described as based on a "Play Written by Wally Reid's Father!" No mention of Hal alone, but as "Wally Reid's Father."[29]

On December 10th *Thirty Days* opened in New York. Theaters ran it for a month. People kept coming while Lasky ads mentioned—*even before he died*—that it was "Wallie Reid's Last Picture."[30] That week was bad for Wally. Dorothy waited too long to bring him to a real hospital. From the 11th to the 17th he almost died three times as his temperature spiked to 103° for days and his pulse rose to 130. His heartbeat was irregular. Weak and emaciated, he fainted every hour or so. His doctors believed Wally suffered from complete nervous exhaustion. Quite simply his body was too tired to rally even though clean of drugs and alcohol. Doctors affirmed, "His present illness has no connection with overindulgences in alcohol or narcotics although such indulgences have undoubtedly undermined his strength and system."[31]

By then he wasn't really

STRAND

THURSDAY AND FRIDAY

Wallace Reid

In His Hilarious Love Comedy

"Thirty Days"

WANDA HAWLEY
IN THE CAST

No Pompus sub-titles, no pageants just fun fast and furious.

Wallie Reid's Last Picture

In ads like this one, Lasky announced *Thirty Days* would be "Wallie Reid's Last Picture," even though it was released a month before he died. Those close to Wally knew the awful truth about his condition.

receiving medical treatment; what Wally went through was hellish. Dorothy said, "A doctor, I was told, looked at him from time to time over the next few weeks he was there, but ... he was only there to make sure Paramount's major investment was still alive, and would be able to return to work as soon as possible. A nurse would leave food only after Wally had spent the first three days virtually alone. All of the patients [*in his condition*] vomited, urinated, and defecated on themselves and on the floor. Only if the patient were deemed safe would anyone venture inside with a mop and a new hospital gown. Most of the patients stayed naked because they sometimes tore their gowns in anguish."[32]

Doctors suggested the only way Wally might rally would be to be put *on* morphine, but when offered the weaning process he simply declined, allegedly saying, "I'll go out clean. I'd rather my body died than go back to the thing that almost killed me. At least, I'm myself now. I'll go out clean."[33] When he asked for Dorothy's advice, she just shook her head and agreed with the death warrant.

During the same week Wally was given the Last Rites of the Catholic Church as his doctors gave him up for dead, but he startled everyone by improving. Dorothy said, "He thought he would die the other night. He was so brave about it, poor boy. For three nights he had expected to die. He isn't afraid to die, but he wants so much to live for Billy and Betty and me."[34] Coincidently, that same week Hays renewed pressure on Lasky to pull Wally's movies and though Lasky refused their discussion made the papers. On December 17th, the *Los Angeles Times* noted, "Hays attempted during the course of the afternoon to get into communication with Jesse Lasky, who finally telephoned him at his Ambassador suite and declared that he would refuse to issue any statement regarding Mr. Reid. Mr. Lasky reminded Mr. Hays that last June he had detailed a physician ... to watch him ... everywhere he went from the cellar to the bathroom."[35] When reporters pressed Hays about the call he said only, "There is nothing for me to say at this time except to say that I join with the others in hoping that Reid will win back his health, and be his old self again."[36]

On December 14th papers confirmed, "WALLACE REID CRITICALLY ILL— 'DOPE' BLAMED!" The article read, "It was no news to Hollywood that Wally Reid was slipping. It was gossip both in Hollywood and Los Angeles. Confirmation came today. A report that Reid had broken away from his nurses and come into Los Angeles and bought morphine for $300 reached the ears of newspapermen." When reporters rushed to DeLongpre early the morning of the 15th, Dorothy denied the story but confirmed his drug use. Wally did not have the strength to get out of bed, let alone leave the hospital. The story also noted that Wally would "have a difficult financial situation when he comes back ... morphine is expensive when a film star buys it. Wally's money, his friends say, went principally to dope peddlers, blackmailers, and bootleggers."[37] Ominously, Dorothy also said, "He is winning the fight ... and I know he will come back and be the old Wally everybody knew and loved. Yes, he will come back—if he survives."[38]

Hays was angered by Dorothy's admissions on the 14th and grew apoplectic at headlines greeting him the 16th and 17th. Every paper in the country seemingly had a front-page interview Dorothy gave to Adela St. Johns' *Los Angeles Herald Examiner*. Under the headline "WALLACE REID'S STRUGGLE AGAINST DRUG ADDICTION" was an interview of Dorothy by reporter William Parker (St. Johns was smart enough to keep her name off of the by-line). Other papers howled, "LIQUOR AND DOPE WRECK SCREEN IDOL—SECRET OF WALLACE REID'S ILLNESS IS REVEALED BY HIS WIFE," or "ADDICTED STAR KEPT OPEN HOUSE," and "GREATER STORY THAN SEEN ON SCREEN THAT OF WALLY REID!"

Parker's story ran from December 18th to the 21st, offering the entire three-year story; from an accident to a hopeless addiction with Paramount's seeming disinterest. It was equal parts biography, excuse, love story, and indictment. But Hollywood was indicted, not "our beloved Wally." The article began, "Mrs. Wallace Reid ... told today for the first time her struggle to save her husband from the grip of the downward pull ... revealed her husband's plan to make public his battle against the modern dragons, dope and booze, that he might save others. 'My husband has traversed the "land of darkness and the shadow of death." The horrors of the hell he has gone through would long ago have broken the heart of an ordinary man. But I know as surely as I know there is a God he will win out.'"[39]

Wally was said to be winning his battle, which was described as "a greater human story than even put on the silver screen," by breaking from what Parker described as his "fair weather friends" and relying on the "love of Dorothy ... who stuck by him through thick and thin." According to Parker, Wally had "conquered the narcotic habit contracted by overwork and insomnia, and is on the upgrade on the road to health...."[40]

It was admitted that Wally was indeed "perilously weak and suffering from collapse" but determined to "stage a 'come-back' both personally and on the screen," and his "cheerfulness [was] unimpaired." Dorothy acknowledged that "My husband is a sick, sick boy" and surprisingly added that she didn't "know if he will recover, but he has broken his habit and won his fight. He made this fight of his own free will and has won it by the strength of his own mind and will. Now he is fighting for his life."[41] It was a shocking admission.

Dorothy said it was Wally's idea to go public: "He recognized ... such a story from him would serve to bring forcibly before the people the dangers of the drug evil. He felt that through such a story he would be able to prompt his thousands of screen 'fans' to use their vote and moral and financial influence in behalf of any campaign being waged against the traffic in drugs and liquor." Wally had nothing to do with going public. By then he was unconscious most of the time; she probably knew he was going to die and was staging her elaborate eulogy. The public would remember the Wally that Dorothy wanted them to remember.

The first installment described her life with "her boy" from their 1911 meeting to their 1913 marriage. The second described her belief that Wally first used morphine in New York and his subsequent admission to his addiction. The third was an impassioned defense of Wally against several stories linking him to the drug trade. Overall, she absolved the movie colony: "His is not ... symptomatic of a community." She denied the

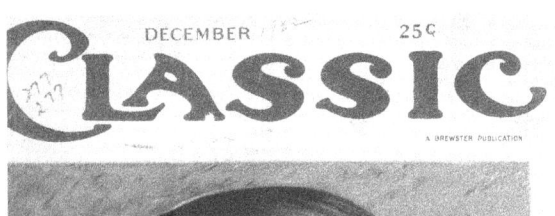

At the time the most popular star in the movies graced the cover of the December, 1922, *Classic* magazine, which featured several studio stills from his films, he was near death.

1919 accident had anything to do with his drug use and again revised *that* story, now saying that a large rock fell from an overhang and hit him in the head. He was knocked out and received eleven stitches and it led to a gradual decline. The fourth offered sanitized versions of several negative stories about Wally and the final installment was her version of Wally's last two years, his roller coaster of drug use and the adoption of Betty, somehow ending up at Banksia Place.

Most papers ran the first installment with a photo of Wally holding his pipe and reading a book titled *A Storybook Hero* over the caption "WALLACE REID ... the 'King of Moviedom.' He was popular because he seemed a regular storybook hero. He was good-looking; he knew how to wear his clothes; he could dance and make love divinely; he was happily married and not afraid to talk about it; he could fix an automobile and come best man in a fight. Wallace Reid; Romance Personified."[42] Strangely, the description was in the past tense, as if he were already gone. At times sad, at times pathetic, at times delusional, Dorothy's pleadings left no secret unbarred. She ended by saying:

> I have told you the truth about Wally, my husband, my boy, because the bare naked truth is so much better, so much cleaner, than the horrible stories which for months, and maybe years, have centered about him. I am not ashamed of anything he has done—sorry, yes. But Wally is not malicious and he is not "bad." He is a big overgrown boy who made a mistake, and who had nerve enough, strength enough to realize his error and to set it right. Can you criticize a man for that?[43]

Privately, Will Hays was furious but publicly he refused comment other than his "hopes that the poor sick boy will regain his health" and his belief that police needed to better control the flow of drugs.[44] But he was concerned the industry would be blamed, and pressured movie magazines to counter Dorothy. *Movie Weekly* published a series in December. The first, "What About Wally Reid?," stated, "until [we] are able to meet with Mr. Reid himself and ask him to speak his side to the public that he has served so valiantly" we would not believe any drug stories.[45] Then "How Wally Reid Is Battling for His Life" blamed the illness and "relapse ... due to overdoing the training stuff."[46] Finally, "Wally Reid's Wife Tells About His Illness" declared, "There is nothing seriously the matter with Wally Reid."[47] Incredibly, they were written *after* Dorothy's confession and not published until January 27, 1923! Zukor had repeatedly warned that Wally's problem was a powder keg and a $2,000,000 investment risk. He and Lasky did not know how to generate public sympathy for the ailing star. Dorothy's interview did that.

The Parker interview created a sensation. A second version—offering much of the same information but allegedly written by Dorothy—was published in other Hearst papers from December 31, 1922, to January 5, 1923. The additions were obviously written by St. Johns, though it ran with the headline "WIFE PENS DRAMATIC STORY OF WALLACE REID'S DRUG RUIN."[48] St. Johns' version was more personal and a stronger defense of the movies so it's likely that Hays, through Lasky, prompted St. Johns to produce this version.

There were several interesting comments in the St. Johns version. She confirmed that Wally was unaware of his condition, that, "He has not been informed yet, and in his present condition we are afraid to tell him. No one outside of his mother and I are allowed to visit him just now." Dorothy was lying; Bertha was still in New York and in the dark about Wally per Dorothy's heartless instructions. Bertha wired Dorothy about the article and Alice replied, "Wally out of danger. Ignore stories."[49] Also, while Dorothy blamed "friends for coming to his home and forcing him to drink," she was insightful that "They were not his friends. None of them are coming around to offer their services now. As soon as Wally is out of the hospital he and I are going to sell our house and move out into the country where we can live real lives. There will be a 'NO WELCOME' sign over the gate, but for the friends who have stuck by us."

Dorothy did not go public for Wally, herself, Hays, or Lasky, though. In her 1978 memoirs St. Johns described taking Dorothy to the noisy, smoky *Examiner* news room and spending "four hours with tears running down her face, telling newsmen the truth, and [convincing] them that she was thinking of all the kids whose idol Wally was."[50] The real reason she went public was that St. Johns was told the paper had incontrovertible proof linking Wally to a ring bringing drugs from New York to L.A. Just the day before a small story of a drug dealer's arrest at his fashionable Greenwich Village apartment appeared in New York papers. William Williams was an erudite, wealthy ex-lawyer from England who sold drugs to the theater and film communities. Police searching his penthouse found 1,500 letters from hundreds of famous actors and actresses and a small red ledger book with the initials "W.R." listed hundreds of times. "W.R.'s addresses and phone numbers" were also listed and they were Wally's. He was one of Williams' biggest customers.[51] The *Herald* was planning to run the story before Dorothy and St. Johns traded her interview to bury the story.

The response to the article was what Dorothy wanted and Lasky needed. Writer DeWitt Bodeen summed it up: "The accounts were not luridly written or sensational in any way; they were honest and sympathetic. The public, awed, was likewise sympathetic ... when *Thirty Days*, Reid's last picture, opened in December, 1922, the audience applauded vigorously when the name of Wallace Reid was flashed upon the screen. His public was rooting for him. His was *never* a scandal; it was pure tragedy."[52] The public was behind him but it was already too late. So he would not be upset the *Examiner* printed a dummy edition and removed any references to Wally. Dorothy took that copy to the hospital every day. He never knew the public was aware of anything. He never really knew himself.

The last photograph Wally sent to his mother, Christmas, 1922, inscribed "To Mother Bertha, Hurry Back Dearest, Wally "Cottontop."

Not everyone was supportive. One writer editorialized, "Another popular idol has been dashed from the lofty pedestal upon which we had in our minds place him, on learning of the serious illness of Wallace Reid due to use of narcotics. Coming as it does before the affairs of Arbuckle and Taylor have been forgotten, the news is already causing no little comment. It is an established fact the talented actor can successfully play a part altogether out of harmony with their own private life. After all, 'The play's the thing.'"[53] Another blamed Hollywood money and the "mad pursuit of pleasure."[54]

Dorothy told the press that Wally was improving. On December 18th headlines read, "WALLACE REID ON MEND—HAS WON FIGHT, WIFE SAYS." Dorothy "BRANDS STORY OF CONNECTION WITH 'DOPE RING' ABSURD, BUT ADMITS HE BECAME ADDICTED TO USE OF DRUGS TO KEEP UP WITH WORK."

> The condition of Wallace Reid ... on the verge of death last night, improved somewhat today and his wife ... said she was hopeful that the crisis was past. "Wally's doctors have about made up their minds it is a case of influenza. If he can throw this off he will be back at work as soon as his strength is regained. He weighs only 130 pounds now. He was making a picture when the collapse came. He was advised at the studio to take a rest and went under treatment. I am satisfied that he has won the fight.[55]

Wally's doctors told a different story. Just a day after Dorothy declared Wally had "won the fight" his doctor told a reporter, "Wally is a little better today after a fairly good night. Wally is able to take a little nourishment now and is able to rise up from his pillow for a few minutes without fainting, as has been the case until now."[56] A man who can't raise his head without fainting is not winning the fight.

Wally's problem became a cause célèbre. California's Republican State Senator Shortridge spoke from the floor of the Senate that "Reid's affliction is a danger signal to the whole world of the frightful punishment inflicted by drugs."[57] He called for stronger anti-drug laws and, remarkably, censorship of movies starring Wally.[58] Civic and morality groups got into the act. The Association of California Methodist Ministers requested on December 18th that the L.A. City Council demand a Grand Jury investigation into moral conditions in the movies. They sent a similar request to Hays, but both fell on deaf ears.[59]

Dorothy did her part, supplying police with the names of three men that supplied Wally drugs. On the 22nd papers reported, "THREE DOPE DEALERS HELD IN LOS ANGELES: Three dope dealers who are believed to have supplied Wally Reid and other people in the film colony with drugs, were arrested today by police narcotics squad. A quantity of narcotics was seized."[60]

As the gravity of Wally's situation grew clear there seemed a tangible effect in Hollywood: more subdued parties, and speakeasies and clubs were less crowded. His friends rallied to his side. Buddy Post offered to give his own blood, a procedure considered dangerous at the time, but doctors declined his offer.[61] Wally's friend Mabel Normand, also a hopeless drug addict, was saddened and probably a little frightened. On December 16th she sailed on a month-long trip to England. Her agent, E.M. Asher, "confirmed Miss Normand sailed on the White Star Line steamship *Majestic* to spend Christmas in England.... Having just returned from Europe in September, she sailed back suddenly 'with a party of friends' and would return two or three days after Christmas. She denied the disclosure of Wally's breakdown had any connection with her sudden departure but admitted she decided on the trip somewhat unexpectedly."[62]

The day before Christmas Wally worsened dramatically and doctors reported, "Wally's condition is not so favorable as in the last two days. He is much weaker and his pulse has increased to 104." Dorothy remained publicly optimistic, saying, "While a setback of this sort would have been exceedingly grave last week, he has recovered enough strength in the past seven days to relieve the extreme danger of a relapse."[63] Dorothy spent Christmas Eve and Day sitting quietly in a chair next to Wally's bed. He was unconscious.

The New Year didn't offer increased hope for Dorothy. Wally's condition was steadily, gradually worsening. He was unconscious most of the time and barely conscious otherwise. And Wally's name arose again when the controversial Dr. John Barker was arrested on January 1st for violating narcotics laws at his Oakland sanitarium. Witnesses alleged that Barker sold patients as much morphine as they wanted and decoy patients purchased morphine at inflated prices, 10 times the street cost by the ounce or by the shot ($5 per).[64] Dorothy denied that Wally was ever a patient at the facility. His stay at C.B. Blessing's L.A. facility just after the October collapse led to the rumor since Blessing offered the same questionable "Barker cure," and the press reported that Wally tried that cure in Oakland. Interestingly, in a November letter to Bertha, Alice Davenport wrote that Wally and Dorothy were on their way home from Oakland. It's possible Wally visited Barker's facility but no proof exists.

Wally weakened further. His respiratory system and kidneys were failing. He was on oxygen 24 hours a day and his weight dipped below 130 pounds. It was clear at the start of the second week in December that he would not survive, but Dorothy still kept Bertha away. Alice sent her a letter on the 15th, probably written the 8th or 9th, saying, "Wally is improving every day and he hopes to be back at work in six weeks. I wish you and the family would write letters he can read. He is shown nothing." Interestingly, Alice also hinted something was amiss in the letters from Dorothy to Bertha.

About the day that letter was written, Wally's beloved Highlands mansion burned to the ground. The entire contents were lost except for a few personal items.[65] Among the items was a box of pictures and keepsakes of Wally. That would be a blessing for Bertha. On January 18th, at about six in the evening, just three days after reading that "Wally is improving every day...." Bertha was handed a telegram. It read, "The boy simply slept away. Died at one o'clock today. Our hearts are together. Dorothy."[66]

Late the evening of the 15th Wally slipped into a coma. Dorothy kept a bedside vigil as he drifted in and out of consciousness and delirium. On the 16th Dorothy asked Teddy Hayes to visit and bring one of Wally's saxophones, which he quietly played as Wally drifted in and out of awareness. She apparently thought Wally might pull through but Dr. Herbert informed her the evening of the 17th that Wally was going to die soon. A few times he awoke and said, "Hi, Dot," and weakly reached for her hand,[67] and early the morning of the 18th Wally allegedly opened his eyes, gave her a ghost of his old quizzical smile and said, "Tell them, Mama, we're going to make it." On Thursday, January 18, 1923, at 1:10 P.M., he momentarily regained consciousness and muttered, "God ... I ... please...," and died. Dorothy was holding him in her arms.[68] Hollywood's best-known and most beloved actor was dead, barely 30 years old. Papers reported that the children were at his bedside but that was untrue.[69]

Wally's doctor Gavin Herbert listed the cause of death as "renal suppression and hypostatic pneumonia," contributed by "nerve exhaustion due to the withdrawal of morphine." It was noted he treated the dead "Motion Picture Actor" from December 6, 1922, to January 18, 1923, and that the informant was Gilbert Heyfron (Wally's attorney and business manager).[70] Herbert's cause of death meant that Wally's body—weighing barely 130 pounds—simply gave out, with his respiratory system and kidneys shutting down and leading to death. Herbert told reporters, "He put up a splendid fight. He gained about 10 pounds since he has been here. But during the last three days he has been quite weak. Yesterday and last night he was in a semi-delirious condition, unconscious most of the time. He was unconscious when he died."[71]

When the news reached Paramount minutes later, everything stopped. Sets were closed, actors retreated to dressing rooms, and directors "put down their megaphones." A grip walked out front and quietly lowered the flag to half-mast. Tears flowed everywhere and Lasky issued a statement, "The motion pictures have lost an artist who held a unique place in the hearts of the patrons of the screen. We have lost one of our brightest stars. Speaking for my organization and myself, I can express only the deepest sorrow and sympathy for the bereaved."[72]

The regular Lasky employees loved Wally. If he were late, workers lied to protect him. If it was known Wally wanted an afternoon off, electricians sabotaged lights, carpenters damaged a set or cameramen their cameras so shooting could not be done. Studio managers knew but were powerless to stop the men from helping the star they called a friend. A crying Mary Pickford told reporters at her Pickfair mansion, "His death is a very great tragedy. I know he would have lived down every mistake he made."[73] Heyfron told reporters, "Well, nobody can call him a quitter. He won his fight and died. But he died at the top of the heap, with the sympathy of all the world going out of him."[74]

After Heyfron arranged for Strather & Dayton Funeral Home, just two blocks from the Lasky lot, to pick up Wally's body, Dorothy sent her telegram to Bertha and returned to DeLongpre. The throng of reporters and photographers saw that she was near collapse. Buddy Post had been helping with the children for a week; they were not told of their father's death. Post and Dorothy told them that Wally was "on location." She told reporters, "There is no reason to sadden the hearts of the children. In time they will learn."[75]

There was the expected media frenzy after Wally's death. The headlines were of a similar theme: "WALLY REID DIES A VICTIM OF NARCOTICS," "WALLY REID SUCCUMBS TO DRUG RAVAGES," "WALLY REID DIES AFTER LONG STRUGGLE TO BREAK DOPE HABIT," or "WALLY REID, MOVIE IDOL, DIES FIGHTING TO CONQUER DRUG HABIT." Articles described his horrific final days with a similar theme, that "Wally Reid has played his last scene. After a long, hard fight against odds ... Wally died in a Hollywood sanitarium, his hand in the hand of his wife. The doctor's certificate says he died from congestion of the lungs, but everybody who knew him knows that the drug habit killed Wally Reid. His strength failed but his courage was with him to the last."[76] Some accounts were fictionalized, like the headline "'TELL THEM I'VE WON,' WALLY'S LAST UTTERANCE," and his last words, "Tell them, Mama, I have won. I have come back."[77]

Sadly, Bertha could not get to California for Wally's funeral. She told reporters, "I pray that his death will accomplish a great purpose and I feel that it will. It probably will accomplish more than columns of sermons, or warnings, or crusades against this horrible drug evil. His death is naturally a terrible shock to me, but Wally has not died in vain. I think his brave struggle to fight off the effects of the habit was a wonderful thing. He had simply made up his mind not to yield. If he had weakened and taken some drugs to still the pangs he suffered he probably would be alive at this moment, but he braved the torment and finally his weakened system succumbed to the ills that were the immediate cause of his death." Bertha's spin, that Wally had actually won the fight even though he died, was echoed in the press. Headlines read, "WITH HIS TRIUMPH CAME DEFEAT," and that "Wally leaves a good name. Had his death been caused by his continued use of the drug, it would have been otherwise."[78]

But Bertha's anger at being lied to by Dorothy and Alice was clear. She said, "What the reason was for my not being taken into the confidence of those who knew the worst,

I do not know. It is too late to matter. Naturally, if I had known the real condition of my beloved boy, I would have been at his bedside long ago. All I learned was from the headlines in the papers that shocked me into insensibility."[79] On this matter, Dorothy's insensitivity is almost mind-boggling.

Wally's body was retrieved on the evening of the 18th and taken back to Glendale to prepare for the funeral service, scheduled for 10:00 Saturday morning the 20th at the First Congregational Church in Hollywood. Wally would lie in state until a funeral service at 2:30 P.M., after which he would be taken to Forest Lawn Memorial Park in Glendale, cremated, and his ashes placed in a large brass urn that reporters noted incorrectly he himself had designed.[80] Tributes streamed to the funeral home, the studio, and to DeLongpre; over 500 floral arrangements and thousands of telegrams from around the world. On the morning of the 20th over 10,000 theaters flew flags at half-staff.

When the hearse bringing Wally's casket arrived early the morning of the 20th there were already 15,000 people lined up around the block. A dozen policemen cleared a path so the purple bronze casket with solid gold fittings could be carried through a side door and placed on a bier in front of the altar. Several hundred floral arrangements, wreaths, baskets, and huge bouquets were laid out around the casket, itself covered with a blanket of maidenhair fern, violets, and dwarf tuberoses. The flowers formed a small stage framed by a purple velvet curtain, adorned with Wally's initials. The casket was open; Wally appeared handsome but thin after hours of studio makeup work, and wore a brown tweed sport coat and tie.

By the time the doors were opened at 10:00 over 20,000 people were in line from every strata of life. A newspaper described the throng: "There was a woman with a baby on one arm. There was a woman 90 years old, holding a tiny black sunshade above her. There one saw a girl in sport clothes; back of her, urging her on, a colored mammy with a brood of girls."[81] For five hours the multitudes slowly inched there way toward the doors and into the church. When the doors were closed at 2:30 only about half the crowd had been able to get in.

Seeing the doors close, the crowd—most of who had been waiting for eight hours—almost rioted. Women screamed and the crowd surged forward up the steps, almost bowling over a line of policemen spread across the front of the church. A few minutes later Dorothy's limousine approached but the dense masses prohibited it from getting within two blocks. Backing up, the car was driven around the block to a side entrance. When the policemen in front explained to the crowd that Dorothy wished to be alone with Wally's body for a half hour, they quieted. Dorothy and Alice exited the limousine swathed in black and accompanied by Buddy Post and Benny Frazee, who would serve as pallbearers along with William S. Hart, Ed Brady, Noah Beery, William Desmond and Eugene Pallette.

Post and Frazee joined the other pallbearers in the lobby while Dorothy sat alone, quietly crying next to Wally's flower-bedecked bier. After about twenty minutes the pallbearers opened the doors to a flow of Hollywood royalty, led by Charlie Chaplin, Pola Negri, Rudolph Valentino, Mary Pickford and Douglas Fairbanks, Harold Lloyd, Bebe Daniels, Theodore Roberts, Jack Holt, Conrad Nagel, Antonio Moreno, Sam Wood and William H. Crane. Among the mourners were other celebrities like golf champion Gene Sarazen, Wally's racing driver friends, and theater owners Sid Grauman and Alexander Pantages. Lasky sent one of his managers, Victor H. Clark, in his place. He did not attend the funeral. Roscoe Arbuckle wanted to attend but was afraid his presence would lead to controversy so he sent his lawyer and manager Frank Dominguez in his place. Adela Rogers St. Johns was also unable to attend; she was in Banff, British Columbia.

The funeral service was a strange combination of religions. Wally was raised Episcopalian but did not practice his faith although he had a strong faith in God. The service was an Episcopalian service for the dead, held in a Congregational church, led by Rev. Neal Dodd, the pastor of St. Mary's of the Angels Catholic Church[82] but given by members of Hollywood's Elks Lodge No. 99, to which Wally belonged. Only once during his final illness had Wally exhibited any interest in religion when he briefly considered meeting with a Christian Scientist practitioner since Dorothy and Bertha were followers. He changed his mind though.[83] Strangely, at one point he asked for Catholic Last Rights, which were administered.

As the service began at 3:30—an hour late due to the crowds—Dorothy, looking drawn and haggard, and Alice, took seats in one front row. On the other side of the aisle sat the pallbearers. Once the Hollywood celebrities had taken their seats police allowed about 1,000 of the mourners outside to fill the remaining rows, sitting within feet of their biggest stars. There was no sermon, no eulogy and no songs. The organist played the mournful "Dead March" from "Saul." The assembled Elks gave their last farewell to their departed brother, a traditional calling of his name aloud and waiting for an answer that would not come. Dodd recited the short funeral service of the Episcopal Church and the organ began to play "Nearer My God to Thee" as the pallbearers rose and escorted the flower-bedecked casket down the aisle and out of the church. The entire service took less than ten minutes.

Dorothy and Alice returned to DeLongpre. Dorothy was close to collapse, unsure of what to do next. Of her plans, Wally's manager Heyfron told reporters, "There aren't any exactly. Everything, you know, is upset. She doesn't know what she is going to do yet. I am going to try and persuade her to take a trip. That is why I selected the cemetery in Glendale instead of the one in Hollywood.[84] If the burial was here in Hollywood it would be a constant reminder."[85]

There was no funeral procession. During the 1920s the Hollywood Chamber of Commerce ordered specific routes to the various cemeteries to avoid processions on Hollywood Boulevard, deeming them too depressing for the community and the movie fans filling sidewalks.[86] The casket was carried out a side door through the remaining fans and loaded into a hearse and taken to Forest Lawn at 1712 South Glendale Avenue in Glendale. The rolling hills in the beautiful 300-acre property held English chapels, a stone church, several huge mausoleums, and hundreds of spectacular statues. Wally's body was cremated later that evening and his ashes placed in a large brass urn in the Great Mausoleum. The urn stands in a wall niche in the Holly Terrace just outside the entrance to the Azalea Corridor. Atop a five-foot brass column, the trophy-shaped urn simply says "WALLACE REID" at the base.

Wally's urn at Forest Lawn Memorial Park, Glendale (courtesy Scott Michaels).

After the funeral, Dorothy released a statement to reporters: "I want the public and our friends to know how much today's tribute to Wally's memory has meant to me and my family. And I want to express, too, my regret that many of the thousands who came to the church, were unable to gain admittance. It means more to me than I can put into the proper phrases that here in our home city the public has shown its friendship, its loyalty, and sympathy in a manner so unmistakable."[87]

The day of the funeral Lasky ran a full-page ad featuring a photo of Wally's favorite dog "Pal" curled up mournfully in his on-set chair, with a headline "HIS PAL IN MOURNING." On the back of the chair was inscribed "WALLY REID—HIS CHAIR," and the caption read, "His friends are welcome when he's not on the set."[88] Another less emotional story began with the comment, "Wallace Reid gave his last performance today. Tonight he is a handful of ashes."[89]

15

Human Wreckage

In the March, 1925, issue of *Photoplay*, James Quirk noted the second anniversary of Wally's death with a description of the fallen star:

> ... his memory is cherished by countless thousands to whom his screen personality and his pictures brought happiness. Wally was intensely human, and lovable in his own personality. He had human weaknesses. He was no saint. But I never heard of him intentionally hurting anyone.... His end was unfortunate, but he was one of the nicest and companionable human beings I ever knew. I never have ceased to marvel how the camera caught that lovable quality in the man and reflected it on the screen. Handsome, accomplished, successful, there wasn't an ounce of personal conceit in him, and the amount of work he could and did perform would be inconceivable to most men.[1]

In the years since Wally's death it has been rumored that Dorothy let doctors "put him to sleep" to end his suffering. That probably did not take place but she may have allowed him to die. Combining versions of Wally's final days the most likely scenario is that Dr. Herbert and Dorothy probably knew that, though Wally had been weaned off drugs in the months since his breakdown, he did not have the strength to survive without at least some morphine. Wally decided, "Then I'll die. At least I'll be clean at last, and free. Only promise me, darling, that somehow you will use this to save others from this horror." Almost plaintively he pleaded, "*Can* you?"[2] The final decision was probably Dorothy's and she decided against using drugs to keep Wally alive. That decision evolved into a persistent rumor that Dorothy had Wally "put to sleep."

Tributes to Wally filled papers and magazines. In death he was no longer the posterchild for Hollywood excess. In death he became a victim. A hero. Even a martyr. One article read, "After two years of whispered rumors about the victims that the narcotic tentacles have claimed among actors, the climax—the death of Reid—caused the film colony to consecrate itself with amazing unanimity of spirit to drive out the menace of the industry."[3] Another, just a week after the funeral, offered, "It had to be Wally! In other words, somebody essentially clean, fine, strong, handsome, and capable had to be offered as a sacrifice in order to convince a callous or gibing world that nobody on earth can 'get away with it.' Wallace Reid has died—a martyr to the cause. Most will pity. Few will condemn. From the ashes will arise a phoenix—clean, bright, enterprising—THE NEW MOVIEDOM!"[4] The writer was the same Chicago writer who Wally had dropped in to visit during his 1918 trip.

A number of famous names offered their own heartfelt tributes. Actor Herbert Howe wrote a *Photoplay* story entitled "A Tribute from a Friend," saying Wally "accepted everyone as a friend and his door was open to all. Who you were or where you came from never mattered to Wally.... He died with the whisper of hope that he might save at least a few from the agony that was his. His last role was the greatest he ever played. Never on screen did he wage such a brave and splendid fight. The loyal love of millions will follow the star that is forever—just Wally."[5]

Picture-Play Magazine published a collection of interviews from earlier issues, noting that "every one [of the writers] loved the man ... utterly unspoiled by his success, always informal, jocular, good-natured—no matter how hard he was working."[6] European magazines like *Pictures* and *Picturegoer* offered photo layouts showing Wally, Dorothy and the children at DeLongpre.[7]

Humorist Will Rogers wrote a wonderful tribute to Wally in his column, the most-read in the U.S. Like Wally, Rogers was universally beloved. He met Wally in 1919 when both were booked at the same one-night Kansas City theater-opening during Rogers' first trip to Hollywood. Their similar personalities led to friendship. Rogers' column was written the day Wally died:

> Just today as I am writing this the sad death of a fellow movie actor is reported. Now I want to say my little of good, for you will no doubt hear people say things who can only see the bad in anything. Four years ago, I was booked to stop off for one night in Kansas City and speak at the opening of a new theater. Wallace Reid had come from the coast to appear also, and I met him for the first time. I am sure I meant nothing to him, still he knew I was new in the business and he wanted to be of any help to me he could. Now, mind you, while he was paying me every attention, he was the admiration of everybody. You can't imagine his popularity. He was the king of a lot of them. ... Now he falls into bad company, though being a good fellow. He sinned. He has paid the highest penalty he can pay. He gave his life. He has left a mother, wife and children—one of them adopted. Now, a bad fellow don't adopt children. He don't even want children. Now don't let a living soul say an unkind word about Wallie Reid. He was just an overgrown kid, who never knowingly harmed a living soul. So let God judge him, not us. I'll bet he will be judged to be way above the average.[8]

Rogers' feelings were written in the homespun style that earned him millions of fans. He was tragically killed in a 1935 Alaskan airplane crash along with his friend and pilot Wiley Post. Coincidently, in that same column Rogers described a New York fundraiser where he met prominent political wives, among them Mrs. Whitelaw Reid! Rogers was unaware of the family relationship.

Of all of the tributes written about Wally perhaps the most heartfelt was from Buddy Post, entitled simply, "Wally Reid, My Friend," for *Movie Weekly*. Wally's closest friend wrote, "Wally did not kill others with kindness but he killed himself with kindness to others. There is no episode of his life which brings forth more admiration and displays the resolute will of the man than the last few weeks he lived. It showed the true Wallace Reid. He could have pursued his course and lived. But he *would* conquer.... The generosity, the unselfishness, the consideration he had for every human and every animal, and his whole-hearted kindness was amazing.... I do not think I shall ever find a more faithful friend, a more genial companion or a more thoro [sic] man than Wallace Reid."[9]

Wally's death had a tragic affect on some of his friends and fans. A February 3rd suicide hit close to home, when sometime actor and writer Claude Tyner Waltman shot himself. His note indicated that he was "discouraged he couldn't make a living in the movies and support his wife and infant child, and his final failure to sell a story about dope written in connection with Wally Reid."[10] Waltman was also known as Thomas H. Tyner and Claude Walton, and was the young man arrested in November, 1920, carrying morphine "for Wally Reid."[11] Found with Waltman's body was a photograph of Wally inscribed "To my pal."

IN MEMORY OF

𝔚𝔞𝔩𝔩𝔞𝔠𝔢 𝔎𝔢𝔦𝔡

BORN IN MARCH, 1892, ST. LOUIS, MO.
DIED JANUARY 18, 1923, HOLLYWOOD, CAL.

A Loving Son, A Faithful Husband and a True Friend

HE WILL MAKE HIS LAST APPEARANCE ON THE SCREEN
at the

Hippodrome Theatre
6th and SOUTH STREET

in His Last Picture

"THIRTY DAYS"

2 DAYS ONLY Fri.-Sat., February 9-10

Lasky re-used the *Nice People* flyers—barely three months old—and printed Wally's memorial card on the reverse.

Sadder was the death of Evelyn Nelson, a beautiful 23 year old from Arizona who shared a tiny bungalow at 1401 North Sanborn Avenue with her father.[12] She arrived in Hollywood in 1920 and was more successful than most, signing with Vitagraph and appearing in four Jimmy Aubrey comedy serials (with Oliver Hardy), western serials with Jack Hoxie, and shorts like *Cyclone Bliss* (1921) and *Desert Bridegroom* (1922). She was successful, leaving one to wonder at the reason behind her suicide on June 15th when her father found her dead. She had turned on the gas in the kitchen stove and put her head inside. One of two pathetic notes appeared to refer to a friendship with Wally. Coming so soon after Wally's death it made studio people wonder if she was one of "Wally's girls." Her first read, "I'm tired, oh so tired. Life has beaten me until it is a hopeless, lonesome, useless struggle. Struggle, disappointment, sadness—what's the use. Good-by." The second, evidently written as the gas began flowing, read, "I'm going—it's nearly over—soon to be with my friends—peace, my pal Wally Reid. Farewell."[13] She was barely 23 and had completed *Desert Rider* just two days previous.

Lasky kept Wally's final pictures in extended release for months and the fans kept filling theaters. In addition to the usual "WALLY REID HERE SUNDAY"[14] headlines, ad text was usually larger than the movie name, and the ads usually ½-page ads. The *Thirty Days* ads reminded fans "This is Wally Reid's last picture and your last chance to see him on the screen!"[15] Original October ads for *Clarence* made no mention that Wally was already dying but post-death ads read, "One of the Last Pictures Ever Starred by WALLACE REID." Locally, papers added, "Probably the Last to be Shown in Reno!"[16] When *Clarence* and *Thirty Days* were both re-released in the weeks after Wally died they were reviewed as if new releases. *Days* ads mentioned, "Wally Smiles Again in His Last Picture," but were subtitled "But Sorrow Subdues Your Joy in Rollicking Film."[17] Theaters ran Wally's films on their own for a year after his death.

Dorothy remained in seclusion at DeLongpre sorting out Wally's financial affairs. Buddy Post remembered, "There was one thing that Wally never worried about, and that was money. He never knew where he stood financially. He would drive Gill Heyfron, his business manager, wild by his thoughtlessness in money matters."[18] Heyfron's first ominous mention that things might not be on solid footing came the day after Wally's death when he noted the family's financial position was "Not so bad. There's a mortgage on the house, of course, but if Wally could have gone back to work he would have cleared that up in a few weeks."[19] A $70,000 life insurance policy was mentioned in every article but no confirmation of such an agreement was ever found.

In fact, Wally's carelessness left Dorothy and the children in perilous financial straits. With stunning insensitivity, during Wally's final 1922 illness Lasky paid Dorothy just $500 a week from Wally's contracted $2,500. That fall she had to sell her diamonds to raise money.[20] Also, he died intestate, without a will, meaning Dorothy had to petition the court for guardianship of the children and appointment as executrix of the estate and then report financial matters. She began the process on February 2nd, petitioning for Letters of Administration naming Wally's heirs "Dorothy D. Reid, your petitioner, age 27 years; William Wallace Reid, Jr., son, age five years, and Betty Anna Reid, daughter, age 3½ years, all of whom now residing at 8327 DeLongpre Avenue, Los Angeles, California."[21] She also petitioned to be appointed guardian of the children, noting that Wally left Bill, Jr. two life insurance policies with Missouri State Life Insurance Company valued at $5,000 apiece and a lot near Universal City worth $1,500 (Wally and Dorothy purchased the lot when they were moving from Morgan Place, intending to build near the studio until buying the DeLongpre property).[22]

On March 6th Dorothy was appointed legal guardian[23] and estate executrix.[24] The estate's estimated worth was $50,000 ($1,000,000 today), but it was noted, "the principal item [was] the Reid home in Hollywood, valued at $40,000.[25] Wally had no cash, made glaringly clear when the court-ordered inventory and appraisal was filed on April 27th. It was whispered that rumors of Wally paying large amounts to blackmailers were true. Indeed, it would have been hard for him to spend *all* of his money simply for the drugs. The Appraisal listed only four items: the DeLongpre house valued at $50,000, two purchase contracts for lots in Arrowhead Woods near Lake Arrowhead (Wally and Dorothy intended to build a vacation cabin there) at $2,050, two automobiles, a 1921 McFarlan Touring Car and a 1920 McFarlan Sedan, a combined $5,000, and "personal property consisting of guns, golf clubs, and furniture," $1,500. The total estate was $58,550. Next to the description "*Moneys belonging to said deceased, which have come into the hands of* [executrix]" was a hand-written "none."[26] Incredibly, Wally was broke. The only cash in the family when he died were two savings accounts at the California State Bank in Hollywood, one for Billy with $381.45, and one for Betty Anna with $54.50.[27] Including insur-

Dorothy and the children in a photo taken at DeLongpre just a few months after Wally's death.

ance policies the children's inheritance was $10,435.95. Dorothy inherited the property, and hundreds of bills.

It was a year and a half before the bills against the $58,550 estate were paid. A final accounting was not concluded until October, 1925. Among the 100-plus creditors were the Strather & Dayton Funeral Home ($498.40), the I.R.S. ($7,840.00), supplies for his beloved cars ($612.05) including $34.00 for a bumper and $67.50 for a carburetor, doctor's bills, and dues at the Hollywood Country Club. His only vices were shown by small amounts due book and record stores. Many of the charges offered insight into the cost of being a movie star: eight wardrobe-makers ($1,946,91), publicity photos from Evans Photography Studio ($135.19), and make-up from the Kress Drug Store ($481.32). Interestingly, Dr. C.B. Blessing billed the estate $1,000 for the failed two-week treatment during Wally's final illness.[28] Creditors were paid $21,214.12 from the $58,550.00 estate; Dorothy had already mortgaged the DeLongpre house to raise cash.

Dorothy couldn't live the life of wealthy movie widow. She had to work; Wally left her essentially broke. She became one of the pioneering women directors, but originally took the job not for creativity but for financial and perhaps emotional survival. Less than two weeks after the funeral Dorothy contracted for Billy to endorse a line of toy cars made by the American National Toy Company. The first ad appeared in the toy industry trade magazine *Playthings* in March for toys to be introduced at the national toy fair in April. The ad read, "WALLACE REID JR. SON OF THE LATE MUCH LOVED

MOVIE STAR LIKES HIS AMERICAN AUTO BEST OF ALL. THIS FELLOWS' UNCLE, JIMMIE MURPHY DOYLE WORLD AUTO'S CHAMPION, WOULD BE SATISFIED WITH NOTHING ELSE THAN THE ALEMITE EQUIPPED AMERICAN AUTO." Doyle was a friend of Wally's, not Bill's uncle.

Also, within weeks Dorothy embarked on an anti-drug crusade for which she is still remembered. If Wally was the martyr, Dorothy would carry the flag. Wally was the "face" of the problem and "Mrs. Wally Reid" the name. She had a banner: a movie that graphically showed the effects of drugs on a family entitled *The Living Dead*. Thomas Ince (she and Ince's wife Elinor were close friends) produced the movie. Lasky apparently didn't want to be involved. She surely would have approached him first but the Inces' Thomas H. Ince Company made the film rather than Paramount.

She invited reporters to DeLongpre for pictures with Ince. Headlines said she was "CARRYING ON FOR WALLIE!!!, TO CARRY ON—TO STAR IN FILM TO FIGHT DOPE!!!" or "WALLACE REID'S WIDOW TO PLAY IN DRUG FILM."[29] Photos showed a doleful-looking Dorothy seated with Ince. Publicly Dorothy said, "It is not my own wish to make a picture. I am very, very tired and I should like to rest from the field for a little while. But during these days since my husband's going, my home has been flooded with appeals for me to *do something* ... to tell what I know for the good of humanity."[30] She was also dreaming of a hospital called the Wallace Reid Anti-Narcotic Sanitarium and announced it would be funded by profits from the film. Those plans began another public feud with Bertha, who with Wally's aunts did not want him remembered for addictions. Bertha said, "The fact that he died because of his fight against the drug habit was merely an incident of his career and should be forgotten."[31] Dorothy replied tersely, "No matter what they think, if naming a sanitarium after Wally will lend impetus to the war against drugs, the sanitarium will be named the Wallace Reid sanitarium."[32]

Dorothy soldiered on, writers mentioning her "plea for help in the fight against the illicit drug traffic throughout the nation, as Mrs. Wallace Reid, widow of the motion picture actor who died recently in his effort to free himself from the habit." She would star in a film to show "the menace"[33] with all proceeds going toward Wally's hospital. Dorothy said it was a condition that she starred but Ince added a requirement that she *appear* with the film as well.[34] She outright begged for money when she and Harold Lloyd formed the Anti-Narcotic League of Los Angeles in March, appointing to their board the Mayor, Chief of Police, President of the California P.T.A., a half dozen judges and the presidents of U.S.C., U.C.L.A., and the California state college system schools. The League was financed from *Living Dead* profits. Mailings and ads asked contributions be sent to "Mrs. Wallace Reid, P.O. Box 617, Los Angeles, Calif."[35]

Production began on March 2nd. The scenario was written by C. Gardner Sullivan and directed by John Griffith Wray (with Dorothy's vocal assistance). Dorothy—billed as "Mrs. Wallace Reid"—starred with James Kirkwood, Bessie Love, George Hackathorne, Claire McDowell, Robert McKim, Harry Northrup, Victory Bateman, Eric Mayne, Otto Hoffman, Philip Sleeman, George Clark and Lucille Ricksen. Also appearing were a dozen L.A. politicians, from Mayor George Cryer to Federal Court Judge Benjamin Bledsoe to Health Commissioner Mrs. Charles F. Gray.[36]

Hackathorne plays Jimmy Browne, a taxi driver driven to addiction by drug ring leader Steve Stone (Northrup). When Browne is arrested for breaking into a pawn shop jewelry case to support his habit his friend Mary Finnegan (Love) approaches Ethel MacFarland (Dorothy) for help. Ethel's lawyer husband (Kirkwood) refuses to help a man he calls a "weak-minded dope addict," but at Ethel's urging arranges for Browne's release to a sanitarium. When he collapses from overwork MacFarland gets drugs from his doctor but is soon hooked himself. Drugs ruin his career and marriage and turn him into a criminal, forced to arrange an acquittal of drug charges for Stone. As he reaches bottom he sees his wife about to succumb to drugs, is miraculously cured and sets out to rid his city of the menace and of Stone. When Stone tries to escape, Browne—taking him away in his taxi—slams his car into a train, killing them both.

The film had several dramatic scenes depicting the wretched lives of drug addicts; Love smearing her breast with opium to quiet her crying baby, drug dealer Northrup enticing children on a school playground and Hackathorne's graphic portrayal of the terrible withdrawal, a difficult scene for Dorothy but frighteningly realistic. Filmed in a beachside bungalow on the Malibu beach, she recreated the Pasadena mountain cabin to which she had taken Wally, and the terrible physical effects of the withdrawal she had seen first-hand.

Lobby card for Dorothy's film *Human Wreckage,* with Bessie Love.

The terrifying taxi ride was filmed on L.A. streets teeming with pedestrians and was described as "one of the most thrilling scenes ever ... whose prominent players ventured almost to the brink of death and came out unscathed."[37] In the days before studios relied on stuntmen players like Hackathorne and Northrup were not important enough to demand one and performed dangerous stunts. At speeds near 90 miles per hour the taxi careened in and out of traffic before a final shot of a head-on crash with a moving train. To facilitate the shot Hackathorne and Northrup sat in the car as the train approached before bailing out at the last second. Not caught on film—their characters died in the fiery crash—were the faces of the actors jumping in terror for their lives seconds before the train demolished their car.

Ince renamed it *Human Wreckage* (papers still called it *The Living Dead* as late as April 5th) and released it on June 17th with gloomy lobby cards and Satan-themed ads with a scowling devil pointing to the reader above the words "YOU WILL NEVER FORGET!!! Mrs. WALLACE REID IN 'HUMAN WRECKAGE!'" In others Kirkwood and Hackathorne are shown with shadows shaped like a hooded Grim Reaper. Reviews were effusive in praise. No writer risked attack by criticizing the movie and many evoked Wally's memory: "A shadowy figure runs through Dorothy Davenport Reid's narcotic crusade film 'Human Wreckage,' although [sic] his name is not in the cast. You get an impression that the film is haunted by the phantom of Wally Reid, to whom it is dedicated."[38] Another said, "Mrs. Wallace Reid takes her first step in an anti-narcotics crusade, and an audience in the Majestic Theater last night sat spellbound ... scenes which this greatest of modern pictures is crowded. Mrs. Reid, who portrays with exquisite pathos the part of the wife of a great lawyer ... is one of the most powerful weapons against the spread of the dope habit in the hands of authorities."[39]

Dorothy appointed herself resident expert on drug abuse and played the role for 30 years. After completing *Wreckage,* on May 1st she and St. Johns left for the National Anti-Narcotics Conference in Washington, D.C., attended by scores of worldwide dignitaries. The first night the anti-drug film *The Greatest Menace* was shown and a reception given for Dorothy, who said, "If my efforts will aid in any way to awaken the public conscience to the peril now knocking at the door and already within, then I shall consider my life effort a success."[40] During her stay she also made the first of thousands of appearances, this one at a Washington church. Papers announced "MRS. WALLIE REID will speak on 'The Menace to the American Home' at the First Congregational Church at 8:00 P.M."[41]

With each appearance she became more melodramatic. Her comments were full of hyperbole and she called drug dealers "fiendish peddlers." She said of *Wreckage,* "Civilization has an enemy, insidious, creeping and hideous—its name is *Dope.* I have met bitter defeat at the hands of this enemy. But I have just begun to fight. The enemy stole from me happiness, contentment—everything, perhaps, save the knowledge that it might be the means unto a ruthless war against the Devourer of Men."[42] She also credited herself with saving "literally dozens" of friends from drugs.

Wearing her signature widow's weeds, Dorothy makes one of her appearances at a *Human Wreckage* filming, this one in Chicago it appears.

During the next five years Dorothy appeared with the movie around the country at every conceivable venue. She appeared at theaters big and small, churches, schools, parks, public buildings and even at New York's Ossining State Prison. A sampling of local headlines include "MRS. REID IN PERSON AT CENTURY THEATER," "MRS. REID HERE FOR OPENING OF DRUG MOVIE," "Wallace Reid's Widow in Church Lecture," and "CONVICTS SEE FILM."[43] Private screenings were also held, like one described "for a group of clergymen, doctors, and welfare societies of this city at the Majestic Theater this morning. The picture is scheduled to start on public performances Sunday and continue through the week."[44]

The story of Lucille Ricksen, who played one of Hackathorne's children, is as sad as the film. She came to Hollywood in 1920 at 10 and began working for Goldwyn in a recurring role in the *Edgar* series based on the Booth Tarkington character Edgar Pomeroy. She did a dozen films in 1920–1921 and graduated to bigger roles, starring with Marie Prevost in *The Married Flapper* (1921) and Colleen Moore in *Forsaking All Others* (1922). A week after completing *Wreckage* she was named the WAMPAS Baby Star of 1924 and was on her way to a major career when she contracted tuberculosis in 1924. She died in early 1925 at barely 16.

There is also an interesting coincidence in the October 11th *Bridgeport Telegram.* Next to a *Wreckage* review was a story about Ambassador George Harvey's return from London with a story about the custom of hanging the outgoing Ambassador's portrait in the embassy. Harvey's portrait hung between those of Joseph H. Choate and Whitelaw Reid.[45]

The movie gave Dorothy something to live for and be identified with and she is most remembered for appearing in her widow's weeds with *Human Wreckage* than for her directing and producing work. The movie was to have financed Dorothy's planned drug sanitarium in Hollywood but never generated nearly enough money for the impressive project. Even so, in 1924 a *Photoplay* story mentioned that "Mrs. Reid's dream of a permanent institution for the cure of unfortunate drug addicts has been realized." Dorothy was photographed standing in the long circular driveway in front of a large bungalow in Loz Feliz. But it was rented, able to allegedly house 16 patients who would be given the DuBry "cure" that Dorothy had negotiated to market.

The William Wallace Reid, Jr. file at the Herrick Library contains Dorothy's agreement with Fred DuBry's Seattle lab to endorse their treatment under the auspices of the re-named Mrs. Wallace Reid Foundation. Dorothy promised DuBry 20 percent of the proceeds from the venture,[46] but it's not known if the hospital ever made money or how long it survived. No mention could be found in the press during the 1920s, and it was not listed in the 1925 L.A. City Directory.

Once the initial hoopla surrounding *Human Wreckage* died down Dorothy was left to raise Bill and Betty. Her position in the public consciousness, initially elevated by Wally's death, diminished with time, as did movie audiences' memories of him. Dorothy never got over Wally's death. Thirty years later she wrote, "I keep busy. And the days pass."[47]

In the years after Wally's death public fascination with the Hollywood drug culture waned. Dorothy and the children remained at the DeLongpre house. Photo layouts of the family ran in *Photoplay* and *Motion Picture Magazine* with the title "Life Must Go On...." Fans remembered Wally for years. A March, 1925 *Photoplay* editorial described his impact on his fans: "Wally brought happiness to thousands of lives in every country where his pictures were shown. His screen personality was his own personality, and the public sensed it. I am thinking not only of the young women who looked on him as the incarnation of their dream hero, or the boys who, in fancy, lived the dashing, romantic and humorous episodes of his pictures, for I can never forget one lonely old lady who once said to me, 'I am always happy when I see Wally's pictures. I never had children, but I keep thinking that he is my boy.'"[48]

Life went on at Paramount. Wally's dressing room was given to Antonio Moreno, a friend and an honorary pallbearer at his funeral. It was "considered to be the most beautiful in all of the Hollywood realm of salons. Wally was particularly proud of the furniture because they were the gift of his bride, who personally selected them."[49]

Lasky's immediate problem was replacing Wally. Dozens of actors jockeyed to become "the Next Wally Reid" and contenders came from everywhere. The first was probably Lloyde Hughes, who writers mentioned "motion picture experts in Hollywood are picking to succeed the late Wallie [sic] Reid as the popular idol of leading man of American movie audiences."[50] Mary Pickford took credit for discovering him in *Tess of Storm Country* (1923) and predicted he "would soon find himself among the foremost ranks of leading men." But fans never accepted Hughes.

Lasky lured Richard Dix from Goldwyn a few months after Wally died. Dix was similar to Wally but more of a wholesome, All-American type than a dashing leading man. He was more athletic and manly on-screen and from 1923 to 1929 made 33 Paramount films but never offered the mix of athleticism and sentiment that Wally offered. In 1925

Lasky even tried Dix in *The Lucky Devil*, one of Wally's type of racing movies. The studio used the exact same ad copy originally used for Wally's movies and the same racing car with the same number—13—used by Wally. But Dix was never the star Wally was.

In 1925 Universal tried Reginald Denny in another racing movie, *California Straight Ahead*. He too was unable to replicate Wally on screen. Lasky even tried to sign University of Illinois football star Harold "Red" Grange. In May, 1925, C.C. Pyle, who owned a string of Paramount-contracted theaters in the Midwest, told the press Grange would be the "new Wallie [sic] Reid, typifying American youth." But after a meeting at a hotel in Milwaukee, Grange decided to remain in college, saying, "the only business I will be in until I finish my college work is my family's ice business."[51] In 1926 Grange came to Hollywood, taking a large mansion at 143 Wilton Place with his father, but he left soon after.

In the late 1920s Lasky brought Richard Arlen in for a last effort to replace Wally. In 1930 Lasky tried yet another racing movie, *Burning Up*, again emulating Wally's films almost exactly. Allen Sigler filmed the racing scenes exactly as Wally's had been done, but like the others Arlen could not bring Wally's imagery to the screen. Little Billy would later get into the act with the 1933 race movie *The Racing Strain*, which was written by Dorothy. Although fans were fascinated at Wally's son in one of his roles, that attempt didn't work with fans either.

A 1926 *Photoplay* fan letter predicted the ultimate failure at replacing Wally when a young girl wrote, "We don't want Wally's pictures back. Our Wally is dead. Do, please, let him rest. We don't want to see his boyish face flashed across the screen again, when we know—well, we know he's lying stiff and cold, six feet under the earth. Don't bring him back. Even the thought is repulsive."[52] By the early 1930s it was apparent to Lasky and Paramount that no actor could ever replace Wally.

The studio continued to battle government antitrust cases after the Federal Trade Commission went after the studio and Lasky and Zukor in 1921 for block booking and studio ownership of theaters. In 1927, after 30,000 pages of testimony and exhibits *Federal Trade Commission v. Famous Players–Lasky Corporation, et al.* resulted in an order prohibiting block booking. When the studio tendered their compliance report in 1928 and denied they engaged in the practice the FTC filed a federal antitrust case. Paramount's perceived arrogance led to charges against *all* members of the original M.M.P.D.A., including Paramount, First National, M-G-M, Universal, United Artists, Fox, Pathé, FBO, Vitagraph, and Educational Films. Resulting decisions would eventually do away with studio control of distribution and forever alter the landscape of the movies.

In 1933 Paramount-Publix was forced into bankruptcy, reorganized as Paramount Pictures, Inc. Adolph Zukor was forced out as president and replaced by Barney Balaban in 1936 but Balaban appointed him Chairman of the Board. For the next 28 years they worked together; Zukor called Balaban "the boy." Balaban himself would be forced out in 1964 and Paramount would later merge with Viacom International, Inc., controlling dozens of companies like the Columbia Broadcasting System (CBS), the UPN, Comedy Central and Black Entertainment networks, Blockbuster, Inc., MTV networks, and the Nickelodeon network. Viacom remains one of the most successful entertainment companies in the world.

Many of the people in Wally's film life had long and distinguished film careers. Jesse Lasky and Cecil B. DeMille are among the most dominant men in the history of the industry, responsible for some of the most important films ever made. Lasky was among the original 36 founders of the Academy of Motion Pictures Arts and Sciences

(AMPAS). He is best remembered for his support of the creative process in filmmaking and his sincere respect for the work of writers, cameramen, artists, etc. He died on January 13, 1958. DeMille was also among the 36 AMPAS founders. His affairs with writer Jeanie Macpherson and actress Julia Faye—he sometimes entertained both simultaneously on his yacht—lasted until their respective deaths. To promote his film *The Ten Commandments* he had stone monuments of the tablets placed in government buildings around the country, some of which are at the center of First Amendment lawsuits today! DeMille kept the suit of armor Wally wore in *Joan the Woman* in his office for the rest of his life. He died on January 21, 1959, outliving Lasky by a year.

Allan Dwan, who probably taught Wally most of what he knew about the movies at Flying A in Santa Barbara, was one of the great influences in his life. Dwan hated most actors, describing them as effeminate "pansies and poseurs," so it's ironic that he liked Wally so much. Dwan's feisty Irish temperament led to lifelong battles with his bosses, but he is a legend who directed 500 films, his last in 1961. He died on December 2, 1981, at 96, in a tiny San Fernando Valley house owned by his long-time housekeeper.[53]

Jack Dempsey, whom Wally befriended during his tragic New York trip to film *Forever*, moved to L.A. in 1923 with his mother and sister and bought a mansion at 24th and Western Avenue. In 1925 he married actress Estelle Taylor, a beautiful woman whose movie career was failing and who told Dempsey that having a prize-fighter husband hurt her socially. They bought a mansion at 5724 Los Feliz Boulevard, and through 1933 he appeared in ten movies, like *The Title Holder* (1924), *Manhattan Madness* (1925) and *A Dozen Socks* (1927). He and Taylor divorced in 1930 and he returned to the ring and appeared in hundreds of exhibitions and fights. In 1940, at age 45 he fought three men in a month and beat them all. He returned to New York where he managed his famous restaurant for 50 years. He died in New York in 1983 at almost 88.

Ann Little remained true to her Christian Science beliefs and never returned to the movies although she stayed in Hollywood. In the late 1920s she anonymously moved into a small bungalow apartment at 1269 North Flores with her mother Mamie Brooks, next door to studio executive Phil Berg and his actress wife Leila and lived there for years. She spent her final years in Hancock Park and on May 21, 1984, died at her home there at 5798 Lindenhurst Drive at the age of 91.

Charles "Buddy" Post was Wally's closest friend although they only appeared in a single film together, *Hell Diggers*, in 1921. Post appeared in another 20 films during the 1920s, mostly small roles in forgettable films like *The Overland Limited* (1925) and *The Satin Woman* (1927). His final role was in 1940s *Lil' Abner*, his only role after 1933. He died in 1952, just 55. He remained close to Dorothy and the children until his death.

Wally's adoring mother Bertha Westbrook Reid died in Newark, New Jersey, on July 30, 1939. Fittingly, her obituaries usually noted first that she was the "mother of silent star Wallace Reid" before noting her marriage to Hal Reid or her early stage career.[54]

Dorothy's father Harry Davenport appeared in over 100 films, working steadily from 1914 until his death on August 9, 1949, at the Hollywood home at 7968 Norton Avenue where he had lived for years. Among his films were *The Hunchback of Notre Dame* (1939), *Meet Me in St. Louis* (1944) and *Little Women* (1949).

Alice Shepard Davenport lived with Dorothy and the children into the 1930s. Her final film, 1930s *The Dude Wrangler*, was her 92nd. Writer Nathaneal West allegedly dated the much older Alice when he first came to Hollywood in the early 1930s and based the character of the amoral Southern woman Alice Sweethorne on her in his 1934 novel *A Cool Million*. Alice died at the Hollywood home she shared with Dorothy and the children on June 24, 1936, at age 72.

By 1926 Dorothy could no longer afford her DeLongpre estate. She left it eerily unchanged after Wally died. It remained exactly as it had that day; his clothes remained hanging in closets, the blue vase he gave her on their second anniversary still on a bookshelf, his Victrolas still scattered around the house. But unable to pay the bills, in 1930 she leased the property to English actor Clive Brook, who paid $300 a month and lived there with his wife Mildred Evelyn and their two children Faith and Lyndon. The former stage actor made 100 films into the 1940s including *A Tale of Two Cities* (1922) and The Sherlock Holmes films *The Return of Sherlock Holmes* (1929) and *Tarnished Lady* (1931).

Chris Davis was a long-time volunteer at the Motion Picture Country Home and Hospital who befriended Dorothy and Bill, Jr. during the 1970s as well as meeting the family that lived at DeLongpre during the 1960s. They told him that they had to be careful when they worked in the backyard gardens because of the presence of buried hypodermic syringes. They unearthed the rusty needles for years.[55]

Wally's beloved DeLongpre house was torn down in the early 1970s to make way for a 6-story apartment building. Among the few 1920s mansions that survive in this block is William S. Hart's colonial house adjacent to the site of the Reid estate. In the early 1930s he turned down $125,000 from a buyer and donated the property to L.A. County for use as a park and museum.[56]

Leaving DeLongpre, Dorothy bought a bungalow just three blocks away at 1330 Crescent Heights Boulevard and moved in along with her mother and children.[57] To make a living and support the children Dorothy formed Mrs. Wallace Reid Productions in the

Dorothy in her 1925 film *Red Kimono*.

According to period Sanford Maps, the Casa de Contenta was a courtyard apartment with a pool in front; this large apartment building is near the location and matches the descriptions.

1920s, the only woman independently producing movies in the era. But after *Human Wreckage* her movies veered from social conscience to exploitation. Historian Kevin Brownlow described her as "a reformer at heart, but she had a showman's outlook ... [and] believed that the primary mission of the screen was to entertain."[58] Subsequent films *Broken Laws* (1924), about the downward spiral of a juvenile delinquent, *Red Kimono* (1925), the story of a young woman forced into white slavery, and *The Earth Woman* (1926), about a family's reaction to the sexual assault of their daughter, were low-budget exploitation pieces, among the first "B" movies. In her final film, *The Satin Woman* (1927), she offered Buddy Post a co-starring role. Without the money to continue producing films on her own, Dorothy joined forces with Willis Kent, who ran the largest independent production company and was an early leader of the exploitation cinema genre, but by 1930 the market for her films seemed gone and Dorothy left the movies.

Her films were only marginally successful financially, and what family money remained by 1932—the childrens' small inheritance—was gone.[59] Dorothy could no longer afford the Crescent Heights house so she sold her properties and bought a lovely courtyard apartment building not far away on Hayworth, just north of Fountain. The Casa de Contenta had a swimming pool and gymnasium and catered to movie people, and Dorothy furnished apartments to suit her tenants. When Roscoe Arbuckle moved in just after she bought the building and admired the Monterey-style lobby furniture she moved it into his apartment. She and the children lived there with Alice. For the first time in a decade she had no servants. She described her move to Casa de Contenta as a "retirement ... until the situation for independents improves."[60]

Owning the apartment did nothing to alleviate the money problems that plagued her throughout the early 1930s. There were dozens of embarrassing lawsuits and financial judgments culminating in a September 22, 1933, bankruptcy filing listing $77,349 in debts and just $2,023 in assets. Her largest debt was a $50,000 note to Sound Picture Finance Company, one of her production partners.[61] About that time she, Alice and the children were forced to sell the Casa de Contenta and the group moved into a large bungalow at 1627 North Martel Avenue, just a few blocks away.

During the next decade she made only casual forays back to the movies. She wrote a few screenplays, produced a final film in 1938, *Rose of the Rio Grande*, and acted in a few forgettable films like 1934's *The Road to Ruin*. In 1942 Louella Parsons reported that Dorothy was working in a defense plant in San Pedro.[62]

In the 1940s and 1950s she wrote several dozen films like the *Curley* series and *Who Killed Doc Robbin?* (1948) and tried unsuccessfully to write for television. Several of her script outlines remain at the Herrick Library. As her children grew she lived in a succession of seemingly ever-smaller apartments and spent part of her final years living with her son. But by the 1970s her failing health led her to move to the Motion Picture and Television Home & Hospital in Woodland Hills, where she died on October 19, 1977, at the age of 82. She was cremated and her ashes placed in Wally's urn at Forest Lawn. She never re-married (though it was rumored she was engaged to director Walter Lang in the 1930s) because "I had over nine years of the best of Wally. It would simply be too difficult to supplant him, for no other man could take his place."[63]

Bill Jr. and Betty attended Fairfax High School in Hollywood and Carl Laemmle, Jr., gave Bill a screen test at the age of 14. In 1932 he debuted in *The Racing Strain* and appeared in small roles in ten films like *The Hoosier Schoolmaster* (1935) and *North West Mounted Police* (1940). He apparently inherited his father's daredevil tendencies; at 19 he spent fifteen days in jail after being sentenced for reckless driving.[64] Arrested for going 60 miles per hour of Franklin Avenue in Hollywood, he later said, "I'd earned $25 doing a high dive for M-G-M and brought it with me. I thought I'd be fined ... and didn't even think to bring a lawyer with me and didn't want to let my mother know I'd been arrested."[65]

He never approached his father's level of stardom and left films in 1943. He became a successful architect with offices in Santa Monica, specializing in large apartment projects. He and his wife—the former Ruth Dugan—had a son and a daughter and lived in a lovely home at 2216 Kelton Avenue in West Los Angeles. For most of the 1960s and 1970s Dorothy lived with them there. In the mid–1960s he accepted a government contract and spent a year in Vietnam building air bases and working in public relations. He also inherited his father's interest in music and was an accomplished saxophone and clarinet player. Also like his father he loved cars, but his real love was the ocean. He was a skilled yachtsman and surfer and also a licensed pilot, flying his own plane. On February 26, 1990, at the age of 72, he was flying about two miles off the Santa Monica beach when his plane crashed into the sea and he died. He was cremated and his ashes scattered over the ocean he so loved.

Betty Anna married at an early age, had a daughter, and was later divorced. In the 1960s she was a successful real estate saleswoman. According to family friend Chris Davis, Betty suffered from severe emotional problems during her entire adult life and died in the 1970s, estranged from the rest of her family.[66]

Although the evidence is circumstantial, as noted, Dorothy also told Davis that Wally was indeed the biological father of little Betty. According to her statements the baby's mother was very young, perhaps 16 or 17, and she was "being a good wife by adopting the child." Lasky and the studio paid a large financial settlement to the "un-named young girl" and she disappeared.[67]

Wally was among the first to receive a star on the Hollywood Walk of Fame, which began celebrating film history in 1958. His star is at 6611 Hollywood Boulevard (though the Hollywood Chamber of Commerce lists 6617½), east of Cherokee Avenue. It is among 2,275 (as of late 2006) stars honoring lifetime achievement in the entertainment industry. Each star is a terrazzo comprising a pink five-pointed star rimmed with bronze and inlaid into a charcoal square. Inside the star is the name engraved in bronze and below a round bronze emblem for the category for which the star was received. Wally's has a motion picture camera.[68] He is between *Wizard of Oz* star Billie Burke on the east and Peter Lorre and Buster Keaton on the west. Nearby are many of his friends and co-workers: D.W. Griffith (6535), Jesse Lasky (6433), Cecil B. DeMille (1725 Vine), Allan Dwan (6263), Charlie Chaplin (6751), Antonio Moreno (6651), and Will Rogers (6608).

Wally's Star on the Hollywood Walk of Fame, located in front of 6811 Hollywood Boulevard, not far from D.W. Griffith.

In her 1978 memoirs Adela Rogers St. Johns, perhaps Wally's closest friend, entitled her chapter about Wally "The Beautiful and the Damned." Wally was indeed both. He was the most famous face in the movies all over the world, but is, surprisingly, virtually forgotten. Dorothy probably described him best, saying in 1966, "Wally died very young—but he gave freely of the gifts of his youth. Most of all, he loved people, and the public responded in kind. He had so many talents—the Gods were overly kind, but they also made him vulnerable, his own worst enemy, to compensate for their divine lavishness. He knew too much ... and not enough."

Filmography

Wallace Reid—Actor

Note: If the film length could not be confirmed, a single reel was estimated at 950–1,000 feet.

1910

The Phoenix Selig Polyscope Company. Writer Milton Nobles. Single reel; 950–1,000 feet. Release date July 18, 1910. Cast: Sam Pickens, Fred Walton, Wallace Reid, Karl King, Barbara Swager.

1911

The Leading Lady Vitagraph Company of America. Director Ned Finley. Writer Allen Johnson. Single reel; 1,079 feet. Release date April 18, 1911. Cast: John Bunny, Van Dyke Brooke, Wallace Reid, Robert Gaillard.

The Reporter Selig Polyscope Company. Single reel; 950–1,000 feet. Release date June 26, 1911. Cast: Sam Pickens, Fred Walton, Wallace Reid, Karl King, Barbara Swager.

His Son Reliance Film Company. Director Milton J. Fahrney. Single reel; 950–1,000 feet. Release date August 5, 1911. Cast: Henry B. Walthall, Wallace Reid, Dorothy Davenport.

War Vitagraph Company of America. Single reel; 1,079 feet. Release date December 8, 1911. Cast: Charles Kent, Rose Tapley, Wallace Reid, Mary Maurice, Edward Brady.

1912

The Seepore Rebellion Vitagraph Company of America, Single reel; 950–1,000 feet. Release date January, 1912. Cast: Wallace Reid, James Morrison.

A Red Cross Martyr; or, On the Firing Lines of Tripoli (aka *A Red Cross Martyr*) Vitagraph Company of America. Director Laurence Trimble. Single reel; 950–1,000 feet. Release date January 2, 1912. Cast: Robert Gaillard, Florence Turner, Anita Stewart, Rosemary Theby, Wallace Reid.

The Course of True Love Vitagraph Company of America. Single reel; 950–1,000 feet. Release date January 6, 1912. Cast: Edith Halleran, James Halleck Reid (as Hal Reid), Wallace Reid, Laurence Trimble, Florence Turner.

Chumps (aka *Chumps: A Fairy Story for Overgrownups*) Vitagraph Company of America. Director George D. Baker. Writer Wallace Reid. Single reel; 1,085 feet. Release date January 16, 1912. Cast: Marshall P. Wilder, John Bunny, Leah Baird, William Shea, Wallace Reid.

Jean Intervenes Vitagraph Company of America. Single reel; 870 feet. Release date January 23, 1912. Cast: Florence Turner, James Halleck Reid (as Hal Reid), Wallace Reid, Edith Halleran, Jean (dog).

Indian Romeo and Juliet Vitagraph Company of America. Director Laurence Trimble. Writer James Halleck Reid (as Hal Reid), based on poem by William Shakespeare. Single reel; 1,092 feet. Release date January 30, 1912. Cast: Wallace Reid, Florence Turner, Harry T. Morey, James Halleck Reid (as Hal Reid), Adelaide Ober, Hal Wilson.

The Telephone Girl Vitagraph Company of America. Single reel; 1,000 feet. Release date March 2, 1912. Cast: Wallace Reid, Edith Storey.

The Seventh Son Vitagraph Company of America. Director James Halleck Reid (as Hal Reid). Writer James Halleck Reid (as Hal Reid; unconfirmed). Single reel; 826 feet. Release date April 3, 1912. Cast: Ralph Ince, Mary Maurice, James Morrison, Tefft Johnson, Robert Gaillard, Earle Williams, William R. Dunn, Wallace Reid.

The Illumination Vitagraph Company of America. Director Charles L. Gaskill. Single reel; 950–1,000 feet. Release date April 5, 1912. Cast: Tom Powers, Rosemary Theby, Helen Gardner, Harry Northrup, Wallace Reid, Rose Tapley.

At Scrogginses' Corner Vitagraph Company of America. Director James Halleck Reid (as Hal Reid). Writer James Halleck Reid (as Hal Reid; unconfirmed). Single reel; 1,095 feet. Release date April 9, 1912. Cast: John Bunny, Leo Delaney, Edith Halleran, James Morrison, Robert Gaillard, Wallace Reid, Julia Swayne Gordon, Hal Wilson, Helene Costello.

Brothers Champion Studios for Motion Pictures Distributors and Sales Company. Director George Field. Single reel; 1,026 feet. Release date April 24, 1912. Cast: Wallace Reid, Frank B. Coigne, Miss Orlamond, Charles Hoskins, Evelyn Francis.

The Victoria Cross (aka *The Charge of the Light Brigade*) Reliance Film Company. Director James Halleck Reid (as Hal Reid). Writer James Halleck Reid (as Hal Reid). Single reel; 1,095 feet. Release date April 27, 1912. Cast: Tefft Johnson, Edith Storey, Wallace Reid, Julia Swayne Gordon, Rose Tapley.

The Hieroglyphic Vitagraph Company of America. Director Charles L. Gaskill. Single reel; 1,069 feet. Release date May 4, 1912. Cast: Tom Powers, Zena Keefe, Harry Northrup, Edwin R. Phillips, Wallace Reid.

Diamond Cut Diamond Vitagraph Company of America. Single reel; 950–1,000 feet. Release date May 24, 1912. Cast: John Bunny, Flora Finch, Mae Costello, Wallace Reid, Richard Rosson, Ray Ford, Kate Price.

Curfew Shall Not Ring Tonight Reliance Film Company. Director James Halleck Reid (as Hal Reid). Writer James Halleck Reid (as Hal Reid). Single reel; 1,072 feet. Release date May 29, 1912. Cast: Wallace Reid.

His Mother's Son (Sometimes attributed as *His Mother's Son* [1913], a different film.) Reliance Film Company. Director William Christie Cabanne. Single reel; 950–1,000 feet. Release date June 1, 1912. Cast: Wallace Reid, Gertrude Robinson.

Kaintuck Reliance Film Company. Director James Halleck Reid (as Hal Reid). Writer Wallace Reid. Single reel; 1,066 feet. Release date June 8, 1912. Cast: Wallace Reid, Gertrude Robinson, Robert Taper, Virginia Westbrook.

Virginius Reliance Film Company. Director James Halleck Reid (as Hal Reid). Writer James Halleck Reid (as Hal Reid), based on play by James Sheridan Knowles. 2 reels; approx. 1,900 feet. Release date June 15, 1912. Cast: James Halleck Reid (as Hal Reid), Wallace Reid.

The Gamblers Vitagraph Company of America. Writer (none confirmed), based on play by Charles Klein. Single reel; 1,079 feet. Release date June 22, 1912. Cast: Wallace Reid, Zena Keefe, Earle Williams, Julia Swayne Gordon, Leah Baird.

Before the White Man Came Reliance Film Company. Director Otis Turner. Writer Wallace Reid. Single reel; 950–1,000 feet. Release date June 29, 1912. Cast: Wallace Reid, Gertrude Robinson.

A Man's Duty Reliance Film Company. Director James Halleck Reid (as Hal Reid). Writer James Halleck Reid (as Hal Reid). Single reel; 1,043 feet. Release date July 3, 1912. Cast: Wallace Reid, Hector Dion, Charles Herman, George Siegmann, Sue Balfour, Edward P. Sullivan.

Cripple Creek Reliance Film Company. Director James Halleck Reid (as Hal Reid). Writer James Halleck Reid (as Hal Reid). 2 reels; 1,950 feet. Release date July 17, 1912. Cast: Wallace Reid, Sue Balfour, Gertrude Robinson.

Making Good Independent Motion Pictures Company (IMP) for Universal Film Manufacturing Company. Single reel; 950–1,000 feet. Release date August 26, 1912. Cast: Wallace Reid, Jane Fearnley, William R. Dunn, Joseph S. Chailee.

The Secret Service Man Reliance Film Company. Single reel, 1,075 feet. Release date August 28, 1912. Cast: Wallace Reid, Rodman Law.

An Unseen Enemy Biograph Company. Director D.W. Griffith. Writer Edward Acker. Cinematographer George W. Bitzer (as G.W. Bitzer). Single reel; 999 feet, 14 minutes. Release date September 9, 1912; re-released September 24, 1915. Cast: Lillian Gish, Dorothy Gish, Robert Harron, Harry Carey, Lionel Barrymore, Mary Gish, Grace Henderson, Adolph Lestina, Charles Hill Mailes, Walter Miller, Antonio Moreno, Wallace Reid, Henry B. Walthall.

The Indian Raiders Bison Motion Pictures for Universal Film Manufacturing Company. Director Tom Ricketts. Cinematographer Charles Rosher. Technical advisor Jack Parsins. 2 reels; approx. 1,900 feet. Release date October 8, 1912. Cast: Wallace Reid.

His Only Son Nestor Film Company for Universal Film Manufacturing Company. Director(s) Jack Conway and Milton J. Fahrney. Single reel; 950–1,000 feet. Release date October 9,

1912. Cast: Wallace Reid, Dorothy Davenport, Jack Conway, Victoria Forde, Hoot Gibson.

Every Inch a Man Vitagraph Company of America. Director William Humphrey. Writer James Halleck Reid (as Hal Reid). Single reel; 925 feet. Release date October 14, 1912. Cast: Wallace Reid, James Halleck Reid (as Hal Reid), Rose Tapley, Robert Gaillard, Morris McGee, Frank Mason.

Early Days in the West Bison Motion Pictures for Universal Film Manufacturing Company. Cinematographer Charles Rosher. 2 reels; approx. 1,900 feet. Release date October 19, 1912. Cast: Wallace Reid, Dolly Larkin, George Field, Ray Francis, W.G. Rice, Paul Machette.

Hunted Down Bison Motion Pictures for Universal Film Manufacturing Company. 2 reels; approx. 1,900 feet. Release date October 22, 1912. Cast: Charles Inslee, William Clifford, Margaret Manners, Wallace Reid, Baby Thorne, Lizette Thorne.

A Daughter of the Redskins Bison Motion Pictures for Universal Film Manufacturing Company. Director Frank Montgomery. 2 reels; approx. 1,900 feet. Release date October 26, 1912. Cast: Charles Inslee, Wallace Reid, Harry Tenbrook, William Messick, Lizette Thorne, Dolly Larkin.

The Cowboy Guardians Bison Motion Pictures for Universal Film Manufacturing Company. Single reel; 950–1,000 feet. Release date October 29, 1912. Cast: Charles Inslee, Sylvia Ashton, Baby Hargraves, Wallace Reid.

The Tribal Law Bison Motion Pictures for Universal Film Manufacturing Company. Director Wallace Reid (other sources note the director as Otis Turner, but period newspapers confirm Wally directed, wrote, and starred in the film). Writer Wallace Reid. 2 reels; 2,109 feet. Release date November 16, 1912. Cast: Charles Inslee, Wallace Reid, Margarita Fischer.

An Indian Outcast Bison Motion Pictures for Universal Film Manufacturing Company. Single reel; 950–1,000 feet. Release date November 26, 1912. Cast: Charles Inslee, Wallace Reid, William Steele, Chief Harvey, Ravena, Margarita Fischer, Edward H. Philbrook, Harry Tenbrook.

Hidden Treasure American Film Company for Mutual Film Corporation. Director Wallace Reid. Cameraman A.G. Heimerl. Single reel; 950–1,000 feet. Release date December, 1912. Cast: Wallace Reid, Lillian Christy, Edward Coxen.

All for a Girl Vitagraph Company of America. Director Frederick A. Thomson. Writer Wallace Reid. Single (split) reel; approx. 500–600 feet. Release date December 14, 1912. Cast: Wallace Reid, Dorothy Kelly, Leah Baird, Harry T. Morey, Kate Price, Earle Foxe, Darwin Carr.

1913

The Picture of Dorian Gray New York Motion Picture Company. Director Phillips Smalley. Writer (none confirmed), scenario based on novel by Oscar Wilde. Single reel; 950–1,000 feet. Release date January, 1913. Cast: Wallace Reid, Lois Weber, Phillips Smalley.

Love and the Law American Film Company for Mutual Film Corporation. Director Wallace Reid. Single reel; 950–1,000 feet. Release date January, 1913. Cast: Wallace Reid, Lillian Christy, Edward Coxen.

Their Masterpiece American Film Company for Mutual Film Corporation. Director Allan Dwan. Single reel; 950–1,000 feet. Release date January 13, 1913. Cast: J. Warren Kerrigan, Pauline Bush, Wallace Reid.

Pirate Gold Biograph Company. Director Wilfred Lucas. Writer George Hennessy. Cinematographer George W. Bitzer. Single reel; 1,080 feet. Release date January 13, 1913. Cast: Blanche Sweet, Charles Hill Mailes, J. Jiquel Lanoe, Hector Sarno, W. Chrystie Miller, Harry Carey, Donald Crisp, Joseph McDermott, Wallace Reid.

A Rose of Old Mexico American Film Company for Mutual Film Corporation. Director(s) Allan Dwan and Wallace Reid. Single reel; 950–1,000 feet. Release date January 25, 1913. Cast: Wallace Reid, Lillian Christy, Edward Coxen, Chester Withey.

When the Light Fades American Film Company for Mutual Film Corporation. Director Allan Dwan. Single reel; 950–1,000 feet. Release date February 24, 1913. Cast: Wallace Reid, Lillian Christy, Eugene Pallette, Edward Coxen.

Near to Earth Biograph Company. Director D.W. Griffith. Writer James Cerr. Cinematographer George W. Bitzer. Single reel; 1,075 feet. Release date March 20, 1913; re-released November 13, 1916. Cast: Lionel Barrymore, Robert Harron, Gertrude Bambrick, Mae Marsh, Kathleen Butler, Walter Miller, Dorothy Bernard, William Christy Cabanne (as Christy Cabanne), Harry Carey, Donald Crisp, Charles Hill Mailes, Joseph McDermott, Mabel Normand, Frank Opperman, Wallace Reid, Blanche Sweet.

The Eye of a God Pyramid Film Company for Warner Features Company. Director Joseph A. Golden. Writer Joseph A. Golden. 3 reels; approx. 2,850 feet. Release date April 5, 1913. Cast: Chester Barnett, Octavia Handworth, Earl Metcalfe, Wallace Reid.

The Ways of Fate American Film Company and Western Feature Productions for Mutual Film Corporation. Producer Allan Dwan. Director Wallace Reid. Single reel; 950–1,000 feet. Release date April 21, 1913. Cast: Wallace Reid, Vivien Rich, Pauline Bush, Lon Chaney, Murdock McQuarrie.

When Jim Returned American Film Company for Mutual Film Corporation. Director Wallace Reid. Writer Wallace Reid. Single reel; 950–1,000 feet. Release date April 24, 1913. Cast: Wallace Reid, Vivien Rich, Eugene Pallette.

The Tattooed Arm American Film Company for Mutual Film Corporation. Director Wallace Reid. Writer Wallace Reid. Single reel; 950–1,000 feet. Release date May 1, 1913. Cast: Wallace Reid, Vivien Rich, Eugene Pallette, George Field.

The Deerslayer Vitagraph Company of America for General Film Company. Director James Halleck Reid (as Hal Reid). Writer(s) Eugene Mullin and James Halleck Reid (as Hal Reid), based upon story by James Fennimore Cooper. 2 reels; 2,309 feet. Release date May 7, 1913. Cast: Harry T. Morey, Wallace Reid, Ethel Dunn, James Halleck Reid (as Hal Reid), Edward Thomas, Evelyn Dominicus, Florence Turner, William F. Cooper, Walter Long. Period newspapers reported that Larry (Laurence) Trimble directed the film.

Youth and Jealousy American Film Company for Mutual Film Corporation. Director Wallace Reid. Writer Theodosia Harris. Single reel; 950–1,000 feet. Release date May 10, 1913. Cast: Wallace Reid, Vivien Rich, Frank Borzage.

The Kiss American Film Company for Mutual Film Corporation. Director Wallace Reid. Writer Theodosia Harris. Single reel; 950–1,000 feet. Release date May 15, 1913. Cast: Wallace Reid, Vivien Rich, Eugene Pallette.

Her Innocent Marriage American Film Company for Mutual Film Corporation. Director(s) Allan Dwan and Wallace Reid. Writer Theodosia Harris. Single reel; 950–1,000 feet. Release date May 19, 1913. Cast: Wallace Reid, Vivien Rich, George Field.

A Modern Snare American Film Company for Mutual Film Corporation. Director Wallace Reid. Single reel; 950–1,000 feet. Release date May 24, 1913. Cast: Wallace Reid, Vivien Rich, George Field.

When Luck Changes American Film Company for Mutual Film Corporation. Director(s) Allan Dwan and Wallace Reid. Writer James Halleck Reid (as Hal Reid). Single reel; 950–1,000 feet. Release date June 2, 1913. Cast: Wallace Reid, Vivien Rich, George Field.

Via Cabaret American Film Company for Mutual Film Corporation. Director Wallace Reid. Writer James Halleck Reid (as Hal Reid). Single reel; 950–1,000 feet. Release date June 7, 1913. Cast: Wallace Reid, Vivien Rich, George Field.

The Spirit of the Flag 101-Bison for Universal Film Manufacturing Company. Director Allan Dwan. Writer Wallace Reid. 2 reels; 2,115 feet. Release date June 7, 1913. Cast: Wallace Reid, Pauline Bush, Jessalyn Van Trump, Arthur Rosson, David Kirkland, Marshall Neilan.

Hearts and Horses American Film Company for Mutual Film Corporation. Director(s) Allan Dwan and Wallace Reid. Single reel; 950–1,000 feet. Release date June 12, 1913. Cast: Wallace Reid, Vivian Rich, George Field.

In Love and War (aka *The Call to Arms*) 101-Bison Motion Pictures for Universal Film Manufacturing Company. Producer(s) Benjamin Chapin and Thomas H. Ince. Director(s) Allan Dwan and Thomas H. Ince. Writer Allan Dwan. 2 reels; 2,030 feet. Release date June 17, 1913. Cast: Wallace Reid, Pauline Bush, Marshall Neilan.

Woman and War 101-Bison Motion Pictures for Universal Film Manufacturing Company. Director Allan Dwan. Writer Wallace Reid. 2 reels; approx. 1,900 feet. Release date June 21, 1913. Cast: Wallace Reid, Pauline Bush, Jessalyn Van Trump, Marshall Neilan.

Dead Man's Shoes American Film Company for Mutual Film Corporation. Director Wallace Reid. Writer Wallace Reid. Single reel; 984 feet. Release date June 28, 1913. Cast: Wallace Reid, Vivian Rich, George Field, Frank Borzage.

The Pride of Lonesome American Film Company for Mutual Film Corporation. Director Wallace Reid. Writer James Halleck Reid (as Hal Reid). Single reel; 984 feet. Release date July 3, 1913. Cast: Wallace Reid, Vivian Rich, Frank Borzage.

The Powder Flash of Death (aka *The Menace*) 101-Bison Film Company for Universal Film Manufacturing Company. Director Allan Dwan. Writer Allan Dwan. Single reel; 1,082 feet (domestic release), also released as 2 reels; 2,023 feet. Release date July 8, 1913; re-released December 28, 1916. Cast: Wallace Reid, Pauline Bush, Jessalyn Van Trump, Marshall Neilan, David Kirkland.

A Foreign Spy American Film Company for Mutual Film Corporation. Director Wallace

Reid. Writer James Halleck Reid (as Hal Reid). Single reel; 950–1,000 feet. Release date July 10, 1913. Cast: Wallace Reid, Vivian Rich, Frank Borzage.

The Picket Guard 101-Bison Film Company for Universal Film Manufacturing Company. Director Allan Dwan. Writer Arthur Rosson, based on poem by Ethelin Eliot Beer. 2 reels; 1,974 feet. Release date July 15, 1913. Cast: Wallace Reid, Pauline Bush, Jessalyn Van Trump, Marshall Neilan, David Kirkland.

Mental Suicide Powers Picture Plays for Universal Film Manufacturing Company. Producer Pat Powers. Director Allan Dwan. Writer Wallace Reid. 2 reels; approx. 1,900 feet. Release date July 25, 1913. Cast: Wallace Reid, Pauline Bush, Jessalyn Van Trump, Marshall Neilan, David Kirkland.

Man's Duty Rex Motion Picture Company for Universal Film Manufacturing Company. Director Allan Dwan. Writer M. de la Parelle. Single reel; 950–1,000 feet. Release date August 10, 1913. Cast: Wallace Reid, Pauline Bush, Jessalyn Van Trump, Marshall Neilan.

The Animal Rex Motion Picture Company for Universal Film Manufacturing Company. Producer Allan Dwan. Director Allan Dwan. Writer Allan Dwan. Single reel; 950–1,000 feet. Release date August 17, 1913. Cast: Wallace Reid, Pauline Bush, Jessalyn Van Trump, Marshall Neilan, D. Barlow.

The Harvest of Flame Rex Motion Picture Company for Universal Film Manufacturing Company. Producer Allan Dwan. Director(s) Wallace Reid and Marshall Neilan. Writer Wallace Reid. 2 reels; 1,623 feet. Release date August 21, 1913. Cast: William Walters, Wallace Reid, Pauline Bush, Marshall Neilan.

The Spark of Manhood Powers Pictures Plays for Universal Film Manufacturing Company. Producer Pat Powers. Director Wallace Reid. Single reel; 950–1,000 feet. Release date August 22, 1913. Cast: Wallace Reid, Dorothy Davenport.

The Mystery of Yellow Aster Mine 101-Bison Film Company for Universal Film Manufacturing Company. Director Frank Borzage. Writer Bess Meredyth. 2 reels; 1,662 feet. Release date August 26, 1913. Cast: Wallace Reid, Pauline Bush, Arthur Rosson, Frank Borzage.

The Gratitude of Wanda 101-Bison Film Company for Universal Film Manufacturing Company. Director Wallace Reid. Writer Bess Meredyth. Single reel; 1,246 feet. Release date August 30, 1913. Cast: Wallace Reid, Pauline Bush, Arthur Rosson, Jessalyn Van Trump, Frank Borzage.

The Wall of Money Rex Motion Picture Company for Universal Film Manufacturing Company. Director Allan Dwan. Writer Marshall Neilan. Single reel; 984 feet, also released as 2 reels; 1,929 feet. Release date September 21, 1913, re-released January 6, 1917. Cast: Wallace Reid, Pauline Bush, Marshall Neilan, Jessalyn Van Trump, James McQuarrie.

The Heart of a Cracksman Powers Picture Plays for Universal Film Manufacturing Company. Producer Pat Powers. Director(s) Wallace Reid and Willis Robards. Writer Wallace Reid. Single reel; 961 feet. Release date November 7, 1914. Cast: Wallace Reid, Cleo Madison, Edward Brady, James Neill, Marcia Moore.

The Cracksman's Reformation Powers Picture Plays for Universal Film Manufacturing Company. Producer Pat Powers. Director Willis Robards. Writer Wallace Reid. Single reel; 1,062 feet. Release date November 14, 1914. Cast: Wallace Reid, Dorothy Davenport, Edward Brady, James Neill.

The Fires of Fate Rex Motion Picture Company for Universal Film Manufacturing Company. Director(s) Wallace Reid and Willis Robards. Writer Wallace Reid. 2 reels; approx. 1,900 feet. Release date November 20, 1914. Cast: Wallace Reid, Dorothy Davenport, Edward Brady.

Cross Purposes Powers Picture Plays for Universal Film Manufacturing Company. Producer Pat Powers. Director(s) Wallace Reid and Willis Robards. Writer Bess Meredyth. Single reel; 902 feet. Release date December 5, 1914. Cast: Wallace Reid, Cleo Madison, James Neill.

Retribution Nestor Film Company for Universal Film Manufacturing Company. Director(s) Wallace Reid and Willis Robards. Single reel; 931 feet. Release date December 10, 1914. Cast: Wallace Reid, Dorothy Davenport, Edward Brady, Frank Borzage, Phil Dunham, Anna Q. Nilsson.

A Cracksman Santa Claus Powers Picture Plays for Universal Film Manufacturing Company. Producer Pat Powers. Director Willis Robards. Writer Wallace Reid. Single reel; 1,118 feet. Release date December 16, 1914. Cast: Wallace Reid, Dorothy Davenport, Gertrude Short, Edward Brady, Frank Borzage.

The Lightning Bolt Nestor Film Company for Universal Film Manufacturing Company. Director Wallace Reid. Single reel; 951 feet. Release date December 24, 1914. Cast: Wallace Reid, Dorothy Davenport, Edward Brady, Phil Dunham.

A Hopi Legend (aka *A Pueblo Romance*) Nestor Film Company for Universal Film Manufacturing Company. Director Wallace Reid. Writer Wallace Reid. Single reel; 990 feet. Release date December 31, 1914. Cast: Wallace Reid, Dorothy Davenport, Edward Brady, Frank Borzage, Phil Dunham.

Song Bird of the North (Reported but unconfirmed.) Vitagraph Company of America. Directed by Ralph Ince. Written by Ralph Ince. Single reel; 1,108 feet. Release date early 1913. Cast: Anita Stewart, Ralph Ince. Wallace Reid is listed in some sources as a cast member of this film, although no archival records remain supporting that claim.

1914

Sierra Jim's Reformation Majestic Motion Picture Corporation for Mutual Film Corporation. Director John B. O'Brien. Single reel; 991 feet, 12 minutes. Release date January, 1914. Cast: Wallace Reid, Gertrude McLynn, Raoul Walsh, Eagle Eye, Dark Cloud, Fred Burns.

The Second Mrs. Roebuck Reliance Film Company and Majestic Motion Picture Corporation for Mutual Film Corporation. Director John B. O'Brien (as Jack O'Brien). Supervising Director D.W. Griffith. Writer W. Carey Wonderly. 2 reels; 2,135 feet. Release date January, 1914. Cast: Mary Alden, Wallace Reid, Blanche Sweet, Raoul Walsh.

A Mother's Influence Majestic Motion Picture Corporation for Mutual Film Corporation. Director John B. O'Brien. Single reel; 1,066 feet. Release date January, 1914. Cast: Wallace Reid, Billie West.

Moonshine Molly Majestic Motion Picture Corporation for Mutual Film Corporation. Director William Christy Cabanne. 2 reels; 2,115 feet. Release date January, 1914. Cast: Wallace Reid, Mae Marsh, Robert Harron, Fred Burns, Eagle Eye.

The Little Country Mouse Majestic Motion Picture Corporation for Mutual Film Corporation. Director Donald Crisp. Single reel; 989 feet. Release date January, 1914. Cast: Blanche Sweet, Wallace Reid, Mary Alden, Raoul Walsh, Howard Gaye.

Her Awakening Majestic Motion Picture Corporation for Mutual Film Corporation. Director William Christy Cabanne. Supervising Director D.W. Griffith. 2 reels; approx. 1,900 feet. Release date January, 1914. Cast: Blanche Sweet, Wallace Reid, Ralph Lewis.

For Those Unborn Majestic Motion Picture Corporation for Mutual Film Corporation. Director William Christy Cabanne. 2 reels; approx. 1,900 feet. Release date January, 1914. Cast: Blanche Sweet, Wallace Reid, Robert Harron, Irene Hunt.

Whoso Diggith a Pit Powers Picture Plays for Universal Film Manufacturing Company. Producer Pat Powers. Single reel; 984 feet. Release date January 9, 1914. Cast: Wallace Reid, Lurline Lyons, James Neill, Edward Brady.

The Intruder Nestor Film Company for Universal Film Manufacturing Company. Director Wallace Reid. Single reel; 1,013 feet. Release date January 14, 1914. Cast: Wallace Reid, Dorothy Davenport, Edward Brady, Phil Dunham.

The Countess Betty's Mine Nestor Film Company for Universal Film Manufacturing Company. Director Wallace Reid. Writer Bess Meredyth. Single reel; 990 feet. Release date January 21, 1914. Cast: Wallace Reid, Dorothy Davenport, Edward Brady, Phil Dunham.

The Wheel of Life Nestor Film Company for Universal Film Manufacturing Company. Director Wallace Reid. Writer James B. Fagan. Single reel; 1,052 feet. Release date January 28, 1914. Cast: Wallace Reid, Dorothy Davenport, Edward Brady, Frank Borzage, John G. Blystone, Lucile Wilson.

Fires of Conscience Nestor Film Company for Universal Film Manufacturing Company. Director Wallace Reid. Writer Henry Christeen Warnack (as Henry C. Warnack). Single reel; 950–1,000 feet. Release date February 4, 1914. Cast: Wallace Reid, Dorothy Davenport, Gertrude Robinson, Edward Brady.

The Greater Devotion Nestor Film Company for Universal Film Manufacturing Company. Director Wallace Reid. Single reel; 984 feet. Release date February 11, 1914. Cast: Wallace Reid, Dorothy Davenport, Fred Gamble, Edward Brady, Phil Dunham.

A Flash in the Dark Nestor Film Company for Universal Film Manufacturing Company. Director Wallace Reid. Writer James Dayton. Single reel; 1,029 feet. Release date February 18, 1914. Cast: Wallace Reid, Dorothy Davenport, Edward Brady, Frank Borzage.

Breed o' the Mountains Nestor Film Company for Universal Film Manufacturing Company. Director Wallace Reid. Writer Harry G. Stafford. Single reel; 950–1,000 feet. Release date February 25, 1914. Cast: Wallace Reid, Dorothy Davenport, Edward Brady, Lucile Wilson.

Regeneration Powers Picture Plays for Universal Film Manufacturing Company. Producer

Pat Powers. Director Wallace Reid. Single reel; 656 feet. Release date February 27, 1914. Cast: Wallace Reid, Helen Taft, Edward Brady, Phil Dunham.

The Voice of the Viola   Nestor Film Company for Universal Film Manufacturing Company. Director Wallace Reid. Writer Bess Meredyth. Single reel; 1,082 feet, also released at 2 reels; approx. 1,900 feet. Release date March 6, 1914. Cast: Wallace Reid, Dorothy Davenport, William Steele, Edward Brady, Phil Dunham.

Heart of the Hills   Rex Motion Picture Company for Universal Film Manufacturing Company. Director Wallace Reid. Writer Wallace Reid. 2 reels; approx. 1,900 feet. Release date March 12, 1914. Cast: Wallace Reid, Dorothy Davenport, Phil Dunham, Edward Brady, Lucile Wilson.

The Way of a Woman   Nestor Film Company for Universal Film Manufacturing Company. Director Wallace Reid. Writer Bess Meredyth. 2 reels; approx. 1,900 feet. Release date March 18, 1914. Cast: Wallace Reid, Dorothy Davenport, Edna Maison, Antrim Short.

The Mountaineer   Nestor Film Company for Universal Film Manufacturing Company. Director Wallace Reid. Writer Wallace Reid. Single reel; 1,000 feet. Release date March 25, 1914. Cast: Wallace Reid, Dorothy Davenport, Phil Dunham, Lucile Wilson, Edward Brady.

The Spider and Her Web   Rex Motion Picture Company for Universal Film Manufacturing Company. Director(s) Phillips Smalley and Lois Weber. Writer Lois Weber. 2 reels; 2,141 feet. Release date March 26, 1914. Cast: Lois Weber, Dorothy Davenport, Phillips Smalley, Rupert Julian, Wallace Reid, William Wolbert.

Cupid Incognito   Nestor Film Company for Universal Film Manufacturing Company. Director Wallace Reid. Writer(s) Bess Meredyth and Wallace Reid. Single reel; 1,072 feet. Release date April 1, 1914. Cast: Wallace Reid, Dorothy Davenport, Phil Dunham, John G. Blystone, Edna Maison, Lucile Wilson, William Wolbert.

A Gypsy Romance   Nestor Film Company for Universal Film Manufacturing Company. Director Wallace Reid. Single reel; 950–1,000 feet. Release date April 8, 1914. Cast: Wallace Reid, Dorothy Davenport, Phil Dunham, Edward Brady, William Steele.

The Test   Nestor Film Company for Universal Film Manufacturing Company. Director Wallace Reid. 2 reels; approx. 1,900 feet. Release date April 15, 1914. Cast: Wallace Reid, Dorothy Davenport, Frank Lloyd, Tom Santschi, Edward Brady, Anrtim Short, Gertrude Short, Gladys Montague.

The Skeleton   Powers Picture Plays for Universal Film Manufacturing Company. Director Wallace Reid. 2 reels; approx. 1,900 feet. Release date April 22, 1914. Cast: Wallace Reid, Dorothy Davenport, Phil Dunham, William Wolbert.

The Fruit of Evil (aka *The Sins of the Fathers*) Nestor Film Company for Universal Film Manufacturing Company. Director Wallace Reid. Writer(s) Wallace Reid and Elaine Stern. 2 reels; approx. 1,900 feet. Release date April 22, 1914. Cast: Wallace Reid, Dorothy Davenport, Edward Brady, Gladys Montague, Antrim Short, Gertrude Short.

The Daughter of a Crook   Victor Film Company for Universal Film Manufacturing Company. 3 reels; approx. 2,850 feet. Release date April 24, 1914. Cast: Wallace Reid, Phyllis Gordon.

Women and Roses   Nestor Film Company for Universal Film Manufacturing Company. Director Wallace Reid. Writer(s) Bess Meredyth and Wallace Reid, based on poem by Robert Browning. 2 reels; approx. 1,900 feet. Release date April 29, 1914. Cast: Wallace Reid, Dorothy Davenport, Phil Dunham, Lillian Brockwell, Vera Sisson.

The Quack   Nestor Film Company for Universal Film Manufacturing Company. Director Wallace Reid. Single reel; 987 feet. Release date May 6, 1914. Cast: Wallace Reid, Dorothy Davenport, Phil Dunham, Lucille Bolton, James Robert Chandler, William Wolbert.

The Siren   Nestor Film Company for Universal Film Manufacturing Company. Director Wallace Reid. Single reel; 1,020 feet. Release date May 13, 1914. Cast: Wallace Reid, Dorothy Davenport, Lillian Brockwell, David Kirkland, Page Peters, Lucille Bolton.

The Man Within   Nestor Film Company for Universal Film Manufacturing Company. Director Wallace Reid. Single reel; 1,056 feet. Release date May 20, 1914. Cast: Wallace Reid, Dorothy Davenport, Phil Dunham, William Steele, Clarence Burton, William Wolbert.

Passing of the Beast   Nestor Film Company for Universal Film Manufacturing Company. Director Wallace Reid. Single reel; 1,020 feet. Release date May 27, 1914. Cast: Wallace Reid, Dorothy Davenport, Joe King, Phil Dunham, John G. Blystone, William Steele, Edgar Keller, William Wolbert.

Love's Western Flight (aka *Children of Fate*) Nestor Film Company for Universal Film Manufacturing Company. Director Wallace Reid. Writer(s) James Oliver Curwood and Harry G. Stafford. Single reel; 1,039 feet. Release date June 3, 1914. Cast: Wallace Reid, Dorothy Davenport, Joe King, Phil Dunham, William Wolbert, Frank Borzage.

A Wife on a Wager (aka *A Wife for a Wager*) Nestor Film Company for Universal Film Manufacturing Company. Director Wallace Reid. Writer Calder Johnstone. Single reel; 1,085 feet. Release date June 10, 1914. Cast: Wallace Reid, Dorothy Davenport, Joe King, John G. Blystone.

'Cross the Mexican Line Nestor Film Company for Universal Film Manufacturing Company. Director Wallace Reid. Writer Harry S. Stafford. Single reel; 1,085 feet. Release date June 17, 1914. Cast: Wallace Reid, Dorothy Davenport, William Steele, Edgar Keller, Phil Dunham.

The Den of Thieves Nestor Film Company for Universal Film Manufacturing Company. Director Wallace Reid. Writer F. McGrew Willis. Single reel; 1,023 feet. Release date June 24, 1914. Cast: Wallace Reid, Dorothy Davenport, Lillian Brockwell, David Kirkland, William Wolbert, Phil Dunham.

Arms and the Gringo (aka *The Rifle Smugglers*) Majestic Motion Picture Company for Mutual Film Corporation. Director William Christy Cabanne. Writer Anna Tupper Wilkes. Single reel; 950–1,000 feet. Release date June 28, 1914. Cast: Wallace Reid, Dorothy Gish, Fred Kelsey, F.A. Lowery, Howard Gaye.

The City Beautiful Majestic Motion Picture Company for Mutual Film Corporation. Director William Christy Cabanne. Single reel; 950–1,000 feet. Release date July 12, 1914. Cast: Wallace Reid, Dorothy Gish.

Down by the Sounding Sea Majestic Motion Picture Company for Mutual Film Corporation. Director William Christy Cabanne. Writer Wallace Reid. Single reel; 1,043 feet. Release date July 28, 1914. Cast: Wallace Reid, Robert Harron, Mae Gaston.

The Avenging Conscience; Thou Shalt Not Kill (working title *The Murderer's Conscience*, original release title *The Telltale Heart*, aka *Thou Shalt Not Kill*) Majestic Motion Picture Company. Producer D.W. Griffith. Director D.W. Griffith. Writer D.W. Griffith, based on the stories "The Pit and the Pendulum" and "The Tell-Tale Heart" by Edgar Allan Poe. Cinematographer George W. Bitzer. Assistant cameraman Karl Brown. Film editor(s) James Smith and Rose Smith. Single reel; 950–1,000 feet. Release date August 2, 1914 (Los Angeles), August 24, 1914 (New York and national). Cast: Henry B. Walthall, Spottiswoode Aitken, Blanche Sweet, George Siegmann, Ralph Lewis, Mae Marsh, Robert Harron, George Beranger, Josephine Crowell, Donald Crisp, Walter Long, Wallace Reid.

Down the Hill to Creditville Majestic Motion Picture Company for Mutual Film Corporation. Director Donald Crisp. Writer George Terwilliger. Single reel; 950–1,000 feet. Release date September 12, 1914. Cast: Donald Crisp, Dorothy Gish, Kate Price, Wallace Reid.

For Her Father's Sins Reliance Film Company. Director John B. O'Brien. Supervising Director D.W. Griffith. Writer Anita Loos. 2 reels; 1,842 feet. Release date October 18, 1914. Cast: Blanche Sweet, Wallace Reid, Billie West, Al W. Wilson.

The Niggard Majestic Motion Picture Company for Mutual Film Corporation. Director Donald Crisp. Single reel; 950–1,000 feet. Release date November 10, 1914. Cast: Wallace Reid, Cora Drew, Billie West, William Lowery, Donald Crisp.

The Odalisque Majestic Motion Picture Company for Mutual Film Corporation. Director William Christy Cabanne. Supervising Director D.W. Griffith. Writer Leroy Scott. 2 reels; 2,066 feet. Release date November 15, 1914. Cast: Blanche Sweet, Miriam Cooper, Robert Harron, Henry B. Walthall, Wallace Reid.

Another Chance Majestic Motion Picture Company for Mutual Film Corporation. Director Donald Crisp. Writer John Halleck Reid (as Hal Reid). Single reel; 950–1,000 feet. Release date November 24, 1914. Cast: Wallace Reid, William Lowery, Mary Alden, Maxfield Stanley, Donald Crisp.

Over the Ledge (aka *On the Ledge*) Reliance Film Company for Mutual Film Corporation. Director Fred Kelsey. 2 reels; 2,066 feet (single reel for United States release). Release date December 12, 1914. Cast: Wallace Reid, Irene Hunt, Ralph Lewis, Donald Crisp.

At Dawn Reliance Film Company for Mutual Film Corporation. Director Donald Crisp. Writer James Halleck Reid (as Hal Reid). Single reel; 950–1,000 feet. Release date December 15, 1914. Cast: Wallace Reid, George Siegmann, Billie West, William Lowery, Claire Anderson, Eagle Eye, Fred Burns.

The Exposure Reliance Film Company for Mutual Film Corporation. Director Fred Kelsey. 2 reels; 2,152 feet. Release date December 26, 1914. Cast: Wallace Reid, Irene Hunt, Howard Gage, Ralph Lewis, William Lowery, Raoul Walsh.

Baby's Ride Majestic Motion Picture Company for Mutual Film Corporation. Director George Geranger. Single reel; 950–1,000 feet. Release date December 29, 1914. Cast: Wallace Reid, Loretta Blake.

1915

The Three Brothers Reliance Film Company for Mutual Film Corporation. Director William Christy Cabanne. 2 reels; 2,016 feet. Release date January, 1915. Cast: Wallace Reid, Allan Sears, William Hinckley, Claire Anderson, Josephine Crowell.

Station Content Reliance Film Company for Mutual Film Corporation. Director Fred Kelsey. 2 reels; 1,804 feet. Release date January, 1915. Cast: Wallace Reid, Catherine Henry, Ben Lewis.

Sheriff for an Hour Mutual Film Corporation. Single reel; 1,148 feet. Release date January, 1915. Cast: Wallace Reid, Arthur Mackley.

The Craven Reliance Film Company for Mutual Film Corporation. Director William Christy Cabanne. Single reel; 1,148 feet. Release date January 23, 1915. Cast: Wallace Reid, Seena Owen, William Hinckley, Allen Sears, Claire Anderson, Josephine Crowell.

The Birth of a Nation D.W. Griffith Corporation for Griffith Feature Films and Epoch Producing Corporation. Producer D.W. Griffith. Director D.W. Griffith. Assistant Director(s) Thomas E. O'Brien, Elmer Clifton, Robert Harron, Joseph Henabery, George Siegmann, Raoul Walsh, Henry B. Walthall, George Andre Beranger, Woodridge Strong Van Dyke, Erich von Stroheim, Jack Conway. Writer(s) D.W. Griffith and Frank E. Woods, based on the novel *The Clansman: An Historical Romance of the Ku Klux Klan* by Thomas Dixon (New York, 1905) and his play of the same name (New York, January 8, 1906). Costume designer Robert Godstein. Set designer Frank Wortman. Cinematographer George W. Bitzer. Assistant cameraman Karl Brown. Film editor(s) D.W. Griffith, Joseph Henabery, James Smith, Rose Smith, and Raoul Walsh. Costumer Robert Goldstein. Music Composer Joseph Carl Breil. 12 reels; 11,586 feet, 110 minutes. Release date February 8, 1915 (Los Angeles), March 3, 1915 (New York and national). Cast: Lillian Gish, Mae Marsh, Henry B. Walthall, Miriam Cooper, Mary Alden, Ralph Lewis, George Siegmann, Walter Long, Robert Harron, Wallace Reid, Joseph Henabery, Elmer Clifton, Josephine Crowell, Spottiswoode Aitken, George Beranger, Maxfield Stanley, Jennie Lee, Donald Crisp, Howard Gaye, Monte Blue, William E. Cassidy, Sam de Grasse, William DeVaull, John Ford, William Freeman, Gibson Howland, Olga Grey, Alberta Lee, Elmo Lincoln, Bessie Love, Eugene Pallette, Charles Stevens, Raoul Walsh, Violet Wilkey, Tom Wilson, Bobby Burns, Edward Burns, Fred Burns, Dark Cloud, Peggy Cartwright, Lenore Cooper, Charles Eagle Eye, Alberta Franklin, D.W. Griffith, Fred Hamer, Russell Hicks, Walter Huston, Charles King, Donna Montran, Vester Pegg, Alma Rubens, Allan Sears, Jules White, Mary Wynn, Eric Campbell, Madame Sul-Te-Wan, Eric von Stroheim.

The Lost House Majestic Motion Picture Company. Director William Christy Cabanne. Based on the short story "The Lost House" by Richard Harding Davis in *The Man Who Could Not Lose* (New York, 1911). Cinematographer William E. Fildew. Four reels; 1,320 feet. Release date March 25, 1915. Cast: Lillian Gish, Wallace Reid, F.A. Turner, Elmer Clifton, Allan Sears.

Enoch Arden (aka *As Fate Ordained* and *The Fatal Marriage*; sometimes described as a D.W. Griffith 1911 release with a cast of Linda Griffith, Jeanie Macpherson and Wallace Reid) Majestic Motion Picture Company. Producer D.W. Griffith. Production Supervisor D.W. Griffith. Director William Christy Cabanne. Inspired by the poem "Enoch Arden" by Alfred, Lord Tennyson (Boston, 1864). Cinematographer William E. Fildew. Four reels; 1,320 feet. Release date April 8, 1915. Cast: Alfred Paget, Lillian Gish, Wallace Reid, D.W. Griffith, Mildred Harris, Betty Marsh.

A Yankee from the West Majestic Motion Picture Company. Director George Siegmann. Writer Mary O'Connor, based on the novel *A Yankee from the West* by Opie Read (Chicago, 1879). Cinematographer B.C. Hayward (as Duke Hayward). Four reels; 1,320 feet. Release date August, 1915. Cast: Wallace Reid, Seena Owen, Tom Wilson, Josephine Crowell, Chris Lynton, William H. Brown, Al W. Filson, George Siegmann.

The Chorus Lady Jesse L. Lasky Feature Play Company, Inc. Producer Jesse L. Lasky. Presenter Jesse L. Lasky. Director Frank Reicher. Assistant Director Frank Lidel. Writer Marion Fairfax, based on the play *The Chorus Lady* by James Forbes (New York, 1 Sep, 1906). Cinematography Walter Stradling. 5 reels; approx. 4,750 feet. Release date October 18, 1915. Cast: Cleo Ridgely, Wallace Reid, Marjorie Daw, Richard Grey, Mrs. Lewis McCord.

Carmen Jesse L. Lasky Feature Play Company, Inc. Producer(s) Jesse L. Lasky, with arrangement with Morris Gest and Cecil B. DeMille. Director Cecil B. DeMille. Assistant Director(s) William Horwitz and Sam Wood.

Writer William C. de Mille, based on the novella *Carmen* by Prosper Mérimée in *La revue des deux mondes* (Paris, 15 Oct, 1845). Cinematography Alvin Wyckoff. Assistant cameraman Charles Rosher. Film editor(s) Anne Bauchens and Cecil B. DeMille. Art Director Wilfred Buckland. Original Music conducted by Hugo Riesenfeld. Original Music Supervision by S.L. Rothapfel. 5 reels; approx. 4,750 feet. Release date November 1, 1915. Cast: Geraldine Farrar, Wallace Reid, Pedro de Cordoba, Horace B. Carpenter, William Elmer, Jeanie Macpherson, Anita King, Milton Brown, Tex Driscoll, Raymond Hatton.

Old Heidelberg Fine Arts Film Company. Producer D.W. Griffith. Director John Emerson. Assistant Director Erich von Stroheim. Writer John Emerson, based on the novel *Karl Heinrich* by Wilhelm Meyer-Förster (Stuttgart, 1902). 5 reels; approx. 4,750 feet. Release date November 14, 1915. Cast: Wallace Reid, Dorothy Gish, Karl Formes, Erich von Stroheim, Raymond Wells, J.W. McDermott, James Gibson, Franklin Arbuckle, Madge Hunt, Erich von Ritzau, Kate Toncray, Francis Carpenter, Harold Goodwin.

1916

The Golden Chance Jesse L. Lasky Feature Play Company, Inc. Producer Cecil B. DeMille. Director Cecil B. DeMille. Writer(s) Jeanie Macpherson and Cecil B. DeMille. Cinematography Alvin Wyckoff. Film Editor Cecil B. DeMille. Art Director Wilfred Buckland. 5 reels; approx. 4,750 feet. Release date January 16, 1916. Cast: Cleo Ridgely, Wallace Reid, Horace B. Carpenter, Ernest Joy, Edythe Chapman, Raymond Hatton.

To Have and to Hold Jesse L. Lasky Feature Play Company, Inc. Director George H. Melford. Writer Margaret Turnbull, based on the novel *To Have and to Hold* by Mary Johnston (Boston, 1900). Cinematographer Percy Hilburn. 5 reels; approx. 4,750 feet. Release date March 5, 1916. Cast: Mae Murray, Wallace Reid, Tom Forman, Ronald Bradbury, Raymond Hatton, James Neill, Lucien Littlefield, Bob Fleming, Camille Astor.

The Love Mask (aka *Under the Mask* and *Behind the Mask*) Jesse L. Lasky Feature Play Company, Inc. Producer Jesse L. Lasky. Director Frank Reicher. Writer(s) Cecil B. DeMille and Jeanie Macpherson. Cinematography Walter Stradling. 5 reels; approx. 4,750 feet. Release date April 13, 1916. Cast: Cleo Ridgely, Wallace Reid, Earle Foxe, Bob Fleming, Dorothy Abril, Lucien Littlefield.

Maria Rosa Jesse L. Lasky Feature Play Company, Inc. Director Cecil B. DeMille. Assistant Director William Horwitz. Writer William C. de Mille, based on the play *Maria Rosa* by Ángel Guimerá (Spain, 1890), and a translation from the Catalan by José Echegaray y Eizaguirre for an English language version of the play by Guido Marburg and Wallace Gillpatrick that premiered in New York on January 19, 1914. Cinematographer Alvin Wyckoff. 5 reels; 4,231 feet. Release date May 8, 1916. Cast: Geraldine Farrar, Wallace Reid, Pedro de Cordoba, James Neill, Ernest Joy, Horace B. Carpenter, Anita King.

The Selfish Woman (aka *The Taming of Helen*) Jesse L. Lasky Feature Play Company, Inc. Director(s) E. Mason Hopper and George H. Melford. Assistant Director Claude H. Mitchell. Writer Hector Turnbull. Cinematographer Percy Hilburn. Art Director Wilfred Buckland. 5 reels; approx. 4,750 feet. Release date July 9, 1916. Cast: Wallace Reid, Cleo Ridgely, Edythe Chapman, Charles Arling, Joe King, Jane Wolf, William Elmer, Horace B. Carpenter, Bob Fleming, Milton Brown.

The House with the Golden Windows (aka *The House of the Golden Windows*) Jesse L. Lasky Feature Play Company, Inc. Director George H. Melford. Assistant Director Claude H. Mitchell. Writer Charles Sarver, from a story by L.V. Jefferson. Cinematographer Percy Hilburn. 5 reels; approx. 4,750 feet. Release date August 3, 1916. Cast: Wallace Reid, Cleo Ridgely, Billy Jacobs, James Neill, Mabel Van Buren, Marjorie Daw, Bob Fleming.

Intolerance: Love's Struggle Through the Ages (working title *The Mother and the Law*, aka *Intolerance* [United States short title], and *Intolerance: A Sun-Play for the Ages* [United States copyright title] D.W. Griffith; Wark Producing Corporation, produced at Fine Arts Studio. Producer D.W. Griffith. Presenter D.W. Griffith. Associate Producer Harry E. Aitken. Research Assistant(s) E. Ellis Wales, Joseph Henabery, Lillian Gish. Director D.W. Griffith. Assistant Director(s) George Siegmann, Erich von Stroheim, Joseph Henabery, Allan Dwan, Edward Dillon, Monte Blue, Elmer Clifton, Mike Siebert, George Hill, Arthur Berthelon, William Christy Cabanne, Jack Conway, George Nichols, Victor Fleming, and Woodridge Strong Van Dyke. Writer(s) D.W. Griffith and Anita Loos. Choreographer Ruth St. Denis. Cinematographer(s) George W. Bitzer and Karl Brown. Film editor(s) D.W. Griffith, James Smith, and Rose Smith. Photographic Reproductions Sam Landers, Joseph Altschuler. Special Effects Hal Sullivan. Film Editor D.W. Griffith. Assistant Film Editor(s) James Smith, Rose Smith, D.W. Griffith. Set Designer(s) Frank Wortman, Walter L. Hall, and Ralph De Lacy. Art Director Walter L. Hall. Title Designer(s) D.W. Griffith, Frank E. Woods, and Anita Loos, inspired by the poem "Out of the Cradle Endlessly Rocking" by Walt Whitman in the third edition of *Leaves of Grass* (New York, 1860). Production Supervisor and Costumer R. Ellis Wales. Costume designer Clare West. Costumes provided by Western Costume Company. Property Master Ralph DeLacy. Assistant Prop Master Hal Sullivan. Carpenter Shorty English. Music Supervisor Joseph Carl Breil. Persian Music themes supplied by Farahanguize Hkanum and Sidney Sprague. Dance Supervisor Ruth St. Denis. Advisor(s) for "The Judean Story" Rabbi L. Myers and Father Dodd. 14 reels filmed; released at 10 reels, 10,957 feet, 210 minutes. Release date August 5, 1916 (Riverside, California), September 5, 1916 (New York and national). Cast: Lillian Gish, Olga Grey, Baron Von Ritzau, Erich von Stroheim (as Count Von Stroheim), Bessie Love, George Walsh, Howard Gaye, William Brown, Margery Wilson, Spottiswoode Aitken, Ruth Handforth, Eugene Pallette, A.D. Sears, Frank Bennett, Maxfield Stanley, Josephine Crowell, Georgia Pearce, W.E. Lawrence, Joseph Henabery, Louise Romaine, Morris Levy, Raymond Wells, George James, Louis Ritz, John Bragdon, Constance Talmadge, Elmer Clifton, Alfred Paget, Seena Owen, Loyola O'Connor, Carl Stockdale, Tully Marshall, George Siegmann, Elmo Lincoln, Robert Lawler, Grace Wilson, Lotta Clifton, George Andre Beranger, Ah Singh, Ranji Singh, James Curley, Ed Burns, James Burns, Kate Bruce, Pauline Stark, Mildred Harris, Winifred Westover, Martin Landry, Howard Scott, Arthur Meyer, Alma Rubens, Ruth Darling, Margaret Mooney, Charles Eagle Eye, William Dark Cloud, Charles Van Cortland, Jack Cosgrove, Ethel Terry, Mae Marsh, Fred Turner, Robert Harron, Sam de Grasse, Clyde Hopkins, Vera Lewis, Mary Alden, Luray Huntley, Lucille Brown, Eleanor Washington, Pearl Elmore, Mrs. Arthur Mackley, Miriam Cooper, Walter Long, Tom Wilson, Ralph Lewis, A.W. McClure, Edward Dillon, Lloyd Ingraham, Max Davidson, Alberta Lee, Frank Brownlee, Barney Bernard, Marguerite Marsh, Tod Browning, Kate Bruce, Sir Herbert Beerbohm Tree, De-Wolf Hopper, Hal Wilson, Francis McDonald, Clarence Geldart, Ernest Butterworth, J.P. McCarthy, Monte Blue, Billy Quirk, Woodridge Strong Van Dyke, Gino Corrado, Wallace Reid, Ted Duncan, Mme. Sul-te-Wan, Carmel Myers, Jewel Carmen, Eve Southern, Natalie Talmadge, Carol Dempster, Daisy Robinson, Anna Mae Walthall, Owen Moore, Wilfred Lucas, Douglas Fairbanks, Frank Campeau, Nigel de Brulier, Donald Crisp, Tammany Young, Ethel Grey Terry, King Vidor, Raymond Wells, Felix Modjeska, Jenny Lee, Clyde E. Hopkins, Dell Henderson, the Denishaw Dancers, George Fawcett, Russell Hicks, William Courtright, Peggy Cartwright, Hazel Childers, Dark Cloud, Virginia Lee Corbin, Jack Cosgrave, David Butler, Frank Borzage, Lillian Langdon, Chandler House, Dore Davidson.

The Yellow Pawn Jesse L. Lasky Feature Play Company. Director George H. Melford. Assistant Director Claude H. Mitchell. Writer Margaret Trumbell, based on the short story "A Close Call" by Frederic Arnold Kummer, allegedly first appearing in *All-Story Magazine* in 1914 (unconfirmed). Cinematographer Percy Hilburn. 5 reels; approx. 4,750 feet. Release date November 23, 1916. Cast: Wallace Reid, Cleo Ridgely, William Conklin, Tom Forman, Irene Aldwyn, Clarence Geldart, George Webb, George Kuwa, Olive Carey.

The Wall of Flame Independent Moving Pictures Company of America. Single reel; 950–1,000 feet. Release date December 3, 1916. Cast: Wallace Reid, Pauline Bush.

The Wrong Heart Big U Production Company for Universal Film Manufacturing Company. Director Wallace Reid. Writer Wallace Reid. Single reel; 950–1,000 feet. Release date December 15, 1916, Cast: Wallace Reid, Dorothy Davenport.

Starlight's Message (Reported but unconfirmed.) Big U Productions for Universal Film Manufacturing Company. Produced in early 1916. Wallace Reid is listed in some sources as a cast member of this film, although no archival records remain pertaining to the title.

1917

Joan the Woman Cardinal Film Corporation for Paramount Pictures Corporation and Famous Players–Lasky Corporation. Producer(s) Cecil B. DeMille and Jesse L. Lasky. Director Cecil B. DeMille. Assistant Director(s) William Horwitz, Claude H. Mitchell, Sterrett Ford, and Cullen B. Tate. Assistant Director(s) Battle Scene(s) William C. de Mille, George Melford, and Donald Crisp. Writer(s) Jeanie Macpherson and William C. de Mille. Cinematographer Alvin Wyckoff. Lighting Howard Ewing. Film Editor Cecil B. DeMille. Film Coloring Cecil B. DeMille, Alvin Wyckoff, Loren Taylor and Max Handscheigl. Art Director Wilfred Buckland. Assistant Art Director Herman Mayers. Prop maker Cullen B. Tate. Construction Supervisor Mr. De Vall. Costumer Alpharetta Hoffman. Costumes provided by Western Costume Company. Film Lab Supervisor Mr. Palm. Original Music William Furst. Stunt Supervisor Leo Nomis. Geraldine Farrar Stunt Double Pansy Perry. Publicity Director Bob McNight. 10–12 reels, 8,292 feet. Release date December 25, 1916 (Los Angeles), January 8, 1917 (New York and national). Cast: Geraldine Farrar, Wallace Reid,

Raymond Hatton, Hobart Bosworth, Theodore Roberts, Charles Clary, James Neill, Tully Marshall, Lawrence Peyton, Horace B. Carpenter, Cleo Ridgley, Lillian Leighton, Marjorie Daw, Stephen Gray, Ernest Joy, John Oaker, Hugo B. Koch, William Conklin, Walter Long, William Elmer, Emilius Jorgensen, Donald Crisp, Jack Hoxie, Lucien Littlefield, Nigel DeBrulier, Jack Holt, Fred Kohler, Ramon Novarro, James Young, Jane Wolfe, Robert Gordon, Pansy Perry, Tex Driscoll, William C. de Mille, George Melford, Donald Crisp.

The Golden Fetter Jesse L. Lasky Feature Play Company, Inc. Director Edward J. LeSaint. Assistant Director Sterrett Ford (as "Capt. Ford"). Writer Charles Maigne, based on the short story "The Golden Fetter" by Charles Tenney Jackson in *Collier's National Weekly* (publication date undetermined). Cinematographer Allen N. Davey. 5 reels; approx. 4,750 feet. Release date January 25, 1917. Cast: Wallace Reid, Anita King, Tully Marshall, Guy Oliver, Walter Long, Mrs. Lewis McCord, Clarence Geldart, Lawrence Peyton, Lucien Littlefield.

Buried Alive Big U Productions for Universal Film Manufacturing Company. Director Wallace Reid. Single reel; 950–1,000 feet. Release date March 4, 1917. Cast: Wallace Reid, Dorothy Davenport.

The Prison Without Walls Jesse L. Lasky Feature Play Company, Inc. Producer Jesse L. Lasky. Presenter Jesse L. Lasky. Director E. Mason Hopper. Assistant Director Sterrett Ford. Writer Beulah Marie Dix, from a story by Robert Emmet MacAlerney. Cinematographer Allen M. Davey. Assistant Cameraman Homer Scott (uncredited; sometimes listed as cinematographer). 5 reels; 4,450 feet. Release date March 15, 1917. Cast: Wallace Reid, Myrtle Stedman, William Conklin, William Elmer, Marcia Manon, James Neill, Lillian Leighton, Clarence Geldart.

A Warrior's Bride Universal Film Manufacturing Company. Single reel; 950–1,000 feet. Release date April 26, 1917. Cast: Wallace Reid.

The Penalty of Silence Big U Productions for Universal Film Manufacturing Company. Director Wallace Reid. Single reel; 950–1,000 feet. Release date April 30, 1917. Cast: Wallace Reid, Dorothy Davenport, Edward Brady.

The World Apart Oliver Morosco Photoplay Company for Paramount Pictures Corporation. Director William Desmond Taylor. Writer Julia Crawford Ivers, from a story by George Middleton. Cinematographer Homer Scott. 5 reels; approx. 4,750 feet. Release date June 4, 1917. Cast: Wallace Reid, Myrtle Stedman, John Burton, Eugene Pallette, Florence Carpenter, Henry A. Barrows, Phyllis Daniels.

Big Timber Oliver Morosco Photoplay Company for Paramount Pictures Corporation. Director William Desmond Taylor. Writer Gardner Hunting, based on the novel *Big Timber* by Bertrand W. Sinclair (Boston, 1916). Cinematographer Homer Scott. Titles and Special Effects Photographer Stewart B. Moss. 5 reels; approx. 4,750 feet. Release date July 5, 1917. Cast: Kathlyn Williams, Wallace Reid, Joe King, Alfred Paget, Helen Bray, John Burton.

The Squaw Man's Son Jesse L. Lasky Feature Film Company. Director E.J. LeSaint. Assistant Director Sterrett Ford. Writer Charles Maigne, based on the novel *The Silent Call* by Edwin Milton Royle (New York, 1910). Cinematographer Allen M. Davey. 5 reels; approx. 4,750 feet. July 26, 1917. Cast: Wallace Reid, Anita King, Dorothy Davenport, Donald Bowles, Clarence Geldart, Frank Lanning, Ernest Joy, Lucien Littlefield, Mabel Van Buren, Raymond Hatton.

The Hostage Jesse L. Lasky Feature Play Company, Inc. Producer Jesse L. Lasky. Director Robert Thornby. Assistant Director Harry Haskin. Writer Beulah Marie Dix, based on her own original story entitled "We and They." Cinematographer Henry Kotani. 5 reels; approx. 4,750 feet. Release date September 10, 1917. Cast: Wallace Reid, Dorothy Abril, Gertrude Short, Clarence Geldart, Guy Oliver, Marcia Manon, Noah Beery, George Spaulding, Lillian Leighton, Lucien Littlefield, Ramon Novarro.

The Woman God Forgot Artcraft Pictures Corporation for Famous Players–Lasky Corporation. Producer(s) Jesse L. Lasky and Cecil B. DeMille. Presenter Jesse L. Lasky. Director Cecil B. DeMille. Assistant Director Cullen B. Tate. Writer(s) William C. de Mille and Jeanie Macpherson. Cinematographer Alvin Wyckoff. Film Editor Cecil B. DeMille. Art Director Wilfred Buckland. Costume Designer Natacha Rambova. 5 reels; approx. 4,750 feet. Release date October 22, 1917. Cast: Wallace Reid, Raymond Hatton, Hobart Bosworth, Theodore Kosloff, Walter Long, Julia Faye, Olga Grey, Geraldine Farrar, Charley Rogers, Ramon Novarro.

Nan of Music Mountain Jesse L. Lasky Feature Play Company, Inc. Director George H. Melford. Assistant Director Claude H. Mitchell. Writer Beulah Marie Dix, based on the novel *Nan of Music Mountain* by Frank H. Spearman (New York, 1916), serialized in *Everybody's Magazine*. Cinematographer Paul Perry. 5 reels; approx. 4,750 feet. Release date December 17, 1917. Cast: Wallace Reid, Ann Little, Theodore Roberts, James Cruze, Charles Ogle, Raymond

Hatton, Jack Hoxie, Ernest Joy, Guy Oliver, Jim Mason, Henry Woodward, Horace B. Carpenter, Alice Marc, Charles McHugh.

The Devil-Stone Artcraft Pictures Corporation for Famous Players–Lasky Corporation. Producer Jesse L. Lasky. Presenter Jesse L. Lasky. Director Cecil B. DeMille. Assistant Director(s) Cullen B. Tate, Charles E. Whitaker (uncredited). Writer Jeanie Macpherson, based on a story by Beatrice C. DeMille and Leighton Osmun. Cinematographer Alvin Wyckoff. Film Editor Cecil B. DeMille. Art Director Wilfred Buckland. 5 reels; approx. 4,750 feet. Release date December 17, 1917. Cast: Geraldine Farrar, Wallace Reid, Hobart Bosworth, Tully Marshall, James Neill, Mabel Van Buren, Lillian Leighton, Gustav von Seyffertitz, Horace B. Carpenter, Ernest Joy, Burwell Hamrick, Raymond Hatton, Theodore Roberts.

A Ram-Bunctious Endeavor American Film Company for Mutual Film Corporation. Wallace Reid is listed in some sources as a cast member of this film, although no archival records remain pertaining to the title.

The Tell-Tale Arm American Film Company for Mutual Film Corporation. Wallace Reid is listed in some sources as a cast member of this film, although no archival records remain pertaining to the title. Kalem Company and General Film Company released a film entitled *The Tell-Tale Message*, a single reel short, on November 20, 1912, with a cast featuring Earle Foxe, Hazel Neason, Stuart Holmes, and Lawrence Wood. Wallace Reid is also listed in some sources as a cast member of this film, although no archival records remain supporting that claim.

The Man Who Saved the Day Wallace Reid is listed in some sources as a cast member of this film, although no archival records remain pertaining to the title. A similar film was produced by Biograph Company in 1913 entitled *How the Day Was Saved*. Directed by Edward Dillon. Written by Anita Loos. Single reel; 950–1,000 feet. Released December 1, 1913. Cast: Charles Murray.

1918

Rimrock Jones Famous Players–Lasky Corporation. Producer Jesse L. Lasky. Presenter Jesse L. Lasky. Director Donald Crisp. Assistant Director Louis Howland. Writer(s) Harvey Thew and Frank X. Finnegan, based on the novel *Rimrock Jones* by Dane Coolidge (New York, 1917). Cinematographer Faxon M. Dean. 5 reels; approx. 4,750 feet. Release date January 21, 1918. Cast: Wallace Reid, Ann Little, Charles Ogle, Paul Hurst, Guy Oliver, Fred Huntley, Edna Mae Cooper, Tote Du Crow, Gustav von Seyffertitz, Ernest Joy, George Kuwa, Mary Mersch.

The Things We Love (original title *Money Mad*) Famous Players–Lasky Corporation. Director Lou Tellegen. Writer Henry Thew. Story by H.B. Daniel and M.G. Daniel. 5 reels; approx. 4,750 feet. Release date February 11, 1918. Cast: Wallace Reid, Kathlyn Williams, Tully Marshall, Mayme Kelso, Charles Ogle, William Elmer.

The House of Silence Famous Players–Lasky Corporation. Producer Jesse L. Lasky. Presenter Jesse L. Lasky. Director Donald Crisp. Assistant Director Nat Deverich. Writer Margaret Turnbull, based on the novel *Marcel Levignet* by Elwyn Alfred Barron (New York, 1906). Cinematographer Henry Kotani. 5 reels; approx. 4,750 feet. Release date April 8, 1918. Cast: Wallace Reid, Ann Little, Adele Farrington, Winter Hall, Ernest Joy, Henry A. Barrows.

Believe Me, Xantippe Famous Players–Lasky Corporation. Producer Jesse L. Lasky. Director Donald Crisp. Writer Olga Printzlau, based on the play *Believe Me Xantippe* by Frederick Ballard (New York, 19 Aug, 1913). Cinematographer Henry Kotani. 5 reels; approx. 4,750 feet. Release date May 22, 1918. Cast: Wallace Reid, Ann Little, Ernest Joy, Henry Woodward, Noah Beery, James Cruze, Winifred Greenwood, Jim Farley, Charles Ogle, Clarence Geldart.

The Firefly of France Famous Players–Lasky Corporation. Producer Jesse L. Lasky. Presenter Jesse L. Lasky. Director Donald Crisp. Assistant Director Nat Deverich. Writer Margaret Turnbull, based on the novel *The Firefly of France* by Marion Polk Angellotti (New York, 1918) serialized in *The Saturday Evening Post*. Cinematographer Henry Kotani. 5 reels; approx. 4,750 feet. Release date June 23, 1918. Cast: Wallace Reid, Ann Little, Charles Ogle, Raymond Hatton, Winter Hall, Ernest Joy, William Elmer, Clarence Geldart, Henry Woodward, Jane Wolfe.

Less Than Kin Famous Players–Lasky Corporation. Producer Jesse L. Lasky. Presenter Jesse L. Lasky. Director Donald Crisp. Assistant Director Nat Deverich. Writer Marion Fairfax, based on the novel *Less Than Kin* by Alice Duer Miller (New York, 1909). Cinematographer Henry Kotani. Art Director Wilfred Buckland. 5 reels; approx. 4,750 feet. Release date July 29, 1918. Cast: Wallace Reid, Ann Little, Raymond Hatton, Noah Beery, James Neill, Charles Ogle, Jane Wolfe, James Cruze, Guy Oliver, Calvert Carter, Jack Herbert, Gustav von Seyffertitz.

The Source Famous Players–Lasky Corporation. Producer Jesse L. Lasky. Presenter Jesse L. Lasky. Director George H. Melford. Assistant Director Claude H. Mitchell. Writer Monte M.

Katterjohn, based on the novel *The Source* by Clarence Budington Kelland (New York, 1918). Cinematographer Paul Perry. Art Director Wilfred Buckland. 5 reels; 4,637 feet. Release date September 1, 1918. Cast: Wallace Reid, Ann Little, Theodore Roberts, Raymond Hatton, James Cruze, Noah Beery, Nina Byron, Charles West, Gustav von Seyffertitz, Charles Ogle.

The Man from Funeral Range   Famous Players–Lasky Corporation. Producer Jesse L. Lasky. Presenter Jesse L. Lasky. Director Walter Edwards. Writer Monte K. Katterjohn, based on the play *Broken Threads* by W. Ernest Wilkes (New York, October 29, 1917). Cinematographer James C. Van Trees. 5 reels; 4,512 feet. Release date October 6, 1918. Cast: Wallace Reid, Ann Little, Lottie Pickford, Willis Marks, Tully Marshall, George A. McDaniel, Phil Ainsworth, Tom Guise.

Too Many Millions   Famous Players–Lasky Corporation. Producer Jesse L. Lasky. Presenter Jesse L. Lasky. Director James Cruze. Assistant Director William Horwitz. Writer Gardner Hunting, based on the novel *Someone and Somebody* by Porter Emerson Browne (New York, 1917). Cinematographer Charles Rosher. 5 reels; 4,517 feet. Release date December 8, 1918. Cast: Wallace Reid, Ora Carew, Tully Marshall, Charles Ogle, James Neill, Winifred Greenwood, Noah Beery, Percy Williams, Ernest Pasque, Richard Wayne.

His Extra Bit   Paramount Pictures Corporation. Produced in early 1918. Wallace Reid is listed in some sources as a cast member of this film, although no archival records remain pertaining to the title.

1919

The Dub   Famous Players–Lasky Corporation. Producer Jesse L. Lasky. Presenter Jesse L. Lasky. Director James Cruze. Assistant Director William Horwitz. Writer Will M. Ritchey, based on the short story "The Dub" by Edgar Franklin (pseudonym of Edgar Franklin Stearns) in *All-Story Weekly* (June 17, 1916). Cinematographer Charles Rosher. 5 reels; 4,401 feet. Release date January 19, 1919. Cast: Wallace Reid, Charles Ogle, Ralph Lewis, Raymond Hatton, Winter Hall, Nina Byron, Guy Oliver, Harry O'Connor, William Elmer.

Alias Mike Moran   Famous Players–Lasky Corporation. Producer Jesse L. Lasky. Presenter Jesse L. Lasky. Director James Cruze. Writer Will M. Ritchey, based on the short story "Open Sesame" by Frederick Orin Bartlett in *The Saturday Evening Post* (August 10–17, 1918). Cinematographer Frank Urson. 5 reels; approx. 4,750 feet. Release date March 2, 1919. Cast: Wallace Reid, Ann Little, Emory Johnson, Charles Ogle, Edythe Chapman, William Elmer, Winter Hall, Jean Calhoun, Guy Oliver.

The Roaring Road   Famous Players–Lasky Corporation. Producer Jesse L. Lasky. Presenter Jesse L. Lasky. Director James Cruze. Assistant Director James Barranger. Second Unit Director Frank Urson. Production Designer Wilfred Buckland. Writer Marion Fairfax, based on the short stories "Junkpile Sweepstakes," "Undertaker's Handicap" and "Roaring Road" by Byron Morgan in *The Saturday Evening Post* (September 28, October 5, October 12, 1918). Cinematographer Frank Urson. Art Director Wilfred Buckland. 5 reels; 4,309 feet. Release date April 27, 1919. Cast: Wallace Reid, Guy Oliver, Gustav von Seyffertitz, Clarence Geldart, Ann Little, Theodore Roberts.

You're Fired   Famous Players–Lasky Corporation. Producer Jesse L. Lasky. Presenter Jesse L. Lasky. Director James Cruze. Assistant Director Cullen B. Tate. Writer Clara G. Kennedy, based on the short story "The Halberdier of the Little Rheinschloss" by O. Henry in *Everybody's Magazine* (May 1907). Cinematographer Frank Urson. Art titles by Wilfred Buckland. 5 reels; 4,183 feet. Release date June 8, 1919. Cast: Wallace Reid, Wanda Hawley, Henry Woodward, Theodore Roberts, Lillian Mason, Herbert Prior, Raymond Hatton, William Lesta.

The Love Burglar   Famous Players–Lasky Corporation. Producer Jesse L. Lasky. Presenter Jesse L. Lasky. Director James Cruze. Assistant Director Cullen B. Tate. Writer Walter Woods, based on the play *One of Us* by Jack Lait and Joseph Swerling (New York, September 9, 1918). Cinematographer Frank Urson. 5 reels; 4,467 feet. Release date July 13, 1919. Cast: Wallace Reid, Anna Q. Nilsson, Raymond Hatton, Wallace Beery, Wilton Taylor, Edmund Burns, Alice Terry, Richard Wayne, Henry Woodward, Loyola O'Connor.

The Valley of the Giants (aka *In the Valley of the Giants*)   Famous Players–Lasky Corporation. Producer Jesse L. Lasky. Presenter Jesse L. Lasky. Director James Cruze. Assistant Director Cullen B. Tate. Writer Marion Fairfax, based on the novel *The Valley of the Giants* by Peter B. Kyne (New York, 1918) which originally appeared in *The Red Book Magazine* (August, 1918). Cinematographer Frank Urson. 5 reels; 4,625 feet. Release date August 31, 1919. Cast: Wallace Reid, Grace Darmond, William Brunton, Charles Ogle, Ralph Lewis, Alice Terry, Kay Laurel, Jack Hoxie, Noah Beery, Guy Oliver, William H. Brown, Richard Cummings, Virginia Foltz, Odgen Crane, Lillian Mason, Speed Hanson.

The Lottery Man Famous Players–Lasky Corporation. Producer Jesse L. Lasky. Director James Cruze. Assistant Director Cullen B. Tate. Writer Elmer Harris, adapted by Frank Urson, based on the play *The Lottery Man* by Rida Johnson Young (New York, December 6, 1909). Cinematographer Frank Urson. 5 reels; 4,404 feet. Release date October 12, 1919. Cast: Wallace Reid, Harrison Ford, Wanda Hawley, Fanny Midgley, Sylvia Ashton, Caroline Rankin, Wilton Taylor, Clarence Geldart, Virginia Foltz, Marcia Manon, Winifred Greenwood, Fred Huntley, Tully Marshall, Lila Lee, Charles Ogle, Guy Oliver.

Hawthorne of the U.S.A. (aka *Hawthorne, the Adventurer*) Famous Players–Lasky Corporation. Producer Jesse L. Lasky. Presenter Jesse L. Lasky. Director James Cruze. Assistant Director Cullen B. Tate. Writer Walter Woods, based on the play *Hawthorne of the U.S.A.* by James B. Fagan (New York, November 4, 1912). Cinematographer Frank Urson. Assistant Cameramen William Marshall and Charles Edgar Schoenbaum. Art Director Wilfred Buckland. 5 reels; 4,780 feet. Release date November 30, 1919. Cast: Wallace Reid, Lila Lee, Harrison Ford, Tully Marshall, Charles Ogle, Guy Oliver, Edwin Stevens, Clarence Burton, Theodore Roberts, Ruth Renick, Robert Brower, Frank Bonner.

1920

Double Speed Famous Players–Lasky Corporation. Director Sam Wood. Writer(s) Clara Genevieve Kennedy and Byron Morgan, from a story by J. Stewart Woodhouse. Cinematographer Alfred Gilks. 5 reels; 4,144 feet. Release date February, 1920. Cast: Wallace Reid, Wanda Hawley, Theodore Roberts, Tully Marshall, Lucien Littlefield, Guy Oliver, Maxine Elliott Hicks.

Excuse My Dust Famous Players–Lasky Corporation. Presenter Jesse L. Lasky. Director Sam Wood. Assistant Director Robert Lee. Writer Will M. Ritchey, based on the story "The Bear Trap" by Byron Morgan in *The Saturday Evening Post* (July 26, 1919). Cinematographer Alfred Gilks. Assistant Cameraman Osmond Borradaile (uncredited). Art Director Wilfred Buckland. 5 reels; 4,330 feet. Release date March 21, 1920. Cast: Wallace Reid, Ann Little, Wallace Reid, Jr., Theodore Roberts, Guy Oliver, Otto Brower, Tully Marshall, Walter Long, James Gordon, Jack Herbert, Fred Huntley, Byron Morgan, Will M. Ritchey.

The Dancin' Fool Famous Players–Lasky Corporation. Producer Jesse L. Lasky. Director Sam Wood. Assistant Director Robert Lee. Writer Clara Genevieve Kennedy, based on the short story "The Dancin' Fool" by Henry Payson Dowst in *The Saturday Evening* Post (May 3–10, 1919). Cinematographer Alfred Gilks. Art Director Wilfred Buckland. 5 reels; 4,124 feet. Release date May 23, 1920. Cast: Wallace Reid, Bebe Daniels, Raymond Hatton, Willis Marks, George B. Williams, Lillian Leighton, Carlos San Martin, William H. Brown, Tully Marshall, Ruth Ashby, Ernest Joy.

Sick Abed Famous Players–Lasky Corporation. Producer Jesse L. Lasky. Presenter Jesse L. Lasky. Director Sam Wood. Writer Clara Genevieve Kennedy, based on the play *Sick Abed* by Ethel Watts Mumford (New York, February 25, 1918). Cinematographer Alfred Gilks. Assistant Cameraman Osmond Borradaile (uncredited). 5 or 6 reels; 4,800 feet. Release date June 27, 1920. Cast: Wallace Reid, Bebe Daniels, John Steppling, Winifred Greenwood, Tully Marshall, Clarence Geldart, Lucien Littlefield, Robert Bolder, Lorenza Lazzarini, George Kuwa.

What's Your Hurry? (aka *The Hippopotamus Parade*) Famous Players–Lasky Corporation. Producer Jesse L. Lasky. Director Sam Wood. Writer Byron Morgan, base on his own short story "The Hippopotamus Parade" in *The Saturday Evening Post* (February 15, 1919). Cinematographer Alfred Gilks. Assistant Cameraman Osmond Borradaile (uncredited). 5 reels; 5,040 feet. Release dates August 15, 1920 (Los Angeles), September 12, 1920 (New York and national). Cast: Wallace Reid, Lois Wilson, Charles Ogle, Clarence Burton, Ernest Butterworth, Ernest Joy, Jack Young.

Mothers of Men Robards-Reid Pictures Company and Robards Players. Director Willis Robards. Writer James Halleck Reid (as Hal Reid), based upon a story by him. 5 reels; approx. 4,750 feet Release date November, 1917. Cast: Willis Robards, Dorothy Davenport, Hal Reid, Marcella Russell (as Mrs. Hal Reid), Katherine Griffith, Arthur Tavares, Billie Bennett, Harry Griffith, Grace Blake, George Utell. *Note:* This film is not typically listed in Wallace Reid filmography materials. However, detailed and otherwise accurate period newspaper articles from several local Santa Cruz, California, newspapers that detailed the daily events during filming repeatedly mentioned Wally as being there during filming, appearing in the film, visiting local retail and food establishments, etc. It would not be surprising that Lasky would allow Wally to work on a film with his father and step-mother, although likely on an uncredited basis.

Always Audacious Famous Players–Lasky Corporation. Producer Jesse L. Lasky. Director James Cruze. Assistant Director Cullen B. Tate.

Writer Thomas J. Geraghty, based on the short story "Toujours de l'Audace" by Ben Ames Williams in *The Saturday Evening Post* (January 3–17, 1920). Cinematographer Charles Edgar Schoenbaum. Assistant Cameraman Karl Brown. Art Director Wilfred Buckland. 5–6 reels; 5,101 feet. Release date November 14, 1920. Cast: Wallace Reid, Margaret Loomis, Clarence Geldart, J.M. Dumont, Rhea Gaines, Carmen Phillips, Guy Oliver, Fanny Midgley, Charles Bennett.

1921

The Charm School Famous Players–Lasky Corporation. Director James Cruze. Writer Thomas J. Geraghty, based on the novel *The Charm School* by Alice Duer Miller (New York, 1919). Cinematographer Charles Edgar Schoenbaum. 5 reels; 4,743 feet. Release date January, 1921. Cast: Wallace Reid, Lila Lee, Adele Farrington, Beulah Bains, Edwin Stevens, Grace Morse, Patricia Magee, Lincoln Stedman, Kate Toncray, Minna Redman, Snitz Edwards, Helen Pillsbury, Tina Marshall.

The Love Special Famous Players–Lasky Corporation. Director Frank Urson. Writer Eugene B. Lewis, based on the novel *The Daughter of a Magnate* by Frank Hamilton Spearman (New York, 1903). Cinematographer Charles Edgar Schoenbaum. 5 reels; 4,855 feet. Release date April 17, 1921. Cast: Wallace Reid, Agnes Ayres, Theodore Roberts, Lloyd Whitlock, Sylvia Ashton, William Gaden, Clarence Burton, Snitz Edwards, Ernest Butterworth, Zelma Maja.

Too Much Speed Famous Players–Lasky Corporation. Producer Jesse L. Lasky. Director Frank Urson. Writer Byron Morgan, based on his own short story "Too Much Speed" in *The Saturday Evening Post* (May 28, 1921). Cinematographer Charles E. Schoenbaum. 5 reels; 4,629 feet. Release date July 10, 1921. Cast: Wallace Reid, Agnes Ayres, Theodore Roberts, Jack Richardson, Lucien Littlefield, Guy Oliver, Henry Johnson, Jack Herbert.

The Hell Diggers Famous Players–Lasky Corporation. Director Frank Urson. Writer Byron Morgan, based on his own story "The Hell Diggers" in *The Saturday Evening Post* (October 2, 1920). Cinematographer Charles Edgar Schoenbaum. 5 reels; 4,277 feet. Release date September 4, 1921. Cast: Wallace Reid, Lois Wilson, Alexander Brown, Frank Leigh, Lucien Littlefield, Clarence Geldart, Charles A. Post.

The Affairs of Anatol (aka *A Prodigal Knight*) Famous Players–Lasky Corporation. Producer Cecil B. DeMille. Presenter Jesse L. Lasky. Director Cecil B. DeMille. Writer(s) Jeanie Macpherson and Lorna Moon (uncredited), based on the novel *Anatol* by Arthur Schnitzer. Cinematographer(s) Karl Struss and Alvin Wyckoff. 9 reels; 8,806 feet. Release date September 25, 1921. Cast: Wallace Reid, Gloria Swanson, Wanda Hawley, Theodore Roberts, Elliott Dexter, Theodore Kosloff, Agnes Ayres, Monte Blue, Bebe Daniels, Alma Bennett, William Boyd, Shannon Day, Elinor Glynn, Winter Hall, Raymond Hatton, Fred Huntley, Lucien Littlefield, Zelma Maja, Ruth Miller, Polly Moran, Charles Ogle, Guy Oliver, Lady Parker, Maude Wayne.

Forever (aka *Peter Ibbetson*) Famous Players–Lasky Corporation. Producer Adolph Zukor. Director George Fitzmaurice. Writer(s) Ouida Bergere and Constance Collier, based on the novel *Peter Ibbetson* by George L. Du Maurier and the play by John Nathaniel Raphael. Cinematographer Arthur C. Miller. 7 reels; 7,236 feet. Release dates October 16, 1921 (New York), March 5, 1922 (Los Angeles and national). Cast: Wallace Reid, Elsie Ferguson, Montagu Love, George Fawcett, Dolores Cassinelli, Paul McAllister, Elliott Dexter, Barbara Dean, Nell Roy Buck, Charles Eaton, Jerome Patrick.

Don't Tell Everything Paramount Pictures. Producer Jesse L. Lasky. Production Supervisor Thompson Buchanan. Director Sam Wood. Assistant Director A.R. Hamm. Writer Albert Shelby Le Vino, based on a story by Lorna Moon. Cinematographer Alfred Gilks. 5 reels; 4,939 feet. Release dates November 13, 1921 (Des Moines, Iowa), December 11, 1921 (Los Angeles and national). Cast: Wallace Reid, Gloria Swanson, Elliott Dexter, Dorothy Cummings, Genevieve Blinn, K.T. Stevens, Baby Gloria Wood, Charles and Raymond De Briac (De Briac Twins).

1922

Rent Free Paramount Pictures. Producer Thompson Buchanan. Director Howard Higgin. Writer(s) Izola Forrester, Mann Page, and Elmer Rice. 5 reels; 4,661 feet. Release date January 1, 1922. Cast: Wallace Reid, Lila Lee, Henry A. Barrows, Gertrude Short, Lucien Littlefield, Lillian Leighton, Claire McDowell, Clarence Geldart.

The World's Champion Famous Players–Lasky Corporation. Producer Jesse L. Lasky. Production supervisor Thompson Buchanan. Presenter Jesse L. Lasky. Director Phil Rosen. Writer Albert S. Le Vino, based on the play *The Champion* by Thomas Louden, and on J.E. Nash's adaptation of the play *The Champion* by Augustus E. Thomas. Cinematographer Charles Edgar Schoenbaum. 5 reels; 5,030 feet. Release date February 25, 1922 (New York), March 12,

1922 (Los Angeles and national). Cast: Wallace Reid, Lois Wilson, Lionel Barrymore, Henry Miller, Jr., Helen Dunbar, Leslie Casey, Tiny Sandford, William J. Ferguson, Guy Oliver.

Across the Continent Paramount Pictures. Director Phil Rosen. Writer Byron Morgan. Cinematographer Charles Edgar Schoenbaum. 6 reels; 5,583 feet; 60 minutes. Release dates April 29, 1922 (New York), June 4, 1922 (Los Angeles and national). Cast: Wallace Reid, Mary MacLaren, Theodore Roberts, Betty Francisco, Walter Long, Lucien Littlefield, Jack Herbert, Guy Oliver, Sidney D'Albrook.

Nice People Famous Players–Lasky Corporation. Producer Adolph Zukor. Director William C. de Mille (as William DeMille). Writer Clara Beranger, based on a play by Rachel Crothers. Cinematographer L. Guy Wilky (as Guy Wilky). 7 reels; 6,300 feet; 70 minutes. Release dates July 2, 1922 (Los Angeles), September 4, 1922 (national). Cast: Wallace Reid, Bebe Daniels, Conrad Nagel, Julia Faye, Claire McDowell, Edward Marindel, Eve Southern, Bertram Johns, William Boyd, Ethel Wales.

The Dictator Famous Players–Lasky Corporation. Producer Jesse L. Lasky. Director James Cruze. Writer Walter Woods, based on a play by Richard Harding Davis. Cinematographer Karl Brown. 5 reels; 5,221 feet; 50 minutes. Release dates October 15, 1922 (Los Angeles), September 10, 1922 (New York and national). Cast: Wallace Reid, Theodore Kosloff, Lila Lee, Kalla Pasha, Sidney Bracey, Fred J. Butler, Walter Long, Alan Hale.

The Ghost Breaker Famous Players–Lasky Corporation. Producer Jesse L. Lasky. Director Alfred E. Green. Writer Walter DeLeon, based on a play by Paul Dickey and Charles W. Goddard. Cinematographer William Marshall. 5 reels; 5,100 feet; 57 minutes. Release dates September 10, 1922 (New York), October 15, 1922 (Los Angeles and national). Cast: Wallace Reid, Lila Lee, Walter Hiers, Arthur Edmund Carewe, J. Farrell MacDonald, Francis Raymond, Snitz Edwards, Richard Arlen, Mervyn LeRoy, George O'Brien.

Clarence Famous Players–Lasky Corporation. Presenter Adolph Zukor. Director William C. de Mille. Writer Clara Beranger, based on a play by Booth Tarkington. Cinematographer L. Guy Wilky (as Guy Wilky). 7 reels; 6,146 feet. Release dates October 15, 1922 (New York), November 19, 1922 (Los Angeles and national). Cast: Wallace Reid, Agnes Ayres, May McAvoy, Kathlyn Williams, Edward Marindel, Robert Agnew, Adolphe Menjou, Bertram Johns, Dorothy Gordon, Mayme Kelso.

Thirty Days Famous Players–Lasky Corporation. Director James Cruze. Writer Walter Woods, based on a play by Clayton Hamilton and Augustus E. Thomas. Cinematographer Karl Brown. 5 reels; 4,979 feet. Release dates December 10, 1922 (New York), January 8, 1923 (Los Angeles and national). Cast: Wallace Reid, Wanda Hawley, Charles Ogle, Cyril Chadwick, Herschel Mayall, Helen Dunbar, Carmen Phillips, Kalla Pasha, Robert Brower.

Wallace Reid—Director

1912

Hidden Treasure American Film Company for Mutual Film Corporation. Director Wallace Reid. Single reel; 950–1,000 feet. Release date November 30, 1912. Cast: (no materials available).

1913

Love and the Law
A Rose of Old Mexico
The Ways of Fate
When Jim Returned
The Tattooed Arm
Youth and Jealousy
The Kiss
Her Innocent Marriage
A Modern Snare
When Luck Changes
Via Cabaret
Hearts and Horses
Dead Man's Shoes
The Pride of Lonesome
A Foreign Spy
The Harvest of Flame
The Spark of Manhood
The Gratitude of Wanda
The Heart of a Cracksman
The Fires of Fate
Cross Purposes
Retribution
The Lightning Bolt
A Hopi Legend (aka *A Pueblo Romance*)

1914

The Intruder
The Countess Betty's Mine
The Wheel of Life
Fires of Conscience
The Greater Devotion
A Flash in the Dark
Breed o' the Mountains
Regeneration
The Voice of the Viola
Heart of the Hills
The Way of a Woman

The Mountaineer
Cupid Incognito
A Gypsy Romance
The Test
The Skeleton
The Fruit of Evil (aka *The Sins of the Fathers*)
Women and Roses
The Quack
The Siren
The Man Within
Passing of the Beast
Love's Western Flight
A Wife on a Wager (aka *A Wife for a Wager*)
'Cross the Mexican Line
The Den of Thieves

1916

The Wrong Heart

1917

Buried Alive
The Penalty of Silence

Wallace Reid—Writer

1912

Chumps (aka *Chumps; A Fairy Story for Overgrownups*)
Kaintuck
Before the White Man Came
All for a Girl

1913

When Jim Returned
The Tattooed Arm
The Spirit of the Flag
Woman and War
Dead Man's Shoes
Mental Suicide
The Harvest of Flame
The Heart of a Cracksman
The Cracksman's Reformation
The Fires of Fate
A Cracksman Santa Claus
A Hopi Legend (aka *A Pueblo Romance*)

1914

Heart of the Hills
The Mountaineer
Cupid Incognito
The Fruit of Evil
Women and Roses
Down by the Sounding Sea

1916

The Wrong Heart

Wallace Reid—As Himself, Other Appearances

1918

United States Fourth Liberty Loan Drive (aka *An Untitled Liberty Loan Film*) Fox Film Corporation. Director Frank Lloyd. Single reel; 950–1,000 feet. Release date November 1, 1918. Cast (as themselves): Dorothy Dalton, William Farnum, William Faversham, Pauline Frederick, Dorothy Gish, William S. Hart, Sessue Hayakawa, Madge Kennedy, Harold Lockwood, Mae Marsh, Tom Moore, Mae Murray, Mabel Normand, Mary Pickford, Wallace Reid, Edith Storey, Norma Talmadge.

This was a short filler film shown in theaters to assist the government in the sales of war bonds.

1922

Night Life in Hollywood (aka *The Shriek of Hollywood*) A.B. Maescher Productions for Arrow Film Corporation. Producer Mrs. A.B. Maescher. Presenter Mrs. A.B. Maescher. Director(s) Fred Caldwell and Jack Pratt. Writer Fred Caldwell. 6 reels; 6,059 feet. Release date November 15, 1922. Cast: J. Frank Glendon, Josephine Gale, Gale Henry, J.L. McComas, Elizabeth Rhodes, Jack Connolly, Delores Hall, (the rest as themselves) Wallace Reid, Theodore Roberts, Sessue Hayakawa, Tsuru Aoki, William Desmond, Bryant Washburn (and the Washburn family), Bessie Love, Will Rogers, J. Warren Kerrigan (and his mother, Mrs. Kerrigan), Johnny Jones, Edward Pell, Jr., Denishawn Dancers.

This film is about a brother and sister from Arkansas who set out for Hollywood, reputed to be a modern-day Babylon. It is something of a Hollywood propaganda film depicting Hollywood (and the movie people) as quiet, unassuming, and certainly not given to partying. When the boy falls in love with an actress, even his parents are shown to approve, since they now know that "Hollywood people" are no different from the folks back home. Among the Hollywood scenes are visits to the homes of J. Warren Kerrigan (with his mother at his side), the Bryant Washburn family home, the Will Rogers home and an Easter service at the Hollywood Bowl.

1931

The Movie Album The Vitaphone Company for Warner Brothers. Single reel; 1,098 feet. Writer Herman Ruby. Film editor Bert Frank. Cast (as themselves): Lionel Barrymore, John Bunny, Harry Carey, Charles Chaplin, Helene Costello, Maurice Costello, Geraldine Farrar, Lillian Gish, Mae Marsh, Antonio Moreno,

Wallace Reid, Norma Shearer, Edith Storey, Leon Trotsky, Clara Kimball Young.

This film was a 10-minute filler shown in theaters between films. It was a compilation of scenes from silent films (most of them not identified) made between 1910 and 1920, accompanied by a humorous commentary. The film highlights early appearances of actors who went on to stardom in the years between the silents and this film's release in 1931. Also featured is a short appearance by soon-to-be Russian revolutionary Leon Trotsky working in an early D.W. Griffith film. He reportedly was an extra in battlefield scenes in *Intolerance*, an interesting coincidence given his later political bent.

Wallace Reid— Archival Footage

1931

The House That Shadows Built Paramount Pictures marked its 20th anniversary in Hollywood with a movie that featured archival film clips and studio history, profiles of its then-current stars, and a group of coming attractions for their 1931–1932 season. A virtual Who's Who of silent stars appear in the film in archival footage, including Sarah Bernhardt in France in *Queen Elizabeth* (1912), Lon Chaney in *The Miracle Man* (1919), Douglas Fairbanks in *Headin' South* (1918), William S. Hart in *Wild Bill Hickock* (1923), John Barrymore in *Dr. Jekyll and Mr. Hyde* (1920), Harold Lloyd in *The Kid Brother* (1927), Mary Pickford in *A Good Little Devil* (1914), Gloria Swanson in *Male and Female* (1919), and Wally in *The Roaring Road* (1919). Among the (at the time of the film's release) contemporary stars that appear are George Bancroft, Clive Brook, Lilyan Tashman, Eleanor Boardman, Miriam Hopkins, Jack Oakie, Ginger Rogers, Tallulah Bankhead, the Marx Brothers (all four: Groucho, Harpo, Chico, and Zeppo), Maurice Chevalier, and Charles Ray. The segment featuring the Marx Brothers, promoting their then-upcoming film *Monkey Business* (1931) was a re-working of the first act of their first successful Broadway play "I'll Say She Is," which was reproduced line for line as it appeared on stage.

1954

Screen Snapshots: Hollywood Stars to Remember Written and Directed by Ralph Staub, this film is a compilation of early interviews, archival footage and photographs, and stories about early stars, including Lon Chaney, Douglas Fairbanks, Carole Lombard, Wally, and Will Rogers.

1980

"Hollywood" (video series) This extremely well-researched 13-part video series was obviously condensed from Kevin Brownlow's groundbreaking book about Hollywood history entitled *The Parade's Gone By* (Ballentine Books, 1968). The series follows the birth, growth and eventual fall of the American silent film industry. Each video episode focuses on a different aspect of the industry—stars, writers, directors, stuntmen, early scandal, producers, and various crew members—with wonderful period and modern interviews.

2004

Cecil B. DeMille: American Epic (television documentary) An excellent documentary by noted Hollywood and movie historian Kevin Brownlow.

Chapter Notes

Acknowledgments

1. St. Johns, Adela Rogers, "The Life Story of Wallace Reid: The Tragedy of an American Idol," *Liberty Magazine*, June 23, 1928.

Preface

1. St. Johns, Adela Rogers, "The Life of Wallace Reid: The Tragedy of an American Idol," *Liberty Magazine*, June 23, 1923, page 11.
2. Bodeen, DeWitt, *From Hollywood*, page 94.

Chapter 1

1. Archives, Valley Forge Historical Site, Muster Roll Data Sheet, no. NA32659.
2. Heitman, Francis B., *Historical Register of Officers of the Continental Army During the War of the Revolution* (Field Officers of Regiments of the Continental Line, Canadian Regiments, Second Canadian), Rev. ed., Washington, D.C., The Rare Book Shop Pub. Co., 1914, page 16.
3. Reid, Bertha Westbrook, *Wallace Reid; His Life Story, by His Mother*, page 7.
4. 1820 U.S. Federal Census, Ohio, Miami County, Dayton Township, page 130.
5. 1840 U.S. Federal Census, Ohio, Greene County, Xenia, page 251.
6. Whitelaw Reid, *Love To Know 1911 Online Encyclopedia* (c) 2004, retrieved March 10, 2005 from http://56.1911encyclopedia.org/R/REID_WHITELAW.htm.
7. 1880 U.S. Federal Census, New York, New York, map 476, page 662B.
8. *Athens Messenger*, March 17, 1881.
9. U.S. Federal Census, 1880, California, San Mateo, Millbrae, District 236, page 32.
10. *Waukesha Freeman*, August 12, 1892.
11. Reid, Bertha Westbrook, *Wallace Reid: His Life Story, by His Mother*, page 8.
12. *Ibid., By His Mother*, page 7.
13. 1870 U.S. Federal Census, Ohio, Green County, Cedarville, page 78.
14. St. Johns, Adela Rogers, "Wallace Reid: The Tragedy of an American Idol," *Liberty Magazine*, June 23, 1928, page 12.
15. *Ibid.*, page 12.
16. *Delphos Daily Herald*, December 2, 1898.
17. 1880 U.S. Federal Census, Ohio, Columbiana County, Madison Township, map 53, page 491D.
18. Kerkhoff, Ingrid, *Contemporary American Drama; History of American Theater* [website research].
19. Henderson, Sue, *An Examination of American Theater Through Two Plays: A Brief Examination of the History of American Theater*, for Historic Fredericksburg Foundation, 2003.
20. *Ibid.*, p. 968, quoted from Henderson.
21. Eyman, Scott, *Mary Pickford: America's Sweetheart*, page 24.
22. *Ibid.*, page 18.
23. In period newspaper stories, Maud's name is sometimes listed as Compster or Compston. No census records were found confirming any of the names.
24. *Bismarck Daily Tribune*, September 6, 1887.
25. *St. Paul Tribune*, September 9, 1887.
26. *Ibid.*, September 10, 1887.
27. *Ibid.*, September 14, 1887.
28. *Bismarck Daily Tribune*, December 1, 1887.
29. *Ibid.*
30. *Ibid.*, December 3, 1887.
31. *Freeborn County Standard*, October 24, 1888.
32. Kerkhoff, Ingrid, *Contemporary American Drama; History of American Theater*, retrieved March 4, 2005 from http://www.fb10.uni-bremen.de/anglistik/kerkhoff/ContempDrama/DR-History.htm.
33. Wilson, Paul F., Methodist College, Fayetteville, North Carolina, from his unpublished dissertation, "North Carolina Opera Houses, 1878–1921: A Sourcebook for Local Theatrical History."
34. *Daily Nevada State Journal*, November 19, 1901.
35. *Trenton Evening Times*, January 31, 1896.
36. *Fort Wayne Sentinel*, April 25, 1901.
37. 1880 U.S. Federal Census, New York, New York, District 173, page 32.
38. *Mansfield News*, February 28, 1889.
39. *New York Dramatic Mirror*, Listings Archives, 1879–1913.
40. Eymann, Scott, *Mary Pickford: America's Sweetheart*, page 17.
41. Quoted from St. Johns, Adela Rogers, "The Life Story of Wallace Reid: The Tragedy of an American Hero," *Liberty Magazine*, June 23, 1928, page 12.
42. St. Johns, Adela Rogers, "Wallace Reid: The Tragedy of an American Idol," *Liberty Magazine*, June 23, 1928, page 12.
43. Reid, Bertha Westbrook, *Wallace Reid: His Life Story, by His Mother*, page 8.
44. *Atlas of the State of Illinois with Historic Statistics and Information*, page 129.
45. All monetary conversions in this text were calculated using a formula taking into account a combination of financial factors, including inflation, the Consumer Price Index, and the relative value of unskilled labor.

46. U.S. 1870 Federal Census, Illinois, Macoupin, Township 8, Range 9, page 225.
47. 1850 U.S. Federal Census, Ohio, Hardin, Dudley, page 135.
48. 1850 U.S. Federal Census, Ohio, Hardin, Goshen, page 152.
49. 1860 U.S. Federal Census, Ohio, Hardin, Dudley, page 83.
50. Reid, Bertha Westbrook, *Wallace Reid: His Life, by His Mother*, page 8.
51. 1890 Census, Veterans Schedules, Missouri, St. Louis City, St. Louis, Roll 27, page 9.
52. 1880 U.S. Federal Census, Missouri, St. Louis City, District 166, page 638B.
53. 1890 Census, Veterans Schedules, Missouri, St. Louis City, St. Louis, Roll 27, page 9.
54. Courteway, Robbi, *Spirits of Saint Louis: A Ghostly Guide to the Mound City's Unearthly Visitors*, page 181.
55. Reid, Bertha Westbrook, *Wallace Reid: His Life Story, by His Mother*, page 9.
56. Thomas, Augustus, *The Print of My Remembrance*, New York, Charles Scribner's Sons, 1922.
57. Reid, Bertha Westbrook, *Wallace Reid: His Life Story by His Mother*, page 10.
58. *Decatur Daily Dispatch*, January 4, 1890.
59. *Daily Herald* (Delphos, Ohio), January 20, 1903.
60. Reid, Bertha Westbrook, *Wallace Reid: His Life Story, by His Mother*, page 11.
61. *Ibid.*
62. Bodeen, DeWitt, *From Hollywood*, page 93.
63. *Picture News,* January 7, 1922, page 21.
64. Quoted from St. Johns, Adela Rogers, "The Life of Wallace Reid: The Tragedy of an American Idol," *Liberty Magazine,* June 17, 1928, page 14.
65. Reid, Wallace, "Wallace Reid: By Himself," *Picture News*, June 7, 1922, page 21.
66. *Ibid.*, page 21.
67. *Waukesha Freeman,* December 12, 1895.
68. *Marion Daily Star*, September 1, 1893.
69. Bodeen, Dewitt, *From Hollywood*, page 93.
70. *Washington Post*, January 19, 1923.
71. *New York Daily Mirror*, June–September records, 1910 summary.
72. Reid, Bertha Westbrook, *Wallace Reid: His Life Story by His Mother*, page 14.
73. St. Johns, Adela Rogers, "The Life Story of Wallace Reid: The Life Story of an American Idol," *Liberty Magazine*, June 23, 1928, page 14.
74. Reid, Bertha, *Wallace Reid: His Life Story, by His Mother*, page 9.
75. St. Johns, Adela Rogers, "The Life Story of Wallace Reid: The Life Story of an American Idol," *Liberty Magazine*, June 23, 1928, page 14.
76. Bodeen, DeWitt, *From Hollywood,* page 93.
77. *Decatur Daily Republican,* January 27, 1897.
78. Bodeen, DeWitt, *From Hollywood,* page 94.
79. *Delphos Daily Herald,* August 7, 1897.
80. 1900 U.S. Federal Census, New York, Manhattan, District 539, page 9-B.
81. *Fort Wayne News,* January 10, 1898.
82. *Delphos Daily Herald,* September 11, 1899.
83. *Ibid.*, November 30, 1898.
84. *Ibid.*, December 2, 1898.
85. *Fort Wayne News,* April 1, 1899.
86. Quoted from St. Johns, Adela Rogers, "The Life of Wallace Reid: The Tragedy of an American Idol," *Liberty Magazine,* June 23, 1923, page 15.
87. *Trenton Evening Times,* February 27, 1899.
88. *Nevada State Journal,* March 11, 1938.
89. Eyman, Scott, *Mary Pickford: America's Sweetheart*, page 17.
90. Smith, Frederick James, *New York Dramatic Mirror*, March 19, 1913.
91. *Elyria Republican*, April 25, 1901.
92. *Elyria Daily Chronicle*, December 23, 1902.
93. *The Washington Post,* February 12, 1911.
94. *The Little Movie Mirror Books: Wallace Reid,* page 2.
95. *Ibid., Wallace Reid,* page 1.
96. Bold print was from the original advertisement; it was not added editorially by the author.
97. Reid, Bertha Westbrook, *Wallace Reid: His Life Story, by His Mother,* page 31.
98. *Ibid.,* page 33.
99. St. Johns, Adela Rogers, "The Life Story of Wallace Reid: The Tragedy of an American Idol," *Liberty Magazine*, June 23, 1928, page 15.
100. Montgomery, Morton, *The History of Berks County*, 1908, page 76.
101. All notes this section from *Perkiomen Griffin*, 1908 edition, pages 62–68.
102. Bodeen, DeWitt, *From Hollywood*, page 94.
103. Reid, Bertha Westbrook, *Wallace Reid: His Life Story, by His Mother*, page 38.
104. St. Johns, Adela Rogers, "The Life Story of Wallace Reid: The Tragedy of an American Idol," *Liberty Magazine*, June 23, 1928, page 15.
105. Reid, Wallace, "Wallace Reid's Life Story: By Himself," *Picture News,* January 7, 1922, page 23.
106. Op cit, page 37.
107. St. Johns, Adela Rogers, "The Life Story of Wallace Reid: The Tragedy of an American Idol," *Liberty Magazine,* June 30, 1928, page 36.
108. York, Scollard, *Wally the Wonderful*, from Academy of Motion Picture Arts & Sciences, Herrick Library, Special Collections Department, William Wallace Reid, Jr. Collection, Folder 7.
109. Albright, Horace M., *Creating the National Park Service: the Missing Years,* not paginated.
110. St. Johns, Adela Rogers, "The Life of Wallace Reid: The Tragedy of an American Idol," *Liberty Magazine,* June 30, 1928, page 37.
111. *Ibid.*
112. *Ibid.*, page 36.
113. Reid, Bertha Westbrook, *Wallace Reid: His Life Story, by His Mother,* page 38.
114. St. Johns, Adela Rogers, "The Life of Wallace Reid: The Tragedy of an American Idol," *Liberty Magazine,* June 30, 1928, page 38.
115. *Ibid.*
116. Reid, Wallace, "Wallace Reid's Life History: By Himself," *Picture Show Magazine*, January 14, 1922, page 16.
117. St. Johns, Adela Rogers, "The Life Story of Wallace Reid: The Tragic Death of an American Idol," *Liberty Magazine*, June 30, 1928, page 40.

Chapter 2

1. Mintz, S. (2003), *The Movies as a Cultural Battleground, Digital History*, retrieved March 15, 2005 from http://www.digitalhistory.uh.edu.
2. *The Sneeze* was apparently filmed on January 7, 1894, although some film historians date the film to 1893.
3. Botnick, Vicki, American Film Institute, *The First Fifty Years of American Film*, Fathom Archives, Columbia University.
4. *The New York Times,* April 21, 1896.
5. *Los Angeles Evening Herald Express,* June 1, 1935.
6. Carr, Harry, "The Untold Tales of Hollywood," *Smart Set Magazine*, December, 1929.
7. Pratt, George, *Spellbound in Darkness,* page 27.
8. Wanamaker, Mark, *The First Studios*, retrieved March 15, 2005, from http://free-culture.org/notes/12.pdf.
9. Cook, Pam (editor), *The Cinema Book*, page 4.
10. Ramsaye, Terry, *A Million and One Nights: A History of the Motion Picture*, page 575.

11. Bogdonovich, Peter, *Allan Dwan: The Last Pioneer*, page 17.
12. Lasky, Jesse L., *I Blow My Own Horn*, page 97.
13. Wanamaker, Mark, *The First Studios*, retrieved March 15, 2005, from http://free-culture.org/notes/12.pdf.
14. Henderson, Robert M., *D.W. Griffith: The Years at Biograph*, page 12.
15. The first Mrs. Roscoe Arbuckle and Charlie Chaplin's first leading lady.
16. Minta Durfee, from an interview with Don Schneider and Stephen Norman, July 21, 1974.
17. Henderson, Robert M., *D.W. Griffith: The Years at Biograph*, page 13.
18. Oderman, Stuart, *Talking to the Piano Player*, page 67.
19. Essanay was not far from Selig, located at 1339 North Argyle Street on Chicago's northwest side.
20. Bodeen, DeWitt, *From Hollywood*, page 94.
21. Bernstein, Arnie, *Hollywood on Lake Michigan: 100 Years of Chicago and the Movies*, page 26.
22. 1900 U.S. Federal Census, Illinois, Chicago, 21st Ward, District 640, page 8.
23. 1910 U.S. Federal Census, Illinois, Chicago, 25th Ward, District 1045, page 2-B.
24. Hobart Van Zandt Bosworth was born in Ohio in 1867, a direct descendant of Miles Standish and John and Priscilla Alden on his father's side, and of the Van Zandts, the first Dutch settlers to settle in America, on his mother's. At 12, he ran away from home and signed on as a cabin boy on the clipper ship *Sovereign of the Seas*, making a five-month voyage around the Horn to San Francisco. He entered the stage and came to movies in 1908 and is credited with almost 260 film roles, although he is rumored to have appeared in close to 500.
25. *Los Angeles Herald*, Dorothy Davenport Reid to William Parker, December 18, 1922.
26. Brownlow, Kevin, *The Parade's Gone By*, page 257.
27. Bodeen, DeWitt, *From Hollywood*, page 95.
28. Reid, Wallace, "Wallace Reid: By Himself," *Picture Show Magazine*, January 21, 1922, page 17.
29. Carr, Harry, "The Untold Tales of Hollywood," *Smart Set Magazine*, December, 1929.
30. St. Johns, Adela Rogers, "The Life Story of Wallace Reid: The Tragedy of an American Idol," *Liberty Magazine*, June 20, 1928, page 40.
31. Quoted from vintage movie magazine article by Scollard York, *Wally the Wonderful*, from Academy of Motion Picture Arts & Sciences, Herrick Library, Special Collections Department, William Wallace Reid, Jr. Collection, Folder 7.
32. Bodeen, DeWitt, *From Hollywood*, page 96.
33. *Ibid.*, page 97.
34. Reid, Wallace, "Wallace Reid: By Himself," *Picture Show Magazine*, January 21, 1922, page 17.
35. Bodeen, DeWitt, *From Hollywood*, page 96.
36. *The Little Movie Mirror Book: Wallace Reid*, page 7.
37. *The New York Times*, April 28, 1915.
38. Theodore Roberts (1861–1928) was one of the best-known of the early silent screen character actors. The son of a sea captain and a veteran stage actor, Roberts was a familiar face in almost 110 films between 1914 and his death in 1928. He debuted in *The Call of the North* (1914), and appeared in dozens of well-known films, including a number of Wally's films, such as *Joan the Woman* (1916), *Nan of Music Mountain* and *The Devil-Stone* (both 1917), *Hawthorne of the U.S.A.* (1919), *Double Speed* and *Excuse My Dust* (1920), and *Across the Continent* (1922). Among Roberts' final roles was his portrayal of Moses in the Cecil B. DeMille 1923 classic *The Ten Commandments*. He died in Hollywood in 1928 of uremic poisoning.
39. Reid, Bertha Westbrook, *Wallace Reid: His Life Story, by His Mother*, page 42.
40. Dorothy collaborated on a filmography with writer DeWitt Bodeen for an article that appeared in the April, 1966, edition of *Films in Review* magazine. Interestingly, the filmography included several heretofore unknown Wally films, as well as details for many others. Most of the film notes for the 1910–1914 films in this text are confirmed in that text.
41. St. Johns, Adela Rogers, "The Life of Wallace Reid: The Tragedy of an American Idol," *Liberty Magazine*, June 30, 1928, page 42.
42. *Ibid.*, page 12.
43. Arnold Bennett (1867–1931) was a prolific English journalist who wrote thirty novels and 3,000 articles on hundreds of topics for magazines and newspapers as varied as *The Realist*, *The Saturday Evening Post*, and *The Evening Standard* during his 40-year career. He died in 1931 from the effect of typhus contracted during a trip to France.
44. St. Johns, Adela Rogers, "The Life of Wallace Reid: The Tragedy of an American Idol," *Liberty Magazine*, June 30, 1928, page 40.
45. Reid, Bertha Westbrook, *Wallace Reid: His Life, by His Mother*, page 44.
46. St. Johns, Adela Rogers, "The Life of Wallace Reid: The Tragedy of an American Idol," *Liberty Magazine*, June 30, 1928, page 37.
47. Mix, Olive Stokes, *The Fabulous Tom Mix*, page 92.
48. Sennett, Mack, *King of Comedy*, page 62.
49. The name was variously mentioned in newspaper accounts as "Minnematsu" or "Minimatso," but the 1910 Census spelled it "Minematsu." 1910 U.S. Federal Census, California, Los Angeles, Los Angeles, District 205, sheet 1-A.
50. *Evening Telegram*, October 28, 1911.
51. *Sheboygan Press*, October 28, 1911.
52. *Stevens Point Daily Journal*, October 28, 1911.
53. Minta Durfee, from an interview with Don Schneider and Stephen Normand, July 21, 1974.
54. Zollo, Paul, *Hollywood Remembered: An Oral History of Its Golden Age*, page 19.
55. Carr, Harry, "The Untold Tales of Hollywood," *Smart Set Magazine*, January, 1930.
56. Sennett, Mack, *The King of Comedy*, page 88.
57. Carr, Harry, "The Untold Tales of Hollywood," *Smart Set Magazine*, February, 1930.
58. Smith, Andrew Brodie, *Shooting Cowboys and Indians: Silent Western Films, American Culture, and the Birth of Hollywood*, page 48.
59. Quoted from *Films in Review*, April, 1966, article by DeWitt Bodeen.
60. Henderson, Robert M., *D.W. Griffith: The Years at Biograph*, Appendix—List of Films, page 191.

Chapter 3

1. *Los Angeles Herald*, Dorothy Davenport Reid to William Parker, December 18, 1922. The quoted text on these pages from Dorothy describing their alleged meeting is from the lengthy William Parker interview with Dorothy that was printed during Wally's final illness.
2. Oderman, Stuart, *Talking to the Piano Player*, page 67.
3. *Fort Wayne News*, March 6, 1897.
4. Library of Congress, Abraham Lincoln Papers, Document: Leonard Grover to Abraham Lincoln, September 28, 1863.
5. *The Atlanta Constitution*, December 3, 1881.
6. 1870 U.S. Federal Census, Massachusetts, Suffolk, Boston, Ward 15, page 298.
7. Tompkins, Eugene, and Quincy Kilby, *The History of the Boston Theatre 1854–1901*, retrieved March 9, 2005 from http://external.oneonta.edu/cooper/drama/stage.html#ss-america.
8. Tice, Joyce M., Tri-Counties Genealogy and His-

tory, retrieved on March 8, 2005, from http://www.rootsweb.com/~srgp./articles/halfway.htm.
  9. Nason & Varney, *Massachusetts Gazetteer*, page 187.
  10. *The Atlanta Constitution*, December 3, 1881.
  11. *The Standard*, Ogden, Utah, September 16, 1891.
  12. *The Trenton Times*, January 26, 1893.
  13. *The New York Times*, August 4, 1895.
  14. *Ibid.*, August 18, 1895.
  15. Beasley, David, interview, Wilfrid Laurier University Press, retrieved March 6, 2005, from www.wlu.ca.
  16. McKee Rankin quotes from this section quoted from interview published in the *Los Angeles Express*, July 3, 1908.
  17. Barrymore, Lionel, *We Barrymores*, page 3.
  18. Retrieved March 28, 2005, from http://www.sparknotes.com/film/birthofanation/context.html.
  19. Sweet, Blanche, interview quoted from Henderson, Robert M., *D.W. Griffith: The Years at Biograph*, page 9.
  20. Between 1908 and 1924 Griffith is credited with writing another 225 films. But he would direct almost 600.
  21. Gauntier, Gene, from autobiography *Blazing the Trail*, retrieved March 28, 2005, from http://www.cinemaweb.com/silentfilm/bookshelf/htm. *Blazing the Trail*, Gauntier's autobiography, was serialized between 1928 and 1929 in the popular magazine *Woman's Home Companion*.
  22. Gauntier quotes from Gauntier, Gene, *Blazing the Trail*, retrieved March 28, 2005, from http://www.cinemaweb.com/silentfilm/bookshelf.htm.
  23. Original Griffith Studio press release circa August, 1928, from Miles, John P., "D.W. Griffith's Twenty-Year Record," *D.W. Griffith Papers, 1897–1954*.
  24. Bitzer was Griffith's favorite cameraman and closest confidant. According to Biograph writer Gene Gauntier, Bitzer and Griffith often sat up all night working together on new photographic effects.
  25. Stanhope, Selwyn A., "The World's Master Picture Producer," *Photoplay Magazine*, January 1915, page 57.
  26. Gauntier, Gene, from autobiography *Blazing the Trail*.
  27. Predmore, Lester, interview quoted from Henderson, Robert M., *D.W. Griffith: The Years at Biograph*, page 77.
  28. Sennett, Mack, *The King of Comedy*, page 73.
  29. Henderson, Robert M., *D.W. Griffith: The Years at Biograph*, page 108.
  30. Horsley, William, "From Pigs to Pictures: The Story of David Horsley," *The International Photographer*, March, 1934, page 2.
  31. Quoted from Brownlow, Kevin, *The Parade's Gone By*, page 257.
  32. Zollo, Paul, *Hollywood Remembered: An Oral History of Its Golden Age*, page 18.
  33. Horsley, William, "From Pigs to Pictures: The Story of David Horsley," *The International Photographer*, March, 1934, page 3.
  34. Harry Herschfeld (1885–1974) would later produce the popular *Can You Top This?* 1940s radio and 1950s television series.
  35. Oderman, Stuart, *Talking to the Piano Player*, page 65.
  36. *San Francisco Chronicle*, June 22, 1936.
  37. St. Johns, Adela Rogers, "The Life of Wallace Reid: The Tragedy of an American Idol," *Liberty Magazine*, June 30, 1928, page 44.
  38. Lasky, Jesse L., *I Blow My Own Horn*, page 95.
  39. Zollo, Paul, *Hollywood Remembered: An Oral History of its Golden Age*, page 22.
  40. *Hollywood Citizen News*, March 20, 1936.
  41. *Los Angeles Evening Herald Express*, August 21, 1939.
  42. Minta Durfee, from interview with Don Schneider and Stephen Norman, July 21, 1974.
  43. St. Johns, Adela Rogers, "The Life of Wallace Reid: The Tragedy of an American Idol," *Liberty Magazine*, July 7, 1928, page 70.
  44. *Los Angeles Herald*, Dorothy Davenport Reid to William Parker, December 18, 1922.
  45. Henderson, Robert M., *D.W. Griffith: The Years at Biograph*, page 110.
  46. Whenever possible, movie plots will be described if the information is available. There are literally thousands of silent films for which no script records or anecdotal evidence remains. There is often no reference other than a title and cast list buried within company or theater archives.
  47. *Ibid.*

Chapter 4

  1. Unless otherwise noted, all Dorothy Davenport quotes from this chapter are taken from Parker, William, *Los Angeles Herald*, December 18–22, 1922.
  2. St. Johns, Adela Rogers, "The Life of Wallace Reid: The Tragedy of an American Idol," *Liberty Magazine*, Jul 20, 1928, page 60.
  3. *Ibid.*
  4. Bodeen, DeWitt, *From Hollywood*, page 96.
  5. St. Johns, Adela Rogers, "The Life of Wallace Reid: The Tragedy of an American Idol," *Liberty Magazine*, July 7, 1928, page 65.
  6. Zollo, Paul, *Hollywood Remembered: An Oral History of Hollywood*, page 21.
  7. *Picture Show Magazine*, "Wallace Reid: By Himself," January 21, 1922, page 17.
  8. Lamb, Blaine P., "Silent Filming in San Diego: 1898–1912," *The Journal of San Diego History*, Fall 1976, Volume 22, No. 4, retrieved March 16, 2005, from http://www.sandiegohistory.org/journal/76fall/film.htm.
  9. *Arizona Daily Star*, December 18, 1910, quoted from Lamb.
  10. Bogdonovich, Peter, *Allan Dwan: The Last Pioneer*, page 17, quoted from Lamb.
  11. During a 50-year career he directed 400-plus films, his last in 1961.
  12. Morris, Gary, "An Interview with Silent Film Pioneer Allan Dwan," *Bright Lights Film Journal*, September 1996, Volume 17, retrieved on March 22, 2005, from http://www.brightlightsfilm.com/17/07_dwan.html.
  13. Bogdonovich, Peter, *Allan Dwan: The Last Pioneer*, page 21, quoted from Lamb.
  14. *Ibid.*, November 5, 1912.
  15. Typed transcript of a recorded interview made with Roy Overbaugh by the Santa Barbara Historical Society, March, 1954, quoted from Lamb.
  16. *Ibid.*, November 5, 1912.
  17. *Ibid.*, November 5, 1912.
  18. St. Johns, Adela Rogers, "The Life of Wallace Reid: The Tragedy of an American Hero," *Liberty Magazine*, July 7, 1928, page 60.
  19. *Ibid.*
  20. Williams, Gregory L., *The Journal of San Diego History*, "San Diego: Hollywood's Backlot, 1898–2002," Spring 2002, Volume 48, Number 2.
  21. Roy Overbaugh was born in Chicago in 1882 and is credited with about 45 films from 1917 to 1935, including *Dr. Jekyll and Mr. Hyde* (1920), Basil Rathbone's *The Bishop Murder Case* (1930), and *Penrod and Sam* (1931). His official filmography does not include any films prior to 1917, but very detailed newspaper accounts of this period in Flying A history mention his work on all of Allan Dwan's productions in Santa Barbara, and hint at work with Dwan in San Diego. He probably worked on another 30 or so films that are not included in his body of work. Overbaugh died in 1966 in Los Angeles.

22. Lillian Christie appeared in 21 films from 1911 to 1913, but after leaving Flying A in 1912 appeared in only a single movie before inexplicably disappearing from film.
23. Albert Edward Coxen was born in London in 1880 and emigrated to the U.S. in 1882. After briefly returning to England with his family he returned to the U.S. in 1897 and moved in with an uncle in San Francisco. After graduating from Berkeley he worked for his family and prospected for gold before joining a San Francisco stage company and moving to Broadway in 1909. He joined Kalem in 1911 and Flying A in 1912, and appeared in almost 200 films between 1911 and 1941, including 160 silents, but was never the star in sound that he was prior. His sound work was mostly small roles, usually as a villain, in westerns like *The Trail Drive* (1933), *Westward Ho* (1935), and *Texas Stampede* (1939). He died in 1954.
24. *Santa Barbara Morning Press*, November 15, 1912.
25. Dwan and his mother moved out of the Edgerly Arms in January and rented a bungalow on De La Vina Street in Santa Barbara, where they stayed until returning to Los Angeles.
26. Tompkins, Walter A., *The Westside*, retrieved June 18, 2005, from http://www.santabarbaraproperties.com/areainfo/neighborhoods/westside.html.
27. *Moving Picture World*, December 14, 1912.
28. During the next eight years, over 1,200 films were made in Santa Barbara by several companies.
29. *Santa Barbara Morning Press*, November 19, 1912.
30. Laurence Trimble (1885–1954) directed almost 100 films from 1900 to 1926 and was married to writers Jane Murfin and Marion Blackton. Murfin later married Wally's pal Donald Crisp.
31. Stewart, John, *Filmarama The Formidable Years, 1893–1919, Volume 1*, page 215.
32. Bodeen, DeWitt, *From Hollywood*, page 97.
33. Bogdonovich, Peter, *Allan Dwan: The Last Pioneer*, page 19.
34. Bodeen, DeWitt, *From Hollywood*, page 97.
35. Lasky, Jesse, *I Blow My Own Horn*, page 93.
36. *Variety*, July 16, 1920.
37. *Santa Barbara Morning Press*, March 18, 1913.
38. *Ibid.*, January 5, 1913.
39. *Motography Magazine*, January 18, 1913.
40. *Santa Barbara Morning Press*, December 28, 1912.
41. *The New York Times*, January 16, 1913.
42. *Santa Barbara Morning Press*, January 18, 1913.
43. *Ibid.*, January 9, 1913.
44. Vivien Rich was born in Philadelphia in 1893 and appeared in 127 films from 1912 to 1931, including 14 alongside Wally, like *Youth and Jealousy* (1913), *The Tell-Tale Arm* (1917) and *The Pride of Lonesome* (1917). She left the movies in 1931 and died in 1957.
45. Jean Durrell appeared in only 9 films between 1913 and 1915.
46. Dorothy Brown did no confirmed work for Flying A, and appeared in only 2 silent films for Universal in 1915, and three later sound films in uncredited roles.
47. *Santa Barbara Morning Press*, February 20, 1913.
48. *Ibid.*, January 23, 1913.
49. Henderson, Robert M., *D.W. Griffith: The Years at Biograph*, pages 214–215.
50. *Santa Barbara Morning Press*, February 22, 1913.
51. *Ibid.*, February 27, 1913.
52. *Ibid.*, April 15, 1913.
53. *Ibid.*, April 16, 1913. Newspaper accounts incorrectly identified Grandon as "F.C. Grandson."
54. With Dana Driskel, a film production instructor at the University of California at Santa Barbara (UCSB) and documentarian.
55. *Santa Barbara Morning Press*, April 17, 1913.
56. Hale directed Louise Lester, who was starring in the popular serial for American.
57. *Santa Barbara Morning Press*, April 20, 1913.
58. *Ibid.*, April 22, 1913.
59. Photographs in period newspapers described "Larry Trimble" (noted director Laurence Trimble, who directed over 100 silent films) as the film's director.
60. *The Freeman's Journal*, September 27, 1911.
61. *Ibid.*, July 5, 1911.
62. *Moving Picture World*, June 3, 1911.
63. *Oneonta Press*, September 6, 1911.
64. Unless otherwise noted, all Dorothy Davenport and Wallace Reid quotes from this chapter taken from Parker, William, *Los Angeles Herald*, December 18–22, 1922.
65. Italics added by author for emphasis.
66. *Chicago Daily Tribune*, December 13, 1914.
67. Dorothy is referring to the Pinecrest Lodge, which was a large mountain retreat near Strawberry Peak in the vicinity of Lake Arrowhead. It was a favorite of early silent film directors who were working in the neighboring mountains. Cecil B. DeMille and his crew stayed at Pinecrest during the filming of his 1913 version of *The Squaw Man*. She probably filmed *The Spark of Flame* there.
68. Dorothy Davenport and Wallace Reid quotes from this chapter taken from Parker, William, *Los Angeles Herald*, December 18–22, 1922.
69. Reid, Bertha Westbrook, *Wallace Reid: His Life Story, by His Mother*, page 47.
70. *Ibid.*
71. Quoted from Bodeen, DeWitt, *From Hollywood*, page 97.
72. Dunham appeared in small roles in 185 films from 1913 to 1951. He died in 1972 in Los Angeles.
73. *Los Angeles Herald*, Dorothy Davenport Reid to William Parker, December 20, 1922.
74. According to Dorothy's recollections, the Bernstein residence was on Morgan Place, but she may have been confused since she later lived on Morgan Place. Period records lists 1525 La Brea as the Bernstein residence during this period.
75. *Moving Picture World*, November 29, 1913.
76. Bodeen, DeWitt, *From Hollywood*, page 97.
77. *Moving Picture World*, November 29, 1913.
78. It is often difficult to determine exact filming locations, given the lack of formal production records for this era. Often the locations are assumed by iteration; following certain crew and cast member lists is often the only confirmation of a filming location. It is known that at least eight of the films noted were made at Lake Arrowhead during this time frame. Since other cast lists are similar, it can be assumed that the filming was done at the same time and at the same location.
79. Bodeen, DeWitt, *From Hollywood*, page 98.
80. From Lake Arrowhead News history website, retrieved March 24, 2005, from http://www.lakearrowheadnews.com/local%20history.htm.
81. Robinson, John W., *The San Bernardinos: The Mountain Country from Cajon Pass to Oak Glen, Two Centuries of Changing Use*, page 127.
82. St. Johns, Adela Rogers, "The Life of Wallace Reid: The Tragedy of an American Idol," *Liberty Magazine*, July 7, 1928, page 62.
83. *Moving Picture World*, January 4, 1913.
84. *Ibid.*, January 25, 1913.
85. *Ibid.*, February 13, 1913.
86. *Los Angeles Times*, February 15, 1913.
87. *Chicago Daily Tribune*, April 15, 1914.
88. *Atlanta Constitution*, April 25, 1914.
89. "The Fruit of Evil," *Moving Picture World*, April 18, 1914.

Chapter 5

1. Retrieved January 1, 2006, from http://www.echopark.net.

2. St. Johns, Adela Rogers, "The Life Story of Wallace Reid: The Tragedy of an American Idol," *Liberty Magazine,* July 7, 1928, page 64.
3. *Motion Picture Magazine,* February, 1917.
4. All address references this section from 1920 U.S. Federal Census, California, Los Angeles County, District 226, pages 1A–16A.
5. *Los Angeles (1914) City Directory*, page 537.
6. *Variety,* September 5, 1928, retrieved April 1, 2005, from http://www.cinemaweb.com/silentfilm/bookshelf.
7. Henderson, Robert M., *D.W. Griffith: The Years at Biograph*, page 153.
8. *New York Dramatic Mirror,* December 3, 1913.
9. St. Johns, Adela Rogers, "The Life of Wallace Reid: The Tragedy of an American Idol," *Liberty Magazine,* July 7, 1928, page 62.
10. Bodeen, DeWitt, *From Hollywood,* page 98.
11. Retrieved on March 26, 2005, from http://www.tvdays.com/silentclassics.htm.
12. It was reported that Wally's first Mutual contract paid him $40 a week.
13. Stanhope, Selwyn A., "The World's Master Picture Producer," *Photoplay Magazine*, January 1915, page 61.
14. "Griffith's 20 Year Record," *Variety,* September 5, 1928, pages 7.
15. He became better known as an actor, appearing in over 360 films from 1912 to the late 1950s. He appeared in a small role in Wally's first movie for Majestic, *Arms and the Gringo*, and built a career playing bumbling policemen, working with everyone from Laurel and Hardy to the Three Stooges. His typical role was a beat cop or detective who either fell asleep on the job or jumped to the wrong conclusion. Often Kelsey's dialogue was one word: "Sayyyyy...!" Animator Tex Avery based the bumbling policeman character in his MGM classic cartoon *Who Killed Who?* on Kelsey, replicating Kelsey down to his mustache, bushy eyebrows, and derby hat.
16. *New York Telegraph,* November 9, 1914.
17. Retrieved March 28, 2005, from http://www.iscriptdb.com/news/cgi-bin/current_view.cgi.
18. Botnick, Vicki, American Film Institute; *The First Fifty Years of American Film*; Fathom Archives, Columbia University.
19. Mintz, S. (2003), *The Movies as a Cultural Battleground, Digital History*, retrieved March 15, 2005, from http://www.digitalhistory.uh.edu.
20. Eyman, Scott, *Mary Pickford: America's Sweetheart*, page 71.
21. Carr, Harry, "The Untold Tales of Hollywood," *Smart Set Magazine,* December, 1929.
22. Kitchen, Karl K., "What They Really Get: A Discussion of Stellar Salaries," *Photoplay Magazine,* October, 1915, pages 139–140.
23. *Chicago Daily Tribune,* December 13, 1914.
24. The writer is describing the typical beautiful but plain-clothes heroines favored by Griffith and Majestic Studios.
25. *Chicago Daily Tribune,* January 11, 1915.
26. *Atlanta Constitution,* May 9, 1915.
27. *The New York Times,* March 3, 1915.
28. Retrieved March 28, 2005, from http://www.sparknotes.com/film/birthofanation/context.html.
29. Carr, Harry, "The Untold Tales of Hollywood," *Smart Set Magazine,* February, 1930.
30. *Ibid.*, December, 1929.
31. Willis, Richard, "David W. Griffith: Genius," *Movie Pictorial Magazine,* September 12, 1914.
32. Rankin, "The Little Colonel Marches Back," *Photoplay,* June 1934, page 96.
33. Bodeen, DeWitt, *From Hollywood,* page 98.
34. Gish, Lillian, *The Movies, Mr. Griffith, and Me,* page 135.
35. Bodeen, DeWitt, *From Hollywood,* page 98.
36. St. Johns, Adela Rogers, quotes in this section from "The Life Story of Wallace Reid: The Tragedy of an American Idol," *Liberty Magazine,* July 7, 1928, page 62.
37. Bodeen, DeWitt, *From Hollywood,* page 98.
38. *Ibid.,* page 98.
39. Stanhope, Selwyn A., "The World's Master Picture Producer," *Photoplay Magazine*, January, 1915, page 57.
40. *Ibid.,* page 58.
41. *Ibid.,* page 61.
42. Carr, Harry, "The Untold Tales of Hollywood," *Smart Set Magazine,* December, 1929.
43. Dirks, Tom (reviewer), *The Birth of a Nation*, retrieved March 3, 2005, from http://www.filmsite.org/birt.html.
44. Retrieved March 29, 2005, from http://www.cas.buffalo.edu/classes/dms/cgkoebel/bc/sil.html.
45. Lasky, Jesse L., *I Blow My Own Horn*, page 112.
46. Retrieved March 6, 2005, from http://www.sparknotes.com/film/birthofanation/context.html.
47. Memo; National Association for the Advancement of Colored People, Boston, 1915.
48. Bodeen, DeWitt, *From Hollywood,* page 98.
49. *Ibid.,* page 99.
50. Retrieved March 3, 2005, from http://www.sparknotes.com/film/birthofanation/context.html.
51. Selling stock to finance a film was an unprecedented strategy, but one that would become a common industry practice decades later.
52. Retrieved March 6, 2005, from http://www.sparknotes.com/film/birthofanation/context.html.
53. Dirks, Tom, *The Birth of a Nation,* retrieved March 1, 2005, from http://www.filmsite.org/birt.html.
54. Bodeen, DeWitt, *From Hollywood,* page 98.
55. Reid, Wallace, "Wallace Reid's Life History: By Himself," *Picture Show Magazine,* January 21, 1922, page 17.

Chapter 6

1. Merrick, Mollie, "Cecil Recalls Early Days in Films," *San Francisco Chronicle,* October 10, 1933.
2. Lasky, Jesse L., *I Blow My Own Horn*, page 93.
3. Zollo, Paul, *Hollywood Remembered: An Oral History of Its Golden Age*, page 19.
4. *Squaw Man* actually made much more money from states' rights sales. Before production began, Sam Goldwyn, Lasky's marketing genius, had sold states' rights deals for almost $90,000.
5. Lasky, Jesse L., *I Blow My Own Horn*, page 103.
6. The DeMille brothers insisted on spelling their individual names differently.
7. Brownlow, Kevin, *The Parade's Gone By*, page 22.
8. It was quite a coup to obtain the services of Turnbull and MacAlarney, who were at the time the Dramatic Critic and City Editor, respectively, of the *New York Herald Tribune*.
9. Lasky, Jesse L., *I Blow My Own Horn*, page 112.
10. *Motography Magazine,* March 6, 1915.
11. New York, 1911.
12. American Film Institute, Catalog of Silent Films, retrieved March 31, 2005, from http://www.afi.com/members/catalog/AbbrView.aspx?s=1&Movie=16535.
13. American Film Institute, Catalog of Silent Films, retrieved March 31, 2005, from http://www.afi.com/members/catalog/AbbrView.aspx?s=1&Movie=16463.
14. Harris' age has been in question since the Chaplin marriage. She was reportedly 18 (the legal age of consent in California) but was clearly younger. Early census records suggest she may have been as young as 14 when they met and she became pregnant, but a more likely age is 15 or just 16. Their son, Norman Spencer, lived only

three days and is buried in an L.A. cemetery under a small headstone reading simply "The Little Mouse." Chaplin's second wife, Lita Grey (real name Lillita MacMurray), was also 15 when she became pregnant and they had to marry.

15. Chicago, 1879.
16. American Film Institute, Catalog of Silent Films, retrieved March 31, 2005, from http://www.afi.com/members/catalog/AbbrView.aspx?s=1&Movie=2126.
17. *Moving Picture World*, May 8, 1915.
18. Stuttgart, 1902.
19. American Film Institute, Catalog of Silent Films, retrieved March 31, 2005, from http://www.afi.com/members/catalog/AbbrView.aspx?s=1&Movie=16578.
20. *Chicago Daily Tribune*, October 12, 1915.
21. Reid, Wallace, "Wallace Reid's Life Story, By Himself," *Picture Show Magazine*, January 22, 1922, page 17.
22. Bodeen, DeWitt, *From Hollywood*, page 100.
23. Carroll, Harrison, *Los Angeles Evening Herald*, November 24, 1930.
24. Parsons, Louella, *New York Telegraph*, March 12, 1922.
25. Brownlow, Kevin, *The Parade's Gone By*, page 209.
26. Reid, Wallace, "Wallace Reid's Life Story, By Himself," *Picture Show Magazine*, January 22, 1922, page 17.
27. St. Johns, Adela Rogers, "The Life Story of Wallace Reid: The Tragedy of an American Idol," *Liberty Magazine*, July 7, 1928, page 62.
28. Real name Ema Kittl (1878–1930), the soprano debuted at the Metropolitan Opera in 1908 and remained there almost a decade. She was one of the most famous opera singers in the world.
29. Farrar, Geraldine, *Such Sweet Compulsion: The Autobiography of Geraldine Farrar*, page 143.
30. Lasky, Jesse L., *I Blow My Own Horn*, page 116.
31. Cohn, Alfred A., "What They Really Get—NOW!" *Photoplay Magazine*, March, 1916, page 28, retrieved March 9, 2005, from http://www.cinemaweb.com/silentfilm/bookshelf.
32. Farrar, Geraldine, *Such Sweet Compulsion: The Autobiography of Geraldine Farrar*, page 144.
33. "Special Studios Built for Geraldine Farrar—Filmdom's Latest Captive," *Photoplay* Magazine, August 1915, page 41, retrieved March 8, 2005, from http://www.cinemaweb.com/silentfilm/bookshelf.
34. "Special Studios Built for Geraldine Farrar—Filmdom's Latest Captive," *Photoplay* Magazine, August 1915, page 42, retrieved March 8, 2005, from http://www.cinemaweb.com/silentfilm/bookshelf.
35. Farrar's father Sid Farrar was a famous National League baseball player.
36. Details of Geraldine Farrar's first days at Lasky from McGaffey, Kenneth, "Jerry on the Job: Geraldine Farrar Came Back to Filmland to Visualize Joan of Arc," *Photoplay Magazine*, January, 1917, pages 33–37.
37. *Photoplay Magazine*, August, 1915.
38. St. Johns, Adela Rogers, "The Life Story of Wallace Reid: The Tragedy of an American Idol," *Liberty Magazine*, July 7, 1928, page 62.
39. Lasky, Jesse L., *I Blow My Own Horn*, page 118.
40. Lou Tellegen (1881–1934) was a Dutch-born stage actor who appeared in 40 films from 1912 to 1934. His accent left him a victim of sound, and he committed suicide in a bizarre hari-kari–like manner in the bathroom of heiress Elizabeth Cudahy's Hollywood mansion. During an October 29, 1934, party, he covered his face with grease paint, laid out dozens of publicity pictures on the floor, and stabbed and slashed himself to death with a pair scissors.
41. St. Johns, Adela Rogers, "The Life Story of Wallace Reid: The Tragedy of an American Idol," *Liberty Magazine*, July 7, 1928, page 62.
42. Quote from St. Johns, Adela Rogers, "The Life Story of Wallace Reid: The Tragedy of an American Idol," *Liberty Magazine*, July 7, 1928, page 62.
43. St. Johns, Adela Rogers, "The Life Story of Wallace Reid: The Tragedy of an American Idol," *Liberty Magazine*, July 7, 1928, page 63.
44. Jeanie Macpherson (1887–1946; sometimes spelled "MacPherson") was an actor and scenario writer when she began working for DeMille, but soon became his long-time mistress as well. Her film credits include acting roles in 128 films from 1908 to 1917 (she only appeared in one more film after *Carmen*) and about 50 writing credits, but it is well known in film history that she worked on every movie that DeMille ever made. He never made a single picture without consulting with her first.
45. Farrar, Geraldine, *Such Sweet Compulsion: The Autobiography of Geraldine Farrar*, page 164.
46. *Ibid.*, page 165.
47. *Chicago Daily Tribune*, October 16, 1915.
48. *Atlanta Constitution*, October 28, 1915.
49. *Chicago Daily Tribune*, October 16, 1915.
50. Burke later became world-famous as Glenda the Good Witch in the 1939 classic film *The Wizard of Oz*.
51. Cohn, Alfred A., "What They Really Get—NOW!" *Photoplay Magazine*, March, 1916, page 28, retrieved March 9, 2005, from http://www.cinemaweb.com/silentfilm/bookshelf.
52. Financial information was among materials discovered in a long-forgotten file cabinet during a 1986 visit by writer David Pierce to DeMille's long-time Laughlin Park home in Hollywood at 2010 DeMille Drive, retrieved March 26, 2005, from http://www.cinemaweb.com/silentfilm/bookshelf.htm.
53. American Film Institute, Catalog of Silent Films, retrieved March 31, 2005, from http://www.afi.com/members/catalog/AbbrView.aspx?s=1&Movie=16430.
54. American Film Institute, Catalog of Silent Films, retrieved March 31, 2005, from http://www.afi.com/members/catalog/AbbrView.aspx?s=1&Movie=14353.
55. Birchard, Robert S., program notes for a Cecil B. DeMille retrospective at the American Museum of the Moving Image, 1989, retrieved March 30, 2005, from www.movingimage.us/film_programs/ program_notes/g/golden_chance.html.
56. *Ibid*.
57. *Los Angeles Evening Herald*, January 22, 1916.
58. Birchard, Robert S., program notes for a Cecil B. DeMille retrospective at the American Museum of the Moving Image, 1989, retrieved March 30, 2005, from www.movingimage.us/film_programs/ program_notes/g/golden_chance.html.
59. *Atlanta Constitution*, January 9, 1916.
60. *Moving Picture World*, November 27, 1915.
61. Boston, 1900.
62. According to studio press releases, this was Mae Murray's first feature film.
63. *Atlanta Constitution*, March 6, 1916.
64. American Film Institute, Catalog of Silent Films, retrieved March 31, 2005, from http://www.afi.com/members/catalog/AbbrView.aspx?s=1&Movie=16872.
65. American Film Institute, Catalog of Silent Films, retrieved March 15, 2005, from http://www.afi.com/members/catalog/AbbrView.aspx?s=1&Movie=14213.
66. *Atlanta Constitution*, April 2, 1916.

Chapter 7

1. Mintz, S. (2003). *The Pre-History of Motion Pictures, Digital History*. Retrieved March 15, 2005, from http://www.digitalhistory.uh.edu.
2. Altman, Diana, *Hollywood East: Louis B. Mayer and the Origins of the Studio System*, page 57.
3. Some texts refer to a "William H. Hodkinson," but Jesse Lasky identifies him as "William W."

4. Siegel, Scott, and Barbara Siegel, *The Encyclopedia of Hollywood*, page 314.
5. Mintz, S. (2003). *The Pre-History of Motion Pictures, Digital History*. Retrieved March 15, 2005, from http://www.digitalhistory.uh.edu.
6. *The New York Dramatic Mirror*, July 7, 1917.
7. *Los Angeles Times*, September 13, 1915.
8. Retrieved June 20, 2005, from http://www.northernstars.ca/directorsal/dwanbio.html.
9. *Atlanta Constitution*, January 2, 1916.
10. In 1912 Wally made 35 films, in 1913, 42, and in 1914, 48.
11. American Film Institute, Catalog of Silent Films, retrieved March 31, 2005, from http://www.afi.com/members/catalog/AbbrView.aspx?s=1&Movie=14336.
12. *Modesto Evening News,* October 5, 1916.
13. American Film Institute, Catalog of Silent Films, retrieved March 31, 2005, from http://www.afi.com/members/catalog/AbbrView.aspx?s=1&Movie=14155.
14. American Film Institute, Catalog of Silent Films, retrieved April 18, 2005, from http://www.afi.com/members/catalog/AbbrView.aspx?s=1&Movie=16950.
15. Drew, William H., "D.W. Griffith (1875–1948)," retrieved April 9, 2005, from http://www.gildasattic.com/dwgriffith.html.
16. Klepper, Robert (reviewer), retrieved April 11, 2005, from http://www.gildasattic.com/intol.html.
17. Schickel, Richard, *D.W. Griffith: An American Life*, quoted from Klepper, Robert.
18. *Variety*, "Griffith's 20 Year Record," September 5, 1928, page 7.
19. Klepper, Robert (reviewer), retrieved April 11, 2005, from http://www.gildasattic.com/intol.html.
20. *Cyrus (550–529 B.C.), King of Persia*.
21. *Catherine de Médicis, (1519–1589), Queen, Consort of Henry II*.
22. *Charles IX (1550–1574), King of France*.
23. On August 24, 1572, a Jesuit priest and spiritual advisor to King Charles IX of France urged him to massacre all Protestants as penance for sins in what was really a strategy to stop the budding Reformation movement in France and ensure that the Vatican retained all of the property and wealth it controlled in the country. Without warning, French soldiers led by Roman Catholic clergymen murdered over 100,000 unarmed peasants, literally filling the countryside with blood and the rivers with corpses. Tens of thousands more were sent into prison or put to work as slaves to row on the King's ships. The massacres continued for almost 200 years, leading eventually to the French Revolution, the Reign of Terror and ultimately the ruin of France. But at the time, Pope Gregory XIII commissioned a special commemorative medal and requested that Italian artist Vasari paint a mural exalting the Massacre which still hangs in the Vatican.
24. Woodbridge "Woody" Strong III (1889–1943) served in World War I, was a mercenary in Africa, a goldminer in Alaska and a lumberjack in Canada. He began as an actor but quickly moved to directing with Essanay, adding "Van Dyke" to his name for a European effect. He was known as "One-Take Van Dyke" because he believed the first take was the best take; he was a studio favorite for bringing films in under budget. He directed *Tarzan, the Ape Man* (1932) after personally picking Johnny Weissmuller for the lead, finished William Powell's *The Thin Man* (1934) in 16 days, Lupe Velez's *Cuban Love Song* (1932), *Manhattan Melodrama* (1935), and the enormously popular Jeanette MacDonald-Nelson Eddy musicals. He was only the second director enshrined at Grauman's Chinese Theater when he and Clark Gable left their prints side by side in the fabled concrete "Forecourt of the Stars" for 1936's *Love on the Run*.
25. Tod Browning (1882–1962) joined the circus at age 16 after falling in love with a circus dancer, and performed as a clown and as "The Living Dead," buried for hours at a time in a specially-designed casket before being dug up for throngs of terrified circus-goers. He was fascinated by the sideshow "geeks," the bearded lady, the midgets, and the dog-faced boy popular at the time. Moving to vaudeville and the movies, he made his acting debut in *Intolerance* before directing Lon Chaney in classics like *The Unholy Three* (1925) and *London After Midnight* (1927). He also directed Lionel Barrymore in *Mark of the Vampire* (1932) and *The Devil-Doll* (1936), Bela Lugosi's *Dracula* (1931), and *Freaks* (1932), a cult classic based upon his own childhood sideshow memories.
26. American Film Institute, Catalog of Silent Films, retrieved March 31, 2005, from http://www.afi.com/members/catalog/AbbrView.aspx?s=1&Movie=16253.
27. Dirks, Tom (reviewer), *Intolerance*, retrieved March 3, 2005, from http://www.filmsite.org/birt.html.
28. The only rival to the *Intolerance* sets is the (reportedly) 40-acre castle built by Wilfred Buckland for Douglas Fairbanks' 1922 *Robin Hood*.
29. Klepper, Robert (reviewer), retrieved April 11, 2005, from http://www.gildasattic.com/intol.html.
30. Dirks, Tom (reviewer), *Intolerance*, retrieved March 3, 2005, from http://www.filmsite.org/birt.html.
31. Drew, William H., *D.W. Griffith (1875–1948)*, retrieved April 9, 2005, from http://www.gildasattic.com/dwgriffith.html.
32. Carr, Harry, "The Untold Tales of Hollywood," *Smart Set Magazine*, February, 1930.
33. St. Johns, Adela Rogers, "The Life Story of Wallace Reid: The Tragedy of an American Idol," *Liberty Magazine*, July 7, 1928, page 63.
34. McGaffey, Kenneth, "Jerry on the Job: Geraldine Farrar Came Back to Filmland to Visualize Joan of Arc," *Photoplay Magazine*, January, 1917, page 39.
35. Lasky, Jesse L., *I Blow My Own Horn*, page 119.
36. Farrar quotes in this section quoted from her autobiography, *Such Sweet Compulsion: The Autobiography of Geraldine Farrar*, pages 164–165.
37. Lasky, Jesse L., *I Blow My Own Horn*, page 119.
38. Friedrich von Schiller (1759–1805) was a leading 18th-century German dramatist, poet, and literary theorist. After studying law and medicine, he began writing in 1780; his plays usually examined the inward freedom of the soul amidst conflict between father and son, government and citizenry, etc. His writings inspired Brahms, Liszt, Mendelssohn, Schubert, Schumann, Richard Strauss and Tchaikovsky.
39. Sources disagree as to the actual length of the film. It was variously reported to be 10, 11 or 12 reels in length. Apparently it was indeed at least 10 reels long at a minimum.
40. Wilfred Buckland (1866–1946) worked on over 80 films from 1915 to 1927, including a number of Wally's films, and was responsible for the original design for interior Kleig lighting. He began with DeMille on the original *The Squaw Man* (1914) and later designed sets for *Carmen* (1915) and *Robin Hood* (1922). In 1946, after his actress wife Vida Buckland died of cancer, he shot his mentally-disturbed son to death and then turned the gun on himself. His suicide note simply said, "I'm taking Bill with me."
41. American Film Institute Catalog of Silent Films, retrieved April 18, 2005, from http://www.afi.com/members/catalog/AbbrView.aspx?s=1&Movie=14176.
42. Retrieved April 19, 2005, from http://www.rottentomatoes.com/m/joan_the_woman/about.php.
43. Alvin Wyckoff (1877–1957) acted in several dozen films from 1909 to 1911 before turning his creative talents to cinematography. He shot almost 75 films from 1914 to 1928, including well-known titles like *Brewster's Millions* and *Carmen* (both 1915), and *Blood and Sand* (1922). But when he led the organization of the cameraman's union

in 1928, he fell out of favor with the studios and only worked sparingly thereafter.

44. Review retrieved April 19, 2005, from http://www.kino.com/video/results.php?search=joan+the+woman.

45. McGaffey, Kenneth, "Jerry on the Job: Geraldine Farrar Came Back to Filmland to Visualize Joan of Arc," *Photoplay Magazine*, January, 1917, page 39.

46. McGaffey, Kenneth, "Jerry on the Job: Geraldine Farrar Came Back to Filmland to Visualize Joan of Arc," *Photoplay Magazine*, January, 1917, page 40.

47. *Ibid*.

48. *Chicago Daily Tribune*, May 29, 1917.

49. McGaffey, Kenneth, "Jerry on the Job: Geraldine Farrar Came Back to Filmland to Visualize Joan of Arc," *Photoplay Magazine*, January, 1917, page 42.

50. McGaffey, Kenneth, "Jerry on the Job: Geraldine Farrar Came Back to Filmland to Visualize Joan of Arc," *Photoplay Magazine*, January, 1917, page 42.

51. *New York Telegraph*, July 9, 1916.

52. *Wichita Daily Times*, July 8, 1917.

53. *Wichita Daily Times*, October 30, 1921.

54. St. Johns, Adela Rogers, "The Life of Wallace Reid: The Tragic Death of an American Idol," *Liberty Magazine*, June 30, 1928, page 42.

55. *Motion Picture World*, August 5, 1916.

56. American Film Institute Catalog of Silent Films, retrieved April 20, 2005, from http://www.afi.com/members/catalog/AbbrView.aspx?s=1&Movie=18213.

57. Sterrett Ford (1882–1955), who worked on five Lasky films in 1916–1917 and acted in a few films in the 1930s.

58. John Ford (1894–1973) directed, acted, and/or wrote almost 300 films from 1915 to 1966, including classics like *Drums Along the Mohawk* (1939), *The Battle of Midway* (1942), and *We Were Expendable* (1945); but he is best-remembered for his westerns, like *She Wore a Yellow Ribbon* (1949), *Rio Grande* (1950), and *The Man Who Shot Liberty Valence* (1962). Ford won 6 Academy Awards during his distinguished career.

59. *Chicago Daily Tribune*, February 9, 1917.

60. American Film Institute Catalog of Silent Films, retrieved April 20, 2005, from http://www.afi.com/members/catalog/AbbrView.aspx?s=1&Movie=15836.

61. *Atlanta Constitution*, March 30, 1917.

62. *Motion Picture Magazine*, February, 1917.

63. Emory Johnson (1894–1960) appeared in almost 80 films between 1913 and 1922, but it was apparent by 1919 that he did not have the star quality that Laemmle had predicted for him, and he was dropped by Universal. He directed about a dozen films between 1922 and 1932 and then left the business. He married actress Ella Hall, and was the father of actor Richard Emory and actress Ellen Hall.

64. Reid, Bertha Westbrook, *Wallace Reid: His Life Story, by His Mother*, page 45.

65. *Motion Picture Magazine*, February, 1917. Author's note: There is no confirmation that Dorothy and Wally lived on Elevado at any time. The L.A. City Directories as late as 1915 had them at Allison Avenue, and the 1917 directory on Morgan Place.

66. Manners, Marjorie, "The House That Wally Built," *Photoplay Magazine*, July, 1917.

67. *Los Angeles (1917) City Directory*, pages 639 & 1683, *Los Angeles (1918) City Directory*, pages 627 & 1638.

68. Harry A. "Nick" Grinde (1893–1979) went on to direct 50-plus films from 1928 to 1945, including Pat O'Brien in *Public Enemy's Wife* (1936) and Betty Grable's *Million Dollar Legs* (1939). He also wrote the Norma Shearer classic *The Divorcee* (1930) and the Laurel and Hardy classic *Babes in Toyland* (1934). Grinde was also briefly married to actress Marie Wilson in the early 1930s.

69. Leider, Emily W., *Dark Lover: The Life and Death of Rudolph Valentino*, page 90.

Chapter 8

1. Mintz, S., (2003), *The Movies as a Cultural Battleground, Digital History*, retrieved March 15, 2005, from http://www.digitalhistory.uh.edu.

2. Roetter, Charles, *The Art of Psychological Warfare 1914–1945*, page 53, quoted from Wells, Robert A.

3. Nurnberger, Ralph D., "Bridling the Passions," *Wilson Quarterly*, Vol. 11, page 103, quoted from Wells, Robert A.

4. Nurnberger, Ralph D., "Bridling the Passions," *Wilson Quarterly*, Vol. 11, page 102, quoted from Wells, Robert A.

5. Knightly, Phillip, *The First Casualty, from the Crimea to Vietnam: The War Correspondent as Hero, Propagandist, and Myth Maker*, page 121, quoted from Wells, Robert A.

6. Ruddenberg, Rob (editor), *The Heritage of the Great War*, retrieved April 25, 2005, from http://www.greatwar.nl.

7. Lasky, Jesse L., *I Blow My Own Horn*, page 126.

8. George E. Middleton (1883–1967) was an early 20th century playwright responsible for well-known plays like *Accused* (1925), *Blood Money* (1927), and *The Big Pond* (1928). He formed California Motion Picture Corporation in 1914 and produced, directed and wrote several dozen films, like *Mignon* (1915), *Always Faithful* (1929), and *A Devil with Women* (1930).

9. American Film Institute, Catalog of Film, retrieved May 18, 2005, from http://www.afi.com/members/catalog/AbbrView.aspx?s=1&Movie=16163.

10. *Exhibitor's Trade Review*, June 2, 1917.

11. *Motion Picture News*, June 9, 1917.

12. *Wichita Daily Times*, July 7, 1917.

13. *Ibid.*, July 8, 1917.

14. *Chicago Daily Tribune*, June 15, 1917.

15. *Ibid.*, June 8, 1917.

16. American Film Institute, Catalog of Film, retrieved May 18, 2005, from http://www.afi.com/members/catalog/AbbrView.aspx?s=1&Movie=16978.

17. *Exhibitor's Daily Review*, May 26, 1917.

18. Walter Lundien, real name Lundien (1892–1954), was the cinematographer on almost 90 films between 1914 and 1940, working with legends like Harold Lloyd, Laurel and Hardy—he filmed their classic *The Music Box* (1932)—and the Little Rascals.

19. *Santa Cruz Morning Sentinel*, March 9, 1917.

20. *Moving Picture World*, October 27, 1917.

21. *Santa Cruz Morning Sentinel*, March 13, 1917, page 5.

22. Carr, Harry, "The Untold Tales of Hollywood," *Smart Set Magazine*, December, 1929

23. *Los Angeles Times*, March 12, 1917.

24. *New York Telegraph*, July 29, 1917.

25. A memo in the Paramount studio archives confirmed that Myrtle Stedman was to co-star in the film in the role which Anita King played. It is not known why she was replaced.

26. The infant role in the original *The Squaw Man* was played by baby Carmen De Rue.

27. American Film Institute, Catalog of Film, retrieved May 18, 2005, from http://www.afi.com/members/catalog/AbbrView.aspx?s=1&Movie=2178.

28. *Ibid.*, August 2, 1917.

29. Scottish-born Eric Campbell (1879–1917) worked with the same Fred Karno Troupe as Chaplin and Stan Laurel, coming to the U.S. in 1916, where he was found on Broadway by Chaplin. Standing over 6 feet tall and weighing 275 pounds, and with a small shaved head, Campbell, his face smeared with black greasepaint for exaggerated eyebrows and darkened eyes, was the menacing bearded ogre opposite Chaplin in a dozen of his most famous silent films, like *The Floorwalker* (1916), *The Rink* (1916), *The Pawnshop* (1916), and *The Immigrant* (1917).

In late 1917 Campbell signed to star in a series of movies with Mary Pickford, the most popular actress in the world. Earlier, on July 9th, his wife suddenly died of a heart attack, and a day later his 14-year-old daughter was hit by a car. On December 20th, returning from a party at the Vernon Country Club, a drunken Campbell ran head-on into another car on Wilshire Boulevard in Hollywood and was killed. Had he lived, he would have become one of the greatest silent screen stars.

30. Charlie Murray, Slim Summerville, Hank Mann, and Chester Conklin were all among the original members of Mack Sennett's "Keystone Kops." Mann was the last surviving member of the Kops, dying in 1971.

31. *Photoplay Magazine,* June, 1917.

32. Ruddenberg, Rob (editor), *The Heritage of the Great War,* retrieved April 25, 2005, from http://www.greatwar.nl.

33. The Fieldstone School United States History Survey, *Imperialism and World War I Timeline,* retrieved June 4, 2005, from http://www.pinzler.com/ushistory/timeline9.html.

34. Fyne, Robert., *The Hollywood Propaganda of World War II,* p.1, quoted from *"Hollywood Goes to War,"* retrieved April 25, 2005, from http://history.sandiego.edu/gen/st.

35. *Los Angeles Evening Herald Examiner,* May 14, 1917.

36. Leider, Emily W., *Dark Lover: The Life and Death of Rudolph Valentino,* page 85.

37. *Motion Picture News,* July 25, 1917.

38. Cornebise, Alfred, *War as Advertised: The Four Minute Men and America's Crusade; 1917–1918,* page 154.

39. Vaughan, Stephen, *Holding Fast the Inner Lines: Democracy, Nationalism, and the Committee on Public Information,* page 32.

40. California State Military Museum, retrieved April 25, 2005, from www.militarymuseum.org/californiahomeguard.html.

41. Period writings mention "prop rifles," but in his autobiography *I Blow My Own Horn,* Jesse Lasky described the rifles as authentic, operational Springfield rifles.

42. Lasky, Jesse L., *I Blow My Own Horn,* page 111.

43. Leider, Emily W., *Dark Lover: The Life and Death of Rudolph Valentino,* page 85.

44. Eyman, Scott, *Mary Pickford: America's Sweetheart,* page 115.

45. *California Home Guard News,* December 22, 1917.

46. *Photoplay Journal,* December, 1917.

47. Whitfield, Eileen, *Pickford, the Woman Who Made Hollywood,* quoted from Lussier, Tim.

48. *Photoplay Magazine,* August, 1918.

49. Eyman, Scott, *Mary Pickford: America's Sweetheart,* page 94.

50. Coincidently, before all of the money could be spent, the war ended, leaving $27,000 in the treasury. Pickford used those funds as seed money for a dream of hers that had already been born: a Motion Picture Home for retired actors in financial need. It still exists today, as the Motion Picture Country Home and Hospital, in Woodland Hills, California.

51. Review of DeBauche, Leslie Midkiff, *Reel Patriotism: The Movies and World War I,* page 195, retrieved April 27, 2005, from http://www.findarticles.com/p/articles.

52. Polakoff, Eileen, *World War I Draft Registration Cards,* retrieved May 19, 2005, from www.ancestry.com.

53. Draft Registration record, William Wallace Reid, California, Precinct 437, No. 133–18, June 5, 1917.

54. Quotes in this section from *Los Angeles Record,* July 12, 1917.

55. Alice Davenport had lived with the couple since they moved to Allison St.

56. Draft Registration record, William Wallace Reid, California, Precinct 437, No. 133–18, June 5, 1917.

57. St. Johns, Adela Rogers, "The Life Story of Wallace Reid: The Tragedy of an American Idol," *Liberty Magazine,* July 14, 1928, page 51.

58. St. Johns, Adela Rogers, "The Life Story of Wallace Reid: The Tragedy of an American Idol," July 14, 1928, pages 50–51.

59. Bodeen, DeWitt, *From Hollywood,* page 101.

60. Reid, Wallace, "Wallace Reid's Life History: By Himself," *Picture Show Magazine,* January 21, 1922, page 19.

61. *Picture-Play Magazine,* December, 1925.

62. *Photoplay Magazine,* August, 1917.

63. At the time, extras were paid $5 a day and had to provide their own wardrobes.

64. *Edwardsville Intelligencer,* October 17, 1928.

65. Reid, Dorothy Davenport, "The Real Wally," *Photoplay Magazine,* January, 1925, page 100.

66. St. Johns, Adela Rogers, "The Life of Wallace Reid: The Tragedy of an American Idol," *Liberty Magazine,* June 30, 1928, page 37.

67. Scalzo, Tom, "Forgotten Stars: Wallace Reid," *Hollywood Studio Magazine,* January, 1987, page 7.

68. *The Little Movie Mirror Books: Wallace Reid,* page 5. The studio usually forced Wally to accept their chauffer-driven cars as a safety precaution, an edict which Wally grudgingly accepted. When he later hired his own driver, he often drove to the vicinity of the studio himself before changing seats for the ride through the gates.

69. Indianan Roscoe Conkling Sarles (1892–1922) was a popular and successful young driver among pre–1920s racers. He won three of the first four Gran Prix races in 1919 driving for the Roamer/Duesenberg racing team before driving for Barney Oldfield in Oldfield's "Golden Submarine" car. Sarles raced in the first four Indianapolis 500 races, finishing 2nd in 1921, and won the Los Angeles Ascot Speedway 150 in 1919, the Beverly Hills 250 in 1920, and the Uniontown 225 and Cotati 150 road races in 1921. On September 17, 1921, he burned to death in a fiery crash during the first race at the new Kansas City Speedway, a wooden-plank track that featured then-unheard-of 35 degree banked turns, which drivers were not used to. He was only 27 when he died.

70. Louvish, Simon, *Keystone: The Life and Clowns of Mack Sennett,* page 74.

71. *New York Telegraph,* June 24, 1917.

72. *Motion Picture News,* September 15, 1917, page 1811.

73. *Hollywood Citizen News,* November 19, 1917.

74. American Film Institute, Catalog of Film, retrieved May 18, 2005, from http://www.afi.com/members/catalog/AbbrView.aspx?s=1&Movie=14865.

75. *Los Angeles Record,* September 15, 1917.

76. St. Johns, Adela Rogers, *Love, Laughter and Tears: My Hollywood Life,* page 142.

77. *Moving Picture World,* May 19, 1917.

78. American Film Institute, Catalog of Film, retrieved May 18, 2005, from http://www.afi.com/members/catalog/AbbrView.aspx?s=1&Movie=16207.

79. *Moving Picture World,* November 17, 1917.

80. Lasky, Jesse L., *I Blow My Own Horn,* page 119.

81. DeMille built an apartment house at 2026 Argyle Avenue in Hollywood for his mother Beatrice and named it DeMille Manor. He visited her almost every day of his life. Just after shooting ended on his classic *The Ten Commandments* in 1924, Beatrice DeMille died in her apartment. DeMille Manor still stands, unchanged.

82. Quote from Farrar, Geraldine, *Such Sweet Compulsion: The Autobiography of Geraldine Farrar,* page 164.

83. American Film Institute, Catalog of Film, retrieved May 18, 2005, from http://www.afi.com/members/catalog/AbbrView.aspx?s=1&Movie=16205.

84. *Moving Picture World,* February 2, 1918.

85. *Woodland Daily Democrat,* August 14, 1919.

86. Real name Erich Oswald Hans Carl Marie Stroheim von Nordenwald.

87. Leider, Emily W., *Dark Lover: The Life and Death of Rudolph Valentino*, page 85.
88. *Chicago Daily Tribune*, December 16, 1917.
89. Little's pioneer upbringing in remote northern California left her with a deep interest in Indian culture, a study she continued the rest of her life. Her faithful and honest depiction of a young Indian girl in *The Squaw Man* (1918) won her the respect and friendship of all of the Indian extras in that film.
90. American Film Institute, Catalog of Film, retrieved June 3, 2005, from http://www.afi.com/members/catalog/AbbrView.aspx?s=1&Movie=16991.
91. *Moving Picture World*, January 5, 1918.
92. *Chillicothe Constitution*, December 21, 1918.
93. Elias Jackson Baldwin would later develop Baldwin Park and the Baldwin Hills areas of Los Angeles County after abandoning his Gold Mountain Mine.
94. Core, Tom, *Isolation Lucky for Valley*, retrieved from http://www.oldminers.org/tom_core.htm.
95. *Atlanta Constitution*, January 7, 1918.
96. The confirmed location of *Rimrock Jones* shooting near Doble makes Wally's suggestion that *Nan of Music Mountain* was filmed in Truckee, almost 525 miles away, less likely, since the two films were made so close together.
97. American Film Institute, Catalog of Film, retrieved May 18, 2005, from http://www.afi.com/members/catalog/AbbrView.aspx?s=1&Movie=17231.
98. *Motion Picture News*, February 9, 1918.
99. Retrieved May 31, 2005, from http://ponderosascenery.homestead.com/baldwin.html.
100. *Los Angeles Evening Herald*, October 12, 1917.
101. Reid, Dorothy Davenport, "The Real Wally," *Photoplay Magazine*, January, 1925, page 100.
102. Reid, Wallace, "Wallace Reid's Life History: By Himself," *Picture Show Magazine*, January 21, 1922, page 17.
103. Reid, Dorothy Davenport, "The Real Wally," *Photoplay Magazine*, March, 1925.
104. Unless otherwise noted, all Wally quotes this section from *Chicago Daily Tribune*, December 16, 1917.

Chapter 9

1. Louvish, Simon, *Keystone: The Life and Clowns of Mack Sennett*, page 139.
2. The Superba was a popular Los Angeles movie theater in the pre-1920s.
3. *Los Angeles Evening Herald*, January 22, 1916.
4. *Los Angeles Times*, November 30, 1916.
5. Lasky, Jesse L., *I Blow My Own Horn*, page 129.
6. *Moving Picture World*, December 29, 1917.
7. Farrar, Geraldine, *Such Sweet Compulsion: The Autobiography of Geraldine Farrar*, page 165. Tellegen previously directed *What Money Can't Buy* for Lasky in 1917.
8. American Film Institute, Catalog of Film, retrieved June 12, 2005, from http://www.afi.com/members/catalog/AbbrView.aspx?s=1&Movie=15213.
9. *Atlanta Constitution*, February 21, 1918.
10. Farrar, Geraldine, *Such Sweet Compulsion: The Autobiography of Geraldine Farrar*, page 165.
11. *Atlanta Constitution*, May 7, 1918.
12. American Film Institute, Catalog of Film, retrieved July 2, 2005, from http://www.afi.com/members/catalog/AbbrView.aspx?s=1&Movie=17114.
13. *Motion Picture News*, April 20, 1918.
14. American Film Institute, Catalog of Film, retrieved July 2, 2005, from http://www.afi.com/members/catalog/AbbrView.aspx?s=1&Movie=17024.
15. Oderman, Stuart, *Talking to the Piano Player*, page 67.
16. *New York Times*, June 3, 1918.
17. *Chicago Daily Tribune*, June 16, 1918.
18. Wally was shirtless for most of his short time onscreen during the D.W. Griffith classic.
19. Oderman, Stuart, *Talking to the Piano Player*, page 67.
20. St. Johns, Adela Rogers, "The Life Story of Wallace Reid: The Tragedy of an American Idol," *Liberty Magazine*, July 7, 1928, page 59.
21. The palatial and elegant Hotel Huntington was built in 1907 as the Wentworth Hotel, but in 1911 was purchased by Henry Edwards Huntington (1850–1927), who hired architect Myron Hunt to transform the 25 acres into a lush manicured garden estate beneath the imposing San Gabriel Mountains. At the time, it was visible for ten miles in any direction, among the biggest resort hotels in the U.S. at the time, housing almost 400 suites on eight extravagantly-decorated floors. Huntington inherited a huge fortune from his uncle in 1900—he married his uncle's widow Arabella in 1913—and became the most successful railroad tycoon in the country, owner of the Southern Pacific Railroad and developer of the Los Angeles street railway system. He was one of the most important—and ruthless—businessmen in California at the turn of the century, perhaps best remembered for his massive 150-acre Huntington Gardens, not far from his hotel in nearby San Marino.
22. *Arcadia Journal*, March 16, 1918.
23. Wally worked with Turner in Chicago at Selig in the days before crewmembers' names were credited, but it is almost a certainty that Wally worked on dozens of Turner's films in Chicago and Edendale before going in front of the camera.
24. *Los Angeles Evening Herald Express*, March 31, 1943.
25. Farnsworth, Elizabeth, *Revisiting the 1918 Flu*, retrieved June 1, 2005, from http://www.pbs.org/newshour.
26. Retrieved June 1, 2005, from http://www.answers.com/topic/spanish-flu.
27. Retrieved June 1, 2005, from http://www.answers.com/topic/spanish-flu.
28. On September 1, 1920, Bobbie died of a self-inflicted bullet wound. Although the death was listed as "accidental," Hollywood has long-rumored that Bobby killed himself in a New York hotel room on the eve of the premiere of D.W. Griffith's *Way Down East* because of depression over his sister's death and at not being cast in the film, which premiered that same evening just down the street.
29. Jarvis, Everett G., *Final Curtain: Deaths of Noted Movie and T.V. Personalities*, page 3.
30. Leiber, Emily W., *Dark Lover: The Life and Death of Rudolph Valentino*, page 90.
31. Allan Forrest, real name Allan Forrest Fisher (1885–1941), was a well-known silent-screen character actor who appeared in small to medium-sized roles in almost 110 movies from 1913 to 1932. Two years after his divorce from Little, Forrest married Mary Pickford's younger sister Lottie.
32. *Atlanta Constitution*, May 8, 1918.
33. *Bridgeport Telegram*, June 26, 1918.
34. American Film Institute, Catalog of Film, retrieved July 8, 2005, from http://www.afi.com/members/catalog/AbbrView.aspx?s=1&Movie=17086.
35. Alice Duer Miller (1874–1942) was a famed early 20th century writer, newspaper columnist, satirist and poet, a suffragist, and member of New York's elite Algonquin Round Table. When her wealthy father lost all of his money in a bank failure, she worked her way through Barnard College selling short stories, essays and poems to national magazines. Famous for her *New York Tribune* column "Are Women People?" she spent much of the 1930s in Hollywood writing scenarios. *Less Than Kin* was the first of 32 films she wrote. Her best known story, 1940s "The White Cliffs," became the famous movie *The White Cliffs of Dover* (1944).

36. With the U.S. deeply involved in the War, von Seyffertitz used one of his Americanized wartime (non–German) pseudonyms, in this film appearing as G. Butler Clonblough.

37. American Film Institute, Catalog of Film, retrieved July 7, 2005, from http://www.afi.com/members/catalog/AbbrView.aspx?s=1&Movie=17188.

38. 1920 U.S. Federal Census, California, Los Angeles County, District 211, page 15-B.

39. William Desmond Taylor, who would later figure prominently in the biggest period of Hollywood scandal.

40. DeMille's hospital was supposed to cost $185,000, maybe $10,000,000 today, and was never realized.

41. *New York Telegraph,* June 9, 1918.

42. *Arcadia Journal,* June 15, 1918.

43. All quotes and descriptions in this section from McGaffey, Kenneth, "Travels with Wally," *Photoplay Magazine,* June, 1918.

44. Wally never really got over the leg injuries suffered when his horse fell on him in Santa Barbara; the nagging injury bothered him for the rest of his life.

45. Norman Selby (1872–1940) changed his boxing name to Charles "Kid" McCoy because Irish names were popular with fans in the late 1800s. The world-renowned middleweight champion won 86 of 98 fights and was best-known for his "corkscrew punch" in which he rotated his fist during impact to create cuts. After his 1916 retirement he came to Hollywood and did a few films. An affair with a wealthy married woman after his acting career flopped led to her filing for divorce, but Theresa Mors was shot to death in the apartment she shared with McCoy in August, 1924. He was charged with murder and injuring 3 others during the shooting spree but was found guilty of manslaughter after offering dramatic testimony that Mors killed herself and was not murdered, and that he was insane due to boxing injuries. Sentenced to 24 years, he served less than 7 before being released from jail, moving to Detroit, and working as a gardener at a Ford Motor plant. In 1940 he committed suicide with an overdose of sleeping pills. The phrase "the Real McCoy" is attributed to him. He often planted phony stories in the press that he was out of shape and not ready to fight; when a fit McCoy showed up, reporters asked, "Is this the real McCoy?"

46. *Los Angeles Times,* June 10, 1918.

47. *Motion Picture Classic,* September, 1918.

48. American Film Institute, Catalog of Film, retrieved April 14, 2005, from http://www.afi.com/members/catalog/AbbrView.aspx?s=1&Movie=2363.

49. James Crawford Van Trees (1890–1973), the son of writer Julia Crawford Ivers, had a prodigious resume of camera work on 170-plus films dating from 1916 to 1963, including silents like *The Road to Love* (1916) and *The Soul of Youth* (1920), sound films including the Cagney classic *Taxi* (1932) and the Marx Brothers' *A Night in Casablanca* (1946), and early television programs *The Many Loves of Dobie Gillis* (1959) and *The New Phil Silvers Show* (1963).

50. *Bridgeport Telegram,* November 27, 1918.

51. American Film Institute, Catalog of Film, retrieved April 14, 2005, from http://www.afi.com/members/catalog/AbbrView.aspx?s=1&Movie=17187.

52. Wakeman, John, *World Film Directors, Volume One, 1890–1945,* pages 159–163.

53. Bodeen, DeWitt, *From Hollywood,* page 101.

54. James Cruze (1884–1942) effectively left acting for directing with *Too Many Millions.* From that time until his death in 1938, Cruze directed almost 75 films, including most of Wally's best-known movies, three of Roscoe "Fatty" Arbuckle's 1920s final pre-scandal films, like *Gasoline Gus* and *Crazy to Marry* (both 1921), the original *Ruggles of Red Gap* (1923), and Gary Cooper's *If I Had a Million* (1932). He also produced another 40. He was married to actresses Betty Compson and Marguerite Snow, and died in Hollywood at the age of 57.

55. American Film Institute, Catalog of Film, retrieved April 16, 2005, from http://www.afi.com/members/catalog/AbbrView.aspx?s=1&Movie=17281.

56. Farrar, Geraldine, *Such Sweet Compulsion: The Autobiography of Geraldine Farrar,* page 144.

57. *London Daily Mail,* July 18, 1921.

58. Quoted from Leider, Emily W., *Dark Lover: The Life and Death of Rudolph Valentino,* page 90.

59. Edgar Franklin was a pseudonym for writer Edgar Franklin Stearns.

60. *Motion Picture Weekly,* January 25, 1919.

61. American Film Institute, Catalog of Film, retrieved April 18, 2005, from http://www.afi.com/members/catalog/AbbrView.aspx?s=1&Movie=17343.

62. *Atlanta Constitution,* January 19, 1919.

63. American Film Institute, Catalog of Film, retrieved April 18, 2005, from http://www.afi.com/members/catalog/AbbrView.aspx?s=1&Movie=17306.

Chapter 10

1. *Manitoba Free Press,* January 18, 1918. In an interesting coincidence, right below Wally's headline was a story of the Marguerite Clark film *Little Miss Hoover,* in which Hal Reid had a small role. Right next to that story was a short piece about a new contract offered to "Mrs. Jack Pickford," Olive Thomas, who would play a role, along with Wally, in the upcoming 1920s scandals that would tear the movie world apart.

2. *Reno Evening Gazette,* April 30, 1919.

3. *Motion Picture Magazine,* February, 1919.

4. *Lima News,* August 7, 1921.

5. *Daily Kennebec Journal,* November 28, 1917.

6. *Wichita Daily Times,* July 8, 1917.

7. St. Johns, Adela, "The Life of Wallace Reid: The Tragedy of an American Idol," *Liberty Magazine,* June 23, 1923, page 11.

8. The diamond necklace was worth $25,000, or about $1,500,000 today.

9. St. Johns, Adela Rogers, "The Life of Wallace Reid: The Tragedy of an American Idol," *Liberty Magazine,* June 23, 1923, page 11.

10. St. Johns, Adela Rogers, *Love, Laughter and Tears: My Hollywood Story,* page 139.

11. St. Johns, Adela, "The Life of Wallace Reid: The Tragedy of an American Idol," *Liberty Magazine,* July 7, 1923, page 65.

12. Reid, Dorothy Davenport, "The Real Wally," *Photoplay Magazine,* January, 1925, page 58.

13. *Photoplay Magazine,* June, 1918.

14. Ibid., page 58.

15. *Los Angeles Herald Examiner,* July 15, 1932.

16. Ibid., July 5, 1928, page 62.

17. Ibid., June 30, 1928, page 40.

18. Reid, Dorothy Davenport, "The Real Wally," *Photoplay Magazine,* January, 1925, page 100.

19. St. Johns, Adela Rogers, "The Life Story of Wallace Reid: The Tragedy of an American Idol," *Liberty Magazine,* July 7, 1928, page 65.

20. Reid, Dorothy Davenport, "The Real Wally," *Photoplay Magazine,* January, 1925, page 100.

21. St. Johns, Adela Rogers, "The Life Story of Wallace Reid: The Tragedy of an American Idol," *Liberty Magazine,* July 14, 1928, page 53.

22. Reid, Dorothy Davenport, "The Real Wally," *Photoplay Magazine,* January, 1925, page 58.

23. St. Johns, Adela Rogers, "The Life Story of Wallace Reid: The Tragedy of an American Idol," *Liberty Magazine,* July 7, 1928, page 65.

24. Reid, Bertha Westbrook, *Wallace Reid: His Life Story, by His Mother,* page 60.

25. *Motion Picture Magazine,* September, 1923.

26. St. Johns is referring to the DeLongpre Avenue mansion that Wally and Dorothy would not move into until 1921.
27. Reid, Dorothy Davenport, "The Real Wally," *Photoplay Magazine,* January, 1925, page 100.
28. St. Johns, Adela Rogers, "The Life of Wallace Reid: The Tragic Death of an American Idol," *Liberty Magazine,* June 30, 1928, page 60.
29. *Los Angeles Herald Examiner,* April 1, 1921.
30. Reid, Wallace, "Wallace Reid's Life Story: By Himself," *Picture Show Magazine,* January 21, 1922, page 17.
31. *Redlands Daily Review,* May 21, 1919.
32. Morgan's serial included three stories, "Junkpile Sweepstakes," "Undertaker's Handicap," and "Roaring Road," published on September 28, October 5, and October 12, 1918.
33. American Film Institute, Catalog of Film, retrieved May 18, 2005, from http://www.afi.com/members/catalog/AbbrView.aspx?s=1&Movie=18263.
34. Early race cars were two-seaters, with a mechanic sitting in the passenger seat, responsible for observing and monitoring engine performance, and, in the event of breakdowns, handling repairs.
35. *Woodland Daily Democrat,* January 24, 1920.
36. *Redlands Daily Review,* May 21, 1919.
37. *Atlanta Constitution,* June 12, 1919.
38. *Newark Advocate,* April 7, 1921.
39. *Photoplay Magazine,* April, 1919.
40. *Newark Advocate,* April 7, 1921.
41. *Motion Picture Magazine,* July, 1919.
42. Bodeen, DeWitt, *From Hollywood,* page 100.
43. Wanda Hawley appeared in almost 85 films from 1917 into the late 1920s, becoming a major star for Cecil B. DeMille, but with the advent of sound her career ended. During the 1930s she was reputed to be working in San Francisco as a high-priced call girl. She died in 1963 in Hollywood.
44. American Film Institute, Catalog of Film, retrieved April 27, 2005, from http://www.afi.com/members/catalog/AbbrView.aspx?s=1&Movie=17722.
45. Anna Q. Nilsson had confirmed roles in 197 films from 1911 to 1954, appearing in every genre with virtually ever major star of the movies. Her accent leveled her stardom, but not her work; she went to smaller roles in almost 50 sound films, like *They Died with Their Boots On* (1941), *The Farmer's Daughter* (1947), *Adam's Rib* (1949) and *An American in Paris* (1951). She died in 1974, the first Swede to earn a star on the Hollywood Walk of Fame.
46. Lovely Alice Taafe was born in 1899 in Vincennes, Indiana, and began appearing as an extra in films at the age of 15, working for New York Motion Picture Company and Thomas Ince, and appearing in almost 50 films from 1916 to 1928, renamed Alice Terry. Her career would no doubt have been much more remembered had she not married director Rex Ingram, whom she met on the set of her first film. They were married in 1921, and she worked only sparingly in the years following before leaving films for good in 1928. She and Ingram remained married until his death in 1950; she died 1987.
47. American Film Institute, Catalog of Film, retrieved May 1, 2005, from http://www.afi.com/members/catalog/AbbrView.aspx?s=1&Movie=17412.
48. *Los Angeles Examiner,* July 14, 1919.
49. Retrieved June 12, 2005, from http://www.hoopansn.gov.
50. Arcata General Plan, Chapter 5, Historic Element, retrieved June 11, 2005, from http://www.arcatacityhall.org/2020/2020/GPfinal/Chapter5/hist_emem.html.
51. Sumner Carson was an early Eureka-area businessman who owned numerous businesses in the area. His large home, built in 1914, was later the home of the local *Times-Standard* Newspaper.
52. *New York Telegraph,* March 7, 1919.
53. Reid, Dorothy Davenport, "The Real Wally," *Photoplay Magazine,* January, 1925, page 100.
54. *Moving Picture World,* March 15, 1919.
55. Reid, Wallace, "Wallace Reid's Life Story: By Himself," *Picture Show Magazine,* January 21, 1922, page 17.
56. St. Johns, Adela Rogers, "The Life Story of Wallace Reid: The Tragedy of an American Idol," *Liberty Magazine,* July 14, 1928, pages 52–53.
57. Morphine was commonly given to soldiers during the Civil War, not only for wounds but to stop the effects of dysentery via the drug's worst side effect: constipation. Some Civil War historians estimate that over 400,000 veterans returned home addicted to the drug.
58. Maxwell, Tonya, "200 Years After Discovery Morphine Still Eases Pain," *Chicago Tribune,* May 22, 2005.
59. *Atlanta Constitution,* August 28, 1921.
60. American Film Institute, Catalog of Film, retrieved May 1, 2005, from http://www.afi.com/members/catalog/AbbrView.aspx?s=1&Movie=18129.
61. *Picture-Play Magazine,* September, 1923.
62. Notes from original sheet music for *The Valley of the Giants,* August 22, 1919.
63. Oderman, Stuart, *Talking to the Piano Player,* page 68.
64. *Los Angeles Times,* December 16, 1922.
65. Oderman, Stuart, *Talking to the Piano Player,* page 68. Author's note: It would not have been strange at all for a doctor to be on-set with a supply of morphine. It was a common practice for studio doctors to administer morphine for the frequent on-set accidents that occurred at the time.
66. *Los Angeles Herald,* Dorothy Davenport Reid to William Parker, December 21, 1922.
67. *Ibid.*
68. *San Francisco Examiner,* December 31, 1922.
69. *Picture Show Magazine,* May 3, 1919.
70. *Ibid.,* page 101.
71. Wally's hip injury had previously re-emerged with the same symptoms—numbness and pain—after he was re-injured on the set of *The Woman God Forgot* the year before.
72. *San Francisco Examiner,* December 31, 1922.
73. *Ibid.,* December 31, 1922.
74. Cronyn, Thoreau, "The Truth About Hollywood," *New York Herald,* April 9, 1922.
75. Dorothy quotes this section from *San Francisco Examiner,* January 3, 1922.
76. Injured during his riding accident in Santa Barbara almost a decade earlier, the injury plagued him with pain even when he wasn't using drugs or alcohol.
77. Bodeen, DeWitt, *From Hollywood,* page 102.
78. Bodeen, DeWitt, *From Hollywood,* page 100.
79. American Film Institute, Catalog of Film, retrieved May 1, 2005, from http://www.afi.com/members/catalog/AbbrView.aspx?s=1&Movie=17432.
80. *Woodland Daily Democrat,* October 26, 1920.
81. *Ibid.,* October 26, 1920.
82. Heimer, Mel, *The Long Count,* retrieved June 16, 2005, from http://www.genetunney.com/long.html.
83. *Moving Picture World,* August 19, 1919.
84. The ever-present Scottish driving cap with which Wally was identified by this time.
85. American Film Institute, Catalog of Film, retrieved May 8, 2005, from http://www.afi.com/members/catalog/AbbrView.aspx?s=1&Movie=17382.
86. *Photoplay Magazine,* February, 1920.
87. *Chicago Daily Tribune,* August 13, 1919.
88. Earl, Harley, interview with Stanley Brams, Detroit, January, 1954.
89. Philadelphia-born Sam Wood left the real estate business to join DeMille's young company in 1917; *Double Speed* was the first of 80 films he directed in a career

that lasted until 1949. Among his notable silents were Jackie Coogan's *Peck's Bad Boy* (1921), Gloria Swanson's *Her Gilded Cage* (1922) and Agnes Ayres' *Bluff* (1924). He was allegedly brought in by Irving Thalberg to salvage *Queen Kelly* (1929) from Erich von Stroheim's extravagances, and later worked on the Marx Brothers' *A Night at the Opera* (1935) and *A Day at the Races* (1936), and classics like *Gone with the Wind* (1939), *Our Town* (1940), *The Pride of the Yankees* (1942) and *Heartbeat* (1946). He died in 1949 in Hollywood, still working.

90. Archival editing records at Paramount use the name "Effie," although most period newspaper reviews mention the name "Sallie" or "Sally."

91. American Film Institute, Catalog of Film, retrieved May 10, 2005, from http://www.afi.com/members/catalog/AbbrView.aspx?s=1&Movie=15728.

92. *Chronicle Telegram* (Elyria, Ohio), February 14, 1920.

93. *New York Telegraph*, December 7, 1919.

94. St. Johns, Adela Rogers, *Los Angeles Examiner*, February 21, 1922.

95. Reid, Bertha Westbrook, *Wallace Reid: His Life Story, by His Mother*, page 48.

Chapter 11

1. 1920 U.S. Federal Census, California, Los Angeles County, Los Angeles, District 106, page 10-A.

2. 1920 U.S. Federal Census, California, Los Angeles County, Los Angeles, District 156, page 9-B.

3. Ingrid Kerkhoff, *Contemporary American Drama (since 1980), History of American Theater* [online research site].

4. *Ibid.*, May 5, 1923.

5. Botnick, Vicki, American Film Institute, *The First Fifty Years of American Film*, Fathom Archives, Columbia University.

6. American Film Institute, Catalog of Film, retrieved May 14, 2005, from http://www.afi.com/members/catalog/AbbrView.aspx?s=1&Movie=17595.

7. St. Johns, Adela Rogers, "The Life of Wallace Reid: The Tragedy of an American Idol," *Liberty Magazine*, June 30, 1928, page 40.

8. American Film Institute, Catalog of Film, retrieved May 18, 2005, from http://www.afi.com/members/catalog/AbbrView.aspx?s=1&Movie=17592.

9. *Wichita Daily Times*, March 27, 1920.

10. Retrieved June 21, 2005, from http://www.classicimages.com/1998/september98.html.

11. Wanaker, Marc, correspondence with author.

12. *Moving Picture World*, April 17, 1920.

13. *Picturegoer Magazine*, March 8, 1920.

14. *Chronicle Telegram*, March 3, 1920.

15. Daniels starred in a number of famous Paramount films, like *The Wild Week* (1921), *The Speed Girl* (1921), *Monsieur Beaucaire* (1924) with Rudolph Valentino, and *Miss Brewster's Millions* (1926). With the advent of sound, she went over to RKO, where she starred in films like *Rio Rita* (1929) and *The Maltese Falcon* (1931). In the 1930s she and her husband toured successfully in England and took up residence in London, where she lived the rest of her life. She died there in 1971. During a late 1920s visit to Chicago, a thief broke into her hotel room and stole $5,000 worth of her jewelry. When Al Capone, one of her biggest fans, heard of the theft, the word went out that whoever had stolen the jewelry had 24 hours to return it. It showed up at the hotel the next morning.

16. American Film Institute, Catalog of Film, retrieved May 18, 2005, from http://www.afi.com/members/catalog/AbbrView.aspx?s=1&Movie=17714.

17. *Bedford Gazette*, February 18, 1921.

18. Bodeen, DeWitt, *From Hollywood*, page 100.

19. *Chillicothe Constitution Tribune*, June 29, 1921.

20. American Film Institute, Catalog of Film, retrieved May 20, 2005, from http://www.afi.com/members/catalog/AbbrView.aspx?s=1&Movie=17947.

21. 1920 U.S. Federal Census, New Jersey, Bergen County, Fort Lee, District 34, page 17B.

22. Reid, Wally, "Wallace Reid's Life History: By Himself," *Picture Show Magazine*, January 14, 1922, page 16.

23. St. Johns, Adela Rogers, "The Life Story of Wallace Reid: The Tragedy of an American Idol," *Liberty Magazine*, June 23, 1928, page 12.

24. *Moving Picture World*, May 29, 1920.

25. Over the years, like many streets in Los Angeles, DeLongpre has been "broken up" by building and now traverses Hollywood in fits and starts, with once-open blocks filled with buildings.

26. Early 1920s city directories list the Reid home as 1581 DeLongpre and the William S. Hart home as 1575, but by 1930 the numbering had been revised to 8327 and 8341, respectively. The former Hart home is now a public park, with the house and grounds open to the public.

27. Bodeen, DeWitt, *From Hollywood*, page 94.

28. *Indianapolis Star*, January 19, 1923.

29. *Photoplay Magazine*, March, 1925.

30. Reid, Bertha Westbrook, *Wallace Reid: His Life Story, by His Mother*, page 53.

31. Lamparski, Richard, *Lamparksi's Hidden Hollywood*, page 100.

32. American Film Institute, Catalog of Film, retrieved May 28, 2005, from http://www.afi.com/members/catalog/AbbrView.aspx?s=1&Movie=17963.

33. *Atlanta Constitution*, August 21, 1920.

34. St. Johns, Adela Rogers, "The Life Story of Wallace Reid: The Tragedy of an American Idol," *Liberty Magazine*, July 7, 1928, page 66.

35. *Ibid.*

36. Frazee is sometimes identified as William Frazee.

37. Released during September, 1920, in the U.S. and U.K. as *One Arabian Night*, *Sumurun* was a German-made film done by *Projektion-AG Union (PAGU) Studio for* First National that starred Negri and Ernst Lubitsch. The post-war German film industry flourished, and PAGU was one of the largest of the German filmmakers.

38. Kovan, Florice Whyte, *Rediscovering Ben Hecht: Selling the Celluloid Serpent*, page 36.

39. American Film Institute, Catalog of Film, retrieved June 1, 2005, from http://www.afi.com/members/catalog/AbbrView.aspx?s=1&Movie=17607.

40. *Manitoba Free Press*, February 16, 1921.

41. *Atlanta Constitution*, January 23, 1921.

42. All quotes this section referencing Howard Theater opening from *Atlanta Constitution*, December 12, 1920.

43. *Atlanta Constitution*, December 15, 1920.

44. American Film Institute, Catalog of Film, retrieved June 5, 2005, from http://www.afi.com/members/catalog/AbbrView.aspx?s=1&Movie=3255.

45. *Lima News*, April 18, 1921.

46. *Los Angeles Herald*, Dorothy Davenport Reid to William Parker, December 21, 1922

47. Dorothy's recollections in this section from *Los Angeles Herald*, Dorothy Davenport Reid to William Parker, December 21, 1922.

48. Dorothy recollections this section from *Los Angeles Herald*, Dorothy Davenport Reid to William Parker, December 21, 1922.

49. Louvish, Simon, *Keystone: The Life and Clowns of Mack Sennett*, page 156.

50. Edmonds, Andy, *Frame-Up!: The Untold Story of Roscoe "Fatty" Arbuckle*, p. 143.

51. Fussell, Betty Harper, *Mabel: Hollywood's First I-Don't-Care Girl*, p. 126.

52. *Photoplay Magazine*, April, 1927, page 37.

53. Brownlow, Kevin, *The Parade's Gone By*, page 41.

54. 1920 U.S. Federal Census, Los Angeles, Los Angeles, District 64, page 2-B.

55. Beauchamp, Cari, *Without Lying Down: Francis Marion and the Powerful Women of Early Hollywood*, page 102.
56. Eyman, Scott, *Mary Pickford: America's Sweetheart*, page 98.
57. *Motion Picture Weekly*, November 22, 1920.
58. Olive Thomas' ghost is said to haunt the New Amsterdam Theater in New York City to this day.
59. *Variety*, November 25, 1920.
60. *Los Angeles Herald*, Dorothy Davenport Reid to William Parker, December 21, 1922.
61. *Atlanta Constitution*, December 20, 1920.
62. Reid, Dorothy Davenport, "The Real Wally," *Photoplay Magazine*, January, 1925.
63. Bodeen, DeWitt, *From Hollywood*, page 101.

Chapter 12

1. It was Urson's first directing job; he was a career cameraman who shot 8 Wally movies, like *The Valley of the Giants* and *Hawthorne of the U.S.A.*
2. American Film Institute, Catalog of Film, retrieved Jun 12, 2005, from http://www.afi.com/members/catalog/AbbrView.aspx?s=1&Movie=10429.
3. *Fayetteville Daily Democrat*, September 19, 1921.
4. *San Francisco Examiner*, January 4, 1922.
5. *Atlanta Constitution*, February 27, 1921.
6. *Motion Picture Magazine*, February, 1921.
7. Wally quotes in this section from Reid, Wallace, "How to Hold a Wife," *Photoplay*, January, 1921.
8. Dorothy quotes in this section from Reid, Dorothy Davenport, "Coming Back at Husband," February, 1921.
9. Kingsley, Grace, *Los Angeles Times*, February 14, 1921.
10. *Moving Picture World*, March 19, 1921.
11. *Atlanta Constitution*, February 5, 1921.
12. *Woodland Daily Democrat*, November 1, 1921.
13. Herbert K. Somborn owned the famous Brown Derby Restaurant from its 1926 founding until his 1934 death. He opened the restaurant after writer Wilson Mizner dared him, "If you know anything about food, you can sell it out of a hat."
14. For several years after Swanson's arrival at Paramount all of her films were directed by former DeMille assistant Sam Wood.
15. Kovan, Florice Whyte, *Rediscovering Ben Hecht: Selling the Celluloid Serpent*, page 36.
16. American Film Institute, Catalog of Film, retrieved June 30, 2005, from http://www.afi.com/members/catalog/AbbrView.aspx?s=1&Movie=2508.
17. *Motion Picture Classic*, September, 1921.
18. Pierce, David, *Costs and Grosses for the Early Films of Cecil B. DeMille*, retrieved June 18, 2005, from http://www.cinemaweb.com/silentfilm/bookshelf/10_dwp_3.htm.
19. *Atlanta Constitution*, August 21, 1921.
20. Swanson, Gloria, *Swanson on Swanson*, quoted from www.silentsaregolden.com/featureholder3.html.
21. The article was written under the pseudonym Cal York, which she used when writing about masculine topics like automobile racing.
22. *Moving Picture World*, March 26, 1921.
23. The Vancouver Courier.com, retrieved June 18, 2005, from http://www.vancourier.com/issues05/042105.
24. *Los Angeles Examiner*, March 16, 1921.
25. *Lima Press*, February 26, 1921.
26. Roberts replaced Charles Ogle, who played Patrick MacMurran in the original *What's Your Hurry*, no doubt at the direction of Lasky, who knew that Wally worked better with his good friends in the cast.
27. American Film Institute, Catalog of Film, retrieved July 1, 2005, from http://www.afi.com/members/catalog/AbbrView.aspx?s=1&Movie=12771.
28. Some archives note a release date of July 10th, but period newspaper advertisements contradict that timing.
29. The American Film Institute archives assign this role to "Frank Geldert." Those archives also list Charles Geldart as "Charles Geldert."
30. American Film Institute, Catalog of Film, retrieved July 5, 2005, from http://www.afi.com/members/catalog/AbbrView.aspx?s=1&Movie=9648.
31. *Atlanta Constitution*, April 24, 1921.
32. *Photoplay Magazine*, May, 1921.
33. Even during prohibition, illegal alcohol flowed freely almost everywhere.
34. *Los Angeles Herald*, May 21, 1921.
35. *Ibid.*, Dorothy Davenport Reid to William Parker, December 21, 1922.
36. St. Johns quotes this section from St. Johns, Adela Rogers, "The Life Story of Wallace Reid: The Tragedy of an American Idol," *Liberty Magazine*, July 14, 1928, pages 52–54.
37. *New York Telegraph*, May 22, 1921.
38. *Ibid.*, May 22, 1921.
39. Reid, Bertha Westbrook, *Wallace Reid: His Life Story, by His Mother*, page 64.
40. Kenneth Webb was a director, writer and composer who began with Vitagraph in 1918 directing Agnes Ayres films in 1918–1919. He worked for Lasky's Realart brand directing stars like Alice Brady, Rod La Rocque, Constance Binney, and Lionel Barrymore, in films like *The Stolen Kiss*, *The Devil's Garden* (both 1920) and *The Great Adventure* (1921). He also wrote the adaptation and music for the RKO classic *The Gay Divorcee* which starred Fred Astaire, Ginger Rogers and Alice Brady. He left the movies in the mid 1930s and died in 1966.
41. *New York Telegraph*, May 20, 1921.
42. *Mansfield News*, May 22, 1921.
43. *New York Telegraph*, May 22, 1921.
44. New York, 1891.
45. Elsie Ferguson was born in New York in 1883, the daughter of a prominent lawyer and a child of wealth and privilege; she grew into something of an elitist and a diva in the truest sense (probably why Wally so disliked her). She was known as the "Aristocrat of the Screen," and her successful 30-year stage career included private performances for Stanford White, who was later murdered by the husband of Evelyn Nesbitt, another actress who gave "private performances" for White. Ferguson was drawn into the 1906 scandal because of the relationship. Entering films in 1917, she was signed by Lasky to a four-picture contract in 1921; her role in *Forever* was considered her finest performance in a career that included just 25 films from 1917 to 1925. She is best known for her Paramount films, which included the William Desmond Taylor–directed *Sacred and Profane Love* (1921) and *Outcast* (both 1921). Only a single Ferguson silent film remains, a copy of her 1919 film *Witness for the Defense*, which remains in the Gosfilmofond archive in Moscow. She left films in 1930 and died in Connecticut in 1966.
46. The children's roles were played by Charles Eaton (Gogo) and Nell Roy Buck (Mimsi).
47. American Film Institute, Catalog of Film, retrieved July 30, 2005, from http://www.afi.com/members/catalog/AbbrView.aspx?s=1&Movie=9197.
48. *Lima News*, June 23, 1921.
49. *Los Angeles Times*, October 15, 1921.
50. *Atlanta Constitution*, July 3, 1921.
51. *Wichita Daily Times*, October 30, 1921.
52. *Ibid.*, October 30, 1921.
53. St. Johns, Adela Rogers, "The Life Story of Wallace Reid: The Tragedy of an American Idol," *Liberty Magazine*, June 28, 1928, page 13.
54. Correspondence, DeWitt Bodeen to Dorothy Davenport Reid, April 5, 1966, AMPAS.
55. *Hollywood Citizen News*, September 30, 1946.
56. Beauchamp, Cari, *Without Lying Down: Francis*

Marion and the Powerful Women of Early Hollywood, page 195.
57. *Mansfield News,* June 26, 1921.
58. Reid, Bertha Westbrook, *Wallace Reid: His Life Story, by His Mother,* page 83.
59. *Los Angeles Evening Herald,* December 21, 1922.
60. All Dorothy quotes this section from *Los Angeles Herald,* Dorothy Davenport Reid to William Parker, December 21, 1922.
61. All St. Johns quotes this section from St. Johns, Adela Rogers, "The Life Story of Wallace Reid: The Tragedy of an American Idol," *Liberty Magazine,* July 14, 1928, pages 51–53.
62. Reid, Dorothy Davenport, *San Francisco Examiner,* December 31, 1922-January 5, 1923.
63. *Los Angeles Herald,* Dorothy Davenport Reid to William Parker, December 21, 1922.
64. *Ibid.,* December 20, 1922.
65. Reid, Dorothy Davenport, *San Francisco Examiner,* December 31, 1922-January 5, 1923.
66. According to a short article in the *Lima News,* the filming was completed on August 22, 1921.
67. Gloria Wood was less than 2 years of age when she appeared in *Don't Tell Everything,* after debuting in the earlier 1921 Jackie Coogan film *Peck's Bad Boy.* She would reappear in the movies in the 1940s as Katherine (or K.T.) Stevens, and appeared in several dozen films and dozens of television series, including *I Love Lucy, Alfred Hitchcock Presents, The Rifleman,* and many others. She died in 1994.
68. American Film Institute, Catalog of Film, retrieved July 18, 2005, from http://www.afi.com/members/catalog/AbbrView.aspx?s=1&Movie=3820.
69. American Film Institute, Catalog of Film, retrieved July 21, 2005, from http://www.afi.com/members/catalog/AbbrView.aspx?s=1&Movie=11636.
70. Lasky, Jesse L., *I Blow My Own Horn,* page 154.
71. *Ibid.,* page 154.
72. Arbuckle's agent and manager Lou Anger.
73. Unless otherwise noted, all quotes this section from Guild, Leo, *The Fatty Arbuckle Case,* pages 48–68.
74. Fussell, Betty Harper, *Mabel: Hollywood's First I-Don't-Care Girl,* p. 139.
75. Giroux, Robert, *A Deed of Death: The Story Behind the Unsolved Murder of Hollywood Director William Desmond Taylor,* p. 37.
76. *Atlanta Constitution,* September 19, 1921.
77. Fussell, Betty Harper, *Mabel: Hollywood's First I-Don't-Care Girl,* page 138.
78. *Ibid.,* page 39.
79. Edmonds, Andy, *Frame-Up!: The Untold Story of Roscoe "Fatty" Arbuckle,* p. 157.
80. Botnick, Vicki, American Film Institute; The First Fifty Years of American Film, Fathom Archives, Columbia University.
81. Unless otherwise noted, quotes concerning this alleged party from *New York American,* September 16, 1921.
82. *Variety,* September 23, 1921.
83. *Photoplay Magazine,* October, 1921.
84. *Atlanta Constitution,* October 2, 1921.
85. *Washington Post,* January 19, 1923.
86. Correspondence, DeWitt Bodeen to Dorothy Davenport Reid, June 5, 1966, AMPAS.
87. *Indiana Evening Gazette,* January 19, 1923.
88. *Photoplay Magazine,* September, 1921.
89. *Ibid.*
90. *Chillicothe Constitution,* October 7, 1922.
91. New York, 1922.
92. American Film Institute, Catalog of Film, retrieved July 20, 2005, from http://www.afi.com/members/catalog/AbbrView.aspx?s=1&Movie=13490.
93. Norman Selby (1872–1940) became Charles "Kid" McCoy because Irish names were popular with boxing fans in the 1890s. He was a world-famous middleweight champion who won 86 of 98 fights, known for a "corkscrew punch" where he rotated his fist during impact to create cuts. After his 1916 retirement he appeared in a few films before wealthy, married Theresa Mars left her husband and moved into McCoy's apartment in 1923. In August, 1924, McCoy shot her to death and wounded 3 neighbors but was convicted of manslaughter after testifying that Mors killed *herself* and that he was insane due to boxing injuries. He served 7 of his 24-year sentence, was paroled and moved to Detroit where he worked as a gardener at the Detroit Ford Motor plant. In 1940 he committed suicide with an overdose of pills. The phrase "the Real McCoy" came from his habit of planting phony stories that he was out of shape and not ready to fight; when he showed up fit, reporters asked, "Is this the real McCoy?"
94. *Appleton Post Crescent,* May 4, 1922.
95. *Los Angeles Times,* November 20, 1921.
96. *Lima News,* February 10, 1922.
97. *Chillicothe Constitution,* October 28, 1922.
98. American Film Institute, Catalog of Film, retrieved August 1, 2005, from http://www.afi.com/members/catalog/AbbrView.aspx?s=1&Movie=2484.
99. Advertisement, Richelieu Theater, Bedford, Pennsylvania, Bedford Gazette, February 23, 1923.
100. *Los Angeles Examiner,* February 17, 1922.
101. Reid, Bertha Westbrook, *Wallace Reid: His Life Story, by His Mother,* page 74.

Chapter 13

1. *Picture Show Magazine,* January 21, 1922.
2. Most filmographies list *The Dictator* immediately after *Across the Continent,* followed by *Nice People,* since *Dictator* was released on June 25th and *Nice People* in July. But according to Bertha Reid's record of her visit, from January to March, 1922, Wally filmed *Across the Continent,* followed by *Nice People,* and then *The Dictator.* He also only had a single day off between *Nice People* and *The Dictator.*
3. Coincidently, Landis was brought in after a scandal, the 1919 "Black Sox" World Series scandal.
4. Fussell, Betty Harper, *Mabel: Hollywood's First I-Don't-Care Girl,* page 145.
5. Lasky, Jesse L., *I Blow My Own Horn,* page 154.
6. Much of the information in the Taylor section was found in Fitzpatrick, Sydney, *A Deed of Death* and the flagship website devoted to the murder, Bruce Long's amazing www.taylorology.com.
7. Giroux, Robert, *A Deed of Death: The Story Behind the Unsolved Murder of Hollywood Director William Desmond Taylor,* page 13.
8. *Ibid.,* page 47.
9. Kirkpatrick, Sidney, *A Cast of Killers,* page 170.
10. *L.A. Examiner,* March 27, 1926.
11. Giroux, Robert, *A Deed of Death: The Story Behind the Unsolved Murder of Hollywood Director William Desmond Taylor,* page 128.
12. *Chicago News,* March 24, 1926, and *Chicago Herald Examiner,* March 25, 1926.
13. *Ibid.,* page 254.
14. Smith, Wallace, *The Chicago American,* February 9, 1922.
15. *Boston Advertiser,* February 20, 1920.
16. *Ibid.,* February 22, 1922.
17. *Movie Weekly Magazine,* March 4, 1922.
18. *Boston Advertiser,* February 20, 1922.
19. *Movie Weekly,* March, 1922.
20. *Kansas City Star,* February 7, 1922.
21. Cronyn, Thoreau, "The Truth About Hollywood," *New York Herald,* April 9, 1922.
22. "What Do They Earn Today?" *Photoplay Magazine,* September 1923.
23. Cronyn, Thoreau, "The Truth About Hollywood," *New York Herald,* April 9, 1922.

24. *Ibid.*
25. Doherty, Edward, *New York News*, February 12, 1922.
26. Lambert, Gavin, *Norma Shearer*, page 48.
27. *Los Angeles Evening Herald*, January 21, 1922.
28. Flamini, Roland, *Thalberg: The Last Tycoon and the World of M-G-M*, page 85.
29. Unless otherwise noted, all Jesse Lasky quotes this section from Lasky, Jesse L., *I Blow My Own Horn*, pages 157–158.
30. Carr, Harry, *Los Angeles Times*, December 24, 1922.
31. Lasky, Jesse L., *I Blow My Own Horn*, page 159. Lasky wrote that Starr stayed with Wally for two weeks, but his report to Lasky was dated March 24, indicating he stayed only one week.
32. American Film Institute, Catalog of Film, retrieved August 2, 2005, from http://www.afi.com/members/catalog/AbbrView.aspx?s=1&Movie=10964.
33. *Los Angeles Times*, October 1, 1922.
34. American Film Institute, Catalog of Film, retrieved August 2, 2005, from http://www.afi.com/members/catalog/AbbrView.aspx?s=1&Movie=3762.
35. Cronyn, Thoreau, *New York Herald*, March 19-April 2, 1922.
36. Unless otherwise noted, all descriptions this section from Reid, Bertha Westbrook, *Wallace Reid: His Life Story, by His Mother*, page 79.
37. *The Ghost Breaker* was Arlen's third film; he went on to appear in over 150 films, including *The Virginian* (1929), *Island of Lost Souls* (1933), and a dozen World War II pictures, like *Torpedo Boat* and *Wildcat* (both 1942), and *Aerial Gunner* (1943). He became a major star and died in 1976.
38. Mervyn LeRoy appeared in only 7 films before turning to directing and producing, and became one of the most successful directors in movie history. Among his 77 films were classics like *Little Caesar* and *Tugboat Annie* (both 1933), *The Wizard of Oz* (1939), *East Side, West Side* (1949), and *Quo Vadis* (1951). LeRoy directed 13 actors in Oscar-winning performances, including Paul Muni, Greer Garson, Ronald Colman, and Walter Pidgeon. He died in 1987.
39. George O'Brien appeared in 84 films from 1922 to 1964, including dozens of westerns like *Hard Rock Harrigan* (1935), *The Painted Desert* (1938) and *Fort Apache* (1948). He was married to actress Marguerite Churchill and died in 1985.
40. American Film Institute, Catalog of Film, retrieved August 2, 2005, from http://www.afi.com/members/catalog/AbbrView.aspx?s=1&Movie=9329.
41. *Appleton Post Crescent*, June 20, 1923.
42. *Chicago Daily Tribune*, November 8, 1922.
43. *Washington Post*, March 16, 1922.
44. *Los Angeles Evening Herald*, April 11, 1922.
45. *Newark Advocate*, April 12, 1922.
46. *Ibid.*, April 15, 1922.
47. *Bridgeport Telegram*, May 12, 1922.
48. *Decatur Review*, May 15, 1922.
49. St. Johns, Adela Rogers, "The Life Story of Wallace Reid: The Tragedy of an American Idol," *Liberty Magazine*, July 14, 1928, page 53.
50. Guild, Leo, *The Fatty Arbuckle Case*, page 132.
51. Transcript, the State of California vs. Roscoe Arbuckle.
52. Letter from Minta Durfee Arbuckle, author's collection.
53. Unless otherwise noted, all quotes this section from Roberts, Ed, *The Sins of Hollywood: An Expose of Movie Vice; A Group of Stories of Actual Happenings Reported and Written by a Hollywood Newspaper Man*.
54. "Revues and other Vanities: The Commodification of Fantasy in the 1920s," retrieved June 16, 2005, from http://www.assumption.edu/ahc/Vanities.

55. *Picture-Play Magazine*, July, 1922.
56. *Woodland Daily Democrat*, March 8, 1923.
57. American Film Institute, Catalog of Film, retrieved August 5, 2005, from http://www.afi.com/members/catalog/AbbrView.aspx?s=1&Movie=3329.
58. *Bridgeport Telegram*, December 11, 1922.
59. American Film Institute, Catalog of Film, retrieved April 22, 2005, from http://www.afi.com/members/catalog/AbbrView.aspx?s=1&Movie=10971.
60. *Moving Picture World*, July 30, 1921.
61. The Canadian Academy of Homeopathy, "To Master a Discipline, We Have to Start from Its Roots Upwards: Interview with André Saine, N.D., F.C.A.H.," Revised, March 2001, retrieved August 8, 2005, from http://www.homeopathy.ca/articles/1_to_master.html.
62. Bryant, C.P., read before the Bureau of Pediatrics, I.H.A., July, 4, 1950, quoted in *The Homeopathic Recorder*, January, 1951, Vol. LXVI, No. 7 Retrieved from http://www.homeoint.org/hompath/articles.
63. Asher, Cash, *Bacteria, Inc.: In Which Is Told the Story of New York's Half Million Dollar Bedbug* (pamphlet), Boston, Bruce Humphries, Inc., 1955, retrieved August 1, 2005, from http://vaclib.org/basic/bacteria.
64. Bryant's treatment notes were found at the Academy of Motion Picture Arts and Sciences, Herrick Library, Special Collections Department, William Wallace Reid, Jr. Collection, Folder 4.
65. AMPAS, William Wallace Reid, Jr. Collection, "CREBO: The Scientific Treatment of NARCOTIC DRUG ADDICTION-DISEASE."
66. At the Academy of Motion Pictures Arts and Sciences, Los Angeles.
67. *Los Angeles Times*, August 26, 1922.
68. *New York Times*, August 26, 1922.
69. Bodeen, DeWitt, *From Hollywood*, page 101. Italics added for emphasis.
70. Reid, Bertha Westbrook, *Wallace Reid; His Life Story, by His Mother*, page 73.
71. *Los Angeles Times*, August 25, 1922.
72. *San Francisco Examiner*, January 5, 1923.
73. *The Fighting Chance* (1920), *Every Woman's Problem* (1921), and *The Masked Avenger* (1922).
74. Reid, Bertha Westbrook, *Wallace Reid: His Life Story, by His Mother*, page 84.
75. *Ibid.*, page 85.
76. *Movie Weekly*, August 18, 1923.
77. State of California, County of Los Angeles, Letters of Guardianship, Petition for Appointment of Guardian, William Wallace Reid, Jr. and Betty Anna Reid, March 6, 1923.
78. Reid, Dorothy Davenport, "The Real Wally," *Photoplay Magazine*, January, 1925.

Chapter 14

1. Unless otherwise noted, all quotes this section from *Los Angeles Herald*, Dorothy Davenport Reid to William Parker, December 21, 1922.
2. St. Johns, Adela Rogers, "The Life Story of Wallace Reid: The Tragedy of an American Idol," *Liberty Magazine*, July 11, 1928.
3. *Indianapolis Star*, January 1, 1923.
4. St. Johns, Adela Rogers, "The Life Story of Wallace Reid: The Tragedy of an American Idol," *Liberty Magazine*, June 23, 1928, page 11.
5. *Ibid.*, June 30, 1928, page 54.
6. *Los Angeles Times*, December 19, 1922.
7. Paramount remade the film in 1931, starring Charles Ruggles, Tamara Geva and Margaret Dumont.
8. American Film Institute, Catalog of Film, retrieved April 22, 2005, from http://www.afi.com/members/catalog/AbbrView.aspx?s=1&Movie=1722.
9. Quoted from Mavromatis, Kally and Glen Pringle, *Wallace Reid: Silent Star of December, 1997*, retrieved

March 2, 2005. from http://www.csse.monash.edu.au/~pringle/silent/ssotm/Dec97.
  10. Hansen, Juanita, *New York American*, March 29-April 4, 1923.
  11. An ounce of morphine cost anywhere from $50 to $80 at the time.
  12. Correspondence, DeWitt Bodeen to Dorothy Davenport Reid, June 5, 1966, AMPAS.
  13. *Los Angeles Herald*, Dorothy Davenport Reid to William Parker, December 18, 1922.
  14. *Bridgeport Telegram*, October 21, 1922.
  15. *Los Angeles Herald Examiner*, October 21, 1922.
  16. *Los Angeles Times*, October 21, 1922.
  17. *Moving Picture World*, October 19, 1921.
  18. *Chicago Daily Tribune*, November 8, 1922.
  19. *Lima News*, November 16, 1922.
  20. *Los Angeles Herald*, December 18, 1922.
  21. Reid, Bertha Westbrook, *Wallace Reid: His Life, by His Mother*, page 87.
  22. *Washington Post*, January 19, 1923.
  23. Reid, Bertha Westbrook, *Wallace Reid: His Life, by His Mother*, page 89.
  24. *Woodland Daily Democrat*, November 3, 1922.
  25. *San Francisco Examiner*, January 3, 1923.
  26. In 1922, Banksia Place was surrounded by bungalows and small apartments. Director Woodridge Strong Van Dyke and actor Martin Bowditch lived in the next block at 5502, and Sennett star Ben Turpin owned an apartment building at 5560; to save money, he lived there, doing all of the janitorial and repair work himself, and took the trolley to the studio every day.
  27. Oderman, Stuart, *Talking to the Piano Player*, page 69.
  28. *Chicago Daily Tribune*, January 19, 1923.
  29. *Iowa City Press Citizen*, December 7, 1922.
  30. *New York Times*, December 14, 1922.
  31. *Los Angeles Herald Examiner*, December 18, 1922.
  32. Oderman, Stuart, *Talking to the Piano Player*, page 69.
  33. St. Johns, Adela Rogers, "The Life Story of Wallace Reid: The Tragedy of an American Idol," *Liberty Magazine*, July 11, 1928.
  34. *Los Angeles Times*, December 19, 1922.
  35. *Ibid.*, December 17, 1922.
  36. *Ibid.*, December 24, 1922.
  37. *Los Angeles Evening Herald Express*, December 14, 1922.
  38. *Chicago Daily Tribune*, December 16, 1922.
  39. Unless otherwise noted, all quotes this section from *Los Angeles Herald*, Dorothy Davenport Reid to William Parker, December 18–24, 1922
  40. *New York Times*, December 17, 1922.
  41. *Chicago Tribune*, December 17, 1922.
  42. *Chicago Daily Tribune*, December 17, 1922.
  43. *Ibid.*
  44. *Chicago Daily Tribune*, December 17, 1922.
  45. Oursler, Fulton, *Movie Weekly*, January 27, 1922.
  46. Kingsley, Grace, *Movie Weekly*, January 27, 1922.
  47. *Movie Weekly*, January 27, 1922.
  48. All Dorothy quotes this section from Reid, Dorothy Davenport, *San Francisco Examiner*, December 31, 1922-January 5, 1923.
  49. Reid, Bertha Westbrook, *Wallace Reid: His Life Story, by His Mother*, page 93.
  50. St. Johns, Adela Rogers, *Love, Laughter and Tears: My Hollywood Story*, page 144.
  51. *Chicago Daily Tribune*, December 16, 1922.
  52. Manuscript notes, Correspondence, DeWitt Bodeen to Dorothy Davenport Reid, June 5, 1966, AMPAS.
  53. *Middlesboro Daily News*, December 20, 1922.
  54. *Fort Wayne Journal Gazette*, December 24, 1922.
  55. *Bridgeport Telegram*, December 19, 1922.
  56. *New York Times*, December 19, 1922.
  57. *Indiana Evening Gazette*, December 19, 1922.
  58. *Washington Post*, December 22, 1923.
  59. *Indiana Evening Gazette*, December 19, 1922.
  60. *Los Angeles Herald Examiner*, December 23, 1922.
  61. Reid, Bertha Westbrook, *Wallace Reid: His Life Story, by His Mother*, page 75.
  62. *Los Angeles Times*, December 22, 1922.
  63. *Lima News*, December 22, 1922.
  64. *Chicago Daily Tribune*, January 2, 1922.
  65. *Newark Star*, February 2, 1922.
  66. Reid, Bertha Westbrook, *Wallace Reid: His Life Story, by His Mother*, page 93.
  67. Louis Weadock, *Los Angeles Examiner*, 19 January 1923.
  68. Correspondence, DeWitt Bodeen to Dorothy Davenport Reid, April 5, 1966, AMPAS.
  69. *Clearfield Progress*, January 19, 1923.
  70. County of Los Angeles, Registrar-Recorder/County Clerk, Death Certificate, no. 617, January 18, 1923.
  71. *Chicago Daily Tribune*, January 19, 1923.
  72. *Los Angeles Times*, January 19, 1923.
  73. Correspondence, DeWitt Bodeen to Dorothy Davenport Reid, April 5, 1966, AMPAS.
  74. *Chicago Daily Tribune*, January 19, 1923.
  75. *Nevada State Journal*, January 20, 1923.
  76. *Indianapolis Star*, January 19, 1923.
  77. *Indiana Evening Gazette*, January 19, 1923.
  78. *Los Angeles Evening Herald Examiner*, January 21, 1923.
  79. *New York American*, January 20, 1923.
  80. *Los Angeles Examiner*, January 20, 1923.
  81. *Chicago Daily Tribune*, January 21, 1923.
  82. Dodd was known as "the Chaplain of the movies," and St. Mary's of the Angels "the little church around the corner."
  83. *Los Angeles Examiner*, January 19, 1923.
  84. Hollywood Memorial Park was the cemetery of choice for the movie crowd during the early 1920s. Wally was one of the first major stars interred at the new Forest Lawn Memorial Park in Glendale. It became the biggest and best-known movie star graveyard in California.
  85. *Los Angeles Evening Herald Examiner*, January 19, 1923.
  86. Zollo, Paul, *Hollywood Remembered: An Oral History of Its Golden Age*, page 355.
  87. *Los Angeles Evening Herald Examiner*, January 20, 1923.
  88. Academy of Motion Picture Arts and Sciences, Herrick Library, Special Collections Department, William Wallace Reid, Jr. Collection, Folder 7.
  89. *Los Angeles Times*, January 21, 1923.

Chapter 15

  1. Quirk, James R., "Speaking of Pictures," *Photoplay Magazine*, March, 1925.
  2. St. Johns, Adela Rogers, *Love, Laughter and Tears: My Hollywood Story*, page 145.
  3. *Woodland Daily Democrat*, January 19, 1923.
  4. *Chicago Daily Tribune*, January 28, 1923.
  5. *Photoplay Magazine*, March, 1923.
  6. *Picture-Play Magazine*, September, 1923.
  7. *Picturegoer Magazine*, February, 1923.
  8. *Washington Post*, January 28, 1923.
  9. *Motion Picture Magazine*, January, 1924.
  10. *Los Angeles Evening Herald Express*, February 3, 1923.
  11. *Variety*, November 25, 1920.
  12. Bureau of the Census, 1920 Federal Census, Map 198, Page 4-A.
  13. *Los Angeles Daily Herald*, June 17, 1923.
  14. *Woodland Daily Democrat*, March 31, 1923.

15. *Decatur Review*, January 30, 1923.
16. *Nevada State Journal*, February 4, 1923.
17. *Chicago Daily Tribune*, January 29, 1923.
18. *Motion Picture Magazine*, September, 1923.
19. *Chicago Daily Tribune*, January 19, 1923.
20. *Indianapolis Star*, January 19, 1923.
21. Petition for Letters of Administration, William Wallace Reid, deceased, February 2, 1923.
22. Petition for Appointment of Guardian, No. 60,383, February 2, 1923.
23. Letters of Guardianship, No. 60,383, Book 18, Page 168, March 6, 1923.
24. Letters of Administration, No. 60,384, March 6, 1923.
25. *Reno State Journal*, February 3, 1923.
26. Inventory and Appraisement, Estate of William Wallace Reid, April 27, 1923.
27. Account Current and Report of Guardian, No. 60,383, August 14, 1924.
28. Settlement of Final Account and Distribution, Estate of William Wallace Reid, June 16, 1925. For a relative value of the costs noted, multiply the amounts by 23.
29. Headlines from *Washington Post*, March 29, 1921, *Mansfield News*, February 15, 1923, and *Appleton Post Crescent*, February 12, 1923.
30. *Chicago Daily Tribune*, February 14, 1923.
31. *Los Angeles Evening Herald Express*, March 23, 1923.
32. *Chicago Daily Tribune*, March 6, 1923.
33. *Washington Post*, February 15, 1923.
34. *Los Angeles Herald Examiner*, January 31, 1923; reference to it being a "condition" from *Indianapolis Star*, May 13, 1923.
35. *Chillicothe Constitution Tribune*, April 20, 1923.
36. The entire twelve-member Board of Dorothy's Anti-Narcotic League of Los Angeles appeared in the film.
37. *Bridgeport Telegram*, October 6, 1923.
38. *Los Angeles Evening Herald*, July 18, 1923.
39. *Bridgeport Telegram*, October 9, 1923.
40. *New York Times*, May 3, 1923.
41. *Washington Post*, May 5, 1923.
42. *Los Angeles Evening Herald Express*, July 15, 1923.
43. Headlines from *Atlanta Constitution*, July 23, 1923, *Appleton Post Crescent*, July 1, 1923, and the *New York Times*, July 7, 1923.
44. *Chillicothe Evening Gazette*, October 5, 1923.
45. *Bridgeport Telegram*, October 9, 1923.
46. Academy of Motion Picture Arts and Sciences, Herrick Library, Special Collections Department, William Wallace Reid, Jr. Collection, Folder 7.
47. *Picture-Play Magazine*, December, 1925.
48. Quirk, James R., "Speaking of Pictures," *Photoplay Magazine*, March, 1925.
49. *Los Angeles Evening Herald Express*, March 2, 1923.
50. *Washington Post*, July 23, 1923.
51. *Chillicothe Constitution*, May 23, 1925.
52. *Photoplay Magazine*, July, 1926.
53. *Bright Lights Film Journal*, September, 1996, Vol. 17.
54. *Long Beach Independent*, July 31, 1939.
55. Davis, Chris, correspondence with author, March, 2006.
56. *Los Angeles Times*, March 7, 1944.
57. 1930 U.S. Federal Census, California, Los Angeles, Beverly Hills, District 831, sheet 21B.
58. Brownlow, Kevin, *Behind the Mask of Innocence: Sex, Violence, Prejudice, Crime: Films of Social Conscience in the Silent Era*, page 175.
59. Account Current and Report of Guardian, and Petition for Exoneration of Bond, No. 60383, January 22, 1934.
60. *Los Angeles Times*, August 12, 1930.
61. *Chicago Tribune*, September 22, 1933.
62. *Los Angeles Herald Examiner*, December 8, 1942.
63. Correspondence, DeWitt Bodeen to Dorothy Davenport Reid, April 5, 1966, AMPAS.
64. *Chicago Tribune*, September 15, 1936.
65. *Los Angeles Times*, April 1, 1936.
66. Davis, Chris, correspondence with author, March, 2006.
67. Davis, Chris, correspondence with author, March, 2006.
68. Retrieved June 18, 2005, from http://www.biography.ms/Hollywood_Walk_of_Fame.html.

Selected Bibliography

Abel, Richard. *The Red Rooster Scare: Making American Cinema, 1900–1910.* Berkeley: University of California, 1999.

Acker, Ally. *Reel Women: Pioneers of the Cinema, 1896 to the Present.* New York: Continuum, 1991.

Albright, Horace M., and Marian Albright Schenck. *Creating the National Park Service: The Missing Years.* Norman: University of Oklahoma Press, 1999.

Alleman, Richard. *The Movie Lover's Guide to Hollywood.* New York: Harper Colophon Books, 1985.

Alpert, Hollis. *The Barrymores.* New York: Dial Press, 1964.

Altman, Diana. *Hollywood East: Louis B. Mayer and the Origins of the Studio System.* New York: Birch Lane Press, 1992.

Anger, Kenneth, *Hollywood Babylon.* New York: Dell, 1981.

———. *Hollywood Babylon II.* New York: Dutton, 1984.

Anthony, Carl S. *As We Remember Her: Jacqueline Kennedy Onassis in the Words of Her Family and Friends.* New York: HarperCollins, 1997.

Ardmore, Frederick Lewis. *Only Yesterday.* New York: Harper & Brothers, 1964.

Asher, Cash. *Bacteria, Inc.: In Which Is Told the Story of New York's Half Million Dollar Bedbug.* Boston: Bruce Humphries, 1955.

Atlas of the State of Illinois with Historic Statistics and Information. Chicago: Union Atlas Company, Warner & Beers Proprietors, 1876.

Austin, John. *Hollywood's Unsolved Mysteries.* New York: Shapolsky, 1990.

Bacon, James. *Hollywood Is a Four-Letter Word.* New York: Avon Books, 1977.

———. *Made in Hollywood.* Chicago: Contemporary Books, 1977.

Banks, Leo W. "Murderous Madam: In the Early Part of This Century, Gabriell Dollie Wiley Left a Long Line of Bodies in Her Wake." *Tucson Weekly,* June 5, 2000.

Barr, Charles. *Laurel & Hardy.* London: Studio Vista, 1967.

Baxter, John. *Hollywood in the 30s.* New York: A.S. Barnes, 1968.

Beasley. David. *McKee Rankin and the Heyday of the American Theater.* Waterloo, Ontario, Canada: Wilfrid Laurier University Press, 2002.

Beauchamp, Cari. *Without Lying Down: Francis Marion and the Powerful Women of Early Hollywood.* New York: Scribner, 1997.

Beaver, Frank. *One Hundred Years of American Film.* New York: Macmillan Library Reference USA, 2000.

Behlmer, Rudy. *Inside Warner Bros. (1935–1951).* New York: Viking Penguin, 1985.

Bengston, John. *Silent Echoes: Discovering Early Hollywood Through the Films of Buster Keaton.* Santa Monica: Santa Monica Press, 2000.

Berg, A. Scott. *Goldwyn: A Biography.* New York: Knopf, 1989.

Bernstein, Arnie. *Hollywood on Lake Michigan: 100 Years of Chicago and the Movies.* Chicago: Lake Claremont Press, 1998.

Blake, Michael F. *Lon Chaney: The Man Behind the Thousand Faces.* Vestal, N.Y.: Vestal Press, 1993.

Bockstruck, Lloyd D. *Revolutionary War Bounty Land Grants: Awarded by State Governments.* Baltimore: Genealogical, 1996.

Bodeen, DeWitt. *From Hollywood.* Cranbury, N.J.: A.S. Barnes, 1976.

Bogdonovich, Peter. *Allen Dwan: The Last Pioneer.* New York: Praeger Press, 1971.

Bowman, William D. *Charlie Chaplin: His Life and Art.* Reprint. New York: Haskell, 1974 (John Day, 1931).

Bowser, Eileen. *The Transformation of Cinema, 1907–1915.* New York: Scribner's, 1990.

Bright Lights Film Journal. September, 1996, Issue 17.

Brody, Richard Clark. unpublished thesis, *Lake level decline, water resource management, and public perception, Lake Arrowhead, CA, Drought Years 1999–2003,* 2004. Water Resources Center Archives, University of California, Berkeley.

Brooks, Louise. *Lulu in Hollywood.* New York: Knopf, 1982.

Brown, T. Allston. *History of the American Stage.* New York: Dick & Fitzgerald, 1870.

Brownlow, Kevin. *Behind the Mask of Innocence: Sex, Violence, Prejudice, Crime: Films of Social Conscience in the Silent Era.* Berkeley: University of California Press, 1990.

———. *Hollywood: The Pioneers.* New York: Knopf, 1980.

———. *The Parade's Gone By.* New York: Knopf, 1968.

———. *The War, the West, and the Wilderness.* New York: Knopf, 1979.
Burroughs, Marie. *Art Portfolio of Stage Celebrities.* Chicago: Marquis, 1894.
Butler, Ivan. *Silent Magic: Rediscovering the Silent Film Era.* New York: Ungar, 1988.
Cahn, William. *The Laugh Makers: A Pictorial History of American Comedians.* New York: Bramhall House, 1957.
Carey, Gary. *All the Stars in Heaven.* New York: E.P. Dutton, 1981.
———. *Anita Loos: A Biography.* New York: Knopf, 1988.
Ceram, C.W. *Archaeology of the Cinema.* London: Thames and Hudson, 1965.
Chaneles, Sol, and Albert Wolsky. *The Movie Makers.* Secaucus, N.J.: Derbibooks, 1974.
Chaplin, Charles. *My Autobiography.* London: Bodley Head, 1964.
———. *My Life in Pictures.* London: Bodley Head, 1974.
Chaplin, Lita Grey, with Morton Cooper. *My Life with Chaplin: An Intimate Memoir.* New York: Bernard Geis Associates, 1966.
Cini, Zelda, and Bob Cran with Peter H. Brown. *Hollywood: Land and Legend.* Westport, CT: Arlington House, 1980.
Coe, Brian. *The History of Movie Photography.* London: Ash & Grant, 1981.
Cohn, Alfred A. "The Reformation of 'Wally.'" *Photoplay.* December 1917.
Cooper, Miriam, and Bonnie Herndon. *Dark Lady of the Silents: My Life in Early Hollywood.* New York: Bobbs-Merrill, 1973.
Corkin, Stanley. *Realism and the Birth of the Modern United States: Cinema, Literature, and Culture.* Athens, Georgia, 1996.
Cornebise, Alfred. *War as Advertised: The Four Minute Men and America's Crusade, 1917–1918.* Philadelphia: The American Philosophical Society, 1984.
Courteway, Robbi. *Spirits of Saint Louis: A Ghostly Guide to the Mound City's Unearthly Visitors.* St. Louis: Virginia, 2003.
Coyle, William, ed. *Ohio Authors and Their Books.* Cleveland: World, 1962.
Creel, George. *Complete Report of the Chairman of the Committee on Public Information, 1917, 1918, 1919.* Washington, D.C.: Government Printing Office, 1920.
———. *How We Advertised America: The First Telling of the Amazing Story of the Committee on Public Information That Carried the Gospel of Americanism to Every Corner of the Globe.* New York: Harper and Brothers, 1920.
Crivello, Kirk. *Fallen Angels: The Lives and Untimely Deaths of 14 Hollywood Beauties.* Secausus: Citadel Press, 1988.
Crowther, Bosley. *Hollywood Rajah: The Life and Times of Louis B. Mayer.* New York: Henry Holt, 1960.
———. *The Lion's Share: The Story of an Entertainment Empire.* New York: Dutton, 1957.
Croy, Homer. *Starmaker: The Story of D.W. Griffith.* New York: Duell, Sloan & Pearce, 1959.
Curtis, Thomas Quinn. *Von Strohiem.* New York: Farrar, Straus & Giroux, 1971.
Curzon, Julian. *The Great Cyclone at St. Louis and East St. Louis.* St. Louis, 1896.
Davis, Dentner. *Jean Harlow, Hollywood Comet.* London: Constable House, 1975.

Day, Beth. *This Was Hollywood.* New York: Doubleday, 1960.
DeMille, Cecil B. *The Autobiography of Cecil B. DeMille.* Englewood Cliffs, N.J.: Prentice-Hall, 1959.
Dictionary of American Biography and Supplements. New York: Scribner's, 1938–58.
Dictionary of National Biography: 1901–1911 Supplement. Oxford: Oxford University Press, 1912.
Donaldson, Norman and Betty Donaldson. *How Did They Die?* New York: St. Martins Press, 1980.
Dowd, Nancy, and David Shepard. *King Vidor.* Metuchen, N.J.: Scarecrow Press, 1988.
Dressler, Marie. *My Own Story.* Boston: Little, Brown, 1934.
Drew, William M. *D.W. Griffith's Intolerance: Its Genesis and Its Vision.* Jefferson, N.C.: McFarland, 1986.
Eames, John Douglas. *The M-G-M Story.* New York: Crown, 1971.
Edmonds, Andy. *Frame-Up!: The Untold Story of Roscoe "Fatty" Arbuckle.* New York: William Morrow, 1991.
Edwards, Anne. *The DeMilles: An American Family.* New York: Abrams, 1988.
Eells, George. *Hedda and Louella.* New York: Putnam, 1972.
Ellis, Frank. *History of Monmouth County, New Jersey.* Philadelphia: Peck, 1885.
Elsaesser, Thomas. *Early Cinema: Space, Frame, Narrative.* London: BFI, 1990.
Endres, Stacy, and Robert Cushman. *Hollywood at Your Feet: The Story of the World-Famous Chinese Theater.* Los Angeles: Pomegranate Press, 1992.
Everson, William K. *American Silent Film.* New York: Da Capo Press, 1998.
———. *The Films of Hal Roach.* New York: Museum of Modern Art, 1971.
———. *The Films of Laurel and Hardy.* New York: Museum of Modern Art, 1967.
Eyman, Scott. *Ernst Lubitsch: Laughter in Paradise.* New York: Simon and Schuster, 1993.
———. *Mary Pickford: America's Sweetheart.* New York: Donald I. Fine, 1990.
Fairbanks, Douglas Jr. *The Salad Days.* New York: Doubleday, 1988.
———, with Richard Schickel. *The Fairbanks Album.* Boston: New York Graphic Society, 1975.
Fairbanks, Letita, and Ralph Hancock. *Douglas Fairbanks: The Fourth Musketeer.* New York: Henry Holt, 1953.
Farber, Stephen, and Marc Green. *Hollywood Dynasties.* New York: Delilah Communications, 1984.
Farrar, Geraldine. *The Autobiography of Geraldine Farrar: Such Sweet Compulsion.* New York: Greystone Press, 1938.
Fell, John L., ed. *Film Before Griffith.* Berkeley: University of California Press, 1983.
Fielding, Raymond, ed. *A Technological History of Motion Pictures and Television.* Berkeley: University of California Press, 1967.
Finler, Joel W. *The Hollywood Story.* New York: Crown, 1988.
Flamini, Roland. *Thalberg: The Last Tycoon and the World of MGM.* New York: Crown, 1994.
Fountain, Leatrice Joy Gilbert. *Dark Star: The Untold Story of the Meteoric Rise and Fall of the Legendary John Gilbert.* New York: St. Martin's Press, 1985.
Fowler, Gene. *Father Goose: The Biography of Mack Sennett.* New York: Crown, 1934.
———. *Good Night Sweet Prince: The Life and Times of*

John Barrymore. New York: Buccaneer Books, 1943.

Freedland, Michael. *The Warner Brothers*. New York: St. Martin's Press, 1983.

Fullerton, John, ed. *Celebrating 1895: The Centenary of Cinema*. Sydney: John Libbey, 1998.

Fyne, Robert. *The Hollywood Propaganda of World War II*. Metuchen, N.J.: Scarecrow, 1994.

Gauntier, Gene. "Blazing the Trail." *Woman's Home Companion*. Volume 55, Number 11, November 1928.

Gifford, Denis. *Chaplin (The Movie-Makers Series)*. Secaucus: Citadel, 1972.

Gilbert, John. "Jack Gilbert Writes His Own Story." *Photoplay*. June-September, 1928.

Glyn, Anthony. *Elinor Glyn: A Biography*. Garden City, N.Y.: Doubleday, 1955.

Golden, Eve. *Platinum Girl—the Life and Legend of Jean Harlow*. New York: Abbeville Press, 1991.

Goodman, Ezra. *The Fifty Year Decline and Fall of Hollywood*. New York: Simon and Schuster, 1961.

Gould, Leo. *The Fatty Arbuckle Case*. New York: Patrick Library, 1962.

Griffith, Richard, and Arthur Mayer. *Movies: The Sixty-Year History of the World of Hollywood*. New York: Bonanza Books, 1957.

"Griffith's 20 Year Record." *Variety*, September 5, 1928.

Guiles, Fred Lawrence. *Stan: The Life of Stan Laurel*. Briarcliff Manor, N.Y.: Stein and Day, 1980.

Gunning, Thomas. *D.W. Griffith and the Rise of the Narrative Film*. Urbana: University of Illinois Press, 1991.

Hall, Lillian Arvida. *Catalogue of Dramatic Portraits, Vol. 4*. Cambridge: Harvard University Press, 1930–1934.

Halliwell, Leslie. *The Filmgoer's Companion. Fourth Edition*. New York: Hill & Wang, 1974.

Hansen, Miriam. *Babel and Babylon: Spectatorship in American Silent Film*. Cambridge: Harvard University Press, 1991.

Harrison, Louis Reeves. "Deerslayer." *The Moving Picture World* 16 (April 5, 1913).

Hartnoll, Phyllis, ed. *The Oxford Companion to the Theatre*. London: Oxford University Press, 1967.

Heimer, Mel. *The Long Count: The Legendary Battle for the World Heavyweight Championship, When Prizefighting was a National Sport and Jack Dempsey and Gene Tunney Were Its Heroes*. New York: Atheneum, 1969.

Heitman, Francis B. *Historical Register of Officers of the Continental Army During the War of the Revolution*. Washington, D.C.: Rare Book Shop, 1914.

Henderson, Robert M. *D.W. Griffith: His Life and Work*. New York: Ferrar, Straus & Giroux, 1972.

Hendricks, Gordon. *Origins of the American Film*. New York: Arno reprint (1972) containing: *The Edison Motion Picture Myth* (University of California, 1961), *Beginnings of the Biograph* (Hendricks, 1964), *The Kinetoscope* (Hendricks, 1966).

Higham, Charles. *Cecil B. DeMille*. New York: Scribner's, 1973.

_____. *Hollywood at Sunset*. New York: Saturday Review Press, 1972.

_____ *Merchant of Dreams: Louis B. Mayer and the Secret Hollywood*. New York: Donald I. Fine, 1993.

_____. *Warner's Brothers*. New York: Scribner's, 1975.

Horsley, William. "From Pigs to Pictures: The Story of David Horsley." *The International Photographer*, March, 1934.

Huff, Theodore. *Intolerance: The film by David Wark Griffith, a Shot-by-Shot Analysis*. New York: Museum of Modern Art, 1966.

Hutton, Laurence. *Curiosities of the American Stage*. New York: Harper & Bros., 1891.

Ireland, Norma Olin. *Index to Women of the World from Ancient to Modern Times: A Supplement*. Metuchen, N.J.: Scarecrow Press, 1988.

Johnson, Claudia. *American Actresses: Perspective on the Nineteenth Century*. Chicago: Nelson-Hall, 1984.

Kanin, Garson. *Hollywood*. New York: Viking Press, 1967.

Katz, Ephraim. *The Film Encyclopedia*. New York: Crowell, 1979.

Kennedy, David M. *Over Here: The First World War and American Society*. New York: Oxford University Press, 1980.

Keylin, Arlene, and Suri Fleischer, eds. *Hollywood Album: Lives and Deaths of Hollywood Stars from the Pages of* The New York Times. New York: Arno Press, 1979.

_____ and _____, eds. *Hollywood Album 2: Lives and Deaths of Hollywood Stars from the Pages of* The New York Times. New York: Arno Press, 1979.

Kingsley, Grace. *Reminiscences of Henry Walthall*. The New Movie Magazine, August 1931.

Kirkpatrick, Sydney D. *A Cast of Killers*. New York: Dutton, 1986.

Knightly, Phillip. *The First Casualty, From the Crimea to Vietnam: The War Correspondent as Hero, Propagandist, and Myth Maker*. New York: Harcourt Brace Jovanovich, 1975.

Kobler, John. *Damned in Paradise: The Life of John Barrymore*. New York: Atheneum, 1977.

Koszarski, Richard. *An Evening's Entertainment: The Age of the Silent Feature Picture, 1915–1928 (History of the American Cinema, Volume 3)*. Berkeley: University of California Press, 1994.

_____. *The Man You Love to Hate: Erich von Stroheim and Hollywood*. New York: Oxford University Press, 1983.

_____. *The Rivals of D.W. Griffith*. New York: Zoetrope, 1980.

Kovan, Florice Whyte. *Rediscovering Ben Hecht: Selling the Celluloid Serpent*. Washington, D.C.: Snickersnee Press, 1999.

Lahue, Kalton C. *Dreams for Sale: The Rise and Fall of Triangle Film Corporation*. Cranbury, N.J.: A.S. Barnes, 1971.

Lambert, Gavin. *Nazimova*. New York: Knopf, 1997.

Lamparski, Richard. *Lamparski's Hidden Hollywood: Where the Stars Lived, Loved and Died*. New York: Fireside Books, 1981.

_____. *Whatever Became Of...?* Third series. New York: Crown, 1971.

_____. *Whatever Became Of...?* Fourth series. New York: Crown, 1973.

_____. *Whatever Became Of...?* Fifth series. New York: Crown, 1974.

Lasky, Jesse L. *I Blow my Own Horn*. Garden City, N.Y.: Doubleday, 1957.

_____. *Whatever Happened to Hollywood?* New York: Funk & Wagnall, 1975.

Lasky, Jesse L., Jr. *Love Scene: The Story of Laurence Olivier and Vivien Leigh*. New York: Crowell, 1978.

Legends in Their Own Time. New York: Prentice Hall General Reference, 1994.

Leider, Emily W. *Dark Lover: The Life and Death of Rudolph Valentino*. New York: Faber and Faber, 2003.

Leondopoulos, Jordan. *Still the Moving World: Intol-*

erance, Modernism, and Heart of Darkness. New York: P. Lang, 1991.
Levin, Martin. *Hollywood and the Great Fan Magazines.* New York: Harrison House, 1970.
Lewton, Lucy. *Alla Nazimova, My Aunt, Tragedienne: A Personal Memoir.* Ventura: Minuteman Press, 1978.
Leyda, Jay, and Charles Musser. *Before Hollywood.* New York: American Federation of the Arts, 1986.
Liebman, Roy. *Silent Film Performers. An Annotated Bibliography of Published, Unpublished, and Archival Sources for Over 350 Actors and Actresses.* Jefferson, N.C.: McFarland, 1996.
Lockwood, Charles. *The Guide to Hollywood and Beverly Hills: The Best.* New York: Crown, 1984.
———. *Dream Palaces: Hollywood at Home.* New York: Viking Press, 1981.
Loos, Anita. *Cast of Thousands.* New York: Viking, 1977.
———. *A Girl Like I.* New York: Viking, 1966.
———. *Kiss Hollywood Good-bye.* New York: Grosset and Dunlap, 1975.
———. *The Talmadge Girls.* New York: Viking, 1978.
Madsen, Axel. *The Sewing Circle: Female Stars Who Loved Other Women.* New York: Birch Lane Press/Carol, 1995.
Maland, Charles J. *Chaplin and American Culture.* Princeton: Princeton University Press, 1989.
Mann, William J. *Wisecracker: The Life and Times of William Haines, Hollywood's First Openly Gay Star.* New York: Viking, 1998.
Marx, Samuel. *Mayer and Thalberg, The Make-Believe Saints.* New York: Random House, 1975.
Marx, Samuel, and Joyce Venderveen. *Deadly Illusions: Jean Harlow and the Murder of Paul Bern.* New York: Random House, 1990.
Mast, Gerald. *A Short History of the Movies.* New York: Macmillan, 1992.
McCabe, John. *Charlie Chaplin.* Garden City, N.Y.: Doubleday, 1978.
———. *The Comedy World of Stan Laurel.* Garden City, N.Y.: Doubleday, 1974.
McClellan, Diana. *Cut to the Chase: A Biography of Buster Keaton.* New York: HarperCollins, 1995.
———. *The Girls: Sappho Goes to Hollywood.* New York: St. Martin's Press, 2000.
McGaffey, Kenneth. "Jerry on the Job." *Photoplay Magazine,* January, 1917.
McLean, Adrienne L., and David A. Cook, eds. *Headline Hollywood: A Century of Film Scandal.* New Brunswick, N.J.: Rutgers University Press, 2000.
Meyers, Jeffrey. *Bogart: A Life in Hollywood.* New York: Fromm, 1997.
Miles, John P. "D.W. Griffith's Twenty-Year Record." *D.W. Griffith Papers, 1897–1954.* Frederick, MD: University Publications of America, 1982.
Mitchell, Lisa. "Ties That Bind: Searching for the Motion Picture Directors Association." *Director's Guild of America Magazine.* November, 2001.
Mix, Olive Stokes, with Eric Heath. *The Fabulous Tom Mix.* Englewood Cliffs, N.J.: Prentice-Hall, 1957.
Montgomery, Morton. *The History of Berks County.* 1908.
Moore, Charles, with Peter Becker and Regula Campbell. *The City Observed: Los Angeles, A Guide to Its Architecture and Landscapes.* New York: Random House, 1984.
Moore, Colleen. *Silent Star.* New York: Doubleday, 1968.
Mordden, Ethan. *Movie Star: A Look at the Women Who Made Hollywood.* New York: St. Martin's Press, 1983.
Morris, Michael. *Madam Valentino: The Many Lives of Natacha Rambova.* New York: Abbeville Press, 1991.
Musser, Charles. *Before the Nickelodeon: Edwin S. Porter and the Edison Manufacturing Company.* Berkeley: University of California Press, 1991.
———. *Edison Motion Pictures, 1890–1900: An Annotated Filmography.* Washington, D.C.: Smithsonian Institution Press, 1997.
———. *The Emergence of Cinema: The American Screen to 1907.* New York: Scribner's, 1990.
———. *Thomas A. Edison and His Kinetographic Motion Pictures.* New Brunswick, N.J.: Rutgers University Press, 1995.
Nasen, M.A., Rev. Elias. *A Gazetteer of the State of Massachusetts.* Revised and enlarged by George J. Varney. Boston: B.B. Russell, 1890.
Negri, Pola. *Memoirs of a Star.* Garden City, N.Y.: Doubleday, 1970.
Norman, Barry. *The Film Greats.* London: Hodder and Stoughton, 1985.
Notable Names in the American Theatre. Clifton, N.J.: White, 1976. Earlier edition published as *The Biographical Encyclopedia and Who's Who of the American Theatre.*
Nurnberger, Ralph D. "Bridling the Passions." *Wilson Quarterly,* Volume 11, 1987.
Odell, George Clinton Densmore. *Annals of the New York Stage, 15 Vols.* New York: Columbia University Press, 1927–1949.
———, Vol. I (to 1798).
———, Vol. IX.
O'Dell, Paul. *Griffith and the Rise of Hollywood.* New York: A.S. Barnes, 1970.
Paris, Barry. *Louise Brooks.* New York: Knopf, 1989.
Parrish, James Robert, with Ronald L. Bowers. *The MGM Stock Company: The Golden Era.* New Rochelle: Arlington House, 1973.
Parsons, Louella. *The Gay Illiterate.* New York: Doubleday, 1944.
———. *Tell It to Louella.* New York: Putnam, 1961.
Pascal, John. *The Jean Harlow Story.* New York: Popular Library, 1965.
Quirk, Lawrence J. *Norma: The Story of Norma Shearer.* New York: St. Martin's Press, 1988.
Ragan, David. *Who's Who in Hollywood, 1900–1976.* New Rochelle: Arlington House, 1976.
Ramsaye, Terry, ed. *1936–37 International Motion Picture Almanac.* New York: Quigley, 1936.
———. *A Million and One Nights: A History of the Motion Picture.* New York: Simon and Schuster, 1926.
Rankin, Ruth. "The Little Colonel Marches Back." *Photoplay,* June 1934.
Reid, Bertha Westbrook. *Wallace Reid: His Life Story.* New York: Sorg Publishing Company, 1923.
Reid, Whitelaw. *Ohio in the War: Her Statesmen, Her Generals and Soldiers.* Volumes 1 & 2. Cincinnati, OH: Baldwin Wilstach, 1868.
Rigdon, Walter. *Biographical Encyclopedia and Who's Who of the American Theatre.* New York: Heinemann, 1966
Roberts, Edward. *The Sins of Hollywood: An Expose of Movie Vice; A Group of Stories of Actual Happenings Reported and Written by a Hollywood Newspaper Man.* Los Angeles: Hollywood, 1922.
Robinson, David. *Chaplin: His Life and Art.* New York: McGraw-Hill, 1985.
———. *From Peep Show to Palace: The Birth of Amer-*

ican Film. New York: Columbia University Press, 1996.

———. *Hollywood in the Twenties*. London/New York: Zwemmer/Barnes, 1968.

Robinson, John W. *The San Bernardinos: The Mountain Country from Cajon Pass to Oak Glen, Two Centuries of Changing Use*. Arcadia, CA: Big Santa Anita Historical Society, 1989.

Ross, Steven J. *Working-Class Hollywood: Silent Film and the Shaping of Class in America*. Princeton, N.J.: Princeton University Press, 1998.

St. Johns, Adela Rogers. *The Honeycomb*. Garden City, N.Y.: Doubleday, 1969.

———. *Love, Laughter and Tears: My Hollywood Story*. New York: Doubleday, 1978.

Scalzo, Tom. "Forgotten Stars: Wallace Reid." *Hollywood Studio Magazine*. June, 1987.

Schickel, Richard. *D.W. Griffith: An American Life*. New York: Simon and Schuster, 1984.

Schulberg, Budd. *Moving Pictures: Memoirs of a Hollywood Prince*. Briarcliff Manor, N.Y.: Stein & Day, 1981.

Sennett, Mack, and Cameron Shipp. *King of Comedy*. Garden City, N.Y.: Doubleday, 1954.

Sennett, Robert S. *Hollywood Hoopla: Creating Stars and Selling Movies in the Golden Age of Hollywood*. New York: Billboard Books, 1988.

Shipman, David. *The Great Movie Stars*. New York: Da Capo Books, 1982.

Shulman, Irving. *Harlow: An Intimate Biography*. New York: Bernard Geis Associates, 1964.

———. *Valentino*. New York: Trident Press, 1967.

Skal, David J., and Elias Savada. *Dark Carnival: The Secret World of Tod Browning, Hollywood's Master of the Macabre*. New York: Anchor Books, 1995.

Slade, Becka; Thesis Outline: *Feminism in Hollywood: The Acceptance of the Woman Director*. Western Connecticut State University. http://people.wcsu.edu/mccarneyh/acad/sladethesis.html

Slide, Anthony. *Early American Cinema*. Metuchen, N.J.: Scarecrow Press, 1994.

Sloan, Kay. *The Loud Silents: Origins of the Social Problem Film*. Urbana: University of Illinois Press, 1988.

Smith, Andrew Brodie. *Shooting Cowboys and Indians: Silent Western Films, American Culture, and the Birth of Hollywood*. Boulder: University of Colorado Press, 1981, 2003.

Sova, Dawn B. *Women in Hollywood: From Vamp to Studio Head*. New York: Fromm International, 1998.

Stenn, David. *Bombshell: The Life and Death of Jean Harlow*. New York: Doubleday, 1993.

———. *Clara Bow: Runnin' Wild*. New York: Doubleday, 1991.

Sternberg, Josef von. *Fun in a Chinese Laundry*. New York: Collier Books, 1965.

Stewart, John, comp. *Filmarama: The Formidable Years, 1893–1919, Volume 1*. Metuchen, N.J.: Scarecrow Press, 1975.

———. *Filmarama. Volume II: The Flaming Years, 1920–1929*. Metuchen, N.J.: Scarecrow Press, 1977.

Strang, Lewis C. *Players and Plays of the Last Quarter Century*. Boston: L. C. Page, 1902.

Thomas, Augustus. *The Print of My Remembrance*. New York: Scribner's, 1922.

Thomas, Bob. *King Cohn: The Life and Times of Harry Cohn*. New York: G.P. Putnam, 1967.

Thomas, Nicholas. *The International Dictionary of Films and Filmmakers. Second edition. Volume 3, Actors and Actresses*. Detroit: St. James Press, 1992.

Thomson, David. *A Biographical Dictionary of Film*. New York: William Morrow, 1976.

Timberlake, Craig. *The Bishop of Broadway: The Life & Work of David Belasco*. New York: Library Publishers, 1954.

Tompkins, Eugene, and Quincy Kilby. *The History of the Boston Theatre 1854–1901*. New York: Benjamin Blom, 1908, 1969.

Torrence, Bruce T. *Hollywood: The First 100 Years*, New York: Zoetrope, 1982.

Truitt, Evelyn Mack. *Who Was Who on Screen. First edition*. New York: R.R. Bowker, 1974.

———. *Who Was Who on Screen. Second edition*. New York: R.R. Bowker, 1977.

———. *Who Was Who on Screen. Third edition*. New York: R.R. Bowker, 1983.

———. *Who Was Who on Screen*. New York: R.R. Bowker, 1984.

Vaughn, Stephen. *Holding Fast the Inner Lines: Democracy, Nationalism, and the Committee on Public Information*. Chapel Hill: University of North Carolina Press, 1980.

Vidor, King. *A Tree Is a Tree*. New York, Hollywood: Samuel French, 1989.

Vinson, James, ed. *The International Dictionary of Films and Filmmakers. First Edition. Volume 3: Actors and Actresses*. Chicago: St. James Press, 1986.

Wakeman, John, ed. *World Film Directors, Volume One, 1890–1945*. New York: Wilson, 1987.

Walker, Alexander. *Rudolph Valentino*. New York: Stein & Day, 1970.

———. *Sex in the Movies*. Middlesex, U.K.: Penguin Books, Harmondsworth, 1968.

———. *Shattered Silents: How the Talkies Came to Stay*. New York: Morrow, 1979.

Wallace, David. *Lost Hollywood*. New York: LA Weekly St. Martin's Press, 2001.

Wallace, W. Stewart (compiler). *A Dictionary of North American Authors Deceased before 1950*. Toronto: Ryerson Press, 1951.

Wearing, J.P. *American and British Theatrical Biography: A Directory*. Metuchen N.J.: Scarecrow Press, 1979.

Weaver, John T. (compiler). *Twenty Years of Silents, 1908–1928*. Metuchen, N.J.: Scarecrow Press, 1971

Webb, Michael, ed. *Hollywood: Legend and Reality*. Boston: Little, Brown, 1986.

Weiss, Ken. *To the Rescue: How Immigrants Saved the American Film Industry, 1896–1912*. San Francisco: Austin & Winfield, 1997.

Who Was Who in America. Chicago: Marquis, 1963–1973.

Wilber, Lillian L. *The Early Schools of Freehold and Vicinity, 1667–1928*. Asbury Park, N.J.: Schuyler Press, 1969.

Williams, Gregory L. "San Diego: Hollywood's Backlot, 1898–2002." *The Journal of San Diego History*, Spring 2002, Volume 48, Number 2.

Willis, Richard. "David W. Griffith: Genius." *Movie Pictorial*. September 12, 1914.

———. "The Edwin Booth of the Screen." *Motion Picture Classic*. June, 1916.

Windeler, Robert. *Sweetheart: The Story of Mary Pickford*. New York: Praeger, 1974.

Wright, Albert Hazen. *The A.H. Wright Papers*. Carl A. Kroch Library, Cornell University.

Yagoda, Ben. *Will Rogers: A Biography*. New York: Knopf, 1993.

Zierold, Norman. *The Moguls*. New York: Coward-McCann, 1969.

_____. *The World of Yesterday.* New York: Viking, 1943.
Zuckor, Adolph. *The Public Is Never Wrong.* New York: Putnam's, 1953.

Newspapers

Atlanta Constitution, Atlanta, Georgia
Baltimore Herald, Baltimore, Maryland
Bedford Gazette, Bedford, Pennsylvania
Bismarck Daily Tribune, Bismarck, North Dakota
Boston Herald, Boston, Massachusetts
Boston Post, Boston, Massachusetts
Bridgeport Telegram, Bridgeport, Connecticut
Chicago American, Chicago, Illinois
Chicago Daily Tribune, Chicago, Illinois
Chicago Sunday Tribune, Chicago, Illinois
Chicago Tribune, Chicago, Illinois
Chillicothe Constitution, Chillicothe, Missouri
Chillicothe Constitution Tribune, Chillicothe, Missouri
Chronicle Telegram, Elyria, Ohio
Clearfield Daily Progress, Clearfield, Pennsylvania
Cleveland Herald, Cleveland, Ohio
Columbus Citizen, Columbus, Ohio
Coshocton Tribune, Coshocton, Ohio
Daily Kennebec Journal, Kennebec, Maine
Decatur Daily Dispatch, Decatur, Illinois
Denton Journal, Denton, Maryland
Des Moines News, Des Moines, Iowa
Freeborn County Standard, Albert Lea, Minnesota
Hollywood Citizen News, Hollywood, California
Hollywood Evening News, Los Angeles, California
Hollywood Reporter, Hollywood, California
Indianapolis Star, Indianapolis, Indiana
Iowa City Press Citizen, Iowa City, Iowa
Kansas City Star, Kansas City, Missouri
Lima News, Lima, Ohio
Los Angeles City News, Los Angeles, California
Los Angeles Downtown News, Los Angeles, California
Los Angeles Evening Herald, Los Angeles, California
Los Angeles Evening Herald Express, Los Angeles, California
Los Angeles Herald, Los Angeles, California
Los Angeles Herald Examiner, Los Angeles, California
Los Angeles Herald Express, Los Angeles, California
Los Angeles Mirror, Los Angeles, California
Los Angeles Post-Record, Los Angeles, California
Los Angeles Sentinel, Los Angeles, California
Los Angeles Times, Los Angeles, California
Los Angeles Tribune, Los Angeles, California
Los Angeles Weekly, Los Angeles, California
Manitoba Free Press, Winnipeg, Manitoba, Canada
Mansfield News, Mansfield, Ohio
Marion Star, Marion, OH
Middlesboro Daily News, Middlesboro, Kentucky
Nashua Telegraph, Nashua, New Hampshire
Naugatuck Daily News, Naugatuck, Connecticut
Nevada State Journal, Reno, Nevada
New York Herald Tribune, New York, New York
New York Times, New York, New York
Newark Daily Advocate, Newark, Ohio
Port Arthur News, Port Arthur, Texas
Port Washington Standard, Port Washington, Wisconsin
Redlands Daily Review, Redlands, California
Topeka Journal, Topeka, Kansas
Trenton Evening Times, Trenton New Jersey
Van Nuys News, Van Nuys, California
Washington Herald, Washington, D.C.
Washington Post, Washington, D.C.
Washington Times-Herald, Washington, D.C.
Waukesha Freeman, Waukesha, Wisconsin
Wichita Beacon, Wichita, Kansas
Wichita Daily Times, Wichita, Texas
Wisconsin Rapids Daily Tribune, Wisconsin Rapids, Wisconsin
Witchita Daily Times, Witchita Falls, Texas
Wyoming State Tribune, Cheyenne, Wyoming

Periodicals

Bioscope, October 13, 1912, July 17, 1913, August 7, 1913, December 10, 1914, October 22, 1914, January 7, 1915, January 14, 1915, January 21, 1915, April 22, 1915, November 11, 1915, September 9, 1915, September 30, 1915, September 7, 1916, April 12, 1917, May 17, 1917, May 24, 1917, June 28, 1917, June 15, 1917, July 12, 1917, August 9, 1917, August 23, 1917, August 30, 1917, July 25, 1918, January 30, 1919, March 27, 1919, May 8, 1919, October 23, 1919, January 22, 1920, May 20, 1920, June 17, 1920, July 29, 1920, February 10, 1921, August 11, 1921
Film Comment, September, 1989
Film Daily, November 4, 1915, September 18, 1921, December 17, 1922
Films in Review, January, 1990, April, 1966
Kinematograph Weekly, January 22, 1920, May 13, 1920, February 3, 1921, August 4, 1921, April 19, 1923, May 31, 1923
Motion Picture Herald, March 14, 1936
Motion Picture News, June 25, 1910, July 23, 1910, January 2, 1915, January 9, 1915, January 30, 1915, February 6, 1915, February 13, 1915, February 20, 1915, March 15, 1915, March 27, 1915, April 3, 1915, April 17, 1915, April 24, 1915, May 1, 1915, May 15, 1915, June 12, 1915, June 19, 1915, June 26, 1915, July 24, 1915, July 17, 1915, July 31, 1915, August 7, 1915, August 14, 1915, August 21, 1915, September 4, 1915, September 11, 1915, October 9, 1915, October 16, 1915, October 30, 1915, November 6, 1915, November 12, 1915, December 4, 1915, December 11, 1915, January 15, 1916, January 22, 1916, February 12, 1916, February 26, 1916, March 11, 1916, April 1, 1916, April 29, 1916, May 13, 1916, June 24, 1916, July 22, 1916, November 25, 1916, December 6, 1916, December 23, 1916, January 6, 1917, February 10, 1917, June 9, 1917, August 4, 1917, August 11, 1917, September 15, 1917, September 29, 1917, November 17, 1917, January 5, 1918, February 9, 1918, April 20, 1918, June 1, 1918, June 22, 1918, July 27, 1918, August 3, 1918, August 24, 1918, November 16, 1918, January 25, 1919, March 29, 1919, April 19, 1919, April 26, 1919, July 5, 1919, August 9, 1919, August 24, 1919, September 13, 1919, October 25, 1919, November 11, 1919, November 29, 1919, December 13, 1919, February 14, 1920, February 21, 1920, March 13, 1920, March 27, 1920, May 15, 1920, June 12, 1920, July 3, 1920, July 24, 1920, November 20, 1920, December 4, 1920, April 17, 1921,
Motography, February 20, 1915, February 27, 1915, March 20, 1915, March 27, 1915, April 3, 1915, April 24, 1915, July 17, 1915, August 21, 1915, August 28, 1915, October 2, 1915, October 16, 1915, October 23, 1915, October 30, 1915, November 20, 1915, April 29, 1916, May 13, 1916, July 22, 1916, October 23, 1916, January 13, 1917, February 17, 1917, November 17, 1917
Moving Picture World, July 9, 1910, July 23, 1910, De-

cember 14, 1912, May 4, 1912, July 27, 1912, November 29, 1913, February 20, 1915, March 13, 1915, March 27, 1915, April 10, 1915, April 24, 1915, May 29, 1915, June 5, 1915, June 12, 1915, July 24, 1915, August 21, 1915, October 9, 1915, October 16, 1915, October 23, 1915, October 30, 1915, November 6, 1915, November 27, 1915, January 8, 1916, January 22, 1916, March 11, 1916, March 18, 1916, April 1, 1916 April 22, 1916, July 15, 1916, August 5, 1916, September 23, 1916, September 30, 1916, October 14, 1916, December 9, 1916, December 30, 1916, January 13, 1917, February 10, 1917, May 19, 1917, June 9, 1917, October 13, 1917, October 20, 1917, December 1, 1917, December 29, 1917, August 11, 1917, August 18, 1917, September 15, 1917, December 22, 1917, December 29, 1917, February 2, 1918, February 9, 1918, February 15, 1918, June 1, 1918, June 22, 1918, July 27, 1918, August 24, 1918, September 7, 1918, September 21, 1918, October 5, 1918, October 12, 1918, October 19, 1918, November 16, 1918, December 21, 1918, January 4, 1919, January 25, 1919, March 15, 1919, March 22, 1919, April 6, 1919, June 20, 1919, August 9, 1919, August 16, 1919, September 13, 1919, November 29, 1919, December 20, 1919, February 7, 1920, March 13, 1920, March 20, 1920, April 17, 1920, May 15, 1920, May 29, 1920, August 14, 1920, August 28, 1920, October 30, 1920, November 22, 1920, March 19, 1921, March 26, 1921, July 31, 1921, August 27, 1921, October 29, 1921, October 27, 1922, December 23, 1922, January 17, 1923, February 3, 1923, February 23, 1923, December 27, 1927, September 10, 1927, November 5, 1927, May 26, 1923, December 29, 1923, August 2, 1924, March 12, 1927, April 23, 1927, May 7, 1927

New York Dramatic Mirror, February 24, 1915, March 10, 1915, April 28, 1915, May 19, 1915, October 30, 1915, November 6, 1915, January 15, 1916, February 5, 1916, April 22, 1916, April 29, 1916, May 6, 1916, September 30, 1916, October 28, 1916, January 13, 1917, December 29, 1917, April 27, 1918, September 22, 1917, March 16, 1918, June 22, 1918, June 29, 1918, August 3, 1918, September 7, 1918, November 16, 1918

Photoplay, September, 1922, November, 1916, December, 1916, February, 1917

Picture Plays, January 10, 1920

Picture Show Magazine, June 14, 1919, August 23, 1919

Picturegoer, February, 1921, May, 1921, November, 1921, June, 1922, October, 1922

Pictures and the Picturegoer, March 13, 1919, September 27, 1919

Quarterly Review of Film Studies, January, 1981.

Variety, March 12, 1915, August 27, 1915, October 16, 1915, October 23, 1915, November 5, 1915, November 20, 1915, December 3, 1915, December 31, 1915, March 3, 1916, April 7, 1916, April 14, 1916, April 29, 1916, July 7, 1916, September 8, 1916, December 29, 1916, March 9, 1917, August 3, 1917, September 14, 1917, November 2, 1917, December 21, 1917, January 25, 1918, April 20, 1918, June 3, 1918, June 14, 1918, July 26, 1918, August 6, 1918, December 13, 1918, January 17, 1919, April 18, 1919, June 20, 1919, July 31, 1919, August 1, 1919, September 5, 1919, October 10, 1919, November 21, 1919, February 6, 1920, March 26, 1920, May 7, 1920, July 9, 1920, August 20, 1920, November 12, 1920, August 26, 1921, December 1, 1922, January 25, 1923, February 8, 1923, December 6, 1954

Internet Research Sites

http://www.afi.com (American Film Institute)
http://www.america-at-war.net (World War I history)
http://www.angelfire.com/mn/hp/minta1 (Don Schneider interview with Minta Durfee; Mabel Normand site)
http://www.archives.gov (National Archives research site)
http://www.assumption.edu/acad/ii/Academic/history/His130/twenties/Taylor (William Desmond Taylor materials)
http://www.beneathlosangeles.com (Los Angeles death background)
http://www.biographcompany.com (Biograph Studio materials)
http://www.busterkeaton.com/Villa (Buster Keaton background materials) http://www.cah.utexas.edu/newspapers/morgues (Newspaper morgue research site)
http://www.cas.buffalo.edu/classes/dms/cgkoebel/bc (Edison film version of *The Kiss*)
http://www.cecilbdemille.com (Cecil B. DeMille materials)
http://www.charliechaplinarchive.org (Charlie Chaplin materials)
http://www.ciajfk.com/barrymore/fr_index.html?/barrymore/lionel (Drew & Barrymore genealogy)
http://www.cinemaweb.com/silentfilm/bookshelf/7_dwg_2 (Silent film history, D.W. Griffith)
http://www.cinema.ucla.edu (UCLA Film & Television Archive)
http://www.citybigbearlake.com (Big Bear Lake Film Commission)
http://www.cmgww.com/historic/rogers (Will Rogers materials)
http://www.csse.monash.edu.au/~pringle/silent (general Wallace Reid materials)
http://www.digitalhistory.uh.edu, Mintz, S. (2003). *Digital History* (silent movie background)
http://www.dotlibrary1.specialcollection.net/scripts/ws.dll?websearch&site=dot_railroads (historic railroad accident reports)
http://ednapurviance.org (Edna Purviance materials)
http://www.eh.net (Money conversion tables)
http://www.employees.oxy.edu/jerry/wselig (history of Wm. Selig studio)
http://www.fathom.com/course/21701779/session1 (Fathom Archives; Columbia University; American Film Institute, The First Fifty Years of American Cinema)
http://www.fb10.uni-bremen.de/anglistik/kerkhoff/ContempDrama/DR-History (history of American theater)
http://www.filmsite.org/birth (Tom Dirks *Birth of a Nation* materials)
http://gdhamann.blogspot.com (Newspaper archive materials)
http://www.geocities.com/murraylar/james (James Murray materials)
http://www.geocities.com/pensacolarice/KingAlfred (Westbrook genealogical materials)
http://www.geocities.com/pfw8015/index (Doc Wilson's *New York Dramatic Mirror* notes)
http://www.greatwar.nl (World War I history)
http://www.gutenberg.org/etext/11827 (book copyright research site)
http://www.henrybwalthall.com (Henry Walthall biographical materials, *Birth of a Nation* background)

http://www.history.sandiego.edu/gen/st (Hollywood and World War I)
http://www.hollywood.com (City of Hollywood background)
http://www.hollywoodreporter.com (Hollywood Reporter magazine background)
http://www.home.comcast.net/~m.chitty/people.htm#drewll (Drew and Barrymore family histories; McKee Rankin background)
http://home.netcom.com/~lippfarr/mugshots (Silent film, forgotten actors site)
http://www.homeoint.org/hompath/articles/2756 (C.P. Bryant homeopathy materials)
http://www.homeopathy.ca/articles/1_to_master (C.P. Bryant biographic information, history of homeopathy)
http://www.hffi.org/event_theater_examtheater (history of American theater)
http://www.ida.liu.se/~juhta/buster (Buster Keaton materials)
http:///www.ifa.org (International Film Institute; film history and reference)
http://www.illinoisbiz.biz/film/film_made_1890 (Illinois Film Office, early 1900s filming in Chicago)
http://www.images.library.uiuc.edu/projects/maps/terms (Historic maps)
http://www.imdb.com (movie history and reference)
http://www.indiana.edu (Black movie history site)
http://www.isanet.org/noarchive/robertwells (World War I background)
http://www.izaak.unh.edu/specoll/mancoll/moviestills (University of New Hampshire Television Stills archive)
http://www.jerre.com (Charles Chaplin background)
http://www.kino.com (Silent film background)
http://www.lapl.org (Los Angeles Public Library)
http://lcweb2.loc.gov/ammem/today/feb08 (Library of Congress, American Memories website)
http://lcweb2.loc.gov/ammem/ed (Library of Congress; The Motion Pictures and Sound Recordings of the Edison Companies)
http://www.lib.byu.edu/~rdh/wwi/1914/wilsonneut (World War I, American involvement)
http://www.library.appstate.edu/appcoll/filmography (Appalachian State University Library, Southern Mountaineers Filmography)
http://www.members.fortunecity.co.uk/annapizzey/blyth (Barrymore genealogy information)
http://members.lycos.co.uk/BARRYMOREMAD (John Barrymore materials)
http://www.montgomerycollege.org/Departments/hpolscrv/cdeibel (Hays Commission)
http://movies.groups.yahoo.com/group/spurr (Melbourne Spurr materials)

http://www.moviesbywomen.com/history (Cari Bauchamp article re: female directors)
http://www.neiu.edu/~rghiggin/ephem/Drew, John (John Drew background)
http://www.newsday.com/community/guide/lihistory/ny-history-hs715a,0,7288771 (Lasata estate history)
http://www.oneonta.edu/~cooper/drama/film (James Fenimore Cooper Society Website, James Fenimore Cooper Society Miscellaneous Papers—Electronic Series No. 2)
http://www.oscars.org (Academy of Motion Pictures Arts & Sciences research site)
http://pages.prodigy.net/vicdru (Los Angeles cemetery materials)
http://www.psychotronicvideo.com/wow/reviews (General films reviews)
http://www.reelclassics.com (Film research site)
http://www.rockingham.k12.va.us/EMS/WWI/WWI (World War I, American involvement)
http://www.santacruzpl.org/history/films/scfilms/surf/3-9-17 (Silent film work in Santa Cruz, CA)
http://www.scplweb.santacruzpl.org/history/films/scfilms/hollywd (filming in Santa Cruz, California)
http://www.scplweb.santacruzpl.org/history/films/scfilms/studios (filming in Santa Cruz, California)
http://www.sharlot.org (Sharlot Hall Museum, Red Kimono background)
http://www.silentladies.com (Silent film research site)
http://www.silent-movies.com/Arbucklemania/home (Misc. silent movie personalities)
http://www.synoptique.ca/core/en/articles/dorothy_davenport (Dorothy Davenport background)
http://www.titansofhollywood.com (Zukor and Leow background)
http://www.uno.edu/~drcom/Griffith/Birth/CW (Movie database for viewing)
http://www.usc.edu/isd/archives/la/scandals/taylor (USC silent movie film site)
http://www.vaclib.org/basic/bacteria (C.P. Bryant homeopathy materials)
http://www.victorian-cinema.net/selig (history of Victorian film era)
http://xroads.virginia.edu/~UG02/wolpert/wdtladies (Shots in the Dark: Sex, Drugs, Women and the Murder of William Desmond Taylor)
http://www.whitleyheights.com (Whitley Heights materials)
http://www.wyomingtalesandtrails.com/cody3 (Cody, Wyoming and Buffalo Bill history)
http://xroads.virginia.edu/~HYPER/HNS/Westfilm/west (Western film history)

Index

Abril, Dorothy 89, 111
Academy of Motion Pictures Arts and Sciences 206, 234, 235, 236, 239
Acord, Art 79
Across the Continent (1922) 189, 190, 191, 192, 197, 199; production details and cast list 257
Adams, Annie 38
Adams, Maude 6, 38
Adams, Samuel 37
The Adventures of Dolly (1908) 40
The Adventures of Kathlyn (1916) 24
The Affairs of Anatol (1921) 145, 170, 174, 182, 183, 191, 199; cost of 170, 171; filming of 172; length of 170, 171, 182; photographic innovations in 171; production details and cast list 256; pushes censors 171; sexual themes of 171
Agnew, Robert 203
Ainsworth, Phil 128
Aitken, Harry 49, 66, 70, 80
Aitken, Spottiswoode 66, 94
Alden, Mary 59, 60, 67, 73, 125
Aldwyn, Irene 93
Alexandria Hotel 151
Alfred "The Great," King 7
Alias Mike Moran (1919) 132, 133; production details and cast list 254
All for a Girl (1912) 49, 51, 258; production details and cast list 243
All the Rivers Meet the Sea (1913) 56
Allison, May 172, 175, 187, 194
All-Star Weekly 130
All-Story Magazine 92
Almost a Suicide (1912) 56
Always Audacious (1920) 161, 162, 163; production details and cast list 255, 256
American Film Manufacturing Company (Flying A) 33, 49, 50, 52, 53, 56, 57, 69, 236
American Mutoscope & Biograph Company 40
American Vitagraph Studio 106; founding of 23; location of 23
Anderson, Claire 67, 69

Anderson, Gilbert M. ("Bronco Billy") 24, 113
Angellotti, Marion Polk 122
Anger, Lewis 185
The Animal (1913) 57, 69; production details and cast list 245
Another Chance (1914) 67; production details and cast list 248
Anti-Narcotics League of Los Angeles 231
Apfel, Oscar 79
Arbuckle, Franklin 81
Arbuckle, Roscoe 1, 2, 24, 59, 79, 150, 151, 175, 185, 193, 197, 213, 220, 223, 238; acquittal of 201, 202; automobile of 185; charged in death of Virginia Rappe 185; death of 202; earnings of 185; first trial of 186; homes of 185; perjured case against 185, 186, 192, 201; second trial of 192; third trial of 201; unfounded rumors about 185, 186, 187
Arch Street Theater Company 37
Arlen, Richard 199, 235
Arling, Charles 91
Armat, Thomas 22
Arms and the Gringo (1914) 66; production details and cast list 248
Arrow Film Company 205
Arrowhead Lake Company 61
Arrowhead Mountain Club 60
Arrowhead Reservoir & Power Company 60
Artcraft Picture Company 102
Arthur, Chester A. 6
Arvidson, Linda 41, 42
Ashby, Ruth 155
Asher, Ephraim M. 220
Ashton, Sylvia 49, 148, 167
Astor, Camille 88, 91
At Cripple Creek (1912) 33
At Dawn (1914) 67; production details and cast list 248
At Scrogginses' Corner (1912) 32, 63; production details and cast list 242
At the Old Crossroads (play) 12
Atlanta Constitution 86, 178
Aubrey, Jimmy 228
The Avenging Conscience: Though Shalt Not Kill (1914) 66, 67;

production details and cast list 248
Ayres, Agnes 167, 168, 169, 170, 171, 173, 180, 195, 203, 204
Ayres, Otto 101

Baby's Ride (1914) 249
The Bachelor and the Baby (1912) 45, 46
Baggott, King 68
Bains, Beulah 162
Baird, Leah 31, 49, 51
Balaban, Barney 235
Balboa Amusement Producing Company 76, 89
Baldwin, Elias Jackson ("Lucky") 114
Balfour, Sue 33
Ballard, Frederick 120
Balshofer, Fred 46
Bancroft, George 259
Bankhead, Tallulah 259
Banksia Place Sanitarium 218
Bara, Theda 105
Barker, Dr. John Scott: arrest of 221; controversial treatment programs of 212
Barlow, Donald 57
Barnes, T. Roy 187
Barranger, James 138
Barriers of Society (1916) 99
Barron, Elwyn Alfred 119
Barrows, Henry [A.] 103, 119, 183
Barrymore, Ethel 6, 35, 68
Barrymore, Georgiana Drew 39
Barrymore, John 90, 198, 259
Barrymore, Lionel 33, 39, 258
Barrymore, Maurice 8, 39
Bartlett, Frederick Orin 132
Bassett, Russell 43
Bateman, Victor 231
The Battle of the Sexes (1914) 67
Bauchens, Luella 152
Baum, L. Frank 25
Bauman, William J. 51
Beal, Frank 49
Beatty, Jerome 162
Beban, George 105
Beery, Noah 111, 120, 124, 128, 129, 141, 223
Beery, Wallace 31, 141
Before the White Man Came (1912)

289

33, 258; production details and cast list 242
Belasco, David 83
Belasco, Jay 89
Believe Me, Xantippe (1918) 120, 121, 129, 154; production details and cast list 253
The Belle of New York (play) 38
Belmore, Lionel 188
Bennett, Alma 170
Bennett, Arnold 27
Bennett, Billie 104
Bennett, Frank 94
Ben's Kid (1909) 24
Beranger, Andre 72
Beranger, Clara 197, 203
Berg, Leila 236
Berg, Phil 236
Bergère, Ouida 89, 178
Bernhardt, Sarah 83, 259
Bernstein, Isador 30, 59
Berst, J.A. 23
The Best Man Wins (1911) 43, 45
Beverly Wilshire Hotel 160
Big Bear Lake 60
Big Timber (1917) 104, 126; production details and cast list 252
Big U Film Company 99
Binney, Constance 177
Binns, George 122
Biograph Company 33, 42, 47, 53, 60, 65, 66, 68; founding of 23; location of 23, 39
The Birth of a Nation (1915) 33, 70, 77, 79, 80, 81, 85, 93, 95, 121; cost of 70, 71; deleted scenes of 74, 76; financial success of 75, 80; impact of rebirth of Ku Klux Klan 76; importance of 70; length of 70, 74; original title of 70, 74; premier of 74; production details and cast list 249; production scope of 70, 71, 72, 74, 76; public reaction to 74, 75; racist content of 73, 74, 75, 76; technical innovations introduced in 74, 75, 76; ticket cost of 74
The Birth of a Race (1918) 76
Bison Film Company 48, 49, 57
Bison Motion Pictures 33
Bitzer, Billy 41, 42, 79, 125; technical innovations of 31, 40, 74
Bixby, Horace, H. 8
Black Entertainment Network 235
Black Friday (1916) 99
A Black Hand Elopement (1912) 56
Black Maria studio 22
Blackton, J. Stuart 23, 106
Blackwell, Carlyle 62, 68, 89
Blair, Montgomery 8
Blake, Grace 104
Blanchard, Kitty 38, 39
Bledsoe, Judge Benjamin 231
Blessing, Dr. C.B. 212, 221, 230
Blinn, Genevieve 183
Block, Ralph 118
Blockbuster, Inc. 235
Blondeau Tavern, Hollywood 43
Blue, Monte 94, 170, 171
Blystone, John 60, 61, 63
Boardman, Eleanor 259
Bodeen, DeWitt 166, 219
Boggs, Francis 24, 29, 33; death of 29, 30, 31
Bolder, Robert 155

Bolton, Lucile 63
Bonanza (television series) 115
Bonner, Frank 149
The Boomerang (1912) 46
Booth, Edwin 4
Booth, John Wilkes 4, 35, 36
Booth, Junius Brutus 35, 36
The Border Parson (1912) 56
Borzage, Frank 54, 56, 57, 58, 59, 60, 61, 63, 82
Bosworth, Hobart 24, 29, 95, 99, 104, 106, 111, 112
Botnick, Vicki 152
Bow, Clara 118
Bowles, Donald 105
Boyd, William 170, 197
Bracey, Sidney 198
Bradbury, Ronald 88, 89
Brady, Alice 177
Brady, Edward 57, 58, 59, 60, 61, 62, 63, 102, 223
Brady, Matthew 192, 201
Brandeis, Justice Louis 8
Braun, Gertrude 74
Brave Little Woman (1912) 45
Bray, Helen 104
Breed o' the Mountains (1914) 61, 257; production details and cast list 246
Bridgeport Telegram 233
Brockwell, Gladys 127
Brockwell, Lillian 63
The Broken Doll (1908) 42
Broken Laws (1925) 238
The Broken Oath (1910) 68
Broken Threads (play) 128
Bronco Film Company 113
Brook, Clive 237, 259
Brook, Faith 237
Brook, Lyndon 237
Brook, Mildred Evelyn 237
Brooke, Van Dyke 26
Brooks, Mamie 236
Brothers (1912) 32; production details and cast list 242
Brower, Robert 149, 150, 212
Brown, Alexander 174, 175
Brown, Dorothy 53, 55
Brown, Henry 7
Brown, Karl 161
Brown, Milton 85, 91
Brown, William H. 80, 94, 141, 155
Browne, Porter Emerson 129
Browning, Tod 56, 94, 98
Brownlow, Kevin 164, 238, 259
Bruce, Kate 41, 42
Brunton, William 141, 143
Bryant, C.P. 205
Buchanan, Thompson 188
Buck, Nell Roy 178
Buckland, Wilfred 88, 96, 111, 112, 124, 128, 138, 149, 155, 161
Bunny, John 26, 31, 32, 68, 258; fame of 26
The Burglar (play) 8
Buried Alive (1917) 102, 258; production details and cast list 252
Burke, Billie 68, 87, 240
Burning Up (1930) 235
Burns, Edward 141
Burns, Fred 60
Burton, Clarence 63, 149, 152, 159, 167
Burton, John 103, 104
Busch, Mae 194

Bush, Pauline 50, 52, 54, 55, 57, 99, 102
Bushman, Francis X. 68, 158
Butler, Fred 198
Butler, William J. 42
Butterworth, Ernest 94, 159, 167
Byron, Nina 128, 131

Cabanne, Christy 59, 60, 66, 67, 69, 79, 98
Caldwell, Fred 205
Calhoun, Jean 132
California Home Guard 106
The California Home Guard News 107
California Straight Ahead (1925) 235
California, S.S. 185
Cameron, Rudy 194
Campbell, Eric 105
Captain Bill's Whiz Bang 110
Carew, Ora 129, 131
Carewe, Arthur Edmund 199
Carey, Harry 33, 258
Carleton, Lloyd B. 99
Carmen (1915) 83, 85, 86, 87, 99; production details and cast list 249, 250
Carmencita (1894) 23
Carnegie, Andrew, pacifism of 102
Carpenter, Florence 103
Carpenter, Horace B. 85, 86, 89, 91, 112, 113
Carpentier, Georges 179, 180
Carr, Harry 23, 25, 30, 68, 71, 95
Carter, Calvert 124
Carter, Lincoln J. 12
Casa de Contenta Apartments 238, 239
Casey, Leslie 188
Cassinelli, Dolores 178
The Cat's Paw (1914) 129
Caudebec Inn 41
Cavell, Edith 102
Cecil B. DeMille: American Epic (television documentary, 2004) 259
censorship, film 185, 196, 220
Centaur Film Company 43, 45, 46
Chadwick, Cyril 212
Champion Film Company 32
Chandler, James Robert 63
Chaney, Lon 259
Chaney, Lon, Sr. 52
Chaplin, Charlie 1, 59, 68, 105, 106, 107, 110, 125, 126, 127, 135, 149, 194, 195, 223, 240, 258; affairs of 80; marriages of 80
Chapman, Edythe 87, 91, 132
Charles Dickson Company 38
Charles, IX, King 94
The Charm School (1921) 161, 162, 163; production details and cast list 256
Chase, Charlie 59, 64
The Cheat (1915) 88
Chevalier, Maurice 259
Chicago American 194
Chicago Daily Tribune 86, 117
Chicago Police Parade (1901) 24
Choate, Joseph H. 234
The Chorus Lady (1915) 83, 87; production details and cast list 249

Christ Episcopal Church, Hollywood, California 59
Christie, Al E. 43, 45, 46, 62
Christy, Lillian 50, 51, 53, 55
Chumps (1912) 31, 258; production details and cast list 241
Church of the Holy Cross, Hollywood, California 59
The City Beautiful (1914) 66; production details and cast list 248
The Clansman (play) 70
Clarence (1922) 202, 203, 204, 205, 229; production details and cast list 257
Clarence: A Comedy in Four Acts (play) 203
Clark, George 231
Clark, Marguerite 68, 90, 125
Clark, Victor H. 223
Clary, Charles 95
Classic (magazine) 217
Clemens, Samuel 8
Clifford, William 49, 56
Clifton, Elmer 72, 79, 94
Clifton, Wallace C. 55
Clume Theater 105
Cody, "Buffalo" Bill 19, 20; friendship with Hal Reid 19
Cody, Lew 82
Cohn, Alfred 179, 180
Coke, Joshua 7
Collier, Constance 178
Collins, John Hancock 122
Columbia Broadcasting System, Inc. (CBS) 235
Comedy Central Network 235
Committee of Public Information 106
Compson, Betty 89, 194, 195
Compson, Maud 5, 11
The Confession (1910) 26
The Confession (play) 13, 24
Conklin, Chester 31, 105
Conklin, William 93, 98
Connick, H.D. 162
Connolly, Jack 205
Connors, Chuck 12
Conway, Jack 45, 46, 47, 56
A Cool Million 236
Coolidge, Dane 114
Coombs, Guy 140
Cooper, Edna Mae 114
Cooper, James Fennimore 12, 51
Cooper, Miriam 67, 72
Corbett, James J. 12, 23
Coronado Hotel 199
Corrigan, Tom 28
corruption, District Attorney's Office, Los Angeles 65
Costello, Helene 258
Costello, Maurice 26, 258
The Count of Monte Cristo (1908) 24, 29
A Counterfeit Santa Claus (1912) 30
The Countess Betty's Mine (1914) 61, 257; production details and cast list 246
The Course of True Love (1912) 32; production details and cast list 241
The Courtship of Miles Standish (1910) 154
The Cowboy Guardians (1912) 49; production details and cast list 243

Coxen, Edward 50, 51, 53, 55
A Cracksman Santa Claus (1913) 58, 258; production details and cast list 245
The Cracksman's Reformation (1913) 57, 258; production details and cast list 245
Crane, Ogden 141, 144
Crane, William H. 223
The Craven (1915) 70; production details and cast list 249
Crawford, Bessie 187
Cripple Creek (1912) 242
Cripple Creek (play) 13
Crisp, Donald 42, 60, 67, 114, 119, 120, 122, 124
Cronyn, Thoreau 195, 198
Cross Purposes (1913) 58, 257; production details and cast list 245
Cross the Mexican Line (1914) 63, 258; production details and cast list 248
Crothers, Rachel 197
Crowell, Josephine 80
Cruze, James 113, 114, 120, 124, 128, 129, 130, 132, 138, 139, 140, 141, 147, 149, 150, 151, 153, 161, 162, 198, 212
Cryer, Mayor George 231
The Cub Reporter's Big Scoop (1912) 46
Culver Military Academy 66
Cumming, Dorothy 171, 182, 183
Cummings, Richard 141
Cunningham, Jack 199
Cupid Incognito (1914) 63, 258; production details and cast list 247
Curfew Shall Not Ring Tonight (1912) 32; production details and cast list 242
Curtis, Allen 97
Curwood, James Oliver 63
Cyclone Bliss (1921) 228

D'Allbrook, Sidney 190
Dalton, Dorothy 105, 127, 258
Daly, Augustin 37
Damon & Pythias (play) 37
Dana, Viola 151
The Dancin' Fool (1920) 154, 155; production details and cast list 255
Daniel, H.B. 119
Daniel, W.B. 119
Daniels, Bebe 103, 151, 154, 155, 156, 170, 171, 194, 195, 197, 223
Daniels, Phyllis 103
Daredevil Jack (1919) 149
Dark Cloud 59
Darmond, Grace 141, 142, 143, 145; injuries from 1919 accident 142
The Daughter of a Crook (1914) 63; production details and cast list 247
Daughter of the Confederacy (play) 9
A Daughter of the Redskins (1912) 49; production details and cast list 243
Davenport, Adele 37; birth of 35; death of 37
Davenport, Alice Shepard 38, 43, 45, 48, 56, 59, 101, 152, 182, 214, 215, 218, 221, 223, 224; death of 236; divorce from Harry Davenport 39; homes of 236, 238; marriage to Harry Davenport 38; roles of 43, 45, 59
Davenport, Blanche (Bianca La Blanche) 36; birth of 35; career of 37, 38
Davenport, Dorothy 23, 24
Davenport, Edgar 37; birth of 35; career of 38
Davenport, Edward Loomis ("E.L.") 35, 36, 38; in Boston, Massachusetts 37; in Canton, Pennsylvania 37; at Drury Lane Theater, New York 35; at Grover Theater, Washington, D.C. 36; at Howard Athenaeum, Boston 35, 37; as influential Bostonian 37; travels of 35
Davenport, Fanny Elizabeth Vining 35, 36, 37, 38; death of 38
Davenport, Florence ("Flo") 37; birth of 35
Davenport, Harry 37, 100; affairs of 38, 39; birth of 35; career of 38; divorce from Alice Shepard 39; at Globe Theater, Boston, Massachusetts 38; at Herald Square Theater 38; homes of 236; marriages of 38, 39
Davenport, Lilly (Fanny): as Fanny Davenport 36, 37; birth of 35; career of 37, 38; death of 36, 37, 39
Davenport, Marion ("May") 37, 38; birth of 35
Davies, Howard 45, 46, 56
Davies, Maitland 105
Davies, Marion 50
Davis, Richard Harding 79, 198
Daw, Marjorie 87, 92, 96
Dead Man's Shoes (1913) 54, 257, 258; production details and cast list 244
Dean, Barbara 178
Dean, Faxon 114
Dean, Jack 88
De Briac, Charles 183
De Briac, Raymond 183
Decker, Lou 19
Decker, May 19, 20
de Cordoba, Pedro 85, 86
de Cordoba, Rudolph 76
The Deerslayer (1913) 51, 55, 56; production details and cast list 244
de Lafayette, Marquis 7
De La Motte, Marguerite 194
DeLeon, Walter 199
Delmont, Bambina Maude 185, 186; criminal life of 186, 192
de Longpre, Paul 44
De Maurier, George 178
de Medicis, Catherine 94
de Mille, Agnes 78, 144, 145
DeMille, Beatrice 112
DeMille, Cecil B. 1, 42, 43, 48, 78, 79, 81, 84, 86, 87, 88, 89, 90, 95, 96, 97, 105, 106, 107, 111, 113, 125, 126, 127, 144, 150, 151, 154, 155, 165, 170, 171, 173, 182, 196, 212, 235, 240; comes to Hollywood 78; death

of 236; legacy of 83; relationship with Julia Faye 236; relationship with Jeanie Macpherson 86, 87, 111, 236; technical innovations of 96, 112, 113, 114
DeMille, Constance 107
de Mille, William 78, 79, 82, 85, 89, 96, 105, 111, 144, 197, 203
Dempsey, Jack 149, 179, 180, 188, 236; death of 236
Dempster, Carol 94
The Den of Thieves (1914) 63, 76, 258; production details and cast list 248
Denny, Reginald 177, 235
DePalma, Ralph 137, 160
Desert Bridegroom (1922) 228
Desert Rider (1922) 228
Desmond, Mary McIvor 170, 191
Desmond, William 105, 191, 205, 223
Desperate Desmond Abducts Raymond (1911) 43
Desperate Desmond at the Cannon's Mouth (1912) 43
Destinn, Emmy 83
Deverich, Nat G. 119, 122, 124
The Devil's Bondwoman (1916) 99
The Devil-Stone (1917) 112, 113; production details and cast list 253
Dewey, George, Admiral 24
Dexter, Elliott 170, 171, 178, 180, 183
Diamond Cut Diamond (1912) 32; production details and cast list 242
Dickey, Paul 89, 199
Dickinson, Stiles 97
Dickson, Charles 38
Dickson, William K.L. 22, 23, 40
The Dictator (1922) 198, 199; production details and cast list 257
The Dictator: A Farce in Three Acts (play) 198
Dillon, Edward 42, 94, 97
Dillon, John 41
Dion, Hector 33
Director's Guild of America, founding of 97
Division of Four Minute Men 106
Dix, Beulah Marie 98, 111, 113
Dix, Richard 234, 235
Dixon, Rev. Thomas 70, 75; racism of 70, 76
Dr. Jekyll and Mr. Hyde (1912) 129
Dr. Jekyll and Mr. Hyde (1920) 259
Doctor Neighbor (1916) 99
Dodd, Rev. Neal 224
Doherty, Edward 195, 196
Dominguez, Frank 223
Dominguez, Stella 110
Dominicus, Evelyn 51, 55
Don't Tell Everything (1921) 174, 182, 183, 191; production details and cast list 256
Dorothy and the Scarecrow of Oz (1910) 25
Dorsey, Hugh 162
Double Speed (1920) 150, 151, 152, 153; production details and cast list 255
Doud, Omar F. 51
Dowlan, William C. 56
Down by the Sounding Sea (1914) 66; production details and cast list 248
Down the Hill to Creditville (1914) 67; production details and cast list 248
Dowst, Henry Parson 155
A Dozen Socks (1927) 236
Drew, Cora 67
Drew, John 6, 35
Drew, John, Sr., Mrs. 39
Drew, Louisa 37, 39
Drew, S. Rankin, death of 62
Drew, Sidney 39, 61; death of 62
drug dealer, "Captain Spaulding" 164
drug dealer, "Mr. Fix-it" 164
drug dealer, "The Man" 164
The Dub (1919) 130, 132; production details and cast list 254
Dubin, Al 16
DuBry, Fred 234
The Dude Wrangler (1933) 236
Dumont, J.M. 161
Dunbar, Helen 188, 212
Duncan, William 28
Dunham, Phil 58, 59, 60, 61, 62, 63, 64
Dunkinson, Harold L. 12
Dunn, Bobby 105
Dunn, William R. 32
Dunne, Ethel 55
Durfee, Minta 23, 30, 202
Durrell, Jean 53, 54, 55
Dwan, Allan 23, 49, 51, 52, 53, 54, 55, 57, 63, 91, 102, 240; career of 236; death of 236; feelings about Hollywood 49, 236; films of 50; fired from American Film Manufacturing Company (Flying A) 55; as mentor to WR 49, 50; in San Diego 50; in Santa Barbara 50

Eagle Eye 59, 60, 67
Eagles, Caryl 47
Earl Carriage Works 150
Early Days in the West (1912) 49; production details and cast list 243
The Earth Woman (1926) 238
East Lynne (play) 13
Eaton, Charles 178
Echo Park 64
Edeson, Robert 17, 38
Edison, Thomas Alva 6, 22, 23, 40, 45; and Edison Manufacturing Company 22; and General Film Company 24; as monopolist 24; and the Motion Pictures Patents Company 23, 24; and the "patent goons" 23, 49; and Projectoscope 9
Edler, Charles 56
Educational Films Corporation of America 235
Edward II, Prince of Wales 7
Edwards, Snitz 162, 167, 199
Edwards, Walter 128
Egan, Gladys 41, 42
Elliott, Frank 89
Elmer, William 85, 98, 119, 122, 123, 131, 132
Elsmore, Margaret 12
Eltinge, Julian 97
Emerson, John 81, 103
The Engagement Ring (1912) 45

Engel, Joseph 46
Enoch Arden (1915) 79, 80; production details and cast list 249
Epoch Producing Corporation 70
Erb, Ludwig 46
Erte, Romaine de Tirtoff 171
The Escape (1914) 67
Essanay Film Manufacturing Company 24, 49, 113
Essanay Film Manufacturing Company, and the MPPC 23
Evans, Frank 41
Evans, Nelson 146
Every Inch a Man (1912) 34, 47, 48; production details and cast list 243
Everybody's Magazine 113, 139
Examination Day at School (1908) 41
Excuse My Dust (1920) 138, 139, 152, 153, 154; production details and cast list 255
Exhibitors Trade Review 103
The Explorer (1915) 89
The Exposure (1914), production details and cast list 248
The Eye of a God (1913) 54; production details and cast list 243
Eyton, Bessie 62
Eyton, Charles 193, 197

F. Ray Comstock Film Company 148
Fagan, Douglas B. 149
Fahrney, Milton 43, 46, 47
The Failure of Success (1913) 56
Fairbanks, Anna Beth 107
Fairbanks, Douglas 1, 66, 80, 94, 97, 102, 105, 107, 110, 125, 127, 149, 150, 164, 170, 173, 195, 223, 259; affair with Pickford, Mary 107, 164
Fairbanks Production Company 108
Fairfax, Marion 123, 138, 141
The Fall of Babylon (1919) 95
A False Friend (1913) 56
Famous Players-Lasky Corporation 68, 90, 104, 118, 149, 198, 199; fire at 91
Fanny Davenport Company 39
Farley, James 120
Farnum, Dustin 78, 79, 105, 125, 126
Farnum, Franklyn 105, 121
Farnum, William 127, 258
Farrar, Geraldine 26, 83, 85, 86, 87, 95, 96, 97, 111, 112, 118, 258; incentives given to 83, 84, 87; popularity of 83; relationship with WR 85, 97; reputation as diva 84
Farrington, Adele 119, 162
Farrow, Mahala 7
Fatty, Round the Clock (unreleased) 202
Fatty's Big Mix-Up (1912) 56
Faversham, William 127, 258
Fawcett, George 178
Faye, Elsie 164
Faye, Hugh ("Hughie") 164
Faye, Julia 111, 170, 197; relationship with DeMille, Cecil B. 236
Fearnley, Jane 33
Federal Trade Commission, anti-

trust case against Paramount Pictures 185, 235
Federated Arts Group 197
Ferguson, Elsie 175, 176, 178
Ferguson, W.J. 188
The Feudal Debt (1912) 45
Field, George 32, 49, 50, 54, 56
Fields, Lew 68
Fields, W.C. 215
Fifth Avenue Theater Company 37
A Fight for Love (play) 12
The Fighting Chance (1920) 105, 152
Film Booking Offices of America 235
film sales, via State's Rights 52
filming locations: Arcata, California 141; Big Bear, California 113; Cuddebackville, New Jersey 42; Eureka, California 142; Fort Bragg, California 104; Holcomb Valley, California 114, 115; Korbel, California 142; Lake Arrowhead, California 60, 62, 128; Lodi, California 174; New York City 116, 118, 175; Pamona College, Claremont, California 162; San Diego, California 50; San Francisco, California 151, 152, 153, 161; Santa Barbara, California 50, 51, 52, 53, 54, 55; Santa Cruz, California 104; Sound View, Connecticut 42; Yosemite National Park 111, 163, 167
filming, cost of 90, 91
Finch, Flora 26, 32, 42
Find, Edythe 101
Fine Arts Film Company 66, 80, 81
Finley, Ned 26
Finnegan, Francis X. 114
The Firefly of France (1918) 122, 123; production details and cast list 253
Fires of Conscience (1914) 61, 257; production details and cast list 246
The Fires of Fate (1913) 58, 257, 258; production details and cast list 245
First National Pictures 191, 195, 235
Fischer, Margarita 47, 49, 56
Fitzgibbons, Bob 12
Fitzmaurice, George 89, 176, 178
$500 Reward (1915) 76
A Flash in the Dark (1914) 61; production details and cast list 246
Fleming, Bob 88, 89, 91, 92
Fleming, Victor 108
Foltz, Virginia 141
For a Human Life (play) 13
For Her Father's Sins (1914) 67; production details and cast list 248
For Those Unborn (1914) 60, 66; production details and cast list 246
Forbes, James 87
Ford, Francis 89
Ford, Harrison 148, 149, 150
Ford, Henry, pacifism of 102
Ford, John 98
Ford, Ray 32
Ford, Sterrett 98, 105

Forde, Eugenie 45, 46
Forde, Victoria 46
A Foreign Spy (1913) 56, 257; production details and cast list 244, 245
Forest Lawn Memorial Park 223, 224, 239
Forever (1921) 135, 175, 178, 191, 199, 236; loss of 179; production details and cast list 256
Forman, Tom 88, 89, 93
Formes, Karl 81
Forrest, Allan 122
Forrester, Izola 183
Forsaking All Others (1922) 233
The Foundling (1915) 91
The Four Horsemen of the Apocalypse (1921) 173
Fox, Della 8
Fox Film Corporation 108, 127, 164, 235
Foxe, Earl 51, 89
Francis, Ray 49
Francisco, Betty 190
Franey, William 108
Frank, Bert 258
Franklin, Edgar 130
Franzen, Nell 52
Frazee, Benjamin ("Benny") 160, 168, 191, 199, 223
Frederick, Pauline 90, 127, 175, 258
Freuler, John 49
Friend, Arthur 78
Frohman, Daniel 17
From Bowery to Broadway (play) 12
The Fruit of Evil (1912) 63
The Fruit of Evil (1914) 258; production details and cast list 247
The Fugitive (1908) 42

Gaden, William 167
Gage, Howard 67
Gaillard, Robert 32, 48
Gale, Josephine 205
Gamble, Fred 60, 61
Gamble, James Morris 60
The Gamblers (1912) 33; production details and cast list 242
Gardner, Helen 32
Gaskill, Charles 32
Gasoline Alley (unreleased) 185
Gaston, Mae 66
Gauntier, Gene 40
Gauzzino, Enrico 65
Gebhardt, George 46
Geldart, Clarence 93, 98, 105, 111, 120, 122, 123, 131, 138, 148, 155, 161, 174, 175, 183
Geraghty, Thomas J. 118, 161, 162
Gest, Morris 83
The Ghost Breaker (1914) 199
The Ghost Breaker (1922) 199, 200, 213; production details and cast list 257
The Ghost Breaker: A Melodramatic Farce in Four Acts (play) 199
Gibson, Edward "Hoot" 24, 47, 48, 173
Gibson, James 81
Gilbert, John 82, 189
Gilks, Alfred 151, 153, 155, 159
Gill, Charles 35
The Girl and the Crisis (1917) 100

The Girl and the Ranger (play) 10, 21, 24
Gish, Dorothy 4, 25, 33, 62, 66, 67, 81, 105, 127, 258
Gish, Lillian 4, 13, 33, 40, 53, 62, 67, 72, 79, 80, 93, 94, 105, 127, 258
Gish, Mary 4
Gismonda (play) 39
Glendon, J. Frank 205
Globe Theater 37
Glyn, Elinor 170, 175
Goddard, Charles W. 199
A Gold Necklace (1908) 42
The Golden Chance (1916) 87, 88, 118; production details and cast list 250
The Golden Fetter (1917) 98; production details and cast list 252
The Golden Supper (1908) 42
Golden, Joseph 54
Goldwyn, Samuel 78, 90, 99, 194
A Good Little Devil (1914) 259
Goodrich, Edna 88
Gordon, Dorothy 203
Gordon, James 153
Gordon, Julia Swayne 32, 33
Gordon, Phyllis 48, 63
Gorman, Charles 43
Grandon, Francis J. 55
Grange, Harold ("Red") 235
The Gratitude of Wanda (1913) 57; production details and cast list 245
Grauman, Sid 223
Gray, Mrs. Charles F. 231
Gray, Robert 89
The Greater Devotion (1914) 61, 257; production details and cast list 246
The Greatest Menace (1923) 233
Greeley, Horace 3
Green, Alfred E. 199
Greenwood, Winifred 120, 129, 148, 155
Grelle, Harry 52
Grey, Jane 76
Grey, Olga 111
Grey, Richard 87
Griffith, David Wark ("D.W.") 1, 29, 31, 33, 39, 42, 45, 53, 54, 63, 65, 69, 77, 79, 80, 81, 93, 94, 95, 105, 118, 122, 125, 126, 240; as actor 40; childhood of 70; directing methods of 70, 72, 73; filming in California 42; filming in Connecticut 40, 42; filming in New Jersey 40, 41, 42; financial success of 65, 67; interest in feature-length films 65; racism of 75, 76; technical innovations of 40, 65, 66, 68, 74, 81, 95
Griffith, Harry 104
Griffith, Jacob ("Roaring Jack") 39
Griffith, Katherine 104
Grinde, Harry A. 101
Grover, Leonard 35, 36
Guimera, Angel 85
Guise, Tom 128
The Gypsy Girl (play) 13
A Gypsy Romance (1914) 63, 258; production details and cast list 247

Haas, Robert H. 178
Hackathorne, George 231, 232, 233
Haines, Rhea 161
Hale, Alan 198
Hale, Albert A. 55
Hall, Delores 205
Hall, Ella 47
Hall, Walter H. 94
Hall, Winter 119, 122, 131, 132, 170
Hallam, Lewis 4
Halleran, Edith 32
Hamilton, Clayton 211
Hamrick, Burwell 112
Handschiegl, Max 96
Hansen, Juanita 212
Hanson, Ariel ("Speed") 141, 142
Hardy, Oliver 148, 180, 228
Harris, Elmer 147
Harris, Henry B. 17
Harris, Mildred 80
Harris, Theodosia 54
Harrison, Benjamin 4
Harrison, Ethel 192
Harron, Johnnie 122
Harron, Robert 25, 41, 60, 66, 67, 72, 94, 122
Harron, Tessie 122
Hart, William S. 80, 82, 102, 105, 107, 125, 127, 157, 187, 195, 223, 237, 258, 259
The Harvest of Flame (1913) 57, 257, 258; production details and cast list 245
Harvey, Chief 49
Harvey, George 234
Harwell, W.D. 153, 154
Hatch, J. Frank 52
Hathaway, Henry 212
Hatton, Raymond 86, 87, 88, 95, 105, 111, 112, 113, 122, 123, 124, 125, 128, 131, 139, 140, 141, 155, 170
Hawks, Howard 118
Hawley, Wanda 139, 140, 148, 151, 170, 187, 194, 212
Haworth Pictures Corporation 191
Hawthorne of the U.S.A. (1919) 149, 198; production details and cast list 255
Hay, John 4
Hayakawa, Sessue 86, 88, 126, 127, 205, 258
Hayes, Teddy 188, 210, 221
Haymarket Theater 35
Hays, Will H. 192, 196, 200, 202, 216, 218, 219
Hays Office, ineffectiveness of 196
Hazel Kirke Company 38
Hazen, Moses 3
Headin' South (1918) 259
Hearne, Eddie 109
The Heart of a Cracksman (1913) 57, 257, 258; production details and cast list 245
Heart of the Hills (1914) 62, 257; production details and cast list 247
Heartaches (1916) 99
Hearts and Horses (1913) 54, 257; production details and cast list 244
Hearts of the World (1917) 105, 122
Hecht, Ben 170
Heimerl, A.G. 51

The Hell Diggers (1921) 170, 174, 175, 191, 236; production details and cast list 256
Henderson, Dell 42, 79
Henderson, Grace 42
Hendricks, Ben 76
Henri, Caroline 38
Henry, Catherine 69
Henry, Gale 205
Henry, Patrick 125
Henry II, King 7
Her Awakening (1914) 60, 66; production details and cast list 246
Her Husband's Faith (1916) 99
Her Indian Hero (1912) 46
Her Innocent Marriage (1913) 54, 257; production details and cast list 244
Herbert, Dr. Gavin S. 215, 221, 226
Herbert, Jack 124, 153, 173, 190
Hermann, Charles 33
Herndon, Agnes 6, 8
Herschfeld, Harry 43
Heyfron, Gilbert 221, 222, 224, 229
Hicks, Maxine Elliott 151
Hidden Treasure (1908) 51
Hidden Treasure (1912) 51, 257; production details and cast list 243
The Hieroglyphic (1912) 32; production details and cast list 242
Hiers, Walter 199
Higgin, Howard 170, 183
Hill, Dale 122
Hill, Lee 89
Hinckley, William 69, 70
His Dream (1911) 43
His Extra Bit (1918) 254
His Mother's Son (1912) 32; production details and cast list 242
His Only Son (1912) 34, 43, 46, 47, 48; production details and cast list 242, 243
His Son (1911) 43, 47; production details and cast list 241
Hite, Charles 49
Hodkinson, William W. 90
Hoffman, Otto 231
Hollywood (television series, 1980) 259
Hollywood, history of 44, 64
Hollywood Hotel 44, 194
Hollywood Walk of Fame 240
Holm, John Cecil 16
Holt, Jack 95, 194, 213, 223
Home and Mother (1912) 56
Home Sweet Home (1914) 67
The Home-spun Heart (play) 9, 13
The Homesteader (1919) 76
The Hoosier Schoolmaster (1935) 239
A Hopi Legend (1913) 59, 258; production details and cast list 246
Hopkins, Miriam 259
Hopper, E. Mason 91, 98
Horning, Bob 89
Horsley, David 42, 43, 46
Horsley, William 43
Horwitz, Richard 130
The Hostage (1917) 110; production details and cast list 252
Hotel Arcata 141, 142, 143
Hotel Irma, Cody, Wyoming 19, 20

The House of Silence (1918) 119, 120; production details and cast list 253
The House That Shadows Built (1931) 259
The House with the Golden Windows (1916) 92, 93; production details and cast list 250
Howe, Herbert 226
Howe, Herbert Riley 111
Howland, Louis 114
Hoxie, Hart *see* Hoxie, Jack
Hoxie, Jack (aka Hoxie, Hart) 113, 141, 143, 228
Hubbard, Lucien 118
Hughes, Lloyde 234
Hughes, Rupert 194
The Human Gamble (1916) 99
Human Hearts (1912) 25, 122, 215
Human Hearts (play) 11, 12, 13; debut of 6; popularity of 6, 8, 9, 10, 13
Human Wreckage (1923) 231, 232, 233, 234, 238
Humphrey, William 47, 48
The Hunchback of Notre Dame (1939) 236
Hunt, Irene 60, 67
Hunted Down (1912) 49; production details and cast list 243
Hunting, Gardner 104, 129
Hunting Big Game in Africa (1909) 29
Huntley, Fred 114, 148, 153, 170
Hurst, Paul 114
Hutchinson, Samuel S. 49, 50, 51, 53, 54, 55, 56
Huygens, Christian 22

The Iconoclast (1908) 41
The Illumination (1912) 32; production details and cast list 242
In Convict Stripes (play) 13
In Humble Guise (1915) 89
In Life's Cycle (1908) 41
In Love and War (1913) 54; production details and cast list 244
In the Long Run (1912) 56
In the Sultan's Power (1909) 29
Inbad the Count (1912) 45
Ince, Elinor ("Nell") 172, 231
Ince, Ralph 32
Ince, Thomas H. 13, 54, 62, 89, 99, 105, 113, 172, 231, 232; and Inceville studio site 111; and Triangle Film Corporation 80; in accident with WR 80, 81
Independent Motion Picture (IMP) Studio 30, 33, 46, 68, 99
The Indian Maiden's Elopement (1911) 113
The Indian Maiden's Lesson (1911) 113
An Indian Outcast (1912) 49; production details and cast list 243
The Indian Raiders (1912) 33; production details and cast list 242
Indian Romeo and Juliet (1912) 32; production details and cast list 241
Indianapolis 500 automobile race 138, 147, 191, 200, 201, 202
Information Series 106
Inslee, Charles 49, 64
Intolerance: Love's Struggle Through the Ages (1916) 93; cast of 93,

94; cost of 93, 95; financial results of 95; length of 93, 95; massive sets of 93, 94, 95; production details and cast list 250, 251; production scope of 93, 95; as response to Griffith critics 93
The Intruder (1914) 61, 257; production details and cast list 246
Ivers, Julia Crawford 103

Jackson, Charles Tenney 98
Jacobs, Billy 92
Jean (animal actor) 32
Jean Intervenes (1913) 32; production details and cast list 241
Jeffries, James J. 106
Jesse L. Lasky Feature Play Company 78, 82, 85, 88, 89
Jim & Joe (1910) 25
Joan the Woman (1917) 95, 96, 97, 102, 106, 108, 130, 236; production details and cast list 251, 252
John Dough and the Cherub (1910) 25
Johns, Bertram 203
Johnson, Emilie 99
Johnson, Emory 99, 132, 133
Johnson, Henry 173
Johnson, Jack 35
Johnson, Julian 118
Johnson, Tefft 32
Johnston, Mary 88
Jones, Bertram 197
Jones, J. Park 64
Joy, Ernest 85, 86, 87, 105, 112, 113, 114, 119, 122, 123, 155, 159
Judith of Bethulia (1914) 53, 65, 69
Julian, Rupert 62, 89

Kaintuck (1912) 32, 258; production details and cast list 242
Kaiser, Fred 101
Kalem Company 33, 140; and the MPPC 23
Katterjohn, Monte M. 128
Kay-Bee Pictures 56
Keaton, Buster 1, 189, 240
Keefe, Zena 32, 33
Kelland, Clarence Buddington 128
Keller, Edgar 63
Keller, Gertrude 89
Kelly, Dorothy 49, 51
Kelly, Kitty 69
Kelsey, Fred 66, 67, 69
Kelso, Mayme 119, 203
Kennedy, Clara Genevieve 139, 151, 155
Kennedy, J.J. 39
Kennedy, Madge 127, 258
Kent, Charles 31
Kent, Willis 238
Kerrigan, J. Warren 49, 50, 51, 52, 59, 62, 68, 205
Kerry, Norman 121
Key, James L. 162
Keyes, Asa 193, 194
Keystone Film Company 45, 59, 64, 98
Keystone Kops, The 30, 31, 106
The Kid Brother (1927) 259
Kinestascope 22, 24
King, Anita 85, 86, 91, 98, 105
King, Joe 63, 91, 104
King, Karl 27
King Lear (1909) 32

The King of Kings (1927) 56
Kinsley, John 7
Kirkland, David 54, 57, 63
Kirkwood, James 47, 175, 231, 232
The Kiss (1913) 54, 257; production details and cast list 244
Kleig eyes, symptoms of 104, 105, 188, 210
Knobs o' Tennessee (play) 12
Knowles, James Sheridan 33
Knox, General Henry 37
Kohn, Ralph 162
Kosloff, Theodore 111, 170, 198
Kotani, Henry 120, 122, 124
Kummer, Frederick Arnold 92
Kuwa, George 93, 114, 155
Kyne, Peter B. 141

La Belle Marie (play) 6
Lackland, John 7
Laemmle, Carl 30, 33, 44, 46, 57, 58, 68, 90, 99, 102; first publicity stunt designed by 68
Lafayette Esquadrille Squadron 62
Lafayette Park, St. Louis, Missouri 8, 11
Lait, Jack 140
Lake Arrowhead, California, travel to 60
Lake Arrowhead Dam 60
The Land of Oz (1910) 25
Lang, Walter 239
Langdon, Lillian 94
Lanning, Frank 105
Larkin, Dolly 49
Larter, Anne 101
Larter, Gertrude 101
Larter, Lucy 101
Lasky, Jesse L. 23, 78, 79, 80, 81, 84, 85, 87, 88, 89, 90, 91, 93, 99, 102, 105, 109, 110, 113, 130, 134, 137, 139, 142, 145, 147, 148, 152, 155, 159, 161, 167, 173, 174, 175, 178, 182, 183, 185, 188, 189, 192, 193, 195, 196, 197, 198, 199, 200, 201, 202, 203, 205, 212, 215, 216, 219, 222, 223, 225, 228, 229, 231, 240; block booking requirements of 118, 185, 235; trying to replace WR 234, 235
Lasky Home Guard, No. 51 106, 107
The Last of the Mohicans (1911) 129
Laurel, Kay 141
Laurel, Stan 180, 228
Law, Rodman 33
Lawrence, Florence 26, 40, 68
Lawrence, Lotta 68
Lazzarini, Lorenza 155
The Leading Lady (1911) 26; production details and cast list 241
LeBaron, William 118
Lee, Lila 148, 150, 162, 183, 198, 199
Lee, Phil 76
Lee, Rev. Baker P. 59
Lee, Robert 153
Le Guerre, George 76
Lehrman, Henry 41, 42, 56, 62, 113, 186
Leider, Emily 106
Leigh, Frank 174

Leighton, Lillian 96, 98, 111, 112, 155, 183
LeRoy, Mervyn 199
LeSaint, Edward 98, 105
Less Than Kin (1918) 123, 124, 125, 129; production details and cast list 253
Lesser, Sol 70
Lesta, William 139, 140
Lester, Louise 50
LeVino, Albert Shelby 183, 188
Levy, Al 135
Lewis, Eugene B. 167
Lewis, Ralph 60, 67, 72, 94, 131, 141, 143
Liberty Magazine 145
Lichtman, Al 162
Liedtke, Henry 189
The Life of an American Fireman (1902) 23
The Lightning Bolt (1913) 58, 59, 257; production details and cast list 245
Lighton, Louis ("Buddy") 118
Lil' Abner (1940) 236
The Lilly and the Rose (play) 10
Lincoln, Abraham 35; death of 36; visits Grover Theater 36; watches Edward Loomis ("E.L.") Davenport 36
Lincoln, Elmo 94
Linder, Max 180
The Little American (1917) 106, 107
The Little Country Mouse (1914) 60; production details and cast list 246
The Little Red Schoolhouse (play) 13
Little Women (1949) 236
Little, Ann 62, 113, 114, 119, 121, 122, 123, 124, 128, 129, 132, 138, 139, 152, 153, 154, 173, 236; Christian Science beliefs of 236; death of 236; homes of 236; physical attributes of 113; relationship with WR 113, 121, 125, 126, 133; resemblance to Dorothy Davenport Reid 113; retirement of 154
Littlefield, Lucien 88, 89, 98, 105, 111, 151, 155, 170, 173, 174, 175, 183, 190
Lloyd, Frank 63, 258
Lloyd, Harold 31, 105, 154, 155, 223, 231, 259
Lockwood, Harold 122, 127, 258
Lockwood, Harry 43, 45
Loew, Marcus 189
Lombard, Carole 259
Lonesome Luke (serial) 155
Long, Walter 94, 98, 111, 153, 190, 198
Loomis, Margaret 161
Loos, Anita 81, 103
Lorre, Peter 240
Los Angeles Herald Examiner 216, 219
Los Angeles Herald Tribune 105
Los Angeles Times 216
The Lost Address (1912) 45
The Lost House (1915) 79, 80; production details and cast list 249
The Lottery Man (1919) 147, 148, 149; production details and cast list 255

Louden, Thomas 188
Louvish, Simon 164
Love and the Law (1913) 51, 52, 257; production details and cast list 243
The Love Burglar (1919) 140, 141; production details and cast list 254
The Love Mask (1916) 89, 91; production details and cast list 250
The Love Special (1921) 161, 167, 168, 169, 170, 174, 191; production details and cast list 256
Love, Bessie 94, 98, 202, 203, 205, 231
Love, Montague 178
The Loves of the Pharaoh (1922) 189
Love's Western Flight (1914) 63, 258; production details and cast list 247, 248
Lowery, F.A. 66
Lowery, William 67
Lubin Film Company 55, 56; and the MPPC 23
Lubitsch, Ernst 161, 189
Lucas, Wilfred 52
The Lucky Devil (1923) 235
Lumière, Auguste 22
Lumière, Louis 22
Lumière Cinématographe 22
Lundin, Walter 104
Lusitania, S.S., sinking of 102, 107
Lynton, Chris 80
Lyons, Edward 56
Lyons, Lurline 60
Lytell, Bert 89, 151

MacAlarney, Robert E. 79, 98
MacDonald, Donald 89
MacDonald, Francis 108
MacDonald, J. Farrell 199
Mace, Fred 45, 62
Machperson, Jeanie 111
Mackley, Arthur 70
MacLaren, Mary 190
MacLean, Douglas 193
MacLean, Faith Cole 193
Macpherson, Jeanie 42, 85, 86, 89, 96, 97, 105, 111, 112, 170, 191; relationship with Cecil B. DeMille 86, 87, 111, 236
MacQuarrie, Murdock 52, 57
MacReady Theater Company 35
Madison, Cleo 57, 79
Madison Square Theater Company 38
Maescher, A.B. 205
Magee, Patricia 162
Magna Carta, signing of 7
Maigne, Charles 98, 105
Mailes, Charles Hill 52
Maison, Edna 62
Maja, Selma 167
Majestic Motion Picture Company 65, 66, 69
Making a Living (1914) 59
Making Good (1912) 33; production details and cast list 242
Male and Female (1919) 52
The Man from Funeral Range (1918) 128; production details and cast list 254
The Man Who Saved the Day (1917) 253
The Man Within (1914) 63, 258; production details and cast list 247
Manhattan Madness (1925) 236
Mann, Herb 105
Mann, Louis 38
Manners, Margaret 49
Manon, Marcia 98, 111, 148
A Man's Duty (1912) 33; production details and cast list 242
Man's Duty (1913) 57; production details and cast list 245
Marc, Alice 113
Maria Rosa (1916) 83, 84, 85, 86, 87, 91; production details and cast list 250
Marks, Willis 128, 155
The Married Flapper (1921) 233
Marsh, Mae 40, 60, 67, 94, 98, 127, 202, 203, 258
Marsh, Marguerite 94, 98, 202, 203
Marshall, George 56, 108
Marshall, Ray 108
Marshall, Tina 162
Marshall, Tully 94, 95, 98, 107, 112, 119, 128, 129, 149, 150, 151, 153, 155
Marshall, William 149
Martin, Vivian 97
Martindel, Edward 197, 203, 204
Marvin, Henry 40, 45
Marx, Adolph ("Harpo") 259
Marx, Herbert ("Zeppo") 259
Marx, Julius Henry ("Groucho") 259
Marx, Leonard ("Chico") 259
Mason, James P. 113
Mason, Lillian 139, 141
Mather, Cotton 37
Mather, Stephen 19
A Matinee Mixup (1912) 45
Maugham, Somerset 89
Maurice, Mary 32
Maxwell, Perriton 13, 26
Mayall, Herschel 64, 212
Mayer, Louis B. 173, 196
Mayne, Eric 231
Mayo, Frank 38
McAllister, Paul 178
McAvoy, May 103, 195, 203, 204
McComas, J.L. 205
McCord, Mrs. Lewis 87
McCoy, Charles ("Kid") 127, 189
McCoy, Harry 45
McCullogh, Philo 76
McCutcheon, Wallace 40, 178
McDaniel, George 128
McDermott, J.W. 81
McDowell, Claire 41, 42, 183, 197, 231
McDowell, Melbourne 39; marriage to Lilly (Fanny) Davenport 39
McGaffey, Kenneth 126, 127, 135
McGee, Morris 48
McKim, Robert 231
McKinley, William 4, 24
McLynn, Gertrude 59
McQuarrie, James 102
McVey, Lucille 62
Meet Me in St. Louis (1944) 236
Meighan, Thomas 175, 177, 180
Melford, George H. 62, 88, 89, 91, 92, 93, 113, 128
Méliès, Georges 23
Méliès Studios, and the MPPC 23
Menjou, Adolphe 203, 204
Mental Suicide (1913) 57, 258; production details and cast list 245
Merch, Mary 114
Meredyth, Bess 62, 63
Messick, William 49
Metro-Goldwyn-Mayer Studio 235, 239
Meyer-Forster, Wilhelm 81
Micheaux, Oscar 76
Mickey (1918) 52
Middleton, George 103
Midgley, Fannie 148, 161
Miller, Alice Duer 123, 162
Miller, Arthur 178
Miller, Betty 43
Miller, Eddie 109, 200
Miller, Henry, Jr. 188
Miller, Ruth 170, 172
Miller, W. Christie 41
Miller Brothers' 101 Ranch & Wild West Show 54
Mills, Darius O. 3
Mills, Elizabeth 3
Minematsu, Frank 29, 30
Miner, Harry C. 10, 12
Minor Theater 142
Minter, Mary Miles 50, 56, 151, 192, 193, 194, 195; relationship with William Desmond Taylor 193, 194
The Miracle Man (1919) 259
Mr. Grex of Monte Carlo (1915) 89
Mitchell, Claude 93, 108, 113, 128
Mix, Tom 24, 28, 47, 62, 67, 79, 159, 173
The Modern Prodigal (1908) 41
A Modern Snare (1913) 54, 257; production details and cast list 244
Modini-Wood, Charles 26, 27; see also Stack, Robert
Modini-Wood, Elizabeth 26, 27
Modini-Wood, Hanna 27
Modini-Wood, Mamie 26, 27
Modini-Wood, Mona 27
Modini-Wood, William 27
A Mohawk's Way (1908) 41
Molly Pitcher (1911) 140
Monkey Business (1931) 259
Montague, Gladys 63
Montgomery, Frank 48
Moon, Lorna 183
Moonshine Molly (1914) 59, 60, 66; production details and cast list 246
Moore, Colleen 233
Moore, Grace 162
Moore, Joyce 76
Moore, Marcia 57
Moore, Owen 29, 94, 164
Moore, Tom 127, 173, 258
Moore, Victor 90, 91
Moran, Polly 170
Moreland, Ned 38
Moreno, Antonio 105, 151, 173, 189, 194, 223, 234, 240, 258
Morey, Harry T. 26, 49, 51, 55
Morgan, Byron 138, 139, 153, 154, 159, 173, 174, 190
Morin, Herman 135
Morris, General Thomas A. 3
Morris, George W. 41
Morrison, James 26, 32

The Mother and the Law (1919) 93, 95
The Mothering Heart (1913) 53
A Mother's Influence (1914) 59; production details and cast list 246
Mothers of Men (1917) 104
Mothers of Men (1920) 255
Motion Picture Classic Magazine 108, 155, 171
Motion Picture Directors Association 192
Motion Picture Magazine 50, 59, 99, 103, 139, 234
Motion Picture News 103
Motion Picture Producers and Distributors of America 196
Motion Picture War Service Association 125
Motion Picture Weekly Magazine 130
Motography 79
A Mountain Romance (play) 13
The Mountaineer (1914) 62, 258; production details and cast list 247
The Movie Album (1931) 258, 259
Movie Weekly Magazine 194, 207, 218, 227
Moving Picture World Magazine 56, 58, 59, 81, 88, 98, 104, 118, 130, 143, 154, 170, 213
moving pictures, history of 22, 23
Mowatt, Anna Cora (Ritchie) 35
Mrs. Jones' Birthday (1909) 24
Mrs. Wallace Reid Productions 237, 238
MTV Networks 235
Mulhall, Jack 110, 175
Mumford, Ethel Watts 155
Murphy, Jimmy (aka Jimmy Murphy Doyle) 109, 137, 160, 231
Murray, Charlie 62, 79, 98, 105, 110, 121, 125, 126, 173
Murray, Mae 88, 126, 127, 258
Musgrove, George 38
The Music Master (1908) 40
Mutoscope & Film Company, founding of 24
Mutt & Jeff (serial) 43
Mutual Film Corporation 56, 59, 65, 66, 67, 69, 76
Muybridge, Eadweard 22
Myers, Carmel 94, 127
Myers, T.E. 200
The Mystery of Yellow Astor Mine (1913) 57; production details and cast list 245

Nagel, Conrad 152, 194, 195, 197, 223
Nan of Music Mountain (1917) 113, 114, 115, 121, 129; production details and cast list 252, 253
Nash, J.E. 188
National Association for the Advancement of Colored People (NAACP) 76
Navajo Films 89
Nazimova, Alla 175
Near to Earth (1913) 53; production details and cast list 243
Negri, Pola 160, 195, 223; misgivings about working with WR 161
Neilan, Marshall 50, 54, 57, 102, 108

Neill, James 57, 60, 85, 88, 89, 92, 95, 98, 107, 111, 112, 124, 128, 129
Nelson, Evelyn 228
Nestor Film Company 33, 42, 43, 44, 45, 46, 47, 58, 59, 61, 62, 63
New York American 187
New York Dramatic Mirror 65, 67, 81, 90
New York Herald 195
New York Journal 43
New York Motion Picture Company 33, 57, 87
New York Telegraph 178
New York Times 185
Nice People (1922) 192, 197, 198, 199; production details and cast list 257
Nichols, George 41
Nickelodeon Network 235
The Niggard (1914) 67; production details and cast list 248
The Night Before Christmas (play) 12
Night Life in Hollywood (1922) 205; production details and cast list 258
Nilsson, Anna Q. 58, 140, 141, 151, 152
Noble, John W. 76
Noble, T.D., Jr. 153
Nobles, Dolly 25
Nobles, Milton 25
Nobody's Money (1922) 212, 213
Normand, Mabel 2, 30, 41, 42, 45, 52, 62, 67, 68, 79, 98, 99, 110, 127, 164, 165, 172, 173, 187, 189, 193, 215, 220, 258; death of 1; as suspect in Taylor murder 1
North West Mounted Police (1940) 239
Northrup, Harry 32, 231, 232
Novarro, Ramon 31

Oakie, Jack 259
Oakley, Florence 125
The Oath and the Man (1908) 41
O'Brien, George 199
O'Brien, John B. 59, 67
O'Connor, H.M. 131
O'Connor, Loyola 141
O'Connor, Mary 80
The Odalisque (1914) 67; production details and cast list 248
Official War Review (newsreel, 1917–1919) 106
Ogle, Charles 113, 114, 119, 120, 122, 123, 124, 128, 129, 131, 132, 141, 143, 144, 148, 149, 159, 170, 171, 212
Old Heidelberg (1915) 80, 81; production details and cast list 250
Old Isaacs the Pawnbroker (1908) 40
Oldfield, Barney 106, 137
Oliver Morosco Productions 103
Oliver, Guy 98, 111, 113, 114, 115, 124, 131, 132, 138, 141, 148, 149, 151, 153, 161, 170, 173, 188, 190
Oliver Twist (1909) 32
101-Bison Films 46, 54, 69, 89, 99
One Hundred Years Ago (1915) 89
One of Us (play) 140
O'Neill, Nance 39
Osborne, Jefferson 45, 46, 56

Over the Ledge (1914) 67; production details and cast list 248
Overbaugh, Roy 50
The Overland Limited (1925) 236
Owen, Seena 70, 72, 80, 94

Page, Mann 183
Paget, Alfred 80, 94, 104
A Pair of Baby Shoes (1912) 46
Pallette, Eugene 48, 53, 54, 94, 103, 105, 223
Pantages, Alexander 223
Paragon Films 76, 89
Paramount Pictures 90, 91, 99, 103, 109, 113, 118, 128, 137, 145, 146, 147, 155, 162, 164, 174, 175, 176, 177, 180, 185, 191, 192, 193, 195, 198, 213, 216, 217, 222, 234, 235; bankruptcy of 235
Paramount-Publix Pictures 90; bankruptcy of 235
Parker, William 180, 216, 217
Parsons, Louella 82, 106, 109, 176, 177, 178, 239
Pasha, Kalla 198, 212
Pasque, Ernest 129
Passing of the Beast (1914) 63, 258; production details and cast list 247
Pathé Exchange 119
Pathé Frères Studio 23
Pathé Studios 191, 235; and the MPPC 23
The Pathfinder (1911) 51
Patrick, Jerome 178
Peck, Vernon 152, 159, 160
Peggy (1916) 87
The Penalty of Silence (1917) 102, 258; production details and cast list 252
The Perils of Pauline (1914 on) 23
Perley, Charles 100
Perry, Pansy 95
Perry, Paul 128
Person, A.Y. 10
Persons, Thomas 24
Peters, Page 63
Peyton, Lawrence 95, 98
The Phantom Island (1916) 89, 99
Phenakistiscope 22
Philbrook, Edward H. 49
Phillips, Carmen 161, 212
The Phoenix (1910) 25; production details and cast list 241
The Phoenix (play) 9
Photoplay Journal 107
Photoplay magazine 106, 107, 109, 126, 127, 145, 150, 164, 168, 172, 175, 180, 187, 188, 202, 205, 226, 234, 235
Photoplayer's Club 62
Pickens, Sam 27
The Picket Guard (1913) 57; production details and cast list 245
Pickford, Jack 13, 25, 29, 41, 42, 105, 121, 151, 164, 165, 173, 202, 203; death of 165
Pickford, Lottie 13, 42, 50, 128, 151, 173
Pickford, Mary 1, 4, 5, 13, 29, 40, 42, 45, 68, 79, 90, 91, 97, 105, 107, 125, 127, 150, 151, 164, 170, 193, 195, 199, 202, 203, 222, 223, 258, 259; affair with Fairbanks, Douglas 107, 164; sleeping habits of 5

The Picture of Dorian Gray (1913) 57; production details and cast list 243
Picture Show Magazine 146, 192
Picturegoer Magazine 146, 154, 189, 227
Picture-Play Magazine 144, 203, 227
Pictures (magazine) 227
Pillsbury, Helen 162
Piper's Opera House 38
Pirate Gold (1913) 51, 52; production details and cast list 243
Pitcher, Molly 14
Playthings (magazine) 230
Polyscope Film Company 24
Porter, Edwin S. 23, 45, 46
Post, Charles A. ("Buddy") 137, 174, 175, 191, 220, 222, 223, 227, 229, 236, 238; death of 236
Post, Wiley 227
The Powder Flash of Death (1913) 54; production details and cast list 244
Powell, Frank 42
Powers Picture Plays 46, 57, 60, 63
Powers, Pat 46
Powers, Tom 32
Pratt, Jack 205
Predmore, Lester 41
Prevost, Marie 233
Price, Kate 49, 51, 67
The Pride of Lonesome (1913) 54, 257; production details and cast list 244
The Prince of Peace (play) 10
Printzlau, Olga 120
The Prison Without Walls (1917) 98, 99, 103; production details and cast list 252
Procter & Gamble Company 60
The Property Man (1914) 59
Provincetown Players 152
Pryor, Herbert 139
Purviance, Edna 151, 193
Pyle, C.C. 235
Pyramid Film Company 54

The Quack (1914) 63, 258; production details and cast list 247
Queen Elizabeth (1912) 259
A Quiet Little Wedding (1913) 59
Quirk, James 226
Quo Vadis (1913) 65

The Racing Strain (1933) 235, 239
A Ram-Buncteous Endeavor (1917) 253
Ramona (1916) 66
Rankin, Carolyn 148
Rankin, Doris 39
Rankin, Gladys 39, 62; death of 61
Rankin, McKee 38, 61; career of 38, 39; childhood of 38; death of 63; marriages of 38, 39; as theater builder 38, 39
Rankin, Phyllis 38, 39
Raphael, John Nathaniel 178
Rappe, Virginia: career of 185, 186; death of 185, 186; funeral of 192; homes of 186; reputation of 185; venereal diseases of 185
Ravena 49

Rawlinson, Herbert 56, 62, 99
Ray, Charles 82, 102, 103, 259
Raymond, Frances 199
Read, Opie 80
Realart Pictures 103
Red Book Magazine 141
A Red Cross Martyr; or, On the Firing Line of Tripoli (1912) 31; production details and cast list 241
Red Feather Pictures 99
Red Kimono (1925) 237, 238
Red, White and Blue 106
Red Wing, Lillian 33
Redman, Minna 162
Regeneration (1914) 61, 62, 257; production details and cast list 246, 247
Reicher, Frank 87, 89
Reid, America 7
Reid, Bertha Westbrook 6, 8, 20, 21, 27, 35, 54, 58, 136, 178, 191, 197, 199, 206, 208; as actor 8; childhood of 8; Christian Science beliefs of 224; death of 236; divorce from James Halleck ("Hal") Reid 19; elopes with James Halleck ("Hal") Reid 8, 9; family history of 6, 7; friendship with Mary Pickford 199; injured in automobile accident 26; meets James Halleck ("Hal") Reid 8; obsession with WR 9; personal travels of 13; pregnancy of 9; reaction to death of WR 222, 223; reconciles with James Halleck ("Hal") Reid 12, 13; scandal caused by elopement 9; self-aggrandizement of 6, 7, 8; separates from James Halleck ("Hal") Reid 11, 13; social aspirations of 8; theatrical touring of 9, 10, 11, 12, 13, 14; writings of 7, 8, 10, 15, 17, 18, 33, 48
Reid, Betty Anna 209, 216, 229, 230, 234; actual arrival at DeLongpre 206, 207, 208; adoption controversy of 206, 207, 208; biological daughter of WR 239, 240; education of 239; emotional problems of 239; family of 239
Reid, Dorothy Davenport 27, 34, 51, 54, 60, 69, 79, 98, 99, 116, 134, 135, 136, 137, 145, 146, 147, 151, 152, 155, 160, 165, 167, 170, 173, 175, 178, 179, 181, 182, 188, 206, 210, 215, 235, 237; accepts WR proposal 57, 58; anti-drug crusades of 232, 233, 234; bankruptcy of 239; at Biograph Company 39, 40; birth of 38; childhood of 39; Christian Science beliefs of 109, 224; death of 239; declines WR proposal 50; as de facto manager of WR 99, 195; earnings of 40, 51, 66; feud with Bertha Westbrook Reid 58, 100, 109, 127, 151, 177, 191; filming in New Jersey 41; financial problems of 237, 238, 239; funeral of 239; grave of 239; hired by Griffith, David Wark ("D.W.") 39; homes of 44, 45, 48, 59, 64, 100, 105, 122, 157, 158, 159, 163, 165, 166, 168, 174, 176, 187, 188, 191, 197, 199, 205, 207, 209, 214, 216, 222, 224, 227, 229, 230, 231, 234, 237, 238, 239; honeymoon at Squirrel Inn, Lake Arrowhead 60; jealousy of 85, 97, 121, 152, 153; keeps details of WR illness from Bertha Westbrook Reid 213, 214, 215, 218, 221, 222, 223; leases DeLongpre house 237; meets WR 43, 46, 47, 48; moves to Hollywood 43; moves to Motion Picture Country Home 239; personality of 121; physical attributes of 48, 121; pregnancy of 100, 104, 108, 168; pride at stage background 35; as producer and director 238; property owned by 60; at Reliance Film Company 42; roles of 40, 41, 42, 43, 44, 45, 46, 47, 48, 56, 57, 58, 59, 60, 61, 62, 63, 76, 77, 89, 99, 102, 104, 105, 122, 231, 232, 237; vacations without WR 163; wedding of 58, 59; William Parker interview 216, 217, 218, 219
Reid, Hazel 4, 11; divorces of 12; joins James Halleck ("Hal") Reid troupe 11; marriage to Harold Dunkinson 11, 12
Reid, Hugh 4, 5, 9; powerful friends of 4
Reid, Hugo 114
Reid, James 3, 7
Reid, James Halleck ("Hal") 4, 24, 26, 32, 33, 35, 47, 48, 51, 54, 55, 56, 67, 104, 215; accused of rape 5; affairs of 4, 9, 11, 13, 27; conviction of 5; death of 156; divorces of 5, 19; friendship with Buffalo Bill Cody 19; marriages of 4, 104, 156; pardon of 6; personality of 4, 13; plays of 6, 9, 10, 12, 13, 21, 24; prison sentence of 5, 6; rape trial of 5; sells rights to *Human Hearts* (play) 12; theatrical touring of 4, 5, 8, 9, 10, 11, 12, 13, 14, 24; tricks WR to leave Wyoming 20; wealth of 12; writes *Human Hearts* (play) 6
Reid, John 3
Reid, John E. 4
Reid, John Harold ("Hal Jr.") 156
Reid, Mae Withers 4, 11
Reid, Robert 3
Reid, Ruth Dugan 239
Reid, Sarah S. 4
Reid, Whitelaw 3, 5, 227, 234; arranges pardon of Hal Reid 6; as Editor in Chief of *New York Tribune* 3; death of 53; estate of 53; homes of 3; marriage of 3; political career of 3, 4, 6; as writer 3
Reid, William Wallace ("Wally") 24, 78; absence from war-related functions 107, 108, 125, 126, 127; academic results of 16; addiction as studio issue 213; adoption of Betty Anna Mummert 206, 207, 208; alcoholism of 121, 136, 145, 147, 151, 163, 174, 179, 181, 182, 191, 213; alternative cures tried by 205,

210; ambivalence toward stardom 97, 98, 117, 134, 135, 178; anger toward David Wark ("D.W.") Griffith 71, 77, 79; on Ann Little 113; artistic talents of 17, 127, 151; athleticism of 2, 16, 17, 18, 28, 106, 168; autobiography of 77, 83; automobiles of 59, 81, 100, 101, 109, 110, 150, 152, 180, 229; autopsy of 221; birth of 9; at Blessing sanitarium 212, 215; as cameraman 25, 31; childhood of 10, 11, 12, 13, 14, 15, 18, 179; at Cody, Wyoming 19; comedic talents of 121, 139, 150, 161; as comic actor 63; creativity of 17, 18; dancing talents of 155, 178; Dorothy Davenport declines proposal 50; death of 2, 185, 221, 222, 229, 234; departs Perkiomen Seminary 18; depression of 147, 181, 187; desire to race at Indianapolis 500 147, 200, 201; as director 34; discovery by Jesse L. Lasky and Cecil B. DeMille 79; dressing room of 234; drug purchases of 219; drug use reported in press 175, 176, 187, 188, 194, 195, 196, 197, 202, 203, 216, 220, 222; earnings of 19, 25, 28, 51, 66, 68, 82, 100, 108, 149, 195, 229; and Elizabeth Modini-Wood 26, 27; endorsement deals of 134, 180, 204; escapes to mountains to rebuild health 188; estate of 229, 230; examined by studio doctor 197; family history of 3; fan mail received by 99, 117, 170; favorite films of 53, 69; favorite foods of 135; fear of blood 143; fear of boats 12; fear of wind 11; fears of military service 108, 119, 125, 132; feelings about acting 21, 24, 31, 47, 62, 134, 135; feelings for father 4, 15, 156, 157; feelings for Highlands homes 12, 13; feelings for time in Wyoming 20; feelings of co-workers 222; female fans of 134; film output of 91; final collapse of 212; final illness of 213, 214, 215, 216, 220, 221; financial affairs of 229, 230; financial problems of 163; at Freehold Military Academy 13, 14, 15, 16; friends of 135 (Jack Dempsey 149, 236; Phil Dunham 58, 59; Allan Dwan 236; Buddy Post 137, 236; Will Rogers 227); funeral of 222, 223, 224, 234; generosity of 136, 137, 166, 180, 191, 199; grave of 223, 224; health of 149, 187, 188, 191; hobbies of 168, 177; homes of, Cody, Wyoming 19; homes of, Highlands, New Jersey (Glory View estate) 12, 13; homes of, Hollywood 134 (Cahuenga Canyon 48; DeLongpre Avenue 157, 158, 159, 163, 165, 166, 168, 174, 176, 179, 187, 188, 189, 191, 197, 199, 205, 206, 207, 214, 216, 222, 223, 237; Las Palmas Avenue 59; Reiter Arms Apartments 56, 59, 98); homes of, Laurel Canyon (Wonderland Avenue hideaway) 151, 202, 203; homes of, Los Angeles (Allison Avenue 64, 81, 99; Morgan Place 100, 101, 105, 109, 115, 116, 122, 151, 152, 163, 229); homes of, New York City 11, 12, 13 (5th Avenue 178, 179); homes of, St. Louis 9, 10, 11; homes of, Santa Barbara 50; honeymoon at Squirrel Inn, Lake Arrowhead 60; as horseman 47, 48, 53; illnesses of 172, 174, 176, 180, 187, 189, 191, 198, 206, 210, 212, 215, 217; image of 144; in Santa Barbara 34; injuries sustained by 53, 54, 81, 111, 112, 115, 126, 143, 145, 146, 147; insecurities of 108, 109; insomnia of 146, 147, 180; intellect of 136; interest in science 136, 158; investigated by police 81; last visit with mother 177; last words of 221; leaves American Film Manufacturing Company (Flying A) 56; leaves Biograph 81; leaves Universal Film Manufacturing Company 66; legacy of 234; lives with Westbrook family 10, 11; love for mother 15; love of automobiles 13, 26, 59, 109, 137, 138, 150, 159, 173, 190; love of books 11, 136, 158; love of parties 110; masculinity of 59; meets Davenport, Dorothy 34, 35, 46, 47, 48; meets Griffith, David Wark ("D.W.") 66; morphine use and addiction of 143–146, 151, 154, 164, 165, 181, 191, 196, 202, 203, 205, 206, 212, 220; moved to Banksia Place Sanitarium 215; musical talents of 2, 59, 105, 108, 109, 127, 168, 177, 178, 180, 194, 204; nervous breakdowns of 188, 213; nicknames of 2, 9, 136, 165; 1919 accident of 141, 142, 143, 145, 218; painting talents of 2, 158; at Perkiomen Seminary 16, 17, 18, 19; personal disappointment of 108, 119, 125, 132, 211; personality of 135; pets of 12; physical appearance and attributes of 14, 16, 17, 69, 150, 154, 160, 161, 172, 180, 181, 185, 188, 196, 198, 200, 205, 210, 211, 215; pilots train 167; popularity of 1, 17, 53, 58, 62, 67, 68, 69, 79, 88, 89, 91, 98, 99, 103, 104, 105, 106, 108, 109, 111, 112, 114, 117, 118, 121, 122, 128, 130, 133, 134, 141, 146, 154, 159, 162, 163, 168, 170, 173, 176, 178, 179, 180, 189, 191, 200, 203, 213, 217, 219, 222, 234; portrait of 97; practical jokes of 161; property owned by 60; as racecar driver 2, 191; reaction to death of father 156; reckless driving of 53, 80, 81, 109, 115, 137, 138, 147, 165, 173, 239; registers for draft 108; relationship with Geraldine Farrar 85, 97; relationship with Ann Little 113, 121, 125, 126, 133; relationship with mother 26, 27, 28, 127, 151, 177, 219; relationship with son 115, 151, 194; relationships with men 28, 59; relationships with women 18, 19, 27, 50, 57, 58, 160, 168, 169, 170; religious beliefs of 216, 224; role in *The Birth of a Nation* (1915) 70, 71, 73, 74, 76, 79; as "Renaissance Man" 3, 218; rumored affairs of 85, 97, 113, 121, 125, 126, 133, 152, 160, 168, 170, 208; rumored euthanasia of 226; as 2nd Unit Director for American Film Manufacturing Company (Flying A) 50, 51, 53, 54, 55; sense of humor of 180; sexuality of 179; spending habits of 100, 109; stabbed by Freehold Military Academy classmate 15; stage appearances of 10, 11, 17, 20, 21, 154; star on Hollywood Walk of Fame 240; stunt work of 47, 48, 59, 173, 188, 189; taken advantage of by friends 160, 163, 167, 168, 199, 203; talents of 2, 81, 82; and tornado of 1896 10, 11, 12; travels with parents 11; at Universal Film Manufacturing Company 55, 56, 58, 63, 81; wedding of 58, 59; works as laborer 20; works as ranch-hand 20; works as reporter 20, 148, 149; works as surveyor 20; works at American Film Manufacturing Company (Flying A) 50, 51; works at Hotel Irma, Cody, Wyoming 19, 20; works at Independent Motion Picture (IMP) 30; works at *Motor Magazine* 26 works at Selig 24, 25, 27; works at Vitagraph 26; writing talents of 15, 17, 18, 21, 24, 26, 31, 32, 33, 136, 192

Reid, William Wallace, Jr. ("Billy") 115, 116, 136, 151, 152, 176, 178, 182, 194, 206, 208, 209, 216, 229, 230, 234, 235, 237; architectural career of 239; arrest of 239; birth of 109, 110; death of 239; education of 239; endorsements of 230, 231; homes of 239; jailing of 239; marriage of 239; reckless driving of 239; roles of 152; stunt work of 239

Reinhardt, John 76
Reliance Film Company 30, 33, 34, 43, 46, 59, 65, 66, 69
Renick, Ruth 149
Rent Free (1922) 174, 183, 185, 187, 191; production details and cast list 256
The Reporter (1911) 27; production details and cast list 241
Retribution (1913) 58, 257; production details and cast list 245
The Return of Sherlock Holmes (1929) 237
Revolutionary War 3
Reward of Courage (1913) 55
Rex Motion Picture Company 46, 57, 58, 62, 99, 102
Rhodes, Elizabeth 205
Rice, Elmer 183
Rice, James 7
Rice, Mary Virginia 7

Rice, Thomas B. 7; moves to Illinois 7; wealth of 7
Rice, W.G. 49
Rich, Vivian 50, 52, 53, 54, 55, 56
Richardson, John 38, 52, 173
Rickenbacker, Eddie 137
Ricketts, Josephine 46
Ricketts, Thomas 33, 43, 45, 46
Ricksen, Lucille 231; death of 233
Ridgely, Cleo 87, 88, 89, 91, 92, 95, 96
Rimrock Jones (1918) 113, 114, 115; production details and cast list 253
Ring, Francis 175
Ritchey, Will M. 130, 132, 153
River Rest estate 13, 14, 26, 27, 177, 221
The Road to Ruin (1934) 239
The Roaring Road (1919) 137, 138, 139, 150, 152, 153, 154, 173, 179, 259; production details and cast list 254
Robards, Willis 58, 104
Robards-Reid Productions 104
Roberts, Edward 202
Roberts, Theodore 26, 62, 86, 89, 91, 95, 112, 113, 121, 128, 135, 138, 139, 140, 149, 151, 152, 153, 167, 169, 170, 173, 190, 205, 223
Robin Hood (1913) 129
Robinson Crusoe (1913) 122
Robinson, Gertrude 32, 33, 41, 43, 60, 61
Robinson, Spike 110
Rogers, Charles B. 111
Rogers, Ginger 259
Rogers, Will 183, 205, 227, 240, 259; death of 227
Roland, Ruth 59, 157
Rooney, James 60
Roosevelt, Theodore 4, 24, 29
A Rose of Old Mexico (1913) 257; production details and cast list 243
Rose of the Rio Grande (1938) 239
Rose, Mayor Henry 84
Rosecrans, General William S. 3
Rosen, Phillip E. 188, 189, 190
Rosher, Charles 25, 43, 129, 131
Rosson, Arthur 54, 57
Rosson, Richard ("Dick") 26, 32
The Rotters (play) 154
Royle, Edwin 105
Rubens, Alma 94, 164, 215
Ruby, Herman 258
Rumer, Elsworth 101
Russell, Lillian 68
Russell, Marcella 104, 156
Russell, William 56
Ryckman, Chester 122
Ryno, William 46

St. Clair, Malcolm 31
St. Francis Hotel 161, 185
St. Johns, Adela Rogers 21, 83, 111, 175, 180, 185, 211, 216, 223, 233; on James Halleck ("Hal") Reid 4; on WR 2, 10, 11, 20, 25, 27, 28, 47, 48, 64, 66, 71, 85, 98, 108, 134, 135, 136, 137, 143, 145, 151, 153, 160, 172, 176, 179, 180, 181, 187, 191, 194, 200, 201, 207, 210, 218, 219, 240
St. Johns, Elaine 176

St. Johns, Ivan 180, 191, 204
St. Rose's Academy 66
Samuel Goldwyn Studio 99, 119, 191, 233, 234
Samuel of Posen (play) 38
San Francisco Examiner 185
San Martin, Charles 155
Sandford, Stanley J. ("Tiny") 188
Sandow (1894) 23
Sands, Dennis 193
The Sanitarium (1910) 24
Santa Monica Road Race 137, 138, 139
Santschi, Thomas 29, 63
Sarazen, Gene 223
Sarles, Roscoe 110; death of 201; friendship with WR 109
The Satin Woman (1927) 236, 238
Saturday Evening Post 122, 128, 132, 138, 153, 155, 159, 160, 161, 162, 173, 174
The Scarlet Crystal (1917) 99, 100
Schenck, Joseph 185
Schnitzler, Arthur 170
Schoenbaum, Charles E. 149, 161, 162, 167, 173, 174, 183, 188, 190
Schwenkfeld, Kaspar von 16
Scott, Homer 103
Screen Snapshots: Hollywood Stars to Remember (1954) 259
Sears, Allan 69, 70, 79, 94
The Second Mrs. Roebuck (1914) 59; production details and cast list 246
The Secret Service Man (1912) 33; production details and cast list 242
The Seepore Rebellion (1912) 32; production details and cast list 241
Selective Service Act, and draft 107, 108
The Selfish Woman (1916) 91, 92; production details and cast list 250
Selig Polyscope Film Company 31, 51, 56, 69, 154; and the MPPC 23; founding of 24
Selig Polyscope Projector 24
Selig Standard Camera 24
Selig, William N. 24, 25, 28, 55, 62; builds California studio 28, 29, 33; and Selig Jungle Zoo 29, 62; shooting of 30; wealth of 24
The Seligettes (Doc Yak series, 1914) 24
Selsor, Lahunta 155
Selwyn, Edgar 99
Sennett, Mack 1, 23, 30, 31, 40, 41, 42, 45, 59, 62, 64, 99, 125, 126, 164, 173, 185
Sertuerner, Friedrich 143
The Seventh Son (1912) 32; production details and cast list 241
Shea, William 31
Shearer, Norma 259
Shelby, Charlotte: bribes paid to district Attorneys 194; as suspect in murder of William Desmond Taylor 193, 194
Sheldon, E. Floyd 118
Shelley, Hazel 203
Sheriff for an Hour (1915) 70; production details and cast list 249
Short, Antrim 62, 63
Short, Gertrude 58, 63, 111, 183

The Shriek of Hollywood (1922) 205
Shulberg, Ben ("B.P.") 118, 185, 193
Shulberg, Budd 193
Sick Abed (1920) 154, 155, 156, 157; production details and cast list 255
Siegmann, George 33, 56, 66, 67, 73, 80, 94
Sierra Jim's Reformation (1913–1914) 59; production details and cast list 246
Sigler, Allen 235
Sinclair, Bertrand W. 104
The Siren (1914) 63, 258; production details and cast list 247
Sisson, Vera 63
The Skeleton (1914) 63, 258; production details and cast list 247
Slaves of Gold (play) 10
Sleeman, Philip 231
Smalley, Phillips 57, 62
Smith, Albert E. 23, 106
Smith, Charlotte 4, 13
Smith, Jim 194
Smith, Nora 109, 152
Smith, Oscar 109, 152, 168; and Harlem Casting agency 109
Somborn, Herbert 170
Song Bird of the North (1913) 246
Sound Picture Finance Company 239
The Source (1918) 128, 129; production details and cast list 253, 254
Southern, Eve 197
A Spanish Dilemma (1912) 45
Spanish Influenza epidemic of 1918 45, 122, 205; impact on movie industry 122
The Spark of Flame (1913) 57
The Spark of Manhood (1913) 257; production details and cast list 245
Spaulding, George 111
Spearman, Frank [H.] 113, 167
The Spider and Her Web (1914) 62; production details and cast list 247
The Spirit of the Flag (1913) 54, 258; production details and cast list 244
The Squaw Man (1914) 78, 105
The Squaw Man (1918) 151
The Squaw Man's Son (1917) 105; production details and cast list 252
Squirrel Inn Club 60, 61
Stack, James Langford 27
Stack, Robert (real name Modini-Wood, Charles Langford) 27
stage and theater in the United States 4; history of 4; touring groups 4, 5, 6; venues 6
The Stage Rustler (1908) 40
Standing, Jack 32
Stanford, Leland 22
Stanhope, Selwyn 72
Stanley, Maxfield 67, 72
Stanton, Frederick 152
Starke, Pauline 94
Starlight's Message (1916) 251
Station Content (1915) 69, 70; production details and cast list 249

Staub, Ralph 259
Steadman, Lincoln 162
Stedman, Myrtle 28, 98, 103, 104
Steele, Murray 43
Steele, William 49, 61, 63
Steppling, John 155, 157
Sterling, Ford 30, 45, 59, 79
Stern, Elaine 63
Stern, Jacob 78
Stevens, Edwin 149, 150, 162
Stewart, Anita 68, 194
Stirling, Major General William Alexander Lord 3
Storey, Edith 32, 127, 258, 259
Strakosch, Maurice 37
Strakosch, Max 37
Strother, Dorothy Savage 7
Strother, William, IV 7; emigration to United States 7; moves to Virginia 7
Struss, Karl 170, 171, 172
studio system, birth of 2
Sullivan, C. Gardner 231
A Summer Idyll (1908) 41
Summerville, George ("Slim") 98, 105
Sumurun (1920) 161
Sutherland, A. Edward 164
Swager, Barbara 27
Swain, Mack 31
Swanson, Gloria 139, 170, 171, 172, 175, 180, 182, 183, 189, 195, 196, 259; misgivings about working with WR 170
Sweet, Blanche 40, 42, 52, 53, 59, 60, 65, 66, 67, 68, 90

Tabor, Robert 32
Taft, Charles P. 4
Taft, Helen 61
Taft, William Howard 4
A Tale of the Sea (1910) 24
A Tale of Two Cities (1911) 32
A Tale of Two Cities (1922) 237
Tally, T.L. 22, 23
Talmadge, Constance 94, 121, 127
Talmadge, Norma 127, 128, 170, 258
Tapley, Rose 31, 32, 47, 48
Tarkington, Booth 203
Tarnished Lady (1931) 237
Tashman, Lilyan 259
Tate, Cullen B. 111, 139, 140, 141, 147, 149, 161
The Tattooed Arm (1913) 54, 257, 258; production details and cast list 244
Tavares, Arthur 104
Taylor, Estelle 236
Taylor, Loren 96
Taylor, William Desmond 2, 39, 79, 103, 104, 125, 185, 194, 197, 213, 220; early life of 192; home of 192; murder of 1, 192, 193, 202; relationship with Mary Miles Minter 193, 194
Taylor, Wilton 141, 148
Teare, Ethel 64
Tearing Down the Spanish Flag (1898) 106
The Telephone Girl (1912) 32; production details and cast list 241
Tellegen, Lou 85, 86, 89, 95, 111, 118
The Tell-Tale Arm (1917) 253
A Telltale Light (1913) 59

Temptation (1915) 86, 87
The Ten Commandments (1956) 236
Tenbrook, Harry 49
Tennyson, Alfred Lord 42, 80
Terry, Alice 141
Tess of Storm Country (1923) 234
The Test (1914) 63, 258; production details and cast list 247
Tetzlaff, Teddy ("Terrible Teddy") 137
Thanhauser, Edwin 46
Thanhauser Film Corporation 129
Thaumatrope 22
Theby, Rosemary 32
Their Masterpiece (1913) 51; production details and cast list 243
Thew, Harvey 114, 119
The Things We Love (1918) 116, 118, 119; production details and cast list 253
Thirty Days (1922) 210, 211, 212, 215, 219, 228, 229; production details and cast list 257
Thomas, A.E. 188, 211
Thomas, Augustus 8
Thomas, Edward 55
Thomas, Olive 1, 121, 164; death of 1, 165
Thomas H. Ince Company 231
Thornby, Robert 110
Thorne, Lizette 49
The Three Brothers (1915) 69; production details and cast list 249
The Three Musketeers (1921) 187
Thurman, Arthur 138
Tiffany, Louis Comfort 52, 53
Till I Come Back to You (1917) 106
Tillie's Punctured Romance (1914) 59
Titanic, RMS, sinking of 17
The Title Holder (1924) 236
To Have and to Hold (1916) 88, 89, 91; production details and cast list 250
To Serve the Cross (play) 13
Toft, Omar 138, 139, 147, 153, 160, 200
The Toilers of the Sea (1915) 76
Told in Colorado (1911) 28
Toncray, Kate 162
Too Many Millions (1918) 129, 130; production details and cast list 254
Too Much Speed (1921) 139, 159, 170, 173, 174, 186, 191; production details and cast list 256
Toplinsky and Company (1913) 56
The Torn Letter (1912) 46
Tourneur, Maurice 125
Triangle Film Corporation 102
The Tribal Law (1912) 49; production details and cast list 243
Trimble, Florence 51
Trimble, Laurence 32, 51
A Trip Around the Union Loop (1903) 24
A Trip to the Moon (1902) 23
Trotsky, Leon 259
The Troublesome Baby (1908) 42
Turnbull, Hector 79, 118
Turnbull, Margaret 78, 88, 119, 122
Turner, F.A. 79
Turner, Florence 31, 32, 55
Turner, Otis 25, 28, 29, 30, 33, 47, 97, 126; death of 122; legacy of 122
Turpin, Ben 31, 105
A Twilight Baby (1920) 186
Two Little Waifs (1908) 42
Two Mothers (1916) 99
Two Orphans (play) 9
Tyner, Thomas H. 165, 227

The Unattainable (1916) 99
Uncle Bill (1912) 46
Uncle Tom's Cabin (1913) 122
Under the Lash (1921) 182
United Artists Corporation 235
United States Fourth Liberty Loan Drive (1918) 258
Universal Film Manufacturing Company 33, 35, 44, 45, 46, 55, 56, 57, 58, 59, 62, 65, 66, 69, 76, 89, 98, 99, 102, 108, 235
University of Notre Dame 49
The Unknown (1915) 89
An Unseen Enemy (1912) 33; production details and cast list 242
Unto the Fourth Generation (play) 17
UPN 235
Urban-Eclipse Studio 51
Uribe, Paul 170, 171
Urson, Frank 132, 138, 140, 141, 147, 149, 161, 167, 173, 174
Utell, George 104

Valentino, Rudolph 101, 122, 135, 149, 170, 173, 189, 194, 195, 202, 223
The Valley of the Giants (1919) 141, 142, 143, 144, 147; production details and cast list 254
Van Buren, Mabel 92, 105, 112
Van Dyke, Woodbridge Strong 94, 149
Van Nuys, J.B. 61
Van Trees, James C. 128
Van Trump, Jessalyn 50, 54, 55, 57, 102
Vargas, Alberto 164
Variety 76, 165, 187
vaudeville, history of 23
Via Cabaret (1913) 54, 257; production details and cast list 244
Viacom International, Inc. 235
Victor Film Company 63, 68
The Victoria Cross (1912) 32; production details and cast list 242
Vidor, King 94
Vining, Frederick 35
Virginius (1912) 33; production details and cast list 242
Vitagraph Company of America 26, 30, 33, 34, 47, 49, 51, 52, 55, 56, 61, 69, 193, 228, 235
Vitascope 22
A Voice from the Sea (1915) 76
The Voice of the Viola (1914) 61, 257; production details and cast list 247
von Schiller, Freidrich 95
von Seyffertitz, Gustav 112, 113, 114, 115, 124, 125; anti-German sentiment felt by 113, 128, 138; uses pseudonym Clonbough, C. Butler 113, 128, 138
von Stroheim, Erich 81, 94, 113; anti-German sentiment felt by 113

Waiter No. 5 (1908) 42
Wales, Ethel 197
The Wall of Flame (1913) 99
The Wall of Flame (1916) 251
The Wall of Money (1913) 57, 102; production details and cast list 245
Wallack, James W., Jr. 35
Walsh, George 105, 106, 108
Walsh, Raoul 59, 60, 67
Walters, William 57
Walthall, Henry B. 29, 41, 43, 47, 65, 66, 67, 71, 72, 79
Wanamaker, Marc 154
War (1911) 31; production details and cast list 241
Ward, Fannie 88
Warner Brothers 202
Warner Features Company 54
Warner's Ranch 44
A Warrior's Bride (1917) 102; production details and cast list 252
Washburn, Bryant 205
Washington Square Players 152
The Way of a Woman (1914) 62, 257; production details and cast list 247
The Way of the World (1916) 99
Wayne, Maude 170
Wayne, Richard 129, 141
The Ways of Fate (1913) 52, 53, 257; production details and cast list 244
Webb, George 93
Webb, Kenneth 178
Webber, "Bull Beef" 5
Webber, Rex 122
Weber, Joe 68
Weber, Lois 57, 62, 125
Wells, Raymond 81
West, Billie 59, 67
West, Charles 41, 42, 128
West, Dorothy 42
West, Nathaneal 236
Westbrook, Chester 7
Westbrook, David 7
Westbrook, Emma 8, 11, 177, 231
Westbrook, Henry ("Harry") 7, 11; childhood of 7; homes of 8; marriage of 7, 8; military service of 8; taken in by farm families after mother's death 7; work of 8
Westbrook, Levi 7
Westbrook, Maloma 7
Westbrook, Mary Virginia Rice 8, 11, 32, 54, 136, 137, 177
Westbrook, Maud 8, 11, 15, 177, 231
Wharton, Leopold 148
Wharton, Theodore 148
What's Your Hurry? (1920) 159, 160, 173; production details and cast list 255

The Wheel of Life (1914) 61, 257; production details and cast list 246
When Jim Returned (1913) 54, 257, 258; production details and cast list 244
When Luck Changes (1913) 54, 257; production details and cast list 244
When the Light Fades (1913) 53; production details and cast list 243
Whitaker, Charles 111
White, Marie 64
White, Pearl 23
Whitfield, Eileen 107
Whitlock, Lloyd 167
Whitman, Fred 76
Whitman, Walt 94
Who Killed Doc Robbin? (1948) 239
Whoso Diggith a Pit (1914) 60; production details and cast list 246
A Wife on a Wager (1914) 63, 258; production details and cast list 248
Wild Bill Hickock (1923) 259
Wilder, Marshall P. 31
Wilkes, Anne Tupper 66
Wilkes, W. Ernest 128
Wilkey, Violet 72
Wilky, Guy 197, 203
Willard, Jess 149
Willful Peggy (1908) 41
William, Kathlyn 24
Williams, Ben Ames 161
Williams, Earle 32, 68
Williams, George B. 155
Williams, Kathlyn 62, 104, 119, 203, 204
Williams, Percy 129
Williams, William 219
Willis, F. McGrew 63
Wilson, Al F. 67
Wilson, Elsie Jane 86, 89
Wilson, Lois 159, 174, 175, 188, 194, 195
Wilson, Lucile 60, 61, 62
Wilson, Margery 94
Wilson, Tom 80
Wilson, Woodrow 75, 106
Windsor, Claire 194
Winship, Beatrice 11
Withey, Chester 51
Within Our Gates (1919) 76
Witzel, Albert 58, 186
The Wizard of Oz (1939) 240
Wodehouse, J. Stuart 151
Wolbert, William 63
Wolfe, Jane 122, 124
The Wolf's Den (1915) 89
Woltan, Fred 27

Woman and War (1913) 54, 258; production details and cast list 244
The Woman God Forgot (1917) 111, 112, 113, 115; production details and cast list 252
Women and Roses (1914) 63, 258; production details and cast list 247
The Wonderful Wizard of Oz (1910) 25, 122, 154
Wood, Gloria 183
Wood, Sam 151, 153, 154, 159, 182, 183, 223
Woods, Frank 42, 67, 118, 125
Woods, Joe 175
Woods, Walter 140, 149, 198, 211
Woodward, Henry 107, 113, 120, 122, 139, 141
Woolwine, Thomas L. 65, 193, 194
The World Apart (1917) 103; production details and cast list 252
The World's Champion (1922) 188, 189, 191, 199; production details and cast list 256, 257
Worsley, Wallace 212
Worthington, Charles 59
Wortman, Frank 94
Wray, John Griffith 231
The Wrong Heart (1913) 99
The Wrong Heart (1916) 258; production details and cast list 251
Wyckoff, Alvin 88, 112, 170, 171, 172; and DeMille-Wyckoff Process 96, 112, 113

A Yankee from the West (1915) 80; production details and cast list 249
The Yellow Pawn (1916) 92, 93; production details and cast list 251
Yellowstone National Park 19, 20
A Yoke of Gold (1916) 99
Young, Clara Kimball 68, 126, 127, 259
Young, Jack 159
Young Deer, James 33
Young, Rida Johnson 148
A Young Squaw's Bravery (1911) 113
You're Fired (1919) 139, 140; production details and cast list 254
Youth and Jealousy (1913) 54, 257; production details and cast list 244

Zukor, Adolph 66, 68, 83, 90, 91, 99, 107, 162, 171, 185, 197, 201, 218, 235

www.ingramcontent.com/pod-product-compliance
Ingram Content Group UK Ltd.
Pitfield, Milton Keynes, MK11 3LW, UK
UKHW050541150426
5217IPUK00026B/2030